# Lecture Notes in Compu[t]  3

*Commenced Publication in 1973*
Founding and Former Series Editors:
Gerhard Goos, Juris Hartmanis, and Jan v[a]

## Editorial Board

Yassine Lakhnech   Sergio Yovine (Eds.)

# Formal Techniques, Modelling and Analysis of Timed and Fault-Tolerant Systems

Joint International Conferences
on Formal Modelling and Analysis of Timed Systems, FORMATS 2004
and Formal Techniques in Real-Time and Fault-Tolerant Systems, FTRTFT 2004
Grenoble, France, September 22-24, 2004
Proceedings

 Springer

Volume Editors

Yassine Lakhnech
Sergio Yovine
Verimag Laboratory
2 av. de Vignate, 38610 Grenoble, France
E-mail:{Yassine.Lakhnech, Sergio.Yovine}@imag.fr

Library of Congress Control Number: 2004112582

CR Subject Classification (1998): D.3.1, F.3.1, C.1.m, C.3, B.3.4, B.1.3, D.2.4

ISSN 0302-9743
ISBN 3-540-23167-6 Springer Berlin Heidelberg New York

Springer is a part of Springer Science+Business Media

springeronline.com

© Springer-Verlag Berlin Heidelberg 2004
Printed in Germany

Typesetting: Camera-ready by author, data conversion by Olgun Computergrafik
Printed on acid-free paper     SPIN: 11324249     06/3142     5 4 3 2 1 0

# Preface

This volume contains the proceedings of the joint conference on *Formal Modelling and Analysis of Timed Systems* (FORMATS) and *Formal Techniques in Real-Time and Fault Tolerant Systems* (FTRTFT), held in Grenoble, France, on September 22–24, 2004. The conference united two previously independently organized conferences FORMATS and FTRTFT. FORMATS 2003 was organized as a satellite workshop of CONCUR 2003 and was related to three independently started workshop series: MTCS (held as a satellite event of CONCUR 2000 and CONCUR 2002), RT-TOOLS (held as a satellite event of CONCUR 2001 and FLoC 2002) and TPTS (held at ETAPS 2002). FTRTFT is a symposium that was held seven times before: in Warwick 1988, Nijmegen 1992, Lübeck 1994, Uppsala 1996, Lyngby 1998, Pune 2000 and Oldenburg 2002. The proceedings of these symposia were published as volumes 331, 571, 863, 1135, 1486, 1926, and 2469 in the LNCS series by Springer.

This joint conference is dedicated to the advancement of the theory and practice of the modelling, design and analysis of real-time and fault-tolerant systems. Indeed, computer systems are becoming increasingly widespread in real-time and safety-critical applications such as embedded systems. Such systems are characterized by the crucial need to manage their complexity in order to produce reliable designs and implementations. The importance of timing aspects, performance and fault-tolerance is continuously growing. Formal techniques offer a foundation for systematic design of complex systems. They have beneficial applications throughout the engineering process, from the capture of requirements through specification, design, coding and compilation, down to the hardware that embeds the system into its environment. The joint conference is devoted to considering the problems and the solutions in designing real-time and/or fault-tolerant systems, and to examining how well the use of advanced design techniques and formal methods for design, analysis and verification serves in relating theory to practice.

We received 70 paper submissions out of which 24 were selected for publication. Each submission received an average of 3 referee reviews. The conference program included three invited talks, by Greg Bollella (Sun Microsystems Laboratories), Paul Feautrier (LIP, École Normale Supérieure de Lyon, France) and Peter Ryan (School of Computing Science, University of Newcastle upon Tyne, UK).

We would like to thank all the Program Committee members and the subreferees. Our thanks also go to the Steering Committee members of FORMATS and FTRTFT. We also thank Claudia Laidet who assisted us in organizing the conference.

July 2004

Yassine Lakhnech and Sergio Yovine
Program Chairs
Joint Conference FORMATS 2004 and FTRTFT 2004

# Organization

The joint conference FORMATS and FTRTFT 2004 was organized by VERIMAG (http://www-verimag.imag.fr) with the support of: IMAG (Institut d'Informatique et Mathématiques Appliquées de Grenoble), CNRS (Centre National de Recherche Scientifique), Université Joseph Fourier, and INPG (Institut National Polytechnique de Grenoble), as well as the city of Grenoble.

## Program Committee

Luca de Alfaro (UCSC, USA)
Eugene Asarin (LIAFA, France)
Patricia Bouyer (LSV, France)
Flavio Corradini (Univ. di L'Aquila Italy)
Jordi Cortadella (UPC Spain)
Pedro D'Argenio (FAMAF, Argentina)
Alain Girault (INRIA, France)
Tom Henzinger (Berkeley, USA)
Mathai Joseph (TCS, India)
Marta Kwiatkowska (Univ. Birmingham, UK)
Yassine Lakhnech (VERIMAG, co-chair, France)
Kim Larsen (Aalborg University, Denmark)
Claude Le Pape (Ilog SA, France)
Ernst-Ruediger Olderog (Univ. Oldenburg)
Jens Palsberg (UCLA, USA)
P. Madhusudan (Univ. Pennsylvania, USA)
Amir Pnueli (NYU, USA)
Jean-Francois Raskin (ULB, Belgium)
Willem-Paul de Roever (Univ. Kiel, Germany)
John Rushby (SRI, USA)
Henny Sipma (Stanford, USA)
Steve Vestal (Honeywell, USA)
Wang Yi (Uppsala University, Sweden)
Sergio Yovine (VERIMAG, co-chair, France)

# Referees

M. Baclet
G. Behrmann
M. Bernardo
P. Bhaduri
I. Bozga
M. Bozga
V. Braberman
M. Bujorianu
D.R. Cacciagrano
P. Caspi
F. Cassez
A. Chakrabarti
S. Chakraborty
R. Clariso
A. Collomb
S. Cotton
R. Culmone
A. David
C. Daws
S. Demri
M. De Wulf
M.R. Di Berardini
H. Dierks
D. Di Ruscio
C. Dima
L. Doyen
D. D'Souza

M. Duflot
E. Dumitrescu
H. Fecher
J.C. Fernandez
E. Fleury
P. Ganty
G. Geeraerts
G. Goessler
O. Grinchtein
D. Guelev
H. Kalla
V. Khomenko
P. Krcal
T. Krilavicius
M. Kyas
F. Laroussinie
L. Lavagno
G. Luettgen
B. Lukoschus
N. Markey
M. Mikucionis
L. Mokrushin
L. Mounier
S. Neuendorffer
B. Nielsen
G. Norman
I. Ober

J. Ober
A. Oliveras
Ju Pang
J. Pearson
P. Pettersson
C. Picaronny
M. Pouzet
V. Prabhu
J.I. Rasmussen
E. Rutten
T.C. Ruys
G. Saiz
C. Sanchez
S. Sankaranarayanan
A. Skou
J. Sproston
M. Steffen
L. Tesei
P.S. Thiagarajan
Ting Zhang
S. Tripakis
R. Venkatesh
N. Wolovick
Wang Xu
T. Yoneda
Yi Zhang

# Table of Contents

## Invited Papers

## Regular Papers

# From Software to Hardware and Back

## (Abstract)

Paul Feautrier

Ecole Normale Supérieure de Lyon

One of the techniques for the formal design of embedded systems is – or should be – Behavioral Synthesis. Among its many advantages, one can quote easier testing and more complete architecture exploration.

Behavioral Synthesis has many aspects in common with another field, Automatic Parallelization. The reason is that, since von Neuman, software is inherently sequential, while hardware, which belongs to the real world, is parallel. The aim in Automatic Parallelization is to transform a sequential program into an equivalent program, suitable for efficient execution on a parallel high performance system. A specification being given, the aim of Behavioral Synthesis is to generate a VLSI circuit which conforms to the specifications. Most often, specifications come in the form of high-level algorithmic languages, like Matlab, C or Fortran. Hence, the outline of a BS system is: - find parallelism in the specification; - while in AP this paralellism is expressed in a form suitable for execution on a parallel computer (Open MP, MPI, fork-join), here it has to be expressed in a form suitable for synthesis (multiple combinatorial circuits, registers, control automata).

It is striking to notice that the two fields share many concepts, sometime under different names. Ressources, schedules and allocations are common objects, but sometime dependences become races or hazards. If we compare the state of the art in the two fields, one observe that Behavioral Synthesis lags behind Automatic Parallelization in the handling of loops and arrays. This is probably due to technological restrictions. It has not be possible to implement large amounts of memory on a chip until the advent of submicronics technologies.

Classical parallelization aimed only at detecting parallel loops, without changing much of the structure of the original program. It was soon noticed that the amount of parallelism that can be found in this way is limited, and that more aggressive methods are needed. Several authors simultaneously noticed, around 1990, that regular programs can be represented as geometric objects (simple set of points in n-space), and that most methods for finding parallelism are just changes of basis in this space. This new outlook allowed one to extend familiar techniques beyond basic blocks, and gave rise to powerful new methods for scheduling, allocation, memory management and code generation. These methods can be directly applied to Behavioral Synthesis, to replace such makeshift techniques as loop unrolling, loop fusion and loop splitting, stripmining and loop coalescing. However, there are many unsolved problems, which would greatly benefit Behavioral Synthesis. One of them is scheduling under resource constraints, which is known to be already NP-complete for basic blocs.

Y. Lakhnech and S. Yovine (Eds.): FORMATS/FTRTFT 2004, LNCS 3253, pp. 1–2, 2004.
© Springer-Verlag Berlin Heidelberg 2004

There are several heuristics which can be applied to loop scheduling, but the results are not satisfactory at present. Similarly, scheduling for a given amount of memory, or, conversely, finding the minimum amount of memory (or registers) to support a given schedule are important problems in synthesis.

Will a good system for Behavioral Synthesis influence software design and implementation? One may notice that general purpose processors are uniformly mediocre for all applications, while specific architectures like vector processors are highly efficient for restricted applications. With the advent of reconfigurable systems (e.g. FPGA) one may be tempted to redesign the architecture according to the needs of each application. The only problem with this idea is that synthesis, especially low level synthesis, is very slow compared to ordinary compilation. Hence, the idea will be limited to stable, high usage programs or to small pieces of big programs.

# Of Elections and Electrons
## (Abstract)

Peter Y. Ryan

University of Newcastle

Digital voting technologies are currently very topical and hotly debated, especially in the US with a presidential election looming. It is essential that voting systems are both trustworthy and trusted. Various schemes and technologies have been proposed, and indeed deployed, that take drastically different approaches to achieving assurance. At one end of the spectrum, we have approaches that claim to achieve assurance through system verification and testing. At the other end, we have the run-time monitoring school. Another way to characterize this dichotomy is to observe that the former approach seeks to verify the electoral system, the latter seeks to verify an actual election.

The first approach is typified by the touch screen (DRE) machines currently widely used in the US. Many researchers are profoundly mistrustful of the claims for verification and trustworthiness of such systems and indeed recent reports indicate that such mistrust is well placed, see for example [1].

The second approach is exemplified by the cryptographic schemes proposed by, for example, Chaum [2] or Neff [3]. These strive for complete transparency, up to the constraints imposed by the ballot secrecy requirements, and seek to achieve assurance via detailed monitoring of the process rather than having to place trust in the system components.

In between we find the paper audit trail approach (the "Mercuri method") that seeks to provide the means to check on the performance of DRE machines and recovery mechanisms [4, 5].

In this talk I discuss the dependability and security requirements of election systems, primarily accuracy and secrecy but also availability and usability. I outline the extent to which these various approaches meet these requirements.

I then discuss in more detail the design philosophy of the Chaum/Neff school and illustrate this with a variant of the Chaum scheme. These schemes support voter verifiability, that is, they provide the voter with a means to verify that their vote has been accurately recorded and counted, whilst at the same time maintaining ballot secrecy. The essence of this scheme is to provide the voter with a receipt that holds their vote in encrypted form. The challenge is to ensure that the decryption of the receipt that the voter sees in the booth is identical to the decryption performed by a sequence of tellers. The scheme combines a cut-and-choose protocol in the booth followed by robust anonymising mixes.

The original scheme uses visual cryptography to generate the encrypted receipts on a pair of transparent sheets. Correctly overlaid in the booth, these sheets reveal the ballot image. Separated they appear just to be random pixels. The voter retains only one of these sheets. The scheme presented here uses a sim-

Y. Lakhnech and S. Yovine (Eds.): FORMATS/FTRTFT 2004, LNCS 3253, pp. 3–4, 2004.

pler mechanism based on the alignment of symbols on adjacent strips of paper. This appears to be both simpler to explain and understand and to implement.

We also note that the dependability of complex computer based systems depends as much on socio-technical factors as the purely technical details of the design. We briefly describe error handling and recovery strategies for this scheme.

Poorly conceived, implemented and maintained voting technology poses a serious threat to democracy. Confidence in the integrity of voting systems appears to be at an all time low in the US for example. Schemes with a high degree of transparency along the lines of the Chaum or Neff proposals hold out the hope of restoring some of that confidence. In the words of Sylvio Micali at the DIMACS workshop on Security Analysis of Protocols. It is our duty as cryptographers to save democracy [7].

# References

1. Avi Rubin et al. http://avirubin.com/vote/analysis/index.html
2. David Chaum, Secret-Ballot Receipts: True Voter-Verifiable Elections.
3. Andy Neff, http:// www.votehere.com
4. Rebecca Mercuri, http://www.notablesoftware.com/evote.html
5. David Dill, http://www.verifiedvoting.org/
6. Peter Y A Ryan and Jeremy W Bryans, The Prêt à Voter Scheme  Newcastle Computer Science Tech Report, to appear.
7. http://dimacs.rutgers.edu/Workshops/Protocols/s.edu/Workshops/Protocols/

# Formal Verification of an Avionics Sensor Voter Using SCADE*

Samar Dajani-Brown[1], Darren Cofer[1], and Amar Bouali[2]

[1] Honeywell Laboratories, Minneapolis, MN, USA
samar.dajani-brown@honeywell.com
[2] Esterel Technologies, Villeneuve-Loubet, France

**Abstract.** Redundancy management is widely utilized in mission critical digital flight control systems. This study focuses on the use of SCADE (Safety Critical Application Development Environment) and its formal verification component, the Design Verifier, to assess the design correctness of a sensor voter algorithm used for management of three redundant sensors. The sensor voter algorithm is representative of embedded software used in many aircraft today. The algorithm, captured as a Simulink diagram, takes input from three sensors and computes an output signal and a hardware flag indicating correctness of the output. This study is part of an overall effort to compare several model checking tools to the same problem. SCADE is used to analyze the voter's correctness in this part of the study. Since synthesis of a correct environment for analysis of the voter's normal and off-normal behavior is a key factor when applying formal verification tools, this paper is focused on 1) the different approaches used for modeling the voter's environment and 2) the strengths and shortcomings of such approaches when applied to the problem under investigation.

## 1 Overview of Sensor Voter Problem

With the advent of digital flight control systems in the mid 1970s came the capability to implement monitoring, redundancy management, and built-in-test functions in software without the need for additional hardware components. The sensors used in these flight control systems exhibit various kinds of deterministic and non-deterministic errors and failure modes including bias offsets, scale factor errors, and sensitivity to spurious input and environmental factors. Redundant sensors are used to compensate for these errors and failures. Sensor failure detection algorithms ("voters") must detect and isolate a sensor whose output departs by more than a specified amount from the normal error spread. Publications such as [8] and [9] describe redundancy management schemes used in flight control systems.

This paper builds on earlier work in [6] and is part of an overall effort to compare several model checking tools when analyzing the correctness of avionics components. We have used as a test case a typical voter algorithm with many

---

* This work has been supported in part by NASA contract NAS1-00079.

Y. Lakhnech and S. Yovine (Eds.): FORMATS/FTRTFT 2004, LNCS 3253, pp. 5–20, 2004.
© Springer-Verlag Berlin Heidelberg 2004

of the features taken from [8]. This class of algorithms is applicable to a variety of sensors used in modern avionics, including rate gyros, linear accelerometers, stick force sensors, surface position sensors, and air data sensors (e.g. static and dynamic pressures and temperature).

Formal methods techniques, though embryonic to software development, have been used in [6] and [7] to analyze or verify safety critical properties of avionic software. We have found that the most challenging aspect of any formal verification effort is the specification of the environment in which the verified system operates. The environment captures all the assumptions about how the system interacts with the rest of the world, including physical constraints, timing considerations, and fault conditions. It should permit all interesting behavior of the system, while prohibiting any unrealistic behaviors. Much of our work has centered on creating good environment models for the sensor voter.

In this study, we use the SCADE, a tool suite for the development of real-time embedded software and its formal verification component, the Design Verifier, to analyze correctness of the voter's algorithm.

### 1.1   Sensor Voter Algorithm

Simulink [13] is a computer aided design tool widely used in the aerospace industry to design, simulate, and auto-code software for avionics equipment. The voter's algorithm was developed in Simulink. It incorporates the typical attributes of a sensor management algorithm and is intended to illustrate the characteristics of such algorithms. The voter takes inputs from three redundant sensors and synthesizes a single reliable sensor output. Each of the redundant sensors produces both a measured data value and self-check bit (validity flag) indicating whether or not the sensor considers itself to be operational. Data flow of the system is shown in Figure 1. A brief description of the voter's design and functionality follows:

1. Sample digitized signals of each sensor measurement at a fixed rate appropriate for the control loop, e.g. 20 Hz. A valid flag supplied by sensor hardware indicating its status is also sampled at the same rate.

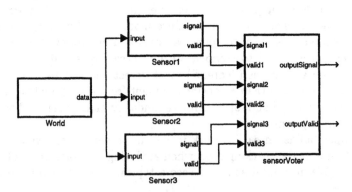

**Fig. 1.** Voter model and environment.

2. Use the valid flag and comparison of redundant sensor measurements to detect and isolate failed sensors.
3. Output at a specified sample rate a signal value computed as a composite average of the signals of non-faulty sensors. Also output, at the same specified rate, the status of the composite output by setting a *ValidOutput* flag.
4. Tolerate "false alarms" due to noise, transients, and small differences in sensor measurements. Sensors are not marked failed if they are operating within acceptable tolerances and noise levels.
5. Maximize the availability of valid output by providing an output whenever possible, even with two failed sensors.
6. The algorithm is not required to deal with simultaneous sensor failures since this is a very low probability event.

A more detailed description appears in earlier work using the symbolic model checker SMV [12] [10] to analyze correctness of the voter's algorithm [6].

## 1.2   Sensor Voter Requirements

Behavioral requirements for the sensor voter fall into two categories:

1. **Computational**, relating to the value of the output signal computed by the voter.
2. **Fault handling**, relating to the mechanisms for detecting and isolating sensor failures. The required fault handling behavior of the voter is shown in Figure 2.

Each of these categories includes requirements for reliability (correctness under normal operation) and robustness (rejection of false alarms).

### Computational Requirements

The main purpose of the sensor voter is to synthesize a reliable output that agrees with the "true" value of the environmental data measured by the redundant sensors. Therefore under normal operation, the output signal should agree with this true value within some small error threshold. In the absence of sensor noise or failures the two values should agree exactly. During the interval between the failure of a sensor and the detection of the failure by the voter, it is expected that the output value will deviate from the true value due to the continued inclusion of the failed sensor in the output average. During this reconfiguration interval the transient error in the output signal must remain within specified bounds, regardless of the type or magnitude of the failure.

### Fault Handling Requirements

The required fault handling behavior for the voter is shown in Figure 2. Initially, all three sensors are assumed to be valid. One of these sensors may be eliminated due to either a false hardware valid signal from the sensor or a miscomparing sensor value, leading to the "2 valid" state. If one of the two remaining sensors sets its hardware valid signal false, it is eliminated leading to the "1 valid" state.

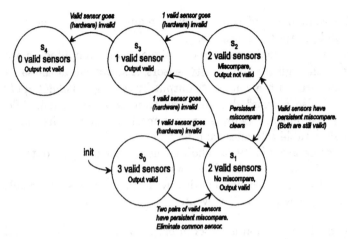

**Fig. 2.** Fault states of the sensor voter.

If this sensor subsequently sets its valid flag false it is eliminated and the voter output is set to not valid. A special situation occurs when there are two valid sensors. If these sensors miscompare, the voter cannot determine which may be faulty. Although there are other possibilities, this voter algorithm continues to keep both sensors in service but it sets its output valid flag false. If the sensors subsequently agree in value, the voter returns to the "2 valid, no miscompare" state and sets its output valid flag to true. Alternatively, if one of the two sensors identifies itself as faulty (via the hardware valid flag) it can be isolated by the voter and the other sensor signal used as the correct output value.

Each of these categories includes requirements for reliability (correctness under normal operation) and robustness (rejection of false alarms).

## 2   Overview of SCADE

SCADE (Safety Critical Application Development Environment)[1] is a tool suite for the development of real-time embedded software. It provides a programming language called SCADE, a simulation environment, automatic code generation, and formal verification.

### 2.1   The SCADE Design Language

SCADE is a graphical deterministic, declarative, and structured data-flow programming language based on the Lustre language [1, 2]. SCADE has a synchronous semantics on a cycle-based and reactive computational model. The node is the basic operator or design block of the language and can be either graphical or textual. A control system is modeled in SCADE via nodes connected to one another in a manner similar to how control systems get modeled

---

[1] SCADE is distributed by Esterel Technologies (www.esterel-technologies.com).

in Simulink. Some of the advantages of SCADE are that while developing the model, the simulator component can be used to check for syntax and semantic correctness of the nodes. SCADE is a strongly typed language with predefined and user defined types. The language allows for arithmetic operations on real and integer values, logical operation on Boolean variables, control flow operations (if then else, case) and temporal operators to access values from the past.

Figure 3 shows a graphical SCADE node programming a simple counter of the occurrence of an event. The occurrence of an event is given as a Boolean input flow called Event. The counter produces an output integer flow called Count. The Lustre textual data-flow equations counter-part of the graphical node are listed in the figure as well. The fby operator is a memory element, whose output

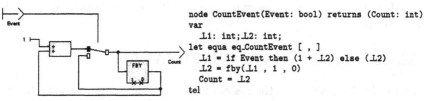

```
node CountEvent(Event: bool) returns (Count: int)
var
    _L1: int;_L2: int;
let equa eq_CountEvent [ , ]
    _L1 = if Event then (1 + _L2) else (_L2)
    _L2 = fby(_L1 , 1 , 0)
    Count = _L2
tel
```

**Fig. 3.** A simple SCADE node.

is equal to its input value after a fixed number of cycles. For instance, _L2 = fby(_L1 , 1 , 0) means _L2 is equal to _L1 after 1 cycle. At the initial cycle, _L2 is equal to 0. The rest of the node behavior is straightforward.

## 2.2   Formal Verification in SCADE

Design Verifier (DV) is the formal verification module of SCADE[2]. DV is a model checker of safety properties. Safety properties are expressed using the SCADE language. There is no specific syntax framework as in SMV to express liveness properties in the form of CTL logic [11]. A SCADE node implementing a property is called an observer [3]. An observer receives as inputs the variables involved in the property and produces an output that should be always true. Figure 4 shows how a new model is built connecting the model to verify to the observer property. DV is used to check if the property observer's output is always true. If it is, the property is said to be Valid, otherwise it is said to be Falsifiable, in which case DV generates a counter-example that can be played back in the SCADE simulator for debugging purposes. DV is able to verify properties mixing Boolean control logic, data-value transformations, and temporal behavior. DV core algorithms are based on Stalmarck's SAT-solving algorithm for dealing with Boolean formulae, surrounded by induction schemes to deal with temporal behavior and state space search [4]. These algorithms are coupled with constraint solving and decision procedures to deal with the data-path. SAT-based model-checking has shown interesting performances compared

---

[2] DV is based on Prover Technology proof engines (www.prover.com).

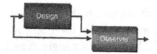

**Fig. 4.** Verification by means of observers.

to BDD-based model-checking [5], in particular for many real-world applications with enormous formulas that could not be handled by current BDD packages [4].

DV, similar to SMV, allows for restriction of the state space while verifying a property through a notion of assertions. A SCADE assertion on an input or output variable is similar to an SMV invariant and prunes the search space to only those instances where the assertion holds true. Therefore, in using SCADE and the DV, our work let us use and compare DV and SMV as applied to the same problem.

## 3   Modeling and Analysis Using SCADE

The overall SCADE model of the system under consideration, as shown in Figure 5, consists of the voter model and the environment model. The voter's model corresponds to the "real" system that we wish to analyze. It is composed of a hierarchal representation of graphical and textual SCADE nodes. The environment model consists of three sensor models and a world model and is intended to be a realistic description of the environment driving the voter's functionality. The distinction between the system under study (voter model) and its environment (the sensors and world models) is an important one. The voter's model should be modeled with the highest possible fidelity, its structure should be traceable to the original design and it should conform as closely as possible to code gener-

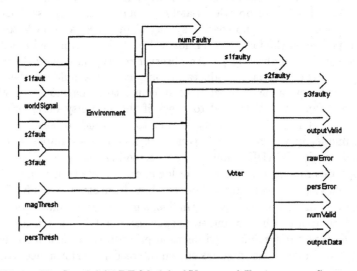

**Fig. 5.** Top Level SCADE Model of Voter and Environment System.

ated from the design. The level of abstraction used in modeling the environment should be carefully optimized; for we must ensure that the environment will exercise all possible behaviors of the voter (including faulty conditions) without introducing any unrealistic behavior [6].

The design of a realistic environment is crucial when verifying "real" system properties using model checking techniques. We can consider the environment as the outside world that interacts with the system under study and the systems' requirements as collections of statements about the outside world that we want the system to help make true. The design of a good environment must model the outside world requirements accurately without introducing erroneous behavior. The environment model must capture all general, including faulty, expected behavior of the outside world that interfaces with the system to be verified.

Design of good environment models is gaining recognition as an important research problem. For example, in [17], automatically generated environment models are used to verify the source code of the Windows kernel. The environment to be modeled is the application programming interface (API). The environment model is generated via a "training" process by taking several programs that use a common API and applying model checking to create abstractions of the API procedures. These abstractions are then reused on subsequent verification runs to model-check different programs utilizing the same API.

In our study, we use knowledge gained from counter examples generated from using an environment model to modify/refine newer environment models that accurately capture the requirements. We expect our system to handle a range of sensor signals some of which are faulty signals but we must not have more than one sensor exhibiting faulty behavior at any given time; it is true about the outside world that no two sensors can become faulty simultaneously as the probability of such an event is very close to zero. As discussed in later sections, we capture this property in two different ways through different environment models. The environment models are developed manually and results of three such models are reported in later sections.

Our SCADE model of the voter was developed based on the voter's original Simulink design. SCADE provides a gateway for automatic translation of Simulink models, but we have not evaluated this capability in our current study.

The sections below list the three approaches used to model the voter's environment. Whenever possible, we compare our modeling approach in SCADE versus our earlier work using SMV. Results to follow were computed using a Pentium III PC with 512 MBytes of RAM running Windows 2000.

## 3.1 Modeling Assumptions and Simplifications

The following assumptions and simplifications have been made in modeling the sensor voter using different environments.

### Fault Injection

A Boolean flag is read from the outside world by the sensor model; such a flag injects non-deterministic faulty behavior in the sensor. The sensor model is designed such that when this flag is set then the sensor is faulty in both hardware and signal. To test correctness of the voter's fault handling and computational requirements when signal or hardware faults occur, we use different values for the persistence value constant; by the voter's design, this constant is the number of cycles that a sensor is allowed to differ in signal prior to being eliminated by the voter. We define a "signal fault" as the fault detected by the voter when a sensor differs in signal from the good expected signal value. To test for a signal fault, we set persistent threshold equal to two. This assumption guarantees that signal failure must be detected and isolated by the voter in two cycles; i.e. in one cycle after the cycle where the fault occurs. We also define a sensor's "hardware fault" as the fault detected by the voter due to hardware failure in the sensor; by the voter's design, the hardware fault should be detected and the faulty sensor should be isolated in three cycles. To test for a hardware fault, we set persistent threshold equal to four. Thus the isolation and detection of hardware fault which requires three cycles to complete; i.e. in two cycles after the cycle where the fault occurs, will occur prior to the detection and isolation of the signal fault which in this case requires four cycles to complete.

## Time Model

The SCADE models do not explicitly model time. Each execution step in the model corresponds to one sample in the Simulink design, independent of the actual sample rate. The only place where time enters into the original Simulink model is a Gain block which multiplies its input by a constant (gain). This gain constant was adjusted so that the model is independent of time. A detailed justification for modeling the voter's algorithm independent of time is described in [6].

## No Simultaneous Sensor Failures

The algorithm assumes that two sensors cannot fail at the same time. In particular, the first sensor failure must be detected and isolated by the voter before it is able to respond to a second failure. This fault hypothesis is reasonable if sensor failures are independent so that the probability of simultaneous failures is sufficiently low.

We approached this single fault hypothesis in two ways: 1) In the first environment model, referred to in later sections as "Environment Model I", we used a similar approach to our earlier work in SMV. Given that it is the case the number of valid sensors plus the number of sensors declared faulty is bounded between three and four inclusive, we used a SCADE assertion to satisfy this bound.

Note that the number of faulty sensors (numFaulty) is computed within the environment as sensors become faulty but the number of valid sensors (numValid) is computed within the voter and its correctness must be verified independently. With this in mind, we developed different environment models, referred to as "Environment Model II" and "Environment Modell III", that handled the single fault hypothesis by asserting that the number of faulty sensors ( a value computed within the environment) is always less than or equal to one.

**Noise Free Signals**
The models developed did not deal with signal noise. In all of our analysis, we assume that any deviation in the sensor signals is a fault. Our verification work focused on the voter's ability to identify and isolate faulty sensors, rather than on robustness requirements.

# 4   Analysis

We will use the following notation to express our properties throughout this section, where HF and SF mean Hardware Failure and Signal failure respectively.

$p \xrightarrow{i \; tick} q$   True iff $q$ is true $i$ cycles after the cycle where $p$ is true.

$VS$   The number of valid sensors.

$F_{h1}, F_{h2}, F_{h3}$ True if there is a HF of one, two, and three sensors respectively.

$F_{s1}, F_{s2}$   True if there is a SF of one and two sensors respectively.

## 4.1   Fault Handling Requirements Properties

The properties extracted from the fault handling requirements of Figure 2 that we want to formally verify can be grouped by the number of sensor failures.

**One Sensor Failure.** Here are the properties when one sensor is detected as faulty.

- **Hardware fault:**
  $(VS = 3 \wedge ValidOutput \wedge F_{h1}) \xrightarrow{2 \; tick} (VS = 2 \wedge ValidOutput)$
  This property means that if the number of valid sensors is 3, and the Voter's output is valid, and there is one hardware faulty sensor, then after 2 cycles the number of valid sensors becomes 2 and the Voter's output is valid.
- **Signal fault:**
  $(VS = 3 \wedge ValidOutput \wedge F_{s1}) \xrightarrow{1 \; tick} (VS = 2 \wedge ValidOutput)$
  This property means that if the number of valid sensors is 3, and the Voter's output is valid, and there is one software faulty sensor, then after 1 cycle the number of valid sensors becomes 2 and the Voter's output is valid.

**Two Sensor Failures.** Here are the same properties when a second sensor is detected as faulty.

- **Hardware fault:**
  $(VS = 2 \wedge ValidOutput \wedge F_{h2}) \xrightarrow{2 \; tick} (VS = 1 \wedge ValidOutput)$.
- **Signal fault:**
  $(VS = 2 \wedge ValidOutput \wedge F_{s2}) \xrightarrow{1 \; tick} (VS = 2 \wedge \neg ValidOutput)$.
  This property means that if 2 valid sensors miscompare in signal, then after 1 cycle the output of the voter is declared invalid. Both sensors remain valid since the voter algorithm is not designed to determine the faulty sensor for this case. However, the faulty sensor will exhibit a faulty behavior in the following cycle and will get eliminated by the voter. This last special case is discussed in more detail in a later section.

**Three Sensor Failures.** Here are the same properties when a third sensor is detected as faulty.

- **Hardware fault:**
  $(VS = 1 \wedge ValidOutput \wedge F_{h3})\ \overset{2\ tick}{\to}\ (VS = 0 \wedge \neg ValidOutput).$
- **Signal fault:**
  If there is only one valid sensor in the system, then the voter can only eliminate this sensor based on a hardware fault, i.e. we cannot test for a signal fault since there is no other valid sensor to compare to.

**Sensor Elimination Property.** When a sensor is eliminated by the Voter it will never be considered in any future computation. We express it as: $((VS = k) \to \neg(VS > k)), k \in [0, 2]$. This property means that if the number of valid sensors becomes $k$ then this value will never become a value greater than $k$.

## 4.2   Environment Model I

### Sensor Model

The sensor model captured as a SCADE graphical node takes as input a non-deterministic Boolean flag from the environment. A signal of one and a hardware valid flag is produced by the sensor if the Boolean flag is false (i.e. sensor not faulty); a signal of five and a hardware invalid flag is broadcasted when the Boolean input flag is true. In addition, logic combination of a single cycle delay and an or-gate are used so that once a sensor becomes faulty (i.e. Boolean input flag is true) it stays faulty and does not recover. This last quantity is also sent as output from the sensor and is used in calculating the numFaulty value. The assumption that a faulty sensor does not recover differs from our sensor model in SMV where we allowed a faulty sensor to recover its faulty behavior. Furthermore, we use only two input signal values {1,5} to indicate the faulty/non-faulty behavior of a sensor which is different than our analysis in SMV where we used a signal range of {1,2,3}. Assuming two input signal values is justifiable since in our analysis of the voter algorithm we only care about the difference between two signals.

### Environment Node

This SCADE node is composed of three sensor nodes, a multiplexer node that groups and outputs the hardware valid flags of the sensors into an array of three Boolean values, a multiplexer that groups and outputs the signals broadcast by the three sensors into an array of three integers and a numFaulty node. The numFaulty node sums the Boolean flags sent by each sensor indicating its faulty/non-faulty status and outputs that sum as numFaulty. We restrict the sum of faulty and valid sensors to be bounded between three and four inclusive. This restriction guarantees our single fault hypothesis because it allows one sensor to become faulty and a second sensor cannot become faulty until the first faulty sensor is detected and eliminated by the voter.

**Table 1.** Verification Results.

| Property | Time(secs) | Result |
|---|---|---|
| One sensor failure | | |
| Hardware fault | 134 | Valid: a faulty sensor on a hardware fault is detected by the voter |
| Signal fault | 3 | Valid |
| Sensor elimination is final | 0.13 | Valid with persistent threshold = 2 (software fault) |
| Sensor elimination is final | 0.14 | Valid with persistent threshold = 4 (hardware fault) |
| Two sensor failures | | |
| Hardware fault | 137 | Valid: a second faulty sensor on a hardware fault is detected by the voter |
| Signal fault | 81 | Valid |
| Sensor elimination is final | 0.11 | Valid with persistent threshold = 2 (software fault) |
| Sensor elimination is final | 0.13 | Valid with persistent threshold = 4 (hardware fault) |
| Three sensor failures | | |
| Hardware fault | 137 | Valid: a second faulty sensor on a hardware fault is detected by the voter |
| Signal fault | | Not relevant, see section 4.1 |
| Sensor elimination is final | 0.14 | Valid |

**Verification of Fault Handling Requirements**

Table 1 summarizes the results we obtain when checking the properties. The first column recalls the name of the property. The second column gives the CPU time in seconds spent by DV to check the property. The third column gives the result of verification, which is either Valid to mean that the property holds, or Falsifiable in the opposite case, and some additional comments when necessary.

Recall that in our sensor model, hardware and signal faults occur simultaneously, therefore, we expect that the signal fault is detected by the voter in a number of cycles equal to the persistence threshold value (i.e. two) where the hardware fault should be detected in three cycles. Therefore, by setting persistence threshold equal to two, not only can we check that a second faulty sensor with a signal fault leads to a state where the voter's output is declared invalid and the number of valid sensors is still equal to two; for we can also check whether this same sensor demonstrates a hardware failure in three cycles; i.e. in one cycle after it reached the state of 2 valid sensors and invalid input, the voter should be in the state of one valid sensor and valid output. We were able to verify that

$$(VS = 2 \wedge \neg ValidOutput) \overset{1 \ tick}{\rightarrow} (VS = 1 \wedge ValidOutput).$$

**Drawbacks to Environment Model I**

1. One drawback to this sensor model is that a failed sensor remains faulty and continues to produce an invalid hardware flag and a bad signal. This means that we cannot test the voter's ability to transition from the state

where the number of valid sensors is two and output is not valid to the state where the number of valid sensors is two and the output is valid as shown in Figure 2. A different sensor model is required to investigate this capability of the voter.

2. The assertion that the number of valid sensors plus the number of faulty sensors is between three and four inclusive, coupled with the sensor design used allows the second faulty sensor on a software fault to manifest its fault as a hardware fault, thus transitioning to the state of 1 valid sensor and valid output. This design eliminates the possibility that the third healthy sensor manifests a faulty hardware behavior before the second fault is detected by the voter.

## 4.3   Environment Model II

### Environment Node

This SCADE node differs from the environment in the previous model in that the numFaulty node sums the Boolean flag read by each sensor from the outside world indicating its faulty/non-faulty status and outputs that sum as numFaulty as opposed to summing up the Boolean flag sent by each sensor indicating its faulty/non-faulty status. Such change is necessary in order to use the assertion that the number of faulty sensors is less than or equal to one (i.e. numFaulty $\leq 1$). This assertion does not make use of the variable numValid which is computed by the voter. The assertion guarantees the single fault hypothesis since it allows only one sensor to be faulty at any given time. The results obtained from this environment model are described below.

### Verification of Fault Handling Requirements

Table 2 summarizes the results we obtain when checking the properties. For one sensor failure the verification attempt resulted in a counter-example where sensor1 is faulty for one cycle (i.e. signal = 5), sensor3 is faulty for the next cycle (i.e. signal = 5) so sensor1 being faulty agrees with sensor3 being faulty in the next cycle instead of being eliminated. Using the assertion that the number of valid and faulty sensors is between three and four inclusive prevented a situation where the second sensor becomes faulty before the first faulty sensor is eliminated by the voter. However, the assertion made use of numValid which is an output of the voter itself. When we avoid using numValid, and instead use the numFaulty $\leq 1$ assertion, we permit more random behavior of the system and receive the counter example above. The problem is that we have not allowed enough time between faults for the voter to eliminate the sensor. For two sensor failures the verification resulted in a counter-example where sensor1 is faulty for two cycles and is eliminated by the voter, after which sensor3 is faulty for one cycle (i.e. signal equals 5), then sensor2 is faulty for the next immediate cycle (signal = 5 also). Therefore, sensor3 and sensor2, though faulty, agree on signal and we do not get to the state where the number of valid sensors is 2 but the output is not valid. The fact that we are not allowing enough time between faults causes this behavior to occur. This problem is addressed in Environment model III described below.

**Table 2.** Verification Results.

| Property | Time(secs) | Result |
|---|---|---|
| One sensor failure ||| 
| Hardware fault | 88 | Valid: a faulty sensor on a hardware fault is detected by the voter |
| Signal fault | | Falsifiable |
| Two sensor failures ||| 
| Hardware fault | 116 | Valid: a second faulty sensor on a hardware fault is detected by the voter |
| Signal fault | | Falsifiable |

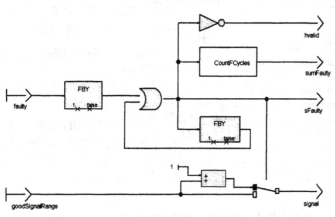

**Fig. 6.** SCADE Model of Sensor used in Environment III.

## 4.4   Environment Model III

### Modifications to Sensor Model

Similar to the previous section, this environment model uses the assertion that numFaulty $<= 1$ and also assumes that a time delay that exceeds the thresholds for detecting a hardware or signal fault exists between sensor faults. The sensor model, Figure 6, is modified such that the fault Boolean flag for faulty sensor remains true for five cycles after which it is set to false thus allowing a second sensor to fail under the assumption that numFaulty $<= 1$ . Recall that a hardware fault must be detected in three cycles and we are using a persistent threshold of two and four for the detection of signal failure, thus the five cycle delay is justified. The sensor model is further modified to receive a signal range between one and five from the outside world; a non-faulty sensor broadcasts the signal received whereas a faulty sensor broadcasts the signal received plus one. Hence a faulty sensor always exhibits faulty behavior in signal. This assumption is valid because we are interested in the voter behavior when the sensors differ in signal. In all the analysis below we use an assertion that numFaulty $<= 1$ and that the sensor signal range is between one and five inclusive.

**Table 3.** Verification Results.

| Property | Time(secs) | Result |
|----------|-----------|--------|
| One sensor failure | | |
| Hardware fault | 204 | Valid: a faulty sensor on a hardware fault is detected by the voter |
| Signal fault | 101.6 | Valid |
| Sensor elimination is final | 0.31 | Valid with persistent threshold = 2 (software fault) |
| Sensor elimination is final | 0.23 | Valid with persistent threshold = 4 (hardware fault) |
| Two sensor failures | | |
| Hardware fault | 225 | Valid: a second faulty sensor on a hardware fault is detected by the voter |
| Signal fault | 122.67 | Valid |
| Sensor elimination is final | 0.19 | Valid with persistent threshold = 2 (software fault) |
| Sensor elimination is final | 0.22 | Valid with persistent threshold = 4 (hardware fault) |
| Three sensor failures | | |
| Hardware fault | 0.22 | Valid: a second faulty sensor on a hardware fault is detected by the voter |
| Signal fault | | Not relevant (see section 4.1) |
| Sensor elimination is final | 0.23 | Valid |

### Verification of Fault Handling Requirements

Table 3 summarizes the results we obtain when checking the fault-handling properties. Table 1 and Table 3 are verification results for the same properties with the exception that the single fault hypothesis used in table 3 is independent of any values computed by the voter.

**Property for the Output Signal Value.** It is expected that there will be a transient condition in which the voter output data may differ from the signal received from the world when a sensor becomes faulty. However, after a certain threshold, the voter output data must agree with the signal received from the world. Using a delay of 2 cycles, a persistent threshold of 4, and asserting that numValid is greater than 0, we verified that:

$$(worldSignal \neq voterdata) \overset{2\ tick}{\rightarrow} (worldSignal = voterdata)$$

The verification completed in 10.4 seconds and produced a valid result.

## 5   Conclusion

In this paper we have used the formal verification capabilities of the SCADE Design Verifier to analyze an embedded avionics software design. Model checking is used to verify the correctness of the design with respect to its high-level fault-handling requirements.

The main contribution of this work is to demonstrate the significance of the environment model in verifying the design requirements of an algorithm. The process of capturing a system's design requirements for algorithm development and subsequent software implementation is never an easy task. The design of a suitable environment model is centered around developing a model that drives the system to be implemented and tests the captured design requirements of the system. Our work shows that capturing and developing the correct environment model is a key issue and can be as hard as verifying correctness of the system itself.

## Acknowledgment

We extend our gratitude to Gary Hartmann and Steve Pratt at Honeywell Laboratories for designing the voter algorithm and providing insight on its behavioral properties and functional requirements.

## References

1. P. Caspi, A. Curic, A. Maignan, C. Sofronis, S. Tripakis, P. Niebert, "From Simulink to SCADE/Lustre to TTA: a layered approach for distributed embedded applications", Proc. of the 2003 ACM SIGPLAN conference on Language, compiler, and tool for embedded systems, San Diego, USA.
2. N. Halbwachs, P. Caspi, P. Raymond, and D. Pilaud, "The Synchronous Data Flow Programming Language Lustre", Proceeding of the IEEE, September, 1991.
3. N. Halbwachs, F. Lagnier, and P. Raymond, "Synchronous observers and the verification of reactive systems", Third Int. Conf. on Algebraic Methodology and Software Technology", AMAST'93, Workshop in Computing, Springer-Verlag.
4. M. Sheeran and G. Stalmarck, "A tutorial on Stalmarck's proof procedure for propositional logic", Prover Technology AB and Chalmers University of Technology, 1998, Sweden.
5. Per Bjesse and Koen Claessen, "SAT-based Verification without State Space Traversal", Formal Methods in Computer-Aided Design, 2000.
6. S. Dajani-Brown, D. Cofer, G. Hartmann, and S. Pratt, "Formal Modeling and Analysis of an Avionics Triplex Sensor Voter", Model Checking Software, 10th International SPIN Workshop, , Springer-Verlag, May 2003.
7. G. Berry, A. Bouali, X. Fornari, E. Ledinot, E. Nassor, R. de Simone, "ESTEREL: a formal method applied to avionic software development", Science of Computer Programming V 36 No 1, January 2000.
8. S. Osder, "Practical View of Redundancy Management Application and Theory", Journal of Guidance and Control, Vol. 22 No. 1 , Jan-Feb 1999.
9. R.P.G. Collinson, Introduction to Avionics, Chapman & Hall, London, 1998.
10. K. McMillan, Symbolic Model Checking , Kluwer Academic Publishers, Boston, Dordrecht, London, 1993.
11. Micheal R A Huth and Mark D Ryan, Logic in Computer Science Modelling and reasoning about systems, University Press, Cambridge, United Kingdom, 2000.
12. SMV web page: http://www-2.cs.cmu.edu/~modelcheck
13. Simulink weg page: http://www.mathworks.com/products/simulink

14. SCADE 4.1.1, Training Manual, Esterel Technologies, Montreal, Canada.
15. SCADE 4.2, Design Verifier User Manual, Esterel Technologies, Montreal, Canada.
16. Gerard Berry, "The effectiveness of Synchronous Languages for the Development of Safety-Critical Systems", white paper, Esterel Technologies 2003
17. T. Ball, V. Levin, and F. Xei, "Automatic Creation of Environment Models via Training", TACAS 2004, Barcelona, Spain

# Mixed Delay and Threshold Voters in Critical Real-Time Systems*

Chiheb Kossentini[1,2] and Paul Caspi[2]

[1] Airbus
[2] Laboratoire Verimag (CNRS)
{kossentini,caspi}@imag.fr
http://www-verimag.imag.fr

**Abstract.** This paper addresses the question of extending the usual approximation and sampling theory of continuous signals and systems to those encompassing discontinuities, such as found in modern complex control systems (mode switches for instance). We provide a topological framework derived from the Skorokhod distance to deal with those cases in a uniform manner. We show how this theoretical framework can be used for voting on hybrid signals in critical real-time systems.

## 1 Introduction

Though the theory of distributed fault-tolerant systems advocates the use of clock synchronisation [9, 7], still many critical real-time systems are based on the GALS (globally asynchronous, locally synchronous) paradigm: in this framework, each computer is time-triggered but the clocks associated with each computer are not synchronised and communication is based on periodic sampling: each computer has its own clock and periodically samples its environment, *i.e.*, the physical environment but, also, the activities of the other computers with which it communicates. When such an architecture is used in critical systems, there is a need for a thorough formalisation of fault tolerance in this framework. In a previous paper [5] we already formalised the concepts of threshold and delay voters. However there was in this paper some lack of symmetry between the two concepts: sampling continuous signals and threshold voting were very simply based on topological notions like uniform continuity and $L_\infty$ distance. On the contrary, sampling discrete event signals and associated delay voting were based on more *ad-hoc* notions.

Later[4], we found that the use of the Skorokhod distance[3] was a way to overcome this lack of symmetry. More precisely, we showed that the discrete signals that could be sampled were those that were uniformly continuous with respect to this distance. This opened the way toward a generalisation to hybrid (mixed continuous-discrete) signals.

---

* This work has been supported by the European Network of Excellence Artist and by the Airbus-Verimag CIFRE grant 2003-2006.

Y. Lakhnech and S. Yovine (Eds.): FORMATS/FTRTFT 2004, LNCS 3253, pp. 21–35, 2004.

Moreover, we remarked that our previous study on voters was incomplete: in practice, it appears that people do not only use threshold voters and delay voters but also, and mainly, mixed threshold and delay voters. In these voters, a failure is detected if two signals differ for more than a given threshold during more than a given time.

This paper is thus devoted to a formalisation of these voters based on the Skorokhod topology. More precisely, we show that if two signals are within a given Skorokhod neighbourhood and if one of them is uniformly Skorokhod continuous, then we can design a 2x2 hybrid voter which will not raise an alarm as long as these conditions are fulfilled. In practice, this result allows us to finely tune the voter parameters as a function of the nominal (non-faulty) errors and delays resulting from:

- the numerical and delay analysis of the sensors,
- the algorithms used for computing outputs[1]
- and the architecture of communication between computing locations.

The paper is organised as follows: in a second section, we provide basic definitions. Section 3 defines an hybrid uniform bounded variability which is an hybrid generalisation of the corresponding notion on piece-wise constant signals. Section 4 recalls basic voting schemes and presents the mixed (hybrid) voter. Then we prove an intermediate (but important) result relating the Skorokhod topology with uniform bounded variability. Finally, we show the formal bases relating the topology and the voting schemes.

## 2   Basic Definitions

### 2.1   Signals and Systems

We consider systems that have to operate continuously for a long time, for instance a nuclear plant control that is in operation for weeks or an aircraft control that flies for several hours. Thus, the horizon of our signals is not bounded. Hence, a *signal* $x$ is for us simply a piece-wise continuous function from $\Re$ to $\Re$, that is to say, a function which is continuous but on a finite or diverging sequence of times $\{t_0, \ldots, t_n, \ldots\}$. This means, in particular, that left and right limits exist at each point in time. Furthermore, we assume that discontinuities are only of the first kind, such that the value at a given time is always within the interval made of left and right limits:

For all t,
$$x(t) \in [\inf(x(t^-), x(t^+)), \sup(x(t^-), x(t^+))]$$

where, as usual, $x(t^-), (x(t^+))$ is the left (right) limit of $x$ at $t$.

Finally, we assume that the signal remains constant before the first discontinuity time $t_0$.

---

[1] We can remark that this kind of method allows the use of diverse programming [2] which is one of the ways for tolerating design and software faults.

A *system* is simply a function $S$ causally transforming signals, that is to say, such that $S(x)(t)$ is only function of $x(t'), t' < t$.

The *delay operator* $\Delta^\tau$ is such that $(\Delta^\tau x)(t) = x(t - \tau)$, and a system is *stationary* (or time invariant) if $\forall \tau, S(\Delta^\tau x) = \Delta^\tau(S x)$.

An even more restricted class of systems is the class of *static or combinational* systems, that is to say, systems that are the "unfolding" of a scalar function:

$$S_f(x)(t) = f(x(t))$$

## 2.2   Retiming and Sampling

A *retiming* function $r \in Ret$ is a non decreasing function from $\Re$ to $\Re$. This is a very general definition which provides many possibilities. For instance, a piece-wise constant retiming function can be seen as a sampler: if $x' = x \circ r$, and if $r$ is piece-wise constant, then, at each jump of $r$, a new value of $x$ is taken and maintained up to the next jump. This allows us to define a periodic sampler $r$, of period $T_r$ by the piece-wise constant function (see figure 1):

$$r(t) = \lfloor t/T_r \rfloor$$

where $\lfloor \rfloor$ is the floor function.

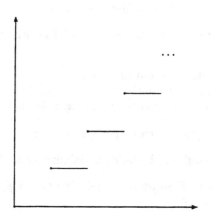

**Fig. 1.** A periodic sampling retiming.

The following well-known lemma state a property of bijective retimings ($BRet$):

**Lemma 1.** *A bijective retiming is both increasing and continuous and its inverse is continuous: it is an homeomorphism.*

Finally, retimings allow us to characterise static (or combinational) systems, that is to say, those systems which commute with retiming:

**Theorem 1 (Static systems).** *A static system $S$ is such that, for any $r \in Ret$,*

$$S \circ r = r \circ S$$

## 3   Hybrid Uniform Bounded Variability

We have already defined in [5] the topological framework of uniform continuity based on the $L_\infty$ distance. This notion finds its application in the continuous signal sampling theory. In the case of piece-wise constant signals, we have formalised the *ad-hoc* concept of *uniform bounded variability*, UBV for short (closely linked to non Zenoness [1]). But the case of hybrid (mixed discrete-continuous) signals remained to be handled. We call hybrid signals those signals which are piece-wise continuous. One can easily remark that this definition encompasses the classical continuous and boolean signals. When trying to generalise the UBV definition of [4] to hybrid signals, we can remark that there can be several such generalisations. In the sequel, we propose two of them, a general and a strict one.

We first remark that, in boolean signals, discontinuities have constant amplitude. Now, discontinuities can have different amplitudes and we introduce the jump function to characterise them:

**Definition 1 (Jump function).** $j_x$ *is the function evaluating the discontinuity amplitude of signal $x$ at point $t$*

$$j_x(t) = |x(t^-) - x(t^+)|$$

The following function counts the number of discontinuities in a given interval:

**Definition 2 (Discontinuity count function).**
  $dc_{x,t1,t2}(\epsilon)$ *is the function counting the number of discontinuity points having discontinuity amplitude larger than $\epsilon$ of a signal $x$ in the interval $[t_1, t_2]$.*

$$dc_{x,t_1,t_2}(\epsilon) = card\{\ t \mid t_1 \le t \le t_2 \land j_x(t) > \epsilon\}$$

We can then define uniform bounded variability for an hybrid signal as:

**Definition 3 (Uniform Bounded Variability (UBV)).** *A signal $x$ has uniform bounded variability if*

1. *there exists a positive (stable time) function $T_x$ such that, for any positive $\epsilon$ and any interval $[t_1, t_2]$,*

$$|t_1 - t_2| \le T_x(\epsilon) \Rightarrow dc_{x,t_1,t_2}(\epsilon) \le 1$$

2. *there exists a positive (error) function $\eta_x$ such that, for any positive $\epsilon$ and any interval $[t_1, t_2]$ not containing a discontinuity point,*

$$|t_1 - t_2| \le \eta_x(\epsilon) \Rightarrow |x(t_2) - x(t_1)| \le \epsilon$$

This also means that, on the one hand, there is at least a time interval larger than $T_x(\epsilon)$ between any two jumps larger than $\epsilon$ and, on the other hand, that $x$ is "piece-wise uniformly continuous".

Yet, we can note that this definition does not ensure the possibility of finding, at any time, a "continuous interval" of minimum length. In this sense, it is a looser definition than the one provided for the Boolean case. This is why we can propose a stricter definition:

**Definition 4 (Strict Uniform Bounded Variability (SUBV)).** *A signal $x$ is SUBV if it is UBV and*

$$lim_{\epsilon \to 0} T_x(\epsilon) = T_x > 0$$

Thus, $T_x$ is now the minimum time interval between any two discontinuities, whatever be the associated jumps.

## 4   Hybrid Voting

In this section we recall the classical threshold and delay voting schemes. Then we propose a 2/2 hybrid voter which is a mixture of these two aspects[2].

### 4.1   Threshold Voting

Knowing bounds on the normal deviation between values that should be equal, easily allows the design of threshold voters. For instance, if $x$ is UBV and continuous and if

$$x' = x \circ r + e$$

with

- $||r - id||_\infty \leq \eta_x(\epsilon)$
- $||e||_\infty \leq \epsilon$

where

- $|| \; ||_\infty$ is the classical $L_\infty$ norm, *i.e.*, for our piece-wise continuous signals with only first kind discontinuities: $||x||_\infty = \sup_t |x(t)|$,
- and *id* is the identity function.

We can find a threshold $\epsilon' = 2\epsilon$ and design a 2/2-voter:

$$voter2/2(x, x', \epsilon') = \mathbf{if} \; |x - x'| \leq \epsilon'$$
$$\mathbf{then} \; x$$
$$\mathbf{else} \; alarm$$

such that the voter delivers a correct output in the absence of failure and, otherwise, delivers an alarm.

---

[2] In the usual terminology for voters, $n_1/n_2$ means that $n_1$ units out of $n_2$ redundant ones should operate correctly in order that the redundant system operates correctly.

*Notations.* In this definition and in the sequel, algorithms are expressed using a functional notation, that is to say by abstracting over time indices, in order to stay consistent with design tools like Simulink[3] or Scade[4]. Thus, a signal definition $x_1 = x_2$ means $\forall n \in N : x_1(nT) = x_2(nT)$ where $T$ is the period of the computing unit running the algorithm.

## 4.2   Delay Voting

Let us consider boolean UBV signals $x$ and $x'$ which is, in normal operation, a delayed image of $x$:

$$x' = x \circ r$$

with a bound on the delay in correct operation:

$$\|r - id\|_\infty \leq \tau_x$$

There signals are received by some unit of period $T$. However, the assumption that correct computers have perfect clocks. is clearly not realistic. To be more realistic, one should consider clock drifts. A frequent assumption is that clock drifts are bounded, either because the mission time is bounded or extra mechanisms allow for detecting exceedingly large drifts. Then there exist lower $(T_m)$ and upper $(T_M)$ bounds for $T$ and, in each condition involving $T$, it should be replaced by the bound which makes it more pessimistic. We thus assume $T_m \leq T \leq T_M$.

We also assume $\tau_x + T_M < T_x(1)$. This assumption guarantees that the joint effect of the delay and the sampling at rate $T$ (which can induce an additional delay) cannot miss any change of input value (which, by assumption last at least $T_x(1)$). Then,

- the maximum time interval where the two signals may continuously disagree is obviously $\tau_x$,
- the maximum number of samples where two correct copies continuously disagree is

$$nmax = \left\lfloor \frac{\tau_x}{T_m} \right\rfloor + 1$$

This allows us to design **delay voters** for delay booleans signals. For instance, a 2/2 voter could be:

**Definition 5 (2/2 delay voter).**

$$voter2/2(x_1, x_2, nmax) = x$$

```
where x,  n        = if x₁ = x₂
                     then x₁, 0
                     else if Δ₀ᵀn < nmax − 1
                          then Δ₀ᵀx, Δ₀ᵀn + 1
                     else alarm
```

---

[3] http://www.mathworks.com
[4] http://www.esterel-technologies.com

where $\Delta_{x_0}^T$ is the *delay operator* such that $\Delta_{x_0}^T x(t) = x(t - \tau)$ with initial value $x_0$.

- this voter maintains a counter $n$ with initial value 0, and its previous output, with some known initial value $x0$,
- whenever the two inputs agree , it outputs one input and resets the counter,
- else, if the counter has not reached $nmax - 1$, it increments it and outputs the previous output,
- else it raises an alarm.

**Theorem 2.** *voter2/2 raises an alarm if the two inputs disagree for more than $nmaxT_M$ and otherwise delivers the correct value with maximum delay $(nmax + 1)T_M$.*

### 4.3   Hybrid Delay-Threshold Voting

Can we mix now the two previous voters, the threshold and the delay one? This would amount to define an hybrid voter:

**Definition 6 (2/2hybrid voter).**

$$hyb\_voter2/2(x, x', nmax, \epsilon') = y$$

```
where y, n                  = if |x − x'| ≤ ε'
                              then x, 0
                              else if Δ₀ᵀn < nmax − 1
                                then Δ_{x₀}ᵀy, Δ₀ᵀn + 1
                              else alarm
```

- this voter maintains a counter $n$ with initial value 0, and its previous output, with some known initial value $x0$,
- whenever the two inputs threshold-agree, it outputs one input and resets the counter,
- else, if the counter has not reached $nmax - 1$, it increments it and outputs the previous output,
- else it raises an alarm.

On which condition could we state the following desirable proposition?

**Theorem 3 (Hybrid voter property).** *hyb_voter2/2 raises an alarm if the two inputs differ for more than $\epsilon'$ during more than $nmaxT_M$ and otherwise delivers the correct value with maximum delay $(nmax + 1)T_M$.*

**The SUBV Case.** Let us consider an hybrid signals $x'$ which is, in normal operation, a delayed and perturbed images of the SUBV signal $x$:

$$x' = x \circ r + e$$

with bounds $\epsilon$ on errors and $\tau$ on delays:

$$||e||_\infty \leq \epsilon$$
$$||r - id||_\infty \leq \tau$$

These two signals are received by some unit of period $T$ ($T_m \leq T \leq T_M$) and we assume $\tau + T_M < \inf\{T_x, \eta_x(\epsilon)\}$.

Then we can find a threshold $\epsilon' = 2\epsilon$ such that (3) holds:

- the maximum time interval where the two signals may continuously differ more than $\epsilon'$ is obviously $\tau$,
- the maximum number of samples where the two signals may continuously differ more than $\epsilon'$ is

$$nmax = \left\lfloor \frac{\tau}{T_m} \right\rfloor + 1$$

**The UBV Case.** On the contrary, in the simpler UBV case, we can find examples for which (3) does not hold. Let us consider the piece-wise constant signal $x_c$ (see Fig.2) with the sequence of discontinuity points and corresponding jumps indexed on $0 < n, p < n$:

$$t_{x_c}(n, p) = n + \frac{p}{n}$$
$$j_{x_c}(t_{x_c}(n, p)) = \frac{1}{\sqrt{n}}$$

On the one hand, it is easy to check that this signal is UBV, with $T_{x_c}(\epsilon) = \epsilon^2$, but not SUBV because $\lim_{\epsilon \to 0} T_{x_c}(\epsilon) = 0$. On the other hand, we cannot find a voter for this signal because its "average" slope is ever increasing. For any $t, T$, we have:

$$\frac{x_c(t + T) - x_c(t)}{T} \geq \sqrt{t}$$

In the following section we present the Skorokhod topology which will let us deal with hybrid signals in a uniform manner. This common framework lets us calculate and finely tune the voter parameters as function of the input properties.

## 5   The Skorokhod Topology

### 5.1   The Skorokhod Distance

This distance [3, 8] has been proposed as a generalisation of the usual $L_\infty$ distance so as to account for discontinuities.

**Definition 7 (Skorokhod distance).**

$$d_S(x, y) = \inf_{r \in BRet} ||r - id||_\infty + ||x - y \circ r||_\infty$$

*where BRet is the set of bijective retimings.*

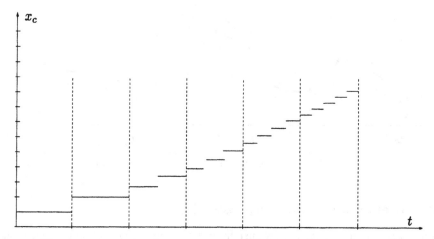

**Fig. 2.** An example where $x_c$ is increasing with an average slope $\sqrt{t}$.

We see here the idea of this definition: instead of comparing the signals at the same times, we allow shifts in time before comparing points, provided the shifts are bijective, i.e., we don't miss any time. In this definition, the use of bijective retimings is fundamental. Otherwise, it could be easily shown that it would not be a distance: for instance symmetry and triangular inequality could be violated.

But this distance is not easy to manipulate because it sums up delays and errors. Hence, we adopt below an equivalent topology which is more flexible.

### 5.2   A Skorokhod Topology

**Definition 8 (Skorokhod tube).** *Let $x$ be a signal, $\tau > 0$ and $\epsilon > 0$. We call* Skorokhod tube *centred at $x$ with $\tau$ and $\epsilon$ as parameters, the set:*

$$\mathcal{B}(\tau, \epsilon, x) = \{y \mid \exists r_y \in Bret, ||r_y - id||_\infty < \tau \wedge ||x - y \circ r_y||_\infty < \epsilon\}$$

It is easy to see that these tubes form a topological basis and define a topology which is equivalent to the one induced by the Skorokhod distance.

**Definition 9 (Uniform Skorokhod Continuity (USC)).** *A signal $x$ is uniformly Skorokhod continuous if there exists a positive function $\theta_x$ from delays and errors to delays such that, for all $\epsilon > 0$, $\tau > 0$ and retiming $r$,*

$$||r - id||_\infty \leq \theta_x(\tau, \epsilon) \Rightarrow x \circ r \in \overline{\mathcal{B}}(\tau, \epsilon, x)$$

where $\overline{\mathcal{B}}$ denotes the closure of $\mathcal{B}$.

In this definition of uniform continuity, we dissociate errors and delays and this allow us to operate separately on these two parameters. But we preserve their dependence through the error function $\theta_x$ which insures that a small distortion of a reference signal $x$ remains in a specified Skorokhod tube (see Fig.3).

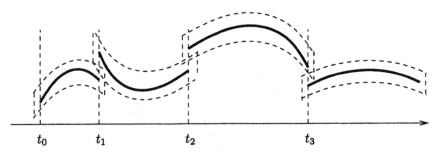

**Fig. 3.** Skorokhod tube around a reference signal.

## 5.3   Relation with Tube Languages [6]

In [6], a topological notion of robust hybrid automata was defined which looks very close to this one. The idea is also to allow both deviations in value and in time and this is achieved by considering a signal $x$ as a set of couples $\{x(t), t \mid t \in \Re\}$. Then the tube distance $d_t$ between two signals $x$ and $y$ is defined as the Hausdorff distance between the two sets[5]:

$$d_t(x, y) = \sup\{\sup_t(\inf_{t'}(|x(t) - y(t')| + |t - t'|), \sup_t(\inf_{t'}(|x(t') - y(t)| + |t - t'|)\}$$

We can, however, state the following proposition:

**Theorem 4.** *The Skorokhod topology is finer than the tube one.*

This is due to the fact that, for any $x, y$, $d_t(x, y) \leq d_S(x, y)$. As a matter of fact, the correspondence between $t$ and $t'$ in the tube distance can be any mapping while, in the Skorokhod distance, it is bound to be a bijective increasing one.

## 5.4   Skorokhod Topology and Bounded Variability

We can now state this important property of USC signals:

**Theorem 5 (USC signal property).** *If the signal $x$ is USC there exists a positive (stable time) $T_x$ and discontinuity number $n_x$ functions such that, for any positive $\epsilon$ and any interval $[t_1, t_2]$,*

$$|t_1 - t_2| \leq T_x(\epsilon) \Rightarrow dc_{x,t_1,t_2}(\epsilon) \leq n_x(\epsilon)$$

*Proof.* Let $\epsilon > 0$, $\tau > 0$, $\alpha = \frac{\epsilon}{3}$ and $n_x = \lceil \frac{\tau}{\theta_x(\tau, \alpha)} + 1 \rceil$. Let us show that if $x$ can have $n_x$ $\epsilon$-discontinuity points[6] arbitrarily close, it cannot be the case that:

---

[5] We present a variation with respect the original presentation which is based on the Euclidian distance, but this deviation is minor as all finite product distances are equivalent.

[6] An $\epsilon$-discontinuity point is a point where the signal yields a jump amplitude larger than $\epsilon$.

$$\forall\, r \in Ret \;\; ||r - id||_\infty \leq \theta_x(\tau, \alpha) \;\Rightarrow\; x \circ r \in \overline{B}(\tau, \alpha, x)$$

Let us show first that we can design a retiming $r$ which erases $(n_x - 1)$ $\alpha$-discontinuity points out of any $n_x$ $\alpha$-discontinuity points closer than $2\theta_x(\tau, \alpha)$. Let $t_1, \ldots t_{n_x}$ such a tuple.

$$t_1 < t_{n_x} < t_1 + 2\theta_x(\tau, \alpha)$$

It suffices to take (see Fig 4):

$$r(t_1^-) = r(t_{n_x}^+)$$

If $x$ were $USC$, we could find a bijective retiming $r'$ such that $||r' - id||_\infty < \tau$ and $||x - x \circ r \circ r'||_\infty \leq \frac{\epsilon}{3}$ .

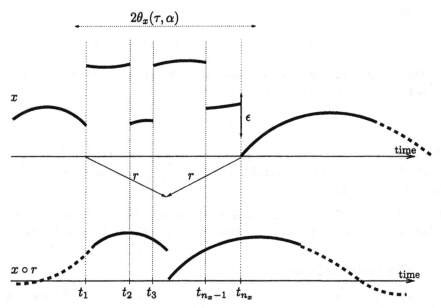

**Fig. 4.** Example of a signal $x$ with $n_x$ discontinuity points closer than $2\theta(\tau, \alpha)$. We show how $r$ reduces the time interval $[t_1, t_{n_x}]$ to a single point. Thus, $r$ erases the signal $x$ on this time interval.

Let us consider $t$, an $\epsilon$-discontinuity point of $x$ which was erased by $r$ in an $n_x$-tuple of $\epsilon$-discontinuity points. Note that, since we assume that $x$ has $n_x$ $\epsilon$-discontinuity points arbitrarily close, it has an unbounded number of $n_x$ $\epsilon$-discontinuity points closer than $2\theta_x(\tau, \alpha)$ and, in any of these $n_x$ tuples, we can choose any of these points as $t$. Then we have:

$$|x(t^-) - x(t^+)| \leq |x(t^-) - x \circ r \circ r'(t^-)| + \\ |x \circ r \circ r'(t^-) - x \circ r \circ r'(t^+)| + \\ |x \circ r \circ r'(t^+) - |x(t^+)|$$

Since $t$ is an $\epsilon$-discontinuity point of $x$,

$$|x(t^-) - x(t^+)| > \epsilon$$

Now, we can remark that $x \circ r \circ r'$ has less than $(n_x - 1)$ $\alpha$-discontinuity points in any $2(\tau + \theta(\tau, \alpha))$ time interval. This is due to the condition on $n_x$ as $n_x - 1$ points cannot partition a $2(\tau + \theta(\tau, \alpha))$ interval into $n_x$ sub-intervals larger than $\frac{2(\tau + \theta(\tau, \alpha))}{n_x} \leq 2\theta_x(\tau, \alpha)$.

Thus, among the $(n_x - 1)$ erased $\epsilon$-discontinuity points of $x$, there is at least one, which cannot be associated with an $\alpha$-discontinuity point of $x \circ r \circ r'$. Let the chosen $t$ be such a point. We have:

$$|x \circ r \circ r'(t^-) - x \circ r \circ r'(t^+)| \leq \frac{\epsilon}{3}$$

Hence,

$$\frac{2\epsilon}{3} < |x(t^-) - x \circ r \circ r'(t^-)| + |x \circ r \circ r'(t^+) - x(t^+)|$$

This lets us state that there is at least one of these two terms which is strictly greater than $\frac{\epsilon}{3}$, which contradicts the hypothesis

$$x \circ r \in \overline{B}(\tau, \frac{\epsilon}{3}, x)$$

**Corollary 1.** *If $x$ is USC, then, for any $\epsilon$, in any time interval larger than $T_x(\epsilon)$, there exists a time interval larger than $\frac{T_x(\epsilon)}{n_x(\epsilon)+1}$ not containing any $\epsilon$-discontinuity point.*

We see here the effect of USC definition: it ensures us to find in the signal infinitely many stable intervals large enough and not too far from each other.

## 5.5  The Voting Scheme

The Skorokhod topology allows us now to give a wider answer to the question raised in 4.3 thanks to the following proposition:

**Theorem 6.** *Let $x$ be a USC signal and $y \in B(\tau, \epsilon, x)$. If*

$$0 < 2\tau < 2\theta_x(\tau, \epsilon) < \frac{T_x(\epsilon)}{n_x(\epsilon) + 1},$$

*there exist positive $T_1, T_2$ such that, for any $t$, there exist $t_1, t_2$ with*

$$t \leq t_1 < t + T_1$$
$$t_1 + T_2 < t_2$$

*such that, for any $t'$ with $t_1 \leq t' \leq t_2$,*

$$|x(t') - y(t')| \leq 4\epsilon$$

*Proof.* We first prove the following lemma:

**Lemma 2.** *Let $x$ be a USC signal. Let $\epsilon > 0$ and $0 < \tau < \theta_x(\tau, \epsilon)$ . If $t_1 \leq t_2$ are two points located within an interval larger than $2\theta_x(\tau, \epsilon)$ not containing any $\epsilon$-discontinuity points and such that*

$$|t_2 - t_1| \leq 2\theta(\tau, \epsilon)$$

*then,*

$$|x(t_1) - x(t_2)| < 3\epsilon$$

*Proof.* Let $T = [\alpha, \beta]$ this interval. Let us define the point $t$ such that:

$$
\begin{cases}
if & t_1 \leq \alpha + \theta_x(\tau, \epsilon) & then & t = \alpha + \theta_x(\tau, \epsilon) \\
else\ if & t_2 \geq \beta - \theta_x(\tau, \epsilon) & then & t = \beta - \theta_x(\tau, \epsilon) \\
else & & & t = \frac{t_1 + t_2}{2}
\end{cases}
$$

We can choose a retiming r with $||r - Id||_\infty \leq \theta_x(\tau, \epsilon)$ satisfying $r(t^-) = t_1$ and $r(t^+) = t_2$

To this r we thus can associate a bijective (hence continuous) r' such that:

$$
\begin{cases}
|r'(t) - t| < \tau \\
|x(t_1) - x(r'(t)^-)| \leq \epsilon \\
|x(t_2) - x(r'(t)^+)| \leq \epsilon
\end{cases}
$$

Then

$$|x(t_1) - x(t_2)| \leq |x(t_1) - x(r'(t)^-)| + |x(r'(t)^-) - x(r'(t)^+)| + |x(t_2) - x(r'(t)^+)|$$

and

$$|x(t_1) - x(t_2)| \leq 2\epsilon + |x(r'(t)^-) - x(r'(t)^+)|$$

The point $t$ that we have chosen lies in all cases in the interval $[\alpha + \tau, \beta - \tau]$. We can then check that $r'(t) \in ]\alpha, \beta[$ holds for any bijective retiming $r'$ verifying $||r - Id||_\infty < \tau$. But, $]\alpha, \beta[ \subset T$ in which $x$ has no jump larger than $\epsilon$, thus, we have obviously $|x(r'(t)^-) - x(r'(t)^+)| \leq \epsilon$.

Hence, the two points $t_1$ and $t_2$ are such that $|x(t_1) - x(t_2)| \leq 3\epsilon$

*Proof of the proposition.* There exists $r_0 \in Bret$ such that $||r_0 - id||_\infty < \tau$ and $||x - y \circ r_0||_\infty < \epsilon$. Let $(a_i)_{i \in N}$ the sequence of $\epsilon$-discontinuities of $x$ and $(b_i)_{i \in N}$ the sequence defined by $b_i = r_0(a_i)$. From the sequence $a_i$, we can extract the subsequence $a_{i_j}$ which begins a stable interval, *i.e.*,

$$a_{i_j} + \frac{T_x(\epsilon)}{n_x(\epsilon) + 1} < a_{i_j+1}$$

We consider the retiming r such that:

$$
r(t) = 
\begin{cases}
t & if\ \ t \in ]\max(a_{i_j}, b_{i_j}), \min(a_{i_j+1}, b_{i_j+1})] \\
\min(a_{i_j}, b_{i_j}) & if\ \ t \in ]\min(a_{i_j}, b_{i_j}), \max(a_{i_j}, b_{i_j})]
\end{cases}
$$

It is easy to remark that $||r - id||_\infty < \tau$. For all $t$ in $]\max(a_{i_j}, b_{i_j}), \min(a_{i_j+1}, b_{i+1})]$ we have:

$$|x \circ r(t) - y \circ r(t)| = |x(t) - y(t)|$$
$$|x \circ r(t) - y \circ r(t)| \leq |x(t) - x \circ r_0^{-1}(t)| + |x \circ r_0^{-1}(t) - y(t)|$$
$$|x \circ r(t) - y \circ r(t)| \leq 4\epsilon$$

because $t$ and $r_0^{-1}(t)$ fulfil the conditions of lemma 2.

We can thus take

$$T_1 = 2T_x(\epsilon)$$

which is the maximum length of any $[\max(a_{i_j}, b_{i_j}), \max(a_{i_{j+1}+1}, b_{i_{j+1}+1})]$ interval, and

$$T_2 = \frac{T_x(\epsilon)}{n_x(\epsilon) + 1} - 2\tau$$

which is the minimum length of any $[\max(a_{i_j}, b_{i_j}), \min(a_{i_j+1}, b_{i_j+1})]$ interval.

This proposition means that if a signal is within some neighbourhood of another USC signal, the two signals cannot continuously differ from more than a given threshold for more than a given time. More precisely, if

$$T_M < T_2$$

then, in normal operation, the two signals cannot differ from more than $4\epsilon$ for more than $nmax$ samples, with:

$$nmax = \left\lfloor \frac{T_1}{T_m} \right\rfloor + 1$$

This property thus explicitly links signal properties to the voter parameters. This allows designing robust voters in critical real time embedded systems.

## 6   Conclusion

This paper has intended to provide a satisfactory theory for merging together threshold voters adapted to continuous signals and delay voters adapted to boolean signals in order to cope with hybrid piece-wise continuous signals. One problem in performing this merge was that, while threshold voters are based on uniform continuity, delay voters are based on a more *ad-hoc* notion of uniform bounded variability. We show in the paper that the Skorokhod topology allows us to perform this merge in a more uniform and also more general manner.

Moreover, this voting problem is clearly related to the more general sampling problem for hybrid systems and the results provided here may also help in defining which hybrid systems can be accurately sampled. This can be a subject for future work.

Yet, we also can notice that our results may not be the last word in the play. First, the relations with the tube distance of [6] have only been partially explored. Moreover, our final result only shows some topological signal properties allowing voters to be designed. But the converse property that signals for which voters can be designed fulfil these properties has not been proved and is likely to be false. This leads us to think that there is perhaps an even more general "votability" property that remains to be defined.

# References

1. M. Abadi and L. Lamport. An old-fashioned recipe for real time. *ACM Transactions on Programming Languages and Systems*, 16(5):1543–1571, 1994.
2. A. Avizienis. The methodology of n-version programming. In M.R. Lyu, editor, *Software Fault Tolerance*, pages 23–46. John Wiley, 1995.
3. P. Billingsley. *Convergence of probability measures*. John Wiley & Sons, 1999.
4. P. Caspi and A. Benveniste. Toward an approximation theory for computerised control. In A. Sangiovanni-Vincentelli and J. Sifakis, editors, *2nd International Wokshop on Embedded Software, EMSOFT02*, volume 2491 of *Lecture Notes in Computer Science*, 2002.
5. P. Caspi and R. Salem. Threshold and bounded-delay voting in critical control systems. In Mathai Joseph, editor, *Formal Techniques in Real-Time and Fault-Tolerant Systems*, volume 1926 of *Lecture Notes in Computer Science*, pages 68–81, September 2000.
6. V. Gupta, T.A. Henzinger, and R. Jagadeesan. Robust timed automata. In O. Maler, editor, *Hybrid and real Time Systems, HART'97*, volume 1201 of *Lecture Notes in Computer Science*, pages 331–345. Springer Verlag, 1997.
7. H. Kopetz. *Real-Time Systems Design Principles for Distributed Embedded Applications*. Kluwer, 1997.
8. M.Broucke. Regularity of solutions and homotopic equivalence for hybrid systems. In *Proceedings of the 37th IEEE Conference on Decision and Control*, volume 4, pages 4283–4288, 1998.
9. J.H. Wensley, L. Lamport, J. Goldberg, M.W. Green, K.N. Lewitt, P.M. Melliar-Smith, R.E Shostak, and Ch.B. Weinstock. SIFT: Design and analysis of a fault-tolerant computer for aircraft control. *Proceedings of the IEEE*, 66(10):1240–1255, 1978.

# Towards a Methodological Approach to Specification and Analysis of Dependable Automation Systems

Simona Bernardi[1], Susanna Donatelli[1], and Giovanna Dondossola[2,*]

[1] Dipartimento di Informatica, Università di Torino, Italy
{susi,bernardi}@di.unito.it
[2] CESI Automation & Information Technology, Milano, Italy
dondossola@cesi.it

**Abstract.** The paper discusses a constructive approach to the temporal logic specification and analysis of dependability requirements of automation systems. The work is based on TRIO formal method, which supports a declarative temporal logic language with a linear notion of time, and makes use of UML class diagrams to describe the automation system. The *general* concepts presented for the automation system *domain* are here *instantiated* on a case study *application* taken from the energy distribution field.

## 1 Introduction

The design of critical systems is faced with the need of devising appropriate "dependability strategies", that is to say the need of choosing and specifying a set of steps that allow to improve the reliability of the system. In the project DepAuDE [6][1] this issue has been investigated and a methodology to support the analyst in collecting and analyzing system dependability requirements, aimed at designing appropriate Fault Tolerance (FT) solutions, has been devised through a collaboration between the CESI[2] company and the University of Torino.

The application *domain* for the methodology is that of distributed cyclic control systems, while the specific *application* considered in the case study presented here is related to the automation system for primary substations of electricity distribution network (called PSAS in the following), proposed by CESI within the DepAuDE project [5]. The PSAS provides the tele-control and protection functions of the Primary Substations (PSs), where PSs are nodes of the electric distribution grid connecting the High Voltage transportation network to the Medium Voltage distribution. The aspects of PSAS that are relevant for this paper concern the cyclic behavior and the synchronization issues of the distributed automation systems local to the PS and they will be introduced, when needed, in Section 4.

Three different formalisms collaborate in a synergic manner in the methodology: UML Class Diagrams [21] (CDs from now on), a static paradigm, TRIO [12] temporal

---

\* Partially funded by Italian Ministry of Productive activities – Rete 21 – SITAR project.
[1] EEC-IST-2000-25434 DepAuDE (Dependability for embedded Automation systems in Dynamic Environment with intra-site and inter-site distribution aspects) project.
[2] CESI is an Italian company providing services and performing research activities for the Electric Power System.

Y. Lakhnech and S. Yovine (Eds.): FORMATS/FTRTFT 2004, LNCS 3253, pp. 36–51, 2004.

logic, and Stochastic Petri nets [19] (PN), an operational paradigm aimed at performance and dependability evaluation. A multi-formalism approach during the dependability process is also advocated by emerging standards like IEC 60300 [4].

Class Diagrams are the "entry level" in the methodology that provides a set of predefined CDs for the automation system domain, called "the *generic* scheme", and guidelines on how to produce from it an *instantiated* one, that refers to the target application. Diagrams are meant as a support for the requirements collection and/or for structuring and/or reviewing for completeness already available requirements. In DepAuDE we have studied how the information available in the scheme can be used as a starting point for the modelling efforts with TRIO and SPN. The role of Stochastic Petri nets in the DepAuDE approach is to evaluate the reliability of the candidate dependability strategies [7, 1], while in this paper we discuss the role of TRIO and its links to the CDs.

TRIO is a linear temporal logic that finds its origins in the nineties as a joint effort of Politecnico di Milano and ENEL as a formal declarative language for real-time systems. Since then several TRIO dialects and validation tools have been prototyped (e.g., [18], [10]) and used in several projects. We use Modular TRIO Language [3] and a tool set developed in the FAST project[3], implemented over the Prover Kernel [9].

In DepAuDE TRIO has been used *for specifying and analysing dependability requirements and fault tolerance strategies in a temporal logic framework*. The choice of a declarative language, and in particular a logic formalism like TRIO, has been driven by the analysis methods followed at CESI, where TRIO is a common practise for system analysis of timed properties. Other choices are indeed possible, like that of using an operational formalism using extended State-charts, as proposed, for example in the embedded system field, in [14]: the advantages and disadvantages of operational versus declarative formalisms are well established, and we shall not discuss them here.

The work on CDs and TRIO in DepAuDE takes its basis from the preliminary work in [11], in which the first ideas on the use of CD in the context of dependability analysis of automation systems and the possibilities of cooperation of TRIO specification with CD models were discussed. The work presented in this paper represents a step forward, by introducing a three steps incremental specification: the *derivation* of the TRIO specification structure from the UML Class Diagrams, a *first completion* of the specification with domain dependent knowledge and the *full formalisation* with application dependent knowledge. Goal of this three steps procedure is to provide the user with a more structured approach to the construction of logic specifications, and to allow reuse of partial specifications.

This paper describes the three steps and demonstrate their efficacy through the PSAS case study. Due to space constraints, the paper concentrates the analysis only on timing properties, while the complete case study can be found in [7].

The paper is structured as follows. Section 2 recalls the language TRIO and its analysis capability, Sect. 3 summarizes the CD scheme proposed in DepAuDE, Sect. 4 introduces the three steps procedure and its application to the PSAS, while Sect. 5 discuss the analysis methodology with examples from the PSAS.

---

[3] ESPRIT FAST Project No. 25581 (Integrating Formal Approaches to Specification, Test case generation and automatic design verification).

## 2   Basic TRIO Methodology

A TRIO specification is structured into classes, and each class includes a declaration session followed by a formulae session. The declaration session defines the signature of TRIO items (atomic propositions, predicates, values and functions), which are grouped into Time Independent (TI) and Time Dependent (TD) items, and the types for the value domains of predicates, values and functions.

TRIO formulae are expressed in a temporal logic language that supports a linear notion of *discrete* time. Beyond the *propositional operators* and, or, xor, implies, iff (&, |, ||, $\rightarrow$, $\leftrightarrow$ in TRIO syntax) and the *quantifiers* $\exists, \forall, \nexists$ (*all, ex, nex* in TRIO), TRIO formulae can be composed using the *primitive* temporal operator *Dist*, and *derived* temporal operators. *Dist* allows to refer to events occurring in the future or in the past with respect to the current, implicit time instant. If $F$ is a TRIO formula and $\delta$ is a term of time type, then $Dist(F, \delta)$ is satisfied at the current time instant if and only if $F$ holds at the instant laying $\delta$ time units ahead (or behind if t is negative) the current one. Derived temporal operators can be defined from *Dist* through propositional composition and first order quantification on variables representing a time distance [3]. The intuitive semantic of the operators used in this paper is as follows: $\mathbf{Alw}(F)$ ( $F$ is always true), $\mathbf{AlwF}(F)$ ( $F$ will be always true in the future), $\mathbf{AlwP}(F)$ ($F$ has been always true in the past), $\mathbf{Becomes}(F)$ ( $F$ is true now and it was false in the instant immediately preceding the current one), $\mathbf{NextTime}(F, \delta)$ ($F$ will become true exactly at $\delta$ time and from now till that instant it will be false). TRIO is linear and time is implicit: all properties refer to a single execution observed at the current time.

The formulae session may include: *definitions, axioms, properties* and *Abstract Test Cases (ATC)*: they are all temporal logic formulae, but they play a different role in the analysis. *Definitions* are a macro-expansion mechanism, *axioms* express system requirements (the description of the system), *properties* express requirements that have to be derivable from the set of axioms (the system properties of interest), and *ATC* are formulae compatible with the axioms that are used to focus the analysis on relevant, more restricted, contexts (a particular behavior of the system).

The TRIO tool supports automatic proof sessions based on three proof techniques: *model generation, property proof*, and *test case generation*. Model generation produces a set of temporal logic models (called TRIO histories) for the selected properties: a model is graphically represented by a set of up/down functions plotting the truth value of a Time Dependent (TD) proposition/predicate on the time line. Property proof computes the validity of a property. If the property is not valid then counter models are produced. Test case generation allows the automatic generation of a set of test cases according to a number of testing criteria. The analysis requires the setup of the "proof session" to specify the portion of the specification to be used for the proof, the choice of the proof technique, and the setting of the time interval considered.

## 3   UML Class Diagrams for Automation Systems

The DepAuDE "generic scheme" consists of a set of UML Class Diagrams (CDs) capturing generic issues considered relevant for a wide class of dependable automation

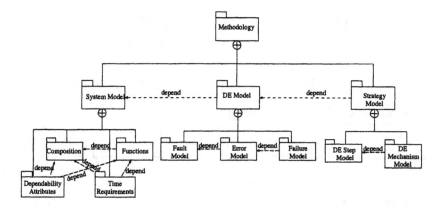

**Fig. 1.** Hierarchical Structure of the packages.

applications. From the generic scheme, an instantiation activity (described in [2]) allows to derive an instantiated CD scheme, that specifies a given application (system description and associated dependability requirements).

The set of CDs are grouped into the hierarchical structure of UML *packages* represented in Fig. 1, where each non-leaf package encapsulates a set of inner packages together with their dependency relationships, that indicates a suggested order of use. For each innermost package one or more CDs are provided that constitute different *views* on the system being described, focusing on aggregation, generalization/specialization, and class definition (associations and attributes) aspects of a portion of the system. In the scheme the class attributes are stereotyped to represent either parameters provided as input to the specifications or measures to be evaluated or upper/lower bounds to be validated. Let us now provide an overview of the scheme, following Fig. 1.

**System Model** addresses the system requirements. It specifies 1) the conceptual structure of an automation system ; 2) the association of automation functions to system components; 3) the association of (real) time requirements to system components and/or functions; and, finally, 4) the association of dependability attributes to system components and/or functions. The CDs that are most relevant for the presented case study are the CD *Structure* in which the whole automated system is decomposed into automation sites connected by an automation communication infrastructure. An automation system residing on a given site is defined as an aggregation of automation components and of automation functions. An automation component may control directly a (set of) plant components through association *control*. The CD *Constraints* allows to identify those temporal attributes which are considered relevant for the specification of automation systems, such as *cycle_time* that refers to the time required by the automation system to execute a complete cycle (i.e., read a sample input from the plant, elaborate to produce the future state and provide output to the plant). The attribute *cycle_time* is defined as a bound to be validated in the generic CD, and as a specific value (100ms) on the instantiated CD.

Figure 2(C) shows a very small portion of the CD that describes the PSAS automation system, made of three Automation Components and with two relevant attributes.

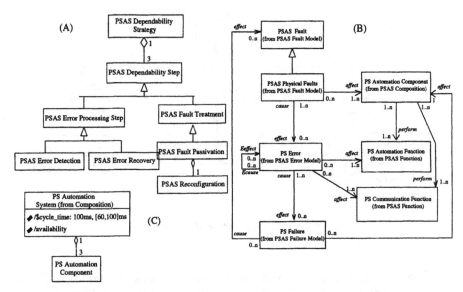

**Fig. 2.** View of the instantiated CD *Strategy* (A) *FEF chain* (B), and *Strategy* (C).

**Dynamic Environment Model.** The package *DE Model* captures several concepts on the fault theory expressed in the literature [16], and its extension to malicious faults, as developed by the European MAFTIA project [24] and partially modified upon CESI experience. It contains three sub-packages (*Fault Model, Error Model* and *Failure Model*) each one characterizing a different view of a fault evolution, from its appearance to its recovery and/or repair. The CDs are connected so as to reflect the propagation effect linking faults to errors and errors to failures (FEF chain).

Once customized on a specific application, the CD of the FEF chain shows which faults provoke which errors and which (set of) errors provoke a failure. The diagram also connects each type of fault, error and failure with the corresponding system components affected by it: a fault may affect an automation component (elaboration, memory or communication unit), and an error may affect an automation function performed by the faulty component. If a function is affected by an error, the error can be propagated to another function thus provoking an error in another function. If errors are not recovered in due time failures may appear. The FEF chain for the PSAS is given in Fig. 2.(B).

**Strategy Model.** This package concerns the representation of the dependability strategy. A dependability strategy is defined as an aggregation of (temporal) steps in which actions have to be undertaken in order to stop the fault evolution. The *Dependability Step* CD supports a classification of those steps and connects them to the fault, error, and failure elements addressed by the step. The PSAS strategy consists of three steps: an error detection followed by an attempt of error recovery and, eventually, a system reconfiguration: the correspondent CD is shown in Fig. 2.(A).

## 4   TRIO Scheme in DepAuDE

The TRIO formalization is aimed at describing and analyzing the logic of a dependability strategy following the requirements collected and structured according to the

UML scheme. The analysis concerns the temporal evolution of an automation system integrating a dependability strategy. The TRIO specification is built incrementally, and each partial specification is validated by several proof sessions.

In the DepAuDE Methodology the TRIO formalisation of dependability requirements is an extension of their representation in UML Class Diagrams. The relation between UML class diagrams and TRIO forms is a partial one: only a subset of the UML class attributes and associations is related with elements of the TRIO scheme and, vice-versa, which is not surprising since the two formalisms play quite different roles in the development of a system. In particular, TRIO classes introduce new time relationships, which are not present in the correspondent CDs.

The approach used to develop a TRIO specification is a *three-steps* procedure. The first step consists of deriving a basic TRIO specification structure, using a set of predefined actions that are applied using information from the instantiated UML scheme (Sect. 4.1). In the second step, domain specific knowledge is introduced leading to partially defined classes that include item declarations and formulae of general usage (Sect. 4.2). In the third step the specification is completed using application dependent knowledge and design level information (Sect. 4.3).

## 4.1   Deriving the Skeleton of the TRIO Scheme from UML Class Diagrams

As a starting point a number of syntactic links have been identified between CDs elements and TRIO elements:

**L1**  Reuse of the structured organization into classes;

**L2**  The objects instances of UML classes are mapped into TRIO types;

**L3**  Class attributes are mapped into TRIO time (in)dependent items;

**L4**  The value of a class attribute is mapped into a TRIO axiom, if the value is unique, or into a TRIO type, otherwise;

**L5**  Associations are mapped into TRIO time (in)dependent predicates and axioms;

**L6**  UML constraints are mapped into TRIO properties.

Each first level package of the UML Dependability Scheme given in Fig. 1 maps to a TRIO class, leading to a TRIO Scheme with three classes: *System, Dynamic Environment* and *Strategy*. In this paper we only provide a partial derivation for the three classes: their full description can be found in [7].

The construction of the classes is described through a set of numbered *actions* that we have defined following the information available in the generic scheme, and that can be applied by the modeller on the specific application using the information available in the instantiated scheme. In the following we present a few examples of actions (again the full set is in [7]), where the numbering respects the original one in [7], for ease of reference, and their application to the PSAS case.

*Derivation of the class System.*  **Sys_Action 1:** in the CD *Structure* the class *Automation System* is composed of a set of *Automation Component* $C_i$. This set is represented as the domain type *Automation_Component_Set* which is an enumerative range identifying class objects (application of **L1** and **L2**). The type *Automation_Component_Set* is then used to define predicates characterising the class *Automation Component*.

**Sys_Action 2.** The attribute *cycle_time* of the UML class *Automation System* in the Class Diagram *Structure* is translated into the TRIO Time Independent (TI) value *cycle_time* taking values over the type *cycle_value* (application of **L3**). The range of values of the UML *cycle_time* attribute defines the type *cycle_value* (application of **L4**). Since a single value is also present for the UML attribute, then the axiom *cycle_time_setting* is introduced assigning that value to the item *cycle_time*. Let us now apply the previous actions to the PSAS case, by considering the set of CDs customised over the PSAS application.

**Application of Sys_Action 1.** According to the customised CD of Fig. 2(A) the PSAS system is composed of three Primary Substation Automation Components. Therefore the domain type *PS_Automation_Component_Set* is introduced which ranges over three values: N1, N2 and N3.

**Application of Sys_Action 2.** According to the instantiated CD of Fig. 2(A) the PSAS cycle_time is set to 100 ms and the range from 60 to 100 ms. Therefore the domain type *PS_cycle_value* and the TI item *cycle_time* are introduced, as well as the axiom *cycle_time_setting*. Fig. 3 shows the partial specification of the class *System* for the PSAS obtained by applying all the actions.

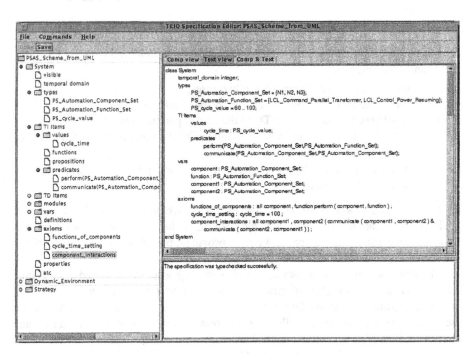

**Fig. 3.** Skeleton of the PSAS System class.

*Derivation of the class DE.* For what concern the class DE, 9 actions have been defined to specify faults, errors, failures, propagation in the FEF chain and relationship with the affected system elements. As an example we present here only those relative to faults and to their propagation into errors.

**DE_Action 1 and its application.** Enumerative types should be introduced for specifying the possible types of faults, errors, and failure. The application of this action for faults, using the information from the *Fault* model in the PSAS instantiated CDs leads to the enumerative type *PS_Fault_Categories* = { *perm_physical, temp_physical* }.

**DE_Action 2, 3 and their application.** These actions relate FEF elements to system elements, following the information of the *affect* CD association, and require to introduce three TI predicates with associated axioms to formalize the predicate. For faults the predicate is called *fault_affect_component (Fault_Categories, Automation_Component_Set)*, and its application to the PSAS leads to the predicate *fault_affect_component (PS_Fault_Categories, PS_Automation_Component_Set)*. Assuming *component* is a variable of
*PS_Automation_Component_Set* type, the axiom is:

fault_model:   **all** component
        (fault_affect_component(perm_physical, component) &
        fault_affect_component(temp_physical, component));

**DE_Action 7.** The axiom *error_causes* is introduced: it traces back to the cause-effect association in the CD of the FEF chain. An error can be directly caused by a fault, or by the propagation of an error. The axiom states that, at a given instant, an error can affect *function1* performed by component1 if some *t* time units before a fault occurred (a fault of a type that can affect *component1*), or if some *t* time units before an error occurred to a *function2* of *component2*, and *component1* and *component2* communicate (thus allowing error propagation).

error_causes:   **Alw(all** component1, function1
      ( Becomes(error(function1,component1)) $\longrightarrow$
        (( perform(component1,function1)  &
          **ex** fault_cat, t ( fault_affect_component(fault_cat,component1)  &
            Dist(Becomes(fault(fault_cat,component1),-t)))  ||
          **ex** component2, function2 (communicate(component1,component2)  &
            perform(component2,function2))  &
            **ex** t Dist(Becomes(error(function2, component2),-t))))));

*Derivation of the class Strategy.* The set of derivation actions for this class introduces a label for each dependability step in the strategy (*error_recovery, error_detection*, and *fault_treatment*), an axiom (*cycle_number*) setting the number of cycles needed to perform the whole strategy, and the property *performance* establishing the duration of the strategy in terms of *cycle_number*.

## 4.2   Completing the Skeleton with Domain Dependent Knowledge

Once the modeller has derived the TRIO skeleton, the methodology proposes a number of *completion actions*, that provide a set of pre-defined predicates and axioms pertinent to the automation system domain. The modeller will then select the actions that he consider relevant for the application, leading to an enrichment of the partial specification produced in the previous step. Again, only a subset of the actual completion steps are shown here, the full description being in [7].

**Sys_Completion1.** In a fault tolerant system, any *Automation_Component* $C_i$ may be operational or not (that is to say it is included in the current configuration). The predicate *included(C)* is therefore introduced: it is a TD predicate since a given *Automation_Component* may change its operational status over time.

**Sys_Completion2.** The axiom *cycle_boundary* is introduced: it formalises which event determines the cyclic evolution of the distributed system. If the cycle is determined by the reception of a periodic_signal, the axiom is naturally expressed by the TRIO operator **NextTime**(F,t), where F is the cycle signal, representing for instance the starting of a new cycle, and *t* is a term set equal to *cycle_time*:

cycle_boundary: **Alw**(periodic_signal_received ⟷
    **ex** cycle_t (cycle_t = cycle_time   &   **NextTime** (periodic_signal_received, cycle_t)) );

**Sys_Completion3.** The (initial, normal, abnormal) behaviour of a distributed automation system is based on message exchange protocols which are formalised by two enumerative types *Received_Messages* and *Sent_Messages* and two TD predicates: *message_received(Received_Messages, Automation_Component_Set)* and *send_message (Sent_ Messages, Automation_Component_Set)*.

**Sys_Completion4.** The axiom label *normal_behavior* is introduced which formalises what the system should do in normal conditions. The actual definition of the axiom will be done at a later stage, when considering application dependent information.

All the completion rules above are considered relevant for the PSAS case and the correspondent axioms and predicates are therefore inserted in the skeleton. This results in the (uncomplete) formalisation of the PSAS *System* class of Fig. 4.

For the completion of the class DE we have chosen to show the definition of temporary fault, that is done in terms of an attribute of faults, called *fault_duration*. A fault is temporary if, given that it occurs at the current time, it will disappear before a time $t1$ smaller than the fault duration parameter, and for all times $t2$ from the current time to $t1$ the fault is active. In TRIO terms:

temporary_faults_persistence: **Alw**(**all** component (
    **Becomes**(fault(temp_physical,component)) ⟶
        ( **ex** t1 ( t1 > 0 &  t1 < fault_duration(temp_physical) &
        **Dist**(**Becomes**(∼fault(temp_physical, component)),t1) &
        **all** t2 (t2 > 0 & t2 < t1 → **Dist**(fault(temp_physical, component),t2)))))));

For the completion of the class *Strategy* we consider the definition of the *error_detection* axiom stating that a component is faulty if there is a potential transient fault in the component, or a permanent fault has been detected.

error_detection: **Alw** ( **all** component faulty(component) ⟷
    potential_transient_fault(component) | permanent_fault_detected(component));

### 4.3   Completing the Specification with Application Dependent Knowledge

The last phase of the TRIO specification construction includes the full definition of axioms introduced only as labels in the previous phase, so as to obtain a complete (or closed) TRIO formalisation, and possibly the addition of new axioms and properties

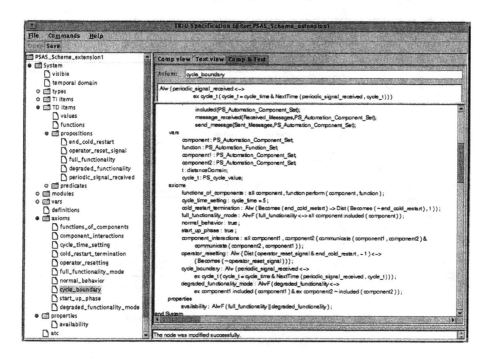

**Fig. 4.** Completion of the PSAS system class.

which are application-specific. Observe that in the first step we have already used application dependent information, but it was information readily available in the instantiated CD scheme (for example the types of faults and components), while in this final step also design level information is needed. As an example consider the following:

**(Re)application of Sys_Action2.** The application of this action in step one led to the assignment of 100 time units to the TRIO item *cycle_time* (see Fig. 3). Considering that the corresponding attribute of the CD has an assigned value of 100ms, a choice of 100 is indeed correct, but it is definitely not the most convenient one from a computational point of view. In TRIO, as in all temporal logic, it is wise to choose the coarsest possible granularity for time. By considering all the events that involve the item *cycle_time* in the design, a choice of 20ms per time unit has been considered appropriate, resulting in an assignment of 5 time units to the item, through the axiom *cycle_time_setting*.

**(Re)application of Completion2.** The definition of axiom *cycle_boundary* is modified, based on a proposition *synch_signal_received*, that represents the external synchronisation signal received by a task coordinating the activities of the *PS Components*:

cycle_boundary:  **Alw** (synch_signal_received ⟷
    **ex** cycle_t (cycle_t = cycle_time & **NextTime** (synch_signal_received, cycle_t)) );

**(Re)application of Completion4.** The normal behaviour of the PSAS is described in terms of a message exchange protocol assuring its correct and consistent evolution. On reception of each synch signal the PSAS component with the master role must receive

**Fig. 5.** Formalization of the normal behavior protocol.

an *end_cycle_OK* message from each slave component at a time *t* which is within a cycle time (**Dist**(message_ received(end_ cycle_ OK, component),t)). If the *end_cycle_OK message* is received by each component, then the master component performs a *confirm_cycle* procedure. The confirmation of the last elaborated cycle consists of sending the orders of *release_outputs* and *perform_cycle* to all the slave *Automation Components*. As formalised in Fig. 5 the order of starting elaboration on a new cycle is sent if and only if each component confirms the correct emission of its output via *released_outputs_OK* messages within 20 ms (i.e., at **Dist** equal to 1 time unit).

# 5   How to Analyze the TRIO Specification

In the previous section we have shown how the logic specification of an application in the automation domain field can be produced re-using the information present in a Class Diagram description of the application, selecting a number of predicates and axioms among a set of predefined ones, and completing the specification with application dependent knowledge made available by the system designers.

Although the construction of a specification is a relevant step in the definition of a dependable automation system, it is also very important to be able to analyze the specification: in TRIO this is realized through model generation and property proof. In this section we show a few examples of model generation. Model generation produces a timed diagram in which the truth values of the selected predicates are plotted against time, and can be considered as an abstract trace of the system execution, concentrating on the predicates of interest, while property proof amount to proving that a property is valid (that is to say, true for any model) for a given temporal window.

In order to perform the analysis of the PSAS behaviour the TRIO models consistent with the specification may be generated automatically by setting up proof sessions in which a subset of axioms, properties and ATC is selected.

For what concerns the class *System* we consider an example on analysis of the normal behaviour of the PSAS (showing its intended functionality in a fault-free setting), specified by the the the axiom *normal_behavior* of Fig. 5, and we ask TRIO to generate all models that represents an execution compatible with the axiom *normal_behavior*. This may lead to too many models: to concentrate on the most interesting ones it is necessary to restrict the focus of the analysis, using Abstract Test Cases. ATCs may be both domain dependent and application dependent. For normal behaviour model generation we concentrate on an initial state characterized by all components being operational, at the instant of time in which the synchronization signal is received (ATC 1), we consider only configurations that are stable (ATC 2) and in a scenario in which all messages are received normally (ATC 3).

(ATC 1) *normal_initialisation*: sets the initial truth-values of system primary attributes, including system configuration (predicates included). The PSAS initialisation establishes that: before the evaluation instant no *PS Automation Components* is included and the synchronization signal is false and that at the evaluation instant all the *PS Automation Components* are included and synchronization signal becomes true.
normal_initialisation:

> **AlwP**(all components ~included(components) & ~synch_signal_received ) &
> all components included (components) & synch_signal_received ;

(ATC 2) *stable_configuration*: it is used to restrict the analysis to models in which the components of the system, once included, will not be removed:
stable_configuration:  **all** components

> (included(components) $\longrightarrow$ **AlwF** (included(components)));

(ATC 3) *normal_scenario*: it focuses the generation process only on cases in which each component sends the expected messages in due time, and it chooses a specific timing for message reception. An example temporally confined to the first cycle is given by the following ATC in which all the *end_cycle_OK* messages are received at time 4 and all the *released_output_OK* messages at time 6:
normal_scenario :   **all** components

> (included( components ) $\longleftrightarrow$
>
> (**Dist**(message_received(end_cycle_OK, components), 4)  &
> **Dist** ( message_received ( released_outputs_OK , components ) , 6 ) &
> **all** t ( t <> 4 $\longleftrightarrow$ **Dist** ( ~message_received ( end_cycle_OK , components ) , t )) &
> **all** t ( t <> 6 $\longleftrightarrow$ **Dist** ( ~ message_received ( released_outputs_OK , components ) , t )))) ;

The set-up of the model generation for the normal behaviour case is done through the TRIO graphical interface. Three axioms have been selected: *normal_behavior* as expected, and *cycle_time_setting* and *cycle_boundary* that define the notion of cycle, and whose definition is given in Fig. 4. The three ATCs defined above are selected, so that only models compatible with the three axioms and the three ATCs will be generated.

At this point the TRIO tool asks for the temporal window of reference of the proof: obviously the larger the window, the more expensive is the analysis. Since with this proof we want to observe the normal behaviour of the system, and since the whole system behaviour is defined in term of cycles, it is a natural choice to choose a temporal domain size that is a multiple *n* of *cycle_time* (that is set to a *cycle_value* equal to 5 for the PSAS). For this proof a value of $n = 2$ has been chosen, leading to a temporal window of 10 time units, that allows to check the behaviour of the system upon the reception of two successive synchronization signal. In general the value of *n* should be the minimal number of cycles needed to check a certain behaviour, for example when checking a complex dependability strategy the value of *n* could be given by the system requirements (recovery has to terminate in within *k* cycle), and we can use model generation to check that this requirement is indeed met.

The model generation of TRIO produces then an execution depicted in Fig. 6: the simulation window shows the truth values over the timeline of the time dependent items of the proof that the modeller has selected for visualization. The model that has been generated corresponds to a "normal_behavior" execution in which each included component has sent an *end_cycle_OK* message, the order *released_output* has been sent to each component, the acknowledge has been received in 20 ms (one time unit) and finally the order to perform the next cycle has been sent to all components.

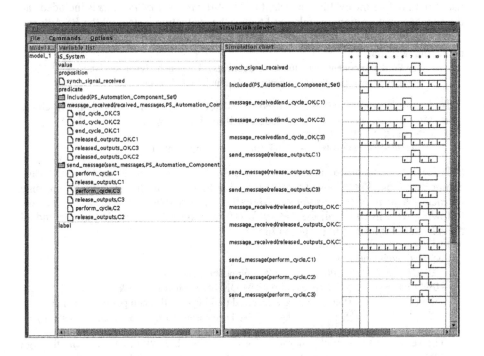

**Fig. 6.** The generated model for the normal_behavior proof.

The TRIO formalisation of the class *Dynamic Environment* allows to study the effect of faults on a system in which a dependability strategy has been deployed, while the analysis of this class together with the class *Strategy* allows to study the effectiveness of the dependability strategy in limiting the damage due to faults.

As an example we consider the case in which PSAS faults are considered (axiom *fault_model*), there is a full communication structure among components (axiom *component_interaction* defined in Fig. 4) each component can perform any function (axiom *functions_of_components* defined in Fig. 4), and the relationship between faults and errors is set according to axiom *error_causes* (defined in the previous section as a result of **DE_Action7**). Since we want to study the effect of faults we concentrate the focus of this first proof on executions that experience a single fault. The model produced (whose window is not shown here for space reasons) depicts a behaviour in which a single fault propagates to all components, and therefore to all functionalities so that the system is not able to deliver the expected service.

The analysis of this class allows therefore to make explicit the global effect of a chain of local actions (as expressed by the *communicate*, *perform*, and *cause_effect* associations that were already present on the UML CDs and that have been translated into TRIO predicates and axioms) under different fault occurence settings.

## 6   Conclusions

In this paper we have presented, with the help of a case study, a support to the specification and analysis of dependable automation systems which makes use of UML class diagrams and of the declarative temporal logic TRIO. In the context of formal analysis tools the peculiarity of TRIO lays on the possibility of analysing temporal scenarios underlying the specification in a uniform framework which makes use of the same language for both specifying and querying the system. The TRIO tool may be classified as a temporal theorem prover, like PVS is for higher order logics.

The combined use of UML with formal methods in the functional specification and analysis of software systems has received a great attention by the research community, with the goal of giving a formal semantics to the UML diagrams, usually through translation into another formal language (there is a very large body of literature on the topic, see for example the work of the Precise UML group [23]).

In this paper we do not propose a translation, but a pre-defined set of temporal logic specifications that have been associated to a pre-defined description of an automation system through a set of UML Class Diagrams. The proposed approach is meant to provide requirement reuse, a topic that, following the work on patterns [8] for design reuse, is gaining increasing interest: in [14] UML based patterns (mainly CD and Statecharts) are defined for embedded system requirements, and the work is extended in [15] to include properties specified in the linear temporal login LTL of SPIN [13].

The novelty of our contribution is in identifying a three-steps approach in which the costruction of the formal specification follows partially a derivative style, and partially a selective style. It is assumed that the analysist still needs to play an important decision role in the analysis, whilst the tool provides him with a methodological support.

The specification support provided here is three steps: the TRIO class structure and a number of initial TRIO items and types are (manually) derived from a UML CD description of the system; this partial specification is then augmented in a second step with a number of domain dependent information; while in the third step the specification is completed using application dependent knowledge. The role of the modeller increases in the three steps: in the first one he only has to apply the predefined actions by extracting information from the instantiated CD diagrams, in the second step he will have to select the subset of predicates and axioms that are considered relevant for the application, while in the third step he has to apply his expertise to define all axioms and additional predicates needed to complete the specification.

Writing TRIO formulae requires indeed a certain skill. To make the use of TRIO transparent to the user the work in [17] proposes the automatic generation of TRIO formulae from annotated UML Statecharts (in the context of real-time systems): this result could be integrated in our approach, especially when the modeller is fluent in UML Statecharts, so that certain parts of the specification can be automatically produced.

The paper also provides a (limited) support to the formal analysis, an activity which requires skill not only to define the system, but also to drive the proof sessions to avoid an explosion of complexity. The methodological lines presented in the paper represents a preliminary result: a support to the identification and definition of ATC, and to the definition of the appropriate temporal window for the analysis is an interesting topic for future research. In particular it is still to be investigated to which extent the "guided approach to specification" described in this paper can be coupled with a "guided approach to analysis". In the paper we have presented examples of analysis: analysis of a logic specification is an incremental activity, and the space limitations allows only the exemplification of limited steps of the analysis activity.

The methodological approach has been exemplified on a case study taken from control systems of electric distribution network. However, it seems reasonable to consider the proposed three steps methods applicable also to other applications in the automation system domain, given the generality of the closed loop execution model considered.

Finally, the TRIO specification has been built starting from an ad-hoc description of the dependability aspects of an automation systems. Following the work on the UML profiler for Performance and Schedulability [20] it is likely that an extension to include dependability aspects will be made available in the near future [22]: it will then be necessary to adapt the proposed CD scheme to the new standard.

# References

1. S. Bernardi and S. Donatelli. Building Petri net scenarios for dependable automation systems. In *Proc. of the 10<sup>th</sup> International Workshop on Petri Nets and Performance Models*, pages 72–81, Urbana-Champain, Illinois (USA), September 2003. IEEE CS.
2. S. Bernardi, S. Donatelli, and G. Dondossola. Methodology for the generation of the modeling scenarios starting from the requisite specifications and its application to the collected requirements. Technical report. Deliverable D1.3b - DepAuDE Project 25434, June 2002.
3. A. Bertani, E. Ciapessoni, and G. Dondossola. Modular TRIO Manual and Guidelines, Tutorial Package. Part I-II, Deliverable D3.4.1 of the FAST Project No. 25581, May 2000.
4. International Electrotechnical Commission. IEC-60300-3-1: Dependability Management. IEC, 3 rue de Varembé CH 1211 Geneva, Switzerland, 2001.
5. G. Deconinck, V. De Florio, R. Belmans, G. Dondossola, and J. Szanto. Integrating recovery strategies into a Primary Substation Automation System. In *Proc. of the International Conference on Dependable Systems and Networks (DSN'03)*, pages 80–85, San Francisco, California (USA), June 2003. IEEE Computer Society ed.

6. DepAuDE. EEC-IST project 2000-25434. http://www.depaude.org.
7. G. Dondossola. Dependability requirements in the development of wide-scale distributed automation systems: a methodological guidance. Technical report. Deliverable D1.4 - DepAuDE IST Project 25434, February 2003.
8. Gamma E. et al. *Design Patterns: Elements of Reusable Object-Oriented Software*. Addison-Wesley, 1995.
9. The FAST toolkit homepage. http://www.prover.com/fast.
10. M. Felder and A. Morzenti. Validating real-time systems by history-checking trio specifications. *ACM Trans. Softw. Eng. Methodol.*, 3(4):308–339, October 1994.
11. Dondossola G. and Botti O. System fault tolerance specification: Proposal of a method combining semi-formal and formal approaches. In *Fundamental Approaches to Software Engineering, FASE 2000*, volume 1783, pages 82–96. Springer, January 2000.
12. C. Ghezzi, D. Mandrioli, and A. Morzenti. TRIO: a logic language for executable specifications of real-time systems. *Journal of Systems and Software*, 12(2):107–123, May 1990.
13. J. Gerard Holzmann. *SPIN Model Checker: the Primer and Reference Manual*. Addison Wesley Professional, 2004.
14. S. Konrad and B.H.C. Cheng. Requirements Patterns for Embedded Systems. In *In Proc. of the Joint International Conference on Requirements Engineering (RE02)*, Essen, Germany, September 2002. IEEE CS.
15. Sascha Konrad, Laura A. Campbell, and Betty H. C. Cheng. Adding formal specifications to requirements patterns. In C. Heitmeyer and N. Mead, editors, *Proceedings of the IEEE Requirements for High Assurance Systems (RHAS02)*, Essen, Germany, September 2002.
16. J. C. Laprie. Dependability – Its attributes, impairments and means. In B. Randell, J.C. Laprie, H. Kopetz, and B. Littlewood, editors, *Predictably Dependable Computing Systems*, pages 3–24. Springer Verlag, 1995.
17. L. Lavazza, G. Quaroni, and M. Venturelli. Combining UML and formal notations for modelling real-time systems. In *Proc. of the 8th European software engineering conference held jointly with 9th ACM SIGSOFT Int. symposium on Foundations of software engineering*, pages 196–206, Vienna, Austria, 2001. ACM Press.
18. D. Mandrioli, S. Morasca, and A. Morzenti. Generating test cases for real-time systems from logic specifications. *ACM Trans. Comput. Syst.*, 13(4):365–398, November 1995.
19. M.K. Molloy. Performance analysis using Stochastic Petri Nets. *IEEE Transaction on Computers*, 31(9):913–917, September 1982.
20. OMG. UML Profile for Schedulability, Performance, and Time Specification. http://www.omg.org, March 2002.
21. OMG. UML Specification: version 1.5. http://www.omg.org, March 2003.
22. A. Pataricza. From the General Ressource Model to a General Fault Modeling Paradigm ? In J. Jürjens, M.V. Cengarle, E.B. Fernandez, B. Rumpe, and R. Sandner, editors, *Critical Systems Development with UML – Proceedings of the UML'02 workshop*, pages 163–170. Technische Universität München, Institut für Informatik, 2002.
23. The Precise UML Group. http://www.puml.org.
24. The European MAFTIA Project. Web page: http://www.research.ec.org/maftia.

# On Two-Sided Approximate Model-Checking: Problem Formulation and Solution via Finite Topologies*

Jennifer M. Davoren[1], Thomas Moor[2], R.P. Goré[3],
Vaughan Coulthard[3,1], and Anil Nerode[4]

[1] Department of Electrical & Electronic Engineering
The University of Melbourne, VIC 3010, Australia
davoren@unimelb.edu.au
[2] Lehrstuhl für Regelungstechnik
Friedrich-Alexander-Universität, Erlangen D-91058, Germany
thomas.moor@rt.eei.uni-erlangen.de
[3] Computer Sciences Laboratory, RSISE
The Australian National University, Canberra ACT 0200, Australia
vaughan@discus.anu.edu.au
[4] Department of Mathematics Cornell University, Ithaca NY 14853, USA
anil@math.cornell.edu

**Abstract.** We give a general formulation of *approximate model-checking*, in which both under- and over-approximations are propagated to give two-sided approximations of the denotation set of an arbitrarily complex formula. As our specification language, we use the *modal $\mu$-calculus*, since it subsumes standard linear and branching temporal logics over transition systems like **LTL**, **CTL** and **CTL***. We give a general construction of a *topological finite approximation scheme* for a Kripke model from a state-space discretization via an A/D-map and its induced finite topology. We further show that under natural *coherence conditions*, any finite approximation scheme can be refined by a topological one.

## 1 Introduction

It is now well established that exact symbolic model-checking of modal and/or temporal logic formulas in transition system models of hybrid and real-time systems is not computationally possible (recursively solvable) except when restricted to some tightly constrained sub-classes of systems. Given these limitations on exactness, a good deal of current research in formal methods for hybrid and real-time systems is devoted to developing algorithms for approximations of various backwards and forwards reachability operators on sets arising from differential inclusions and equations. Such approximations are typically based on

* Research support from Aust. Research Council, Grants DP0208553, LX0242359. We thank Bryn Humberstone at Univ. of Melbourne for many valuable discussions.

Y. Lakhnech and S. Yovine (Eds.): FORMATS/FTRTFT 2004, LNCS 3253, pp. 52–67, 2004.
© Springer-Verlag Berlin Heidelberg 2004

a discretization of the state space by a finite partition or cover, e.g. consisting of a regular array of rectangular boxes, or of convex polyhedra or ellipsoids. Recent contributions focus attention on application relevant classes of reachability relations and include algorithms for the efficient computation of over-approximations of sets of reachable states [1–3, 8, 10].

For example, in seeking to verify a safety property of a hybrid system model, such as expressed by "*From given initial conditions, the system never reaches a danger state*", one can use an *over-approximation* of the true reach-set and its disjointness from the danger states to conclude "*definitely YES*" to the verification question. Now suppose instead that one is asking *control* questions, such as "*From which set of states can the system be steered to reach a given target region, and up until then, always remain within designated safe states?*" Here, a guaranteed *under-approximation* of this backwards reachability set will let us identify a set of states of which we can answer "*definitely YES*" to this controllability question, with respect to the particular dynamics of the steered system.

In this paper, we address the task of giving *two-sided approximate evaluations* of the denotation set $[\![\varphi]\!]^{\mathcal{M}} \subseteq X$ of a logic formula $\varphi$, where $[\![\varphi]\!]^{\mathcal{M}}$ is the set of all states of a Kripke model $\mathcal{M}$ at which $\varphi$ is satisfied – with $\mathcal{M} = (X, R, v)$, $X$ the state space, $R \subseteq X \times X$ the transition relation, and $v : P \to 2^X$ a valuation of atomic propositions $p \in P$ as subsets of $X$. We consider the general problem of constructing maps $Un^{\mathcal{M}}$ and $Ov^{\mathcal{M}}$ which, when applied to a formula $\varphi$, return explicit computable descriptions of subsets of $X$ with the property that $Un^{\mathcal{M}}(\varphi) \subseteq [\![\varphi]\!]^{\mathcal{M}} \subseteq Ov^{\mathcal{M}}(\varphi)$. As our specification language, we take the *modal $\mu$-calculus*, since all the standard linear and branching temporal logics interpreted over transition systems (**LTL**, and **CTL** and **CTL***, respectively) are subsumed by the $\mu$-calculus. We actually work with the *tense logic* extension, with modal operators for both the one-step future and past along the transition relation, as both constructs naturally rise in control and verification problems.

Building on the foundations of Cousot and Cousot's *abstract interpretation* [5], questions of approximation and abstraction for model-checking of large but finite state systems have been addressed by Grumberg and colleagues in [4, 6, 12]. In the recent [12], they develop a framework for abstraction using three-valued semantics, working say with $\mathbb{T} := \{\text{yes}, \text{no}, \text{indf}\}$ (the latter abbreviating "*indefinite*"); working over bi-relational "must-may" Kripke models $\mathcal{M}$, they give a disjoint pair of affirmation and refutation denotation sets $[\![\varphi]\!]^{\mathcal{M}}_{\text{yes}} \subseteq X$ and $[\![\varphi]\!]^{\mathcal{M}}_{\text{no}} \subseteq X$ such that $[\![\varphi]\!]^{\mathcal{M}}_{\text{yes}} \cap [\![\varphi]\!]^{\mathcal{M}}_{\text{no}} = \varnothing$, and take $[\![\varphi]\!]^{\mathcal{M}}_{\text{indf}} = X - ([\![\varphi]\!]^{\mathcal{M}}_{\text{yes}} \cup [\![\varphi]\!]^{\mathcal{M}}_{\text{no}})$. As we discuss below, the basic framework in [12] gives rise to a particular solution to our problem of two-sided approximate model-checking: given a standard Kripke model $\mathcal{M}$ that is abstracted under a suitable *mixed simulation relation* by a bi-relational "must-may" Kripke model $\mathcal{N}$, an under-approximation set $Un^{\mathcal{M}}(\varphi)$ can be obtained from $[\![\varphi]\!]^{\mathcal{N}}_{\text{yes}}$ and an over-approximation set $Ov^{\mathcal{M}}(\varphi)$ can be obtained from the set-complement of $[\![\varphi]\!]^{\mathcal{N}}_{\text{no}}$. The main results in [4, 6, 12] all assume that one has available an explicit first-order description of the true transition relation $R$ on the concrete model $\mathcal{M}$, with exact point-wise knowledge of $R$. While these are reasonable assumptions for the very large but still finite state systems considered in these papers, they are quite restrictive in the setting of hybrid and real-time systems.

Technically, we develop a simple set-theoretic notion of a *finite approximation scheme* (f.a.s.) for $\mu$-calculus formulas interpreted in a Kripke model, and establish the naturalness of our notion by showing that a model has a maximally refined f.a.s. if and only if it has a finite bisimulation quotient. We then give a general construction of an f.a.s. for a Kripke model from the topology generated from a finite cover or discretization of the state space under an A/D-map. In contrast to [4, 6, 12], we do not assume exact point-wise knowledge of the concrete transition relation $R$ in order to construct approximations of the modal/tense operators; instead, we make do with a weaker assumption of having under- and over-approximations of the $R$-reachability (post-image) operator applied to the cells of the A/D map, which fits much better with current algorithms for approximating sets of reachable states in papers such as [1–3, 10]. We conclude the paper by proving a comprehensiveness result that every f.a.s. satisfying natural coherence conditions can be refined to give a topological f.a.s..

*Structure of paper:* Section 2 contains preliminaries from mathematics and logic. In Section 3, we formulate a general notion of a finite approximation scheme, and of refinements of schemes. Section 4 gives the basics of covers, A/D maps, and their Alexandroff topologies. The main results are in Section 5, and Section 6 gives a brief summary and discussion.

## 2   Preliminaries

### 2.1   Mathematical Preliminaries

We write $r : X \rightsquigarrow Y$ to mean both that $r : X \rightarrow 2^Y$ is a *set-valued map*, with (possibly empty) set-values $r(x) \subseteq Y$ for each $x \in X$, and equivalently, that $r \subseteq X \times Y$ is a *relation*. (Total and single-valued) functions $r : X \rightarrow Y$ are a special case of set-valued maps. We write $r^{-1} : Y \rightsquigarrow X$ for the relational inverse/converse; $dom(r) := \{x \in X \mid r(x) \neq \varnothing\}$ and $ran(r) := dom(r^{-1})$. For maps $r_1 : X \rightsquigarrow Y$ and $r_2 : Y \rightsquigarrow Z$, we write their relational composition as $r_1 \bullet r_2 : X \rightsquigarrow Z$ given by $(r_1 \bullet r_2)(x) := \{z \in Z \mid (\exists y \in Y)\,[y \in r_1(x) \wedge z \in r_2(y)]\}$, in sequential left-to-right application order.

A relation $r : X \rightsquigarrow Y$ determines two *pre-image operators* (predicate transformers): the *existential* pre-image function $r^{-\exists} : 2^Y \rightarrow 2^X$ and the set-theoretic dual *universal* pre-image $r^{-\forall} : 2^Y \rightarrow 2^X$. Formally,

$$r^{-\exists}(W) := \{x \in X \mid W \cap r(x) \neq \varnothing\}$$
$$r^{-\forall}(W) := X - r^{-\exists}(Y - W) = \{x \in X \mid r(x) \subseteq W\}$$

for $W \subseteq Y$. The corresponding adjoint pair of *post-image operators* $r^\forall, r^\exists : 2^X \rightarrow 2^Y$ are given by $r^\forall := (r^{-1})^{-\forall}$ and $r^\exists := (r^{-1})^{-\exists}$, respectively. The adjoint relationships are: $r^{-\exists}(W) \subseteq V$ iff $W \subseteq r^\forall(V)$ and $r^\exists(V) \subseteq W$ iff $V \subseteq r^{-\forall}(W)$, for all $V \subseteq X$ and $W \subseteq Y$.

Recall that a *topology* $\mathcal{T} \subseteq 2^X$ on a set $X$ is a family of subsets of $X$ that is closed under arbitrary unions and finite intersections. So $\mathcal{T}$ is a distributive lattice of sets. The *interior operator* $int_\mathcal{T} : 2^X \rightarrow 2^X$ determined by $\mathcal{T}$ is given by $int_\mathcal{T}(W) := \bigcup \{U \in \mathcal{T} \mid U \subseteq W\}$. Sets $W \in \mathcal{T}$ are called *open* w.r.t. $\mathcal{T}$, and this is so iff $W = int_\mathcal{T}(W)$. A sub-family of open sets $\mathcal{B} \subseteq \mathcal{T}$ constitutes a *basis* for the topology $\mathcal{T}$ on $X$ if every open set $W \in \mathcal{T}$ is a union of basic opens in $\mathcal{B}$, and for every $x \in X$ and every pair of basic opens $U_1, U_2 \in \mathcal{B}$ such that $x \in U_1 \cap U_2$, there exists $U_3 \in \mathcal{B}$ such that $x \in U_3 \subseteq (U_1 \cap U_2)$.

A topology $\mathcal{T}$ on $X$ is called Alexandroff if for every $x \in X$, there is a *smallest* open set $U \in \mathcal{T}$ such that $x \in U$. In particular, every *finite* topology (i.e. only finitely many open sets) is Alexandroff. There is a one-to-one correspondence between pre-orders on $X$ and Alexandroff topologies on $X$. Any pre-order $\preccurlyeq$ on $X$ induces an Alexandroff topology $\mathcal{T}_\preccurlyeq$ by taking $int_{\mathcal{T}_\preccurlyeq}(W) := (\preccurlyeq)^{-\forall}(W)$, which means $U \in \mathcal{T}_\preccurlyeq$ iff $U$ is upwards-$\preccurlyeq$-closed, and $V$ is closed in $\mathcal{T}_\preccurlyeq$ iff $V$ is downwards-$\preccurlyeq$-closed, and $cl_{\mathcal{T}_\preccurlyeq}(W) = (\preccurlyeq)^{-\exists}(W)$. Conversely, for any topology, define a pre-order $\preccurlyeq_\mathcal{T}$ on $X$, known as the *specialisation pre-order*: $x \preccurlyeq_\mathcal{T} y$ iff $(\forall U \in \mathcal{T})[x \in U \Rightarrow y \in U]$. For any pre-order, $\preccurlyeq_{\mathcal{T}_\preccurlyeq} = \preccurlyeq$, and for any topology, $\mathcal{T}_{\preccurlyeq_\mathcal{T}} = \mathcal{T}$ iff $\mathcal{T}$ is Alexandroff.

Given two topological spaces $(X, \mathcal{T})$ and $(Y, \mathcal{S})$, a relation $R : X \rightsquigarrow Y$ is called: *lower semi-continuous* (l.s.c.) if for every $\mathcal{S}$-open set $U$ in $Y$, $R^{-\exists}(U)$ is $\mathcal{T}$-open in $X$; *upper semi-continuous* (u.s.c.) if for every $\mathcal{S}$-open set $U$ in $Y$, $R^{-\forall}(U)$ is $\mathcal{T}$-open in $X$; and *continuous* if it is both l.s.c. and u.s.c. [9].

## 2.2 Logic Preliminaries: Syntax

Fix a finite set $P$ of atomic propositions, and let *Var* be a countable set of propositional variables. Let $\mathcal{F}_\mu^t(P)$ be the $\mu$-calculus (fixed-point) language generated by the grammar:

$$\varphi ::= p \mid z \mid \bot \mid \top \mid \neg\varphi \mid \varphi_1 \vee \varphi_2 \mid \varphi_1 \wedge \varphi_2 \mid \Diamond\varphi \mid \blacklozenge\varphi \mid \mu z.\varphi$$

where $p \in P$, $z \in Var$, and a least fixed-point formula $\mu z.\varphi$ is well-formed only when every occurrence of the variable $z$ within $\varphi$ occurs within the scope of an even number of negations. A formula $\varphi$ is a *sentence* of the language $\mathcal{F}_\mu^t(P)$ if every occurrence of a propositional variable in $\varphi$ is bound by (within the scope of) a fixed-point operator $\mu$; let $\mathcal{L}_\mu^t(P)$ denote the set of all such sentences.

The superscript $^t$ indicates our use of *tense logic*, with the temporally dual *future* and *past* modal diamond operators $\Diamond$ and $\blacklozenge$ operators, respectively, and their negation-dual box operators $\Box\varphi := \neg\Diamond\neg\varphi$ and $\blacksquare\varphi := \neg\blacklozenge\neg\varphi$. A formula $\Diamond\varphi$ is read "*At some state in the future, $\varphi$ will hold*", while $\blacklozenge\varphi$ is read "*At some state in the past, $\varphi$ has held*".

For formulas $\varphi, \psi \in \mathcal{F}^t(P)$, and propositions $p \in P$, we write $\varphi[p := \psi]$ to mean the formula resulting from the simultaneous substitution of $\psi$ for each occurrence of $p$ in $\varphi$. Likewise, for propositional variables $z \in Var$, we write $\varphi[z := \psi]$ to mean the formula resulting from the simultaneous substitution of $\psi$ for each occurrence of $z$ in $\varphi$ that is not bound by a $\mu$, and with preliminary renaming of any occurrences of $z$ in $\psi$ that are bound by a $\mu$. The $\mu$ operator is a *least* fixed-point constructor, and its dual *greatest* fixed-point constructor $\nu$ is defined by $\nu z.\varphi := \neg\mu z.\neg\varphi[z := \neg z]$.

## 2.3   Logic Preliminaries: Semantics

A *Kripke model* for the language $\mathcal{F}_\mu^t(P)$ is a structure $\mathcal{M} = (X, R, v)$, where $X$ is any non-empty set, $R : X \rightsquigarrow X$ is a binary relation, and $v : P \rightsquigarrow X$ is a set-valued map (atomic valuation). A *variable assignment* in $\mathcal{M}$ is a set-valued map $\xi : Var \rightsquigarrow X$. A model $\mathcal{M}$ and a variable assignment $\xi$ together determine the (classical, two-valued) *denotation map* $[\![\,\cdot\,]\!]_\xi^\mathcal{M} : \mathcal{F}_\mu^t(P) \rightsquigarrow X$, defined by induction on formulas:

$$[\![\, p \,]\!]_\xi^\mathcal{M} := v(p) \qquad\qquad [\![\, z \,]\!]_\xi^\mathcal{M} := \xi(z)$$
$$[\![\, \bot \,]\!]_\xi^\mathcal{M} := \varnothing \qquad\qquad [\![\, \top \,]\!]_\xi^\mathcal{M} := X$$
$$[\![\, \neg\varphi \,]\!]_\xi^\mathcal{M} := X - [\![\, \varphi \,]\!]_\xi^\mathcal{M}$$
$$[\![\, \varphi_1 \vee \varphi_2 \,]\!]_\xi^\mathcal{M} := [\![\, \varphi_1 \,]\!]_\xi^\mathcal{M} \cup [\![\, \varphi_2 \,]\!]_\xi^\mathcal{M} \qquad [\![\, \varphi_1 \wedge \varphi_2 \,]\!]_\xi^\mathcal{M} := [\![\, \varphi_1 \,]\!]_\xi^\mathcal{M} \cap [\![\, \varphi_2 \,]\!]_\xi^\mathcal{M}$$
$$[\![\, \Diamond\varphi \,]\!]_\xi^\mathcal{M} := R^{-\exists}([\![\, \varphi \,]\!]_\xi^\mathcal{M}) \qquad\qquad [\![\, \blacklozenge\varphi \,]\!]_\xi^\mathcal{M} := R^\exists([\![\, \varphi \,]\!]_\xi^\mathcal{M})$$
$$[\![\, \mu z.\varphi \,]\!]_\xi^\mathcal{M} := \bigcap \{ W \in 2^X \mid [\![\, \varphi \,]\!]_{\xi[z/W]}^\mathcal{M} \subseteq W \}$$

where $\xi[z/W]$ is the assignment that is the same as $\xi$ except for assigning the set $W$ to the variable $z$. For sentences $\varphi \in \mathcal{L}_\mu^t(P)$, the denotation set is independent of the variable assignment: $[\![\, \varphi \,]\!]_{\xi_1}^\mathcal{M} = [\![\, \varphi \,]\!]_{\xi_2}^\mathcal{M}$ for any two assignments $\xi_1, \xi_2 : Var \rightsquigarrow X$. Thus a model determines a (sentence) denotation map $[\![\,\cdot\,]\!]^\mathcal{M} : \mathcal{L}_\mu^t(P) \rightsquigarrow X$ by $[\![\, \varphi \,]\!]^\mathcal{M} := [\![\, \varphi \,]\!]_\xi^\mathcal{M}$ for any assignment $\xi$. A sentence $\varphi \in \mathcal{L}_\mu^t(P)$ is *true* (respectively, *satisfiable*) in a model $\mathcal{M}$ if $[\![\, \varphi \,]\!]^\mathcal{M} = X$ (respectively, $[\![\, \varphi \,]\!]^\mathcal{M} \neq \varnothing$).

Let $\mathcal{M} = (X, R, v)$ and $\mathcal{N} = (Z, S, u)$ be two Kripke models for the tense language $\mathcal{F}_\mu^t(P)$. A relation $h : X \rightsquigarrow Z$ constitutes a *simulation* (respectively, *tense simulation*) of model $\mathcal{M}$ by model $\mathcal{N}$ if:

-  the set inclusion $h^\exists(v(p)) \subseteq u(p)$ holds for each $p \in P$, and
-  the relational inclusion $(h^{-1} \bullet R) \subseteq (S \bullet h^{-1})$ holds (respectively, the relational inclusion $(R \bullet h) \subseteq (h \bullet S)$ also holds).

A relation $h : X \rightsquigarrow Z$ is a *bisimulation* (respectively, *tense bisimulation*) between models $\mathcal{M}$ and $\mathcal{N}$ if $h : X \rightsquigarrow Z$ is a simulation (respectively, tense simulation) of $\mathcal{M}$ by $\mathcal{N}$, and additionally $h^{-1} : Z \rightsquigarrow X$ is a simulation (respectively, tense simulation) of $\mathcal{N}$ by $\mathcal{M}$. In particular, for a single model $\mathcal{M} = (X, R, v)$, if $h$ is an equivalence relation on $X$, then $h$ is a tense bisimulation between $\mathcal{M}$ and itself iff for each equivalence class $V$ of $h$, both $R^{-\exists}(V)$ and $R^\exists(V)$ are (possibly empty) unions of $h$-equivalence classes, and for each atomic $p \in P$, the set $v(p)$ is a (possibly empty) union of $h$-equivalence classes.

## 2.4   Logic Preliminaries: Three-Valued Semantics

Let $\mathbb{T} := \{\mathsf{yes}, \mathsf{no}, \mathsf{indf}\}$ denote a set of three values, with partial order $\trianglelefteq$ defined by $\mathsf{indf} \trianglelefteq \omega$ and $\omega \trianglelefteq \omega$ for all $\omega \in \mathbb{T}$. A *three-valued must-may Kripke model* (in [7, 12], a *Kripke modal transition system* or *KMTS*) for the language $\mathcal{F}_\mu^t(P)$ is a structure $\mathcal{M} = (X, R_{\mathsf{must}}, R_{\mathsf{may}}, v_{\mathsf{yes}}, v_{\mathsf{no}})$, where $X$ is any non-empty set, $R_{\mathsf{must}}$ and $R_{\mathsf{may}}$ are two binary relations on $X$ with $R_{\mathsf{must}} \subseteq R_{\mathsf{may}}$, and $v_{\mathsf{yes}}, v_{\mathsf{no}} : P \rightsquigarrow X$ are atomic valuations such that $v_{\mathsf{yes}}(p) \cap v_{\mathsf{no}}(p) = \varnothing$. A (standard)

Kipke model $\mathcal{M} = (X, R, v)$ can be viewed as a three-valued must-may Kripke model in which $R = R_{\text{must}} = R_{\text{may}}$ and $v(p) = v_{\text{yes}}(p) = X - v_{\text{no}}(p)$. A three-valued Kripke model $\mathcal{M}$ naturally determines two standard Kripke models $\mathcal{M}_{un} := (X, R_{\text{must}}, v_{\text{yes}})$ where $v_{un}(p) := v_{\text{yes}}(p)$, and $\mathcal{M}_{ov} := (X, R_{\text{may}}, v_{ov})$ where $v_{ov}(p) := X - v_{\text{no}}(p)$, for all atomic $p \in P$.

Extending [12], §2.2, a three-valued must-may Kripke model $\mathcal{M}$ determines three sentence denotation maps $[\![ \cdot ]\!]^{\mathcal{M}}_{\omega} : \mathcal{L}^{\text{t}}_{\mu}(P) \rightsquigarrow X$, one for each of the three values $\omega \in \mathbb{T}$, defined by induction on sentences:

$$[\![ p ]\!]^{\mathcal{M}}_{\text{yes}} := v_{\text{yes}}(p) \qquad\qquad [\![ p ]\!]^{\mathcal{M}}_{\text{no}} := v_{\text{no}}(p)$$

$$[\![ \bot ]\!]^{\mathcal{M}}_{\text{yes}} = [\![ \top ]\!]^{\mathcal{M}}_{\text{no}} := \varnothing \qquad\qquad [\![ \top ]\!]^{\mathcal{M}}_{\text{yes}} = [\![ \bot ]\!]^{\mathcal{M}}_{\text{no}} := X$$

$$[\![ \neg\varphi ]\!]^{\mathcal{M}}_{\text{yes}} := [\![ \varphi ]\!]^{\mathcal{M}}_{\text{no}} \qquad\qquad [\![ \neg\varphi ]\!]^{\mathcal{M}}_{\text{no}} := [\![ \varphi ]\!]^{\mathcal{M}}_{\text{yes}}$$

$$[\![ \varphi_1 \vee \varphi_2 ]\!]^{\mathcal{M}}_{\text{yes}} := [\![ \varphi_1 ]\!]^{\mathcal{M}}_{\text{yes}} \cup [\![ \varphi_2 ]\!]^{\mathcal{M}}_{\text{yes}} \qquad [\![ \varphi_1 \vee \varphi_2 ]\!]^{\mathcal{M}}_{\text{no}} := [\![ \varphi_1 ]\!]^{\mathcal{M}}_{\text{no}} \cap [\![ \varphi_2 ]\!]^{\mathcal{M}}_{\text{no}}$$

$$[\![ \varphi_1 \wedge \varphi_2 ]\!]^{\mathcal{M}}_{\text{yes}} := [\![ \varphi_1 ]\!]^{\mathcal{M}}_{\text{yes}} \cap [\![ \varphi_2 ]\!]^{\mathcal{M}}_{\text{yes}} \qquad [\![ \varphi_1 \wedge \varphi_2 ]\!]^{\mathcal{M}}_{\text{no}} := [\![ \varphi_1 ]\!]^{\mathcal{M}}_{\text{no}} \cup [\![ \varphi_2 ]\!]^{\mathcal{M}}_{\text{no}}$$

$$[\![ \Diamond\varphi ]\!]^{\mathcal{M}}_{\text{yes}} := R^{-\exists}_{\text{must}}([\![ \varphi ]\!]^{\mathcal{M}}_{\text{yes}}) \qquad\qquad [\![ \Diamond\varphi ]\!]^{\mathcal{M}}_{\text{no}} := R^{-\forall}_{\text{may}}([\![ \varphi ]\!]^{\mathcal{M}}_{\text{no}})$$

$$[\![ \blacklozenge\varphi ]\!]^{\mathcal{M}}_{\text{yes}} := R^{\exists}_{\text{must}}([\![ \varphi ]\!]^{\mathcal{M}}_{\text{yes}}) \qquad\qquad [\![ \blacklozenge\varphi ]\!]^{\mathcal{M}}_{\text{no}} := R^{\forall}_{\text{may}}([\![ \varphi ]\!]^{\mathcal{M}}_{\text{no}})$$

$$[\![ \mu z.\varphi ]\!]^{\mathcal{M}}_{\text{yes}} := \bigcup_{\lambda < \eta_{\mathcal{M}}} W^{(\lambda)} \qquad\qquad [\![ \mu z.\varphi ]\!]^{\mathcal{M}}_{\text{no}} := \bigcap_{\lambda < \eta_{\mathcal{M}}} V^{(\lambda)}$$

and $[\![ \varphi ]\!]^{\mathcal{M}}_{\text{indf}} := X - ([\![ \varphi ]\!]^{\mathcal{M}}_{\text{yes}} \cup [\![ \varphi ]\!]^{\mathcal{M}}_{\text{no}})$ for all sentences $\varphi \in \mathcal{L}^{\text{t}}_{\mu}(P)$. For the fixed-point constructor, one appeals as in [12] to the alternative iterative formulation of the Tarski fixed-point theorem for monotone operators on a complete lattice. The iteration bound $\eta_{\mathcal{M}}$ is the ordinal of the cardinality of $2^X$; the affirming iteration sets $W^{(\lambda)}$ are defined by $W^{(0)} := \varnothing$, and $W^{(\eta)} := \bigcup_{\lambda < \eta} W^{(\lambda)}$ for limit ordinals $\eta \le \eta_{\mathcal{M}}$, and for successor ordinals, $W^{(\lambda+1)} := ([\![ \varphi ]\!]^{\mathcal{M}}_{\text{yes}})_{\xi}$, where $\xi$ is any variable assignment such that $\xi(z) = W^{(\lambda)}$ ($z$ is the *sole* free variable in $\varphi$). The refuting iteration sets $V^{(\lambda)}$ are defined by $V^{(0)} := X$, and $V^{(\eta)} := \bigcap_{\lambda < \eta} V^{(\lambda)}$ for limit ordinals $\eta \le \eta_{\mathcal{M}}$, and for successor ordinals, $V^{(\lambda+1)} := ([\![ \widetilde{\varphi} ]\!]^{\mathcal{M}}_{\text{no}})_{\xi}$, where $\xi$ is any assignment such that $\xi(z) = V^{(\lambda)}$ and $\widetilde{\varphi} := \neg\varphi[z := \neg z]$.

Let $\mathcal{M} = (X, R_{\text{must}}, R_{\text{may}}, v_{\text{yes}}, v_{\text{no}})$ and $\mathcal{N} = (Z, S_{\text{must}}, S_{\text{may}}, u_{\text{yes}}, u_{\text{no}})$ be three-valued must-may Kripke models. A relation $h : X \rightsquigarrow Z$ is a *mixed simulation* (respectively, *mixed tense simulation*) of model $\mathcal{M}$ by model $\mathcal{N}$, or model $\mathcal{N}$ is a *three-valued abstraction* of $\mathcal{M}$ under $h$ [7,12] if: (a) $h : X \rightsquigarrow Z$ is a simulation (respectively, tense simulation) of $\mathcal{M}_{ov}$ by $\mathcal{N}_{ov}$; and (b) $h^{-1} : Z \rightsquigarrow X$ is a simulation (respectively, tense simulation) of $\mathcal{N}_{un}$ by $\mathcal{M}_{un}$. In particular, if $\mathcal{M} = (X, R, v)$ is a standard Kripke model, and $\mathcal{N}$ is a three-valued abstraction of $\mathcal{M}$ under mixed tense simulation $h : X \rightsquigarrow Z$, then for each $p \in P$, we have the two-sided approximation inclusions $h^{-\exists}(u_{\text{yes}}(p) \subseteq v(p) \subseteq h^{-\forall}(Z - v_{\text{no}}(p))$ for the atomic denotation sets $v(p)$ in the concrete model $\mathcal{M}$. Consequently, it follows by induction on sentences that if $\mathcal{N}$ is a *finite* three-valued abstraction of $\mathcal{M}$ under $h$, then for all $\mu$-calculus sentences $\varphi \in \mathcal{L}^{\text{t}}_{\mu}(P)$, we have:

$$h^{-\exists}([\![ \varphi ]\!]^{\mathcal{N}}_{\text{yes}}) \subseteq [\![ \varphi ]\!]^{\mathcal{M}} \subseteq h^{-\forall}(Z - [\![ \varphi ]\!]^{\mathcal{N}}_{\text{no}}) \qquad\qquad (1)$$

## 3   Finite Approximation Schemes for Model-Checking

We begin by developing a generic notion of a *scheme* for approximate evaluation of $[\![\varphi]\!]^{\mathcal{M}}$ which makes central the task of fulfilling the two-sided approximation inclusions.

**Definition 1.** [Schemes for approximate model-checking]
*Given a Kripke model $\mathcal{M} = (X, R, v)$ for the language $\mathcal{F}_\mu^t(P)$ generated from a finite set $P$ of atomic propositions, a finite approximation scheme (f.a.s.) for $\mathcal{M}$ over $P$ is a pair of structures $\Sigma = (\Sigma_{un}, \Sigma_{ov})$ with $\Sigma_{un} = (\mathcal{A}_{un}, \mathbf{un}, k_{un})$ and $\Sigma_{ov} = (\mathcal{A}_{ov}, \mathbf{ov}, k_{ov})$, where $\mathcal{A}_{un}$ and $\mathcal{A}_{ov}$ are non-empty finite sets, and the functions $\mathbf{un} : \mathcal{L}_\mu^t(P) \to \mathcal{A}_{un}$ and $k_{un} : \mathcal{A}_{un} \to 2^X$, and $\mathbf{ov} : \mathcal{L}_\mu^t(P) \to \mathcal{A}_{ov}$ and $k_{ov} : \mathcal{A}_{ov} \to 2^X$, are such that for all sentences $\varphi \in \mathcal{L}_\mu^t(P)$:*

$$k_{un}\,(\mathbf{un}(\varphi)) \ \subseteq \ [\![\varphi]\!]^{\mathcal{M}} \ \subseteq \ k_{ov}\,(\mathbf{ov}(\varphi)) \tag{2}$$

The following diagram indicates the types of the maps (but it is not a commutative diagram):

$$\mathcal{A}_{un} \xrightarrow{\ k_{un} \ \subseteq\ } 2^X \xleftarrow{\ \subseteq\ k_{ov}\ } \mathcal{A}_{ov}$$
$$\mathbf{un} \searrow \quad \downarrow [\![\cdot]\!]^{\mathcal{M}} \quad \swarrow \mathbf{ov}$$
$$\mathcal{L}_\mu^t(P)$$

The idea is that elements $a \in \mathcal{A}_{un}$ or $a \in \mathcal{A}_{ov}$ are *abstract* or *symbolic* representatives for state sets $W \subseteq X$, and the *concretization* maps $k_{un} : \mathcal{A}_{un} \to 2^X$ and $k_{ov} : \mathcal{A}_{ov} \to 2^X$ realize or decode the abstract representation. The propositional and modal operators on sentences should be semantically interpreted via $\mathbf{un}$ and $\mathbf{ov}$ by functions on the finite sets $\mathcal{A}_{un}$ or $\mathcal{A}_{ov}$. More specifically, these functions should constitute the semantics of computer programs implementing specific approximation algorithms for the various operators/functions on $2^X$: the Boolean set-theoretic operations and the relational pre-/post-image operators $R^{-\exists}, R^{\exists} : 2^X \to 2^X$, and the least fixed points of $\subseteq$-monotone operators $F : 2^X \to 2^X$ built up from them.

Note that, as for the work on abstraction via three-valued must-may models in [7,12], our two-sided approach of giving both under- and over-approximation values does provide substantial information about the unknown or unknowable denotation set $[\![\varphi]\!]^{\mathcal{M}}$. When we have values for both $k_{ov}\,(\mathbf{ov}(\varphi))$ and $k_{un}\,(\mathbf{un}(\varphi))$ from an f.a.s. $\Sigma$, then we know the true set $[\![\varphi]\!]^{\mathcal{M}}$ lies somewhere in between, and the set difference $k_{ov}\,(\mathbf{ov}(\varphi)) - k_{un}\,(\mathbf{un}(\varphi))$ is the set of all states in $X$ at which the sentence $\varphi$ does not have a determinate truth value under $\Sigma$. In contrast, if one has only a one-sided approximation scheme returning values $Over([\![\varphi]\!]^{\mathcal{M}})$ and satisfying the single inclusion $[\![\varphi]\!]^{\mathcal{M}} \subseteq Over([\![\varphi]\!]^{\mathcal{M}})$, then one has no further knowledge of accuracy when, *prima facie*, the exact set $[\![\varphi]\!]^{\mathcal{M}}$ is not known.

Clearly, there are better and worse approximation schemes, where the natural notion of "better" for a scheme is to return set values closer to that of the exact denotation set. We also identify further desirable properties of schemes, such as a scheme $\Sigma$ behaving "reasonably" or "coherently".

**Definition 2.** *Given two finite approximation schemes* $\Sigma^1 = (\Sigma^1_{un}, \Sigma^1_{ov})$ *and* $\Sigma^2 = (\Sigma^2_{un}, \Sigma^2_{ov})$ *for a model* $\mathcal{M}$ *over* $P$, *we say that* $\Sigma^2$ *is a* refinement *of* $\Sigma^1$, *and we write* $\Sigma^1 \leqslant \Sigma^2$, *if for all sentences* $\varphi \in \mathcal{L}^t_\mu(P)$:

$$k^1_{un}\left(\mathbf{un}^1(\varphi)\right) \subseteq k^2_{un}\left(\mathbf{un}^2(\varphi)\right) \subseteq [\![\varphi]\!]^\mathcal{M} \subseteq k^2_{ov}\left(\mathbf{ov}^2(\varphi)\right) \subseteq k^1_{ov}\left(\mathbf{ov}^1(\varphi)\right)$$

*A refinement is* proper, *written* $\Sigma^1 < \Sigma^2$, *if for some sentence* $\varphi \in \mathcal{L}^t_\mu(P)$, *either* $k^1_{un}\left(\mathbf{un}^1(\varphi)\right) \subset k^2_{un}\left(\mathbf{un}^2(\varphi)\right)$, *or* $k^2_{ov}\left(\mathbf{ov}^2(\varphi)\right) \subset k^1_{ov}\left(\mathbf{ov}^1(\varphi)\right)$.
*Two f.a. schemes* $\Sigma^1$ *and* $\Sigma^2$ *will be called* bijectively equivalent *if there exist two bijective functions* $f_{un} : ran(\mathbf{un}^1) \to ran(\mathbf{un}^2)$ *and* $f_{ov} : ran(\mathbf{ov}^1) \to ran(\mathbf{ov}^2)$, *such that for all* $\varphi \in \mathcal{L}^t_\mu(P)$, $k^1_{un}\left(\mathbf{un}^1(\varphi)\right) = k^2_{un}\left(f_{un}(\mathbf{un}^1(\varphi))\right)$, $k^2_{un}\left(\mathbf{un}^2(\varphi)\right) = k^1_{un}\left(f^{-1}_{un}(\mathbf{un}^2(\varphi))\right)$, $k^1_{ov}\left(\mathbf{ov}^1(\varphi)\right) = k^2_{ov}\left(f_{ov}(\mathbf{ov}^1(\varphi))\right)$, *and* $k^2_{ov}\left(\mathbf{ov}^2(\varphi)\right) = k^1_{ov}\left(f^{-1}_{ov}(\mathbf{ov}^2(\varphi))\right)$.
*An f.a.s.* $\Sigma$ *is* non-degenerate *if both* $\mathcal{A}_{un}$ *and* $\mathcal{A}_{ov}$ *have at least two elements, and* $\mathbf{un}(\top) \neq \mathbf{un}(\bot)$ *and* $\mathbf{ov}(\top) \neq \mathbf{ov}(\bot)$. *A non-degenerate f.a.s.* $\Sigma$ *is:*
–   trivial *if both* $\mathcal{A}_{un}$ *and* $\mathcal{A}_{ov}$ *have exactly two elements;*
–   extremal-coherent *if* $k_{un}\left(\mathbf{un}(\top)\right) = X$, *and* $k_{ov}\left(\mathbf{ov}(\bot)\right) = \varnothing$;
–   full *if* $ran(\mathbf{un}) = \mathcal{A}_{un}$ *and* $ran(\mathbf{ov}) = \mathcal{A}_{ov}$;
–   substitution-coherent *if for all sentences* $\varphi, \psi_1, \psi_2 \in \mathcal{L}^t_\mu(P)$, *and all* $p \in P$,
    *if* $\mathbf{un}(\psi_1) = \mathbf{un}(\psi_2)$ *then* $\mathbf{un}\left(\varphi[p := \psi_1]\right) = \mathbf{un}\left(\varphi[p := \psi_2]\right)$, *and*
    *if* $\mathbf{ov}(\psi_1) = \mathbf{ov}(\psi_2)$ *then* $\mathbf{ov}\left(\varphi[p := \psi_1]\right) = \mathbf{ov}\left(\varphi[p := \psi_2]\right)$;
–   exact *if* $k_{un}\left(\mathbf{un}(\varphi)\right) = [\![\varphi]\!]^\mathcal{M} = k_{ov}\left(\mathbf{ov}(\varphi)\right)$, *for all sentences* $\varphi \in \mathcal{L}^t_\mu(P)$.
*Henceforth, we will treat as equal any two schemes that are bijectively equivalent. Let* FAS($\mathcal{M}, P$) *denote the set of all extremal-coherent and substitution-coherent f.a.s. for* $\mathcal{M}$ *over* $P$.

The refinement relation $\leqslant$ defines a partial order on the set FAS($\mathcal{M}, P$), under our standing convention of identifying bijectively equivalent schemes. There is a unique trivial f.a.s. $\Sigma_\varnothing$ that is non-degenerate, extremal-coherent, full, and substitution-coherent: each of $\mathcal{A}_{un}$ and $\mathcal{A}_{ov}$ have exactly two elements, and take $\mathbf{un}(\varphi) = \mathbf{un}(\bot)$ for all sentences $\varphi \neq \top$; $\mathbf{ov}(\varphi) = \mathbf{ov}(\top)$ for all sentences $\varphi \neq \bot$; $k_{un}\left(\mathbf{un}(\bot)\right) = \varnothing = k_{ov}\left(\mathbf{ov}(\bot)\right)$; and $k_{un}\left(\mathbf{un}(\top)\right) = X = k_{ov}\left(\mathbf{ov}(\top)\right)$. This scheme $\Sigma_\varnothing$ is the $\leqslant$-minimal element of the set FAS($\mathcal{M}, P$).

Regarding $\leqslant$-maximal schemes in FAS($\mathcal{M}, P$), it is intuitively plausible that any scheme short of exact can always be further refined. The following result confirms the intuition: having an exact scheme is equivalent to having a finite bisimulation quotient.

**Proposition 1.** *For a model* $\mathcal{M}$ *over* $P$, *the following are equivalent:*
(a.)   *there is an* $\leqslant$-maximal scheme in FAS($\mathcal{M}, P$);
(b.)   *there is an exact scheme in* FAS($\mathcal{M}, P$);
(c.)   $\mathcal{M}$ *has a finite tense bisimulation quotient.*

So for infinite models $\mathcal{M}$ that don't have finite bisimulation quotients, there will no maximal schemes in FAS($\mathcal{M}, P$) under the refinement partial order $\leqslant$. This is a typical situation for hybrid systems and real-time systems, where the state-space is the product of a finite set and a real vector space.

As noted in the introduction, and developed in Section 2.4 leading to Equation 1, abstraction via three-valued must-may Kripke models in [12,7] naturally gives rise to a finite approximation scheme.

**Proposition 2.** *If $Z$ is a finite set, and $\mathcal{N} = (Z, S_{\text{must}}, S_{\text{may}}, u_{\text{yes}}, u_{\text{no}})$ is a three-valued must-may Kripke model that gives an abstraction of a standard Kripke model $\mathcal{M} = (X, R, v)$ under map $h : X \rightsquigarrow Z$, then $\Sigma^{\mathcal{N}}$ is in $\mathsf{FAS}(\mathcal{M}, P)$, where $\Sigma^{\mathcal{N}} := (\Sigma_{un}^{\mathcal{N}}, \Sigma_{ov}^{\mathcal{N}})$ with $\Sigma_{un}^{\mathcal{N}} = (\mathcal{A}_{un}, \mathbf{un}, k_{un})$ and $\Sigma_{ov}^{\mathcal{N}} = (\mathcal{A}_{ov}, \mathbf{ov}, k_{ov})$, where: $\mathbf{un}(\varphi) := [\![ \varphi ]\!]_{\text{yes}}^{\mathcal{N}}$, and $\mathbf{ov}(\varphi) := X - [\![ \varphi ]\!]_{\text{no}}^{\mathcal{N}}$; $\mathcal{A}_{un} := ran(\mathbf{un}) \subseteq 2^Z$ and $\mathcal{A}_{ov} := ran(\mathbf{ov}) \subseteq 2^Z$; and $k_{un} := h^{-\exists}$ and $k_{ov} := h^{-\forall}$.*

In the remainder of the paper, we focus on finite approximation schemes that arise from *finite topologies* $\mathcal{T}$ on the state space $X$ of the target concrete model $\mathcal{M}$. We say that $\Sigma \in \mathsf{FAS}(\mathcal{M}, P)$ is *topological* with respect to a topology $\mathcal{T}$ on $X$ if for each sentence $\varphi \in \mathcal{L}_\mu^t(P)$, the set $k_{un}(\mathbf{un}(\varphi))$ is $\mathcal{T}$-open, and $k_{un}(\mathbf{un}(\varphi)) \subseteq int_{\mathcal{T}}([\![ \varphi ]\!]^{\mathcal{M}})$, and on the other side, $k_{ov}(\mathbf{ov}(\varphi))$ is $\mathcal{T}$-closed, and $cl_{\mathcal{T}}([\![ \varphi ]\!]^{\mathcal{M}}) \subseteq k_{ov}(\mathbf{ov}(\varphi))$.

# 4 Covers, A/D Maps and Their Alexandroff Topologies

An initial study of covers, A/D maps (*analog-to-digital* maps) and their topologies was made by Nerode and Kohn in [11]. In this section, we build on that work to develop just enough of the general topology of A/D maps and their Alexandroff spaces for use in addressing the task of building approximation schemes.

**Definition 3.** *A cover of a set $X$ is any total relation $\alpha: X \rightsquigarrow S$. We call $S$ the index set or observation set of the cover. The cells of $\alpha$ are the subsets $\alpha^{-1}(s)$ of $X$; define $\mathsf{Cells}(\alpha) := \{\alpha^{-1}(s) \in 2^X \mid s \in ran(\alpha)\}$. Let $\mathcal{T}_\alpha$ be the topology generated by $\alpha$, i.e. the smallest subset of $2^X$ containing $\mathsf{Cells}(\alpha)$ and closed under arbitrary unions and finite intersections.*

The totality condition on $\alpha$ ensures that $X = \bigcup_{s \in S} \alpha^{-1}(s)$, so the cells of $\alpha$ do constitute a *cover* of $X$ in the usual sense. In general, the $\alpha$-cells constitute a *sub-basis* for the topology $\mathcal{T}_\alpha$; i.e. every open set is a union of finite intersections of $\alpha$-cells. In the special case where $\alpha: X \to S$ is actually a function, then $\alpha$ can be thinned, by eliminating any excess elements of $S$, to give a surjective quotient map. In this case, the $\alpha$-cells constitute a partition of $X$, and we have the "classical collapse" of $\mathcal{T}_\alpha$ to a complete Boolean algebra.

**Definition 4.** *Given covers $\alpha: X \rightsquigarrow S$ and $\beta: X \rightsquigarrow T$, we say $\alpha$ is refined by $\beta$, and write $\alpha \leqslant \beta$ if there exists a map $\theta: S \rightsquigarrow T$ such that $\alpha = \beta \bullet \theta^{-1}$.*

This means $\alpha \leqslant \beta$ iff each $\alpha$-cell indexed by $s \in ran(\alpha)$ breaks up into a union of $\beta$-cells indexed by $t \in \theta(s)$: $\alpha^{-1}(s) = \bigcup\{\beta^{-1}(t) \mid t \in \theta(s)\}$. Thus $\alpha \leqslant \beta$ iff $\mathcal{T}_\alpha \subseteq \mathcal{T}_\beta$. The transfer map $\theta$ describes how each cell/observation $s$ of the original $\alpha$ is broken up into a union of $\beta$ cells or converted into a set of observations $\theta(s) \subseteq T$. So $\beta$ allows us to make at least as many distinctions between states in $X$, as does $\alpha$.

The refinement relation $\leqslant$ is a *pre-order* on the collection (proper class) of all covers of $X$. One can have *equi-refinements* $\alpha \leqslant \beta$ and $\beta \leqslant \alpha$ for distinct covers $\alpha \colon X \rightsquigarrow S$ and $\beta \colon X \rightsquigarrow T$, related by transfer maps $\theta_0 : S \rightsquigarrow T$ and $\theta_1 : T \rightsquigarrow S$ such that $\alpha = \alpha \bullet \theta_1^{-1} \bullet \theta_0^{-1}$ and $\beta = \beta \bullet \theta_0^{-1} \bullet \theta_1^{-1}$, and having the same topology $T_\alpha = T_\beta$ on $X$.

For any cover $\alpha$, we can find a minimally coarse refinement $\alpha'$ such that $T_\alpha = T_{\alpha'}$ and the $\alpha'$-cells constitute a basis for the topology $T_\alpha$: take the closure under non-empty finite intersections of the family $\mathsf{Cells}(\alpha)$. In our application to finite discretization and approximation, our interest is in *finite* covers: if $\mathsf{Cells}(\alpha)$ has finite cardinality $k$, then for such a topological refinement $\alpha'$, the cardinality of $\mathsf{Cells}(\alpha')$ is bounded by $2^k - 1$, and the cardinality of $T_\alpha = T_{\alpha'}$ is bounded by $2^{2^k-1}$.

**Definition 5.** *An A/D map on a set $X$ is a cover $\alpha : X \rightsquigarrow \mathbb{N}$ such that the converse map $\alpha^{-1}$ is injective and the family $\mathsf{Cells}(\alpha)$ is finite and constitutes a minimal basis for the topology $T_\alpha$. Let $Z_\alpha := ran(\alpha) \subset \mathbb{N}$ be the finite range and let $A := \alpha^{-1} : \mathbb{N} \rightsquigarrow X$ denote the converse map, so $A(z) \subseteq X$ is the $\alpha$-cell indexed by $z \in Z_\alpha$. Let $\mathsf{ADmap}(X)$ denote the set of all A/D maps on $X$.*

An A/D map $\alpha$ determines a topology $T_\alpha$ on $X$ that has only a finite number of open sets, and is thus Alexandroff. Further clarifying the definition, by *minimal basis* we mean that any proper sub-family of $\mathsf{Cells}(\alpha)$ fails to constitute a basis for $T_\alpha$, which implies that no $\alpha$-cell $A(z)$ is the union of two or more strictly smaller open sets of $T_\alpha$. To see this, suppose otherwise, so $A(z) = U_1 \cup U_2$ where $U_1, U_2 \in T_\alpha$ are both proper subsets of $A(z)$. Since $\mathsf{Cells}(\alpha)$ is a basis, each $U_i$ is a union of basic opens in $\mathsf{Cells}(\alpha)$. But then $\mathsf{Cells}(\alpha) - \{A(z)\}$ will be a proper sub-family constituting a basis for $T_\alpha$, contradicting the minimality of $\mathsf{Cells}(\alpha)$ as a basis. In particular, no $\alpha$-cell is *disconnected*, by being a disjoint union of two smaller open sets of $T_\alpha$. The requirement that $A = \alpha^{-1}$ be injective simply means that there is no redundancy in $Z_\alpha$: $z \neq w$ implies $A(z) \neq A(w)$.

A pair of maps $\alpha, \beta \in \mathsf{ADmap}(X)$ are equi-refinements $\alpha \leqslant \beta$ and $\beta \leqslant \alpha$ iff there exists a bijective function $\tau : Z_\alpha \to Z_\beta$ such that $A(z) = B(\tau(z))$ and $B(w) = A(\tau^{-1}(w))$ for all $z \in Z_\alpha$ and $w \in Z_\beta$. Hence we can consider the set $\mathsf{ADmap}(X)$ to be *partially ordered* by the refinement relation $\leqslant$, up to re-labeling of cell indices via bijective functions.

In signal processing, analog-to-digital conversion is almost invariably modeled by a finite partition of the analog state space. This gives single-valued and total functions $\alpha : X \to \mathbb{N}$ with finite range, where the $\alpha$-cells are partition blocks (and so will trivially form a minimal basis for the Boolean algebra $T_\alpha$). One of the arguments in [11] is that in looking for *continuity* in the process of analog-to-digital conversion, one won't find it in the Euclidean topology on the analog state space, so look instead at the finite topology on that space generated by the cells of an A/D map. The definition of an A/D map here is essentially equivalent to that in [11], which also briefly considers the non-finite case; there, a *generalized A/D map* has as its cells the fully join-irreducible elements in the lattice of open sets of an Alexandroff topology, which is equivalent to requiring the cells form a minimal basis.

For $\alpha \in \mathsf{ADmap}(X)$, we will write $\preccurlyeq_\alpha$ and $\approx_\alpha$, respectively, for the pre-order $\preccurlyeq_{\mathcal{T}_\alpha}$ on $X$, and equivalence relation $\approx_{\mathcal{T}_\alpha} := (\preccurlyeq_{\mathcal{T}_\alpha} \cap \succcurlyeq_{\mathcal{T}_\alpha})$ on $X$ determined by $\mathcal{T}_\alpha$. We will also write $int_\alpha$ and $cl_\alpha$ for $int_{\mathcal{T}_\alpha}$ and $cl_{\mathcal{T}_\alpha}$. Let $s_\alpha : X \to X/\!\approx_\alpha$ be the Stone $T_0$ quotient map $s_\alpha(x) := [x]_{\approx_\alpha}$ mapping $x$ to its topological equivalence class $[x]_{\approx_\alpha} \subseteq X$. The following result gives clean characterizations of the $\approx_\alpha$-classes, and of the topological operators $int_\alpha$ and $cl_\alpha$.

**Proposition 3.** *Let $\alpha : X \rightsquigarrow Z_\alpha$ be any non-trivial A/D map on $X$.*

*(1.) The function $F : X/\!\approx_\alpha \to Z_\alpha$ defined by*

$$F(s_\alpha(x)) = z \quad \text{iff} \quad s_\alpha(x) = A(z) - \bigcup\{\, A(w) \mid A(w) \subset A(z)\,\}$$

*is a bijection, hence the function $q_\alpha : X \to Z_\alpha$ defined by $q_\alpha(x) := F(s_\alpha(x))$ is surjective. Let $Q_\alpha := q_\alpha^{-1} : Z_\alpha \rightsquigarrow X$ denote the converse map. Then for all $z \in Z_\alpha$, we have $Q_\alpha(z) \subseteq A(z)$, and $Q_\alpha(z)$ is the $\approx_\alpha$ partition block with the property that $x \in Q_\alpha(z)$ iff $A(z)$ is the smallest $\alpha$-cell containing $x$.*

*(2.) The finite quotient space $(Z_\alpha, \mathcal{T}_q)$ under the surjection $q_\alpha : X \to Z_\alpha$ from $(X, \mathcal{T}_\alpha)$ has as its specialization pre-order $z \sqsubseteq w$ iff $A(w) \subseteq A(z)$.*

*(3.) For each $z \in Z_\alpha$, the $\alpha$-cell $A(z)$ satisfies $A(z) = \bigcup\{\, Q_\alpha(w) \mid z \sqsubseteq w\,\}$; equivalently, $\alpha = \sqsubseteq \bullet q_\alpha$ and $A = Q_\alpha \bullet \sqsupseteq$.*

*(4.) The topological operators of $\mathcal{T}_\alpha$ are expressible in terms of unions of $\approx_\alpha$ equivalence classes. Specifically, for subsets $W \subseteq X$:*

$$int_\alpha(W) = \bigcup\{\, Q_\alpha(z) \mid A(z) \subseteq W\,\}$$

$$cl_\alpha(W) = \bigcup\{\, Q_\alpha(z) \mid A(z) \cap W \neq \varnothing\,\} \tag{3}$$

$$bd_\alpha(W) = \bigcup\{\, Q_\alpha(z) \mid A(z) \cap W \neq \varnothing \text{ and } A(z) \cap (X - W) \neq \varnothing\,\}$$

*(5.) The maps have the following semi-continuity properties respect to $(X, \mathcal{T}_\alpha)$ and $(Z_\alpha, \mathcal{T}_q)$:*
  - *$q_\alpha : X \to Z_\alpha$ is both l.s.c. and u.s.c., and a continuous function;*
  - *$Q_\alpha = q_\alpha^{-1} : Z_\alpha \rightsquigarrow X$ is both l.s.c. and u.s.c., and thus continuous;*
  - *$\alpha : X \rightsquigarrow Z_\alpha$ is l.s.c.; and*
  - *$A = \alpha^{-1} : Z_\alpha \rightsquigarrow X$ is u.s.c.*

In Figure 1, we illustrate an A/D map $\alpha$ on a bounded region of $\mathbb{R}^2$, where the $\alpha$-cells $A(z)$ consist of the following four types of sets:

basic larger squares: $\mathbf{Sq}(i, j)$          for $i < 9$ and $j < 14$

horizontal overlaps: $\mathbf{HO}(i, j) := \mathbf{Sq}(i, j) \cap \mathbf{Sq}(i, j+1)$ for $i < 9$ and $j < 13$

vertical overlaps:    $\mathbf{VO}(i, j) := \mathbf{Sq}(i, j) \cap \mathbf{Sq}(i+1, j)$ for $i < 8$ and $j < 14$

diagonal overlaps:    $\mathbf{DO}(i, j) := \mathbf{HO}(i, j) \cap \mathbf{VO}(i, j)$    for $i < 8$ and $j < 13$

Take the index set $Z_\alpha \subset \mathbb{N}$ to be the result of some coding of pairs and pairs of pairs. For this example, $Z_\alpha$ has cardinality 459; more generally, for a regular cover $\alpha$ of a bounded region of $\mathbb{R}^2$ such as this, of size $N \times M$, the cardinality of $Z_\alpha$ will be at most $3k^2$, where $k = \max\{N, M\}$.

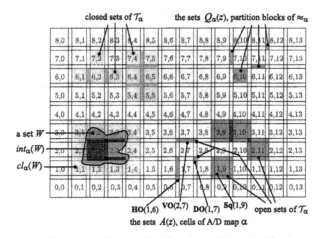

**Fig. 1.** Example of A/D map $\alpha$ from regular cover of bounded region of $\mathbb{R}^2$.

## 5   Topological f.a.s. from A/D Maps

We will use an A/D map $\alpha$ and its topology $\mathcal{T}_\alpha$ to construct a topological finite approximation scheme $\Sigma^\alpha$ for a concrete Kripke model $\mathcal{M} = (X, R, v)$. To satisfy the conditions that $k_{un}(\mathbf{un}(\varphi))$ is $\mathcal{T}_\alpha$-open and $k_{ov}(\mathbf{ov}(\varphi))$ is $\mathcal{T}_\alpha$-closed, we will need to enforce various semi-continuity properties on relations $S_{un}, S_{ov} : Z_\alpha \rightsquigarrow Z_\alpha$ used in the approximation of $R$ modal/tense operators, and need to draw on semi-continuity properties established in Proposition 3.

In what follows, we are given a model $\mathcal{M} = (X, R, v)$, and we need to have available an A/D map $\alpha \in \mathsf{ADmap}(X)$ and a pair of operators on sets $upo_\alpha, opo_\alpha : \mathsf{Cells}(\alpha) \to 2^X$ such that $upo_\alpha(A(z)) \subseteq R^\exists(A(z)) \subseteq opo_\alpha(A(z))$ for every $\alpha$-cell $A(z) \in \mathsf{Cells}(\alpha)$. Moreover, we must be able to determine by finite computation whether $A(w) \subseteq upo_\alpha(A(z))$ and whether $A(w) \cap opo_\alpha(A(z)) \neq \varnothing$. So for example, if all the cells of the A/D map as well as the approximated values of $upo_\alpha$ and $opo_\alpha$ on cells are all first-order definable in a decidable structure (such as $\mathbb{R}$ as a real-closed field), then the computational pre-conditions will be met.

**Definition 6.** *For a Kripke model $\mathcal{M} = (X, R, v)$ over $P$, a triple $(\alpha, upo_\alpha, opo_\alpha)$ will be called A/D adequate if $\alpha : X \rightsquigarrow Z_\alpha$ is a non-degenerate A/D map on $X$, and the operators on sets $upo_\alpha, opo_\alpha : \mathsf{Cells}(\alpha) \to 2^X$ satisfy:*

(i)   *for all $p \in P$, either $v(p) = \varnothing$, or there exists $z \in Z_\alpha$ such that $A(z) \subseteq v(p)$;*
(ii)   *for all $z, w \in Z_\alpha$, if $A(z) \subseteq A(w)$ (i.e. $w \sqsubseteq z$), then*
    *$upo_\alpha(A(z)) \subseteq upo_\alpha(A(w))$, and $opo_\alpha(A(z)) \subseteq opo_\alpha(A(w))$;*
(iii)   *$upo_\alpha(A(z)) \subseteq R^\exists(A(z)) \subseteq opo_\alpha(A(z))$ for every $\alpha$-cell $A(z) \in \mathsf{Cells}(\alpha)$;*
(iv)   *for all $z, z', w \in Z_\alpha$, if $A(z') \subseteq A(z)$ and $A(w) \subseteq upo_\alpha(A(z))$, then there exists $w' \in Z_\alpha$ such that $A(w') \subseteq A(w) \cap upo_\alpha(A(z'))$.*

The first adequacy condition (i) says that $\alpha$ has to be fine enough to fit a cell inside every non-empty atomic denotation set. Condition (ii) asks that the oper-

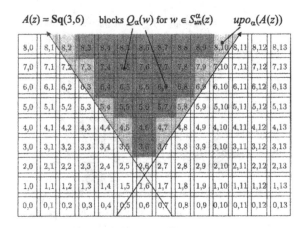

**Fig. 2.** Finite relation $S_{un}^{\alpha}$ from A/D map $\alpha$ and known operator $upo_{\alpha}$ on $\alpha$-cells.

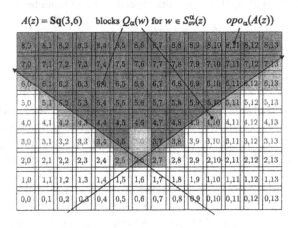

**Fig. 3.** Finite relation $S_{ov}^{\alpha}$ from A/D map $\alpha$ and known operator $opo_{\alpha}$ on $\alpha$-cells.

ators $upo_{\alpha}$ and $opo_{\alpha}$ should be inclusion-monotone on $\alpha$-cells, and (iii) requires that they give correct approximations of the post-image operator $R^{\exists}$ applied to $\alpha$-cells. Condition (iv) amounts to asking for a semi-continuity property of a relation on the finite index set $Z_{\alpha}$ derived from $upo_{\alpha}$.

**Proposition 4.** [Construction of finite approximating Kripke models]
*Given a Kripke model $\mathcal{M} = (X, R, v)$ over $P$, suppose $(\alpha, upo_{\alpha}, opo_{\alpha})$ is A/D adequate for $\mathcal{M}$. Define two finite Kripke models $\mathcal{N}_{un}^{\alpha} = (Z_{\alpha}, S_{un}^{\alpha}, u_{un})$ and $\mathcal{N}_{ov}^{\alpha} = (Z_{\alpha}, S_{ov}^{\alpha}, u_{ov})$ by:*

$$S_{un}^{\alpha}(z) := \{w \in Z_{\alpha} \mid A(w) \subseteq upo_{\alpha}(A(z))\} \quad u_{ov}(p) := \{z \in Z_{\alpha} \mid A(z) \cap v(p) \neq \varnothing\}$$

$$S_{ov}^{\alpha}(z) := \{w \in Z_{\alpha} \mid A(w) \cap opo_{\alpha}(A(z)) \neq \varnothing\} \quad u_{un}(p) := \{z \in Z_{\alpha} \mid A(z) \subseteq v(p)\}$$

*Consider the set $Z_\alpha$ equipped with the quotient topology $\mathcal{T}_{\mathrm{q}} = \mathcal{T}_{\sqsubseteq}$. Then the maps $S_{un} : Z_\alpha \rightsquigarrow Z_\alpha$ and $S_{un}^{-1} : Z_\alpha \rightsquigarrow Z_\alpha$ are both l.s.c. and each atomic set $u_{un}(p)$ is $\mathcal{T}_{\mathrm{q}}$-open, and the maps $S_{ov} : Z_\alpha \rightsquigarrow Z_\alpha$ and $S_{ov}^{-1} : Z_\alpha \rightsquigarrow Z_\alpha$ are both u.s.c. and each atomic set $u_{ov}(p)$ is $\mathcal{T}_{\mathrm{q}}$-closed.*

In Figures 2 and 3, we illustrate the process of "blockifying" a pair of known approximating operators $upo_\alpha$ and $opo_\alpha$ through an A/D map $\alpha$ to produce the relations $S_{un}^\alpha$ and $S_{ov}^\alpha$ in the models $\mathcal{N}_{un}^\alpha$ and $\mathcal{N}_{ov}^\alpha$, as defined in Proposition 4.

**Proposition 5.** [Topological f.a.s. from A/D maps]
*Given a Kripke model $\mathcal{M} = (X, R, v)$ for $\mathcal{L}_\mu^t(P)$, suppose $(\alpha, upo_\alpha, opo_\alpha)$ is A/D adequate for $\mathcal{M}$, and let $\mathcal{N}_{un}^\alpha = (Z_\alpha, S_{un}^\alpha, u_{un})$ and $\mathcal{N}_{ov}^\alpha = (Z_\alpha, S_{ov}^\alpha, u_{ov})$ be the finite models defined in Proposition 4. Define two maps $\mathbf{un} : \mathcal{L}_\mu^t(P) \to 2^{Z_\alpha}$ and $\mathbf{ov} : \mathcal{L}_\mu^t(P) \to 2^{Z_\alpha}$ by mutual induction on sentences:*

$$
\begin{aligned}
\mathbf{un}(p) &:= u_{un}(p) & \mathbf{ov}(p) &:= u_{ov}(p) \\
\mathbf{un}(\bot) &:= \varnothing & \mathbf{ov}(\bot) &:= \varnothing \\
\mathbf{un}(\top) &:= Z_\alpha & \mathbf{ov}(\top) &:= Z_\alpha \\
\mathbf{un}(\neg\varphi) &:= Z_\alpha - \mathbf{ov}(\varphi) & \mathbf{ov}(\neg\varphi) &:= Z_\alpha - \mathbf{un}(\varphi) \\
\mathbf{un}(\varphi_1 \vee \varphi_2) &:= \mathbf{un}(\varphi_1) \cup \mathbf{un}(\varphi_2) & \mathbf{ov}(\varphi_1 \vee \varphi_2) &:= \mathbf{ov}(\varphi_1) \cup \mathbf{ov}(\varphi_2) \\
\mathbf{un}(\varphi_1 \wedge \varphi_2) &:= \mathbf{un}(\varphi_1) \cap \mathbf{un}(\varphi_2) & \mathbf{ov}(\varphi_1 \wedge \varphi_2) &:= \mathbf{ov}(\varphi_1) \cap \mathbf{ov}(\varphi_2) \\
\mathbf{un}(\Diamond\varphi) &:= (S_{un}^\alpha)^{-\exists}(\mathbf{un}(\varphi)) & \mathbf{ov}(\Diamond\varphi) &:= (S_{ov}^\alpha)^{-\exists}(\mathbf{ov}(\varphi)) \\
\mathbf{un}(\blacklozenge\varphi) &:= (S_{un}^\alpha)^{\exists}(\mathbf{un}(\varphi)) & \mathbf{ov}(\blacklozenge\varphi) &:= (S_{ov}^\alpha)^{\exists}(\mathbf{ov}(\varphi)) \\
\mathbf{un}(\mu z.\varphi) &:= \bigcup_{n \leq K_\alpha} \mathbf{un}(\varphi^n) & \mathbf{ov}(\mu z.\varphi) &:= \bigcup_{n \leq K_\alpha} \mathbf{ov}(\varphi^n)
\end{aligned}
$$

*where $\varphi^0 := \bot$ and $\varphi^{n+1} := \varphi[z := \varphi^n]$ and the iteration bound is $K_\alpha := |\mathcal{T}_{\mathrm{q}}|$. Then $\Sigma_\alpha := (\Sigma_{un}^\alpha, \Sigma_{ov}^\alpha)$ is in $\mathsf{FAS}(\mathcal{M}, P)$, and is a topological f.a.s. with respect to the finite topology $\mathcal{T}_\alpha$ on $X$, where $\Sigma_{un}^\alpha := (\mathcal{T}_{\sqsubseteq}, \mathbf{un}, k_{un}^\alpha)$ and $\Sigma_{ov}^\alpha := (\mathcal{T}_{\sqsupseteq}, \mathbf{ov}, k_{ov}^\alpha)$, and $k_{un}^\alpha : \mathcal{T}_{\sqsubseteq} \to 2^X$ and $k_{ov}^\alpha : \mathcal{T}_{\sqsupseteq} \to 2^X$ are given by $k_{un}^\alpha := q_\alpha^{-1}$ and $k_{ov}^\alpha := q_\alpha^{-1}$.*

*In addition, if $\beta \in \mathsf{ADmap}(X)$, $\alpha \leqslant \beta$, $(\beta, upo_\beta, opo_\beta)$ is A/D adequate for $\mathcal{M}$, and $upo_\alpha(B(w)) \subseteq upo_\beta(B(w)) \subseteq R^\exists(B(w)) \subseteq opo_\beta(B(w)) \subseteq opo_\alpha(B(w))$ for all $\beta$-cells $B(w)$ for $w \in Z_\beta$, then $\Sigma_\alpha \leqslant \Sigma_\beta$.*

This work emerged from a study by the authors of topological semantics for intuitionistic modal and tense logics, and their relationship under the *Gödel translation* to classical multi-modal logics equipped with additional **S4** modal operators $\Box$ and $\Diamond$ interpreted by topological interior and closure, respectively. In the light of this background, we are led to consider Gödel-inspired translation maps from the base language $\mathcal{L}_\mu^t(P)$ into a multi-modal extension, which allows us to formally express and reason about not only the "real thing", but also our under- and over-approximations.

Let $\mathcal{L}_\Box^\star(P)$ be the multi-modal language which extends $\mathcal{L}^t(P)$ (the tense language generated from $P$ *without* the $\mu$ operator) by the addition of further pairs of tense diamonds, $\Diamond_\circ$ and $\blacklozenge_\circ$, and $\Diamond^\bullet$ and $\blacklozenge^\bullet$, and a plain box modality $\Box$. As before, we treat $\to$, $\Diamond$, and the now three pairs of tense box modalities $\boxdot$ and $\blacksquare$, $\boxdot_\circ$ and $\blacksquare_\circ$, and $\boxdot^\bullet$ and $\blacksquare^\bullet$, as all classically definable.

**Proposition 6.** *Given a Kripke model* $\mathcal{M} = (X, R, v)$ *over* $P$, *suppose the triple* $(\alpha, upo_\alpha, opo_\alpha)$ *is A/D adequate for* $\mathcal{M}$, *and let* $\mathcal{N}_{un}^\alpha = (Z_\alpha, S_{un}^\alpha, u_{un})$, *and* $\mathcal{N}_{ov}^\alpha = (Z_\alpha, S_{ov}^\alpha, u_{ov})$ *be the finite models defined in Proposition 4.*
*Define a multi-relational topological model* $\mathcal{M}_\alpha^\star := (X, \mathcal{T}_\alpha, R, R_{un}^\alpha, R_{ov}^\alpha, v)$ *for the language* $\mathcal{L}_\square^\star(P)$, *with* $int_\alpha$ *interpreting* $\square$, *relation* $R$ *interpreting* $\diamondsuit$ *and* $\blacklozenge$, *and relations* $R_{un}^\alpha$ *interpreting* $\diamondsuit_\circ$ *and* $\blacklozenge_\circ$, *and* $R_{ov}^\alpha$ *interpreting* $\diamondsuit^\bullet$ *and* $\blacklozenge^\bullet$, *where:*

$$R_{un}^\alpha := q_\alpha \bullet S_{un}^\alpha \bullet q_\alpha^{-1} \quad and \quad R_{ov}^\alpha := q_\alpha \bullet S_{ov}^\alpha \bullet q_\alpha^{-1}$$

*Then there are two Gödel-like translation maps* $\mathrm{UT}, \mathrm{OT} \colon \mathcal{L}_\mu^{\mathrm{t}}(P) \to \mathcal{L}_\square^\star(P)$ *such that the approximation values generated by the f.a.s.* $\Sigma_\alpha$ *are (classically) expressible in* $\mathcal{L}_\square^\star(P)$, *over the model* $\mathcal{M}_\alpha^\star$, *in the sense that, for all sentences* $\varphi \in \mathcal{L}_\mu^{\mathrm{t}}(P)$:

$$q_\alpha^{-1}(\mathbf{un}(\varphi)) = [\![ \mathrm{UT}(\varphi) ]\!]^{\mathcal{M}_\alpha^\star} \quad and \quad q_\alpha^{-1}(\mathbf{ov}(\varphi)) = [\![ \mathrm{OT}(\varphi) ]\!]^{\mathcal{M}_\alpha^\star}$$

$$\mathcal{M}_\alpha^\star \models \mathrm{UT}(\varphi) \to \varphi \quad and \quad \mathcal{M}_\alpha^\star \models \varphi \to \mathrm{OT}(\varphi)$$

$$\mathcal{M}_\alpha^\star \models \mathrm{UT}(\varphi) \leftrightarrow \square \mathrm{UT}(\varphi) \quad and \quad \mathcal{M}_\alpha^\star \models \mathrm{OT}(\varphi) \leftrightarrow \diamondsuit \mathrm{OT}(\varphi)$$

*The mutually recursive translation maps are defined as follows:*

$$\mathrm{UT}(p) := \square p \qquad\qquad \mathrm{OT}(p) := \diamondsuit p$$
$$\mathrm{UT}(\bot) := \bot \qquad\qquad \mathrm{OT}(\bot) := \bot$$
$$\mathrm{UT}(\top) := \top \qquad\qquad \mathrm{OT}(\top) := \top$$
$$\mathrm{UT}(\neg\varphi) := \neg\mathrm{OT}(\varphi) \qquad\qquad \mathrm{OT}(\neg\varphi) := \neg\mathrm{UT}(\varphi)$$
$$\mathrm{UT}(\varphi_1 \vee \varphi_2) := \mathrm{UT}(\varphi_1) \vee \mathrm{UT}(\varphi_2) \qquad \mathrm{OT}(\varphi_1 \vee \varphi_2) := \mathrm{OT}(\varphi_1) \vee \mathrm{OT}(\varphi_2)$$
$$\mathrm{UT}(\varphi_1 \wedge \varphi_2) := \mathrm{UT}(\varphi_1) \wedge \mathrm{UT}(\varphi_2) \qquad \mathrm{OT}(\varphi_1 \wedge \varphi_2) := \mathrm{OT}(\varphi_1) \wedge \mathrm{OT}(\varphi_2)$$
$$\mathrm{UT}(\diamondsuit\varphi) := \diamondsuit_\circ \mathrm{UT}(\varphi) \qquad\qquad \mathrm{OT}(\diamondsuit\varphi) := \diamondsuit^\bullet \mathrm{OT}(\varphi)$$
$$\mathrm{UT}(\blacklozenge\varphi) := \blacklozenge_\circ \mathrm{UT}(\varphi) \qquad\qquad \mathrm{OT}(\blacklozenge\varphi) := \blacklozenge^\bullet \mathrm{OT}(\varphi)$$
$$\mathrm{UT}(\mu z.\varphi) := \bigvee_{n \le K_\alpha} \mathrm{UT}(\varphi^n) \qquad \mathrm{OT}(\mu z.\varphi) := \bigvee_{n \le K_\alpha} \mathrm{OT}(\varphi^n)$$

*where the iteration bound is* $K_\alpha = |\mathcal{T}_{\mathsf{q}}|$.

For example, in the extended language $\mathcal{L}_\square^\star(P)$, the formula $\mathrm{OT}(\varphi) \wedge \neg\mathrm{UT}(\varphi)$ denotes in $\mathcal{M}_\alpha^\star$ the set of all states $x \in X$ that do not have a determinate truth value under the scheme $\Sigma_\alpha$.

We conclude the paper with a comprehensiveness result: from any finite approximation scheme $\Sigma \in \mathsf{FAS}(\mathcal{M}, P)$, we can construct an A/D map $\alpha$ and a topological f.a.s. $\Sigma_\alpha$ that is a refinement of the given scheme $\Sigma$.

**Proposition 7.** [Comprehensiveness of topological finite approximation schemes]
*Given any f.a.s.* $\Sigma \in \mathsf{FAS}(\mathcal{M}, P)$ *for a model* $\mathcal{M} = (X, R, v)$, *there exists an A/D map* $\alpha \colon X \rightsquigarrow Z_\alpha$, *and a pair of finite models* $\mathcal{N}_{un}^\alpha = (Z_\alpha, S_{un}^\alpha, u_{un})$ *and* $\mathcal{N}_{ov}^\alpha = (Z_\alpha, S_{ov}^\alpha, u_{ov})$ *which determine a topological finite approximation scheme* $\Sigma_\alpha$, *as given in Proposition 5, such that* $\Sigma \leqslant \Sigma_\alpha$.
*Moreover, the A/D map* $\alpha$ *and the models* $\mathcal{N}_{un}^\alpha$ *and* $\mathcal{N}_{ov}^\alpha$ *are such that the construction and conclusions of Proposition 6 hold of them.*

# 6   Conclusions

This paper gives clear focus to the problem of approximate model-checking in modal and tense logics, calling for two-sided approximations propogated to arbitrarily complex formulas. We have developed a generic notion of a finite approximation scheme for a model, and of a partial ordering on such schemes, and we have established the naturalness of the notion by proving that a model has a maximally refined finite approximation scheme if and only if it has a finite bisimulation quotient. We then gave a general construction of finite approximation schemes from A/D maps and their finite topologies plus a pair of basic approximation operators defined on the cells of the A/D map. We showed this sub-class of topological schemes to be comprehensive in the sense that, given any finite approximation scheme $\Sigma$ satisfying minimal coherence conditions, we can construct an A/D map $\alpha$ and a topological finite approximation scheme $\Sigma_\alpha$ that refines the given scheme $\Sigma$. Future work will investigate efficient implementation for reasonable classes of continuous dynamics based on [10, 1–3, 8].

# References

1. R. Alur, T. Dang, and F. Ivancic. Progress on reachability analysis of hybrid systems. In *Hybrid Systems: Computation and Control* (HSCC'03), LNCS 2623, pages 20–35. Springer.
2. E. Asarin, T. Dang, and O. Maler. The d/dt tool for verification of hybrid systems. In *Computer Aided Verification 2002*, LNCS 2404, pages 365–370. Springer.
3. A. Chutinam and B. Krogh. Computational techniques for hybrid system verification. *IEEE Transactions on Automatic Control*, 48:64–75, 2003.
4. E. M. Clarke, O. Grumberg, and D. Long. Model checking and abstraction. *ACM Trans. on Prog. Lang. and Systems*, 16(5):1512–, 1994.
5. P. Cousot and R. Cousot. Abstract interpretation: a unified lattice model for static analysis of programs by construction of fixpoints. In *Proc. 4th ACM Symp on Principles of Prog Lang* (POPL'77), pages 238–252. ACM Press, 1977.
6. D.Dams, R.Gerth, and O.Grumberg. Abstract interpretation of reactive systems. *ACM Trans on Prog Langs and Systems (TOPLAS)*, 19(2), 1997.
7. P. Godefroid, M. Huth, and R. Jagadeesan. Abstraction-based model checking using modal transition systems. In *Proc International Conf on Concurrency* (CONCUR 2001), LNCS 2154, pages 426–440. Springer-Verlag, 2001.
8. B.H Krogh and O. Stursberg. Efficient representation and computation of reachable sets for hybrid systems. In *Hybrid Systems: Computation and Control* (HSCC'03), volume 2623 of *LNCS*, pages 498–513. Springer, 2003.
9. K. Kuratowski. *Topology*. Academic Press, 1966. (Vol 1, 1966; Vol 2, 1968.).
10. A.B. Kurzhanski and P. Varaiya. Reachability analysis for uncertain systems – the ellipsoidal technique. *Control and optimization. Dyn. Contin. Discrete Impuls. Syst. Ser. B Appl. Algorithms*, 9(3):347–367, 2002.
11. A. Nerode and W. Kohn. Models for hybrid systems: Automata, topologies, controllability, observability. In R. L. Grossman, editor, *Hybrid Systems* (HSI), LNCS 736, pages 297–316. Springer-Verlag, 1993.
12. S. Shoham and O. Grumberg. Monotonic abstraction-refinement for **CTL**. In *Proc Int Conf on Tools and Algorithms for the Construction and Analysis of Systems* (TACAS'04), LNCS 2988, pages 546 – 560. Springer, 2004.

# On Timed Automata
# with Input-Determined Guards

Deepak D'Souza[1] and Nicolas Tabareau[2]

[1] Dept. of Computer Science & Automation
Indian Institute of Science, Bangalore, India
deepakd@csa.iisc.ernet.in
[2] Ecole Normale Superieure de Cachan, Cachan, France
Nicolas.Tabareau@dptmaths.ens-cachan.fr

**Abstract.** We consider a general notion of timed automata with *input-determined* guards and show that they admit a robust logical framework along the lines of [6], in terms of a monadic second order logic characterisation and an expressively complete timed temporal logic. We then generalize these automata using the notion of recursive operators introduced by Henzinger, Raskin, and Schobbens [10], and show that they admit a similar logical framework. These results hold in the "pointwise" semantics. We finally use this framework to show that the real-time logic MITL of Alur et al [2] is expressively complete with respect to an MSO corresponding to an appropriate set of input-determined operators.

## 1  Introduction

The timed automata of Alur and Dill [1] are a popular model for describing timed behaviours. While these automata have the plus point of being very expressive and having a decidable emptiness problem, they are neither determinizable nor closed under complementation. This is a drawback from a couple of points of view. Firstly, one cannot carry out model checking in the framework where a system is modeled as a timed transition system $T$ and a specification of timed behaviours as a timed automaton $A$, and where one asks "is $L(T) \subseteq L(A)$?". This would normally involve *complementing* $A$ and then checking if its intersection with $T$ is non-empty. One can get around this problem to some extent by using determinizable specifications, or specifying directly the negation of the required property. A second reason why lack of closure properties may concern us is that it precludes the existence of an unrestricted logical characterisation of the class of languages accepted by timed automata. The existence of a monadic second order logic (MSO) characterisation of a class of languages is a strong endorsement of the "regularity" of the class. It also helps in identifying expressively complete temporal logics, which are natural to use as specification languages and have relatively efficient model checking algorithms.

The event clock automata of [3] was one of the first steps towards identifying a subclass of timed automata with the required closure properties. They were shown to be determinizable in [3], and later to admit a robust logical framework in terms of an MSO characterisation and an expressively complete timed temporal logic [6]. Similar results were shown in [15], [10] and [8]. A common technique used in all these results was the idea of "implicit" clocks, whose values are determined solely by the timed word being read. For example the event recording clock $x_a$ records the time since the last $a$ action w.r.t. the current position in a timed word, and is thus implicitly reset with each $a$ action. The truth of a guard over these clocks at a point in a timed word is thus completely determined by the word itself, unlike in a timed automaton where the value of a clock depends on the path taken in the automaton.

In this paper we generalize the notion of an implicit clock to that of an *input determined operator*. An input determined operator $\Delta$ identifies for a given timed word and position in it, a set of intervals in which it is "satisfied". The guard $I \in \Delta$ is then satisfied at a point in a timed word if the set of intervals identified by $\Delta$ contains $I$. For example, the event recording clock $x_a$ can be modeled as an input determined operator $\lhd_a$ which identifies at a given point in a timed word, the (infinite) set of intervals containing the distance to the last $a$ action. The guard $(x_a \in I)$ now translates to $(I \in \lhd_a)$. As an example to show that this framework is more general than implicit clocks, consider the input determined operator $\Diamond_a$ inspired by the Metric Temporal logic (MTL) of [12, 4]. This operator identifies the set of all intervals $I$ for which there is a future occurrence of an $a$ at a distance which lies in $I$. The guard $I \in \Diamond_a$ is now true iff there is a future occurrence of an $a$ action, at a distance which lies in $I$.

Timed automata which use guards based on a set of input determined operators are what we call *input determined automata*. We show that input determined automata form a robust class of timed languages, in that they are (a) determinizable, (b) effectively closed under boolean operations, (c) admit a logical characterisation via an unrestricted MSO, and (d) identify a natural expressively complete timed temporal logic.

We then go over to a more expressive framework using the idea of *recursive* event clocks from [10]. In the recursive version of our input determined operator, the operators now expect a third parameter (apart from the timed word and a position in it) which identifies a set of positions in the timed word. This argument could be (recursively) another input determined automaton, or as is better illustrated, a temporal logic formula $\theta$. The formula $\theta$ naturally identifies a set of positions in a timed word where the formula is satisfied. Thus a recursive operator $\Delta$ along with the formula $\theta$, written $\Delta_\theta$, behaves like an input determined operator above, and the guard $I \in \Delta_\theta$ is true iff the set of intervals identified by $\Delta_\theta$ contains $I$. These recursive input determined automata are also shown to admit similar robust logical properties as above.

We should be careful to point out here that, firstly, these results hold in the *pointwise* semantics, where formulas are evaluated only at the "action points" in a timed word (used e.g. in [17]), and not at arbitrary points in between actions in a timed word as allowed in the *continuous* semantics of [2, 10]. Secondly, we make no claims about the existence of *decision procedures* for these automata and logics. In fact it can be seen that the operator $\Diamond_a$ above takes us out of the class of timed automata as we can define the language of timed sequences of $a$'s in which no two $a$'s are a distance 1 apart, with a single state input determined automaton with a loop guarded by $\neg([1,1] \in \Diamond_a)$. Similar versions can be seen to have undecidable emptiness problems and correspondingly undecidable logics [4]. Thus the contribution of this paper should be seen more in terms of a general framework for displaying logical characterisations of timed automata, and proving expressive completeness of temporal logics related to these automata. Many of the results along these lines from [8, 6] and some in the pointwise semantics from [14] follow from the results in this paper.

As a new application of this framework, we provide an expressive completeness result for MITL in the pointwise semantics, by showing that it is expressively equivalent to the first order fragment of an MSO based on recursive operators. This answers an open question from [14], apart from identifying an interesting class of timed automata.

The techniques used in this paper essentially build on those from [8] and [6] which use the notion of *proper* symbolic alphabets and factor through the results of Büchi [5] and Kamp [11]. The idea of using recursive operators comes from [10], who show a variety of expressiveness results, including an expressive completeness for MITL in the continuous semantics. Their result for MITL is more interesting in that it uses event-clock modalities, while we use essentially the same modalities as MITL. However, our MSO is more natural as it is *unrestricted*, unlike the MSO in [10] which has restricted second order quantification.

## 2    Input Determined Automata

We use $\mathbb{N}$ to denote the set of natural numbers $\{0, 1, \ldots\}$, and $\mathbb{R}^{\geq 0}$ and $\mathbb{Q}^{\geq 0}$ to denote the set of non-negative reals and rationals respectively. The set of finite and infinite words over an alphabet $A$ will be denoted by $A^*$ and $A^\omega$ respectively. We use the notation $X \to Y$ to denote the set of functions from $X$ to $Y$.

An *(infinite) timed word* over an alphabet $\Sigma$ is an element $\sigma$ of $(\Sigma \times \mathbb{R}^{\geq 0})^\omega$ satisfying the following conditions. Let $\sigma = (a_0, t_0)(a_1, t_1) \cdots$. Then:

1. *(monotonicity)* for each $i \in \mathbb{N}$, $t_i \leq t_{i+1}$,
2. *(progressiveness)* for each $t \in \mathbb{R}^{\geq 0}$ there exists $i \in \mathbb{N}$ such that $t_i > t$.

Let $T\Sigma^\omega$ denote the set of infinite timed words over $\Sigma$. Where convenient, we will use the representation of $\sigma$ as $(\alpha, \tau)$ where $\alpha \in \Sigma^\omega$ and $\tau : \mathbb{N} \to \mathbb{R}^{\geq 0}$ is a time sequence satisfying the conditions above.

We will use rational bounded intervals to specify timing constraints. These intervals can be open or closed, and we allow $\infty$ as an open right end. These intervals denote a subset of reals in the usual manner – for example $[2, \infty)$ denotes the set $\{t \in \mathbb{R}^{\geq 0} \mid 2 \leq t\}$. The set of all intervals is denoted $\mathcal{I}_\mathbb{Q}$.

Our input determined automata will use guards of the form "$I \in \Delta$", where $I$ is an interval and $\Delta$ is an operator which determines for a given timed word $\sigma$ and a position $i$ in it, a set of intervals "satisfying" it at that point. We then say that $\sigma$ at position $i$ satisfies the guard "$I \in \Delta$" if $I$ belongs to the set of intervals identified by $\Delta$. By a "position" in the timed word we mean one of the "action points" or instants given by the time-stamp sequence, and use natural numbers $i$ (instead of the time $\tau(i)$) to denote these positions. More formally, an input determined operator $\Delta$ (w.r.t. the alphabet $\Sigma$) has a semantic function $[\![\Delta]\!] : (T\Sigma^\omega \times \mathbb{N}) \to 2^{\mathcal{I}_\mathbb{Q}}$. The guard $I \in \Delta$ is satisfied at position $i$ in $\sigma \in T\Sigma^\omega$ iff $I \in [\![\Delta]\!](\sigma, i)$.

The transitions of our input determined automata are labeled by symbolic actions of the form $(a, g)$ where $a$ is an action, and $g$ is a guard which is a boolean combination of atomic guards of the form $I \in \Delta$. The set of guards over a finite set of input determined operators $Op$ is denoted by $\mathcal{G}(Op)$ and given by the syntax $g ::= \top \mid I \in \Delta \mid \neg g \mid g \vee g \mid g \wedge g$. The satisfaction of a guard $g$ in a timed word $\sigma$ at position $i$, written $\sigma, i \models g$, is given in the expected way: we have $\sigma, i \models \top$ always, $\sigma, i \models I \in \Delta$ as above, and the boolean operators $\neg$, $\vee$, and $\wedge$ interpreted as usual.

A *symbolic alphabet* $\Gamma$ based on $(\Sigma, Op)$ is a finite subset of $\Sigma \times \mathcal{G}(Op)$. An infinite word $\gamma$ in $\Gamma^\omega$ specifies in a natural way a subset of timed words $tw(\gamma)$ defined as follows. Let $\gamma(i) = (a_i, g_i)$ for each $i \in \mathbb{N}$. Let $\sigma \in T\Sigma^\omega$ with $\sigma(i) = (b_i, t_i)$ for each $i \in \mathbb{N}$. Then $\sigma \in tw(\gamma)$ iff for each $i \in \mathbb{N}$, $b_i = a_i$ and $\sigma, i \models g_i$. We extend the map $tw$ to work on subsets of $\Gamma^\omega$ in the natural way. Thus, for $\widehat{L} \subseteq \Gamma^\omega$, we define $tw(\widehat{L}) = \bigcup_{\gamma \in \widehat{L}} tw(\gamma)$. Finally, we denote the vocabulary of intervals mentioned in $\Gamma$ by $ivoc(\Gamma)$.

Recall that a Büchi automaton over an alphabet $A$ is a structure $\mathcal{A} = (Q, s, \longrightarrow, F)$ where $Q$ is a finite set of states, $s \in Q$ is an initial state, $\longrightarrow \subseteq Q \times A \times Q$ is the transition relation, and $F \subseteq Q$ is a set of accepting states. Let $\alpha \in A^\omega$. A run of $\mathcal{A}$ over $\alpha$ is a map $\rho : \mathbb{N} \to Q$ which satisfies: $\rho(0) = s$ and $\rho(i) \xrightarrow{\alpha(i)} \rho(i+1)$ for every $i \in \mathbb{N}$. We say $\rho$ is an *accepting* run of $\mathcal{A}$ on $\alpha$ if $\rho(i) \in F$ for infinitely many $i \in \mathbb{N}$. The set of words accepted by $\mathcal{A}$, denoted here as $L_{sym}(\mathcal{A})$ (for the "symbolic" language accepted by $\mathcal{A}$), is defined to be the set of words in $A^\omega$ on which $\mathcal{A}$ has an accepting run.

We are now in a position to define an input determined automaton. An *input determined automaton* (IDA for short) over an alphabet $\Sigma$ and a set of operators $Op$, is simply a Büchi automaton over a symbolic alphabet based on $(\Sigma, Op)$. Viewed as a Büchi automaton over a symbolic alphabet $\Gamma$, an input determined automaton $\mathcal{A}$ accepts the language $L_{sym}(\mathcal{A}) \subseteq \Gamma^\omega$ which we call the symbolic language accepted by $\mathcal{A}$. However, we will be more interested in the timed language accepted by $\mathcal{A}$: this is denoted $L(\mathcal{A})$ and is defined to be $tw(L_{sym}(\mathcal{A}))$.

To give a concrete illustration of input determined automata, we show how the event clock automata of [3] can be realized in the above framework. Take $Op$ to be the set of operators $\{\triangleleft_a, \triangleright_a \mid a \in \Sigma\}$, where the operators $\triangleleft_a$ and $\triangleright_a$ record respectively the time since the last $a$ action, and the time to the next $a$ action. The operator $\triangleleft_a$ (and similarly $\triangleright_a$) can be defined here by setting $[\![\triangleleft_a]\!](\sigma, i)$ to be

$$\{I \in \mathcal{I}_\mathbb{Q} \mid \exists j < i : \sigma(j) = a, \tau(i) - \tau(j) \in I, \text{ and } \forall k : j < k < i, \sigma(k) \neq a\}.$$

As another example which we will use later in the paper, consider the operator $\diamondsuit_a$ related to the logic MTL [12, 4]. The guard $\diamondsuit_a \in I$ is meant to be true in a word $\sigma$ at time $i$ iff there is a future instant $j$ labeled $a$ and the distance to it lies in $I$ – i.e. $\tau(j) - \tau(i) \in I$. The guard $\diamondsuit_a \in I$ makes a similar assertion about the *past* of $\sigma$ w.r.t. the current position. An input determined automaton based on these operators can be defined by taking $Op = \{\diamondsuit_a, \diamondsuit_a \mid a \in \Sigma\}$, and where, for example, $[\![\diamondsuit_a]\!](\sigma, i) = \{I \mid \exists j \geq i : \sigma(j) = a, \text{ and } \tau(j) - \tau(i) \in I\}$.

## 3    Closure Under Boolean Operations

We now want to show that the class of timed languages accepted by input determined automata (for a given choice of $\Sigma$ and $Op$) is closed under boolean operations. The notion of a *proper* symbolic alphabet will play an important role here and subsequently. A *proper symbolic alphabet* based on $(\Sigma, Op)$ is of the form $\Gamma = \Sigma \times (Op \rightarrow 2^{\mathcal{I}})$ where $\mathcal{I}$ is a finite subset of $\mathcal{I}_\mathbb{Q}$. An element of $\Gamma$ is thus of the form $(a, h)$, where the set of intervals specified by $h(\Delta)$ is interpreted as the *exact* subset of intervals in $ivoc(\Gamma)$ which are satisfied by $\Delta$. This is formalised in the following definition of $tw_\Gamma$ for a proper symbolic alphabet $\Gamma$. Let $\gamma \in \Gamma^\omega$ with $\gamma(i) = (a_i, h_i)$. Let $\sigma \in T\Sigma^\omega$ with $\sigma(i) = (b_i, t_i)$. Then $\sigma \in tw_\Gamma(\gamma)$ iff for each $i \in \mathbb{N}$: $b_i = a_i$ and for each $\Delta \in Op$, $h_i(\Delta) = [\![\Delta]\!](\sigma, i) \cap ivoc(\Gamma)$.

Let $\Gamma$ be a proper symbolic alphabet based on $(\Sigma, Op)$. Then a Büchi automaton $\mathcal{A}$ over $\Gamma$, which we call a *proper* IDA over $(\Sigma, Op)$, determines a timed language over $\Sigma$ given by $tw_\Gamma(L_{sym}(\mathcal{A}))$.

The class of timed languages defined by IDA's and proper IDA's over $(\Sigma, Op)$ coincide. An IDA over a symbolic alphabet $\Gamma$ can be converted to an equivalent one (in terms of the timed language they define) over a proper symbolic alphabet $\Gamma' = \Sigma \times (Op \rightarrow 2^{ivoc(\Gamma)})$. Firstly, each transition label $(a, g)$ in $\Gamma$ can be written in a disjunctive normal form $(c_1 \vee \cdots \vee c_k)$, with each $c_i$ being a conjunction of literals $I \in \Delta$ or $\neg(I \in \Delta)$. Thus each transition labeled $(a, g)$ can be replaced by a set of transitions labeled $(a, c_i)$, one for each $i$. Now each transition labeled $(a, c)$, with $c$ a conjunct guard, can be replaced by a set of transitions $(a, h)$, one for each $h$ "consistent" with $c$: i.e. $h$ should satisfy the condition that if $I \in \Delta$ is one of the conjuncts in $c$ then $I \in h(\Delta)$, and if $\neg(I \in \Delta)$ is one of the conjuncts in $c$ then $I \notin h(\Delta)$. In the other direction, to go from a proper IDA to an IDA, a label $(a, h)$ of a proper symbolic alphabet can be replaced by the guard

$$\bigwedge_{\Delta \in Op} ( \bigwedge_{I \in h(\Delta)} (I \in \Delta) \wedge \bigwedge_{I \in ivoc(\Gamma) - h(\Delta)} \neg(I \in \Delta)).$$

The following property of proper symbolic alphabets will play a crucial role.

**Lemma 1.** *Let $\Gamma$ be a proper symbolic alphabet based on $(\Sigma, Op)$. Then for any $\sigma \in T\Sigma^\omega$ there is a* unique *symbolic word $\gamma$ in $\Gamma^\omega$ such that $\sigma \in tw_\Gamma(\gamma)$.*

*Proof.* Let $\sigma(i) = (a_i, t_i)$. The only possible candidate symbolic word $\gamma$ must be given by $\gamma(i) = (a_i, h_i)$, where for each $\Delta \in Op$, $h_i(\Delta) = [\![\Delta]\!](\sigma, i) \cap ivoc(\Gamma)$.    $\square$

In the light of lemma 1, going from a symbolic alphabet to a proper one can be viewed as a step towards determinizing the automaton with respect to its timed language. From here one can simply use classical automata theoretic techniques to determinize the automaton w.r.t. its *symbolic* language to obtain a time-deterministic one. (Of course, since we deal with infinite words we will need to go from a Büchi to a Muller or Rabin acceptance condition [16]).

**Theorem 1.** *The class of IDA's over $(\Sigma, Op)$ are effectively closed under the boolean operations of union, intersection, and complement.*

*Proof.* It is sufficient to address union and complementation. Given automata $\mathcal{A}$ and $\mathcal{B}$ over symbolic alphabets $\Gamma$ and $\Lambda$ respectively, we can simply construct an automaton over $\Gamma \cup \Lambda$ which accepts the union of the two symbolic languages. For complementing the timed language of $\mathcal{A}$, we can go over to an equivalent proper IDA $\mathcal{A}'$ over a proper symbolic alphabet $\Gamma'$, and now simply complement the symbolic language accepted by $\mathcal{A}'$ to get an automaton $\mathcal{C}$. It is easy to verify, using the uniqueness property of proper alphabets given in Lemma 1, that $L(\mathcal{C}) = T\Sigma^\omega - L(\mathcal{A}')$. In the constructions above we have made use of the closure properties of classical $\omega$-regular languages [16]. □

We emphasize that no claim is made here about *decidability* of these classes.

# 4    A Logical Characterisation of IDA's

We now show that input determined automata admit a natural characterisation via a timed MSO in the spirit of [5]. Recall that for an alphabet $A$, Büchi's monadic second order logic (denoted here by $\mathrm{MSO}(A)$) is given as follows:

$$\varphi ::= Q_a(x) \mid x \in X \mid x < y \mid \neg\varphi \mid (\varphi \vee \varphi) \mid \exists x\varphi \mid \exists X\varphi.$$

The logic is interpreted over a word $\alpha \in A^\omega$, along with an interpretation $\mathbb{I}$ which assigns individual variables $x$ a position in $\alpha$ (i.e. an $i \in \mathbb{N}$), and to set variables $X$ a set of positions $S \subseteq \mathbb{N}$. The relation $<$ is interpreted as the usual ordering of natural numbers, and the predicate $Q_a$ (one for each $a \in A$) as the set of positions in $\alpha$ labeled $a$.

The formal semantics of the logic is given below. For an interpretation $\mathbb{I}$ we use the notation $\mathbb{I}[i/x]$ to denote the interpretation which sends $x$ to $i$ and agrees with $\mathbb{I}$ on all other variables. Similarly, $\mathbb{I}[S/X]$ denotes the modification of $\mathbb{I}$ which maps the set variable $X$ to a subset $S$ of $\mathbb{N}$. Later we will also use the notation $[i/x]$ to denote an interpretation which sends $x$ to $i$ when the rest of the interpretation is irrelevant.

$$
\begin{aligned}
\alpha, \mathbb{I} &\models Q_a(x) \quad \text{iff} \quad \alpha(\mathbb{I}(x)) = a. \\
\alpha, \mathbb{I} &\models x \in X \quad \text{iff} \quad \mathbb{I}(x) \in \mathbb{I}(X). \\
\alpha, \mathbb{I} &\models x < y \quad \text{iff} \quad \mathbb{I}(x) < \mathbb{I}(y). \\
\alpha, \mathbb{I} &\models \exists x\varphi \quad \text{iff} \quad \text{there exists } i \in \mathbb{N} \text{ such that } \sigma, \mathbb{I}[i/x] \models \varphi. \\
\alpha, \mathbb{I} &\models \exists X\varphi \quad \text{iff} \quad \text{there exists } S \subseteq \mathbb{N} \text{ such that } \sigma, \mathbb{I}[S/X] \models \varphi.
\end{aligned}
$$

For a sentence $\varphi$ (i.e. a formula without free variables) in $MSO(A)$ we set $L(\varphi) = \{\sigma \in A^\omega \mid \sigma \models \varphi\}$. Büchi's result then states that a language $L \subseteq A^\omega$ is accepted by a Büchi automaton over $A$ iff $L = L(\varphi)$ for a sentence $\varphi$ in $MSO(A)$.

We define a timed MSO called $TMSO(\Sigma, Op)$, parameterised by the alphabet $\Sigma$ and set of input determined operators $Op$, whose syntax is given by:

$$\varphi ::= Q_a(x) \mid I \in \Delta(x) \mid x \in X \mid x < y \mid \neg\varphi \mid (\varphi \vee \varphi) \mid \exists x\varphi \mid \exists X\varphi.$$

In the predicate "$I \in \Delta(x)$", $I$ is an interval in $\mathcal{I}_\mathbb{Q}$, $\Delta \in Op$, and $x$ is a variable.

The logic is interpreted in a similar manner to MSO, except that models are now timed words over $\Sigma$. In particular, for a timed word $\sigma = (\alpha, \tau)$, we have:

$$\sigma, \mathbb{I} \models Q_a(x) \quad \text{iff } \alpha(\mathbb{I}(x)) = a$$
$$\sigma, \mathbb{I} \models I \in \Delta(x) \text{ iff } I \in [\![\Delta]\!](\sigma, \mathbb{I}(x)).$$

Given a sentence $\varphi$ in $TMSO(\Sigma, Op)$ we define $L(\varphi) = \{\sigma \in T\Sigma^\omega \mid \sigma \models \varphi\}$.

**Theorem 2.** *A timed language $L \subseteq T\Sigma^\omega$ is accepted by an input determined automaton over $(\Sigma, Op)$ iff $L = L(\varphi)$ for some sentence $\varphi$ in $TMSO(\Sigma, Op)$.*

*Proof.* Given an IDA $\mathcal{A}$ over $(\Sigma, Op)$ we can give a TMSO sentence $\varphi$ which describes the existence of an accepting run of $\mathcal{A}$ on a timed word. Following [16], for $\mathcal{A} = (Q, q_0, \longrightarrow, F)$ with $Q = \{q_0, \ldots q_n\}$, we can take $\varphi$ to be the sentence

$$\exists X_0 \cdots \exists X_n \, ( \, 0 \in X_0 \, \wedge \, \bigwedge_{i \neq j} \forall x (x \in X_i \Rightarrow \neg(x \in X_j))$$

$$(*) \qquad \wedge \, \forall x \bigvee_{q_i \xrightarrow{(a,g)} q_j} (x \in X_i \, \wedge \, (x+1) \in X_j \, \wedge Q_a(x) \wedge g')$$

$$\wedge \bigvee_{q_i \in F} \forall x \exists y (x < y \wedge y \in X_i)).$$

Here $g'$ denotes the formula obtained by replacing each $I \in \Delta$ in $g$ by $I \in \Delta(x)$. Further, "$0 \in X_0$" abbreviates $\forall x \, (zero(x) \Rightarrow x \in X_0)$ where $zero(x)$ in turn stands for $\neg\exists y(y < x)$. Similarly $x+1 \in X_j$ can be expressed via $\forall y(succ_x(y) \Rightarrow y \in X_j)$, where $succ_x(y)$ is the formula $x < y \, \wedge \, \neg\exists z(x < z \, \wedge \, z < y)$.

In the converse direction we take the route used in [6] as it will be useful in the sequel. Let $\varphi$ be a formula in $TMSO(\Sigma, Op)$, and let $\Gamma$ be the (unique) *proper* symbolic alphabet with the same interval vocabulary as $\varphi$. We give a way of translating $\varphi$ to a formula $t\text{-}s(\varphi)$ in $MSO(\Gamma)$ in such a way that the timed languages are preserved. The translation $t\text{-}s$ is done with respect to $\Gamma$ and simply replaces each occurrence of

$$Q_a(x) \text{ by } \bigvee_{(b,h)\in\Gamma, \, b=a} Q_{(b,h)}(x) \text{ and } I \in \Delta(x) \text{ by } \bigvee_{(a,h)\in\Gamma, \, I\in h(\Delta)} Q_{(a,h)}(x).$$

The translation preserves the timed models of a formula $\varphi$ in the following sense:

**Lemma 2.** *Let* $\sigma \in T\Sigma^\omega$, $\gamma \in \Gamma^\omega$, *and* $\sigma \in tw_\Gamma(\gamma)$. *Let* $\mathbb{I}$ *be an interpretation for variables. Then* $\sigma, \mathbb{I} \models \varphi$ *iff* $\gamma, \mathbb{I} \models t\text{-}s(\varphi)$.           □

The lemma is easy to prove using induction on the structure of the formula $\varphi$ and making use of the properties of proper symbolic alphabets. From the lemma it immediately follows now that for a sentence $\varphi$ in TMSO($\Sigma$, $Op$), we have $L(\varphi) = tw_\Gamma(L(t\text{-}s(\varphi)))$, and this is the sense in which the translation preserves timed languages.

We can now argue the converse direction of Theorem 2 using this translation and factoring through Büchi's theorem. Let $\varphi$ be a sentence in TMSO($\Sigma$, $Op$) and let $\widehat{\varphi} = t\text{-}s(\varphi)$. Then by Büchi's theorem we have an automaton $\mathcal{A}$ over $\Gamma$ which recognizes exactly $L(\widehat{\varphi})$. Thus $\mathcal{A}$ is our required proper IDA since $L(\mathcal{A}) = tw_\Gamma(L_{sym}(\mathcal{A})) = tw_\Gamma(L(\widehat{\varphi})) = L(\varphi)$.           □

# 5   An Expressively Complete Timed LTL

In this section we identify a natural, expressively complete, timed temporal logic based on input determined operators. The logic is denoted TLTL($\Sigma$, $Op$), parameterized by the alphabet $\Sigma$ and set of input determined operators $Op$. The formulas of TLTL($\Sigma$, $Op$) are given by:

$$\theta ::= a \mid I \in \Delta \mid O\theta \mid \Theta\theta \mid (\theta U\theta) \mid (\theta S\theta) \mid \neg\theta \mid (\theta \vee \theta).$$

Here we require $a \in \Sigma$, $I \in \mathcal{I}_\mathbb{Q}$, and $\Delta \in Op$. The models for TLTL($\Sigma$, $Op$) formulas are timed words over $\Sigma$. Let $\sigma \in T\Sigma^\omega$, with $\sigma = (\alpha, \tau)$, and let $i \in \mathbb{N}$. Then the satisfaction relation $\sigma, i \models \varphi$ is given by

$$\begin{aligned}
\sigma, i &\models a & &\text{iff} \quad \alpha(i) = a \\
\sigma, i &\models I \in \Delta & &\text{iff} \quad I \in [\![\Delta]\!](\sigma, i) \\
\sigma, i &\models O\theta & &\text{iff} \quad \sigma, i+1 \models \theta \\
\sigma, i &\models \Theta\theta & &\text{iff} \quad i > 0 \text{ and } \sigma, i-1 \models \theta \\
\sigma, i &\models \theta U\eta & &\text{iff} \quad \exists k \geq i : \sigma, k \models \eta \text{ and } \forall j : i \leq j < k, \ \sigma, j \models \theta \\
\sigma, i &\models \theta S\eta & &\text{iff} \quad \exists k \leq i : \sigma, k \models \eta \text{ and } \forall j : k < j \leq i, \ \sigma, j \models \theta.
\end{aligned}$$

We define $L(\theta) = \{\sigma \in T\Sigma^\omega \mid \sigma, 0 \models \varphi\}$.

Let us denote by TFO($\Sigma$, $Op$) the first-order fragment of TMSO($\Sigma$, $Op$) (i.e. the fragment we get by disallowing quantification over set variables). The logics TLTL and TFO are *expressively equivalent* in the following sense:

**Theorem 3.** *A timed language* $L \subseteq T\Sigma^\omega$ *is definable by a* TLTL($\Sigma$, $Op$) *formula* $\theta$ *iff it is definable by a sentence* $\varphi$ *in* TFO($\Sigma$, $Op$).

*Proof.* Given a TLTL($\Sigma$, $Op$) formula $\theta$ we can associate a TFO($\Sigma$, $Op$) formula $\varphi$ which has a single free variable $x$, and satisfies the property that $\sigma, i \models \theta$ iff $\sigma, [i/x] \models \varphi$. This can be done in a straightforward inductive manner as follows. For the atomic formulas $a$ and $I \in \Delta$ we can take $\varphi$ to be $Q_a(x)$ and $I \in \Delta(x)$

respectively. In the inductive step, assuming we have already translated $\theta$ and $\eta$ into $\varphi$ and $\psi$ respectively, we can translate $\theta U \eta$ into

$$\exists y (x \leq y \wedge \psi[y/x] \wedge \forall z((x \leq z \wedge z \leq y) \Rightarrow \varphi[z/x])).$$

Here $\psi[y/x]$ denotes the standard renaming of the free variable $x$ by $y$ in $\psi$. The remaining modalities are handled in a similar way, and we can verify that if $\varphi$ is the above translation of $\theta$ then $\sigma, i \models \theta$ iff $\sigma, [i/x] \models \varphi$. It also follows that $\sigma, 0$ satisfies $\theta$ iff $\sigma$ satisfies the sentence $\varphi_0$ given by $\forall x(zero(x) \Rightarrow \varphi)$. Hence we have that $L(\theta) = L(\varphi_0)$.

In the converse direction a more transparent proof is obtained by factoring through Kamp's result for classical LTL. Recall that the syntax of LTL$(A)$ is given by:

$$\theta ::= a \mid O\theta \mid \Theta\theta \mid (\theta U \theta) \mid (\theta S \theta) \mid \neg\theta \mid (\theta \vee \theta)$$

where $a \in A$. The semantics is given in a similar manner to TLTL, except that models are words in $A^\omega$. In particular the satisfaction relation $\alpha, i \models \theta$ for the atomic formula $a$ is given by: $\sigma, i \models a$ iff $\alpha(i) = a$. Let FO$(A)$ denote the first-order fragment of MSO$(A)$. Then the result due to Kamp [11] states that:

**Theorem 4 ([11]).** LTL$(A)$ *is expressively equivalent to* FO$(A)$.     □

Consider now a proper symbolic alphabet $\Gamma$ based on $(\Sigma, Op)$. We can define a timed language preserving translation of an LTL$(\Gamma)$ formula $\widehat{\theta}$ to a formula $s\text{-}t(\widehat{\theta})$ in TLTL$(\Sigma, Op)$. In the translation $s\text{-}t$ we replace subformulas $(a, h)$ by

$$a \wedge \bigwedge_{\Delta \in Op} (\bigwedge_{I \in h(\Delta)} (I \in \Delta) \wedge \bigwedge_{I \in ivoc(\Gamma) - h(\Delta)} \neg(I \in \Delta)).$$

It is easy to argue along the lines of Lemma 1 that

**Lemma 3.** *Let* $\sigma \in T\Sigma^\omega$ *and* $\gamma \in \Gamma^\omega$ *with* $\sigma \in tw_\Gamma(\gamma)$. *Then* $\sigma, i \models s\text{-}t(\widehat{\theta})$ *iff* $\gamma, i \models \widehat{\theta}$.     □

Hence we have $L(s\text{-}t(\widehat{\theta})) = tw_\Gamma(L(\widehat{\theta}))$.

We can now translate a sentence $\varphi$ in TFO$(\Sigma, Op)$ to an equivalent formula $\theta$ in TLTL$(\Sigma, Op)$, according to the diagram below.

This completes the proof of Theorem 3.     □

We point out here that the past temporal operators of $\Theta$ ("previous") and $S$ ("since") can be dropped from our logic without affecting the expressiveness of the logic. This follows since it is shown in [9] that Theorem 4 also holds for the future fragment of LTL. The reason we retain the past operators is because they are needed when we consider a recursive version of the logic in Section 8.

## 6    Recursive Input Determined Automata

We now consider "recursive" input determined operators. The main motivation is to increase the expressive power of our automata, as well as to characterise the expressiveness of recursive temporal logics which occur naturally in the real-time setting.

To introduce recursion in our operators, we need to consider *parameterised* (or *recursive*) input determined operators. These operators, which we continue to denote by $\Delta$, have a semantic function $[\![\Delta]\!] : (2^N \times T\Sigma^\omega \times \mathbb{N}) \to 2^{\mathcal{I}_\mathbb{Q}}$, whose first argument is a subset of positions $X$. Thus $\Delta$ with the parameter $X$ determines an input determined operator of the type introduced earlier, whose semantic function is given by the map $(\sigma, i) \mapsto [\![\Delta]\!](X, \sigma, i)$. The set of positions $X$ will typically be specified by a temporal logic formula or a "floating" automaton, in the sense that given a timed word $\sigma$, the formula (resp. automaton) will identify a set of positions in $\sigma$ where the formula is satisfied (resp. automaton accepts). These ideas will soon be made more precise.

We first recall the idea of a "floating" automaton introduced in [10]. These are automata which accept pairs of the form $(\sigma, i)$ with $\sigma$ a timed word, and $i$ a position (i.e. $i \in \mathbb{N}$). We will represent a "floating" word $(\sigma, i)$ as a timed word over $\Sigma \times \{0, 1\}$. Thus a timed word $\nu$ over $\Sigma \times \{0, 1\}$ represents the floating word $(\sigma, i)$, iff $\nu = (\alpha, \beta, \tau)$, with $\beta \in \{0, 1\}^\omega$ with a *single* 1 in the $i$-th position, and $\sigma = (\alpha, \tau)$. We use $fw$ to denote the (partial) map which given a timed word $\nu$ over $\Sigma \times \{0, 1\}$ returns the floating word $(\sigma, i)$ corresponding to $\nu$, and extend it to apply to timed languages over $\Sigma \times \{0, 1\}$ in the natural way.

Let $Op$ be a set of input determined operators w.r.t. $\Sigma$. Then a *floating IDA* over $(\Sigma, Op)$ is an IDA over $(\Sigma \times \{0, 1\}, Op')$, where the set of operators $Op'$ w.r.t. $\Sigma \times \{0, 1\}$ is defined to be $\{\Delta' \mid \Delta \in Op\}$, with the semantics

$$[\![\Delta']\!](\sigma', i) = [\![\Delta]\!](\sigma, i),$$

where $\sigma'$ is a timed word over $\Sigma \times \{0, 1\}$, with $\sigma' = (\alpha, \beta, \tau)$ and $\sigma = (\alpha, \tau)$. Thus the operator $\Delta'$ simply ignores the $\{0, 1\}$ component of $\sigma'$ and behaves like $\Delta$ on the $\Sigma$ component. A floating IDA $\mathcal{B}$ accepts the floating timed language $L^f(\mathcal{B}) = fw(L(\mathcal{B}))$.

We now give a more precise definition of recursive input determined automata (rec-IDA's) and their floating counterparts frec-IDA's. Let $Rop$ be a finite set of recursive input determined operators. Then the class of rec-IDA's over $(\Sigma, Rop)$, and the timed languages they accept, are defined as follows.

- Every IDA $\mathcal{A}$ over $\Sigma$ that uses only the guard $\top$ is a rec-IDA over $(\Sigma, Rop)$, and accepts the timed language $L(\mathcal{A})$.

Similarly, every floating IDA $\mathcal{B}$ over $\Sigma$ which uses only the guard $\top$ is a frec-IDA over $(\Sigma, Rop)$, and accepts the floating language $L^f(\mathcal{B})$.

- Let $C$ be a finite collection of frec-IDA's over $(\Sigma, Rop)$. Let $Op$ be the set of input determined operators $\{\Delta_{\mathcal{B}} \mid \Delta \in Rop,\ \mathcal{B} \in C\}$, where the semantic function of each $\Delta_{\mathcal{B}}$ is given as follows. Let $pos(\sigma, \mathcal{B})$ denote the set of positions $i$ such that $(\sigma, i) \in L^f(\mathcal{B})$. Then $[\![\Delta_{\mathcal{B}}]\!](\sigma, i) = [\![\Delta]\!](pos(\sigma, \mathcal{B}), \sigma, i)$. Then any IDA $\mathcal{A}$ over $(\Sigma, Op)$ is a rec-IDA over $(\Sigma, Rop)$, and accepts the timed language $L(\mathcal{A})$ (as defined in Section 2).
  Similarly every floating IDA $\mathcal{B}$ over $(\Sigma, Op)$ is a frec-IDA over $(\Sigma, Rop)$, and accepts the floating language $L^f(\mathcal{B})$.

Recursive automata fall into a natural "level" based on the level of nesting of operators they use. A rec-IDA is of *level* 0 if the only guard it uses is $\top$. Similarly a frec-IDA is of level 0, if the only guard it uses is $\top$. A rec-IDA is of *level* (i+1) if it uses an operator $\Delta_{\mathcal{B}}$, with $\Delta \in Rop$ and $\mathcal{B}$ a frec-IDA of level $i$, and no operator $\Delta'_C$ with $\Delta' \in Rop$ and $C$ of level greater than $i$. A similar definition of level applies to frec-IDA's.

As an example consider the level 1 rec-IDA $\mathcal{A}$ below over the alphabet $\{a, b\}$ and recursive input determined operators $\Diamond$ and $\diamondsuit$ given by (as usual $\sigma \in T\Sigma^\omega$ with $\sigma = (\alpha, \tau)$):

$$[\![\Diamond]\!](X, \sigma, i) = \{I \in \mathcal{I}_{\mathbb{Q}} \mid \exists j \in X : j \geq i,\ \text{and } \tau_j - \tau_i \in I\}$$
$$[\![\diamondsuit]\!](X, \sigma, i) = \{I \in \mathcal{I}_{\mathbb{Q}} \mid \exists j \in X : j \leq i,\ \text{and } \tau_i - \tau_j \in I\}.$$

The floating automaton $\mathcal{B}$ accepts a floating word $(\sigma, i)$ iff the position $i$ is labeled $b$ and the previous and next positions are labeled $a$. The rec-IDA $\mathcal{A}$ thus recognizes the set of timed words $\sigma$ over $\{a, b\}$ which begin with an $a$ and have an occurrence of $b$ – with $a$'s on its left and right – exactly 1 time unit later.

**Theorem 5.** *The class of rec-IDA's over $(\Sigma, Rop)$ is closed under boolean operations. In fact, for each $i$, the class of level $i$ rec-IDA's is closed under boolean operations.*

*Proof.* It is sufficient to prove the latter statement, since a rec-IDA can always be promoted to a higher level using a vacuous guard. Let $\mathcal{A}$ and $\mathcal{A}'$ be two rec-IDA's of level $i$. Let $Op$ be the union of operators used in $\mathcal{A}$ and $\mathcal{A}'$. Then both $\mathcal{A}$ and $\mathcal{A}'$ are IDA's over $(\Sigma, Op)$, and hence by Theorem 1 there exists an IDA $\mathcal{B}$ over $(\Sigma, Op)$ which accepts $L(\mathcal{A}) \cup L(\mathcal{A}')$. Similarly there exists an IDA $C$ over $(\Sigma, Op)$, which accepts the language $T\Sigma^\omega - L(\mathcal{A})$. Notice that $\mathcal{B}$ and $C$ use the same set of operators $Op$, and hence are also level $i$ automata.     □

We note that IDA's over $(\Sigma, Op)$ are a special case of level 1 rec-IDA's over $(\Sigma, Rop)$, where the set of recursive operators $Rop$ is taken to be $\{\Delta' \mid \Delta \in Op\}$ with $[\![\Delta']\!](X, \sigma, i) = [\![\Delta]\!](\sigma, i)$. Thus each guard $I \in \Delta$ in an IDA over $(\Sigma, Op)$ can be replaced by the guard $I \in \Delta'_{\mathcal{B}}$, for any "dummy" level 0 frec-IDA $\mathcal{B}$.

# 7    MSO Characterisation of rec-IDA's

We now introduce a recursive version of TMSO which will characterise the class of timed languages defined by rec-IDA's. The logic is parameterised by an alphabet $\Sigma$ and a set of recursive input determined operators $Rop$, and denoted rec-TMSO$(\Sigma, Rop)$. The syntax of the logic is given by

$$\varphi ::= Q_a(x) \mid I \in \Delta_\psi(x) \mid x \in X \mid x < y \mid \neg\varphi \mid (\varphi \vee \varphi) \mid \exists x\varphi \mid \exists X\varphi.$$

In the predicate $I \in \Delta_\psi(x)$, we have $I \in \mathcal{I}_\mathbb{Q}$, $\Delta \in Rop$, and $\psi$ a rec-TMSO$(\Sigma, Rop)$ formula with a single free variable $z$.

The logic is interpreted over timed words in $T\Sigma^\omega$. Its semantics is similar to TMSO except for the predicate "$I \in \Delta_\psi(x)$" which is defined inductively as follows. If $\psi$ is a formula which uses no $\Delta$ predicates, then the satisfaction relation $\sigma, \mathbb{I} \models \psi$ is defined as for TMSO. Inductively, assuming the semantics of $\psi$ has already been defined, $\Delta_\psi$ is interpreted as an input determined operator as follows. Let $pos(\sigma, \psi)$ denote the set of interpretations for $z$ that make $\psi$ true in the timed word $\sigma$ – i.e. $pos(\sigma, \psi) = \{i \mid \sigma, [i/z] \models \psi\}$. Then

$$[\![\Delta_\psi]\!](\sigma, i) = [\![\Delta]\!](pos(\sigma, \psi), \sigma, i).$$

Thus we have

$$\sigma, \mathbb{I} \models I \in \Delta_\psi(x) \text{ iff } I \in [\![\Delta]\!](pos(\sigma, \psi), \sigma, \mathbb{I}(x)).$$

Note that the variable $z$, which is free in $\psi$, is *not* free in the formula $I \in \Delta_\psi(x)$. A sentence $\varphi$ in rec-TMSO$(\Sigma, Rop)$ defines the language $L(\varphi) = \{\sigma \in T\Sigma^\omega \mid \sigma \models \varphi\}$, and a rec-TMSO$(\Sigma, Rop)$ formula $\psi$ with one free variable $z$ defines a floating language $L^f(\psi) = \{(\sigma, i) \mid \sigma, [i/z] \models \psi\}$.

We note that each rec-TMSO$(\Sigma, Rop)$ formula $\varphi$ can be viewed as a formula in TMSO$(\Sigma, Op)$, for a suitably defined set of input determined operators $Op$. We say an operator $\Delta_\psi$ has a *top-level* occurrence in $\varphi$ if there is an occurrence of $\Delta_\psi$ in $\varphi$ which is *not* in the scope of any $\Delta'$ operator. We can now take $Op$ to be the set of all top-level operators $\Delta_\psi$ in $\varphi$.

Analogous to the notion of level for rec-IDA's we can define the *level* of a rec-TMSO formula $\varphi$. The level of $\varphi$ is 0 if $\varphi$ uses no $\Delta$ predicates; $\varphi$ has level $i + 1$ if it uses a predicate of the form $I \in \Delta_\psi(x)$ with $\psi$ a level $i$ formula, and *no* predicate of the form $I \in \Delta'_\phi(x)$ with $\phi$ of level greater than $i$.

As an example the level 1 sentence $\varphi$ below defines the same timed language as the level 1 rec-IDA $\mathcal{A}$ defined in Section 2. We can take $\varphi$ to be $Q_a(0) \wedge ([1,1] \in \Diamond_\psi(0))$, where $\psi$ is the level 0 formula $Q_b(z) \wedge Q_a(z-1) \wedge Q_a(z+1)$.

**Theorem 6.** $L \subseteq T\Sigma^\omega$ *is accepted by a rec-IDA over $(\Sigma, Rop)$ iff $L$ is definable by a rec-TMSO$(\Sigma, Rop)$ sentence.*

In fact, we will show that for each $i$, the class of rec-IDA's of level $i$ correspond to the sentences of rec-TMSO$(\Sigma, Rop)$ of level $i$. But first it will be useful to state a characterisation of floating languages along the lines of Theorem 2.

**Theorem 7.** *Let $L$ be a a floating language over $\Sigma$. Then $L = L^f(\mathcal{B})$ for some floating IDA $\mathcal{B}$ over $(\Sigma, Op)$ iff $L = L^f(\psi)$, for some TMSO$(\Sigma, Op)$ formula $\psi$ with one free variable.*

*Proof.* Let $\mathcal{B}$ be a floating IDA over $(\Sigma, Op)$. Keeping in mind that $\mathcal{B}$ runs over the alphabet $\Sigma \times \{0, 1\}$, we define a formula $\psi$ with one free variable $z$ as follows. $\psi$ is the formula $\varphi$ given in the proof of Theorem 2, except for the clause (*) which we replace by

$$\wedge \; \forall x((x = z) \Rightarrow \bigvee_{q_i \xrightarrow{((a,1),g)} q_j} (x \in X_i \; \wedge \; (x+1) \in X_j \; \wedge Q_a(x) \wedge g')$$

$$\wedge \; (x \neq z) \Rightarrow \bigvee_{q_i \xrightarrow{((a,0),g)} q_j} (x \in X_i \; \wedge \; (x+1) \in X_j \; \wedge Q_a(x) \wedge g')).$$

The formula $\psi$ satisfies $(\sigma, i) \in L^f(\mathcal{B})$ iff $\sigma, [i/z] \models \psi$.

In the converse direction, let $\varphi(m, n)$ denote a TMSO$(\Sigma, Op)$ formula with free variables $x_1, \ldots, x_m, X_1 \ldots X_n$. An interpretation $\mathbb{I}$ for these variables is encoded (along with $\sigma$) as a timed word over $\Sigma \times \{0, 1\}^{m+n}$. We extend the definition of a floating IDA to an IDA which works over such an alphabet, where, in particular, the $\Delta$ operators apply only to the $\Sigma$ component of the timed word. Then we can inductively associate with $\varphi(m, n)$ a floating IDA $\mathcal{B}$ over $\Sigma \times \{0, 1\}^{m+n}$ such that $L^f(\mathcal{B}) = L^f(\varphi)$. In the inductive step for $\exists X_n(\varphi(m, n))$ we make use of the fact that the class of languages accepted by floating IDA's over $(\Sigma, Op)$ are closed under the restricted renaming operation required in this case. The reader is referred to [6] for a similar argument. □

Returning now to the proof of Theorem 6, we use induction on the level of automata and formulas to argue that

1. $L \subseteq T\Sigma^\omega$ is accepted by a level $i$ rec-IDA over $(\Sigma, Rop)$ iff $L$ is definable by a level $i$ rec-TMSO$(\Sigma, Rop)$ sentence $\varphi$. And
2. A floating language $L$ over $\Sigma$ is accepted by a level $i$ frec-IDA over $(\Sigma, Rop)$ iff $L$ is definable by a level $i$ rec-TMSO$(\Sigma, Rop)$ formula $\psi$ with one free variable.

For the base case we consider level 0 automata and sentences. Since level 0 automata only make use of the guard $\top$, they are simply Büchi automata over $\Sigma$. Similarly, level 0 sentences don't use any $\Delta$ predicates and hence they are simply MSO$(\Sigma)$ sentences. By Büchi's theorem, we have that level 0 automata and sentences are expressively equivalent.

For the base case for the second part of the claim, given a level 0 floating automaton $\mathcal{B}$ we can apply the construction in the proof of Theorem 7 to get a TMSO$(\Sigma)$ formula $\psi$ with one free variable. Since the construction preserves the guards used, $\psi$ has no $\Delta$ operators, and hence is a level 0 rec-TMSO$(\Sigma, Rop)$ formula. Conversely, for a level 0 formula $\psi$ we can apply the construction of

Theorem 7 to obtain a floating automaton $\mathcal{B}$ such that $L^f(\mathcal{B}) = L^f(\psi)$. The construction preserves the $\Delta$ operators used, and hence $\mathcal{B}$ is a level 0 automaton.

Turning now to the induction step, let $\mathcal{A}$ be a level $i + 1$ automaton over $(\Sigma, Rop)$. Let $Op$ be the set of top-level $\Delta$ operators in $\mathcal{A}$. Now since $\mathcal{A}$ is an IDA over $(\Sigma, Op)$, by Theorem 2, we have a TMSO$(\Sigma, Op)$ sentence $\varphi$ such that $L(\mathcal{A}) = L(\varphi)$. Now for each $\Delta_{\mathcal{B}}$ in $Op$, $\mathcal{B}$ is of level $i$ or lower, and by our induction hypothesis there is a corresponding rec-TMSO$(\Sigma, Rop)$ formula $\psi$ with one free variable, of the same level as $\mathcal{B}$, with $L^f(\mathcal{B}) = L^f(\psi)$. Hence for each $\Delta_{\mathcal{B}}$ we have a semantically equivalent operator $\Delta_\psi$. This is because $L^f(\mathcal{B}) = L^f(\psi)$, which implies $pos(\sigma, \mathcal{B}) = pos(\sigma, \psi)$, which in turn implies $[\![\Delta_{\mathcal{B}}]\!] = [\![\Delta_\psi]\!]$. We can now simply replace each occurrence of $\Delta_{\mathcal{B}}$ in $\varphi$ to get an equivalent sentence $\varphi'$ which is in rec-TMSO$(\Sigma, Rop)$. Further, by construction, $\varphi'$ is of level $i + 1$.

Conversely, let $\varphi$ be a level $i + 1$ sentence in rec-TMSO$(\Sigma, Rop)$. Let $Op$ be the set of top level $\Delta$ operators in $\varphi$. Then $\varphi$ is a TMSO$(\Sigma, Op)$ sentence, and hence by Theorem 2 we have an equivalent input determined automaton $\mathcal{A}$ over $(\Sigma, Op)$. Once again, for each $\Delta_\psi$ in $Op$, the formula $\psi$ is of level $i$ or lower, and hence by induction hypothesis we have a frec-IDA $\mathcal{B}$ over $(\Sigma, Rop)$, of the same level as $\psi$, and accepting the same floating language. The operators $\Delta_\psi$ and $\Delta_{\mathcal{B}}$ are now equivalent, and we can replace each $\Delta_\psi$ in $\mathcal{A}$ by the corresponding $\Delta_{\mathcal{B}}$ to get a language equivalent input determined automaton. This automaton is now the required level $i + 1$ rec-IDA over $(\Sigma, Rop)$ which accepts the same language as $L(\varphi)$.

The induction step for part 2 is proved similarly, making use of Theorem 7 and the induction hypothesis. This completes the proof of Theorem 6.    $\square$

## 8    Expressive Completeness of rec-TLTL

We now define a recursive timed temporal logic along the lines of [10]. The logic is similar to the logic TLTL defined in Sec. 5. It is parameterized by an alphabet $\Sigma$ and a set of recursive input determined operators $Rop$, and denoted rec-TLTL$(\Sigma, Rop)$. The syntax of the logic is given by

$$\theta ::= a \mid I \in \Delta_\theta \mid O\theta \mid \Theta\theta \mid (\theta U \theta) \mid (\theta S \theta) \mid \neg\theta \mid (\theta \vee \theta),$$

where $a \in \Sigma$, and $\Delta \in Rop$.

The logic is interpreted over timed words in a similar manner to TLTL. The predicate $I \in \Delta_\theta$ is interpreted as follows. If $\theta$ does not use a $\Delta$ predicate, then the satisfaction relation $\sigma, i \models \theta$ is defined as for TLTL. Inductively assuming the semantics of a rec-TLTL$(\Sigma, Rop)$ formula $\theta$ has been defined, and setting $pos(\sigma, \theta) = \{i \in \mathbb{N} \mid \sigma, i \models \theta\}$, the operator $\Delta_\theta$ is interpreted as an input determined operator with the semantic function

$$[\![\Delta_\theta]\!](\sigma, i) = [\![\Delta]\!](pos(\sigma, \theta), \sigma, i).$$

The satisfaction relation $\sigma, i \models I \in \Delta_\theta$ is then defined as in TLTL.

Once again, since $\Delta_\theta$ behaves like an input determined operator, each formula in rec-TLTL$(\Sigma, Rop)$ is also a TLTL$(\Sigma, Op)$ formula, for an appropriately chosen set of input determined operators $Op$, containing operators of the form $\Delta_\theta$. A rec-TLTL($\Sigma, Rop$) formula $\theta$ naturally defines both a timed language $L(\theta) = \{\sigma \in T\Sigma^\omega \mid \sigma, 0 \models \theta\}$ and a floating language $L^f(\theta) = \{(\sigma, i) \mid \sigma, i \models \theta\}$.

As an example, the formula $a \wedge ([1,1] \in \Diamond_\theta)$ where $\theta = b \wedge \Theta a \wedge Oa$, restates the property expressed by the rec-TMSO formula in Sec. 7.

Let us denote by rec-TFO($\Sigma, Rop$) the first-order fragment of the logic rec-TMSO($\Sigma, Rop$). Then we have the following expressive completeness result:

**Theorem 8.** rec-TLTL($\Sigma, Rop$) *is expressively equivalent to* rec-TFO($\Sigma, Rop$).

*Proof.* We show by induction on $i$ that (1) A timed language $L \subseteq T\Sigma^\omega$ is definable by a level $i$ rec-TLTL($\Sigma, Rop$) formula iff it is definable by a level $i$ rec-TFO($\Sigma, Rop$) sentence. (2) A floating timed language over $\Sigma$ is definable by a level $i$ rec-TLTL($\Sigma, Rop$) formula iff it is definable by a level $i$ rec-TFO($\Sigma, Rop$) formula with one free variable. We need to make use of the following result due to Kamp:

**Theorem 9 ([11]).** *For any* FO($A$) *formula* $\psi$ *with one free variable* $z$, *there is a* LTL($A$) *formula* $\theta$ *s.t. for each* $\alpha \in A^\omega$ *and* $i \in \mathbb{N}$, $\alpha, [i/z] \models \psi$ *iff* $\alpha, i \models \theta$.

The proof now proceeds similarly to that of Theorem 6, and Theorem 3 where we make use of the translations $s$-$t$ and $t$-$s$. The details can be found in [7]. $\square$

## 9   Expressive Completeness of MITL

As an application of the results in this paper we show that the logic MITL introduced in [2] is expressively equivalent to rec-TFO for a suitably defined set of recursive input determined operators. We point out here that this result is shown for the pointwise semantics of MITL given below. We begin with the logic MTL($\Sigma$) which has the following syntax [4]:

$$\theta ::= a \mid O\theta \mid \Theta\theta \mid (\theta U_I \theta) \mid (\theta S_I \theta) \mid \neg\theta \mid (\theta \vee \theta).$$

Here $I$ is an interval in $\mathcal{I}_\mathbb{Q}$. When $I$ is restricted to be *non-singular* (i.e. not of the form $[r,r]$) then we get the logic MITL($\Sigma$). The logic is interpreted over timed words in $T\Sigma^\omega$ similarly to TLTL. The modalities $U_I$ and $S_I$ are interpreted as follows, for a timed word $\sigma = (\alpha, \tau)$.

$\sigma, i \models \theta U_I \eta$ iff $\exists k \geq i : \sigma, k \models \eta, \tau(k) - \tau(i) \in I$, and $\forall j : i \leq j < k, \sigma, j \models \theta$
$\sigma, i \models \theta S_I \eta$ iff $\exists k \leq i : \sigma, k \models \eta, \tau(i) - \tau(k) \in I$, and $\forall j : k < j \leq i, \sigma, j \models \theta$.

We first observe that MTL($\Sigma$) is expressively equivalent to its sublogic MTL$^\Diamond(\Sigma)$ in which the modalities $U_I$ and $S_I$ are replaced by the modalities $U$, $S$, $\Diamond_I$ and $\Diamondblack_I$, where $U$ and $S$ are as usual and $\Diamond_I\theta = \top U_I\theta$ and $\Diamondblack_I\theta = \top S_I\theta$. This is because the formula $\theta U_I\eta$ (and dually $\theta S_I\eta$) can be translated as follows. Here '$\rangle$' denotes either a ']' or ')' interval bracket.

$$\theta U_I \eta = \begin{cases} \Diamond_I\eta \wedge \square_{[0,a)}(\theta U(\theta \wedge O\eta)) & \text{if } I = [a, b\rangle, a > 0 \\ \Diamond_I\eta \wedge \square_{[0,a]}(\theta U(\theta \wedge O\eta)) & \text{if } I = (a, b\rangle, a > 0 \\ \Diamond_I\eta \wedge (\theta U\eta) & \text{if } I = [0, b\rangle \\ \Diamond_I\eta \wedge (\theta U(\theta \wedge O\eta)) & \text{if } I = (0, b\rangle. \end{cases}$$

Next we consider the logic rec-TLTL($\Sigma, \{\Diamond, \diamondsuit\}$). The logic MTL$^{\Diamond}(\Sigma)$ is clearly expressively equivalent to rec-TLTL($\Sigma, \{\Diamond, \diamondsuit\}$) since the predicates $\Diamond_I \theta$ and $I \in \Diamond_{\theta}$ are equivalent. Using Theorem 8 we can now conclude that

**Theorem 10.** MTL($\Sigma$) *is expressively equivalent to* rec-TFO($\Sigma, \{\Diamond, \diamondsuit\}$).

Let rec-TFO$_{\neq}$ denote the restriction of rec-TFO to non-singular intervals. Then since the translation of MTL to MTL$^{\Diamond}$ does not introduce any singular intervals, and the constructions in Theorem 8 preserve the interval vocabulary of the formulas, we conclude that the logics MITL($\Sigma$) and rec-TFO$_{\neq}(\Sigma, \{\Diamond, \diamondsuit\})$ are expressively equivalent.

# References

1. R. Alur, D. L. Dill: A theory of timed automata, *Theoretical Computer Science* **126**: 183–235 (1994).
2. R. Alur, T. Feder, T. A. Henzinger: The benefits of relaxing punctuality, *J. ACM* **43**, 116–146 (1996).
3. R. Alur, L. Fix, T. A. Henzinger: Event-clock automata: a determinizable class of timed automata, *Proc. 6th CAV*, LNCS **818**, 1–13, Springer-Verlag (1994).
4. R. Alur, T. A. Henzinger: Real-time logics: complexity and expressiveness, *Information and Computation* **104**, 35–77 (1993).
5. J. R. Büchi: Weak second-order arithmetic and finite automata, *Zeitschrift für Math. Logik und Grundlagen der Mathematik*, **6**, 66–92 (1960).
6. D. D'Souza: A Logical Characterisation of Event Clock Automata, in *J. Foundations of Computer Science*, **14**, No. 4, World Scientific (2003).
7. D. D'Souza, N. Tabareau: On timed automata with input-determined guards, Technical report TR-2004-1, CSA/IISc, (http://archive.csa.iisc.ernet.in/TR).
8. D. D'Souza, P. S. Thiagarajan: Product Interval Automata: A Subclass of Timed Automata, *Proc. 19th FSTTCS*, LNCS **1732** (1999).
9. D. Gabbay, A. Pnueli, S. Shelah, J. Stavi: The Temporal Analysis of Fairness, *Seventh ACM Symposium on Principles of Programming Languages*, 163–173 (1980).
10. T. A. Henzinger, J.-F. Raskin, and P.-Y. Schobbens: The regular real-time languages, *Proc. 25th ICALP 1998*, LNCS **1443**, 580–591 (1998).
11. H. Kamp: Tense Logic and the Theory of Linear Order, PhD Thesis, University of California (1968).
12. R. Koymans: Specifying real-time properties with metric temporal logic, *Real-time Systems*, **2**(4), 255–299 (1990).
13. A. Pnueli: The temporal logic of programs, *Proc. 18th IEEE FOCS*, 46–57 (1977).
14. J. -F. Raskin: Logics, Automata and Classical Theories for Deciding Real Time, Ph.D Thesis, FUNDP, Belgium (1999).
15. J. -F. Raskin, P. -Y. Schobbens: State-clock Logic: A Decidable Real-Time Logic, *Proc. HART '97: Hybrid and Real-Time Systems*, LNCS **1201**, 33–47 (1997).
16. W. Thomas: Automata on Infinite Objects, in J. V. Leeuwen (Ed.), *Handbook of Theoretical Computer Science*, Vol. B, 133–191, Elsevier (1990).
17. Th. Wilke: Specifying Timed State Sequences in Powerful Decidable Logics and Timed Automata, in *Proc. 3rd FTRTFT*, LNCS **863**, 694–715 (1994).

# Decomposing Verification
# of Timed I/O Automata

Dilsun Kırlı Kaynar and Nancy Lynch

MIT Computer Science and Artificial Intelligence Laboratory
{dilsun,lynch}@csail.mit.edu

**Abstract.** This paper presents assume-guarantee style substitutivity results for the recently published timed I/O automaton modeling framework. These results are useful for decomposing verification of systems where the implementation and the specification are represented as timed I/O automata. We first present a theorem that is applicable in verification tasks in which system specifications express safety properties. This theorem has an interesting corollary that involves the use of auxiliary automata in simplifying the proof obligations. We then derive a new result that shows how the same technique can be applied to the case where system specifications express liveness properties.

## 1   Introduction

The timed I/O automata (TIOA) modeling framework [KLSV03a,KLSV03b] provides a *composition operation*, by which TIOAs modeling individual timed system components can be combined to produce a model for a larger timed system. The model for the composed system can describe interactions among the components, which involves joint participation in discrete transitions. Composition requires certain "compatibility" conditions, namely, that each output action be controlled by at most one automaton, and that internal actions of one automaton cannot be shared by any other automaton.

The composition operation for TIOAs satisfies *projection* and *pasting* results, which are fundamental for compositional design and verification of systems: a trace of a composition of TIOAs "projects" to give traces of the individual TIOAs, and traces of components are "pastable" to give behaviors of the composition. This allows one to derive conclusions about the behavior of a large system by combining the results obtained from the analysis of each individual component.

The composition operation for TIOAs also satisfies a basic substitutivity result that states that the composition operation respects the implementation relation for TIOAs. An automaton $\mathcal{A}_1$ is said to *implement* an automaton $\mathcal{A}_2$ if the set of traces of $\mathcal{A}_1$ is included in the the set of traces of $\mathcal{A}_2$. The implementation relation is a congruence with respect to parallel composition. That is, given an automaton $\mathcal{B}$, if $\mathcal{A}_1$ implements $\mathcal{A}_2$ then the composition $\mathcal{A}_1\|\mathcal{B}$ implements the composition $\mathcal{A}_2\|\mathcal{B}$. A corollary of this basic substitutivity result is that, if

Y. Lakhnech and S. Yovine (Eds.): FORMATS/FTRTFT 2004, LNCS 3253, pp. 84–101, 2004.
© Springer-Verlag Berlin Heidelberg 2004

$\mathcal{A}_1$ implements a specification $\mathcal{A}_2$ and $\mathcal{B}_1$ implements a specification $\mathcal{B}_2$ then $\mathcal{A}_1\|\mathcal{B}_1$ implements $\mathcal{A}_2\|\mathcal{B}_2$.

The basic substitutivity property described above is desirable for any formalism for interacting processes. For design purposes, it enables one to refine individual components without violating the correctness of the system as a whole. For verification purposes, it enables one to prove that a composite system satisfies its specification by proving that each component satisfies its specification, thereby breaking down the verification task into more manageable pieces. However, it might not always be possible or easy to show that each component $\mathcal{A}_1$ (resp. $\mathcal{B}_1$) satisfies its specification $\mathcal{A}_2$ (resp. $\mathcal{B}_2$) without using any assumptions about the environment of the component. *Assume-guarantee* style results such as those presented in [Jon83,Pnu84,Sta85,AL93,AL95,HQR00,TAKB96] are special kinds of substitutivity results that state what *guarantees* are expected from each component in an environment constrained by certain *assumptions*. Since the environment of each component consists of the other components in the system, assume-guarantee style results need to break the circular dependencies between the assumptions and guarantees for components.

This paper presents assume-guarantee style theorems for use in verification and analysis of timed systems within the TIOA framework. The first theorem allows one to conclude that $\mathcal{A}_1\|\mathcal{B}_1$ implements $\mathcal{A}_2\|\mathcal{B}_2$ provided that $\mathcal{A}_1$ implements $\mathcal{A}_2$ in the context of $\mathcal{B}_2$ and $\mathcal{B}_1$ implements $\mathcal{B}_2$ in the context of $\mathcal{A}_2$, where $\mathcal{A}_2$ and $\mathcal{B}_2$ express safety constraints and admit arbitrary time-passage. This theorem has an interesting corollary that involves the use of auxiliary automata $\mathcal{A}_3$ and $\mathcal{B}_3$ in decomposing the proof that $\mathcal{A}_1\|\mathcal{B}_1$ implements $\mathcal{A}_2\|\mathcal{B}_2$. The main idea behind this corollary is to capture, by means of $\mathcal{A}_3$ and $\mathcal{B}_3$, what is essential about the behavior of the contexts $\mathcal{A}_2$ and $\mathcal{B}_2$ in proving the implementation relationship. The second theorem extends this corollary to the case where liveness conditions are added to automaton specifications. This theorem requires one to find the appropriate auxiliary liveness properties for $\mathcal{A}_3$ and $\mathcal{B}_3$, in addition to what is already needed for proving the safety part of the specification. The liveness properties devised for $\mathcal{A}_3$ and $\mathcal{B}_3$ are supposed to capture what liveness guarantees of the contexts $\mathcal{A}_2$ and $\mathcal{B}_2$ are essential in showing the implementation relationship.

*Related Work.* The results of this paper constitute the first assume-guarantee style results for timed I/O automata. Assume-guarantee reasoning has been previously investigated in various formal frameworks, most commonly, in frameworks based on temporal logics [Pnu84,Sta85,AL93,AL95] and reactive modules [HQR00,HQR02]. Although some of these frameworks such as TLA and reactive modules can be extended to support modeling of timed system behavior [AL94,AH97], it is hard to understand whether all of the results and reasoning techniques obtained for their untimed versions generalize to the timed setting. The work presented in [TAKB96] considers a framework based on timed processes that underlies the language of the tool COSPAN [AK96]. The focus of that paper is timed simulation relations, how they relate to verification based on language inclusion and algorithmic aspects of checking for timed simulations.

The topic of assume-guarantee reasoning is visited only for a single theorem, which is akin to the first theorem of this paper. Our other theorems that involve the use of auxiliary automata and liveness properties appear to incorporate novel and simple ideas that have not been investigated before in decomposing verification of timed systems.

*Organization of the Paper.* Section 2 introduces the basic concepts of the TIOA framework, and gives the basic definitions and results relevant to what its presented in the rest of the paper. This section also states the notational conventions used in writing the TIOA specifications that appear in the examples. Section 3 gives a theorem and its corollary that can be used in decomposing verification of systems where the TIOAs express safety properties. Section 4 shows how the ideas of Section 3 can be applied to decomposition of verification where TIOAs express liveness properties as well as safety properties. Section 5 summarizes the contributions of the paper and discusses possible directions for future work.

## 2    Timed I/O Automata

In this section, we present briefly the basic definitions and results from the timed I/O modeling framework that are necessary to understand the material in this paper. The reader is referred to [KLSV03a] for the details.

### 2.1    Describing Timed System Behavior

We use the set R of real numbers as the domain (in [KLSV03a] other time domains are also considered). A time interval is a nonempty, convex subset of R. An interval is *left-closed (right-closed)* if it has a minimum (resp., maximum) element, and *left-open (right-open)* otherwise. It is *closed* if it is both left-closed and right-closed.

States of automata will consist of valuations of *variables*. Each variable has both a *static type*, which defines the set of values it may assume, and a *dynamic type*, which gives the set of trajectories it may follow. We assume that dynamic types are closed under some simple operations: shifting the time domain, taking subintervals and pasting together intervals. We call a variable *discrete* if its dynamic type equals the pasting-closure of a set of constant-valued functions (i.e., the step-functions), and *analog* if its dynamic type equals the pasting-closure of a set of continuous functions (i.e., the piecewise-continuous functions).

A *valuation* for a set $V$ of variables is a function that associates with each variable $v \in V$ a value in its static type. We write $val(V)$ for the set of all valuations for $V$. A *trajectory* for a set $V$ of variables describes the evolution of the variables in $V$ over time; formally, it is a function from a time interval that starts with 0 to valuations of $V$, that is, a trajectory defines a value for each variable at each time in the interval. We write $trajs(V)$ for the set of all trajectories for $V$. A *point trajectory* is one with the trivial domain $\{0\}$. The *limit time* of a trajectory $\tau$, $\tau.ltime$, is the supremum of the times in its domain. We say that a trajectory is *closed* if its domain is a closed interval. $\tau.fval$ is defined to be the first valuation of $\tau$, and if $\tau$ is closed, $\tau.lval$ is the last valuation. Suppose $\tau$ and $\tau'$ are trajectories for $V$, with $\tau$ closed. The *concatenation* of $\tau$ and $\tau'$, denoted by $\tau \frown \tau'$, is the trajectory obtained by taking the union of the first trajectory and the function obtained by shifting the domain of the second trajectory until the start time agrees with the limit time of the first trajectory; the last valuation of the first trajectory, which may not be the same as the first valuation of the second trajectory, is the one that appears in the concatenation.

The notion of a *hybrid sequence* is used to model a combination of changes that occur instantaneously and changes that occur over intervals of time. Our definition is parameterized by a set $A$ of discrete actions and a set $V$ of variables. Thus, an $(A, V)$-*sequence* is a finite or infinite alternating sequence, $\tau_0\, a_1\, \tau_1\, a_2\, \tau_2$ ..., of trajectories over $V$ and actions in $A$. A *hybrid sequence* is any $(A, V)$-sequence. The *limit time* of a hybrid sequence $\alpha$, denoted by $\alpha.ltime$, is defined by adding the limit times of all its trajectories. Hybrid sequence $\alpha$ is defined to be *admissible* if $\alpha.ltime = \infty$, and *closed* if it is a finite sequence and the domain of its final trajectory is a closed interval. Like trajectories, hybrid sequences can be concatenated, and one can be a prefix of another. If $\alpha$ is a closed $(A, V)$-sequence, where $V = \emptyset$ and $\beta \in trajs(\emptyset)$, we call $\alpha \frown \beta$ a *time-extension* of $\alpha$. A hybrid sequence can also be restricted to smaller sets of actions and variables: the $(A', V')$-*restriction* of an $(A, V)$-sequence $\alpha$ is obtained by first projecting all trajectories of $\alpha$ on the variables in $V'$, then removing the actions not in $A'$, and finally concatenating all adjacent trajectories.

A set $S$ of hybrid sequences is said to be *closed under limits* if for each chain (with respect to prefix ordering) of closed hybrid sequences in $S$, the limit of the chain is in $S$.

## 2.2   Timed I/O Automata Definition

Formally, a *timed I/O automaton (TIOA)* consists of:

- A set $X$ of *internal variables*.
- A set $Q \subseteq val(X)$ of *states*.
- A nonempty set $\Theta \subseteq Q$ of *start states*.
- A set $H$ of *internal actions*, a set $I$ of *input* actions and a set $O$ of *output actions*. We write $E \triangleq I \cup O$ for the set of external actions and $A \triangleq E \cup H$ for the set of all actions. Actions in $L \triangleq H \cup O$ are called *locally controlled*.
- A set $\mathcal{D} \subseteq Q \times A \times Q$ of *discrete transitions*.
  We use $\mathbf{x} \xrightarrow{a} \mathbf{x}'$ as shorthand for $(\mathbf{x}, a, \mathbf{x}') \in \mathcal{D}$. We say that $a$ is *enabled* in $\mathbf{x}$ if $(\mathbf{x}, a, \mathbf{x}') \in \mathcal{D}$ for some $\mathbf{x}'$.
- A set $\mathcal{T}$ of *trajectories* for $X$ such that $\tau(t) \in Q$ for every $\tau \in \mathcal{T}$ and every $t$ in the domain of $\tau$. Given a trajectory $\tau \in \mathcal{T}$ we denote $\tau.fval$ by $\tau.fstate$ and, if $\tau$ is closed, we denote $\tau.lval$ by $\tau.lstate$.

We require that the set of trajectories be closed under the operations of prefix, suffix, and concatenation and that there is a point trajectory for every state of the automaton. Moreover, the following axioms are satisfied:

**E1** (Input action enabling)

For every $\mathbf{x} \in Q$ and every $a \in I$, there exists $\mathbf{x}' \in Q$ such that $\mathbf{x} \xrightarrow{a} \mathbf{x}'$.

**E2** (Time-passage enabling)

For every $\mathbf{x} \in Q$, there exists $\tau \in \mathcal{T}$ such that $\tau.fstate = \mathbf{x}$ and either $\tau.ltime = \infty$, or $\tau$ is closed and some $l \in L$ is enabled in $\tau.lstate$.

*Executions and Traces.* An *execution fragment* of a TIOA $\mathcal{A}$ is an $(A, V)$-sequence $\alpha = \tau_0\, a_1\, \tau_1\, a_2\, \tau_2 \ldots$, where $A$ and $V$ are all the actions and variables of $\mathcal{A}$, respectively, where each $\tau_i$ is a trajectory of $\mathcal{A}$, and for every $i$, $\tau_i.lval \xrightarrow{a_{i+1}} \tau_{i+1}.fval$. An execution fragment records what happens during a particular run of a system, including all the discrete state changes and all the changes that occur while time advances. An *execution* is an execution fragment whose first state is a start state of $\mathcal{A}$. We write *frags*$_\mathcal{A}$ for the set of all execution fragments of $\mathcal{A}$ and *execs*$_\mathcal{A}$ for the set of all executions of $\mathcal{A}$.

The external behavior of a TIOA is captured by the set of "traces" of its execution fragments, which record external actions and the intervening passage of time. Formally, the *trace* of an execution fragment $\alpha$ is the $(E, \emptyset)$-restriction of $\alpha$. Thus, a trace is a hybrid sequence consisting of external actions of $\mathcal{A}$ and trajectories over the empty set of variables. The only interesting information contained in these trajectories is the amount of time that elapses. A *trace fragment* of $\mathcal{A}$ is the trace of an execution fragment of $\mathcal{A}$, and a *trace* of $\mathcal{A}$ is the trace of an execution of $\mathcal{A}$. We write *tracefrags*$_\mathcal{A}(\mathbf{x})$ for the set of trace fragments of $\mathcal{A}$ from $\mathbf{x}$ and *traces*$_\mathcal{A}$ for the set of traces of $\mathcal{A}$.

*Implementation Relationships.* Timed I/O automata $\mathcal{A}$ and $\mathcal{B}$ are *comparable* if they have the same external actions. If $\mathcal{A}$ and $\mathcal{B}$ are comparable then $\mathcal{A}$ *implements* $\mathcal{B}$, denoted by $\mathcal{A} \leq \mathcal{B}$, if *traces*$_\mathcal{A} \subseteq$ *traces*$_\mathcal{B}$.

*Composition.* We say that TIOAs $\mathcal{A}_1$ and $\mathcal{A}_2$ are *compatible* if, for $i \neq j$, $X_i \cap X_j = H_i \cap A_j = O_i \cap O_j = \emptyset$. If $\mathcal{A}_1$ and $\mathcal{A}_2$ are compatible TIOAs then their *composition* $\mathcal{A}_1 \| \mathcal{A}_2$ is defined to be the tuple $\mathcal{A} = (X, Q, \Theta, H, I, O, \mathcal{D}, \mathcal{T})$ where

- $X = X_1 \cup X_2$.
- $Q = \{\mathbf{x} \in val(X) \mid \mathbf{x} \lceil X_1 \in Q_1 \wedge \mathbf{x} \lceil X_2 \in Q_2\}$ [1].
- $\Theta = \{\mathbf{x} \in Q \mid \mathbf{x} \lceil X_1 \in \Theta_1 \wedge \mathbf{x} \lceil X_2 \in \Theta_2\}$.
- $H = H_1 \cup H_2$.
- $I = (I_1 \cup I_2) - (O_1 \cup O_2)$
- $O = O_1 \cup O_2$.
- For each $\mathbf{x}, \mathbf{x}' \in Q$ and each $a \in A$, $\mathbf{x} \xrightarrow{a}_\mathcal{A} \mathbf{x}'$ iff for $i \in \{1, 2\}$, either (1) $a \in A_i$ and $\mathbf{x} \lceil X_i \xrightarrow{a}_i \mathbf{x}' \lceil X_i$, or (2) $a \notin A_i$ and $\mathbf{x} \lceil X_i = \mathbf{x}' \lceil X_i$.
- $\mathcal{T} = \{\tau \in trajs(X) \mid \tau \downarrow X_1 \in \mathcal{T}_1 \wedge \tau \downarrow X_2 \in \mathcal{T}_2\}$ [2].

---

[1] If $f$ is a function and $S$ is a set, then we write $f \lceil S$ for the restriction of $f$ to $S$, that is, the function $g$ with $dom(g) = dom(f) \cap S$ such that $g(c) = f(c)$ for each $c \in dom(g)$.

[2] If $f$ is a function whose range is a set of functions and $S$ is a set, then we write $f \downarrow S$ for the function $g$ with $dom(g) = dom(f)$ such that $g(c) = f(c) \lceil S$ for each $c \in dom(g)$.

The following theorem is a fundamental theorem that relates the set of traces of a composed automaton to the sets of traces of its components. Set inclusion in one direction expresses the idea that a trace of a composition "projects" to yield traces of the components. Set inclusion in the other direction expresses the idea that traces of components can be "pasted" to yield a trace of the composition.

**Theorem 1.** *Let $A_1$ and $A_2$ be comparable TIOAs, and let $A = A_1 \| A_2$. Then $traces_A$ is exactly the set of $(E, \emptyset)$-sequences whose restrictions to $A_1$ and $A_2$ are traces of $A_1$ and $A_2$, respectively. That is, $traces_A = \{\beta \mid \beta$ is an $(E, \emptyset)$-sequence and $\beta \lceil (E_i, \emptyset) \in traces_{A_i}, i = \{1, 2\}\}$.*

## 2.3 Properties

A *property* $P$ for a timed I/O automaton $A$ is defined to be any subset of the execution fragments of $A$. We write $execs_{(A,P)}$ for the set of executions of $A$ in $P$ and $traces_{(A,P)}$ for the set of traces of executions of $A$ in $P$.

A property $P$ for a TIOA $A$ is said to be a *safety* property if it is closed under prefix and limits of execution fragments. A property $P$ for $A$ is defined to be a *liveness* property provided that for any closed execution fragment $\alpha$ of $A$, there exists an execution fragment $\beta$ such that $\alpha \frown \beta \in P$.

In the TIOA modeling framework safety properties are typically specified as all of the execution fragments of a TIOA. That is, no extra machinery other than the automaton specification itself is necessary to specify a safety property. The set of execution fragments of a TIOA is closed under prefix and limits. When the external behavior sets (trace sets), rather than execution fragments are taken as a basis for specification, an automaton is said to specify a safety property only if its trace set is closed under limits (trace sets are closed under prefixes by definition).

Liveness properties are typically specified by coupling a TIOA $A$ with a property $P$ where $P$ is a liveness property. A pair $(A, P)$ can be viewed as a two-part specification: a safety condition expressed by the automaton $A$ and a liveness condition expressed by $P$. It is in general desirable that $P$ does not itself impose safety constraints, beyond those already imposed by the execution fragments of $A$. To achieve this, $P$ should be defined so that every closed execution in $P$ can be extended to some execution that is in both $execs_A$ and $P$. The notion of machine-closure is used to formalize this condition. A detailed discussion can be found in [KLSV03a].

*Implementation Relationships.* In analogy with basic TIOAs, we define another preorder for automata with properties: $(A_1, P_1) \leq (A_2, P_2)$ provided that $traces_{(A_1, P_1)} \subseteq traces_{(A_2, P_2)}$.

*Composition.* If $A_1$ and $A_2$ are two compatible timed I/O automata and $P_1$ and $P_2$ are properties for $A_1$ and $A_2$, respectively, then we define $P_1 \| P_2$ to be $\{\alpha \in frags_{A_1 \| A_2} \mid \alpha \lceil (A_i, X_i) \in P_i, i \in \{1, 2\}\}$. Using this, we define composition of automata with properties $(A_1, P_1) \| (A_2, P_2)$ as $(A_1 \| A_2, P_1 \| P_2)$.

**Theorem 2.** *Let $\mathcal{A}_1$ and $\mathcal{A}_2$ be two compatible TIOAs and $P_1$ and $P_2$ be properties for $\mathcal{A}_1$ and $\mathcal{A}_2$, respectively. Then $traces_{(\mathcal{A}_1 \| \mathcal{A}_2, P_1 \| P_2)}$ is exactly the set of $(E, \emptyset)$-sequences whose restrictions to $\mathcal{A}_1$ and $\mathcal{A}_2$ are $traces_{(\mathcal{A}_1, P_1)}$ and $traces_{(\mathcal{A}_2, P_2)}$, respectively. That is, $traces_{(\mathcal{A}_1 \| \mathcal{A}_2, P_1 \| P_2)} = \{\beta \mid \beta$ is an $(E, \emptyset)$ -sequence and $\beta \lceil (E_i, \emptyset) \in traces_{(\mathcal{A}_i, P_i)}, i \in \{1, 2\}\}$.*

## 2.4   Conventions for Writing TIOA Specifications

We typically specify sets of trajectories using differential and algebraic equations and inclusions. Suppose the time domain T is R, $\tau$ is a (fixed) trajectory over some set of variables $V$, and $v \in V$. With some abuse of notation, we use the variable name $v$ to denote the function that gives the value of $v$ at all times during trajectory $\tau$. Similarly, we view any expression $e$ containing variables from $V$ as a function with $dom(\tau)$ (the domain of $\tau$). Suppose that $v$ is a variable and $e$ is a real-valued expression containing variables from $V$. We say that $\tau$ satisfies the algebraic equation $v = e$ which means that, for every $t \in dom(\tau)$, $v(t) = e(t)$, that is, the constraint on the variables expressed by the equation $v = e$ holds for each state on trajectory $\tau$. Suppose also that $e$, when viewed as a function, is integrable. Then we say that $\tau$ satisfies $d(v) = e$ if, for every $t \in dom(\tau)$, $v(t) = v(0) + \int_0^t e(t')dt'$. This way of specifying trajectories generalizes to differential inclusions as explained in [KLSV03a].

In the rest of the paper, we use examples to illustrate our theorems. These examples are based on TIOA specifications written using certain notational conventions (see Appendix B). The transitions are specified in precondition-effect style. A **precondition** clause specifies the enabling condition for an action. The **effect** clause contains a list of statements that specify the effect of performing that action on the state. All the statements in an effect clause are assumed to be executed sequentially in a single indivisible step. The absence of a specified precondition for an action means that the action is always enabled and the absence of a specified effect means that performing the action does not change the state.

The trajectories are specified by using a variation of the language presented in [MWLF03]. A **satisfies** clause contains a list of predicates that must be satisfied by all the trajectories. This clause is followed by a **stops when** clause. If the predicate in this clause becomes true at a point $t$ in time, then $t$ must be the limit time of the trajectory. When there is no stopping condition for trajectories we omit the **stops when** clause. In our examples, we write $\mathbf{d}(v) = e$ for $d(v) = e$. If the value of a variable is constant throughout a trajectory then we write $\mathbf{constant}(v)$.

## 3   Decomposition Theorem for TIOAs

In this section we present two assume/guarantee style results, Theorem 3 and Corollary 1, which can used for proving that a system specified as a composite automaton $\mathcal{A}_1 \| \mathcal{B}_1$ implements a specification represented by a composite automaton $\mathcal{A}_2 \| \mathcal{B}_2$ .

The main idea behind Theorem 3 is to assume that $\mathcal{A}_1$ implements $\mathcal{A}_2$ in a context represented by $\mathcal{B}_2$, and symmetrically that $\mathcal{B}_1$ implements $\mathcal{B}_2$ in a context represented by $\mathcal{A}_2$ where $\mathcal{A}_2$ and $\mathcal{B}_2$ are automata whose trace sets are closed under limits. The requirement about limit-closure implies that $\mathcal{A}_2$ and $\mathcal{B}_2$ specify trace safety properties. Moreover, we assume that $\mathcal{A}_2$ and $\mathcal{B}_2$ allow arbitrary time-passage. This is the most general assumption one could make to ensure that $\mathcal{A}_2 \| \mathcal{B}_2$ does not impose stronger constraints on time-passage than $\mathcal{A}_1 \| \mathcal{B}_1$.

**Theorem 3.** *Suppose $\mathcal{A}_1$, $\mathcal{A}_2$, $\mathcal{B}_1$, $\mathcal{B}_2$ are TIOAs such that $\mathcal{A}_1$ and $\mathcal{A}_2$ are comparable, $\mathcal{B}_1$ and $\mathcal{B}_2$ are comparable, and $\mathcal{A}_i$ is compatible with $\mathcal{B}_i$ for $i \in \{1,2\}$. Suppose further that:*

1. *The sets $traces_{\mathcal{A}_2}$ and $traces_{\mathcal{B}_2}$ are closed under limits.*
2. *The sets $traces_{\mathcal{A}_2}$ and $traces_{\mathcal{B}_2}$ are closed under time-extension.*
3. *$\mathcal{A}_1 \| \mathcal{B}_2 \leq \mathcal{A}_2 \| \mathcal{B}_2$ and $\mathcal{A}_2 \| \mathcal{B}_1 \leq \mathcal{A}_2 \| \mathcal{B}_2$.*

*Then $\mathcal{A}_1 \| \mathcal{B}_1 \leq \mathcal{A}_2 \| \mathcal{B}_2$.*

Theorem 3 has a corollary, Corollary 1 below, which can be used in the decomposition of proofs even when $\mathcal{A}_2$ and $\mathcal{B}_2$ neither admit arbitrary time-passage nor have limit-closed trace sets. The main idea behind this corollary is to assume that $\mathcal{A}_1$ implements $\mathcal{A}_2$ in a context $\mathcal{B}_3$ that is a variant of $\mathcal{B}_2$, and symmetrically that $\mathcal{B}_1$ implements $\mathcal{B}_2$ in a context that is a variant of $\mathcal{A}_2$. That is, the correctness of implementation relationship between $\mathcal{A}_1$ and $\mathcal{A}_2$ does not depend on all the environment constraints, just on those expressed by $\mathcal{B}_3$ (symmetrically for $\mathcal{B}_1, \mathcal{B}_2$, and $\mathcal{A}_3$). In order to use this corollary to prove $\mathcal{A}_1 \| \mathcal{B}_1 \leq \mathcal{A}_2 \| \mathcal{B}_2$ one needs to be able to find appropriate variants of $\mathcal{A}_2$ and $\mathcal{B}_2$ that meet the required closure properties. This corollary prompts one to pin down what is essential about the behavior of the environment in proving the intended implementation relationship, and also allows one to avoid the unnecessary details of the environment in proofs.

**Corollary 1.** *Suppose $\mathcal{A}_1$, $\mathcal{A}_2$, $\mathcal{A}_3$, $\mathcal{B}_1$, $\mathcal{B}_2$, $\mathcal{B}_3$ are TIOAs such that $\mathcal{A}_1$, $\mathcal{A}_2$, and $\mathcal{A}_3$ are comparable, $\mathcal{B}_1$, $\mathcal{B}_2$, and $\mathcal{B}_3$ are comparable, and $\mathcal{A}_i$ is compatible with $\mathcal{B}_i$ for $i \in \{1,2,3\}$. Suppose further that:*

1. *The sets $traces_{\mathcal{A}_3}$ and $traces_{\mathcal{B}_3}$ are closed under limits.*
2. *The sets $traces_{\mathcal{A}_3}$ and $traces_{\mathcal{B}_3}$ are closed under time-extension.*
3. *$\mathcal{A}_2 \| \mathcal{B}_3 \leq \mathcal{A}_3 \| \mathcal{B}_3$ and $\mathcal{A}_3 \| \mathcal{B}_2 \leq \mathcal{A}_3 \| \mathcal{B}_3$.*
4. *$\mathcal{A}_1 \| \mathcal{B}_3 \leq \mathcal{A}_2 \| \mathcal{B}_3$ and $\mathcal{A}_3 \| \mathcal{B}_1 \leq \mathcal{A}_3 \| \mathcal{B}_2$.*

*Then $\mathcal{A}_1 \| \mathcal{B}_1 \leq \mathcal{A}_2 \| \mathcal{B}_2$.*

The proofs for Theorem 3 and Corollary 1 can be found in [KLSV03a].

*Example 1.* This example illustrates that, in cases where specifications $\mathcal{A}_2$ and $\mathcal{B}_2$ satisfy certain closure properties, it is possible to decompose the proof of

$\mathcal{A}_1 \| \mathcal{B}_1 \leq \mathcal{A}_2 \| \mathcal{B}_2$ by using Theorem 3, even if it is not the case that $\mathcal{A}_1 \leq \mathcal{A}_2$ or $\mathcal{B}_1 \leq \mathcal{B}_2$.

The automata *AlternateA* and *AlternateB* in Figure 1 are timing-independent automata in which no consecutive outputs occur without inputs happening in between. *AlternateA* and *AlternateB* perform a handshake, outputting an alternating sequence of $a$ and $b$ actions when they are composed. The automata *CatchUpA* and *CatchUpB* in Figure 2 are timing-dependent automata that do not necessarily alternate inputs and outputs as *AlternateA* and *AlternateB*. *CatchUpA* can perform an arbitrary number of $b$ actions, and can perform an $a$ provided that *counta* $\leq$ *countb*. It allows *counta* to increase to one more than *countb*. *CatchUpB* can perform an arbitrary number of $a$ actions, and can perform a $b$ provided that *counta* $\geq$ *countb* $+ 1$. It allows *countb* to reach *counta*. Timing constraints require each output to occur exactly one time unit after the last action. *CatchUpA* and *CatchUpB* perform an alternating sequence of $a$ actions and $b$ actions when they are composed.

Suppose that we want to prove that *CatchUpA* $\|$ *CatchUpB* $\leq$ *AlternateA* $\|$ *AlternateB*. We cannot apply the basic substitutivity theorem since the assertions *CatchUpA* $\leq$ *AlternateA* and *CatchUpB* $\leq$ *AlternateB* are not true. Consider the trace $\tau_0 \, b \, \tau_1 \, a \, \tau_2 \, a \, \tau_3$ of *CatchUpA* where $\tau_0$, $\tau_1$, $\tau_2$ and $\tau_3$ are trajectories with limit time 1. After having performed one $b$ and one $a$, *CatchUpA* can perform another $a$. But, this is impossible for *AlternateA* which needs an input to enable the second $a$. *AlternateA* and *CatchUpA* behave similarly only when put in a context that imposes alternation.

It is easy to check that *AlternateA* and *AlternateB* satisfy the closure properties required by Assumptions 1 and 2 of Theorem 3 and, hence can be substituted for $\mathcal{A}_2$ and $\mathcal{B}_2$ respectively. Similarly, we can easily check that Assumption 3 is satisfied if we substitute *CatchUpA* for $\mathcal{A}_1$ and *CatchUpB* for $\mathcal{B}_1$.

*Example 2.* This example illustrates that it may be possible to decompose verification, using Corollary 1, in cases where Theorem 3 is not applicable. If the aim is to show $\mathcal{A}_1 \| \mathcal{B}_1 \leq \mathcal{A}_2 \| \mathcal{B}_2$ where $\mathcal{A}_2$ and $\mathcal{B}_2$ do not satisfy the assumptions of Theorem 3, then we find appropriate context automata $A_3$ and $\mathcal{B}_3$ that abstract from those details of $\mathcal{A}_2$ and $\mathcal{B}_2$ that are not essential in proving $\mathcal{A}_1 \| \mathcal{B}_1 \leq \mathcal{A}_2 \| \mathcal{B}_2$.

Consider the automata *UseOldInputA* and *UseOldInputB* in Figure 3. *UseOldInputA* keeps track of whether or not it is *UseOldInputA*'s turn, and when it is *UseOldInputA*'s turn, it keeps track of the next time it is supposed to perform an output. The number of outputs that *UseOldInputA* can perform is bounded by a natural number. In the case of repeated $b$ inputs, it is the oldest input that determines when the next output will occur. The automaton *UseOldInputB* is the same as *UseOldInputA* (inputs and outputs reversed) except that the turn variable of *UseOldInputB* is set to false initially. Note that *UseOldInputA* and *UseOldInputA* are not timing-independent and their trace sets are not limit-closed. For each automaton, there are infinitely many start states, one for each natural number. We can build an infinite chain of traces, where each element in the chain corresponds to an execution starting from a distinct start state. The limit of such a chain, which contains infinitely many outputs, cannot be a trace of *UseOldInputA* or *UseOldInputA* since the number of outputs they can perform is bounded by a natural number. The automaton *UseNewInputA* in Figure 4 behaves similarly to *UseOldInputA* except for the handling of inputs. In the case of repeated $b$ inputs, it is the most recent input that determines when the next output will occur. The automaton *UseNewInputB* in Figure 4 is the same as *UseNewInputA* (inputs and outputs reversed) except that the turn variable of *UseNewInputB* is set to false initially.

Suppose that we want to prove that *UseNewInputA* $\parallel$ *UseNewInputB* $\leq$ *UseOldInputA* $\parallel$ *UseOldInputB*. Theorem 3 is not applicable here because the high-level automata *UseOldInputA* and *UseOldInputB* do not satisfy the required closure properties. However, we can use Corollary 1 to decompose verification. It requires us to find auxiliary automata that are less restrictive than *UseOldInputA* and *UseOldInputB* but that are restrictive enough to express the constaints that should be satisfied by the environment, for *UseNewInputA* to implement *UseOldInputA* and for *UseNewInputB* to implement *UseOldInputB*.

The automata *AlternateA* and *AlternateB* in Figure 1 can be used as auxiliary automata in this example. They satisfy the closure properties required by Corollary 1 and impose alternation, which is the only additional condition to ensure the needed trace inclusion.

We can define a forward simulation relation (see [KLSV03a]) from *UseNewInputA* $\parallel$ *UseNewInputB* to *UseOldInputA* $\parallel$ *UseOldInputB*, which is based on the equality of the turn variables of the implementation and the specification automata. The fact that this simulation relation only uses the equality of turn variables reinforces the idea that the auxiliary contexts, which only keep track of their turn, capture exactly what is needed for the proof of *UseNewInputA* $\parallel$ *UseNewInputB* $\leq$ *UseOldInputA* $\parallel$ *UseOldInputB*. We can observe that a direct proof of this assertion would require one to deal with state variables such as *maxout* and *next* of both *UseOldInputA* and *UseOldInputB*, which do not play any essential role in the proof. On the other hand, by decomposing the proof along the lines of Corollary 1 some of the unnecessary details can be avoided. Even though, this is a toy example with an easy proof it should not be hard to observe how this simplification would scale to large proofs.

# 4   Decomposition Theorem with TIOAs with Properties

Theorem 3 and its corollary presented in Section 3 assume specification automata whose trace sets are closed under limits, and hence express safety constraints. In this section we present a theorem that can be used in the decomposition of verification where the specification automata may also express liveness properties.

The decomposition of a proof of the assertion $(\mathcal{A}_1, P_1) \parallel (\mathcal{B}_1, Q_1) \leq (\mathcal{A}_2, P_2) \parallel (\mathcal{B}_2, Q_2)$ can be viewed as consisting of two parts. The first part involves the decomposition of the proof that $(\mathcal{A}_1, P_1)$ and $(\mathcal{B}_1, Q_1)$ satisfy their safety properties and the second part involves the decomposition of the proof that $(\mathcal{A}_1, P_1)$ and $(\mathcal{B}_1, Q_1)$ satisfy their liveness properties. Theorem 4 uses Corollary 1 for the safety part of proofs; the first four hypotheses of Theorem 4 imply those of

Corollary 1. The remaining two hypotheses involve the liveness part of proofs. It requires one to find auxiliary automata with properties, $(\mathcal{A}_3, P_3)$ and $(\mathcal{B}_3, Q_3)$, such that $(\mathcal{A}_1, P_1)$ implements $(\mathcal{A}_3, P_3)$ in the context of $\mathcal{B}_3$ without relying on the liveness property of $\mathcal{B}_3$, and $(\mathcal{B}_1, Q_1)$ implements $(\mathcal{B}_3, Q_3)$ in the context of $\mathcal{A}_3$ without relying on the liveness property of $\mathcal{A}_3$. Moreover, $(\mathcal{A}_1, P_1)$ must implement $(\mathcal{A}_2, P_2)$ in the context of $(\mathcal{B}_3, Q_3)$ and $(\mathcal{B}_1, Q_1)$ must implement $(\mathcal{B}_2, Q_2)$ in the context of $(\mathcal{A}_3, P_3)$. That is, the implementation relation between $(\mathcal{A}_1, P_1)$ and $(\mathcal{A}_2, P_2)$ depend on the liveness property $Q_3$ of the auxiliary context, and the implementation relation between $(\mathcal{B}_1, Q_1)$ and $(\mathcal{B}_2, Q_2)$ depend on the liveness property $P_3$ of the auxiliary context.

**Theorem 4.** *Suppose $\mathcal{A}_1$, $\mathcal{A}_2$, $\mathcal{A}_3$, $\mathcal{B}_1$, $\mathcal{B}_2$, $\mathcal{B}_3$ are TIOAs such that $\mathcal{A}_1$, $\mathcal{A}_2$, and $\mathcal{A}_3$ are comparable, $\mathcal{B}_1$, $\mathcal{B}_2$, and $\mathcal{B}_3$ are comparable, and $\mathcal{A}_i$ is compatible with $\mathcal{B}_i$ for $i \in \{1, 2, 3\}$. Suppose that $P_i$ is a property for $\mathcal{A}_i$ and $Q_i$ is a property for $\mathcal{B}_i$ for $i \in \{1, 2, 3\}$. Suppose further that:*

1. *The sets $traces_{\mathcal{A}_3}$ and $traces_{\mathcal{B}_3}$ are closed under limits.*
2. *The sets $traces_{\mathcal{A}_3}$ and $traces_{\mathcal{B}_3}$ are closed under time-extension.*
3. *$\mathcal{A}_2 \leq \mathcal{A}_3$ and $\mathcal{B}_2 \leq \mathcal{B}_3$.*
4. *$\mathcal{A}_1 \| \mathcal{B}_3 \leq \mathcal{A}_2 \| \mathcal{B}_3$ and $\mathcal{A}_3 \| \mathcal{B}_1 \leq \mathcal{A}_3 \| \mathcal{B}_2$.*
5. *$(\mathcal{A}_1, P_1) \| (\mathcal{B}_3, frags_{\mathcal{B}_3}) \leq (\mathcal{A}_3, P_3) \| (\mathcal{B}_3, frags_{\mathcal{B}_3})$ and*
   *$(\mathcal{A}_3, frags_{\mathcal{A}_3}) \| (\mathcal{B}_1, Q_1) \leq (\mathcal{A}_3, frags_{\mathcal{A}_3}) \| (\mathcal{B}_3, Q_3)$.*
6. *$(\mathcal{A}_1, P_1) \| (\mathcal{B}_3, Q_3) \leq (\mathcal{A}_2, P_2) \| (\mathcal{B}_3, Q_3)$ and*
   *$(\mathcal{A}_3, P_3) \| (\mathcal{B}_1, Q_1) \leq (\mathcal{A}_3, P_3) \| (\mathcal{B}_2, Q_2)$.*

*Then $(\mathcal{A}_1, P_1) \| (\mathcal{B}_1, Q_1) \leq (\mathcal{A}_2, P_2) \| (\mathcal{B}_2, Q_2)$.*

The proof sketch for Theorem 4 is given in Appendix A.

*Example 3.* This example illustrates the use of Theorem 4 in decomposing the proof of an implementation relationship where the implementation and specification are not merely composition of automata but composition of automata that satisfy some liveness property.

Let *UseOldInputA'*, *UseOldInputB'*, *UseNewInputA'*, and *UseNewInputB'* be automata which are defined exactly as automata *UseOldInputA*, *UseOldInputB*, *UseNewInputA*, and *UseNewInputB* from Example 2 except that there is no bound on the number of outputs that the automata can perform. That is, *maxout* is removed from their sets of state variables. Let $P_1, P_2, Q_1$ and $Q_2$ be properties for, respectively, *UseNewInputA'*, *UseOldInputA'*, *UseNewInputB'* and *UseOldInputB'* defined as follows:

- $P_1$ consists of the admissible execution fragments of *UseNewInputA'*.
- $Q_1$ consists of the admissible execution fragments of *UseNewInputB'*.
- $P_2$ consists of the execution fragments of *UseOldInputA'* that contain infinitely many $a$ actions.
- $Q_2$ consists of the execution fragments of *UseOldInputB'* that contain infinitely many $b$ actions.

Suppose that we want to prove that:

$(UseNewInputA',P_1) \parallel (UseNewInputB',Q_1) \leq (UseOldInputA',P_2) \parallel (UseOldInputB',Q_2)$.

The automata $UseNewInputA' \parallel UseNewInputB'$ and $UseOldInputA' \parallel UseOldInputB'$ perform an alternating sequence of $a$ and $b$ actions. The properties express the additional condition that as time goes to infinity the composite automaton $UseNewInputA' \parallel UseNewInputB'$ performs infinitely many $a$ and infinitely many $b$ actions where $a$ and $b$ actions alternate.

As in Example 2 automata $AlternateA$ and $AlternateB$ from Figure 1 satisfy the required closure properties for auxiliary automata and capture what is essential about the safety part of the proof, namely that the environments of $UseNewInputA'$ and $UseNewInputB'$ impose alternation. The essential point in the proof of the liveness part is that each automaton responds to each input it receives from its environment. Therefore, we need to pair $AlternateA$ and $AlternateB$ with properties that eliminate non-responding behavior. The properties $P_3$ and $Q_3$ defined below satisfy this condition:

- $P_3$ consists of execution fragments $\alpha$ of $AlternateA$ that satisfy the following condition: if $\alpha$ has finitely many actions then the last action in $\alpha$ is $a$.
- $Q_3$ consists of execution fragments $\alpha$ of $AlternateB$ that satisfy the following condition: if $\alpha$ has finitely many actions and contains at least one $a$ then the last action in $\alpha$ is $b$.

In order to see why the first part of Assumption 5 is satisfied we can inspect the definition of $UseNewInputA$ and observe that $UseNewInputA$ performs an output $a$ one time unit after each input $b$, when it is composed with $AlternateB$. This implies that in any admissible execution fragment of $UseNewInputA \parallel AlternateB$ with finitely many actions the last action must be $a$. This is exactly the liveness constraint expressed by $P_3$. The second part of Assumption 5 can be seen to hold using a symmetric argument.

In order to see why the first part of Assumption 6 holds consider any execution fragment $\beta$ of $UseNewInputA \parallel AlternateB$. For $\beta$ to satisfy $P_1$ and $Q_3$ at the same time, it must consist of an infinite sequence in which $a$ and $b$ actions alternate. It is not possible for $UseNewInputA \parallel AlternateB$ to have an admissible execution fragment with finitely many actions because the definition of $UseNewInputA$ requires such a sequence to end in $a$ while this is ruled out by $Q_3$, which requires $AlternateB$ to respond to $a$. The second part of Assumption 6 can be seen to hold using a symmetric argument.

Note that in our explanations we refer to execution fragments rather than traces of execution fragments. This is because our examples do not include any internal actions and our arguments for execution fragments extend to trace fragments in a straightforward way.

## 5    Conclusions and Future Work

In this paper we have focused on compositionality for timed I/O automata. In particular, we have presented three assume-guarantee style substitutivity results for the composition operation of timed I/O automata. We believe that these results are simple and easy to understand; they build upon the basic concepts about TIOAs and the fundamental results for the composition operation. Unlike many of the related results obtained for other formal frameworks, no complex logical operators or induction principles are needed for our theorem statements and their proofs.

Theorem 4 suggests a useful way of separating out proof obligations for safety and liveness in decomposing verification tasks that involve TIOAs paired with liveness properties. A proof based on Theorem 1 that shows that an implementation satisfies a safety specification can in large part be reused when liveness conditions are added to the specification.

Our main goal in this line of work was to obtain simple and general compositionality results. As future work we intend to explore the implications on our results of considering special kinds of automata and properties that we have defined in [KLSV03a]. For example, it would be interesting to know if any of the assumptions of our theorems would be implied if we considered receptive TIOAs, I/O feasible TIOAs or I/O liveness properties.

Our current results apply to trace inclusion preorder. Another interesting direction for future work would be to extend these results to other preorders based on various notions of simulations relations defined in [KLSV03a].

## Acknowledgements

This work is supported by DARPA/AFOSR MURI Contract F49620-02-1-0325. We thank Frits Vaandrager and Roberto Segala for their comments on the preliminary versions of our results.

## References

[AH97]    R. Alur and T. Henzinger. Modularity for timed and hybrid systems. In *Proceedings of the 8th International Conference on Concurrency Theory (CONCUR)*, volume 1243 of *LNCS*, pages 74–88. Springer-Verlag, 1997.

[AK96]    R. Alur and R. P. Kurshan. Timing analysis in COSPAN. In *Hybrid Systems III: Verification and Control*. Springer-Verlag, 1996.

[AL93]    M. Abadi and L. Lamport. Composing specifications. *ACM Transactions on Programming Languages and Systems*, 1(15):73–132, 1993.

[AL94]    Martin Abadi and Leslie Lamport. An old-fashioned recipe for real time. *ACM Transactions on Programming Languages and Systems*, 16(5):1543–1571, 1994.

[AL95]    M. Abadi and L. Lamport. Conjoining specifications. *ACM Transactions on Programming Languages and Systems*, 17(3):507–534, 1995.

[HQR00]    T. A. Henzinger, S. Qadeer, and S. K. Rajamani. Decomposing refinement proofs using assume-guarantee reasoning. In *Proceedings of the International Conference on Computer-Aided Design (ICCAD)*, pages 245–252. IEEE Computer Society Press, 2000.

[HQR02]  T. Henzinger, S. Qadeer, and S. K. Rajamani. An assume-guarantee rule for checking simulation. *ACM Transactions on Programming Languages and Systems*, 24:51–64, 2002.

[Jon83]  C. B. Jones. Specification and design of parallel programs. In R. E. A. Mason, editor, *Information Processing 83: Proceedings of the IFIP 9th World Congress*, pages 321–332. North-Holland, 1983.

[KLSV03a]  D. Kaynar, N. Lynch, R. Segala, and F. Vaandrager. The theory of timed I/O automata. Technical Report MIT/LCS/TR-917, MIT Laboratory for Computer Science, 2003. Available at http://theory.lcs.mit.edu/tds/reflist.html.

[KLSV03b]  D. Kaynar, N. Lynch, R. Segala, and F. Vaandrager. Timed I/O automata: A mathematical framework for modeling and analyzing real-time systems. In *Proceedings of the 24th IEEE International Real-Time Systems Symposium*, pages 166–177, Cancun, Mexico, 2003. IEEE Computer Society. Full version available as Technical Report MIT/LCS/TR-917.

[MWLF03]  S. Mitra, Y. Wang, N. Lynch, and E. Feron. Safety verification of pitch controller for model helicopter. In O. Maler and A. Pnueli, editors, *Proc. of Hybrid Systems: Computation and Control*, volume 2623 of *Lecture Notes in Computer Science*, pages 343–358, Prague, the Czech Republic April 3-5, 2003.

[Pnu84]  A. Pnueli. In transition from global to modular temporal reasoning about programs. In K. R. Apt, editor, *Logis and Models of Concurret Systems*, NATO ASI, pages 123–144. Springer-Verlag, 1984.

[Sta85]  E. W. Stark. A proof technique for rely/guarantee properties. In S. N. Maheshwari, editor, *Foundations of Software Technology and Theoretical Computer Science*, volume 206 of *LNCS*, pages 369–391. Springer-Verlag, 1985.

[TAKB96]  S. Tasiran, R. Alur, R.P. Kurshan, and R.K. Brayton. Verifying abstractions of timed systems. In *Proceedings of the Seventh Conference on Concurrency Theory (CONCUR)*, volume 1119 of *LNCS*, 1996.

# A   Proofs

*Proof of Theorem 4:* Let $\beta \in traces_{(\mathcal{A}_1, P_1)\|(\mathcal{B}_1, Q_1)}$. By definition of composition for automata with properties, $\beta \in traces_{(\mathcal{A}_1\|\mathcal{B}_1)}$. By Assumptions 1, 2, 3 and 4 and Theorem 1, we have $\beta \in traces_{(\mathcal{A}_2\|\mathcal{B}_2)}$. By projection using Theorem 1, $\beta\lceil(E_{\mathcal{A}_2}, \emptyset) \in traces_{\mathcal{A}_2}$ and $\beta\lceil(E_{\mathcal{B}_2}, \emptyset) \in traces_{\mathcal{B}_2}$. By Assumption 3, $\beta\lceil(E_{\mathcal{A}_2}, \emptyset) \in traces_{\mathcal{A}_3}$ and $\beta\lceil(E_{\mathcal{B}_2}, \emptyset) \in traces_{\mathcal{B}_3}$. Since $\mathcal{A}_2$ and $\mathcal{A}_3$ are comparable, $\beta\lceil(E_{\mathcal{A}_2}, \emptyset) = \beta\lceil(E_{\mathcal{A}_3}, \emptyset)$ and $\beta\lceil(E_{\mathcal{B}_2}, \emptyset) = \beta\lceil(E_{\mathcal{B}_3}, \emptyset)$. Therefore, $\beta\lceil(E_{\mathcal{A}_3}, \emptyset) \in traces_{\mathcal{A}_3}$ and $\beta\lceil(E_{\mathcal{B}_3}, \emptyset) \in traces_{\mathcal{B}_3}$.

By projection using Theorem 2, we have $\beta\lceil(E_{\mathcal{A}_1}, \emptyset) \in traces_{(\mathcal{A}_1, P_1)}$ and $\beta\lceil(E_{\mathcal{B}_1}, \emptyset) \in traces_{(\mathcal{B}_1, Q_1)}$. By pasting using Theorem 2, we have $\beta \in traces_{(\mathcal{A}_1, P_1)\|(\mathcal{B}_3, frags_{\mathcal{B}_3})}$ and $\beta \in traces_{(\mathcal{B}_1, Q_1)\|(\mathcal{A}_3, frags_{\mathcal{A}_3})}$. By Assumption 5, we have $\beta \in traces_{(\mathcal{A}_3, P_3)\|(\mathcal{B}_3, frags_{\mathcal{B}_3})}$ and $\beta \in traces_{(\mathcal{B}_3, Q_3)\|(\mathcal{A}_3, frags_{\mathcal{A}_3})}$. By projection using Theorem 2, we get $\beta\lceil(E_{\mathcal{A}_3}, \emptyset) \in traces_{(\mathcal{A}_3, P_3)}$ and $\beta\lceil(E_{\mathcal{B}_3}, \emptyset) \in traces_{(\mathcal{B}_3, Q_3)}$. Since $\beta\lceil(E_{\mathcal{A}_1}, \emptyset) \in traces_{(\mathcal{A}_1, P_1)}$, by pasting using Theorem 2, we have $\beta \in traces_{(\mathcal{A}_1, P_1)\|(\mathcal{B}_3, Q_3)}$, similarly since $\beta\lceil(E_{\mathcal{B}_1}, \emptyset) \in traces_{(\mathcal{B}_1, Q_1)}$, we have

$\beta \in traces_{(\mathcal{B}_1,Q_1)\|(\mathcal{A}_3,P_3)}$. By Assumption 6, we have $\beta \in (\mathcal{A}_2,P_2)\|(\mathcal{B}_3,Q_3)$ and $\beta \in (\mathcal{A}_3,P_3)\|(\mathcal{B}_2,Q_2)$. By projection pasting using Theorem 2, $\beta \lceil (E_{\mathcal{A}_2},\emptyset) \in traces_{(\mathcal{A}_2,P_2)}$ and $\beta \lceil (E_{\mathcal{B}_2},\emptyset) \in traces_{(\mathcal{B}_2,Q_2)}$. By pasting using Theorem 2, it follows that $\beta \in (\mathcal{A}_2,P_2)\|(\mathcal{B}_2,Q_2)$, as needed.

# B    Specifications of Automata Used in Examples

---

**Automaton** *AlternateA*

**Variables** $X$ :     **discrete** $myturn \in Bool$ **initially** true

**States** $Q$ :     $val(X)$

**Actions** $A$ :     **input** $b$, **output** $a$

**Transitions** $\mathcal{D}$ :   **input** $b$                 **output** $a$
                   **effect**                **precondition**
                       $myturn := true$           $myturn$
                                         **effect**
                                             $myturn := false$

**Trajectories** $\mathcal{T}$ : **satisfies**
                   **constant**$(myturn)$

---

**Automaton** *AlternateB*

**Variables** $X$ :     **discrete** $myturn \in Bool$ **initially** false

**States** $Q$ :     $val(X)$

**Actions** $A$ :     **input** $a$, **output** $b$

**Transitions** $\mathcal{D}$ :   **input** $a$                 **output** $b$
                   **effect**                **precondition**
                       $myturn := true$           $myturn$
                                         **effect**
                                             $myturn := false$

**Trajectories** $\mathcal{T}$ : **satisfies**
                   **constant**$(myturn)$

---

**Fig. 1.** Example automata for $\mathcal{A}_2$ and $\mathcal{B}_2$ in Theorem 3.

**Automaton** *CatchUpA*

**Variables** $X$ :    **discrete** *counta, countb* $\in$ N **initially** 0
                    **analog** *now* $\in$ R$^{\geq 0}$ **initially** 0
                    **analog** *next* $\in$ R$^{\geq 0} \cup \{\infty\}$ **initially** 0

**States** $Q$ :    $val(X)$

**Actions** $A$ :    **input** $b$, **output** $a$

**Transitions** $\mathcal{D}$ :    **input** $b$                          **output** $a$
                    **effect**                           **precondition**
                        *countb* := *countb* + 1             *counta* $\leq$ *countb* $\wedge$
                        *next* := *now* + 1                      *now* = *next*
                                                        **effect**
                                                            *counta* := *counta*
                                                                        $+1$
                                                            *next* := *now* + 1

**Trajectories** $\mathcal{T}$ :    **satisfies**
                        **constant**(counta,countb)
                    **stops when**
                        *now* = *next*

---

**Automaton** *CatchUpB*

**Variables** $X$ :    **discrete** *counta, countb* $\in$ N **initially** 0
                    **analog** *now* $\in$ R$^{\geq 0}$ **initially** 0
                    **analog** *next* $\in$ R$^{\geq 0} \cup \{\infty\}$ **initially** 0

**States** $Q$ :    $val(X)$

**Actions** $A$ :    **input** $a$, **output** $b$, **internal** $c$

**Transitions** $\mathcal{D}$ :    **input** $a$                          **output** $b$
                    **effect**                           **precondition**
                        *counta* := *counta* + 1             *countb* + 1 $\leq$ *counta*
                        *next* := *now* + 1                      $\wedge now$ = *next*
                                                        **effect**
                                                            *countb* := *countb* + 1
                                                            *next* = *now* + 1

**Trajectories** $\mathcal{T}$ :    **satisfies**
                        **constant**(counta,countb)
                    **stops when**
                        *now* = *next*

**Fig. 2.** Example automata $\mathcal{A}_1$ and $\mathcal{B}_1$ for Theorem 3.

---

**Automaton** *UseOldInputA*

**Variables** $X$ :     **discrete** *myturn* $\in$ *Bool* **initially** true
                        **discrete** *maxout* $\in$ N **initially** arbitrary
                        **analog** *now* $\in$ R$^{\geq 0}$ **initially** 0
                        **analog** *next* $\in$ R$^{\geq 0}$ $\cup$ {$\infty$} **initially** 0

**States** $Q$ :     *val(X)*

**Actions** $A$ :     **input** *b*, **output** *a*

**Transitions** $\mathcal{D}$ :     **input** *b*                                     **output** *a*
                                        **effect**                               **precondition**
                                          *myturn* := *true*                  *myturn* $\wedge$ (*maxout* > 0)
                                          **if** *next* = $\infty$               $\wedge$ (*now* = *next*)
                                          **then** *next* := *now* + 1       **effect**
                                                                                        *myturn* := *false*
                                                                                        *maxout* := *maxout* − 1
                                                                                        *next* := $\infty$

**Trajectories** $\mathcal{T}$ :     **satisfies**
                                         **constant**(*myturn*, *maxout*, *next*)
                                         **d**(*now*) = 1
                                       **stops when**
                                         *now* = *next*

---

**Automaton** *UseOldInputB*

**Variables** $X$ :     **discrete** *myturn* $\in$ *Bool* **initially** false
                        **discrete** *maxout* $\in$ N **initially** arbitrary
                        **analog** *now* $\in$ R$^{\geq 0}$ **initially** 0
                        **analog** *next* $\in$ R$^{\geq 0}$ $\cup$ {$\infty$} **initially** 0

**States** $Q$ :     *val(X)*

**Actions** $A$ :     **input** *a*, **output** *b*

**Transitions** $\mathcal{D}$ :     **input** *a*                                     **output** *b*
                                        **effect**                               **precondition**
                                          *myturn* := *true*                  *myturn* $\wedge$ (*maxout* > 0)
                                          **if** *next* = $\infty$               $\wedge$ (*now* = *next*)
                                          **then** *next* := *now* + 1       **effect**
                                                                                        *myturn* := *false*
                                                                                        *maxout* := *maxout* − 1
                                                                                        *next* := $\infty$

**Trajectories** $\mathcal{T}$ :     **satisfies**
                                         **constant**(*myturn*, *maxout*, *next*)
                                         **d**(*now*) = 1
                                       **stops when**
                                         *now* = *next*

---

**Fig. 3.** Example automata for $\mathcal{A}_2$ and $\mathcal{B}_2$ in Theorem 1.

---

**Automaton** *UseNewInputA*

**Variables** $X$ :    **discrete** *myturn* $\in$ *Bool* **initially** true
**discrete** *maxout* $\in$ N **initially** arbitrary
**analog** *now* $\in$ R$^{\geq 0}$ **initially** 0
**analog** *next* $\in$ R$^{\geq 0} \cup \{\infty\}$ **initially** 0

**States** $Q$ :    $val(X)$

**Actions** $A$ :    **input** $b$, **output** $a$

**Transitions** $\mathcal{D}$ :   **input** $b$                    **output** $a$
        **effect**                      **precondition**
            *myturn* := *true*            *myturn* $\wedge$ (*maxout* > 0)
            *next* := *now* + 1                $\wedge$ (*now* = *next*)
                                     **effect**
                                         *myturn* := *false*
                                         *maxout* := *maxout* $-$ 1
                                         *next* := $\infty$

**Trajectories** $\mathcal{T}$ : **satisfies**
            **constant**(*myturn*, *maxout*, *next*)
            **d**(*now*) = 1
            **stops when**
                *now* = *next*

---

**Automaton** *UseNewInputA*

**Variables** $X$ :    **discrete** *myturn* $\in$ *Bool* **initially** false
**discrete** *maxout* $\in$ N **initially** arbitrary
**analog** *now* $\in$ R$^{\geq 0}$ **initially** 0
**analog** *next* $\in$ R$^{\geq 0} \cup \{\infty\}$ **initially** 0

**States** $Q$ :    $val(X)$

**Actions** $A$ :    **input** $a$, **output** $b$

**Transitions** $\mathcal{D}$ :   **input** $a$                    **output** $b$
        **effect**                      **precondition**
            *myturn* := *true*                *myturn* $\wedge$ (*count* > 0)
            *next* := *now* + 1                $\wedge$ (*now* = *next*)
                                 **effect**
                                     *myturn* := *false*
                                     *maxout* := *maxout* $-$ 1
                                     *next* := $\infty$

**Trajectories** $\mathcal{T}$ : **satisfies**
            **constant**(*myturn*, *maxout*, *next*)
            **d**(*now*) = 1
            **stops when**
                *now* = *next*

---

**Fig. 4.** Example automata for $\mathcal{A}_1$ and $\mathcal{B}_1$ in Theorem 1.

# Symbolic Model Checking
# for Simply-Timed Systems

Nicolas Markey[1,2] and Philippe Schnoebelen[2]

[1] Département d'Informatique
Université Libre de Bruxelles
nmarkey@ulb.ac.be
[2] Lab. Spécification & Vérification
ENS de Cachan & CNRS UMR 8643
{markey,phs}@lsv.ens-cachan.fr

**Abstract.** We describe OBDD-based symbolic model checking algorithms for *simply-timed systems*, i.e. finite state graphs where transitions
carry a duration. These durations can be arbitrary natural numbers. A
simple and natural semantics for these systems opens the way for improved efficiency. Our algorithms have been implemented in NuSMV
and perform well in practice (on standard case studies).

## 1 Introduction

*Symbolic verification of timed systems.* Formal verification tools play an ever-
increasing role in the design of complex systems. Using OBDD technology, *symbolic model checking* techniques [3,17], are able to analyze larger and larger
models [12,1]. Symbolic model checking techniques are not so successful with
*time-critical systems*. A popular approach to these systems is based on *timed
automata*, for which several model checkers exist (e.g. [22,16]). Timed automata
raise difficult problems: the existing symbolic representations for sets of clock
valuations (including DBMs, CDDs and REDs) are not as simple and convenient as OBDDs and do not mix well with the OBDDs used for the control part.
Finally fixpoint computations are notably tricky for timed automata [2].

*State graphs as timed models.* Time-critical systems do not always have to be
modeled with timed automata. Indeed, labeled state graphs, a.k.a. *Kripke structures* (KS's), have been used for such purposes. If we assume that each transition
in a KS takes one time unit, RTCTL model checking is not harder than CTL
model checking [13] [1]. Symbolic OBDD-based model checking extends easily to
RTCTL on KS's [6]. The corresponding algorithms have been implemented (*e.g.*
in NuSMV [11], Verus [4]) and perform quite efficiently. This approach combines
simplicity and efficiency. Its limitation is the restricted expressive power of the
KS model, even disregarding the issue of discrete *vs.* dense time.

---

[1] RTCTL, or "Real Time CTL", is the extension of CTL where temporal modalities
may carry numerical time bounds.

Y. Lakhnech and S. Yovine (Eds.): FORMATS/FTRTFT 2004, LNCS 3253, pp. 102–117, 2004.
© Springer-Verlag Berlin Heidelberg 2004

*Our contribution.* We extend symbolic RTCTL model checking to *timed Kripke structures* (TKS's), *i.e.* Kripke structures where each transition carries a *duration*, that can be any integer value (including zero). Thus the difference between KS's and TKS's is that we do not assume that each transition takes one and only one time unit. We provide algorithms for symbolic model checking on TKS's against RTCTL specifications. We also compute quantitative information, answering queries of the kind "what is the minimum (resp. maximum) delay between a state satisfying some *Start* property and a state satisfying some *Final* property?" [9].

Durations in TKS's are *atomic* and do not reduce to a sequence of unit steps, contrary to the model used in RAVEN [19], for instance. Our model checking algorithms take advantage of this semantics of time and, for models that would naturally be described with long transitions, they perform better than the algorithms offered in NuSMV (see Section 6). Thus, while our approach builds on earlier research by Campos, Clarke *et al.* [5–10], there are nevertheless some clear differences between the two approaches: differences in the models, in the algorithms, and in the running times. A more detailed comparison is provided in section 7.

We implemented our algorithms on top of NuSMV. This readily provides a symbolic model checker for TKS's, called TSMV and available at http://www.lsv.ens-cachan.fr/~markey/TSMV/. Our experiments indicate that our tool TSMV provides appreciable gain in expressive power and improved running time (when compared with the verification of "equivalent" unit-steps KS's).

Finally, TSMV improves the available set of solutions for model checking *simply-timed systems*, i.e. systems where the control part is too large for a timed-automaton approach, and where the timing aspects are simple enough to be described with durations on transitions.

*What use are arbitrary durations?* Compared to plain KS's, there are three main ways where TKS's provide increased expressive power:

**Long steps:** TKS's allow considering that some transitions take a long time, *e.g.* 1000 time units. Such transitions could be encoded in KS's by inserting 999 intermediate states (*e.g.* using a simple counter) as advocated in [7, p.106]. But this encoding is tedious, and leads to quite costly extra verification work. It is better to have algorithms that understand arbitrary durations.

**Instantaneous steps:** TKS's allow considering that some transitions have *zero duration*. This is very convenient in models where some steps are described indirectly, as a short succession of micro-steps.

**Counting specific events only:** Zero-length transitions are also a convenient way of abstracting away (for timing aspects only) from some internal transitions. Then the RTCTL formulae count the durations of the other, time-relevant, transitions. This can also be used in models where transitions carry some "cost", a notion more general than elapsed time. For example, when verifying a communication protocol, one can wish to only count the sendings and receivings of messages. When checking a model of an elevator system, one can wish to count cabin moves, or door closings and openings, and use these in cost-constrained CTL formulae.

## 2    Basic Notions

We assume familiarity with CTL model checking on finite Kripke structures (KS's). Furthermore, we assume the reader understands the working of OBDD-based symbolic model checking, as implemented *e.g.* in (Nu)SMV [3, 17, 11]. These notions are available in several textbooks, for instance [12, 1].

### 2.1    Kripke Structures with Durations on Transitions

Simply-timed Kripke Structures (TKS's) are an extension of KS's where each transition is labeled by a nonnegative integer. Formally, given a set $AP = \{p_1, p_2, \ldots\}$ of *atomic propositions*, a TKS is a tuple $M = \langle S, S_0, R, L \rangle$ where $S = \{s, s', \ldots\}$ is a finite set of states, $S_0 \subseteq S$ is a set of initial states, and $L : S \mapsto 2^{AP}$ is a labeling of states with atomic propositions. The difference with KS's is that here $R \subseteq S \times \mathbb{N} \times S$ is a finite set of *transitions* labeled by a natural number, called the *duration* of the transition. We require that the untimed relation $\overline{R}$, obtained from $R$ by dropping durations, is total.

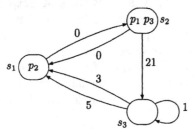

**Fig. 1.** A simple TKS

Fig. 1 displays a simple example. Note that, between two states, there may exist several transitions with different durations. In graphical representations, such sets of transitions are sometimes depicted with several labels on one arrow.

A path $\pi$ in $M$ is an infinite sequence $s_0 \xrightarrow{d_1} s_1 \xrightarrow{d_2} s_2 \xrightarrow{d_3} \cdots$ of linked transitions. For such a path, and for $n \in \mathbb{N}$, we let $\pi(n)$ denote the $n$th state $s_n$, and $\pi^n$ denote the $n$th suffix $s_n \xrightarrow{d_{n+1}} s_{n+1} \xrightarrow{d_{n+2}} \cdots$. Finally, for $n \leq m \in \mathbb{N}$, we let $\pi[n..m]$ denotes the finite sequence $s_n \xrightarrow{d_{n+1}} s_{n+1} \xrightarrow{d_{n+2}} \cdots s_m$ with $m - n$ transitions and $m - n + 1$ states. The (cumulative) *duration* $\mathrm{D}\pi[n..m]$ of such a finite sequence is $d_n + \cdots + d_{m-1}$ (hence 0 when $n = m$). We write $\Pi(s)$ for the set of paths that start from $s$: since $R$ is total, $\Pi(s)$ is never empty.

### 2.2    RTCTL: A Temporal Logic with Timing Constraints

RTCTL formulae are the state formulae built according to the following syntax:

$$\varphi_s ::= \neg\varphi_s \mid \varphi_s \wedge \psi_s \mid \mathsf{E}\,\varphi_p \mid p_1 \mid p_2 \mid \cdots \qquad \text{(state formulae)}$$
$$\varphi_p ::= \neg\varphi_p \mid \mathsf{X}\varphi_s \mid \varphi_s \mathsf{U}_\alpha \psi_s \qquad \text{(path formulae)}$$

where $\alpha$, called the *timing constraint*, is a predicate on durations. All constraints of the form "$\leq k$", "$= k$", "$\geq k$" and "$[k..l]$" for $k$ and $l$ values in the relevant domain (here $\mathbb{N}$) are allowed. We write $n \models \alpha$ when duration $n \in \mathbb{N}$ satisfies the constraint $\alpha$ (definition omitted). We write $s \models \varphi_s$ and $\pi \models \varphi_p$ when a state $s \in S$ satisfies a state formula $\varphi_s$ (resp. a path $\pi$ satisfies a path formula $\varphi_p$). The definition is as expected, and we only spell out the few cases that are specific to RTCTL and TKS's:

$$s \models \mathsf{E}\,\varphi_p \quad \stackrel{\text{def}}{\Leftrightarrow}\quad \text{there exists a } \pi \in \Pi(s) \text{ s.t. } \pi \models \varphi_p,$$

$$\pi \models \mathsf{X}\varphi_s \quad \stackrel{\text{def}}{\Leftrightarrow}\quad \pi(1) \models \varphi_s,$$

$$\pi \models \varphi_s \mathsf{U}_\alpha \psi_s \quad \stackrel{\text{def}}{\Leftrightarrow}\quad \begin{cases} \text{there exists } i \in \mathbb{N} \text{ s.t. } \mathrm{D}\pi[0..i] \models \alpha, \\ \pi(i) \models \psi_s, \text{ and } \pi(j) \models \varphi_s \text{ for all } 0 \le j < i. \end{cases}$$

We use all the classical abbreviations: $\top$, $\bot$, $\varphi_s \vee \psi_s$, $\varphi_s \Rightarrow \psi_s$, $\mathsf{A}\,\varphi_p$ (for $\neg\mathsf{E}\neg\varphi_p$), $\mathsf{F}_\alpha\varphi_s$ (for $\top\mathsf{U}_\alpha\varphi_s$), and $\mathsf{G}_\alpha\varphi_s$ (for $\neg\mathsf{F}_\alpha\neg\varphi_s$). Then $\mathsf{EF}_\alpha\varphi$ means that it is possible to reach a state satisfying $\varphi$ via a finite path whose cumulative duration satisfies $\alpha$, and $\mathsf{EG}_\alpha\varphi$ means that there is a path along which $\varphi$ holds at all states visited after a cumulative duration satisfying $\alpha$.

### 2.3 Some Comments on Semantics

Our semantics for TKS's is the simplest and most natural way of reading state graphs like the one in Fig. 1. However, it differs from the semantics commonly found with other models (like timed automata). Disregarding the well-known issue of discrete vs. dense time, the important differences are:

**Zeno behaviors:** we admit infinite paths where time stays forever bounded. This simplifies the exposition, and lets us use durations for counting things other than elapsed time. It is however possible to rule our Zeno behaviors with fairness constraints (see Section 5.3).

**Atomicity of durations:** during a transition $s \xrightarrow{10} s'$, the system moves from "$s$ at some time $t$" to "$s'$ at $t + 10$": between $t$ and $t + 10$, there is no state (or time) where the system is in. Hence $s_1 \models \mathsf{AG}_{=2}\bot$ in Fig. 1 since no path starting from $s_1$ encounters a cumulative duration of 2. See section 7 for a comparison with other semantics of durations.

## 3 Symbolic Computation of Minimum and Maximum Delays

In this section, we present a symbolic algorithm for computing the minimum delay between two sets of states. An algorithm for maximum delay would be similar. As we explain below, this algorithm improves on earlier proposals in its strategy for handling the durations that appear in the model.

The *minimum delay* between a set $Start \subseteq S$ of starting states and a set $Final \subseteq S$ of final states is the minimum $d$ s.t. there is a finite path $s_0 \xrightarrow{d_1} s_1 \ldots \xrightarrow{d_n} s_n$ in $S$ with $s_0 \in Start$, $s_n \in Final$, and $d = d_1 + \cdots + d_n$ [9]. The minimum is $\infty$ if no such path exists. It is 0 when $Start \cap Final$ is non-empty, or when $Final$ can be reached from $Start$ using only zero-transitions.

Assume $M = \langle S, S_0, R, L \rangle$ is a TKS. Let $d_{max}$ denote the highest duration occurring as a label in $R$. For $d = 0, \ldots, d_{max}$, write $R_d$ for the relation $\{(s, s') \in S^2 \mid s \xrightarrow{d} s'\}$ and $R'_d$ for $R_d \backslash \bigcup_{e<d} R_e$. Hence $R_d$ relates states that are connected by a transition with duration $d$ and $R'_d$ also relates these states provided they are not related by a "shorter" transition. Finally, write $Dur$ for the set $\{d_1, \ldots, d_l\}$ (in increasing order) of all durations $d$ with non-empty $R_d$ and $Dur'$ for the set $\{d'_1, \ldots, d'_m\}$ of all durations for which $R'_d$ is non-empty. Note that $Dur$ contains exactly the labels appearing in $R$ (thus $d_l = d_{max}$) and that $Dur' \subseteq Dur$.

*The procedure and its correctness proof.* Algorithm 1 is a backward chaining procedure computing minimum delays (Algorithms for modalities $EF_{=0}$ and $EU_{=0}$

```
 1  function min_delay(Start, Final)
 2    n ← 0;
 3    Incr[0], Diff[0] ← EF₌₀( Final );
 4    repeat {
 5        if ( Start ∩ Diff[n] ≠ ∅ ) { return(n); }
 6        n++;
 7        aux ← ⋃{Pre[R'_d](Diff[n-d]) | d ∈ Dur' ∧ 0 < d ≤n};
 8        Diff[n] ← EU₌₀( ¬Incr[n-1], ¬Incr[n-1] ∩ aux );
 9        Incr[n] ← Incr[n-1] ∪ Diff[n];
10    } until (n≥ d_max ∧ Incr[n] = Incr[n-d_max]);
11  return(∞);
```

**Algorithm 1.** Algorithm for computing minimum delay

are discussed later, in section 4.1.) We prove correctness by showing that the following two invariants hold whenever we enter the **repeat** loop:

$$0 \le i \le \text{n} \Rightarrow \left[ s \in \text{Incr}[i] \text{ iff } s \models EF_{\le i} Final \right] \tag{Inv1}$$

$$0 \le i \le \text{n} \Rightarrow \left[ s \in \text{Diff}[i] \text{ iff } s \in (\text{Incr}[i] \setminus \text{Incr}[i-1]) \right] \tag{Inv2}$$

- (Inv1) and (Inv2) clearly hold the first time the loop is entered: n is 0 and both Incr[0] and Diff[0] have been initialized correctly (by convention Incr[−1] is empty).
- Once we are inside the loop, n is incremented. The last three lines of the loop compute Incr[n] and Diff[n] for that new value. The following key Lemma ensures that (Inv1) and (Inv2) are maintained.

**Lemma 3.1.** *Assume $n > 0$. The following are equivalent:*
*(a)* $s \models EF_{\le n} \varphi \wedge \neg EF_{<n} \varphi$.

*(b)* $\exists d \in \{1, \ldots, n\}, \exists s', s'' \in S : \begin{cases} 1. \ s' \xrightarrow{d} s'', \text{ and} \\ 2. \ s'' \models EF_{\le n-d} \varphi \wedge \neg EF_{<n-d} \varphi, \text{ and} \\ 3. \ s \models E(\neg EF_{<n} \varphi) U_{=0}(s' \wedge \neg EF_{<n} \varphi). \end{cases}$

*Additionally, (b) implies that there is no* $s' \xrightarrow{d'} s''$ *with* $d' < d$.

- Once the invariants are established, we can check the return values. The algorithm returns a number n iff it is the smallest value s.t. *Start* intersects Diff[n]. This is correct by (Inv1) and (Inv2).
- The algorithm returns $\infty$ iff Incr[n] = Incr[n-$d_{max}$] for some n $\geq d_{max}$ s.t. *Start* does not intersect Incr[n]. In such a case, all Incr[m] for $m \geq$ n are equal (stabilization has been reached at index n and detected at index n + $d_{max}$) and *Final* is not reachable from *Start*. Hence the returned value is correct.
- Finally, the algorithm must terminate since, as can be seen from (Inv1), the Incr[n]'s are increasing.

*Some comments on the algorithm.* When comparing this algorithm to the standard one (assuming durations are encoded as sequences of unit-length transitions between intermediate states), it could be noted that we compute more Pre's: The standard algorithm computes one Pre and one union of BDDs per iteration of the loop computing min, while Algorithm 1 computes (at most) $d_{max}$ Pre's and as many unions per iteration. However, our computations use much smaller BDDs:

- When considering unit-length transitions, the sets of states computed by the standard algorithm contain some "fake" intermediate states, leading to larger BDDs and unnecessary computations that are not performed with our algorithm;
- We split the transition relation into one transition BDD for each duration occuring in the model.

Also, a specific feature of our algorithm is that it uses the $R'_d$ relations instead of the $R_d$'s. This is correct in situations where shorter transitions have no disadvantages (*e.g.* when looking for minimum delays, or for evaluating $EU_{\leq k}$ modalities). In practice, using $R'_d$ results in using smaller relations and a smaller $Dur'$ set. The difference between $R_d$ and $R'_d$ can be dramatic in examples where the system can nondeterministically pick any large enough duration for its steps, as in the **bridge** benchmark (see Section 6);

*OBDD-based implementation.* Algorithm 1 leads naturally to an OBDD-based implementation. As usual, we assume a state is given by the values of state variables $x_1, \ldots, x_m$. The transition relation is an OBDD-encoded predicate $R(x_1, \ldots, x_m, d, x'_1, \ldots, x'_m)$. Our implementation precomputes $Dur'$ and the $R'_k$ relations for $k \in Dur'$. This only requires simple Boolean operations on OBDDs. An OBDD for $R'$ is obtained via

$$R' := \forall d'[R \wedge (d \leq d' \vee \neg R[d/d'])]. \tag{1}$$

(Here $R[d/d']$ is $R$ where $d'$ has been substituted for $d$.) Then $Dur$ and $Dur'$ (in predicate form) are obtained with:

$$Dur := \exists x_1, \ldots, x_m, x'_1, \ldots, x'_m R, \quad Dur' := \exists x_1, \ldots, x_m, x'_1, \ldots, x'_m R'. \tag{2}$$

And, for $k \in Dur$ (resp. in $Dur'$), the relations $R_k$ and $R'_k$ are obtained with:

$$R_k := \exists d(R \wedge d = k), \qquad\qquad R'_k := \exists d(R' \wedge d = k). \tag{3}$$

Some other implementation details are not so relevant. For example, observe that it is not necessary to store all previous Incr$[i]$ and Diff$[i]$: Our implementation only stores the last $1 + d_{\max}$ values.

# 4    Symbolic Model Checking of RTCTL Properties

We describe algorithms for the main RTCTL modalities. As is usual in symbolic model checking, these algorithms accept sets of states (corresponding to the subformulae that are combined by the modality) and return a set of states, where the compound formula holds.

## 4.1    Zero-Duration Conditions

Modalities with "=0" constraints play a special role, as seen in Section 3.

$EU_{=0}$: Formula $E\varphi U_{=0}\psi$ holds in all states where it is possible to reach a state satisfying $\psi$ all the while visiting only states satisfying $\varphi$ *and only using zero-length steps*. Our procedure for the $EU_{=0}$ modality mimics the standard NuSMV routine for the (untimed) CTL modality EU, with the difference that $R_0$ rather than $R$ is taken as the underlying transition relation.

$EG_{=0}$: This modality can be seen as a weak until: $EG_{=0}\varphi$ means that $\varphi$ must hold until we (possibly) reach a state by firing a non-zero duration transition. We use the modality $EU_{=0}$ above for the strong until case, and add states from which there exists a path verifying $G\varphi$ and only using zero-steps.

$AU_{=0}$: Formula $A\varphi U_{=0}\psi$ is equivalent to $AF_{=0}\psi \wedge A\varphi U\psi$, and $AF_{=0}\psi$ is equivalent to $\neg EG_{=0}\neg\psi$.

## 4.2    RTCTL Modalities with $\leq k$ Constraints

The procedures for the $EU_{\leq k}$ and the $EG_{\leq k}$ modalities work by computing iteratively a sequence Incr$[0]$, Incr$[1]$, ..., Incr$[k]$ of sets associated with $E\varphi U_{\leq i}\psi$ (resp. $EG_{\leq i}\varphi$) for $i = 0, 1, \ldots, k$, and returning Incr$[k]$ Other modalities with $\leq k$ constraints are readily obtained from the above ones.

We do not describe these procedures in more detail here since they are very similar to the functions that compute minimum delays: Compare the specification for the sequence Incr$[0]$, Incr$[1]$, ... and the invariant (Inv1).

## 4.3    RTCTL Modalities with Interval Constraints

**The $EU_{[k..l]}$ Modality.** For $EU_{[k..l]}$ we use Algorithm 2. Write $w$ for the *width* $l - k + 1$ of the interval $[k..l]$ (and assume that both $w$ and $l$ are nonnegative). Algorithm 2 performs $l+1$ steps, computing intermediary results. The same comments as for the minimum delay algorithm could be issued here: this algorithm computes more Pre's and unions than an equivalent algorithm with unit-length transition, but they involve much smaller BDDs.

The correctness of the algorithm relies on the following Lemma:

```
 1  function EUint(S₁, S₂, k, l)
 2  w ← l − k + 1; i ← 0;
 3  if (w≤0 || l<0) { return(FALSE) }
 4  /* Initialization (step i=0)*/
 5  for (j←1; j ≤min(w, d_max); j++) {
 6    Incr[j] ← EU_{=0}( S₁, S₂ ∩ EF_{=0}( ⋃{Pre[R_d](⊤) | d ≥j} ) )
 7  }
 8  for (j← w+1; j≤d_max; j++) { Incr[j] ← ∅ }
 9  Incr[d_max + 1] ← ∅
10  aux0, Res ← EU_{=0}( S₁, S₂ );
11  /* Loop (steps i=1..l)*/
12  for (i←1; i≤ l; i++) {
13    for (j←1; j≤ d_max; j++) {
14      Incr[j] ← Incr[j+1] ∪ EU_{=0}( S₁, S₁ ∩ Pre[R_j](Res) ) ;
15    }
16    Res ← Incr[1];
17    if (i<w) { Res ← Res ∪ aux0 }
18  }
19  return(Res);
```

**Algorithm 2.** Algorithm for $EU_{[k..l]}$

**Lemma 4.1.** *After step $i$, the following invariants hold for all $j$ between $1$ and $d_{max} + 1$:*

$$s \in \text{Incr}[j] \;\; iff \;\; \begin{bmatrix} there\ is\ a\ path\ \pi = s \xrightarrow{0} \cdots \xrightarrow{0} s' \xrightarrow{d} s'' \cdots\ s.t. \\ (a)\ d \geq j,\ and \\ (b)\ \pi \models S_1 U_{[i+j-w..i+j-1]} S_2. \end{bmatrix} \qquad (\text{Inv4})$$

$$s \in \text{Res}\ iff\ s \models E S_1 U_{[i+1-w..i]} S_2. \qquad (\text{Inv5})$$

**Other Modalities.** The algorithm for modality $EG_{[k..l]}$ is similar to the previous one, and also has to consider "border case" paths never reaching an interesting cumulative duration.

The modality $AU_{[k..l]}$ is handled using previous algorithms: We use the following equivalence, which holds whenever $k > 0$:

$$A(\varphi U_{[k..l]} \psi) \equiv AF_{[k..l]} \psi \wedge AG_{<k}(\varphi \wedge AX(A\varphi U\psi))$$

Algorithms for modalities for "$\geq k$"-constraints are not described in the paper, but they are very similar to the above ones.

## 5 TSMV: Embedding Our Algorithms on Top of NuSMV

We now describe how we implemented our algorithms on top of NuSMV [11]. The resulting model checker is called TSMV and is available at http://www.lsv.ens-cachan.fr/~markey/TSMV/, together with all the examples of Section 6.

Extending NuSMV was quite easy and, essentially, we added about 3.500 lines of C code in the model checking section of the tool. These implement the procedures described in earlier sections (Algorithms 1, 2 and other timed modalities described in section 4), and the computations of sets $Dur, Dur', Dur''$ and relations $R_d, R'_d$ described in section 3.

## 5.1 Defining TKS's

For describing TKS's, we opted for the simplest and most practical solution. When describing a model, we use normal NuSMV syntax and reserve an additional state variable, called duration, for specifying the duration of steps. Hence, instead of specifying durational TKS steps of the form

$$\langle v_1, \ldots, v_m \rangle \xrightarrow{d} \langle v'_1, \ldots, v'_m \rangle \qquad \text{(TKS step)}$$

we describe simple KS steps of the form

$$\langle v_1, \ldots, v_m, \star \rangle \rightarrow \langle v'_1, \ldots, v'_m, d \rangle \qquad \text{(extended KS step)}$$

For example, the TKS from Fig. 1 could be defined with

```
VAR
  state: 1..3;
  duration: 0..21;
TRANS
    (state = 1 & next(state)=2 & next(duration) = 0)
  | (state = 2 & next(state)=1 & next(duration) = 0)
  | (state = 2 & next(state)=3 & next(duration) = 21)
  ...
```

More realistic examples can be found in Section 6.

Using this scheme has a number of benefits. It lets us reuse all the NuSMV machinery for assembling and instantiating modules. Furthermore, it allows using symbolic constraints when defining sets of possible durations between states (see e.g. the bridge example).

Once NuSMV has computed an OBDD for the transition relation of the extended KS, it is easy to extract the relations of the underlying TKS, with the projections and other Boolean operations described in Section 3.

## 5.2 Querying the TKS

TSMV reuses NuSMV syntax for RTCTL formulae. Additionally, we support RTCTL modalities with right-open intervals. Computing minimum and maximum delays reuses NuSMV syntax too. For example, one would write:

```
SPEC AG>=4 (p2 -> AF<=21 ! p1)
COMPUTE MAX[p1 | p2, state = 2]
```

## 5.3  Extra Features

As much as possible, TSMV reuses features from NuSMV. For example:

**Fairness:** For simplicity, our exposition in Section 2 did not mention fairness issues. But fairness constraints à la SMV are allowed in TSMV, and only fair paths are considered. Fairness constraints can involve the `duration` variable, thus TSMV can express the so-called "non-Zeno" behavior.

**Counter-example generation:** In some cases, it is possible to reuse NuSMV counter-example generation features. This could be done e.g. with "=0" constraints, that can easily be expressed in pure RTCTL (using the subformula `duration=0`). For other modalities, our algorithms do not rely enough on NuSMV temporal primitives and we are developping our own counter-example generation functions for these cases.

# 6  Experimental Results

## 6.1  The Bridge-Crossing Problem

*The problem.* The bridge-crossing problem is a famous mathematical puzzle with time critical aspects [21, 18]. A group of four persons, called P1, P2, P3 and P4, cross a bridge at night. It is dark and one can only cross the bridge with a lamp. Only one lamp is available and at most two persons can cross at the same time. Therefore any solution requires that, after the first two persons cross the bridge, one of them returns, carrying back the lamp for the remaining persons. The four persons have different maximal speeds: here P1 crosses in 5 time units (t.u.), P2 in 10 t.u., P3 in 20 t.u. and P4 in 25 t.u. When a pair crosses the bridge, they move at the speed of the slowest person in the pair. Now, how much time is required before the whole group is on the other side?

*Bridge-crossing in TSMV.* A person is described as an SMV module with his crossing time as a parameter. His possible steps are to stay where he is, or move to the other side. He can only cross when the lamp is on his side (and then the lamp crosses with him). When he crosses, the transition takes at least his crossing time. This way, when four persons are synchronized, the crossing time is any integer greater or equal to the maximum crossing time of the crossing persons. The complete system is obtained by combining four persons (four instances of the same `person` module, with different crossing times) with a Boolean `lamp` value keeping track of the position of the lamp, and adding a further constraint (an `INVAR` in SMV) telling that at most two persons cross in one move. The system is further labeled with two propositions: `initial` for the initial configuration, and `safe` for the configurations where everyone is on the other side of the bridge. We can ask how much time is required for crossing:

```
COMPUTE MIN[initial, safe]
```

The answer (60 t.u.) is obtained in a few milliseconds.

It turns out that 60 t.u. is the best total crossing time *from the initial configuration.* But if we let people move freely and at some time ask them to cross quickly, can it happen that they are in a configuration where more than 60 t.u. are required? We ask

```
SPEC  AG EF<=60 safe
```

and get a negative answer: in some reachable configurations, more than 60 t.u. are required.

Indeed, if we start after just one person has crossed, that person will have to come back before we can implement the 60 t.u. solution. Hence 85 t.u. (=25+60) are sometimes required. We check that this is indeed the worst case with

```
SPEC  (AG EF<=85 safe) & !(AG EF<=84 safe)
```

*Comparison with related tools.* The same example can be treated with NuSMV, Verus or RAVEN. Since NuSMV and Verus only handle unit steps, we use the method advocated in [7, p.106] and introduce a counter forcing several t.u. between actual system moves. It can be argued that these models are slightly more cumbersome. With RAVEN, we can directly specify duration intervals for each transitions, even though it internally considers the semi-continuous semantics.

The command COMPUTE MIN[initial, safe] produces the (correct) answer but takes significantly more time with NuSMV, Verus and RAVEN than with TSMV (see Table 1).

When verifying SPEC (AG EF<=85 safe) & !(AG EF<=84 safe) we obtain a negative answer! This is because the semantical models are different. With all three tools, the semi-continuous semantics introduces intermediary positions along what are long steps in our TKS's, and the AG modality quantifies over these intermediate positions too.

It can be argued that the semi-continuous semantics is "better", or closer to specifier's purposes. However, it makes verification more costly. Furthermore, it is slightly less general: our TKS's generalize unit-steps KS's, while TKS semantics can only be simulated akwardly in KS's. The previous example shows that a counter-based encoding is not enough: one further has to adapt the RTCTL formulae. For example, in the bridge problem, we can introduce a new proposition, crossing, labeling intermediate configurations that should not exist in the TKS. Then the following formula is satisfied:

```
SPEC  AG (!crossing -> EF<= 85 (safe & !crossing)).
```

## 6.2  TSMV and Sensitivity to Scaling up the Durations

The bridge problem is an example of a system where durations are mostly "long" (greater than 1). Our algorithms are designed in such a way that only useful durations are considered. As a result, TSMV is mostly insensitive to scaling up the durations. When we define a model "bridge x 10" by replacing 5, 10, 20 and 25 with (resp.) 50, 100, 200, and 250, TSMV computes the minimum delay of 600 t.u. in more or less the same time it needed for the initial problem[2].

---

[2] The TKS defined with bridge x 10 is not *exactly* a scaling up of bridge. It uses conditions of the form "duration >= 100" that allow all values $100, 101, 102, \ldots, d_{max}$.

**Table 1.** Scale up (in)sensitivity.

| | TSMV | | NuSMV | | Verus | | RAVEN | |
|---|---|---|---|---|---|---|---|---|
| | time | mem | time | mem | time | mem | time | mem |
| bridge | 0.02 s | 1.3 M | 0.21 s | 9.5 M | 7.14 s | 16.5 M | 4.01 s | 5.9 M |
| bridge×10 | 0.04 s | 1.3 M | 23.24 s | 18.5 M | 259.54 s | 39.2 M | 3 098 s | 371 M |
| bridge×20 | 0.07 s | 1.3 M | 120.13 s | 18.5 M | 573.05 s | 44.1 M | | |
| bridge×50 | 0.22 s | 9.0 M | 2 209 s | 35.0 M | 3 626 s | 55.0 M | | |
| bridge×100 | 0.45 s | 11.0 M | 14 296 s | 65.0 M | 17 870 s | 59.2 M | | |

By contrast, the computation time for NuSMV, Verus and RAVEN increases dramatically when we scale up the durations. In fact, there is no way to avoid this: These tools do not know about TKS's and are bound to compute all sets associated with different values of the counter for intermediate states. Computing these sets is a tedious and mostly repetitive task that cannot be avoided unless a notion of TKS is introduced.

Table 1 shows how running time and memory requirements grow when we scale up the timing parameters of the bridge problem.

## 6.3   Verifying the PCI Local Bus

A model of the PCI local bus was analyzed by Campos *et al.* in [8], computing minimum and maximum delays with symbolic model checking techniques. This model is a standard example that comes with the NuSMV distribution. We refer to [8] for more explanations on this case study. The reader only needs to know that it is a large example where NuSMV can show that a complete transaction might take up to 244 steps, from the request of the bus to the end of the transaction.

First of all, we added duration 1 to all transitions. This allows a direct comparison with NuSMV. In that case, we were able to prove the aforementioned maximal time for a complete transaction, by adding the following lines to the main module of the PCI model:

```
VAR  duration: 0..1;
TRANS  next(duration)=1
COMPUTE MAX[ req0, isa_bridge.end_transaction ]
COMPUTE MAX[ req1, scsi_ctrl.end_transaction ]              (E₁)
COMPUTE MAX[ req2, vga_ctrl.end_transaction ]
COMPUTE MAX[ req4, processor.end_transaction ]
```

For the isa_bridge and scsi_ctrl components, the result is 244. It is 130 for the other two components (see explanations for this difference in [8]).

Counting specific kinds of events is possible. For instance, one can use durations to count the number of transactions issued on the PCI bus between a request and a grant of each of the masters.

```
DEFINE start_tr := processor.start_transaction |
                   vga_ctrl.start_transaction |
                   scsi_ctrl.start_transaction |
                   isa_bridge.start_transaction ;
VAR  duration: 0..1;
TRANS  next(duration)=case
              start_tr: 1;
              1          : 0;
         esac
COMPUTE MAX[ req0, grant=0 ]
COMPUTE MAX[ req1, grant=1 ]
COMPUTE MAX[ req2, grant=2 ]
COMPUTE MAX[ req4, grant=4 ]
```
$$(E_2)$$

TSMV answers that up to 5 transactions might start between request and grant for both the isa_bridge and the scsi_ctrl components, and 2 for the other two masters. These are the values given in [8], where they were obtained with a special condition counting Algorithm.

With the following lines, we count the amount of data the processor can transfer between a request and its corresponding grant:

```
(in module bus_master)
  VAR transmitting: boolean;
  ASSIGN init(transmitting) := FALSE;
         next(transmitting) := (count>next(count));
(in module main)
  VAR  duration: 0..1;
  TRANS  next(duration)=case
              processor.transmitting : 1;
              1                      : 0;
         esac
COMPUTE MAX[ req0, grant=0 ]
COMPUTE MAX[ req1, grant=1 ]
COMPUTE MAX[ req2, grant=2 ]
COMPUTE MAX[ req4, grant=4 ]
```
$$(E_3)$$

The result is 30 for the isa_bridge, the scsi_ctrl and the vga_ctrl, and 15 for the processor (the total amount of data that a master can transmit in one "session" is limited to 15 in this model).

Last, we verify that, when a transaction is aborted, the component has to request for the bus before being able to transmit anew. We verify this property for the processor by counting only data transfers of the processor, and specifying that, after abortion, he can transmit at most one bit of data if it does not assert a new grant. This is achieved with the following additions to pci4p.smv:

```
(in module bus_master)
   VAR transmitting: boolean;
   ASSIGN init(transmitting) := FALSE;
          next(transmitting) := (count>next(count));
(in module main)
   VAR  duration: 0..1;
   TRANS  next(duration)=case
               processor.transmitting : 1;
               1                       : 0;
          esac
SPEC AG ((processor.transmitting & abort) -> !E [ (!req4) U>=2 TRUE ] )
SPEC EF ((processor.transmitting & abort) -> E [ (!req4) U= 1 TRUE ] )
SPEC EF ((processor.transmitting & abort) -> E [ (!req4) U= 0 TRUE ] )
```
$$(E_4)$$

The table below summarizes the total time and memory consumption for the four examples above. Since NuSMV does not handle zero-duration transitions, it could only be applied in the first example:

**Table 2.** Verification of the PCI local bus.

|  | NuSMV | | TSMV | |
|---|---|---|---|---|
|  | time | memory | time | memory |
| $(E_1)$ | 178.37 sec. | 21 228KB | 186.34 sec. | 26 932KB |
| $(E_2)$ | | | 69.59 sec. | 24 340KB |
| $(E_3)$ | | | 306.74 sec. | 31 780KB |
| $(E_4)$ | | | 13.56 sec. | 33 900KB |

## 7   Comparison with Other Work

*On the semantics of time.* Emerson *et al.* [13] pioneered the investigation of RTCTL model checking on KS's with unit-length transitions. Campos, Clarke *et al.* [5, 10] and Kropf, Ruf *et al.* [14, 20] considered more general Timed Transition Systems (TTGs) where durations can be arbitrary (sets of) natural numbers. The difference between these models and our TKS's is that time in TTGs elapses "semi-continuously", *i.e.* using intermediate states, while TKS's transitions are atomic (see section 2.3). We chose atomic durations because they lead to more efficient model checking algorithms [15]. When it comes to modeling actual systems, the semi-continuous semantics is perhaps more natural (but we did not feel hampered by atomic durations in our case studies). Observe that it is easy to simulate semi-continuous durations in atomic durations (by adding intermediate states) while designing a simulation the other way around is more involved.

Another major issue is that consecutive zero-length transitions in TKS's are not amalgamated (which would make intermediate states disappear). Amalgamating these can make verification more efficient when zero-length transitions are just internal micro-steps, as in [7]. But when zero-length transitions are used in condition-counting applications, amalgamating them is costly (sometimes infeasible). Additionally, this loses a lot of the branching-time aspects that *CTL* talks about. Finally, these two different ways of treating zero-length transitions have very different applications.

*On algorithmics.* It may seem that our symbolic algorithms are not very different from earlier algorithms for RTCTL model checking: these procedures all compute fixed-points iteratively. However, an important difference exists: all our algorithms use information on what durations really appear in the model. In connection with the atomicity of durations, this leads to more efficient algorithms. In particular, it makes model checking mostly insensitive to scaling up the durations, as illustrated in section 6.2. Additionally, the algorithms we designed for the "$\geq k$" and "$\leq k$" constraints benefit from considering a derived transition relation where only maximal (resp. minimal) durations appear (see Section 3).

*On implementations.* Several symbolic algorithms for discrete-time models have been published, and some of them consider models with arbitrary durations on transitions. However, not all published algorithms have been implemented. NuSMV and Verus only support unit-length durations. RAVEN uses the semi-continuous semantics and does not allow null durations. TSMV is, to our knowledge, the first tool dealing with (general) integer durations in discrete time models. Similarly, "$\geq k$" constraints are not available in the other tools.

## 8    Conclusion

We proposed OBDD-based symbolic verification procedures for model checking RTCTL properties and for computing extremum delays. The underlying models are (symbolic descriptions of) TKS's, or state graphs where transitions carry an arbitrary duration.

For the analysis of timed systems, this extends the verification facilities that are offered in NuSMV (based on earlier work by Campos, Clarke *et al.*). Our algorithms are implemented on top of NuSMV, and allow all combinations of long, unit and zero-length steps. We also deal with an enlarged set of RTCTL modalities, and offer procedures for computing extremum delays.

The procedures we propose take advantage of the TKS model: we do not reduce a long step (e.g. 10 time units) to an implicit sequence of 10 unit steps. A consequence is that the behavior of our model checking algorithm enjoys a kind of insensitivity to scaling up of durations (a feature of tools based on timed automata). This suggests that there exist ways of bridging the gap that still exists between approaches à la SMV where clocks are considered like any other discrete variable, and approaches based on timed automata, à la UPPAAL and Kronos, still in need of efficient symbolic representations handling combinatorial control and clock valuations.

## References

1. B. Bérard, M. Bidoit, A. Finkel, F. Laroussinie, A. Petit, L. Petrucci, and Ph. Schnoebelen. *Systems and Software Verification. Model-Checking Techniques and Tools.* Springer, 2001.
2. P. Bouyer. Forward analysis of updatable timed automata. *Formal Methods in System Design*, 24(3):281–320, 2004.
3. J. R. Burch, E. M. Clarke, K. L. McMillan, D. L. Dill, and L. J. Hwang. Symbolic model checking: $10^{20}$ states and beyond. *Inf. & Comp.*, 98(2):142–170, 1992.
4. S. Campos. *Verus 0.9 – Reference Manual.* Pittsburgh, PA, USA, March 1997.
5. S. Campos and E. M. Clarke. Real-time symbolic model checking for discrete time models. In T. Rus and C. Rattray, editors, *Theories and Experiences for Real-Time System Development*, vol. 2 of *AMAST Series in Computing*, pp. 129–145. World Scientific, 1995.

6. S. Campos and E. M. Clarke. Analysis and verification of real-time systems using quantitative symbolic algorithms. *J. Software Tools for Technology Transfer*, 2(3):260–269, 1999.
7. S. Campos and E. M. Clarke. The Verus language: representing time efficiently with BDDs. *Theor. Comp. Sci.*, 253(1):95–118, 2001.
8. S. Campos, E. M. Clarke, W. R. Marrero, and M. Minea. Verifying the performance of the PCI local bus using symbolic techniques. In *Proc. 1995 Int. Conf. on Computer Design (ICCD '95), VLSI in Computers and Processors, Austin, TX, USA, Oct. 1995*, pp. 72–78. IEEE Comp. Soc. Press, 1995.
9. S. Campos, E. M. Clarke, W. R. Marrero, M. Minea, and H. Hiraishi. Computing quantitative characteristics of finite-state real-time systems. In *Proc. 15th IEEE Real-Time Systems Symposium (RTSS'94), San Juan, Puerto Rico, Dec. 1994*, pp. 266–270. IEEE Comp. Soc. Press, 1994.
10. S. Campos, M. Teixeira, M. Minea, A. Kuehlmann, and E. M. Clarke. Model checking semi-continuous time models using BDDs. In *Proc. 1st Int. Workshop on Symbolic Model Checking (SMC'99), Trento, Italy, July 1999*, vol. 23(2) of *Electronic Notes Theor. Comp. Sci.* Elsevier Science, 1999.
11. A. Cimatti, E. M. Clarke, F. Giunchiglia, and M. Roveri. NuSMV: a new symbolic model checker. *J. Software Tools for Technology Transfer*, 2(4):410–425, 2000.
12. E. M. Clarke, O. Grumberg, and D. A. Peled. *Model Checking*. MIT Press, 1999.
13. E. A. Emerson, A. K. Mok, A. P. Sistla, and J. Srinivasan. Quantitative temporal reasoning. *Real-Time Systems*, 4(4):331–352, 1992.
14. J. Frößl, J. Gerlach, and Th. Kropf. An efficient algorithm for real-time symbolic model checking. In *Proc. European Design and Test Conference (ED&TC'96), Paris, France, Mar. 1996*, pp. 15–21. IEEE Comp. Soc. Press, 1996.
15. F. Laroussinie, N. Markey, and Ph. Schnoebelen. On model checking durational Kripke structures (extended abstract). In *Proc. 5th Int. Conf. Foundations of Software Science and Computation Structures (FOSSACS'2002), Grenoble, France, Apr. 2002*, vol. 2303 of *Lect. Notes Comp. Sci.*, pp. 264–279. Springer, 2002.
16. K. G. Larsen, P. Pettersson, and Wang Yi. UPPAAL in a nutshell. *J. Software Tools for Technology Transfer*, 1(1–2):134–152, 1997.
17. K. L. McMillan. *Symbolic Model Checking*. Kluwer Academic, 1993.
18. G. Rote. Crossing the bridge at night. *EATCS Bull.*, 78:241–246, 2002.
19. J. Ruf. RAVEN: Real-time analyzing and verification environment. *J. Universal Comp. Sci.*, 7(1):89–104, 2001.
20. J. Ruf and Th. Kropf. A new algorithm for discrete timed symbolic model checking. In *Proc. Int. Workshop Hybrid and Real-Time Systems (HART'97), Grenoble, France, Mar. 1997*, vol. 1201 of *Lect. Notes Comp. Sci.*, pp. 18–32. Springer, 1997.
21. T. C. Ruys and E. Brinksma. Experience with literate programming in the modelling and validation of systems. In *Proc. 4th Int. Conf. Tools and Algorithms for the Construction and Analysis of Systems (TACAS'98), Lisbon, Portugal, Mar. 1998*, vol. 1384 of *Lect. Notes Comp. Sci.*, pp. 393–407. Springer, 1998.
22. S. Yovine. Kronos: A verification tool for real-time systems. *J. Software Tools for Technology Transfer*, 1(1–2):123–133, 1997.

# Robustness and Implementability of Timed Automata[*]

Martin De Wulf, Laurent Doyen[**], Nicolas Markey, and Jean-François Raskin

Computer Science Departement, Université Libre de Bruxelles, Belgium

**Abstract.** In a former paper, we defined a new semantics for timed automata, the Almost ASAP semantics, which is parameterized by $\Delta$ to cope with the reaction delay of the controller. We showed that this semantics is implementable provided there exists a strictly positive value for the parameter $\Delta$ for which the strategy is correct. In this paper, we define the implementability problem to be the question of existence of such a $\Delta$. We show that this question is closely related to a notion of robustness for timed automata defined in [Pur98] and prove that the implementability problem is decidable.

## 1   Introduction

Timed automata are an important formal model for the specification and analysis of real-time systems. Formalisms like timed automata and hybrid automata are central in the so-called *model-based development methodology for embedded controllers*. The steps underlying that methodology can be summarized as follows: (*i*) construct a (timed/hybrid automaton) model Env of the environment in which the controller will be embedded; (*ii*) make clear what is the control objective: for example, prevent the environment to enter a set of Bad states; (*iii*) design a (timed automata) model Cont of the control strategy; (*iv*) verify that Reach([[Env ∥ Cont]]) ∩ Bad = ∅ (where Reach([[Env ∥ Cont]]) denotes the set of states reachable in the transition system associated to the synchronized product of the automaton for the environment and the automaton for the controller). When Cont has been proven correct, it would be valuable to ensure that an implementation Impl of that model can be obtained in a systematic way in order to ensure the conservation of correctness, that is to ensure that Reach([[Env ∥ Impl]]) ∩ Bad = ∅ is obtained by construction.

Unfortunately, this is often not possible for several *fundamental* and/or *technical* reasons. First, the notion of time used in the traditional semantics of timed automata is *continuous* and defines *perfect clocks* with *infinite precision* while implementations can only access time through *digital* and *finitely precise* clocks. Second, timed automata react *instantaneously* to events and time-outs while implementations can only react within a given, usually small but not zero, *reaction*

---

[*] Supported by the FRFC project "Centre Fédéré en Vérification" funded by the Belgian National Science Foundation (FNRS) under grant nr 2.4530.02.
[**] Research fellow supported by the Belgian National Science Foundation (FNRS).

Y. Lakhnech and S. Yovine (Eds.): FORMATS/FTRTFT 2004, LNCS 3253, pp. 118–133, 2004.

*delay.* Third, timed automata may describe control strategies that are *unrealistic*, like *zeno-strategies* or strategies that ask the controller *to act faster and faster* [CHR02]. For one of those three reasons, a model for a digital controller that has been proven correct may not be implementable (at all) or it may not be possible to turn it systematically into an implementation that is proven correct w.r.t. this model.

To overcome those problems, we recently proposed in [DDR04] an alternative semantics to timed automata. This semantics is called the Almost ASAP semantics, AASAP for short. The AASAP-semantics of a timed automaton $A$, noted $[\![A]\!]_\Delta^{\text{AASAP}}$, is a parametric semantics that leaves as a parameter $\Delta \in \mathbb{Q}^{\geq 0}$ the *reaction delay* of the controller. This semantics relaxes the classical semantics of timed automata in that it does not impose on the controller to react instantaneously but imposes on the controller to react *within $\Delta$ time units*. We have proven that a timed controller is implementable with a *sufficiently fast* hardware if and only if there exists $\Delta \in \mathbb{Q}^{>0}$ such that $\text{Reach}([\![\text{Env} \parallel \text{Cont}]\!]_\Delta) \cap \text{Bad} = \varnothing$. Details on the notion of implementability can be found in [DDR04]. The *implementability problem* is to determine the existence of such a $\Delta$. The decidability of that important problem is open. We will close this open question here.

The use of the AASAP-semantics in the verification phase can be understood intuitively as follows. When we verify a control strategy using the AASAP-semantics, we test if the proposed strategy is *robust* in the following sense[1]: *"Is the strategy still correct if it is perturbed a little bit when executed on a device that has a finite speed and uses finitely precise clocks ?"*

In this paper, we show that this intuition relating robustness and implementability allows us to draw an interesting and important link with a paper by Puri [Pur98] and allows us to answer *positively* the open question about the decidability of the implementability problem.

*Related works.* In this paper, we focus on timed controllers and environments that can be modeled using timed automata. There exist related works where the interested reader will find other ideas about implementability.

In [AFILS03], Rajeev Alur et al consider the more general problem of generating code from hybrid automata, but they only sketch a solution and state interesting research questions. The work in this paper should be useful in that context.

In [AFM+02,AFP+03], Wang Yi et al present a tool called TIMES that generates executable code from timed automata models. However, they make the synchrony hypothesis and so they *assume* that the hardware on which the code is executed is infinitely fast and precise.

In [HKSP03], Tom Henzinger et al introduce a programming model for real-time embedded controllers called GIOTTO. GIOTTO is an embedded software model that can be used to specify a solution to a given control problem independently of an execution platform but which is closer to executable code than

---

[1] Our notion of robustness is different from another interseting one introduced in [GHJ97].

a mathematical model. So, GIOTTO can be seen an intermediary step between mathematical models like hybrid automata and real execution platforms.

Our paper is structured as follows. In Section 2, we recall some classical definitions related to timed automata and we introduce a general notion of enlarged semantics for those automata. In Section 3, we recall the essential notions and problems related to the AASAP-semantics, and we recall the notion of robustness as introduced by Puri in [Pur98]. In Section 4, we present a small example that illustrates the enlarged semantics and the problems that we want to solve on this semantics. In Section 5, we make formal the link between our notion of implementability and the notion of robustness introduced by Puri. In Section 6, we give a direct proof that the implementability problem is decidable. Finally, we close the paper by a conclusion.

Complete proofs can be found in a longer version of this paper at the following web page: http://www.ulb.ac.be/di/ssd/cfv/publications.html.

## 2   Preliminaries

**Definition 1** [TTS] A *timed transition system* $T$ is a tuple $\langle S, \iota, \Sigma, \rightarrow \rangle$ where $S$ is a (possibly infinite) set of states, $\iota \in S$ is the initial state, $\Sigma$ is a finite set of labels, and $\rightarrow \subseteq S \times \Sigma \cup \mathbb{R}^{\geq 0} \times S$ is the transition relation where $\mathbb{R}^{\geq 0}$ is the set of positive real numbers. If $(q, \sigma, q') \in \rightarrow$ we write $q \xrightarrow{\sigma} q'$.     □

A *trajectory* of a TTS $T = \langle S, \iota, \Sigma, \rightarrow \rangle$ is a sequence $\pi = (s_0, t_0) \ldots (s_k, t_k)$ such that for $0 \leq i \leq k$, $(s_i, t_i) \in S \times \mathbb{R}$ and for $0 \leq i < k$, $s_i \xrightarrow{\sigma} s_{i+1}$ and either $\sigma \in \Sigma$ and $t_{i+1} = t_i$, or $\sigma \in \mathbb{R}^{>0}$ and $t_{i+1} = t_i + \sigma$. We sometimes refer to this trajectory as $\pi[t_0, t_k]$ and write $\pi(t_i)$ instead of $q_i$. A trajectory is *stutter-free* iff it is not the case for any $i$ that $q_i \xrightarrow{\tau_i} q_{i+1}$ and $q_{i+1} \xrightarrow{\tau_{i+1}} q_{i+2}$ with $\tau_i, \tau_{i+1} \in \mathbb{R}^{>0}$. A state $s$ of $T$ is *reachable* if there exists a trajectory $\pi = (s_0, t_0) \ldots (s_k, t_k)$ such that $s_0 = \iota$ and $s_n = s$. The set of reachable states of $T$ is noted $\mathsf{Reach}(T)$.

Given a set $\mathsf{Var} = \{x_1, \ldots, x_n\}$ of clocks, a *clock valuation* is a function $v \colon \mathsf{Var} \rightarrow \mathbb{R}^{\geq 0}$. In the sequel, we often say that a clock valuation is a point in $\mathbb{R}^n$. If $R \subseteq \mathsf{Var}$, then $v[R := 0]$ denotes the valuation $v'$ such that

$$v'(x) = \begin{cases} 0 & \text{if } x \in R \\ v(x) & \text{if } x \notin R \end{cases}$$

A *closed rectangular guard* $g$ over $\{x_1, \ldots, x_n\}$ is a set of inequalities of the form $a_i \leq x_i \leq b_i$, one for each $x_i$ where $a_i, b_i \in \mathbb{Q}^{\geq 0} \cup \{+\infty\}$ and $a_i \leq b_i$. We write $\mathsf{Rect}_c(\mathsf{Var})$ for the set of closed rectangular guards over $\mathsf{Var}$. For $\Delta \geq 0$, we define $\llbracket g \rrbracket_\Delta = \{(x_1, \ldots, x_n) \mid a_i - \Delta \leq x_i \leq b_i + \Delta\} \subseteq \mathbb{R}^n$. When $\Delta = 0$, we write $\llbracket g \rrbracket$ instead of $\llbracket g \rrbracket_0$.

We slightly modify the classical definitions related to timed automata [AD94]. In particular, guards on edges are rectangular and closed[2]. Also the value of

---

[2] In the sequel, the guards are enlarged by strictly positive parameter $\Delta$, and so it is natural to consider them closed.

their clock is bounded by $M$, the largest constant appearing in guards. The last restriction does not reduce the expressive power of timed automata.

**Definition 2** [Timed automaton] A *timed automaton* is a tuple $A = \langle \mathsf{Loc}, \mathsf{Var}, q_0, \mathsf{Lab}, \mathsf{Edg} \rangle$ where

- $\mathsf{Loc}$ is a finite set of locations representing the discrete states of the automaton.
- $\mathsf{Var} = \{x_1, \ldots, x_n\}$ is a finite set of real-valued variables.
- $q_0 = (l_0, v_0)$ where $l_0 \in \mathsf{Loc}$ is the initial location and $v_0$ is the initial clock valuation such that $\forall x \in \mathsf{Var} : v_0(x) \in \mathbb{N} \wedge v_0(x) \leq M$.
- $\mathsf{Lab}$ is a finite alphabet of labels.
- $\mathsf{Edg} \subseteq \mathsf{Loc} \times \mathsf{Loc} \times \mathsf{Rect}_c(\mathsf{Var}) \times \mathsf{Lab} \times 2^{\mathsf{Var}}$ is a set of edges. An edge $(l, l', g, \sigma, R)$ represents a jump from location $l$ to location $l'$ with guard $g$, event $\sigma$ and a subset $R \subseteq \mathsf{Var}$ of variables to be reset. $\qquad \square$

We now define a family of semantics for timed automata that is parameterized by $\epsilon \in \mathbb{Q}^{\geq 0}$ (drift on clocks) and $\Delta \in \mathbb{Q}^{\geq 0}$ (imprecision on guards).

**Definition 3** [Enlarged semantics of timed automata] The semantics of a timed automaton $A = \langle \mathsf{Loc}, \mathsf{Var}, q_0, \mathsf{Lab}, \mathsf{Edg} \rangle$, when the two parameters $\epsilon$ and $\Delta$ are fixed is given by the TTS $[\![A]\!]_\Delta^\epsilon = \langle S, \iota, \Sigma, \rightarrow \rangle$ where

1. $S = \{(l, v) \mid l \in \mathsf{Loc} \wedge v : \mathsf{Var} \rightarrow [0, M]\}$.
2. $\iota = q_0$.
3. $\Sigma = \mathsf{Lab}$.
4. The transition relation $\rightarrow$ is defined by
   (a) For the discrete transitions: $((l, v), \sigma, (l', v')) \in \rightarrow$ iff there exists an edge $(l, l', g, \sigma, R) \in \mathsf{Edg}$ such that $v \in [\![g]\!]_\Delta$ and $v' = v[R := 0]$.
   (b) For the continuous transitions: $((l, v), t, (l', v')) \in \rightarrow$ iff $l = l'$ and $v'(x_i) - v(x_i) \in [(1 - \epsilon)t, (1 + \epsilon)t]$ for $i = 1 \ldots n$. $\qquad \square$

In the sequel, we write $[\![A]\!]$ for $[\![A]\!]_0^0$, which is the classical semantics of timed automata.

*Remark.* Our definition of timed automata does not use strict inequalities; this simplifies the presentation and is not restrictive. Indeed, consider a timed automaton $A$ with (possibly open) rectangular guards and the closure automaton $\widehat{A}$ resulting from $A$ by replacing strict inequalities by non-strict ones. It appears obviously that $\mathsf{Reach}([\![\widehat{A}]\!]_{\frac{\epsilon}{2}}^\epsilon) \subseteq \mathsf{Reach}([\![A]\!]_\Delta^\epsilon)$ and $\mathsf{Reach}([\![A]\!]_\Delta^\epsilon) \subseteq \mathsf{Reach}([\![\widehat{A}]\!]_\Delta^\epsilon)$, and hence the implementability problem on $A$ *"Does there exist $\Delta \in \mathbb{Q}^{>0}$ such that $\mathsf{Reach}([\![A]\!]_\Delta^\epsilon) \cap \mathsf{Bad} = \varnothing$ ?"* is equivalent to the the implementability problem on $\widehat{A}$.

We now recall some additional classical notions related to timed automata.

Let $\lfloor x \rfloor$ denote the integer part of $x$ (the greatest integer $k \leq x$), and $\langle x \rangle$ denote its fractional part.

**Definition 4** [Clock regions] A *clock region* is an equivalence class of the relation $\sim$ defined over the clock valuations in $\mathsf{Var} \to [0, M]$. We have $v \sim w$ iff all the following conditions hold:

- $\forall x \in \mathsf{Var} : \lfloor v(x) \rfloor = \lfloor w(x) \rfloor$.
- $\forall x, y \in \mathsf{Var} : \langle v(x) \rangle \leq \langle v(y) \rangle$ iff $\langle w(x) \rangle \leq \langle w(y) \rangle$.
- $\forall x \in \mathsf{Var} : \langle v(x) \rangle = 0$ iff $\langle w(x) \rangle = 0$.    $\square$

We write $]v[$ for the clock region containing $v$. It is easy to see that $]v[$ contains the valuations that agree with $v$ on the integer part of the variables, and on the ordering of their fractional part and 0. The closure of the region containing $v$ is noted $[v]$. Such a set is called a *closed region*.

**Definition 5** [Region graph] Given the TTS $[\![A]\!] = \langle S, s_0, \Sigma, \to_A \rangle$ of a timed automaton $A$, we define the corresponding *region graph* $G = \langle \mathcal{C}, \to_G \rangle$ of $A$ :

- $\mathcal{C} = \{(l, [v]) \mid (l, v) \in S\}$ is the set of closed regions.
- $\to_G \subseteq \mathcal{C} \times \mathcal{C}$. $((l, [v]), (l', [v'])) \in \to_G$ if $(l, v) \to_A (l', v')$ and $(l, [v]) \neq (l', [v'])$.    $\square$

This definition is meaningful since $\mathcal{C}$ is finite and whenever $(l, [v]) \to_G (l', [v'])$, for any $s \in [v]$ there exists $s' \in [v']$ such that $(l, s) \to_A (l', s')$, and for any $s' \in [v']$ there exists $s \in [v]$ such that $(l, s) \to_A (l', s')$ [AD94].

Let $W = |\mathcal{C}|$ be the total number of regions.

**Definition 6** [Zones] A *zone* $Z \subseteq \mathbb{R}^n$ is a *closed set* defined by inequalities of the form

$$x_i - x_j \leq m_{ij}, \quad \alpha_i \leq x_i \leq \beta_i$$

where $1 \leq i, j \leq n$ and $m_{ij}, \alpha_i, \beta_i \in \mathbb{Z}$.    $\square$

A set of states is called a *zone-set* if it is a finite union of sets of the form $\{l\} \times Z$ where $l$ is a location and $Z$ is a zone.

**Definition 7** [Progress cycle] A *progress cycle* in the region graph of a timed automaton is a cycle in which each clock is reset at least once.    $\square$

**Assumption 8** We make the assumption that every cycle in the region graph of the timed automata we consider is a progress cycle.

This assumption, made by Puri in his paper [Pur98], is not a very restrictive assumption, since it is weaker than classical non-Zeno assumptions in the literature (for example in [AMPS98], they impose that "in every cycle in the transition graph of the automaton, there is at least one transition which resets a clock variable $x_i$ to zero, and at least one transition which can be taken only if $x_i \geq 1$").

# 3   AASAP Semantics and Enlarged Semantics

In [DDR04], we introduced the Almost ASAP semantics. This semantics relaxes the usual semantics of timed automata, its main characteristics are summarized as follows:

- any transition that can be taken becomes urgent only after a small delay $\Delta$ (which may be left as a parameter);
- a distinction is made between the occurrence of an event in the environment (sent) and in the controller (received), however the time difference between the two events is bounded by $\Delta$;
- guards are enlarged by some small amount depending on $\Delta$.

In the same paper, in Theorem 6, we show that this semantics can be encoded using a syntactical transformation of the automaton controller and by enlarging the guards by the parameter $\Delta$ which takes its value in the positive rationals. So we can study the AASAP-semantics of Env ∥ Cont by considering the semantics $[\![\text{Env} \parallel \text{Cont}']\!]^0_\Delta$ where Cont' is obtained syntactically from Cont. So in the rest of this paper, we will consider the $\Delta$-enlarged semantics instead of the AASAP-semantics.

In this previous work, we have shown that the AASAP-semantics and so the $\Delta$-enlarged semantics allow us to reason about the implementability of a control strategy defined by a timed automaton. The problems that we want to solve algorithmically on the $\Delta$-enlarged semantics are the following ones:

- [Fixed] given a zone-set of Bad states, the timed automata Env and Cont, and a fixed value of $\Delta \in \mathbb{Q}^{>0}$ decide whether $\text{Reach}([\![\text{Env} \parallel \text{Cont}']\!]^0_\Delta) \cap \text{Bad} = \varnothing$;
- [Existence] given a zone-set of Bad states, Env and Cont, decide whether there exists $\Delta \in \mathbb{Q}^{>0}$ such that $\text{Reach}([\![\text{Env} \parallel \text{Cont}']\!]^0_\Delta) \cap \text{Bad} = \varnothing$. This is also called the implementability problem.
- [Maximization] given a zone-set of Bad states, Env and Cont, compute the least upper bound of the set of $\Delta \in \mathbb{Q}^{>0}$ such that $\text{Reach}([\![\text{Env} \parallel \text{Cont}']\!]^0_\Delta) \cap \text{Bad} = \varnothing$. Intuitively, this gives us the information about the slowest hardware that can implement correctly the strategy.

To solve the fixed version, we use the usual reachability algorithm for timed automaton defined in [AD94]. To solve the maximization version (in an approximative way), we observe that for any timed automaton $A$, any two positive rational numbers $\Delta_1$, $\Delta_2$, if $\Delta_1 \leq \Delta_2$ then $\text{Reach}([\![A]\!]^0_{\Delta_1}) \subseteq \text{Reach}([\![A]\!]^0_{\Delta_2})$. So, given a tolerance $\eta \in \mathbb{Q}^{>0}$, the maximal value of $\Delta$ can be approached by $\eta$ as follows: assuming Bad is reachable in $[\![A]\!]^0_{\Delta=1}$, it suffices to solve the [Fixed] problems with values $\Delta_i = i\eta$ $(0 \leq i \leq \lceil \frac{1}{\eta} \rceil)$, and take as approximation of the maximal $\Delta$ the value $\Delta_i$ such that the answer of the [Fixed] problem is YES for $\Delta_i$ and No for $\Delta_{i+1}$, which can be found more efficiently with a dichotomy search.

The decidability of the implementability problem is established in the next sections. To achieve this, we draw a strong link with a robust semantics defined by Puri in [Pur98]. In that paper, Puri shows that the traditional reachability analysis defined in [AD94] is not correct when the clocks drift even by a very small amount. He then reformulates the reachability problem as follows: given a timed automaton $A$, instead of computing $\mathsf{Reach}(\llbracket A \rrbracket_0^0)$, he proposes an algorithm that computes $\cap_{\epsilon \in \mathbb{Q}^{>0}} \mathsf{Reach}(\llbracket A \rrbracket_0^\epsilon)$. When $A$ is clear from the context, this set is denoted by $R_\epsilon^*$. This is the set of states that can be reached when the clocks drift by an infinitesimally small amount. He shows that this set has nice robustness properties with respect to modeling errors. In particular, he establishes that if the clocks are drifting, then guards can be checked with some small imprecisions (see [Pur98] for details).

In our paper, in order to make the link with the implementability problem, we study a variant of this robust semantics where only small imprecisions on guards checking are allowed: the set of reachable states in this semantics is the set $\cap_{\Delta \in \mathbb{Q}^{>0}} \mathsf{Reach}(\llbracket A \rrbracket_\Delta^0)$. When $A$ is clear from the context, this set is abbreviated by $R_\Delta^*$. We first show that for any timed automaton $A$, any zone-set $\mathsf{Bad}$, we have that: $\cap_{\Delta \in \mathbb{Q}^{>0}} \mathsf{Reach}(\llbracket A \rrbracket_\Delta^0) \cap \mathsf{Bad} = \varnothing$ iff there exists $\Delta \in \mathbb{Q}^{>0}$ such that $\mathsf{Reach}(\llbracket A \rrbracket_\Delta^0) \cap \mathsf{Bad} = \varnothing$. After, we establish that the algorithm proposed by Puri to compute the set $\cap_{\epsilon \in \mathbb{Q}^{>0}} \mathsf{Reach}(\llbracket A \rrbracket_0^\epsilon)$ is also valid to compute the set of states $\cap_{\Delta \in \mathbb{Q}^{>0}} \mathsf{Reach}(\llbracket A \rrbracket_\Delta^0)$. As corollaries, we obtain that $\cap_{\epsilon \in \mathbb{Q}^{>0}} \mathsf{Reach}(\llbracket A \rrbracket_0^\epsilon) = \cap_{\Delta \in \mathbb{Q}^{>0}} \mathsf{Reach}(\llbracket A \rrbracket_\Delta^0)$ and so we obtain an algorithm to decide the implementability problem.

The proofs of our results follow the general ideas of the proofs of Puri and are based on the structure of limit cycles of timed automata (a fundamental notion introduced by Puri) but we needed new techniques to treat the imprecisions on guards instead of the drifts of clocks as in the original paper. Also the proofs in the paper of Puri are not always convincing, so we reproved a large number of his lemmas that are needed to establish our proof and had to correct one of them.

## 4   Example

Consider automaton $A$ of Fig. 1. We examine two cases : $\alpha = 2$ and $\alpha = 3$. For both cases, the reachable states of the classical semantics $\llbracket A \rrbracket$ are the same and are depicted in Fig. 2 (the points $v_0 \ldots v_7$ will be used later in the paper). The safety property we want to verify is that the location $err$ is not reachable. Note that in the classical semantics this is true in both cases.

Consider now the enlarged semantics $\llbracket A \rrbracket_\Delta^0$ with $\Delta > 0$. In this semantics, guards are enlarged by the amount $\Delta$. The edge from $l_1$ to $l_2$ has the guard $a \leq 2 + \Delta$ and the edge from $l_2$ to $l_1$ has the guard $b \geq 2 - \Delta$. Starting from the initial state $(l_1, a = 1, b = 0)$, the jump to $l_2$ can occur $\Delta$ time units later, so that the states $(l_2, a = 0, b \leq 1 + \Delta)$ are reached. Similarly, the transition from $l_2$ back to $l_1$ is enabled $\Delta$ time units earlier and the states $(l_1, a \geq 1 - 2\Delta, b = 0)$ can be reached. By iterating the cycle, the states $(l_1, a \geq 1 - 2k\Delta, b = 0)$ and $(l_2, a = 0, b \leq 1 + (2k - 1)\Delta)$ are reachable. So, for any $\Delta > 0$ some new states are reachable in $\llbracket A \rrbracket_\Delta^0$ that were not reachable in the classical semantics. Those states are represented in Fig. 3.

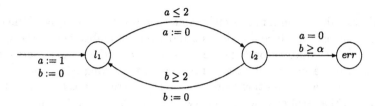

**Fig. 1.** A timed automaton $A$.

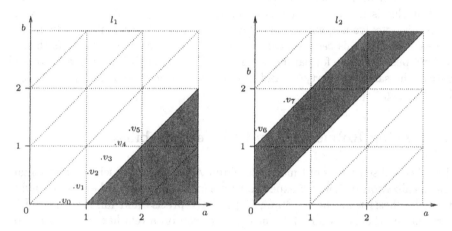

**Fig. 2.** Reach($[\![A]\!]$) for the timed automaton $A$ of Fig. 1.

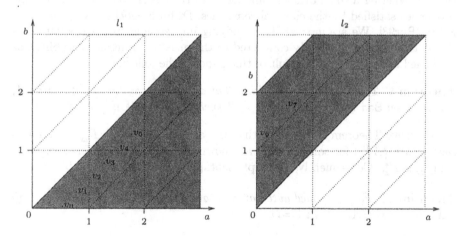

**Fig. 3.** The set $R_\Delta^*$ for the timed automaton $A$ of Fig. 1.

From those new states that become reachable in location $l_2$, if $\alpha = 3$, the location *err* remains unreachable but if $\alpha = 2$ it becomes reachable.

Clearly, from this example, one sees that a correct timed system (in the sense of the classical semantics) could have a completely different (and potentially bad) behavior due to an infinitesimally small inaccuracy in testing of the clocks (which is unavoidable since the clocks are discrete in embedded systems). This is the case for the automaton of figure 1. When $\alpha = 2$, the classical semantics is not robust since even the slightest error in guard checking allows new discrete transition to be taken. In other words, there is no strictly positive value for the parameter $\Delta$ that still ensures the safety property for $[\![A]\!]_\Delta^0$. Systems with such features cannot have a correct implementation because their correctness relies on the idealization of the mathematical model.

But this is not always the case: for the same automaton when $\alpha = 3$, no more discrete transitions are possible in the enlarged semantics than in the classical one. In this case, we can answer positively to the question "Is there a strictly positive value for parameter $\Delta$ that allows the enlarged semantics to still satisfy the safety property?". And indeed, we can prove that any value $\Delta < \frac{1}{3}$ is satisfying.

## 5    Linking Robustness and Implementability

The classical semantics of timed automaton $A$ is $[\![A]\!]_{\Delta=0}^{\epsilon=0}$, which is a mathematical idealization of how we expect an implementation would behave: it makes the hypothesis that the hardware is perfectly precise and infinitely fast. Unfortunately, the execution of a timed automaton on a real hardware cannot be considered as ideal in the mathematical sense. It is thus an interesting question to know whether a small drift or imprecision of the clocks could invalidate some properties satisfied by the classical semantics. Drifts in clocks have been studied in [Pur98]. We are interested in studying imprecisions in the evaluation of the guards since it is directly connected to the question of implementability, as explained above. The main result of this paper is the following.

**Theorem 9** *There exists an algorithm that decide for any timed automaton $A$, any zone-set* Bad *if there exists $\Delta \in \mathbb{Q}^{>0}$ such that* Reach($[\![A]\!]_\Delta^0$) $\cap$ Bad $= \varnothing$.

To prove Theorem 9, we show that the set Bad intersects $R_\Delta^*$ iff it intersects Reach($[\![A]\!]_\Delta^0$) for some $\Delta > 0$. As shown in the next section, Algorithm 1 computes $R_\Delta^*$. Consequently, the implementability problem is decidable.

**Theorem 10** *For any timed automaton $A$, any zone-set* Bad, $R_\Delta^* \cap$ Bad $= \varnothing$ *iff* $\exists \Delta > 0 :$ Reach($[\![A]\!]_\Delta^0$) $\cap$ Bad $= \varnothing$.

The proof of Theorem 10 relies on two intermediate lemmas, one of which corrects a wrong claim in [Pur98]: it gives a bound on the distance between two zones with empty intersection. This bound is claimed to be $\frac{1}{2}$. We show that $\frac{1}{n}$ where $n$ is the dimension of the space is the tightest bound. However the final results of [Pur98] are not deeply affected by this mistake. The distance considered is defined by $d_\infty(x,y) = \|x - y\|_\infty = \max_{1 \leq i \leq n}(|x_i - y_i|)$. Let us reformulate that lemma.

---

**Algorithm 1:** Algorithm from [Pur98] for computing $R_\epsilon^*(A)$ for a timed automaton $A$.

---

**Data** : A timed automaton $A = \langle \mathsf{Loc}, \mathsf{Var}, q_0, \mathsf{Lab}, \mathsf{Edg} \rangle$

**Result** : The set $J^* = R_\epsilon^*$

**begin**

    1. Construct the region graph $G = (R_A, \longrightarrow_A)$ of $A$ ;

    2. Compute $SCC(G) = $ strongly connected components of $G$;

    3. $J^* \leftarrow [(q_0)]$ ;

    4. $J^* \leftarrow \mathsf{Reach}(G, J^*)$ ;

    5. if for some $S \in SCC(G)$, $S \nsubseteq J^*$ and $J^* \cap S \neq \varnothing$ then

        | $J^* := J^* \cup S$ ;

        | Goto 4 ;

**end**

---

**Lemma 11 (Corrected from [Pur98, Lemma 6.4])** *Let $Z_1 \subseteq \mathbb{R}^n$ and $Z_2 \subseteq \mathbb{R}^n$ be two zones such that $Z_1 \cap Z_2 = \varnothing$. Then, for any $x \in Z_1$ and $y \in Z_2$, $d_\infty(x, y) \geq \frac{1}{n}$. This bound is tight.*

In the sequel, when a distance $d$ or a norm $\| \ \|$ is used, we always refer to $d_\infty$ and $\| \ \|_\infty$. The following lemma relies on the theory of real numbers and the basics of topology.

**Lemma 12** *Let $A_\Delta (\Delta \in \mathbb{R}^{>0})$ be a collection of sets such that $A_{\Delta_1} \subseteq A_{\Delta_2}$ if $\Delta_1 \leq \Delta_2$. Let $A = \bigcap_{\Delta > 0} A_\Delta$ be nonempty. If $d(A, B) > 0$, then there exists $\Delta > 0$ such that $A_\Delta \cap B = \varnothing$.*

**Proof of theorem 10.** If $R_\Delta^* \cap \mathsf{Bad} = \varnothing$, since $R_\Delta^*$ and $\mathsf{Bad}$ are unions of sets of the form $\{l\} \times Z_l$ where $Z_l$ is a zone, Lemma 11 applies and we have $d(R_\Delta^*, \mathsf{Bad}) > 0$. From Lemma 12, we obtain that there exists $\Delta > 0$ such that $\mathsf{Reach}(\llbracket A \rrbracket_\Delta^0) \cap \mathsf{Bad} = \varnothing$.

If there exists $\Delta > 0$ such that $\mathsf{Reach}(\llbracket A \rrbracket_\Delta^0) \cap \mathsf{Bad} = \varnothing$, then trivially $R_\Delta^* \cap \mathsf{Bad} = \varnothing$. ∎

# 6  Algorithm for Computing $R_\Delta^*$

In this section, we prove that the algorithm proposed in [Pur98] computes $R_\Delta^*$. This implies that $R_\epsilon^* = R_\Delta^*$. The algorithm is shown as Algorithm 1.

Let us first examine how Algorithm 1 performs on the example of section 4. In the region graph of the timed automaton of Fig. 1, there is a cycle that runs from valuation $v_0$ to itself through $v_1$ to $v_7$ (see Fig. 2). Thus there is a cycle through the regions containing valuations $v_0$ to $v_7$. Furthermore, these regions have an intersection with the set of reachable states in the classical semantics (in gray). Indeed since we consider closed regions, the intersection of two adjacent regions is not empty. Since those regions form a strongly connected component of the region graph and their intersection with the reachable states in the classical semantics is not empty, the algorithm adds all those regions to the set $J^*$.

One can check that all regions of $R^*_\Delta$ for the automaton $A$ of figure 1 will be correctly added by Algorithm 1 (see figure 3).

In the rest of this section, we prove that this algorithm computes $R^*_\Delta$, by proving $J^* \subseteq R^*_\Delta$ on the one hand, and $R^*_\Delta \subseteq J^*$ on the other hand.

## 6.1   Limit Cycles

This section studies the behavior of limit cycles. A *limit cycle* of a timed automaton $A$ is a trajectory $\pi = (q_0, t_0)(q_1, t_1) \ldots (q_k, t_k)$ of $[\![A]\!]$ such that $t_k > t_0$ and $q_k = q_0$. As suggested in [Pur98], given a progress cycle in the region graph and a region on this cycle, we focus on the subset of points of this region having a limit cycle. We first define this subset:

**Definition 13** [See [Pur98, Section 7.1]] Consider a cyclic path $p = p_0 p_1 \ldots p_N$ with $p_N = p_0$ in the region graph of a timed automaton $A$. We define the *return map* $R_p : 2^{p_0} \to 2^{p_0}$ by $R_p(S) = \cup_{q \in S} R_p(\{q\})$ for $S \subseteq p_0$, and, for singletons,

$$R_p(\{q_0\}) = \left\{ q_N \left| \begin{array}{l} \text{there exists a trajectory } \pi \text{ in } [\![A]\!] \text{ s.t.} \\ \pi = (q_0, t_0)(q_1, t_1) \ldots (q_N, t_N) \text{ and } \forall i.\ q_i \in p_i \end{array} \right. \right\}.$$

The set $L_{i,p}$ of points which can return back to themselves after $i$ cycles through $p$, is defined as follows: $L_{i,p} = \{q \mid q \in R^i_p(q)\}$. The set of points with limit cycles through $p$ is $L_p = \cup_{i \in \mathbb{N}} L_{i,p}$. $\qquad\square$

In the sequel, we write $R$ or $L$ instead of $R_p$ or $L_p$ when the path $p$ is clear from the context. The interesting property of $L_p$ is that it is always reachable from any valuation in $p$:

**Theorem 14 ([Pur98, Lemma 7.10])** *Let $p = p_0 p_1 \ldots p_N$ be a cycle in $G$. Then for any $z \in p_0$, there exists $z', z'' \in L$ s.t. there exist trajectories in $[\![A]\!]$ from $z$ to $z'$ and from $z''$ to $z$.*

## 6.2   Soundness of Algorithm 1: $J^* \subseteq R^*_\Delta$

Let $r \in \mathbb{R}^{\geq 0}$ and $x \in \mathbb{R}^n$. The *closed ball* of radius $r$ centered in $x$ is the set $B(x, r) = \{x' \mid d(x, x') \leq r\}$. The following Lemma shows how a trajectory may be modified when enlarging guards in timed automata:

**Lemma 15** *Let $A$ be a timed automaton with $n$ clocks, $\Delta \in \mathbb{Q}^{>0}$, and $\delta = \frac{\Delta}{n}$. Let $p = p_0 p_1 p_2 \ldots p_N$ be a cycle in the region graph of $A$. Let $u$ be a valuation in $p_0$ having a limit cycle, i.e. for which there exists a trajectory $\pi[0, T]$ in $[\![A]\!]^0_0$ following $p$ and with $\pi(0) = \pi(T) = u$. Let $v \in p_0 \cap B(u, \delta)$ be a neighbor valuation. Then there exists a trajectory from $u$ to $v$ in $[\![A]\!]^0_\Delta$.*

Intuitively, the result is proved by slightly anticipating or delaying the transition dates when a clock is reset.

Consider for instance the following path:

$$(x = a, y = b) \xrightarrow[x:=0]{\tau_1} (x = 0, y = b + \tau_1) \xrightarrow{\tau_2} (x = a', y = b').$$

with $a' = \tau_2$ and $b' = b + \tau_1 + \tau_2$. By slightly modifying the continuous transition labels $\tau_i$, we get

$$(x = a, y = b) \xrightarrow[x:=0]{\tau_1 - \delta} (x = 0, y = b + \tau_1 - \delta) \xrightarrow{\tau_2 + \delta} (x = a' + \delta, y = b').$$

Thus the final value of clock $y$ is identical in both cases, while the final value of $x$ has been slightly modified. By carefully repeating this procedure, we can independently modify the final valuations of each clock. This corresponds to the idea behind Lemma 15.

**Theorem 16** *Let $A$ be a timed automaton. Let $p = p_0 p_1 \ldots p_N$ be a cyclic path in the region graph of $A$, and let $x$ and $y$ be two valuations in $p_0$. For any $\Delta \in \mathbb{Q}^{>0}$, there exists a trajectory from $x$ to $y$ in $[\![A]\!]_\Delta^0$.*

**Proof.** From Lemma 14, there exists $u, v \in L$ s.t. $x \to u$ and $v \to y$ in $[\![A]\!]$. Then $u$ satisfies the conditions of Lemma 15, and thus any $w \in L$ "close to" $u$ is reachable from $u$ in $[\![A]\!]_\Delta^0$. Since $L$ is convex, by recursively applying the previous argument, any $w \in L$ is reachable from $u$ in $[\![A]\!]_\Delta^0$. In particular, $v$ is reachable from $u$ in $[\![A]\!]_\Delta^0$, and $y$ is reachable from $x$ in $[\![A]\!]_\Delta^0$. ∎

As a consequence:

**Theorem 17** *The set $J^*$ computed by Algorithm 1 is a subset of $R_\Delta^*$, i.e. $J^* \subseteq R_\Delta^*$.*

**Proof.** Let $\Delta > 0$. If a set of regions $J$ is a subset of $\mathsf{Reach}([\![A]\!]_\Delta^0)$, then so is the set of reachable regions from $J$ in the region graph $G$. Moreover, whenever a state of $J$ appears in a cyclic region path $p$, then Theorem 16 ensures that any state in that region path is reachable in $[\![A]\!]_\Delta^0$. Thus $J \cup p \subseteq \mathsf{Reach}([\![A]\!]_\Delta^0)$. Since $J^*$ is built by successively applying the above two operations, this ensures that $J^* \subseteq \mathsf{Reach}([\![A]\!]_\Delta^0)$. This holds for any $\Delta > 0$, thus $J^* \subseteq R_\Delta^*$. ∎

## 6.3  Completeness of Algorithm 1: $R_\Delta^* \subseteq J^*$

To prove the completeness of Algorithm 1, we need to better understand the relationship between trajectories of $[\![A]\!]_\Delta^0$ and those of $[\![A]\!]$. In particular, Theorem 18 states that any trajectory $\pi'$ of $[\![A]\!]_\Delta^0$ can be approached by a trajectory $\pi$ of $[\![A]\!]$, making the same discrete transitions and passing by the same regions.

**Theorem 18** *For any distance $\delta \in \mathbb{R}^{>0}$, for any number of steps $k \in \mathbb{N}$, there exists $\Delta \in \mathbb{Q}^{>0}$ such that for any $k$-step trajectory $\pi' = (q_0', t_0') \dots (q_k', t_k')$ of $[\![A]\!]_\Delta^0$, there exists a $k$-step trajectory $\pi = (q_0, t_0) \dots (q_k, t_k)$ of $[\![A]\!]$ such that for any position $i$ $(0 \le i \le k)$*

- *$q_i \in [q_i']$, that is the two trajectories cross the same regions,*
- *and the distance between corresponding states $q_i$ and $q_i'$ is bounded by $\delta$, that is $q_i = (l_i, v_i)$, $q_i' = (l_i', v_i')$ where $l_i = l_i'$ and $\|v_i - v_i'\| \le \delta$.*

Below, we give the general ideas underlying the proof. It uses the following lemma, stating that if $v$ is reachable from $u$ by letting time elapse, then any point $x \in [u]$ in the neighborhood of $u$ can reach some point $y \in [v]$ in the neighborhood of $v$. More precisely:

**Lemma 19** *Suppose $r \to_G r'$ in the region graph $G$ of a timed automaton, and $u \xrightarrow{\tau} v$ with $u \in r$, $v \in r'$ and $\tau \in \mathbb{R}^{\ge 0}$. Then for any $x \in B(u, R) \cap r$, there exists $y \in B(v, 2R) \cap r'$ such that $x \xrightarrow{\tau'} y$ for some $\tau'$ with $|\tau - \tau'| \le R$.*

**Proof (Sketch) of theorem 18.**

The outline of the proof is as follows. We define a "simulation" relation $\mathcal{R}$ between valuations, which is a subset of $\mathbb{R}^n \times \mathbb{N} \times \mathbb{R}^n$ and we write $\mathcal{R}_a(x', x)$ if $(x', a, x) \in \mathcal{R}$. We show that

$$\text{If } \begin{cases} a \le k \\ \mathcal{R}_a(x', x) \\ x' \xrightarrow{t'} y' \xrightarrow{\sigma} z' \text{ in } [\![A]\!]_\Delta^0 \end{cases} \quad \text{then } \exists y, z : \begin{cases} x \xrightarrow{t} y \xrightarrow{\sigma} z \text{ in } [\![A]\!] \\ \mathcal{R}_{a+1}(z', z) \\ \|z - z'\| \le \|y - y'\| \le \delta \end{cases}$$

The relation $\mathcal{R}_a$ takes into account the current position in the trajectory: if $x'$ is the $a^{\text{th}}$ state in the trajectory, then $x$ is in a neighborhood of size parameterized by $a$. This size increases with $a$, because the longer is the trajectory, the greater is the possible deviation (Fig. 4). This is not a classical simulation relation because it only works for a fixed trajectory length $k$ (which is sufficient for proving Theorem 18).

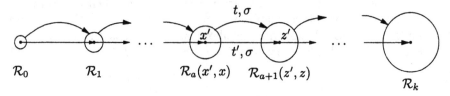

**Fig. 4.** Simulation of the trajectory $\pi'$ of $[\![A]\!]_\Delta^0$.

Intuitively, $\mathcal{R}$ links a valuation $x$ with a valuation $x'$ if whenever two clock have *close* fractional parts in $x'$ (for a special distance $\mathcal{D}$), those clocks have *identical* fractional parts in $x$.

Fig. 5 illustrates the necessity of this choice: consider the trajectory $(x', 0)$ $(y', t')(z', t')$ of $[\![A]\!]^0_\Delta$. We must construct a trajectory $(x, 0)(y, t)(z, t)$ of $[\![A]\!]$ taking the same discrete transition (labeled with $\sigma$). In the enlarged semantics, the guard on this transition is satisfied by $y'$ (*i.e.* $y' \in [\![g]\!]_\Delta$).

The only possible choice for $y$ is to both lie in the region $[y']$ and in $[\![g]\!]_0$ as shown in the figure. This imposes the choice of $x$ on the diagonal (*i.e.* with identical fractional parts for $x_i$ and $x_j$).

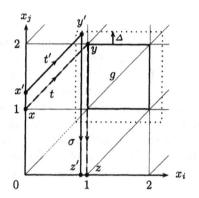

**Fig. 5.** Simulating $x' \xrightarrow{t'} y' \xrightarrow{\sigma} z'$ enforces to take $x$ with $\langle x_i \rangle = \langle x_j \rangle$. This is because $\langle x_i' \rangle$ and $\langle x_j' \rangle$ are too close.

$\mathcal{R}$ is formally defined in the complete proof, and it is shown that the $\Delta$ can be chosen such that $\Delta < \frac{\delta}{2^k(2+4n)}$. ∎

The following theorem is a direct consequence of Theorem 18. It says that points in $J^*$ cannot reach points that are more than distance $\alpha$ away from $J^*$ in $[\![A]\!]^0_\Delta$ for sufficiently small $\Delta$.

**Theorem 20** *Suppose $x \in J^*$ and there exists a trajectory from $x$ to $y$ in $[\![A]\!]^0_\Delta$ with $\Delta < \frac{\alpha}{2^{W+1}(2+4n)}$ where $\alpha < \frac{1}{2n}$, and $W$ is the total number of regions. Then $d(y, J^*) < \alpha$.*

Finally, we can establish the completeness of Algorithm 1.

**Theorem 21** *The set $J^*$ computed by Algorithm 1 contains $R^*_\Delta$, i.e. $R^*_\Delta \subseteq J^*$.*

**Proof.** Since $J^*$ is a closed set containing the initial state, from Theorem 20, for any $y \in \mathsf{Reach}([\![A]\!]^0_\Delta)$, $d(y, J^*) \leq \alpha$ where $\alpha$ can be made arbitrarily small. It follows that $R^*_\Delta \subseteq J^*$. ∎

This concludes the proof that Algorithm 1 computes $R^*_\Delta$. According to [Pur98], we have the corollary that $R^*_\Delta = R^*_\epsilon = R^*$ where $R^* = \cap_{\Delta \in \mathbb{Q}>0} \cap_{\epsilon \in \mathbb{Q}>0}$ $\mathsf{Reach}([\![A]\!]^\epsilon_\Delta)$ so that the enlarged semantics $R^*_\Delta$ is also robust against drifts in clocks.

## 6.4   Complexity

Complexity issues have been studied in [Pur98], so we recall the main result.

**Theorem 22 ([Pur98])** *Given a timed automaton $A = \langle \mathsf{Loc}, \mathsf{Var}, q_0, \mathsf{Lab}, \mathsf{Edg} \rangle$ and a location $l_f \in \mathsf{Loc}$, determining whether a state $(l_f, v) \in R_\Delta^*$ for some valuation $v$ is PSPACE-Complete.*

## 7   Conclusion

In this paper, we have shown that a notion of robustness defined by Puri [Pur98] is closely related to a notion of implementability that we recently introduced in [DDR04]. Making this link formal allowed us to show that our notion of implementability is decidable for the class of timed automata. To establish this link, we have proved that the algorithm proposed by Puri computes the set of reachable states of timed automata where guards are enlarged by an infinitesimally small rational value. The existence of such a value implies the implementability as shown in our previous paper. The proofs of the decidability result rely on non trivial adaptations of the main ideas underlying the study of drift in the rate of clocks made by Puri.

The algorithm that is used to check implementability manipulates strongly connected components of the region graph. It can be seen as defining exact accelerations of cycles of the timed automaton.

We will work in the future on making those accelerations practical and as a consequence, we will work on to turn the theoretical algorithm proposed in this paper into a practical one. If we succeed in this task, the results of this paper and of our previous paper [DDR04] will allow us to propose a practical procedure to produce provably correct code from proved correct controller modeled as timed automata.

## References

[AD94]     Rajeev Alur and David L. Dill. A theory of timed automata. *Theoretical Computer Science*, 126(2):183–235, 1994.

[AFILS03]  R. Alur, J. Kim F. Ivancic, I. Lee, and O. Sokolsky. Generating embedded software from hierarchical hybrid models. In *ACM Symposium on Languages, Compilers, and Tools for Embedded Systems*, 2003.

[AFM+02]   Tobias Amnell, Elena Fersman, Leonid Mokrushin, Paul Pettersson, and Wang Yi. Times: A tool for modelling and implementation of embedded systems. In J.-P. Katoen and P. Stevens, editors, *Proc. Of The 8 Th International Conference On Tools And Algorithms For The Construction And Analysis Of Systems*, number 2280 in Lecture Notes In Computer Science, pages 460–464. Springer–Verlag, 2002.

[AFP+03]   Tobias Amnell, Elena Fersman, Paul Pettersson, Hongyan Sun, and Wang Yi. Code synthesis for timed automata. *Nordic Journal of Computing(NJC)*, 9, 2003.

[AMPS98]  E. Asarin, O. Maler, A. Pnueli, and J. Sifakis. Controller synthesis for timed automata. In *Proc. System Structure and Control.* Elsevier, 1998.

[CHR02]   F. Cassez, T.A. Henzinger, and J.-F. Raskin. A comparison of control problems for timed and hybrid systems. In *HSCC 02: Hybrid Systems— Computation and Control*, Lecture Notes in Computer Science 2289, pages 134–148. Springer-Verlag, 2002.

[DDR04]   M. De Wulf, L. Doyen, and J.-F. Raskin. Almost ASAP semantics: From timed models to timed implementations. In *HSCC 04: Hybrid Systems— Computation and Control*, Lecture Notes in Computer Science 2993, pages 296–310. Springer-Verlag, 2004.

[GHJ97]   Vineet Gupta, Thomas A. Henzinger, and Radha Jagadeesan. Robust timed automata. In O. Maler, editor, *Hybrid and Real-Time Systems*, Lecture Notes in Computer Science, pages 331–345. Springer Verlag, March 1997.

[HKSP03]  T.A. Henzinger, C.M. Kirsch, M.A. Sanvido, and W. Pree. From control models to real-time code using GIOTTO. *IEEE Control Systems Magazine*, 23(1):50–64, 2003.

[Pur98]   Anuj Puri. Dynamical properties of timed automata. In *Proceedings of Formal Techniques in Real-Time and Fault-Tolerant Systems, 5th International Symposium, FTRTFT'98, Lyngby, Denmark, September 14-18, 1998*, volume 1486 of *Lecture Notes in Computer Science*, pages 210–227. Springer, 1998.

# Real-Time Testing
# with Timed Automata Testers
# and Coverage Criteria*

Moez Krichen and Stavros Tripakis

VERIMAG
Centre Equation, 2, avenue de Vignate, 38610 Gières, France
www-verimag.imag.fr

**Abstract.** In previous work, we have proposed a framework for black-box conformance testing of real-time systems based on timed automata specifications and two types of tests: analog-clock or digital-clock. Our algorithm to generate analog-clock tests is based on an on-the-fly determinization of the specification automaton during the execution of the test, which in turn relies on reachability computations. The latter can sometimes be costly, thus problematic, since the tester must quickly react to the actions of the system under test. In this paper, we provide techniques which allow analog-clock testers to be represented as deterministic timed automata, thus minimizing the reaction time to a simple state jump. We also provide a method for (statically) generating a suite of digital-clock tests which covers the specification with respect to a number of criteria: location, edge or state coverage. This can dramatically reduce the number of generated tests, as can be evidenced on a small example.

## 1 Introduction

Testing is a fundamental step in any development process. It consists in applying a set of experiments to a system (*system under test − SUT*), with multiple aims, from checking correct functionality to measuring performance. In this paper, we are interested in so-called *black-box conformance testing*, where the aim is to check conformance of the SUT to a given specification. The SUT is a "black box" in the sense that we do not have a model of it, thus, can only rely on its observable input/output behavior.

Our work targets *real-time* systems, that is, systems which operate in an environment with strict timing constraints. Examples of such systems are many: embedded systems (e.g., automotive, avionic and robotic controllers, mobile phones), communication protocols, multimedia systems, and so on. When testing real-time systems, one must pay attention to two important facts. First, it is not sufficient to check whether the SUT produces the correct outputs; it must also be checked that the timing of the outputs is correct. Second, the timing of

---

* Work partially supported by CNRS STIC project "CORTOS".

Y. Lakhnech and S. Yovine (Eds.): FORMATS/FTRTFT 2004, LNCS 3253, pp. 134–151, 2004.

the inputs determines which outputs will be produced as well as the timing of these outputs.

Classical testing frameworks are based on Mealy machines (e.g., see [13, 24]) or finite labeled transition systems − LTSs (e.g., see [30, 11, 18, 3, 14]). These frameworks are not well-suited for real-time systems. In Mealy machines, inputs and outputs are synchronous, which is a reasonable assumption when modeling synchronous hardware, but not when outputs are produced with variable delays, governed by complex timing constraints. In testing methods based on LTSs, time is typically abstracted away and timeouts are modeled by special $\delta$ actions [29] which can be interpreted as "no output will be observed". This is problematic, because timeouts need to be instantiated with concrete values upon testing (e.g., "if nothing happens for 10 seconds, output FAIL"). However, there is no systematic way to derive the timeout values (indeed, durations are not expressed in the specification). Thus, one must rely on empirical, ad-hoc methods.

In previous work [22] we have proposed a testing framework for real-time systems based on specifications modeled as *timed automata* − *TA* [1] with inputs, outputs and unobservable actions. We have presented techniques for generating two types of tests: *analog-clock* tests which measure real-time precisely and *digital-clock* tests which can only count the ticks of a digital clock.

Our technique for generating analog-clock tests is based on an *on-the-fly determinization* of the specification automaton during the execution of the test. This technique, introduced in [31] for purposes of fault detection, is essential in order to avoid two problems. First, the fact that timed automata cannot always be determinized [1] and it is undecidable to check determinizability [32]. Second, the problem that analog-clock tests cannot be represented (statically) as finite trees. This is because the response delays of the SUT are unknown and in dense-time, which requires a tree of infinite branching.

On-the-fly testing avoids both problems above, by generating the test strategy during the execution of the test (when the response delays become known). The on-the-fly determinization algorithm is essentially a reachability computation on the specification automaton. This can be problematic: timed automata reachability can be costly; but the tester must quickly respond to the inputs it receives from the SUT since the two interact in real-time.

Digital-clock tests, on the other hand, *can* be represented statically as finite trees. A special input, tick, models the reaction of the tester to the ticks of its own clock. This reaction is simply "jumping" to a successor node in the tree, thus, fast. However, a new problem arises, namely, how many tests to generate and which ones. A simple approach is to generate all possible tests up to a given depth, defined by the user. However, this quickly leads to explosion, even for small examples, as shown in [22].

In this paper, we show how to improve the testing framework by providing solutions to the two problems discussed above. First, we provide techniques which allow analog-clock tests to be represented as deterministic timed automata. This results in minimizing the reaction time of the tester to a simple state jump. Since timed automata determinization is undecidable [32], we take a pragmatic approach. We suppose that the tester disposes of a single clock and that this clock is reset every time the tester receives an observable input[1]. Then, we provide techniques to compute the locations, edges, guards and deadlines of the tester automaton. Naturally, having only one clock implies that the tester will not be *complete* in general, i.e., it might accept behaviors of the SUT which should be rejected. However, we guarantee that the tester is *sound* (i.e., when it announces "FAIL", the SUT is indeed non-conforming). We can also show that the tester "does its best" given the information that it has, that is, the tester is in a sense the optimal one-clock tester (which resets its clock at every transition).

The second contribution of this paper is a method to statically generate a suite of digital-clock tests which covers the specification with respect to a number of criteria, namely, *location, edge or state coverage*. The benefits can be significant. For the example considered in [22], suites of less than ten tests suffice to achieve coverage, whereas exhaustive suites contain several thousands of tests even for small depths.

The rest of this paper is organized as follows. Section 2 reviews our testing framework, namely, the specification model, the conformance relation and the types of tests we consider. Section 3 presents our technique for generating timed automata testers. Section 4 presents our coverage technique. Section 5 discusses our tool and two case studies. Section 6 presents the conclusions and future work plans.

### Related Work

Most existing real-time testing frameworks [15, 12, 21, 25, 28, 26, 20] consider only restricted subclasses of the TA model. For instance, TA with *isolated* and *urgent* outputs in [28, 20] or event-recording automata in [25]. Our framework can fully handle non-deterministic and partially observable specifications. This is essential for ease of modeling, expressiveness and implementability. Specifications are often built in a *compositional* way, from many components. This greatly simplifies modeling[2]. In such cases, internal component interactions are typically unobservable to the external world, thus, also to the tester. Abstractions can also result in non-determinism and partial observability. The latter is also essential for implementability, since it may be hard, in practice, to export all events to the tester. Other differences of our work with other frameworks include the conformance relation used and the types of tests generated. For an extensive comparison the reader is referred to [22].

To our knowledge, there is no work on generating testers represented as timed automata. The closest in spirit is the work on timed controller synthesis reported in [9]. There, it is shown that the problem of synthesizing a timed automaton

---

[1] The technique can be extended to more than one clocks, assuming we fix the points where each clock is reset.

[2] Notice that a compositional specification does not require that the SUT be implemented following the same structure. Composition is merely a way of modeling the specification.

controller is decidable iff the *resources* of the controller are fixed, where the resources are the number of clocks, their granularity and the maximal constant that can be used in the guards of the controller. The decidability result relies on a region-graph construction and also uses the notion of symbolic alphabet, which essentially encodes all possible reset/guard combinations for the given resources. Our approach fixes the number of clocks, maximal constant and points where the clocks are reset. Our generation algorithm does not rely on the region graph but on symbolic reachability.

Regarding coverage, [20] provides techniques for generating tests covering edges, locations or definition-use pairs for clock variables of the specification. These techniques rely on the assumption that outputs are urgent and isolated. Thanks to this assumption, every input sequence results in a unique output sequence. This means that tests are *sequences* rather than trees. Thus, finding a test can be reduced to a standard reachability problem for timed automata.

## 2    The Testing Framework

We briefly present our testing framework. See [22] for more details and examples.

### 2.1    Timed Automata with Inputs, Outputs and Unobservable Actions

To model the specification, we use timed automata [1] with *deadlines* to capture urgency [27,7], and input, output and unobservable actions, to capture inputs, outputs and internal actions of the SUT.

Let R be the set of non-negative reals. Given a finite set of *actions* Act, the set $(\text{Act} \cup \text{R})^*$ of all finite *real-time sequences* over Act will be denoted $\text{RT}(\text{Act})$. $\epsilon \in \text{RT}(\text{Act})$ is the empty sequence. Given $\text{Act}' \subseteq \text{Act}$ and $\rho \in \text{RT}(\text{Act})$, $P_{\text{Act}'}(\rho)$ denotes the *projection* of $\rho$ to $\text{Act}'$, obtained by "erasing" from $\rho$ all actions not in $\text{Act}'$. For example, if $\text{Act} = \{a, b\}$, $\text{Act}' = \{a\}$ and $\rho = a\,1\,b\,2\,a\,3$, then $P_{\text{Act}'}(\rho) = a\,3\,a\,3$. The time spent in a sequence $\rho$, denoted $\text{time}(\rho)$ is the sum of all delays in $\rho$, for example, $\text{time}(\epsilon) = 0$ and $\text{time}(a\,1\,b\,0.5) = 1.5$.

A *timed automaton over* Act is a tuple $(Q, q_0, X, \text{Act}, E)$ where $Q$ is a finite set of *locations*; $q_0 \in Q$ is the initial location; $X$ is a finite set of *clocks*; E is a finite set of *edges*. Each edge is a tuple $(q, q', \psi, r, d, a)$, where $q, q' \in Q$ are the source and destination locations; $\psi$ is the *guard*, a conjunction of constraints of the form $x \# c$, where $x \in X$, $c$ is an integer constant and $\# \in \{<, \leq, =, \geq, >\}$; $r \subseteq X$ is the set of clocks to be *reset*; $d \in \{\text{lazy}, \text{delayable}, \text{eager}\}$ is the *deadline*; and $a \in \text{Act}$ is the action. We will not allow eager edges with guards of the form $x > c$.

A TA $A$ defines an infinite labeled transition system (LTS). Its states are pairs $s = (q, v) \in Q \times \text{R}^X$, where $q \in Q$ is a location and $v : X \to \text{R}$ is a clock *valuation*. Given state $s = (q, v)$ and clock $x$, we write $x(s)$ to denote the value of $x$ at $s$, i.e., $v(x)$. $\mathbf{0}$ is the valuation assigning 0 to every clock of $A$. $S_A$ is the set of all states and $s_0^A = (q_0, \mathbf{0})$ is the initial state. There are two types of transitions, discrete and timed. Discrete transitions are of the form $s = (q, v) \xrightarrow{a} s' = (q', v')$, where $a \in$ Act and there is an edge $e = (q, q', \psi, r, d, a)$, such that $v$ satisfies $\psi$ and $v'$ is obtained by resetting to zero all clocks in $r$ and leaving the others unchanged. We say that $e$ is enabled at $s$ and write $s \models e$ (or $s \models \psi$). Timed transitions are of the form $(q, v) \xrightarrow{t} (q, v + t)$, where $t \in$ R, $t > 0$ and there is no edge $(q, q'', \psi, r, d, a)$, such that: either $d =$ delayable and there exist $0 \leq t_1 < t_2 \leq t$ such that $v + t_1 \models \psi$ and $v + t_2 \not\models \psi$; or $d =$ eager and there exists $0 \leq t_1 < t$ such that $v + t_1 \models \psi$. We use notation such as $s \xrightarrow{a}$, $s \xrightarrow{a}\!\!\!\!/\,$, ..., to denote that there exists $s'$ such that $s \xrightarrow{a} s'$, there is no such $s'$, and so on. This notation naturally extends to timed sequences. For example, $s \xrightarrow{a1b} s'$ if there exist $s_1, s_2$ such that $s \xrightarrow{a} s_1 \xrightarrow{1} s_2 \xrightarrow{b} s'$. A state $s \in S_A$ is *reachable* if there exists $\rho \in$ RT(Act) such that $s_0^A \xrightarrow{\rho} s$. The set of reachable states of $A$ is denoted Reach($A$).

In the rest of the paper, we assume given a set of actions Act, partitioned in two disjoint sets: a set of *input actions* Act$_{in}$ and a set of *output actions* Act$_{out}$. We also assume there is an *unobservable action* $\tau \notin$ Act. Let Act$_\tau =$ Act $\cup \{\tau\}$.

A *timed automaton with inputs and outputs* (TAIO) is a timed automaton over Act$_\tau$. A TAIO is called *observable* if none of its edges is labeled by $\tau$. A TAIO $A$ is called *input-complete* if it can accept any input at any state: $\forall s \in$ Reach($A$) . $\forall a \in$ Act$_{in}$ . $s \xrightarrow{a}$. It is called *deterministic* if $\forall s, s', s'' \in$ Reach($A$) . $\forall a \in$ Act$_\tau$ . $s \xrightarrow{a} s' \wedge s \xrightarrow{a} s'' \Rightarrow s' = s''$. It is called *non-blocking* if

$$\forall s \in \text{Reach}(A) . \forall t \in \text{R} . \exists \rho \in \text{RT(Act}_{out} \cup \{\tau\}) . \text{time}(\rho) = t \wedge s \xrightarrow{\rho} . \quad (1)$$

The non-blocking property states that at any state, $A$ can let time pass forever, even if it does not receive any input. This is a sanity property which ensures that a TAIO does not "force" its environment to provide an input by blocking time.

The set of *observable timed traces* of $A$ is defined to be

$$\text{Traces}(A) = \{P_{\text{Act}}(\rho) \mid \rho \in \text{RT(Act}_\tau) \wedge s_0^A \xrightarrow{\rho}\}. \quad (2)$$

Finally, given a set of states $S \subseteq S_A$ and $a \in$ Act, we define the following operator:

$$\text{succ}(S, a) = \{s' \in S_A \mid \exists s \in S . \exists \rho \in \text{RT}(\{\tau\}) . s \xrightarrow{a \cdot \rho} s'\} \quad (3)$$

$\text{succ}(S, a)$ contains all states that can be reached from some state in $S$ by performing $a$ followed by an unobservable sequence $\rho$.

## 2.2   Specifications, Implementations and Conformance

We assume that the specification of the system to be tested is given as a non-blocking TAIO $A_S$. We assume that the SUT, also called *implementation*, can be modeled as a non-blocking, input-complete TAIO $A_I$. Notice that we do not assume that $A_I$ is known, simply that it exists. The assumption of $A_S$ and

$A_I$ being non-blocking is natural, since in reality time cannot be blocked. The assumption of $A_I$ being input-complete is also reasonable, since a system usually accepts all inputs at any time, possibly ignoring them or issuing an error message when the input is not valid. Notice that we do not assume, as is often done, that the specification $A_S$ is input-complete. This is because $A_S$ needs to be able to model assumptions on the environment, i.e., restrictions on the inputs. For instance, a guard $x \leq 2$ on an edge labeled with input $a$ is interpreted as "*if $a$ is received while $x \leq 2$ then* it must be guaranteed that ...".

In order to formally define the conformance relation, we introduce a number of operators. In the definitions that follow, $A$ is a TAIO, $\sigma \in \text{RT}(\text{Act})$, $s$ is a state of $A$ and $S$ is a set of states of $A$.

$$
\begin{aligned}
\sigma(A) \quad &= \{s \in S_A \mid \exists \rho \in \text{RT}(\text{Act}_\tau) \ . \ s_0^A \xrightarrow{\rho} s \land P_{\text{Act}}(\rho) = \sigma\} \\
\text{elapse}(s) &= \{t > 0 \mid \exists \rho \in \text{RT}(\{\tau\}) \ . \ \text{time}(\rho) = t \land s \xrightarrow{\rho}\} \\
\text{out}(s) \quad &= \{a \in \text{Act}_{\text{out}} \mid s \xrightarrow{a}\} \cup \text{elapse}(s) \\
\text{out}(S) \quad &= \bigcup_{s \in S} \text{out}(s).
\end{aligned}
$$

$\sigma(A)$ is the set of all states of $A$ that can be reached by some timed sequence $\rho$ whose projection to observable actions is $\sigma$. $\text{elapse}(s)$ is the set of all delays which can elapse from $s$ without $A$ making any observable action. $\text{out}(s)$ is the set of all observable "events" (outputs or delays) that can occur when the system is at state $s$.

The *timed input-output conformance relation*, denoted tioco, requires that after any observable sequence specified in $A_S$, every possible observable output of $A_I$ (including delays) is also a possible output of $A_S$. Notice that this requirement only refers to outputs, thus, the fact that $A_I$ accepts generally "more inputs" than $A_S$ does not pose problems of non-conformance: it simply means that the implementation is required to be conforming only with respect to the input assumptions given in the specification. tioco is inspired from its "untimed" counterpart, ioco [29]. The key idea is that delays are considered to be observable events, along with output actions. Formally, $A_I$ conforms to $A_S$, denoted $A_I$ tioco $A_S$, if

$$\forall \sigma \in \text{Traces}(A_S) \ . \ \text{out}(\sigma(A_I)) \subseteq \text{out}(\sigma(A_S)). \tag{4}$$

Due to the fact that implementations are assumed to be input-complete, it can be easily shown that tioco is a transitive relation, that is, if $A$ tioco $B$ and $B$ tioco $C$ then $A$ tioco $C$. It can be also shown that checking tioco is undecidable. This is not a problem for black-box testing: since $A_I$ is unknown, we cannot check conformance directly, anyway.

tioco permits to express most useful types of requirements for real-time systems, such as the requirements that an output must be generated neither too late nor too early. It can also capture "observable deadlocks", that is, situations where no output is generated for a "long" time[3]. Finally, it can capture as-

---

[3] The requirement "*output $b$ must be emitted* **sometime** *after input $a$ is received*" cannot be expressed by tioco. However, this requirement is hardly testable: if we do not have an upper bound on the time that it takes to emit $b$, how can we check conformance within a finite amount of time?

sumptions on the environment. For examples illustrating these features of tioco, see [22].

## 2.3    Analog-Clock and Digital-Clock Tests

A test (or *test case*) is an experiment performed on the implementation by an agent (the *tester*). There are different types of tests, depending on the capabilities of the tester to observe and react to events. Here, we consider two types of tests (the terminology is borrowed from [19]). *Analog-clock* tests can measure precisely the real-time delay between two observed actions. *Digital-clock* tests can only count how many "ticks" of a finite-granularity clock have occurred between two actions. For simplicity, we assume that the tester and the implementation are started precisely at the same time. In practice, this can be achieved by having the tester issuing the start command to the implementation.

It should be noted that we consider *adaptive* tests (following the terminology of [24]), where the action the tester takes depends on the observation history. Adaptive tests can be seen as *trees* representing the strategy of the tester in a game against the implementation. Due to restrictions in the specification model, which essentially remove non-determinism from the implementation strategy, some existing methods [28, 20] generate non-adaptive test *sequences*.

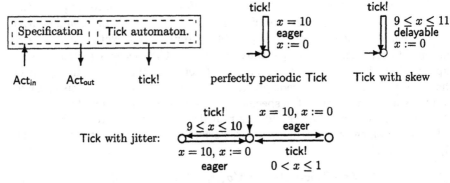

**Fig. 1.** Extending the specification with a tester clock model and possible such models.

An analog-clock test can be defined as a total function $T : RT(Act) \rightarrow Act_{in} \cup \{\bot, \text{pass}, \text{fail}\}$ specifying the action the tester must take given its current observation (if $a \in Act_{in}$ then the tester emits $a$; if $\bot$ then the tester waits; if $\{\text{pass}, \text{fail}\}$ then the tester produces a verdict and stops). For the purpose of this paper, which is to represent analog-clock testers as timed automata, it makes more sense to define an analog-clock test directly as a TAIO $T$. $T$ has as inputs (resp. outputs) the outputs (resp. inputs) of the specification $A_S$. $T$ is observable (i.e., has no $\tau$ actions), deterministic and non-blocking. Locations of $T$ are marked are either "input" or "output". In an input location, the tester waits for an input from the SUT (i.e., some $a \in Act_{out}$). In an output location, the tester emits an output (i.e., some $b \in \mathsf{Act_{in}}$). Input locations of $T$ are input-complete with respect to $\mathsf{Act_{out}}$, that is, for each input location $q$, for any $a \in \mathsf{Act_{out}}$ and any state $s = (q, \bar{v})$, $s \xrightarrow{a}$. $T$ must also satisfy the *urgent* and *isolated* output condition of [28] with respect to $\mathsf{Act_{in}}$. This means that if $s \xrightarrow{a}$ for some state $s$ and $a \in \mathsf{Act_{in}}$ then (a) time cannot elapse at $s$ and (b) there is no other $b \in \mathsf{Act_{in}}$ such that $s \xrightarrow{b}$. Thus, there is no ambiguity as to which output must be emitted and when. The states of $T$ will be partitioned into *accepting* and *rejecting*, corresponding to "PASS" and "FAIL" verdicts, respectively.

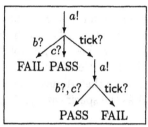

**Fig. 2.** A digital-clock test represented as a finite tree.

A digital-clock test can also be defined as a function $D : (\mathsf{Act} \cup \{\mathsf{tick}\})^* \rightarrow \mathsf{Act_{in}} \cup \{\perp, \mathsf{pass}, \mathsf{fail}\}$, where tick is a new output action, not in $\mathsf{Act}_\tau$, modeling the tick of the tester's clock. In fact, the clock of the tester can be modeled directly by extending the specification automaton with a Tick automaton, as shown in Figure 1 (we use notation ! for outputs and ? for inputs). The Tick automaton models the digital clock of the tester. Different Tick automata can be used, depending on whether we want to model a clock which is assumed to be perfectly periodic, or a clock with skew, and so on. At the end, we obtain an extended specification model, denoted $A_S^{\mathsf{tick}}$, and the objective becomes to generate an *untimed* test for $A_S^{\mathsf{tick}}$. The test is untimed because it only has access to discrete observable actions, namely, all actions in the set $\mathsf{Act} \cup \{\mathsf{tick}\}$. The test has no direct access to time, it merely observes tick actions. Such a test can be represented as a finite tree, like the one shown in Figure 2. Nodes in this tree are marked either "input" or "output". In an input node, the tester waits for an input or the next tick of its clock. In an output node, the tester emits an output. Leaves are labeled PASS or FAIL.

## 3    Generating Timed Automata Testers

The problem of generating an analog-clock test represented as a TAIO can be anything from trivial to undecidable, depending on its precise definition. If we require a test which is only sound, then the problem is trivial, because a test always announcing PASS is sound. On the other hand, if we require a test which is also complete, then we face two problems: (a) such a test may not exist because the specification is non-deterministic whereas the test has to be deterministic, but TA are not determinizable; (b) checking and producing a deterministic test when it exists can be shown to be an undecidable problem [32].

To avoid these difficulties, we take a pragmatic approach. We suppose that the tester has only one clock which is reset every time the tester observes an action, that is, at any edge of the tester TAIO. We then provide techniques to compute the locations and edges of the tester automaton and the guards and deadlines of the edges.

It should be noted that the above technique can be easily extended to generate testers with more than one clock, provided the *skeleton* of the tester is given. The skeleton is a deterministic finite automaton the transitions of which are labeled with resets of the clocks of the tester. This information is necessary since, for a given number of clocks (even for one clock) there exist many possible testers which differ in their logic of resetting clocks. A special case is an *event-clock* tester which has one clock for each observable action, reset when this action occurs, as in *event-clock automata* [2].

## 3.1  "One-Clock Determinization" of Timed Automata

For pedagogical reasons, we first explain our technique for plain timed automata, which can be seen as TAIO with an empty set of input actions. For such an automaton $A$, the technique amounts to determinizing $A$ "as best as possible", given that we can only use one clock. Formally, the deterministic counterpart of $A$, denoted $A_{mon}$, will accept a superset of $\mathsf{Traces}(A)$. Notice that $A$ may contain unobservable actions and non-determinism. Viewing $A$ as the specification, $A_{mon}$ is a *monitor* for $A$.

$A_{mon}$ is a TAIO which has as inputs the outputs of $A$. $A_{mon}$ is observable, deterministic and input-complete. All its locations are input locations. $A_{mon}$ uses a single clock, $y$, which is reset to zero every time an action is observed. $A_{mon}$ tries to estimate the state of $A$ based on its current observation (including the value of its own clock $y$). $A_{mon}$ has no urgency constraints: all its deadlines are lazy, thus, $A_{mon}$ is non-blocking. $A_{mon}$ needs no urgency because it acts as an "acceptor" rather than a "generator" of traces. On the other hand, the states of $A_{mon}$ (including locations and values of the clock $y$) are divided into accepting and rejecting.

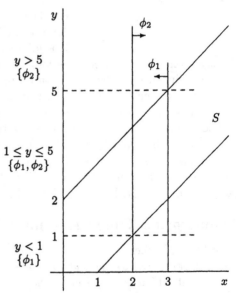

**Fig. 3.** Illustration of the $\sim_S^a$ equivalence.

Let $A = (Q, q_0, X, \mathsf{Act}, \mathsf{E})$ and suppose $y$ is a new clock, not in $X$. Let $S_A^y$ be the set of states of $A$ extended with the clock $y$, that is, $S_A^y = Q \times \mathsf{R}^{X \cup \{y\}}$. For an action $a \in \mathsf{Act}$, let $\mathsf{E}_a \subseteq \mathsf{E}$ be the set of edges of $A$ which are labeled with $a$. For a given set of extended states $S \subseteq S_A^y$ and a value $u \in \mathsf{R}$ of clock $y$, we define the set of edges:

$$\mathsf{E}_a(S, u) = \{e \in \mathsf{E}_a \mid \exists s \in S \,.\, y(s) = u \wedge s \models e\}. \tag{5}$$

$E_a(S, u)$ contains all edges labeled $a$ which are satisfied by a state in $S$ where $y$ equals $u$. Finally, we define the following equivalence on values $u_1, u_2 \in \mathsf{R}$ of the clock $y$:

$$u_1 \sim_S^a u_2 \quad \text{iff} \quad E_a(S, u_1) = E_a(S, u_2). \tag{6}$$

The intuition is as follows. Two values of $y$ are equivalent if they give the same information on the enabledness of an edge labeled with $a$, assuming $S$ holds. $S$ captures the current "knowledge" of the monitor. In particular, it captures the relation between values of $y$ and possible states where $A$ can be in.

Let us illustrate the meaning of $\sim_S^a$ with the example shown in Figure 3. We assume that

$$S = (q, -2 \le x - y \le 1)$$

and that $q$ has two outgoing edges $e_1$ and $e_2$ labeled $a$, with guards $\phi_1 \equiv x \le 3$ and $\phi_2 \equiv x \ge 2$, respectively. Then, $\sim_S^a$ induces three equivalence classes, namely, $y < 1$, $1 \le y \le 5$ and $y > 5$. Indeed, given the assumption $-2 \le x - y \le 1$, $y < 1$ implies $x < 2$. Thus, when $y < 1$ we know that $\phi_2$ does not hold, therefore, $e_2$ is not enabled. Similarly, when $y > 5$ we know that $e_1$ is not enabled. When $1 \le y \le 5$, both $e_1$ and $e_2$ may be enabled. It is important to note that *not all* states in $S$ for which $1 \le y \le 5$ satisfy $\phi_1$, and similarly for $\phi_2$. However, given our information on $y$, we cannot be sure. Thus, we need to include both $e_1$ and $e_2$ in the set of possible enabled edges, given the constraint $1 \le y \le 5$.

We now explain the construction of the monitor automaton $A_{\mathsf{mon}}$. A location of $A_{\mathsf{mon}}$ is associated with a set of extended states of $A$, $S \subseteq S_A^y$. For each action $a$, for each equivalence class $\psi$ in the (coarsest) partition induced by $\sim_S^a$, $A_{\mathsf{mon}}$ has an edge $e = (S, S', \psi, \{y\}, \mathsf{lazy}, a)$, where the destination location $S'$ is computed as follows:

$$S' = \mathsf{succ}(S \cap \psi, a) \tag{7}$$

where $S \cap \psi$ denotes the set of all states $s \in S$ such that $y(s) \models \psi$. Notice that $S'$ can be empty, even when $S$ is non-empty. This is because $\psi$ may be unsatisfied in $S$. Also note that $S'$ is the "best" possible estimate, in the sense that $S'$ is the smallest set possible, given the knowledge the monitor has when $a$ arrives. This knowledge is captured by $S \cap \psi$. Indeed, the monitor knows that $A$ cannot be in a state outside $S$. It also knows that clock $y$ satisfies $\psi$, which further restricts the possible states $A$ can be in.

Let $A^y$ be the automaton $A$ extended with clock $y$ and recall that $s_0^{A^y}$ denotes the initial state of $A^y$. Then, the initial location of $A_{\mathsf{mon}}$ is defined to be $S_0 = \{s \in S_{A^y} \mid \exists \rho \in \mathsf{RT}(\{\tau\}) . s_0^{A^y} \xrightarrow{\rho} s\}$. $S_0$ captures the initial knowledge of the monitor. The latter knows that initially $y$ and all clocks of $A$ equal zero. However, $S_0$ must also include all states that $A$ can move to by performing unobservable sequences.

It remains to define the accepting and rejecting states of $A_{\mathsf{mon}}$. Given $S \subseteq S_A^y$, let $S_{/y}$ be the projection of $S$ on clock $y$, that is, $S_{/y} = \{u \in \mathsf{R} \mid \exists s \in S . y(s) = u\}$. Then, all states $(S, S_{/y})$ of $A_{\mathsf{mon}}$ are accepting, provided $S \ne \emptyset$. The rest of the states are rejecting. The above algorithm is essentially a *subset construction* for $A$, with the addition that clock $y$ is used to infer knowledge about states that $A$ can possibly be in. The construction relies on repeating two basic steps: (a) computing the partition induced by equivalences $\sim_S^a$, and (b) computing successor locations $S'$ using reachability. We show how step (a) can be implemented below. As for step (b), standard symbolic reachability techniques, coupled with so-called *extrapolation abstractions* can be used to ensure that the number of possible locations of $A_{\text{mon}}$ remains finite [16, 4, 8].

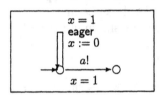

**Fig. 4.** A TAIO which can produce $a!$ at times 1, 2, 3, ...

In such abstractions, the maximal constants compared with each clock play an essential role. These constants are known in the case of the clocks of $A$ but must be specified by the user for the monitor clock $y$. Indeed, increasing the maximal constant for $y$ amounts to increasing the observational power of the monitor. In fact, there are cases where there is no optimal monitor: the greater the maximal constant allowed for $y$ is, the more precise $A_{\text{mon}}$ will be, in the sense of how "close" the language of $A_{\text{mon}}$ is to the language of $A$. An example is shown in Figure 4. The TAIO shown in the figure can produce a single output $a$ at any time $k$, where $k \in \{1, 2, ...\}$. It can be seen that for any such $k$, a monitor able to compare $y$ to constants up to $k$ is "less accurate" than a monitor able to compare $y$ to constants up to $k + 1$. Indeed, the former cannot distinguish between $a!$ happening precisely at time $k$ or at time strictly greater than $k$, while the latter can.

A simple algorithm for computing the coarsest partition induced by $\sim_S^a$ is the following. Given a constraint $\psi$ on clock $y$, let $\mathsf{E}_a^{S,\psi} = \{e \in \mathsf{E}_a \mid S \cap (\psi \wedge \text{guard}(e)) \neq \emptyset\}$, where $\text{guard}(e)$ is the guard of edge $e$. $\mathsf{E}_a^{S,\psi}$ contains all edges labeled $a$ whose guards may be satisfied by a state in $S$ where $y$ lies in the interval $\psi$. In other words, $\mathsf{E}_a^{S,\psi}$ is the union of $\mathsf{E}_a(S, u)$ over all values $u$ satisfying $\psi$. Now, let $K$ be the greatest constant appearing in a constraint defining $S$ or a guard of an edge in $\mathsf{E}_a$. For each $\psi$ in the set of intervals $\{[0, 0], (0, 1), [1, 1], (1, 2), ..., [K, K], (K, \infty)\}$, compute $\mathsf{E}_a^{S,\psi}$. For this, the condition $S \cap (\psi \wedge \text{guard}(e)) \neq \emptyset$ needs to be checked. This can be done symbolically, using standard techniques and data structures such as DBMs [6, 17]. Once $\mathsf{E}_a^{S,\psi}$ is computed for all intervals $\psi$, the coarsest partition is obtained by "merging" (i.e., taking the union of) intervals having the same set $\mathsf{E}_a^{S,\psi}$. For the example of Figure 3, $\mathsf{E}_a^{S,y<1} = \{e_1\}$, $\mathsf{E}_a^{S,1\leq y\leq 5} = \{e_1, e_2\}$ and $\mathsf{E}_a^{S,y>5} = \{e_2\}$. Notice that the correctness of the above algorithm relies on the fact that all values in an interval $(i, i + 1)$ are equivalent, and the same is true for the interval $(K, \infty)$. This is because constraints only have integer constants.

Let us give an example illustrating the construction of $A_{\text{mon}}$. Consider the non-deterministic timed automaton shown in Figure 5. All its edges are lazy, except the one from location 2 to location 4, which is delayable. Its one-clock monitor automaton is shown in Figure 6. Not all locations and edges of the monitor are shown, in order not to overload the figure. In particular, the empty location and all edges leading to it are not shown. For instance, there is an edge labeled $a$ with guard $y > 5$ from the initial location to the empty location, since $a$ is not accepted if it arrives after 5 time units from start.

All states of the monitor are accepting, except from the empty location and the states of location $S = (2, x = y \leq 2)$ where $y > 2$ (notice that $S_{/y}$ is the constraint $y \leq 2$). This is because $c$ must be received at most 2 time units after $a$, in order to be accepted. Note that there are no such rejecting states at location $S' = (1, 1 \leq x - y \leq 2) \cup (2, x = y \leq 2)$. This is because the monitor does not know whether the original automaton is at location 1 or 2, and there is no urgency at location 1. Indeed, $S'_{/y}$ is the constraint *true*.

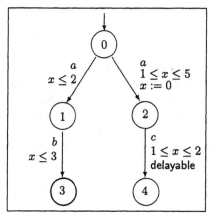

**Fig. 5.** A non-deterministic timed automaton.

## 3.2 From Monitors to Testers

We now consider the general case of TAIO with both input and output actions. In this case, the monitor becomes a tester, since it must supply inputs to the SUT. Formally, the tester is an analog-clock test TAIO, denoted $A_{\text{test}}$, as defined in Section 2.3.

The algorithm for constructing $A_{\text{test}}$ is a generalization of the algorithm for building $A_{\text{mon}}$. As with $A_{\text{mon}}$, each location of $A_{\text{test}}$ is a set $S \subseteq S_A^y$. The choice of marking a location as input or output is made by the algorithm non-

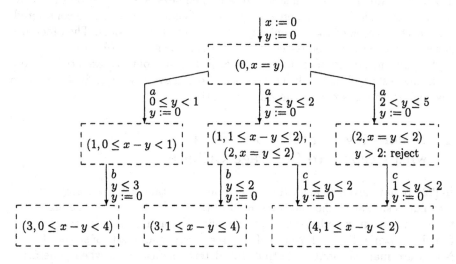

**Fig. 6.** The one-clock deterministic monitor of the automaton of Figure 5.

deterministically. For locations marked as input, their outgoing edges are computed as shown in the previous section, using the equivalence $\sim_S^a$, where, in this case, $a \in \mathsf{Act_{out}}$. In order to mark a location $S$ as output, there must exist $a \in \mathsf{Act_{in}}$ and $u \in R$ such that

$$\forall s \in S \, . \, y(s) = u \Rightarrow s \xrightarrow{a} .$$

This condition guarantees that when $y = u$ then $a$ is a relevant input, that is, it satisfies the environment assumptions given in the specification. If $S$ is indeed marked as output, then the edge $(S, S', y = u, \mathsf{eager}, a)$ is added to $A_{\mathsf{test}}$, where $S'$ is computed as shown in the previous section. Notice that the deadline of the edge is eager: this is because we want the output to be emitted at a precise point in time, otherwise the tester is not time-deterministic. To find a $u$ satisfying the condition above, we first compute the constraint $P_{S,a}(y)$ on clock $y$:

$$P_{S,a}(y) \equiv \forall q, \forall x \, . \, (q, x, y) \in S \Rightarrow \exists e \in \mathsf{E}_a \, . \, (q, x) \models \mathsf{guard}(e)$$

where $q$ and $x$ are variables denoting the location and clocks of $A$, respectively (we slightly abuse notation and write $\forall x$ instead of $\forall v \in R^X$). $P_{S,a}(y)$ can be computed symbolically by using quantifier elimination to eliminate variables $q$ and $x$. $P_{S,a}(y)$ is a linear constraint on $y$. Thus, we can check satisfiability in a constructive way and find the value $u$ we seek. If we cannot find an integer value $u$, then we pick a rational value and multiply at the end of the construction all constants in the automaton with a sufficiently large constant to make them integer.

The states of $A_{\mathsf{test}}$ are defined to be either accepting or rejecting, as with $A_{\mathsf{mon}}$. Rejecting states correspond to the tester emitting a "FAIL" verdict. On the other hand, there is no specific point in time where the tester emits a "PASS". Indeed, the execution of the test can go on as long as the tester remains in an accepting state. The user can stop the test when he/she is tired of waiting. Coverage criteria, similar to the ones discussed in Section 4 can also be considered, since each location of $A_{\mathsf{test}}$ essentially covers a set of states of $A$. The difference is that in this case the book-keeping of coverage must be performed on-the-fly, that is, during execution of the test. Also, since tester outputs are urgent, more than one tests will generally be necessary to achieve coverage. Studying such coverage methods is part of our ongoing work.

## 4    Generating Digital-Clock Tests with Respect to Coverage Criteria

In [22] we have given an algorithm to generate a digital-clock test using symbolic techniques similar to the ones presented in the previous section. The algorithm takes as input an extended specification model $A_S^{\mathsf{tick}}$ and generates a test tree like the one shown in Figure 2. Nodes of the tree correspond to sets of states of $A_S^{\mathsf{tick}}$. Nodes are marked input or output non-deterministically, as when generating timed automata testers. In order for a node $S$ to be marked output, there must exist an action $a \in \mathsf{Act}_{\mathsf{in}}$ such that $S' = \mathsf{succ}(S, a) \neq \emptyset$. In this case, the algorithm chooses such an action and generates an edge $S \xrightarrow{a} S'$. For each input node $S$ and every action $b \in \mathsf{Act}_{\mathsf{out}} \cup \{\mathsf{tick}\}$, the algorithm generates an edge $S \xrightarrow{b} S''$ in the test tree, with $S'' = \mathsf{succ}(S, b)$. If $S'' = \emptyset$, then $S''$ is marked "FAIL". Otherwise, the algorithm continues to extend the test from $S''$.

The above algorithm is only partially specified. It must be completed by specifying a policy for marking nodes as input or output, for choosing which of the possible outputs to emit and for choosing when to stop the test. An easy way is to resolve these choices randomly. This may not be satisfactory when some completeness guarantees are required or when repetitions must be avoided as much as possible. Another possibility is to generate an *exhaustive* test suite up to a depth $k$ specified by the user. This approach suffers from the *explosion* problem, since the number of tests is generally exponential in $k$.

To remedy the above problems, many approaches have been proposed for generating test suites with respect to a given *coverage criterion*. Different coverage criteria have been proposed for software, such as statement coverage, branch coverage, and so on [33]. In the TA case existing methods attempt to cover either finite abstractions of the state space (e.g., the region graph [28] or a time-abstracting quotient graph [25]) or structural elements of the specification such as edges or locations [20].

Here, we propose a new technique for covering states, locations or edges of the specification[4]. Our technique relies on the concept of *observable graph* of the composed automaton $A_S^{\mathsf{tick}}$, denoted OG. This graph is generated as follows. The initial node of the graph is $S_0 = \{s \mid \exists \rho \in \mathsf{RT}(\{\tau\}) . s_0^{A_S^{\mathsf{tick}}} \xrightarrow{\rho} s\}$. For each generated node $S$ and each $a \in \mathsf{Act} \cup \{\mathsf{tick}\}$, a successor node $S' = \mathsf{succ}(S, a)$ is generated and an edge $S \xrightarrow{a} S'$ is added to the graph. Extrapolation abstractions can be used here as well, to ensure that the graph remains finite.

Every node of OG corresponds to a set of states $S$ of $A_S^{\mathsf{tick}}$. We say that the node *covers* $S$. On the other hand, every static test tree is essentially a sub-graph of OG. We say that such a test covers the union of all sets of states covered by its nodes. We say that a set of tests (or *test suite*) achieves *state coverage* if every reachable state of $A_S$ is covered by some test in the suite[5].

Similarly, a node $S$ of OG covers a location $q$ of $A_S$ if $S$ contains some state $s = (q, v)$. A test suite achieves *location coverage* if every reachable location of $A_S$ is covered by some test in the suite. When $A_S$ is built compositionally, we can distinguish between *global* and *local* location coverage. In global location coverage, we require that all reachable global locations be covered. A global location is a vector $(q_1, ..., q_n)$ where $n$ is the number of components and $q_i$ is the local location of component $i$. In local location coverage, we simply require that all reachable individual locations of components be covered. Clearly, a test

---

[4] As mentioned in the introduction, we cannot use the technique of [20] because it relies on the assumption that outputs in the specification are urgent and isolated.

[5] Unreachable states of $A_S$ can be ignored, since they play no role regarding conformance.

suite achieving global location coverage also achieves local location coverage, but the converse is not generally true. Similarly, a test suite achieving state coverage also achieves both local and global location coverage, but the converse is not always true.

Every edge of OG can be associated to a set of edges of $A_S$. In particular, an edge $S \xrightarrow{a} S'$ will be associated to all edges which are visited during the reachability algorithm which computes $S'$ from $S$. Formally, if $s \in S$, $s' \in S'$ and $s \xrightarrow{\rho \cdot a} s'$ for an unobservable sequence $\rho$, all edges in the path from $s$ to $s'$ are covered by the edge $S \xrightarrow{a} S'$. We say that a test suite achieves *edge coverage* if every reachable edge of $A_S$ (i.e., an edge enabled at a reachable state of $A_S$) is covered by some test in the suite. A test suite achieving edge coverage also achieves local location coverage. However, it may not achieve global location (or state) coverage.

We now give an algorithm to generate a test suite achieving coverage with respect to a given criterion. The first step is to build the observation graph of $A_S^{\text{tick}}$. Then, tests are extracted statically from OG, until coverage is achieved. We first consider location coverage. Tests are extracted as follows.

While there are reachable locations not covered, the algorithm picks such a location, say $q$. Next, it picks a node $v$ of OG associated with $q$ (such a node exists since $q$ is reachable) and finds a path in OG from the initial node to $v$. Then, it extends this path into a test tree. This can be done by completing the path with the missing edges, labeled with tester inputs. For instance, if there is an edge $v_1 \xrightarrow{a} v_2$ in the path, with $a \in \text{Act}_{\text{out}} \cup \{\text{tick}\}$, then every outgoing edge of $v_1$ labeled with a tester input $b$, i.e., every edge $v_1 \xrightarrow{b} v'$, $b \in \text{Act}_{\text{out}} \cup \{\text{tick}\}$, must be added[6]. The leaves of the tree are labeled PASS, except if a leaf is empty, in which case it is labeled FAIL. This new test is added to the set of tests already generated and the algorithm repeats choosing a new uncovered location, until all locations are covered. Notice that the algorithm is essentially an AND/OR search in a finite graph, AND nodes being input nodes and OR nodes being output nodes.

A state-covering suite can be extracted in a similar way. If some state $s$ is not covered, we first find a node $v$ of OG covering $s$. Then we extract a test including $v$ as above. Notice that this test will cover not only $s$, but a set of states containing $s$. It will at least cover the region in which $s$ belongs. This guarantees that the algorithm terminates with a finite test suite, even though the set of states is infinite. The algorithm is also similar for edge coverage, with the difference that instead of finding a path reaching a target node of OG, the algorithm finds a path reaching a target edge (the so-far uncovered edge).

It can be shown that for every reachable state of $A_S$ there exists a node $S$ of OG covering this state, and similarly for locations and edges. Thus, covering all nodes in OG suffices to achieve coverage for each of the three criteria above. Since OG is finite, a finite number of tests suffices to achieve coverage, thus, the algorithm terminates. The worst-case complexity of the algorithm is polynomial

---

[6] In general, it is a good idea to continue extending the test tree in this way. This is because, using such a policy, a single test will cover as many locations as possible.

in the size of OG. Indeed, finding a node (or edge) of OG associated with a location (or edge) of $A_S$ is linear. Finding a path in OG and extending the path into a test tree is also linear. These steps are performed at most as many times as there are nodes in OG.

One drawback of the algorithm is that it does not always generate *minimal* test suites. A test suite is minimal in the sense that if any test is removed from the suite, then coverage is no longer achieved. In general the minimal suite is not unique. Moreover, adding a new test to the suite may result in making one or more previously generated tests redundant. We are currently studying methods of generating minimal test suites.

## 5   Prototype Tool and Experiments

We have built a prototype test-generation tool, called TTG, on top of the IF environment [10]. The IF modeling language allows to specify systems consisting of many processes communicating through message passing or shared variables and includes features such as hierarchy, priorities, dynamic creation and complex data types. Currently, TTG allows the user to generate digital tests interactively, randomly or exhaustively up to a given length. TTG can also generate analog on-the-fly testers or monitors for a given time granularity. Generation of timed automata testers and coverage criteria are being implemented.

We have used TTG on a number of examples, including a modification of the light switch example presented in [20] and the executive subsystem of the Mars rover controller K9, developed at NASA Ames. Due to lack of space, we omit description of these case studies and refer the reader to [22, 5].

In [22] we have reported on using TTG to generate the exhaustive digital-clock test suite for the light switch specification, with parameter set $D = 1, m = 1, M = 2$ and for various depths. We have obtained 68, 180, 591 and 2243 tests, for depth levels 5, 6, 7 and 8, respectively. It can be seen that the number of tests grows exponentially with the depth and is very large, even for such a small example. On the other hand, a very small test suite (less than ten tests of depth no more than 20) suffices to cover this specification with respect to any of the three criteria of Section 4. Examples of such tests can be found in the full version of this paper, available on-line as a technical report [23].

## 6   Conclusions and Future Work

The main contributions of this paper are two techniques for improving on-the-fly analog-clock testing and static digital-clock test generation. First, we have provided an algorithm to generate analog-clock testers which are represented as timed automata with one clock. This permits to minimize the reaction time of on-the-fly testing from a reachability computation to a simple state jump. Second, we have provided an algorithm to generate digital-clock test suites with respect to several coverage criteria, namely, state, location and edge coverage. Compared to generating an exhaustive test suite up to a given depth, coverage can dramatically reduce the number of generated tests, as evidenced on a small case study.

We are currently implementing on TTG the test generation technique with respect to coverage criteria of Section 4 and studying methods to generate minimal test suites. We are also implementing the timed automata tester generation technique of Section 3 and examining notions of coverage in this context as well.

# References

1. R. Alur and D. Dill. A theory of timed automata. *Theoretical Computer Science*, 126:183–235, 1994.
2. R. Alur, L. Fix, and T. Henzinger. A determinizable class of timed automata. In *CAV'94*, volume 818 of *LNCS*. Springer, 1994.
3. A. Belinfante, J. Feenstra, R.G. de Vries, J. Tretmans, N. Goga, L. Feijs, S. Mauw, and L. Heerink. Formal test automation: A simple experiment. In 12<sup>th</sup> *Int. Workshop on Testing of Communicating Systems*. Kluwer, 1999.
4. J. Bengtsson and W. Yi. On clock difference constraints and termination in reachability analysis of timed automata. In *ICFEM'03*, volume 2885 of *LNCS*. Springer, 2003.
5. S. Bensalem, M. Bozga, M. Krichen, and S. Tripakis. Testing conformance of real-time applications by automatic generation of observers. In *4th International Workshop on Runtime Verification (RV'04)*, 2004. To appear in ENTCS series by Elsevier.
6. B. Berthomieu and M. Menasche. An enumerative approach for analyzing time Petri nets. *IFIP Congress Series*, 9:41–46, 1983.
7. S. Bornot, J. Sifakis, and S. Tripakis. Modeling urgency in timed systems. In *Compositionality*, volume 1536 of *LNCS*. Springer, 1998.
8. P. Bouyer. Untameable timed automata! In *STACS'03*, volume 2607 of *LNCS*. Springer, 2003.
9. P. Bouyer, D. D'Souza, P. Madhusudan, and A. Petit. Timed control with partial observability. In *CAV'03*, 2003.
10. M. Bozga, J.C. Fernandez, L. Ghirvu, S. Graf, J.P. Krimm, and L. Mounier. IF: a validation environment for timed asynchronous systems. In E.A. Emerson and A.P. Sistla, editors, *Proc. CAV'00*, volume 1855 of *LNCS*, pages 543–547. Springer Verlag, 2000.
11. E. Brinksma and J. Tretmans. Testing transition systems: An annotated bibliography. In *MOVEP 2000*, volume 2067 of *LNCS*. Springer, 2001.
12. R. Cardell-Oliver and T. Glover. A practical and complete algorithm for testing real-time systems. In *FTRTFT'98*, volume 1486 of *LNCS*, 1998.
13. T.S. Chow. Testing software design modeled by finite-state machines. *IEEE Transactions on Software Engineering*, 4(1), 1978.
14. D. Clarke, T. Jéron, V. Rusu, and E. Zinovieva. STG: A symbolic test generation tool. In *TACAS'02*, volume 2280 of *LNCS*. Springer, 2002.
15. D. Clarke and I. Lee. Automatic generation of tests for timing constraints from requirements. In *3rd Workshop on Object-Oriented Real-Time Dependable Systems (WORDS'97)*, 1997.
16. C. Daws and S. Tripakis. Model checking of real-time reachability properties using abstractions. In *Tools and Algorithms for the Construction and Analysis of Systems '98, Lisbon, Portugal*, volume 1384 of *LNCS*. Springer-Verlag, 1998.

17. D.L. Dill. Timing assumptions and verification of finite-state concurrent systems. In J. Sifakis, editor, *Automatic Verification Methods for Finite State Systems*, volume 407 of *Lecture Notes in Computer Science*, pages 197–212. Springer–Verlag, 1989.

18. J.C. Fernandez, C. Jard, T. Jéron, and G. Viho. Using on-the-fly verification techniques for the generation of test suites. In *CAV'96*, LNCS 1102, 1996.

19. T. Henzinger, Z. Manna, and A. Pnueli. What good are digital clocks? In *ICALP'92*, LNCS 623, 1992.

20. A. Hessel, K. Larsen, B. Nielsen, P. Pettersson, and A. Skou. Time-optimal real-time test case generation using UPPAAL. In *FATES'03*, Montreal, October 2003.

21. T. Higashino, A. Nakata, K. Taniguchi, and A. Cavalli. Generating test cases for a timed I/O automaton model. In *IFIP Int'l Work. Test. Communicat. Syst.* Kluwer, 1999.

22. M. Krichen and S. Tripakis. Black-box conformance testing for real-time systems. In *11th International SPIN Workshop on Model Checking of Software (SPIN'04)*, volume 2989 of *LNCS*. Springer, 2004.

23. Moez Krichen and Stavros Tripakis. Real-time testing with timed automata testers and coverage criteria. Technical Report TR-2004-15, Verimag, Centre Équation, 38610 Gières, June 2004.

24. D. Lee and M. Yannakakis. Principles and methods of testing finite state machines - A survey. *Proceedings of the IEEE*, 84:1090–1126, 1996.

25. B. Nielsen and A. Skou. Automated test generation from timed automata. In *TACAS'01*. LNCS 2031, Springer, 2001.

26. J. Peleska. Formal methods for test automation - hard real-time testing of controllers for the airbus aircraft family. In *IDPT'02*, 2002.

27. J. Sifakis and S. Yovine. Compositional specification of timed systems. In *13th Annual Symposium on Theoretical Aspects of Computer Science, STACS'96*, pages 347–359, Grenoble, France, February 1996. Lecture Notes in Computer Science 1046, Spinger-Verlag.

28. J. Springintveld, F. Vaandrager, and P. D'Argenio. Testing timed automata. *Theoretical Computer Science*, 254, 2001.

29. J. Tretmans. Testing concurrent systems: A formal approach. In J.C.M Baeten and S. Mauw, editors, *CONCUR'99 - 10$^{th}$ Int. Conference on Concurrency Theory*, volume 1664 of *Lecture Notes in Computer Science*, pages 46–65. Springer-Verlag, 1999.

30. J. Tretmans. Testing techniques. Lecture notes, University of Twente, The Netherlands, 2002.

31. S. Tripakis. Fault diagnosis for timed automata. In *Formal Techniques in Real Time and Fault Tolerant Systems (FTRTFT'02)*, volume 2469 of *LNCS*. Springer, 2002.

32. S. Tripakis. Folk theorems on the determinization and minimization of timed automata. In *Formal Modeling and Analysis of Timed Systems (FORMATS'03)*, volume 2791 of *LNCS*. Springer, 2004.

33. H. Zhu, P. Hall, and J. May. Software unit test coverage and adequacy. *ACM Computing Surveys*, 29(4), 1997.

# Monitoring Temporal Properties of Continuous Signals*

Oded Maler and Dejan Nickovic

VERIMAG, 2 Av. de Vignate, 38610 Gières, France
{Dejan.Nickovic,Oded.Maler}@imag.fr

**Abstract.** In this paper we introduce a variant of temporal logic tailored for specifying desired properties of continuous signals. The logic is based on a bounded subset of the real-time logic MITL, augmented with a static mapping from continuous domains into propositions. From formulae in this logic we create automatically property monitors that can check whether a given signal of bounded length and finite variability satisfies the property. A prototype implementation of this procedure was used to check properties of simulation traces generated by Matlab/Simulink.

## 1 Introduction

Temporal logic [MP95] is a rigorous formalism for specifying desired behaviors of discrete systems such as programs or digital circuits. The algorithmic approach to verification [Kur94,CGP99,BBF$^+$01,VW86] consists of checking whether all (finite and infinite) state-event sequences generated by a system $S$ satisfy a formula $\varphi$, that is, effectively deciding the language inclusion $[\![S]\!] \subseteq [\![\varphi]\!]$. Recently a version of a temporal logic-based specification formalism, PSL-Sugar [BBDE$^+$02], has been adopted by the hardware industry as a standard specification language.

For systems which are outside the scope of automatic verification tools, either due to the incorporation of unbounded variables (numbers, queues) or simply due to size, simulation/testing is still the preferred validation method. It has been suggested by several authors that the specification component of verification can be exported toward simulation through property monitors (observers, testers). In the software context this is called *run-time verification* [HR02a,SV03]. The idea is simple: unlike the inclusion test $[\![S]\!] \subseteq [\![\varphi]\!]$ used in verification, in monitoring one performs each time a much simpler *membership* test $\xi \in [\![\varphi]\!]$ on an individual simulation trace $\xi \in [\![S]\!]$ and the responsibility for exhaustive coverage is delegated to the test generation procedure (or abandoned altogether).

The essence of this approach is the automatic construction of a monitor from the formula in the form of a program that can be interfaced with the simulator and alert the user if the property is violated by a simulation trace. This process is much more reliable than manual (visual or textual) inspection of simulation traces, or manual construction of property monitors.

---

* This work was partially supported by the EC projects IST-2001-33520 CC (Control and Computation), IST-2001-35302 AMETIST (Advanced Methods for Timed Systems) and IST-2003-507219 PROSYD (Property-Based System Design).

Y. Lakhnech and S. Yovine (Eds.): FORMATS/FTRTFT 2004, LNCS 3253, pp. 152–166, 2004.

Temporal logic has been used as the specification language in a number of monitoring tools, including Temporal Rover (TR) [Dru00], FoCs [ABG+00], Java PathExplorer (JPaX) [HR01] and MaCS [KLS+02]. TR is a commercial tool that allows to annotate programs with temporal logic formulae and then monitor them. FoCs is a monitoring system developed at IBM that automatically transforms PSL-Sugar properties into deterministic property checkers in the form of simulation blocks compatible with various HDL simulators. JPaX is a software-oriented runtime verification system for data race analysis, deadlock detection and temporal specifications. MaCS is another software-oriented monitoring framework aimed at runtime checking (and steering) of real-time programs.

Unlike verification, where the availability of the system model allows one to reason about infinite computations (carried by cycles in the transition graph), monitoring is usually restricted to finite traces. One thread of monitoring research attempts to redefine the semantics of temporal formulae on finite (truncated) runs [EFH+03]. We avoid this problem altogether by considering a temporal logic with *bounded* time modalities which interprets naturally over finite traces.

The main contribution of this work is the definition of a temporal logic for specifying properties of *dense-time real-valued signals* and the automatic generation of property monitors for this language. The motivation to do so stems from the need to improve validation methodology for *continuous and hybrid systems*. Two prime examples of such systems are *control* systems, where the continuous variables are used to model the physical plant under control, and *analog* and *mixed-signal circuits* where such variables represent currents and voltages throughout the circuit. The natural models for such systems are differential equations, for purely continuous systems, or hybrid automata, a combination of automata with differential equations, when the dynamics is mixed and contains mode switching, saturation, etc. The exact exhaustive verification of continuous and hybrid systems is impossible due to undecidability except for some trivial sub-classes. Even approximate verification is very hard, restricted in the current state-of-the-art to systems with very few continuous variables. Consequently, numerical simulation is the commonly-used method to validate such systems and our work can be seen as a step toward making this process more systematic and rigorous. Some primitive forms of monitoring do exist in certain numerical simulation tools but their temporal ("sequential") sophistication is very limited.

The rest of the paper is organized as follows. In Section 2 we introduce the real-time temporal logic $\text{MITL}_{[a,b]}$, a restricted version of the logic MITL of Alur and Henzinger [AFH96] along with its semantic domain, Boolean signals of finite variability defined over finite prefixes of the positive real time axis. In Section 3 we describe a simple offline monitoring procedure which reads a formula $\varphi$ and a signal $s$ of a sufficient length (relative to the formula) and determines whether $s$ satisfies $\varphi$. This procedure by itself can be used to monitor dense real-time properties of digital circuits and programs. In section 4 we introduce the logic STL (Signal Temporal Logic), discuss its semantic domain and show how monitoring for its formulae can be reduced, via static Boolean abstraction, to monitoring of $\text{MITL}_{[a,b]}$ formulae. The behavior of a prototype implementation on simulation traces generated by Matlab/Simulink is illustrated in Section 5, followed by discussions of related and future work.

# 2 Signals and Their Temporal Logic

## 2.1 Signals

Let the time domain $\mathbb{T}$ be the set $\mathbb{R}_{\geq 0}$ of non-negative real numbers. A finite length signal $s$ over a domain $\mathbb{D}$ is a partial function $s : \mathbb{T} \to \mathbb{D}$ whose domain of definition is the interval $I = [0, r)$, $r \in \mathbb{Q}_{\geq 0}$. We say that the length of the signal is $r$ and denote this fact by $|s| = r$. We use the notation $s[t] = \bot$ for every $t \geq |s|$.

Signals over different domains can be combined and separated using the standard pairing and projection operators as well as any pointwise operation. Let $s_1 : \mathbb{T} \to \mathbb{D}_1$, $s_2 : \mathbb{T} \to \mathbb{D}_2$, $s_{12} : \mathbb{T} \to \mathbb{D}_1 \times \mathbb{D}_2$ and $s_3 : \mathbb{T} \to \mathbb{D}_3$ be signals and let $f : \mathbb{D}_1 \times \mathbb{D}_2 \to \mathbb{D}_3$ be a function. The pairing function is defined as

$$s_1 \parallel s_2 = s_{12} \text{ if } \forall t \ s_{12}[t] = (s_1[t], s_2[t]).$$

and its inverse operation, projection as:

$$s_1 = \pi_1(s_{12}) \qquad s_2 = \pi_2(s_{12}).$$

The lifting of $f$ to signals is defined as

$$s_3 = f(s_1, s_2) \text{ if } \forall t \ s_3[t] = f(s_1[t], s_2[t]).$$

Note that if $s_1$ and $s_2$ differ in length, the convention $f(x, \bot) = f(\bot, x) = \bot$ guarantees that $|s_3| = \min(|s_1|, |s_2|)$.

In the rest of this paper, unless otherwise stated, we restrict our attention to Boolean signals, $\mathbb{D} = \mathbb{B}$. In this case (and for discrete domains in general) all reasonable signals are piecewise-constant[1] and can be represented by their values on a countable number of intervals. An *interval covering* for an interval $I = [0, r)$ is a sequence $\mathcal{I} = I_1, I_2 \ldots$ of left-closed right-open intervals such that $\bigcup I_i = I$ and $I_i \cap I_j = \emptyset$ for every $i \neq j$.

An interval covering $\mathcal{I}$ is said to be *consistent* with a signal $s$ if $s[t] = s[t']$ for every $t, t'$ belonging to the same interval $I_i$. In that case we can abuse notation and write $s(I_i)$. We say that a signal $s$ is of *finite variability* if it has a finite interval covering [AFH96]. It is not hard to see that such signals are closed under pointwise operations, pairing and projection. We restrict ourselves to signals of finite variability which are, by definition, non-Zeno. An interval covering $\mathcal{I}$ is said to refine $\mathcal{I}'$, denoted by $\mathcal{I} \prec \mathcal{I}'$ if $\forall I \in \mathcal{I} \ \exists I' \in \mathcal{I}'$ such that $I \subseteq I'$. Clearly, if $\mathcal{I}'$ is consistent with $s$, so is $\mathcal{I}$.

We denote by $\mathcal{I}_s$ the minimal interval covering consistent with a finite variability signal $s$. The set of positive intervals of $s$ is $\mathcal{I}_s^+ = \{I \in \mathcal{I}_s : s(I) = 1\}$ and the set of negative intervals is $\mathcal{I}_s^- = \mathcal{I}_s - \mathcal{I}_s^+$. A Boolean signal $s : \mathbb{T} \to \mathbb{B}$ can be represented by the pair $(|s|, \mathcal{I}_s^+)$. Such a signal is said to be *unitary* if $\mathcal{I}_s^+$ is a singleton. Clearly any Boolean signal $s$ of finite variability can be written as $s = s_1 \vee s_2 \vee \ldots \vee s_k$ where all $s_i$ are unitary and the boundaries of their corresponding positive intervals do not intersect.

---

[1] Pathological signals which are 1 on rationals and 0 on irrationals are out of the scope of this work.

## 2.2  Real-Time Temporal Logic

We consider the logic $\text{MITL}_{[a,b]}$ as a fragment of the real-time temporal logic MITL [AFH96], such that all temporal modalities are restricted to intervals of the form $[a,b]$ with $0 \le a < b$ and $a, b \in \mathbb{Q}_{\ge 0}$. More on various dialects of real-time logic can be found in [AH92,Hen98]. The use of bounded temporal properties is justified by the nature of monitoring where the behavior of a system is observed for a finite time interval. The basic formulae of $\text{MITL}_{[a,b]}$ are defined by the grammar

$$\varphi := p \mid \neg\varphi \mid \varphi_1 \vee \varphi_2 \mid \varphi_1 \mathcal{U}_{[a,b]}\varphi_2$$

where $p$ belongs to a set $P = \{p_1, \ldots, p_n\}$ of propositions. From basic $\text{MITL}_{[a,b]}$ operators one can derive other standard Boolean and temporal operators, in particular the time-constrained *eventually* and *always* operators:

$$\Diamond_{[a,b]}\varphi = \top\,\mathcal{U}_{[a,b]}\varphi \quad \text{and} \quad \Box_{[a,b]}\varphi = \neg\Diamond_{[a,b]}\neg\varphi$$

In this paper, $\text{MITL}_{[a,b]}$ formulae are interpreted over $n$-dimensional Boolean signals. The satisfaction relation $(s,t) \models \varphi$, indicating that signal $s$ satisfies $\varphi$ starting from position $t$, is defined inductively as follows:

$$
\begin{aligned}
(s,t) &\models p &&\leftrightarrow \pi_p(s)[t] = \top \\
(s,t) &\models \neg\varphi &&\leftrightarrow (s,t) \not\models \varphi \\
(s,t) &\models \varphi_1 \vee \varphi_2 &&\leftrightarrow (s,t) \models \varphi_1 \text{ or } (s,t) \models \varphi_2 \\
(s,t) &\models \varphi_1 \mathcal{U}_{[a,b]}\varphi_2 &&\leftrightarrow \exists t' \in [t+a, t+b]\ (s,t') \models \varphi_2 \text{ and } \forall t'' \in [t,t'], (s,t'') \models \varphi_1
\end{aligned}
$$

Note that our definition of the semantics of the time-bounded *until* operator differs slightly from its conventional definition since it requires a time instant $t' \in [t+a, t+b]$ where *both* $(s,t') \models \varphi_2$ and $(s,t') \models \varphi_1$. This definition does not have any repercussion on the derived *eventually* and *always* operators which retain their usual semantics:

$$
\begin{aligned}
(s,t) &\models \Diamond_{[a,b]}\varphi \leftrightarrow \exists t' \in t + [a,b]\ (s,t') \models \varphi \\
(s,t) &\models \Box_{[a,b]}\varphi \leftrightarrow \forall t' \in t + [a,b]\ (s,t') \models \varphi
\end{aligned}
$$

A signal $s$ satisfies the formula $\varphi$ iff $(s,0) \models \varphi$.

According to the standard semantics for temporal logic, the satisfaction of a formula with unbounded modalities can rarely be determined with respect to a finite signal or sequence. In fact, only the satisfaction of $\Diamond p$ or the violation of $\Box p$ can be detected in finite time. By using bounded modalities we avoid the problems related to the ambiguity of $\models$ when applied to finite signals or sequences. Nevertheless, even for $\text{MITL}_{[a,b]}$ certain signals are too short to determine satisfaction of the formula, for example the property $\Box_{[a,b]}\Diamond_{[c,d]}p$ cannot be evaluated on signals shorter than $b + d$. Hence we restrict ourselves to signals which are sufficiently long. The necessary length associated with a formula $\varphi$, denoted by $\|\varphi\|$, is defined inductively on the structure of the formula:

$$
\begin{aligned}
\|p\| &= 0 \\
\|\neg\varphi\| &= \|\varphi\| \\
\|\varphi_1 \vee \varphi_2\| &= \max(\|\varphi_1\|, \|\varphi_2\|) \\
\|\varphi_1 \mathcal{U}_{[a,b]}\varphi_2\| &= \max(\|\varphi_1\|, \|\varphi_2\|) + b
\end{aligned}
$$

The reader can verify that $s \models \varphi$ is well defined whenever $|s| > \|\varphi\|$.

## 3   Monitoring MITL$_{[a,b]}$ Formulae

In this section we present a procedure for deciding the satisfiability of an MITL$_{[a,b]}$ formula by a sufficiently long signal. This procedure, partly inspired by [Pnu03] and [HR02b], is very simple. It works in a bottom-up fashion on the parse tree of the formula. Starting from the leaves we construct for every sub-formula $\psi$ a signal $s_\psi$ such that $s_\psi[t] = 1$ iff $(s, t) \models \psi$. When the process is completed we have the signal $s_\varphi$ for the formula whose value at 0 determines satisfiability. Since future temporal modalities talk about truth *now* as a function of some truth in the future, it is natural that our procedure goes *backwards*, propagating, for example, the truth value of $p$ at time $t$, toward the truth of $\Diamond_{[a,b]}p$ at $[t - b, t - a]$. This procedure is not causal and has to wait for the termination of the simulation before starting the evaluation of the signal with respect to the formula.

For Boolean operators the computation of (a representation of) a signal for a formula from (the representations of) the signals of its sub-formulae is rather straightforward. For negation we have $\mathcal{I}^+_{\neg p} = \mathcal{I}^-_p$. For disjunction $\psi = p \vee q$ we first construct a refined interval covering $\mathcal{I} = \{I_1, \dots I_k\}$ for $p\|q$ and then for each $I_i$, let $\psi(I_i) = p(I_i) \vee q(I_i)$. Finally we merge adjacent positive intervals to obtain $\mathcal{I}^+_\psi$ (see Figure 1).

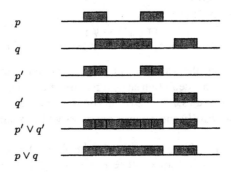

**Fig. 1.** To compute $p \vee q$ we first refine the interval covering to obtain the a representation of the signals by $p'$ and $q'$, then perform interval-wise operations to obtain $p' \vee q'$ and then merge adjacent positive intervals.

To treat the *until* we need to shift intervals backwards. Let $I = [m, n)$ and $[a, b]$ be intervals in $\mathbb{T}$. The $[a, b]$-back shifting of $I$, is

$$I \ominus [a, b] = [m - b, n - a) \cap \mathbb{T}.$$

This is essentially the inverse of the Minkowski sum with saturation at zero (see Figure 2).

*Claim (Unitary Until).* Let $p$ and $q$ be two unitary signals with $\mathcal{I}^+_p = \{I_p\}$ and $\mathcal{I}^+_q = \{I_q\}$. Then the signal $\psi = p\mathcal{U}_{[a,b]}q$ is a unitary signal satisfying

$$\mathcal{I}^+_\psi = \{((I_p \cap I_q) \ominus [a, b]) \cap I_p\}.$$

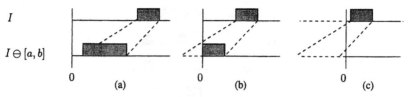

**Fig. 2.** Three instances of back shifting $I' = [m, n) \ominus [a, b]$: (a) $I' = [m - b, n - a)$; (b) $I' = [0, n - a]$ because $m - b < 0$; (c) $I' = \emptyset$ because $n - a < 0$.

*Proof.* This follows directly from the definition of $\mathcal{U}_{[a,b]}$ semantics. Let $t$ be point in $((I_p \cap I_q) \ominus [a, b]) \cap I_p$. This means that there is a time $t' \in [t + a, t + b]$ where $q$ and $p$ are satisfied and that $p$ is satisfied also at $t$. Since $p$ is unitary, this implies that $p$ holds throughout the interval $[t, t']$. A point $t$ not belonging to $I_\psi$ will either not have such a point $t'$ or will not satisfy $p$ and hence will not satisfy $\psi$.　　⌐

*Claim (General Until).* Let $p = p_1 \vee \ldots \vee p_m$ and $q = q_1 \vee \ldots \vee q_n$ be two signals, each written as a union of unitary signals. Then

$$p\mathcal{U}_{[a,b]}q = \bigvee_{i=1}^{m} \bigvee_{j=1}^{n} p_i\mathcal{U}_{[a,b]}q_j.$$

*Proof.* First, observe that $p\mathcal{U}_{[a,b]}(q_1 \vee q_2) = p\mathcal{U}_{[a,b]}q_1 \vee p\mathcal{U}_{[a,b]}q_2$. This is because $q[t]$ is quantified existentially in the semantic definition. Secondly, when the positive intervals of $p_1$ and $p_2$ are separated we have $(p_1 \vee p_2)\mathcal{U}_{[a,b]}q = p_1\mathcal{U}_{[a,b]}q \vee p_1\mathcal{U}_{[a,b]}q$.　　⌐

In practice this should be computed only for $p_i$ and $q_j$ such that their respective positive intervals intersect, and the number of such pairs is at most $m + n$. Figure 3 demonstrates why we cannot work directly on $\mathcal{I}_p^+$ and $\mathcal{I}_q^+$ but rather need to go through unitary decomposition.

These claims imply the correctness of our procedure[2] whose complexity is $O(k \cdot n)$ where $k$ is the number of sub-formulae and $n$ is the maximal number of positive intervals in the atomic signals. As an example, the execution of our procedure is illustrated in Figure 4 on the formula $\square_{[0,10]}(p \rightarrow \Diamond_{[1,2]}q)$. We have implemented this procedure.

## 4   Real-Valued Signals

In this section we extend our semantic domain and logic to real-valued signals. While Boolean signals of finite variability admit a finite representation, this is typically not the case for real-valued signals which are often represented via sampling, that is a sequence of time stamped values of the form $(t, s[t])$. Although we define the semantics of the

---

[2] Note that the design decision to allow only closed intervals in the time modalities contributed significantly to its simplicity, because we can restrict our attention to left-closed right-open intervals without the annoying case splitting associated with different types of intervals.

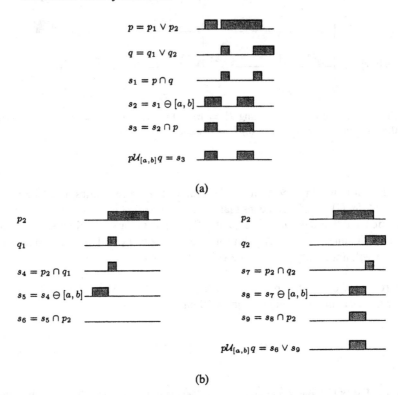

$$p = p_1 \vee p_2$$

$$q = q_1 \vee q_2$$

$$s_1 = p \cap q$$

$$s_2 = s_1 \ominus [a, b]$$

$$s_3 = s_2 \cap p$$

$$p\,\mathcal{U}_{[a,b]}\,q = s_3$$

(a)

$$p_2$$

$$q_1$$

$$s_4 = p_2 \cap q_1$$

$$s_5 = s_4 \ominus [a, b]$$

$$s_6 = s_5 \cap p_2$$

$$p_2$$

$$q_2$$

$$s_7 = p_2 \cap q_2$$

$$s_8 = s_7 \ominus [a, b]$$

$$s_9 = s_8 \cap p_2$$

$$p\,\mathcal{U}_{[a,b]}\,q = s_6 \vee s_9$$

(b)

**Fig. 3.** (a) Applying back shifting to non-unitary signals leads to wrong results for $p\,\mathcal{U}_{[a,b]}q$; (b) Applying back shifting to the unitary decomposition of $p$ and $q$ leads to correct results. The computation with $p_1$ is omitted as it has an empty intersection with $q$.

logic in terms of the mathematical objects, signals of the from $s : \mathbb{T} \to \mathbb{R}^m$, we cannot ignore issues related to their effective representation based on the output of some numerical simulator.

Our logic, to be defined in the sequel, does not speak about continuous signals directly but rather via a set of static abstractions of the from $\mu : \mathbb{R}^m \to \mathbb{B}$. Typically $\mu$ will partition the continuous state-space according to the satisfaction of some inequality constraints on the real variables. As long as $\mu(s[t])$ remains constant we do not really care about the exact value of $s[t]$. However, in order to evaluate formulae we need the sampling to be sufficiently dense so that all such transitions can be detected when they happen. The problem of "event detection" in numerical simulation is well-known (see a survey in [Mos99]) and can be resolved using variable step adaptive methods for numerical integration.

However this may raise problems related to finite variability and Zenoness. Consider an abstraction $\mu : \mathbb{R} \to \mathbb{B}$ defined as $\mu(x) = 1$ iff $x > 0$ and consider a signal $s$ that oscillates with an unbounded frequency near the origin. Such a signal will cross zero too often and its abstraction may lead to Boolean signals of infinite variability. These are eternal problems that need to be solved pragmatically according to the context.

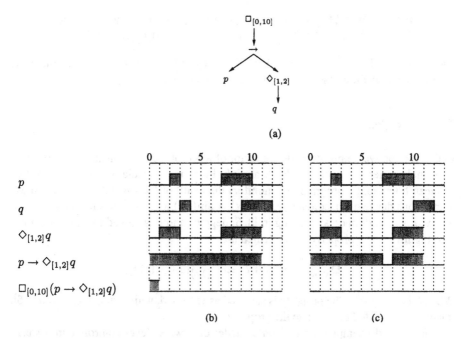

**Fig. 4.** Monitoring two 2-dimensional signals against the formula $\Box_{[0,10]}(p \to \Diamond_{[1,2]}q)$: (a) The formula parse tree; (b) The property is satisfied; (c) The formula is violated.

In any case the dynamics of most reasonable systems have a bounded frequency, and even if we add white noise to a system, the frequency remains bounded by the size of the integration step used by the simulator. From now on we assume that we deal with signals that are well-behaving with respect to every $\mu$, that is, $\mu(s)$ has a bounded variability and every change in $\mu(s)$ is detected in the sense that every point $t$ such that $\mu(s[t]) \neq \lim_{t' \to t} \mu(s[t'])$ is included in the sampling.

**Definition 1 (Signal Temporal Logic).** *Let $U = \{\mu_1, \ldots, \mu_n\}$ be a collection of predicates, effective functions of the form $\mu_i : \mathbb{R}^m \to \mathbb{B}$. An STL$(U)$ formula is an MITL$_{[a,b]}$ formula over the atomic propositions $\mu_1(x), \ldots \mu_n(x)$.*

Any signal which is well-behaving with respect to $U$ can be transformed into a Boolean signal $s' : \mathbb{T} \to \mathbb{B}^n$ such that $s' = \mu_1(s)\|\mu_2(s)\| \ldots \|\mu_n(s)$ is of bounded variability. By construction, for every signal $s$ and STL formula $\varphi$, $s \models \varphi$ iff $s' \models \varphi'$ in the MITL$_{[a,b]}$ sense where $\varphi'$ is obtained from $\varphi$ by replacing every $\mu_i(x)$ by a propositional variable $p_i$.

The monitoring process for STL formulae decomposes hence into two parts. First we construct a Boolean "filter" for every $\mu_i \in U$ which transforms $s$ into a Boolean signal $p_i = \mu_i(s)$. Consider, for example, the signal $\sin[t]$ where $t$ is given in degrees and $\mu(x) = x > 0$. The signal is of length 400 and is sampled every 50 time units plus two additional sampling points to detect zero crossing at 180 and 360. The input to the Boolean filter is

$(0, 0.0), (50, 0.766), (100, 0.984), (150, 0.5), (180, 0.0), (200, -0.342),$
$(250, -0.939), (300, -0.866), (350, -0.173), (360, 0), (400, 0.643)$

and the output is a signal $p$ such that $\mathcal{I}_p^+ = \{[0, 180), [360, 400]\}$. From there the monitoring procedure described in the previous section can be applied.

## 5 Examples

In this section we demonstrate the behavior of a prototype implementation of our tool on signals generated using Matlab/Simulink. From the formula we generate a set of Boolean filters and a program that monitors the result of the simulation. As a first example consider two sinusoidal signals $x_1[t] = \sin(\omega t)$ and $x_2[t] = \sin(\omega(t + d)) + \theta$ where $d$ is a random delay ranging in $[3, 5]$ degrees and $\theta$ is an additive random noise (see Figure 5). The property to be verified is

$$\Box_{[0,300]}((x_1 > 0.7) \Rightarrow \Diamond_{[3,5]}(x_2 > 0.7)).$$

When $\theta$ is negligible, the property is satisfied as expected, while when $\theta \in [-0.5, 0.5]$, traces are generated that violate the property.

The second example is based on a model of a water level controller in a steam generator of a nuclear plant [Ben02,Don03]. The plant is modeled by a hybrid system with each discrete state having a linear dynamics. There are 5 state variables, among which the variable of disturbance (electricity demand), a control variable (steam flow) and an output variable (the water level). The controller is modeled as a hybrid PI controller whose coefficients depend on the system state. A high-level block diagram of the system is depicted in Figure 6-(a).

The property that we want to check is a typical stabilizability property for control systems. We want the output stay always in the interval $[-30, 30]$ (except, possibly, for an initialization period of length 300) and if, due to a disturbance, it goes outside the interval $[-0.5, 0.5]$, it will return to it within 150 time units and will stay there for at least 20 time units. The whole property is

$$\Box_{[300,2500]}((|y| \leq 30) \wedge ((|y| > 0.5) \Rightarrow \Diamond_{[0,150]}\Box_{[0,20]}(|y| \leq 0.5))))$$

The result of monitoring for this formula appear on Figure 6-(b). When the disturbance is well-behaving the property is verified while when the disturbance changes too fast, the property is violated both by over-shooting below $-30$ and by taking more than 150 time to return to $[-0.5, 0.5]$.

To demonstrate the complexity of our procedure as a function of signal length we applied it to increasingly longer signals ranging from 5000 to one million seconds. We use variable integration/sampling step with average step size of 2 seconds so the number of sampling point in the input is roughly half the number of seconds. The results are depicted in Table 1 and one can see that monitoring can be done very quickly and it adds a negligible overhead to the simulation of complex systems. For example, the simulation of the water level controller for a time horizon of million seconds takes 45 minutes while monitoring the output takes less than 3 seconds.

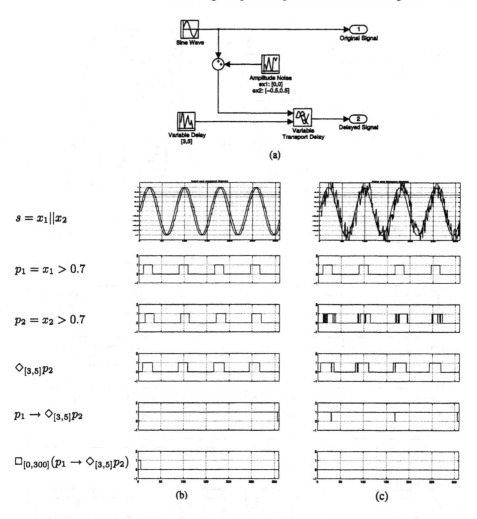

**Fig. 5.** Monitoring two 2-dimensional continuous signals against the property $\Box_{[0,300]}((x_1 > 0.7) \Rightarrow \Diamond_{[3,5]}(x_2 > 0.7))$: (a) The generating system; (b) The property is satisfied; (c) The property is violated.

## 6   Related Work

In this section we mention some work related to the extension of monitoring to real-time properties and to generation of models from real-time logics in general. Some restricted versions of real-time temporal logic already appear in some tools, for example, the specification of real-time properties in MaCS is based on a logic that supports time-stamped instantaneous *events* and *conditions* which have a duration between two events. The TemporalRover allows formulae in the discrete time temporal logic MTL.

TimeChecker [KPA03] is a real-time monitoring system with properties written in $LTL_t$ which uses a *freeze quantifier* to specify time constraints. The time notion in

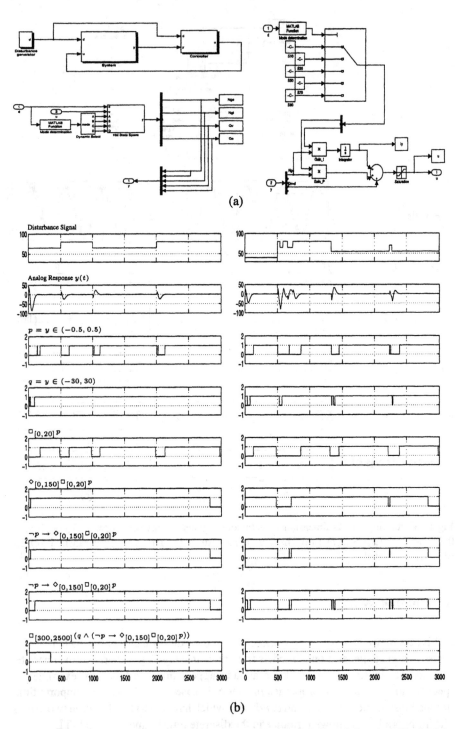

**Fig. 6.** (a) The water level controller: general scheme, the plant (left) and the controller (right); (b) Monitoring results: property satisfied (left) and violated (right).

**Table 1.** CPU time of monitoring the water level controller example as a function of the time horizon (signal length). The number of positive intervals in the Boolean abstractions is given as another indication for the complexity of the problem.

| sig length | $|\mathcal{I}_p^+|$ | $|\mathcal{I}_q^+|$ | time(sec) |
|---|---|---|---|
| 5000 | 98 | 82 | 0.01 |
| 50000 | 970 | 802 | 0.13 |
| 100000 | 1920 | 1602 | 0.25 |
| 200000 | 3872 | 3202 | 0.49 |
| 500000 | 9732 | 8002 | 1.36 |
| 1000000 | 19410 | 16002 | 2.84 |

TimeChecker is discrete. Despite the discrete sampling, the runtime verification steps are not done at the chosen resolution but are rather event-based, i.e. performed only at relevant points of time. This approach allows efficient monitoring of applications where the sampling period is required to be very small, but the period between two relevant events may be large.

Another runtime monitoring method based on discrete-time temporal specifications is presented in [TR04] who use Metric Temporal Logic (MTL). Like TimeChecker, this method is event-based and can be seen as an on-the-fly adaptation of tableau construction. The efficiency of the algorithm is based mainly on a procedure that keeps transformed MTL formulae in a canonical form that retains its size relatively small.

The only work we are aware of concerning monitoring of dense time properties is that of [BBKT04] who propose an automatic generation of real-time (analog or digital) observers from timed automaton specifications. They use the method of state-estimation to check whether an observed timed trace satisfies the specified property. This technique corresponds to an on-the-fly determinization of the timed automaton by computing all possible states that can be reached by the observed trace. No logic is used in this work.

Geilen [Gei02,GD00,Gei03] identifies MITL$_<$ as an interesting portion of MITL with the restriction that all the temporal operators have to be bounded by an interval of the form $[0, d]$. He proposes an on-the-fly tableau construction algorithm that converts any MITL$_<$ formula into a timed automaton. Dense time does not admit a natural notion of discrete states needed for a tableau construction algorithm. Hence, the idea of $\varphi$-fine intervals is used to separate the dense timed sequences into a finite number of interesting "portions" (states). An important feature of this method is that the constructed timed automaton requires only one timer per temporal operator in the formula (unlike the timed automata generated from full MITL). However, his automata are still non-deterministic and would require an on-the-fly subset construction in order to be able to monitor a timed sequence. In [Gei02], a restricted fragment of MITL$_<$ is introduced which yields deterministic timed automata suitable for observing finite paths. However, this restriction is strong since it does not allow an arbitrary nesting of *until* and *release* temporal operators.

## 7   Conclusions and Future Work

This work is, to the best of our knowledge, the first application of temporal logic monitoring to continuous and hybrid systems and we hope it will help in promoting formal methods beyond their traditional application domains. The simple and elegant offline monitoring procedure for MITL$_{[a,b]}$ is interesting by itself and can be readily applied to monitoring of timed systems such as asynchronous circuits or real-time programs. We are now working on the following improvements:

- *Online monitoring*: online monitoring has the following advantages over an offline procedure. The first is that it may sometimes declare satisfaction or violation before the simulation terminates when the automaton associated with the formula reaches a sink state (either accepting or rejecting) after reading a prefix of the trace. This can be advantageous when simulation is costly. The second reason to prefer an on-line procedure is when the simulation traces are too big to store in memory [TR04]. Finally, for monitoring real (rather then virtual) systems offline monitoring is not an option. For discrete systems there are various ways to obtain a deterministic ac-ceptor for a formula, e.g. by applying subset construction to the non-deterministic automaton obtained using a tableau-based translation method. Although, in gen-eral, timed automata are not determinizable, monitoring for bounded variability signals is probably possible without generating more and more clocks (see related discussions in [KT04,Tri02,GD00,MP04]).

- *Extending the logic with events*: Adding new atoms such as $p^\uparrow$ and $p^\downarrow$ which hold exactly at times where the signal changes its value, can add expressive power without making monitoring harder. With such atoms we can express properties of bounded variability such as $\Box_{[a,b]}(p^\uparrow \Rightarrow \Box_{[0,d]}p)$ indicating that after becoming true $p$ holds for at least $d$ time.

- *Richer temporal properties*: in the current version of STL, values of $s$ at different time instances can "communicate" only through their Boolean abstractions. This means that one cannot express properties such as $\forall t, t' \cdot (s[t'] - s[t])/(t' - t) < d$. To treat such properties we need to extend the architecture of the monitor beyond Boolean filters to include arithmetical blocks, integrators, etc.

- *Frequency domain properties*: these properties are not temporal in our sense but speak about the spectrum of the signal via some transform such as Fourier or wavelets. It is not hard to construct a simple (non-temporal) logic to express such spectral properties. To monitor them we need to pass the signal first through the transform in question and then check whether the result satisfies the formula. Some of these transforms can be done only offline and some can be dome partially online using a shifting time window.

- *Tighter integration with simulators*: the current implementation is still in the "proof of concept" stage. The monitor is a stand-alone program which interacts with the simulator through the Matlab workspace. In the future versions we will develop a tighter coupling between the monitor and the simulator where the monitor is a Matlab block that can influence the choice of sampling points in order to detect changes in the Boolean abstractions. We will also work on integration with other simulators used in control and circuit design.

**Acknowledgments.** This work benefited from discussions with M. Geilen, S. Tripakis and Y. Lakhnech and from comments of anonymous referees. We thank A. Donzé for his help with the water level controller example.

# References

[ABG⁺00]   Y. Abarbanel, I. Beer, L. Glushovsky, S. Keidar, and Y. Wolfsthal. FoCs: Automatic Generation of Simulation Checkers from Formal Specifications. In *Proc. CAV'00*, pages 538–542. LNCS 1855, Springer, 2000.

[AFH96]   R. Alur, T. Feder, and T.A. Henzinger. The Benefits of Relaxing Punctuality. *Journal of the ACM*, 43(1):116–146, 1996.

[AH92]   R. Alur and T.A. Henzinger. Logics and Models of Real-Time: A Survey. In *Proc. REX Workshop, Real-time: Theory in Practice*, pages 74–106. LNCS 600, Springer, 1992.

[BBDE⁺02]   I. Beer, S. Ben David, C. Eisner, D. Fisman, A. Gringauze, and Y. Rodeh. The Temporal Logic Sugar. In *Proc. CAV'01*. LNCS 2102, Springer, 2102.

[BBF⁺01]   B. Berard, M. Bidoit, A. Finkel, F. Laroussinie, A. Petit, L. Petrucci, Ph. Schnoebelen, and P. McKenzie. *Systems and Software Verification: Model-Checking Techniques and Tools*. Springer, 2001.

[BBKT04]   S. Bensalem, M. Bozga, M. Krichen, and S. Tripakis. Testing Conformance of Real-time Applications with Automatic Generation of Observers. In *Proc. RV'04*. (to appear in ENTCS), 2004.

[Ben02]   P. Bendotti. Steam Generator Water Level Control Problem. Technical report, CC project, 2002.

[CGP99]   E.M. Clarke, O. Grumberg, and D.A. Peled. *Model Checking*. The MIT Press, 1999.

[Don03]   A. Donzé. Etude d'un Modèle de Contrôleur Hybride. Master's thesis, INPG, 2003.

[Dru00]   D. Drusinsky. The Temporal Rover and the ATG Rover. In *Proc. SPIN'00*, pages 323–330. LNCS 1885, Springer, 2000.

[EFH⁺03]   C. Eisner, D. Fisman, J. Havlicek, Y. Lustig, A. McIsaac, and D. Van Campenhout. Reasoning with Temporal Logic on Truncated Paths. In *Proc. CAV'03*, pages 27–39. LNCS 2725, Springer, 2003.

[GD00]   M.C.W. Geilen and D.R. Dams. An On-the-fly Tableau Construction for a Real-time Temporal Logic. In *Proc. FTRTFT'00*, pages 276–290. LNCS 1926, Springer, 2000.

[Gei02]   M.C.W. Geilen. *Formal Techniques for Verification of Complex Real-time Systems*. PhD thesis, Eindhoven University of Technology, 2002.

[Gei03]   M.C.W. Geilen. An Improved On-the-fly Tableau Construction for a Real-time Temporal Logic. In *Proc. CAV'03*, pages 394–406. LNCS 2725, Springer, 2003.

[Hen98]   T.A. Henzinger. It's about Time: Real-time Logics Reviewed. In *Proc. CONCUR'98*, pages 439–454. LNCS 1466, Springer, 1998.

[HR01]   K. Havelund and G. Rosu. Java PathExplorer - a Runtime Verification Tool. In *Proc. ISAIRAS'01*, 2001.

[HR02a]   K. Havelund and G. Rosu, editors. *Runtime Verification RV'02*. ENTCS 70(4), 2002.

[HR02b]   K. Havelund and G. Rosu. Synthesizing Monitors for Safety Properties. In *Proc. TACAS'02*, pages 342–356. LNCS 2280, Springer, 2002.

[KLS⁺02]   M. Kim, I. Lee, U. Sammapun, J. Shin, and O. Sokolsky. Monitoring, Checking, and Steering of Real-time Systems. In *Proc. RV'02*. ENTCS 70(4), 2002.

[KPA03]   K.J. Kristoffersen, C. Pedersen, and H.R. Andersen. Runtime Verification of Timed LTL using Disjunctive Normalized Equation Systems. In *Proc. RV'03*. ENTCS 89(2), 2003.

[KT04]   M. Krichen and S. Tripakis. Black-box Conformance Testing for Real-time Systems. In *Proc. SPIN'04*, pages 109–126. LNCS 2989, Springer, 2004.

[Kur94]    R. Kurshan. *Computer-aided Verification of Coordinating Processes: The Automata-theoretic Approach*. Princeton University Press, 1994.

[Mos99]    P.J. Mosterman. An Overview of Hybrid Simulation Phenomena and their Support by Simulation Packages. In *Proc. HSCC'99*, pages 165–177. LNCS 1569, Springer, 1999.

[MP95]     Z. Manna and A. Pnueli. *Temporal Verification of Reactive Systems: Safety*. Springer, 1995.

[MP04]     O. Maler and A. Pnueli. On Recognizable Timed Languages. In *Proc. FOSSACS'04*, pages 348–362. LNCS 2987, Springer, 2004.

[Pnu03]    A. Pnueli. Verification of Reactive Systems. Lecture Notes, NYU, 2003. http://cs.nyu.edu/courses/fall03/G22.3033-007/lecture4.pdf.

[SV03]     O. Sokolsky and M. Viswanathan, editors. *Runtime Verification RV'03*. ENTCS 89(2), 2003.

[TR04]     P. Thati and G. Rosu. Monitoring Algorithms for Metric Temporal Logic Specifications. In *Proc. of RV'04*, 2004.

[Tri02]    S. Tripakis. Fault Diagnosis for Timed Automata. In *Proc. FTRTFT'02*, pages 205–224. LNCS 2469, Springer, 2002.

[VW86]     M.Y. Vardi and P. Wolper. An Automata-theoretic Approach to Automatic Program Verification. In *Proc. LICS'86*, pages 322–331. IEEE, 1986.

# A Unified Fault-Tolerance Protocol[*]

Paul Miner[1], Alfons Geser[2], Lee Pike[1], and Jeffrey Maddalon[1]

[1] Mail Stop 130, NASA Langley Research Center, Hampton, VA 23681-2199, USA
{paul.s.miner,lee.s.pike,j.m.maddalon}@nasa.gov
[2] National Institute of Aerospace, 144 Research Drive, Hampton, VA 23666, USA
geser@nianet.org

**Abstract.** Davies and Wakerly show that Byzantine fault tolerance can be achieved by a cascade of broadcasts and middle value select functions. We present an extension of the Davies and Wakerly protocol, the *unified protocol*, and its proof of correctness. We prove that it satisfies validity and agreement properties for communication of exact values. We then introduce bounded communication error into the model. Inexact communication is inherent for clock synchronization protocols. We prove that validity and agreement properties hold for inexact communication, and that exact communication is a special case. As a running example, we illustrate the unified protocol using the SPIDER family of fault-tolerant architectures. In particular we demonstrate that the SPIDER interactive consistency, distributed diagnosis, and clock synchronization protocols are instances of the unified protocol.

**Keywords:** fault tolerance, protocol, SPIDER, Byzantine, reliability, Diagnosis, Interactive Consistency.

## 1 Introduction

Safety-critical real-time applications rely on basic fault-tolerant services such as interactive consistency (IC), clock synchronization (CS), and distributed diagnosis (DD, also called group membership). These services are usually rendered by distinct protocols that are designed, implemented, and validated separately. Examples of systems that provide these services are SAFEbus [HD92], TTA [Kop97], and MAFT [KWFT88]. Rushby presents an overview of how several architectures realize these fundamental services [Rus03].

Davies and Wakerly, in their ground-breaking paper [DW78], observed that Byzantine fault tolerance can be achieved through a cascade of middle value select functions. This is true when exact values are communicated, such as the payload messages in IC or the accusations in DD. It is also true when inexact values are communicated. By inexact values we mean values that range over the real numbers that may change by a bounded error during communication.

---

[*] This work was supported by the National Aeronautics and Space Administration under NASA Contract No. NAS1-97046 while the second author was in residence at the National Institute of Aerospace, Hampton, VA 23666, USA.

Y. Lakhnech and S. Yovine (Eds.): FORMATS/FTRTFT 2004, LNCS 3253, pp. 167–182, 2004.

Timing values for CS or analog sensor values are typical examples. Correct operation of a system crucially depends on both exact and inexact communication satisfying suitable validity and agreement properties.

We introduce a generalization and extension of the Davies and Wakerly protocol, which we call the *unified protocol*. Instances of this general protocol provide the core set of fault-tolerant services. We model the unified protocol formally and prove validity and agreement results for both exact and inexact data, under suitable fault assumptions. The exact case is precisely the inexact case with zero accumulated error. We then demonstrate how the unified protocol can be used as a basis for the IC, DD, and CS protocols for the SPIDER fault-tolerant architecture [MMTP02]. We have verified the unified protocol using PVS [ORSvH95], a semi-automated theorem-proving system developed at SRI. The PVS proof files are available on the web [SPI].

The original contributions of this paper include a formally verified generalization of the Davies and Wakerly protocol, adapted to exploit diagnostic information in the context of a hybrid fault model. In addition, we hope to rekindle interest in Davies and Wakerly's results, which provide an effective approach for Byzantine fault tolerance for real-time embedded applications.

The structure of this paper is as follows. Section 2 presents the unified protocol. Section 3 presents the assumptions and requirements for the protocols described in this paper. Section 4 presents the analysis of the protocol for exact communication, and then illustrates how the SPIDER IC and DD protocols are instances of the unified protocol. Section 5 presents the analysis when the communication can introduce error, then demonstrates how the SPIDER CS protocol is an instance of the unified protocol.

## 2    The Unified Protocol

The unified protocol is a multiple stage protocol which is constructed from a single basic operation: a middle value select. In this section, we describe the middle value select function and then present the unified protocol using it. We conclude with a mapping of the unified protocol to the SPIDER fault-tolerant architecture.

A *distributed system* is modeled as a graph with directed edges. Vertices are called *nodes* and directed edges are called *links*. We call $s$ the *source* node, and $d$ the *destination* node of the link $(s, d)$. A *communication stage* is a set of source nodes, a set of destination nodes, and a set of of links between them. The absence of a link is modeled conservatively as a link fault. We allow both nodes and links to fail. However, we abstractly model link failures as failures of the source node [PMMG04].

### 2.1    Notation

We use $i$ or $j$ to refer to an arbitrary stage and $k$ to refer to the total number of stages. In the first stage of a $k$-stage protocol, each member of the set $N^0$ of nodes broadcasts to all members of the set $N^1$ of nodes; in the second stage, each member of $N^1$ broadcasts to all members of $N^2$, and so forth, up through the $k^{th}$ stage. Let us now fix an arbitrary stage $i+1$ for $0 \le i < k$. The set of source nodes is $N^i$, and the set of destination nodes is $N^{i+1}$. We use $s, s_1, s_2, \ldots \in N^i$ to denote source nodes and $d, d_1, d_2, \ldots \in N^{i+1}$ for destination nodes. When we refer to a node without refering to a communication stage, we use $n \in N^i$. In the trivial example of a 0-stage protocol, no communication takes place and $N^0$ is the only set of nodes.

Now we turn our attention to the values that are transfered at each stage. We model payload data using real numbers. We augment the set of reals with certain special values to indicate error conditions. Specifically we define a type $T$ by

$$T = \{receive\_error\} \cup \{source\_error^i \mid i \in \mathbb{N}\} \cup \mathbb{R}.$$

Let $v^i(s) \in T$ denote the value that $s \in N^i$ intends to broadcast in stage $i+1$. After communication in this stage, each destination $d$ has a vector of values $v_d^i$, such that $v_d^i(s)$ is $d$'s estimate of $v^i(s)$. If the message that $d$ receives from $s$ is obviously incorrect (for example, it does not arrive within the expected window or fails a cyclical redundancy check), then $v_d^i(s) = receive\_error$. The value $source\_error^i$ is a special message that is used to report the total absence of credible sources in stage $i+1$.

## 2.2   Middle Value Select

The main computation during the execution of a single stage of the protocol is a middle value select voting algorithm. This algorithm chooses the middle value from the vector of received values, $v_d^i$. For the data type $T$, we extend the natural order on the reals by the relations:

- $receive\_error < source\_error^0$,
- $source\_error^i < source\_error^j$ if $i < j$,
- $source\_error^i < x$ for all $x \in \mathbb{R}$.

Values from sources that are known to be faulty can be excluded from consideration. For this purpose, we define the *filtered eligible sources*, $F_d^i$, to be the set of sources whose values are included in the vote computed by node $d$. If the cardinality of $F_d^i$ is even, any value between the two middle eligible values is an acceptable result, provided that all good nodes implement the same selection function. Let $mvs(F_d^i, v_d^i)$ denote the middle value of the received values from the filtered eligible sources.

## 2.3   Protocol

The unified protocol is composed of a cascade of individual communication stages. A $k$-stage protocol operates on the node sets $N^0, \ldots, N^k$. These sets may or may not be disjoint. For $0 \le i < k$, the algorithm for stage $i+1$ is shown in Figure 1. Each destination node $d$ maintains a set $E_d^i \subseteq N^i$ of *eligible* sources.

The set $E_d^i$ is based, in part, on $d$'s view of the failure status of the sources. Recognize that because of faults and errors during communication, $v_d^i(s)$ may differ from $v^i(s)$.

---

For stage $i + 1$, let $s \in N^i$ and $d \in N^{i+1}$

**Communication:** Each source $s$ broadcasts $v^i(s)$ to all destination nodes. For each destination $d$, $v_d^i(s)$ denotes the value received from source $s$.

**Computation:** Each $d$ computes
1. $I_d^i = \{s \mid v_d^i(s) = receive\_error\}$
2. $F_d^i = E_d^i \setminus I_d^i$
3. $v^{i+1}(d) = \begin{cases} source\_error^i, & \text{if } F_d^i = \emptyset, \\ mvs(F_d^i, v_d^i), & \text{otherwise.} \end{cases}$

---

**Fig. 1.** Unified Protocol.

We assume that all correctly operating nodes share common knowledge of the communication schedule. In order to maintain integrity of the communication schedule, we require that correctly operating nodes be synchronized within a known precision. This synchrony provides a global time reference to manage the system's time-triggered communication. Synchrony is maintained by a CS protocol.

The protocol presented in Figure 1 generalizes the Davies and Wakerly (DW) protocol [DW78]. In the DW protocol, every stage has the same number of nodes. There is no such restriction on the unified protocol. Furthermore, the DW protocol does not use accumulated diagnostic information. At each stage, all nodes vote using identical sets of inputs. In the unified protocol, distinct nodes may compute the vote using nonintersecting vote sets. This capability enables the unified protocol to be analyzed using a weak hybrid fault assumption (see Section 3.4).

## 2.4   Application: SPIDER

The Scalable Processor-Independent Design for Electromagnetic Resilience (SPIDER) is a family of general-purpose fault-tolerant architectures. The SPIDER is designed at NASA Langley Research Center to support laboratory investigations into various recovery strategies from transient failures caused by electromagnetic effects [MMTP02]. The unified protocol is used in SPIDER to implement the IC, CS, and DD protocols. One instance of the SPIDER architecture consists of several Processing Elements (PE) communicating over a Reliable Optical Bus (ROBUS). All application-level functions take place on the PEs. To the PEs, the ROBUS operates as a Time Division Multiple Access (TDMA) broadcast bus.

The topology of the ROBUS is depicted in Figure 2. There are two types of nodes internal to the ROBUS. The Bus Interface Units (BIU) provide the only interface to the PEs. The Redundancy Management Units (RMU) provide the necessary replication for fault tolerance. There is no direct link between any pair of BIUs nor any pair of RMUs.

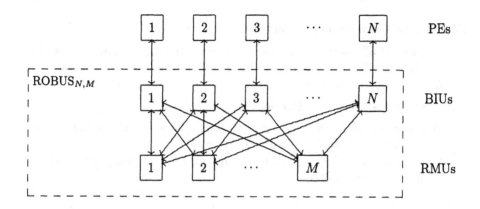

**Fig. 2.** ROBUS architecture.

The primary uses of the unified protocol in the ROBUS are as 2- or 3-stage protocol instances. In a 2-stage instance, three sets of nodes are involved: $N^0, N^1$ and $N^2$. For our subsequent discussions of the ROBUS protocols, $N^0$ corresponds to a subset of the BIUs, $N^1$ corresponds to the RMUs, and $N^2$ corresponds to the BIUs. Communication is initiated from the BIUs (using information from their attached PE) who send their values to the RMUs. The RMUs apply the middle value select and send their results back to the BIUs. The BIUs then apply another middle value select and forward the result to the PEs. Provided the system fault assumptions are maintained, the unified protocol allows the ROBUS to provide strong guarantees about the timeliness and correctness of the communication between the various PEs.

## 3   Protocol Analysis

In this section, we explain the properties the unified protocol must satisfy: validity and agreement. After a description of the fault model, i.e., the covered kinds of faults, we define a fault assumption which constrains the number of faults of each kind. In the succeeding sections, we prove that the correctness conditions hold under this fault assumption.

### 3.1   Correctness Conditions

The unified protocol solves both the distributed consensus problem and the approximate agreement problem, as defined in [Lyn96]. The IC and DD protocols solve specific instances of the distributed consensus problem, and the CS protocol solves a specific instance of the approximate agreement problem. Validity, agreement, and termination conditions are specified for each kind of problem. The unified protocol obviously terminates for a finite number of stages, so we do not formally state or prove this condition.

### Distributed Consensus Properties

**Validity** If all nonfaulty processes start with the same initial value $v \in V$, then $v$ is the only possible decision value for nonfaulty processes.

**Agreement** No two nonfaulty processes decide on different values.

### Approximate Agreement Properties

**Validity** Any decision value for a nonfaulty process is within the range of the initial values of the nonfaulty processes.

**Agreement** The decision values of any pair of nonfaulty processes are within $\varepsilon$ of each other.

### 3.2    Fault Classification

Faults are classified according to the effect they have on the nodes of the system. We use a hybrid fault model from Thambidurai and Park [TP88] with one modification: benign nodes can sometimes behave as good nodes. The particular advantage of this modification is that many intermittent faults are now counted as benign, whence they are easy to mask. The nodes of the system are classified as follows:

**Good** Each good node behaves according to specification; that is, it always sends valid messages.

**Benign** Each benign faulty node either sends detectably incorrect messages to every receiver, or sends valid messages to every receiver.

**Symmetric** A symmetric faulty node may send arbitrary messages, but each receiver receives the same message.

**Asymmetric** An asymmetric (Byzantine) faulty node may send arbitrary messages that may differ for the various receivers.

A node that is not good is called *faulty*. A node is classified according to its worst error manifestation during the classification period. For example, it is possible for an asymmetric faulty node to behave in a manner that is observationally indistinguishable from a good node at times during this period. These classifications form a "behavioral hierarchy" such that benign nodes can behave as if they are good; symmetric nodes can behave as if they are benign or good, etc. We let $G$, $B$, $S$, and $A$ denote the sets of good, benign, symmetric, and asymmetric nodes, respectively.

Good nodes always provide valid messages. Similarly, benign faulty nodes never provide misleading information. We define a set of nodes $C$, such that the worst case error manifestation of a source in $C$ is ommissive[1]. That is, a node in $C$ can send a valid message or an obviously incorrect message, but can never communicate an invalid message. From the definitions above, we know that $G \cup B \subseteq C$.

We attribute all faults to the communication, i.e., we assume that the processing of values by destination nodes is fault-free. We have described the rationale for this abstraction in [PMMG04].

For the analyses presented in sections 4 and 5, we introduce the following definitions and supporting facts. Unless we explicitly state otherwise, we assume $C \cap N^i \neq \emptyset$.

$$v_{max}^i \stackrel{df}{=} \max(\{v^i(n) \mid n \in C \cap N^i\})$$

$$v_{min}^i \stackrel{df}{=} \min(\{v^i(n) \mid n \in C \cap N^i\})$$

**Lemma 1.** *For all $n \in C \cap N^i$, if $v_{min}^i \in \mathbb{R}$, then $v^i(n) \in \mathbb{R}$ .*

**Lemma 2.** *For all $s \in C \cap N^i$ and $d \in C \cap N^j$, if $v_{min}^i, v_{min}^j \in \mathbb{R}$, then*

$$|v^i(s) - v^j(d)| \leq \max(v_{max}^i - v_{min}^i, v_{max}^j - v_{min}^i) .$$

### 3.3   Eligibility Assumptions

In order to have a basis for agreement, we require that the sets of eligible sources differ only with respect to asymmetric sources.

Let $\mathcal{X}$ be a family of sets of nodes. We say that $\mathcal{X}$ satisfies the Eligible Sources Property if all its members differ only in asymmetric nodes.

**Definition 1 (Eligible Sources Property (ESP)).**

$$ESP(\mathcal{X}) \stackrel{df}{=} \forall X_1, X_2 \in \mathcal{X} : n \notin A \implies (n \in X_1 \iff n \in X_2) .$$

Let $I_d^i, F_d^i$ be computed as in Figure 1. The families $\mathcal{E}^i, \mathcal{I}^i, \mathcal{F}^i, 0 \leq i < k$ of sets of *eligible sources*, *ignored sources*, and *filtered eligible sources* are respectively defined as follows:

- $\mathcal{E}^i \stackrel{df}{=} \{E_d^i \mid d \in N^{i+1}\}$ ,
- $\mathcal{I}^i \stackrel{df}{=} \{I_d^i \mid d \in N^{i+1}\}$ ,
- $\mathcal{F}^i \stackrel{df}{=} \{E_d^i \setminus I_d^i \mid d \in N^{i+1}\}$ .

By definition, the filtered eligible sources inherit the Eligible Sources Property from their constituents:

**Lemma 3.** *If $ESP(\mathcal{E}^i)$ and $ESP(\mathcal{I}^i)$, then $ESP(\mathcal{F}^i)$.*

We expect that $\mathcal{E}^i$ is derived from accumulated knowledge about the $s \in N^i$, such that $ESP(\mathcal{E}^i)$. In addition, we expect that the models of communication be analyzed to ensure $ESP(\mathcal{I}^i)$ for all $i$. The property $ESP(\mathcal{F}^i)$ can then be deduced by Lemma 3.

---

[1] Azadmanesh and Kieckhafer [AK00] introduce the notion of a *strictly ommissive asymmetric* faulty node. In future work, we expect to extend our fault model to include this additional classification.

## 3.4  Fault Assumption

Nodes can exhibit incorrect behavior; that is, they can fail. We require an independence of failure between nodes. Moreover we assume that a certain minimum number of nodes are operating correctly. Engineering design and analysis has to guarantee the satisfaction of these assumptions to a specified probability. A DD protocol provides mechanisms that can increase the probability that a sufficient number of nodes are operating correctly [LMK04].

Our fault assumption contains two clauses. Each clause is an assumption used to guarantee that validity and agreement hold. Agreement is established using two different fault assumptions: *agreement propagation* and *agreement generation*. We name the clauses after the proofs in which they play a role.

The first clause is called the *Validity and Propagation Fault Assumption* (VPFA). It states that for each destination and each stage between $j$ and $k$, the majority of eligible, non-benign nodes are good. Formally,

**Definition 2 (Validity and Propagation Fault Assumption (VPFA)).**

$$VPFA(j,k) \stackrel{\mathrm{df}}{=} \forall i : j \leq i < k \implies \forall d \in N^{i+1} : 2|G \cap E_d^i| > |E_d^i \setminus B|.$$

The second clause is called the *Agreement Generation Fault Assumption* (AGFA). It states that some stage between $j$ and $k$ is free of asymmetric, eligible nodes, and that the subsequent stages satisfy the VPFA. Formally,

**Definition 3 (Agreement Generation Fault Assumption(AGFA)).**

$$AGFA(j,k) \stackrel{\mathrm{df}}{=} \exists i : j \leq i < k \wedge ESP(\mathcal{E}^i) \wedge VPFA(i+1,k) \wedge \forall d \in N^{i+1} :$$

$$|A \cap E_d^i| = 0 .$$

We have the following supporting lemmas:

**Lemma 4.** *For $d \in N^{i+1}$, if $2|G \cap E_d^i| > |E_d^i \setminus B|$, then $2|C \cap F_d^i| > |F_d^i|$.*

**Lemma 5.** *For $d_1, d_2 \in N^{i+1}$, if $|A \cap E_{d_1}^i| = |A \cap E_{d_2}^i| = 0$, $ESP(\mathcal{E}^i)$, and $ESP(\mathcal{I}^i)$, then $F_{d_1}^i = F_{d_2}^i$.*

## 3.5  Application: SPIDER

For the ROBUS architecture described in Section 2.4, we let $N^{2i}$ denote the BIUs and $N^{2i+1}$ denote the RMUs, for any $k$-stage SPIDER protocol and $0 \leq i < k$. For $k \geq 2$, the SPIDER Maximum Fault Assumption is $VPFA(j, j+k) \wedge AGFA(j, j+k)$. This is equivalent to the following restatement of the SPIDER Maximum Fault Assumption [GM03]:

1. $2|G \cap E_r| > |E_r \setminus B|$ for all RMUs $r$, and
2. $2|G \cap E_b| > |E_b \setminus B|$ for all BIUs $b$, and
3. $|A \cap E_r| = 0$ for all RMUs $r$, or $|A \cap E_b| = 0$ for all BIUs $b$.

## 4   Exact Agreement

In this section, we analyze the unified protocol assuming exact communications. We prove validity, agreement propagation and agreement generation under two assumptions on the communication. This framework is a special case of inexact communication, addressed in the next section. However, this special case is simpler, so we present it first.

### 4.1   A Model of Exact Communication

For exact communication we assume that destinations receive exactly the messages sent by good sources, that messages from benign faulty sources are either correct or ignored, and that all destinations receive exactly the same messages from non-asymmetric sources.

More formally, we assume the following properties for the communication step in stage $i + 1$:

**Assumption 1** *For all $s \in C \cap N^i$ and $d \in N^{i+1}$,*

- *$s \notin G$ and $v_d^i(s) = receive\_error$, or*
- *$v_d^i(s) = v^i(s)$.*

**Assumption 2** *For all $s \in N^i \setminus A$ and $d_1, d_2 \in N^{i+1}$, $v_{d_1}^i(s) = v_{d_2}^i(s)$.*

These assumptions define an implementation requirement for the communication subsystem for any consensus protocol based on exact communication. The assumptions were constructed to ensure $ESP(\mathcal{I}^i)$.

### 4.2   Exact Agreement Results

In this section, we present the properties of the $k$-stage protocol presented in Section 2.3 using the communication assumptions presented in Section 4.1.

**Theorem 1 (Upper Validity).** *If $VPFA(j, j + k)$, then $v_{\max}^{j+k} \leq v_{\max}^j$.*

*Proof.* By induction on $k$.

The base case, $k = 0$, is trivial, so assume $k > 0$. By the induction hypothesis, we know that $v_{\max}^{j+k-1} \leq v_{\max}^j$. It remains to show that $v_{\max}^{j+k} \leq v_{\max}^{j+k-1}$. Choose $d \in C \cap N^{j+k}$ such that $v^{j+k}(d) = v_{\max}^{j+k}$. By $VPFA(j, j + k)$, we know that $2|G \cap E_d^{j+k-1}| > |E_d^{j+k-1} \setminus B|$. By Lemma 4, we know that $2|C \cap F_d^{j+k-1}| > |F_d^{j+k-1}|$. The pigeonhole principle ensures that there is an $s \in C \cap F_d^{j+k-1}$ such that $v^{j+k}(d) \leq v_d^{j+k-1}(s)$. Assumption 1 ensures that $v_d^{j+k-1}(s) = v^{j+k-1}(s)$. The definition of $v_{\max}^{j+k-1}$ ensures that $v^{j+k-1}(s) \leq v_{\max}^{j+k-1}$. □

**Theorem 2 (Lower Validity).** *If $VPFA(j, j + k)$, then $v_{\min}^j \leq v_{\min}^{j+k}$.*

*Proof.* Similar to the proof of Theorem 1. □

The following corollaries are direct consequences of Theorems 1 and 2.

**Corollary 1 (Consensus Validity).** *If VPFA$(j, j + k)$ and $v_{max}^j = v_{min}^j = v$, then $v_{max}^{j+k} = v_{min}^{j+k} = v$.*

**Corollary 2 (Master-Slave).** *If VPFA$(j, j + k)$, $v_{min}^j \in \mathbb{R}$, and $v_{max}^j - v_{min}^j \leq \Delta$, then for all $s \in C \cap N^j$, $d \in C \cap N^{j+k}$ we have $|v^j(s) - v^{j+k}(d)| \leq \Delta$.*

**Corollary 3 (Agreement Propagation).** *If VPFA$(j, j + k)$, $v_{min}^j \in \mathbb{R}$, and $v_{max}^j - v_{min}^j \leq \Delta$, then $v_{max}^{j+k} - v_{min}^{j+k} \leq \Delta$.*

Corollary 3 ensures that agreement among receivers will be at least as good as the agreement among the sources. However, it does not provide assurance that exact agreement will ever be achieved. Specifically, the presence of an eligible asymmetric faulty node in every stage can prevent exact agreement.

**Theorem 3 (Agreement Generation).** *If AGFA$(j, j + k)$ then $v_{max}^{j+k} = v_{min}^{j+k}$.*

*Proof.* By AGFA$(j, j + k)$, there is a $i < k$ such that VPFA$(j + i + 1, j + k)$, and $|A \cap E_d^{j+i}| = 0$, for all $d \in C \cap N^{j+i+1}$. By Lemma 5, we know that $F_{d_1}^{j+i} = F_{d_2}^{j+i} = F$, for $d_1, d_2 \in C \cap N^{j+i+1}$. Since $F \subseteq N^{j+i} \setminus A$, Assumption 2 ensures that $v_{d_1}^{j+i}(s) = v_{d_2}^{j+i}(s)$ for all $s \in F$. Thus, $v_{max}^{j+i+1} = v_{min}^{j+i+1}$. From Corollary 1, we get $v_{max}^{j+k} = v_{min}^{j+k}$.    □

## 4.3    Application: SPIDER Interactive Consistency

The SPIDER interactive consistency protocol [MMTP02] is an instance of the 2-stage unified protocol. The properties we require of interactive consistency are the distributed consensus properties as defined in Section 3.1.

Let $s$ be some BIU that intends to send a value to all other BIUs. Next let $v^2$ be computed using a 2-stage exchange with $N^0 = \{s\}$, $N^1$ the set of all RMUs, and $N^2$ the set of all BIUs. The interactive consistency protocol for $d \in N^2$ is:

$$ic(d) = \begin{cases} v^2(d), & \text{if } v^2(d) = majority(F_d^1, v_d^1), \\ no\_majority, & \text{otherwise,} \end{cases}$$

where *no_majority* is a distinguished constant.

**Theorem 4 (IC validity).** *If $s \in G$ and VPFA$(0, 2)$, then $ic(d) = v(s)$.*

*Proof.* Since we have a singleton source set, $v_{min}^0 = v_{max}^0 = v(s)$. The result follows directly from Corollary 1 for $k = 2$.    □

**Theorem 5 (IC agreement).** *If AGFA$(0, 2)$, then $ic(d_1) = ic(d_2)$.*

*Proof.* The result follows from Theorem 3 for $k = 2$.    □

In addition, we are able to gather some diagnostic information about the source BIU, $s$. The following corollaries follow from Theorems 4 and 5, respectively.

**Corollary 4.** *If VPFA$(0,2)$ and $ic(d) = source\_error^0$, then $s \notin G$.*

**Corollary 5.** *If AGFA$(0,2)$ and $ic(d) = no\_majority$, then $s \in A$.*

## 4.4    Application: SPIDER Distributed Diagnosis

Distributed on-line diagnosis consists of two main parts. First, nodes accumulate evidence of faulty behavior by other nodes. Second, this local evidence must be reliably distributed to allow for global decisions.

There are several mechanisms for accumulating evidence of faulty behavior. There are indirect mechanisms, such as those provided by Corollaries 4 and 5. There are also several direct accusation mechanisms. These include communication resulting in *receive\_error* and disagreement with results during an agreement propagation stage.

We let $D_n(def) \in \mathbb{N}$ represent node $n$'s accumulated evidence against defendant $def$. If $D_n(def) = 0$, then $n$ has no recent evidence of faulty behavior by $def$. A larger $D_n(def)$ indicates more severe misbehavior by $def$.

We require that a good node can never make a false accusation. Formally, if $n \in C$ and $D_n(def) > 0$, then $def \notin G$. The role of the distributed diagnosis protocol is to achieve global consensus from locally gathered accusations. Strictly speaking, SPIDER does not require a distributed diagnosis protocol. It is possible for the locally gathered accusations to satisfy the required assumptions. However, by periodically exchanging diagnostic information, we can remove accumulated disagreement caused by asymmetric faults. This can increase the probability that our fault assumptions are true, thus increasing the predicted reliability of the system [LMK04].

The SPIDER DD protocol is a 3-stage instance of the unified protocol. The first two stages are to assure agreement among the BIUs. The third stage is to propagate this consensus diagnostic information to the RMUs.

Let $v^0(b) = D_b(def)$, and $v^2$ and $v^3$ be computed using the 3-stage unified protocol. Thus, $v^0_{max}$ is the most severe correct local accusation against $def$ and $v^0_{min}$ is the least severe accusation.

**Theorem 6 (DD Validity).** *If VPFA$(0,3)$, then for $b \in C \cap N^2$, $r \in C \cap N^3$,*

- *If $v^2(b) > 0$, then $def \notin G$.*
- *If $v^3(r) > 0$, then $def \notin G$.*

*Proof.* Both clauses are direct consequences of Theorems 1 and 2.    □

**Theorem 7 (DD Agreement).** *If AGFA$(0,3)$ then for $b \in C \cap N^2$, $r \in C \cap N^3$, $v^2(b) = v^3(r)$.*

*Proof.* Follows from Theorem 3 and Corollary 1.    □

The preceding results ensure consensus based on the BIUs local accusations against *def*. A similar protocol beginning with the RMUs ensures consensus based on the RMUs accusations against *def*. The maximum of the two results also satisfies validity and agreement.

## 5   Approximate Agreement

In this section we generalize the exact communication assumptions to accommodate error introduced in the communication phase. The results in Section 4 are all special cases of the results introduced in this section.

Analog information can be understood as a real valued, uniformly continuous function of time [Ros68]. Uniform continuity roughly means that the rate of change is bounded. For processing in a digital system, a digital approximation of the function value at a given moment is determined: the function is *sampled*. There are various sources of imprecision. For instance, the actual time of sampling may vary or the sampled value may be superposed with noise. The purpose of the inexact protocol is to reliably communicate values that may vary and may be further distorted during communication.

### 5.1   A Model of Inexact Communication

We model communication as in the exact case, but add terms representing the inherent imprecision of broadcasting inexact information. The error terms $\varepsilon_l, \varepsilon_u$, and $\varepsilon$ are nonnegative reals. We define $\varepsilon \stackrel{\mathrm{df}}{=} \varepsilon_l + \varepsilon_u$.

We assume that messages from good nodes are correctly received within a known error tolerance, that messages from benign faulty nodes are either ignored or are correctly received within a known tolerance, and that only asymmetric nodes may introduce disagreement beyond $\varepsilon$ in the communication phase. We allow the communication error bounds, $\varepsilon_l$ and $\varepsilon_u$, to differ as the error may be biased. Formally, the assumptions for stage $i + 1$ are:

**Assumption 3** *For all $s \in C \cap N^i$ and $d \in N^{i+1}$:*

  - $s \notin G$ *and* $v^i_d(s) = receive\_error$,
  - $receive\_error < v^i_d(s) = v^i(s) < source\_error^i$, *or*
  - $v^i(s) \in \mathbb{R}$ *and* $v^i(s) - \varepsilon_l \leq v^i_d(s) \leq v^i(s) + \varepsilon_u$.

**Assumption 4** *If $s \in N^i \setminus A$, then for $d_1, d_2 \in N^{i+1}$:*

  - $v^i_{d_1}(s) = v^i_{d_2}(s) < source\_error^i$, *or*
  - $v^i_{d_1}(s), v^i_{d_2}(s) \in \mathbb{R}$ *and* $|v^i_{d_1}(s) - v^i_{d_2}(s)| \leq \varepsilon$.

When $\varepsilon = \varepsilon_l = \varepsilon_u = 0$, Assumptions 3 and 4 reduce to Assumptions 1 and 2. Thus, exact communication is a special case of inexact communication.

## 5.2    Approximate Agreement Results

The following results generalize the results from Section 4.2, by introducing the effects of bounded errors. By requiring $v_{min}^j \in \mathbb{R}$ for these results, we avoid the clutter of defining arithmetic involving *source_error*. These results can be extended to handle such special cases.

**Theorem 8 (Inexact Upper Validity).** *If VPFA$(j, j+k)$ and $v_{min}^j \in \mathbb{R}$, then*

$$v_{max}^{j+k} \leq v_{max}^j + k\varepsilon_u.$$

*Proof.* Similar to proof of Theorem 1.                                                       □

**Theorem 9 (Inexact Lower Validity).** *If VPFA$(j, j+k)$ and $v_{min}^j \in \mathbb{R}$, then*

$$v_{min}^j - k\varepsilon_l \leq v_{min}^{j+k}.$$

*Proof.* Similar to proof of Theorem 1.                                                       □

**Corollary 6 (Inexact Master-Slave).** *If VPFA$(j, j + k)$, $v_{min}^j \in \mathbb{R}$, and $v_{max}^j - v_{min}^j \leq \Delta$, then for all $s \in C \cap N^j$, $d \in C \cap N^{j+k}$ we have*

$$|v^j(s) - v^{j+k}(d)| \leq \Delta + \max(k\varepsilon_l, k\varepsilon_u).$$

*Proof.* Follows directly from Lemma 2 and Theorems 8 and 9.                                 □

**Corollary 7 (Inexact Agreement Propagation).** *If VPFA$(j, j+k)$, $v_{min}^j \in \mathbb{R}$, and $v_{max}^j - v_{min}^j \leq \Delta$, then*

$$v_{max}^{j+k} - v_{min}^{j+k} \leq \Delta + k\varepsilon.$$

*Proof.* From Theorems 8 and 9, we have $v_{max}^{j+k} - v_{min}^{j+k} \leq (v_{max}^j + k\varepsilon_u) - (v_{min}^j - k\varepsilon_l) \leq \Delta + k\varepsilon$.                                                       □

**Theorem 10 (Inexact Agreement Generation).** *If AGFA$(j, j + k)$ and $v_{min}^{j+k} \in \mathbb{R}$, then*

$$v_{max}^{j+k} - v_{min}^{j+k} \leq k\varepsilon.$$

*Proof.* Similar to proof of Theorem 3.                                                       □

## 5.3    Application: SPIDER Synchronization Protocol

A clock is formalized as a function from clock time to real time. Clocks distributed in a system need to be re-synchronized periodically in order to prevent them from drifting too far apart. The two goals of synchronization are:

**Accuracy.** All good clock readings are within a linear envelope of real time.
**Precision.** At all times, the clock times of all good clocks differ by a bounded amount.

Prior formal models of fault tolerant clock synchronization [SvH98,Min93,Sha92] have established a systematic way to derive accuracy and precision from the following properties:

**Accuracy Preservation.** The resynchronization time of a good clock is within the expected resynchronization times of good clocks, up to an error margin.

**Precision Enhancement.** If the skew of good clocks is within a known bound at the time of protocol execution, then all good clocks are synchronized to within a tighter skew after protocol execution

Below we show how to prove accuracy preservation and precision enhancement, using validity and agreement properties of the unified protocol. The values communicated during this protocol are estimates of the real time that nodes should reset their clocks for the next period.

Let $c_n(T^{p+1}) \in \mathbb{R}$ denote the real time that node $n$ expects to begin synchronization period $p + 1$. Let $c'_n(T^{p+1})$ denote the real time that node $n$ actually begins period $p + 1$. Put another way, $c_n$ models $n$'s clock before resynchronization, and $c'_n$ models $n$'s clock after resynchronization.

The SPIDER synchronization protocol is a 3-stage instance of the unified protocol. The BIUs are $N^0$ and $N^2$, the RMUs are $N^1$ and $N^3$. Let $v^0(b_0) = c_{b_0}(T^{p+1})$, for BIU $b_0 \in N^0$. Then, for all $b \in N^2$, $r \in N^3$, define

$$c'_b(T^{p+1}) \stackrel{\text{df}}{=} v^2(b)$$

$$c'_r(T^{p+1}) \stackrel{\text{df}}{=} v^3(r)$$

The values $\varepsilon_l$ and $\varepsilon_u$ bound the variation of clock readings caused by drift, jitter, and differences in communication delay. Let $c_{\min}(p)$ and $c_{\max}(p)$ denote the minimal and maximal values of all $c_b(T^{p+1})$ such that $c_b$ is a correct BIU clock at round $p$.

Within the ROBUS, we are principally concerned with the accuracy of the BIUs, as these provide time references for the PEs. If needed, a similar argument can be used to bound the accuracy of the RMUs.

**Theorem 11 (BIU Accuracy Preservation).** *If VPFA(0, 2) holds during synchronization period $p$, then for all good BIU clocks $c'_b$:*

$$c_{\min}(p) - 2\varepsilon_l \leq c'_b(T^{p+1}) \leq c_{\max}(p) + 2\varepsilon_u.$$

*Proof.* Follows immediately from Theorems 8 and 9.     □

Precision results are given for the set of BIUs, the set of RMUs, and between the BIUs and RMUs. This last result provides the skew bounds necessary to reliably communicate within the ROBUS.

**Theorem 12 (Precision Enhancement).** *If AGFA(0, 3) then*

1. $|c'_{b_1}(T^{p+1}) - c'_{b_2}(T^{p+1})| \leq 2\varepsilon,$
2. $|c'_{r_1}(T^{p+1}) - c'_{r_2}(T^{p+1})| \leq 2\varepsilon,$
3. $|c'_b(T^{p+1}) - c'_r(T^{p+1})| \leq 2\varepsilon + \max(\varepsilon_l, \varepsilon_u).$

*Proof.* Clauses 1 and 2 each follow from Theorem 10 (Clause 1 using $AGFA(0,2)$, and Clause 2 using $AGFA(1,3)$). Clause 3 is a consequence of Clause 1 and Corollary 6.                                                                          □

## 6    Concluding Remarks

We introduce a formal model of an extension of the Davies and Wakerly protocol, called the *unified protocol*. We prove that under a weak hybrid fault assumption, the unified protocol satisfies validity and agreement, both for exact and inexact communication. Three fundamental fault-tolerant protocols are shown to be instances of the unified protocol.

With the unified protocol, the analysis of fault-tolerance properties can be restricted to one general protocol. In this way, the unified protocol provides a useful abstraction layer: the analysis of the fault tolerance is not complicated by specific concerns of individual protocols. For the SPIDER architecture, this has resulted in simpler specifications. This in turn yields a simpler implementation and more transparent treatment of the separate functions. Although we have not yet performed the analysis, we believe that the SPIDER transient recovery and restart protocols are also instances of the unified protocol.

The unified protocol is flexible and can be adapted to other fault tolerant applications. In particular, it should be possible to adapt some of the arguments provided by Caspi and Salem [CS00] to bound the effects of computation error for locally computed control functions between communication stages.

In addition, we expect that our results may be extended to analyze other architectures. Similar arguments may be constructed under weaker fault assumptions. In particular, we intend to explore the benefits of extending our analysis to incorporate the strictly ommissive asymmetric classification introduced by Azadmanesh and Kieckhafer [AK00]. We also plan to explore a wider range of fault tolerant averaging functions within our PVS framework. Ultimately, we intend to provide a PVS library of reusable fault tolerance results.

## References

[AK00]    Mohammad H. Azadmanesh and Roger M. Kieckhafer. Exploiting omissive faults in synchronous approximate agreement. *IEEE Transactions on Computers*, 49(10):1031–1042, 2000.

[CS00]    Paul Caspi and Rym Salem. Threshold and bounded-delay voting in critical control systems. In Mathai Joseph, editor, *FTRTFT*, volume 1926 of *Lecture Notes in Computer Science*, pages 70–81. Springer, 2000.

[DW78]    Daniel Davies and John F. Wakerly. Synchronization and matching in redundant systems. *IEEE Transactions on Computers*, 27(6):531–539, June 1978.

[GM03]    Alfons Geser and Paul S. Miner. A new on-line diagnosis protocol for the SPIDER family of Byzantine fault tolerant architectures. Technical Memorandum NASA/TM-2003-212432, NASA Langley Research Center, Hampton, VA, December 2003. In print.

[HD92]      Kenneth Hoyme and Kevin Driscoll. SAFEbus$^{TM}$. In *11th AIAA/IEEE Digital Avionics Systems Conference*, pages 68–73, Seattle, WA, October 1992.

[Kop97]     Hermann Kopetz. *Real-Time Systems*. Kluwer Academic Publishers, 1997.

[KWFT88]    R. M. Kieckhafer, C. J. Walter, A. M. Finn, and P. M. Thambidurai. The MAFT architecture for distributed fault tolerance. *IEEE Transactions on Computers*, 37(4):398–405, April 1988.

[LMK04]     Elizabeth Latronico, Paul Miner, and Philip Koopman. Quantifying the reliability of proven SPIDER group membership service guarantees. In *Proceedings of the International Conference on Dependable Systems and Networks*, June 2004.

[Lyn96]     Nancy A. Lynch. *Distributed Algorithms*. Morgan Kaufmann, 1996.

[Min93]     Paul S. Miner. Verification of fault-tolerant clock synchronization systems. NASA Technical Paper 3349, NASA Langley Research Center, Hampton, VA, November 1993.

[MMTP02]    Paul S. Miner, Mahyar Malekpour, and Wilfredo Torres-Pomales. Conceptual design of a Reliable Optical BUS (ROBUS). In *21st AIAA/IEEE Digital Avionics Systems Conference DASC*, Irvine, CA, October 2002.

[ORSvH95]   Sam Owre, John Rushby, Natarajan Shankar, and Friedrich von Henke. Formal verification for fault-tolerant architectures: Prolegomena to the design of PVS. *IEEE Transactions on Software Engineering*, 21(2):107–125, February 1995.

[PMMG04]    Lee Pike, Jeffrey Maddalon, Paul Miner, and Alfons Geser. Abstractions for fault-tolerant distributed system verification. In *Proceedings of Theorem-Proving in Higher-Order Logics (TPHOLs)*. Theorem Proving in Higher-Order Logics (TPHOLs), 2004. Accepted. Available at http://shemesh.larc.nasa.gov/fm/spider/spider_pubs.html.

[Ros68]     Maxwell Rosenlicht. *Introduction to Analysis*. Dover Publications, Inc., 1968.

[Rus03]     John Rushby. A comparison of bus architectures for safety-critical embedded systems. Technical Report NASA/CR-2003-212161, NASA Langley Research Center, Hampton, VA, March 2003.

[Sha92]     Natarajan Shankar. Mechanical verification of a generalized protocol for Byzantine fault-tolerant clock synchronization. In J. Vytopil, editor, *Formal Techniques in Real-Time and Fault-Tolerant Systems*, volume 571 of *Lecture Notes in Computer Science*, pages 217–236, Nijmegen, The Netherlands, January 1992. Springer-Verlag.

[SPI]       SPIDER homepage, NASA Langley Research Center, Formal Methods Team. Available at http://shemesh.larc.nasa.gov/fm/spider/.

[SvH98]     Detlef Schwier and Friedrich von Henke. Mechanical verification of clock synchronization algorithms. In Anders P. Ravn and Hans Rischel, editors, *Formal Techniques in Real-Time and Fault-Tolerant Systems*, number 1486 in LNCS, pages 262–271. Springer, September 1998.

[TP88]      Philip Thambidurai and You-Keun Park. Interactive consistency with multiple failure modes. In *7th Reliable Distributed Systems Symposium*, pages 93–100, October 1988.

# Automating the Addition
# of Fail-Safe Fault-Tolerance:
# Beyond Fusion-Closed Specifications

Felix C. Gärtner[1,*] and Arshad Jhumka[2]

[1] RWTH Aachen, Lehr- und Forschungsgebiet Informatik 4
D-52056 Aachen, Germany
fcg@acm.org
[2] Chalmers University of Technology, Department of Computer Science
41296, Göteborg, Sweden
arshad@cs.chalmers.se

**Abstract.** The fault tolerance theories by Arora and Kulkarni [3] and by Jhumka *et al.* [8] view a fault-tolerant program as the composition of a fault-intolerant program with fault tolerance components called *detectors* and *correctors*. At their core, the theories assume that the correctness specifications under consideration are *fusion closed*. In general, fusion closure of specifications can be achieved by adding *history variables*. However, the addition of history variables causes an exponential growth of the state space of the program, causing addition of fault tolerance to be expensive. To redress this problem, we present a method which can be used to add history information to a program in a way that significantly reduces the number of additional states. Hence, automated methods that add fault tolerance can be efficiently applied in environments where specifications are not necessarily fusion closed.

## 1 Introduction

It is an established engineering method in computer science to generate complicated things from simpler things. This technique has been applied in the area of fault-tolerant distributed systems. The goal is to start off with a system which is not fault-tolerant for certain kinds of faults and use a sound procedure to transform it into a program which is fault-tolerant. To this end, Arora and Kulkarni [3] developed a theory of fault tolerance, whereby fault tolerance is achieved by composing a fault-intolerant program with two types of fault tolerance components called *detectors* and *correctors*. Intuitively, a detector is used to detect a certain (error) condition on the system state and a corrector is used to bring the system into a valid state again. Since common fault tolerance methods like triple modular redundancy or error correcting codes can be modeled by using detectors and correctors, the theory can be viewed as an abstraction of many existing fault tolerance techniques.

---

* Felix Gärtner was supported by Deutsche Forschungsgemeinschaft (DFG) as part of "Graduiertenkolleg ISIA" at TU Darmstadt and by an Emmy Noether postdoc scholarship at the Distributed Programming Laboratory, EPFL, Switzerland.

Y. Lakhnech and S. Yovine (Eds.): FORMATS/FTRTFT 2004, LNCS 3253, pp. 183–198, 2004.

Kulkarni and Arora [9] and more recently Jhumka *et al.* [8] proposed methods to automate the addition of detectors and correctors to a fault-intolerant program. The basic idea of these methods is to perform a state space analysis of the fault-affected program and change its transition relation in such a way that it still satisfies its (weakened) specification in the presence of faults. These changes result in either the removal of transitions to satisfy a safety specification or the addition of transitions to satisfy a liveness specification. A critical prerequisite for this to work is the assumption that the correctness specifications are *fusion closed*.

Fusion closure means that the next step of a program merely depends on the current state and not on the previous history of the execution. For example, given a program with a single variable $x \in \mathbb{N}$, then the specification "never $x = 1$" is fusion closed while the specification "$x = 4$ implies that previously $x = 2$" is not. Specifications written in the popular Unity Logic [5] are fusion closed [7], as are specifications consisting of state transition systems (like C programs). But general temporal logic formulas which are usually used in the area of fault-tolerant program synthesis and refinement [4, 11, 12] are not. Arora and Kulkarni [3, p. 75] originally argued that this assumption is not restrictive in the sense that for every non-fusion closed specification there exists an "equivalent" specification which is fusion closed if it is allowed to add *history variables* to the program. History variables are additional control variables which are used to record the previous state sequence of an execution and hence can be used to answer the question of, e.g., "has the program been in state $x = 2$?". Using such a history variable $h$ the example above which was not fusion closed can be rephrased in a fusion-closed fashion as "never $(x = 4$ and $(x = 2) \notin h)$". However, these history variables add states to the program.

There are obvious "brute force" approaches on how to add history information like the one sketched above where the history variable remembers the entire previous state sequence of an execution. However, history variables must be implemented which is costly since they exponentially enlarge the state space of the fault-intolerant program. So, we are interested in adding as little additional states as possible.

In this paper, we present a method to add history states to a program in a way which avoids exponential growth of the state space, but rather causes a polynomial increase in the size of the state space in the worst case. More specifically, we start with a problem specification $SPEC_1$ which is *not* fusion closed, a program $\Sigma_1$ which satisfies $SPEC_1$ and a class of faults $F$. Depending on $F$ we show how to transform $SPEC_1$ and $\Sigma_1$ into $SPEC_2$ and $\Sigma_2$ in such a way that (a) $SPEC_2$ is fusion closed, (b) $\Sigma_2$ can be made fault tolerant for $SPEC_2$ iff $\Sigma_1$ can be made fault tolerant for $SPEC_1$, and (c) $\Sigma_2$ is (in a certain sense) minimal with respect to the added states. We restrict our attention to cases where $SPEC$ is a safety property and therefore are only concerned with what Arora and Kulkarni call *fail-safe fault tolerance* [3]. The programs which we consider are non-deterministic state machines and so our application domain is that of distributed or concurrent systems.

The benefit of the proposed method is the following: Firstly, it makes the methods which automatically add detectors [8, 9] amendable to specifications which are not fusion closed and closes a gap in the applicability of the detector/corrector theory [3]. And secondly, the presented method offers further insight into the efficiency of the basic mechanisms which are applied in fault tolerance.

The paper is structured as follows: We first present some preliminary definitions in Section 2 and then discuss the assumption of fusion closure in Section 3. In Section 4 we study specifications which are not fusion closed and sketch a method which makes these types of specifications efficiently manageable in the context of automated methods which add fault tolerance. Finally, Section 5 presents some open problems and directions for future work. For lack of space, we only give proof sketches for theorems and lemmas. The detailed proofs can be found in the full version of this work [6].

## 2    Formal Preliminaries

*States, Traces and Properties.* The *state space* of a program is an unstructured finite nonempty set $C$ of states. A *state predicate over* $C$ is a boolean predicate over $C$. A *state transition over* $C$ is a pair $(r, s)$ of states from $C$.

In the following, let $C$ be a state set and $T$ be a state transition set. We define a *trace over* $C$ to be a non-empty sequence $s_1, s_2, s_3, \ldots$ of states over $C$. We sometimes use the notation $s_i$ to refer to the $i$-th element of a trace. Note that traces can be finite or infinite. We will always use Greek letters to denote traces and normal lowercase letters to denote states. For two traces $\alpha$ and $\beta$, we write $\alpha \cdot \beta$ to mean the concatenation of the two traces. We say that a transition $t$ occurs in some trace $\sigma$ if there exists an $i$ such that $(s_i, s_{i+1}) = t$.

We define a *property over* $C$ to be a set of traces over $C$. A trace $\sigma$ *satisfies* a property $P$ iff $\sigma \in P$. If $\sigma$ does not satisfy $P$ we say that $\sigma$ *violates* $P$. There are two important types of properties called *safety* and *liveness* [2, 10]. In this paper, we are only concerned with safety properties. Informally spoken, a safety property demands that "something bad never happens" [10], i.e., it rules out a set of unwanted trace prefixes. Mutual exclusion and deadlock freedom are two prominent examples of safety properties. Formally, a property $S$ over $C$ is a *safety property* iff for each trace $\sigma$ which violates $S$ there exists a prefix $\alpha$ of $\sigma$ such that for all traces $\beta$, $\alpha \cdot \beta$ violates $S$.

*Programs, Specifications and Correctness.* We define programs as state transition systems consisting of a state set $C$, a set of initial states $I \subseteq C$ and a transition relation $T$ over $C$, i.e., a *program* (sometimes also called *system*) is a triple $\Sigma = (C, I, T)$. The state predicate $I$ together with the state transition set $T$ describe a safety property $S$, i.e., all traces which are constructable by starting in a state in $I$ and using only state transitions from $T$. We denote this property by *safety-prop*$(\Sigma)$. For brevity, we sometimes write $\Sigma$ instead of *safety-prop*$(\Sigma)$. A state $s \in C$ of a program $\Sigma$ is *reachable* iff there exists a trace $\sigma \in \Sigma$ such that $s$ occurs in $\sigma$. Otherwise $s$ is *non-reachable*. Sometimes we will call a non-reachable state *redundant*.

We define specifications to be properties, i.e., a *specification over $C$* is a property over $C$. A *safety specification* is a specification which is a safety property. Unlike Arora and Kulkarni [3], we do *not* assume that problem specifications are fusion closed. Fusion closure is defined as follows: Let $C$ be a state set, $s \in C$, $X$ be property over $C$, $\alpha$, $\gamma$ finite state sequences, and $\beta$, $\delta$, $\sigma$ be state sequences over $C$. A set $X$ is *fusion closed* if the following holds: If $\alpha \cdot s \cdot \beta$ and $\gamma \cdot s \cdot \delta$ are in $X$ then $\alpha \cdot s \cdot \delta$ and $\gamma \cdot s \cdot \beta$ are also in $X$.

It is easy to see that for every program $\Sigma$ holds that *safety-prop*$(\Sigma)$ is fusion closed. Intuitively, fusion closure means that the entire history of every trace is present in every state of the trace. We will give examples for fusion closed and not fusion closed specifications later.

We say that program $\Sigma$ *satisfies* specification *SPEC* iff all traces in $\Sigma$ satisfy *SPEC*. Consequently, we say that $\Sigma$ *violates* *SPEC* iff there exists a trace $\sigma \in \Sigma$ which violates *SPEC*.

*Extensions.* Given some program $\Sigma_1 = (C_1, I_1, T_1)$ our goal is to define the notion of a fault-tolerant version $\Sigma_2$ of $\Sigma_1$ meaning that $\Sigma_2$ does exactly what $\Sigma_1$ does in fault-free scenarios and has additional fault tolerance abilities which $\Sigma_1$ lacks. Sometimes, $\Sigma_2 = (C_2, I_2, T_2)$ will have additional states (i.e., $C_2 \supset C_1$) and for this case we must define what these states "mean" with respect to the original program $\Sigma_1$. This is done using a *state projection function* $\pi : C_2 \mapsto C_1$ which tells which states of $\Sigma_2$ are "the same" with respect to states of $\Sigma_1$. A state projection function can be naturally extended to traces and properties, e.g., for a trace $s_1, s_2, \ldots$ over $C_2$ holds that $\pi(s_1, s_2, \ldots) = \pi(s_1), \pi(s_2), \ldots$

We say that a program $\Sigma_1 = (C_1, I_1, T_1)$ *extends* a program $\Sigma_2 = (C_2, I_2, T_2)$ using state projection $\pi$ iff the following conditions hold[1]:

1. $C_2 \supseteq C_1$,
2. $\pi$ is a total mapping from $C_2$ to $C_1$ (for simplicity we assume that for any $s \in C_1$ holds that $\pi(s) = s$), and
3. $\pi(\textit{safety-prop}(\Sigma_2)) = \textit{safety-prop}(\Sigma_1)$.

If $\Sigma_2$ extends $\Sigma_1$ using $\pi$ and $\Sigma_1$ satisfies *SPEC* then obviously $\pi(\Sigma_2)$ satisfies *SPEC*. When it is clear from the context that $\Sigma_2$ extends $\Sigma_1$ we will simply say that $\Sigma_2$ satisfies *SPEC* instead of "$\pi(\Sigma_2)$ satisfies *SPEC*".

*Fault Models.* We define a fault model $F$ as being a program transformation, i.e., a mapping $F$ from programs to programs. We require that a fault model does not tamper with the set of initial states, i.e., we rule out "immediate" faults that occur before the system is switched on. We also restrict ourselves to the case where $F$ "adds" transitions, since this is the only way to violate a safety

---

[1] The concept of extension is related to the notion of *refinement* [1]. Extensions are refinements with the additional property that the original state space is preserved and that there is no notion of *stuttering* [1].

specification. Formally, a *fault model* is a mapping $F$ which maps a program $\Sigma = (C, I, T)$ to a program $F(\Sigma) = (F(C), F(I), F(T))$ such that the following conditions hold:

1. $F(C) = C$
2. $F(I) = I$
3. $F(T) \supset T$

The resulting program is called the *fault-affected version* or the *program in the presence of faults*. We say that a program $\Sigma$ is *F-intolerant with respect to SPEC* iff $\Sigma$ satisfies *SPEC* but $F(\Sigma)$ violates *SPEC*.

Given two programs $\Sigma_1$ and $\Sigma_2$ such that $\Sigma_2$ extends $\Sigma_1$ and a fault model $F$, it makes sense to assume that $F$ treats $\Sigma_1$ and $\Sigma_2$ in a "similar way". Basically, this means that $F$ should at least add the same transitions to $\Sigma_1$ and $\Sigma_2$. But with respect to the possible new states of $\Sigma_2$ it can possibly add new fault transitions. This models faults which occur within the error detection and correction mechanisms. Formally, a fault model $F$ must be *extension monotonic*, i.e., for any two programs $\Sigma_1 = (C_1, I_1, T_1)$ and $\Sigma_2 = (C_2, I_2, T_2)$ such that $\Sigma_2$ extends $\Sigma_1$ using $\pi$ holds:

$$F(T_1) \setminus T_1 \subseteq F(T_2) \setminus T_2$$

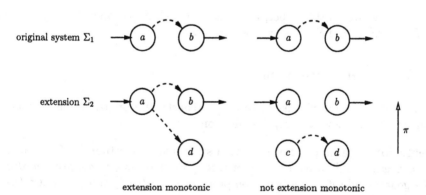

extension monotonic          not extension monotonic

**Fig. 1.** Examples for extension monotonic and not extension monotonic fault models.

An example is given in Fig. 1. The original system is given at the top and the extension is given below (the state projection is implied by vertical orientation, i.e., states which are vertically aligned are mapped to the same state by $\pi$). In the left example the fault model is extension monotonic since all fault transitions in $\Sigma_1$ are also in $\Sigma_2$. The right example is not extension monotonic. Intuitively, an extension monotonic fault model maintains at least its original transitions over extensions.

The extension monotonicity requirement does not restrict faulty behavior on the new states of the extension. However, we have to restrict this type of behavior since it would be impossible to build fault-tolerant versions otherwise. In this paper we assume a very general type of restriction: it basically states that in any infinite sequence of extensions of the original program there is always some point where $F$ does not introduce new fault transitions anymore. Formally, an extension monotonic fault model $F$ is *finite* iff for any infinite sequence of programs $\Sigma_1, \Sigma_2, \ldots$ such that for all $i$, $\Sigma_{i+1}$ extends $\Sigma_i$ holds that there exists a $j$ such that for all $k \geq j$ no new fault transition is introduced in $\Sigma_k$, i.e., $F(T_{k+1}) \setminus T_{k+1} = F(T_k) \setminus T_k$. Finite fault models are those for which infinite redundancy is not needed for fault tolerance. We assume our fault model to be finite and extension monotonic.

*Fault-tolerant Versions.* Now we are able to define a *fault-tolerant version*. It captures the idea of starting with some program $\Sigma_1$ which is fault-intolerant regarding a specification *SPEC* and some fault model $F$. A fault-tolerant version $\Sigma_2$ of $\Sigma_1$ is a program which has the same behavior as $\Sigma_1$ if no faults occur, but additionally satisfies *SPEC* in the presence of faults. Formally, a program $\Sigma_2$ the *F-tolerant version* of program $\Sigma_1$ for *SPEC* using state projection $\pi$ iff the following conditions hold:

1. $\Sigma_1$ is $F$-intolerant with respect to $F$,
2. $\Sigma_2$ extends $\Sigma_1$ using $\pi$,
3. $F(\Sigma_2)$ satisfies *SPEC*.

In the remainder of this paper, $F$ is a fault model, $\Sigma$, $\Sigma_1$ and $\Sigma_2$ are programs, *SPEC*, $SPEC_1$ and $SPEC_2$ are specifications.

## 3   Problem Statement

The basic task we would like to solve is to construct a fault-tolerant version for a given program and a safety specification.

**Definition 1 (general fail-safe transformation problem).** *Given a program $\Sigma$ which is F-intolerant with respect to a general safety specification SPEC. The general fail-safe transformation problem consists of finding a fault-tolerant version of $\Sigma$.*

*Solutions for Fusion-Closed Specifications.* The basic mechanism which Kulkarni and Arora [9] and Jhumka et al. [8] apply is the creation of non-reachable transitions. Both approaches assume that *SPEC* is fusion closed which implies that safety specifications can be concisely represented by a set of "bad" transitions [3, 7]. Since $F(\Sigma)$ violates *SPEC*, there must exist executions in which a specified bad transition occurs, which must be prevented. So, for all bad transitions $t = (d, b)$ the mentioned approaches make either state $d$ or state $b$ unreachable in $F(\Sigma_2)$. If this is impossible without changing the behavior of $\Sigma$, then no fault-tolerant version exists.

*Adding History Variables.* Consider program with one variable $x$ which can take five different values (integers 0 to 4) and simply proceeds from state $x = 0$ to $x = 4$ through all intermediate states. The fault assumption $F$ has added one transition from $x = 1$ to $x = 3$ to the transition relation. Now consider the correctness specification $SPEC =$ "always ($x = 4$ implies that previously $x = 2$)". Note that $F(\Sigma)$ does not satisfy $SPEC$ (i.e., $F(\Sigma)$ can reach state $x = 4$ without having been in state $x = 2$), and that $SPEC$ is not fusion closed. To see the latter, consider the two traces $0, 3, 2, 4$ and $2, 3, 4$ from $SPEC$. The fusion at state $x = 3$ yields trace $0, 3, 4$ which is not in $SPEC$. Since $SPEC$ is not fusion closed, we cannot apply the known transformation methods [8, 9].

The specification can be made fusion closed by adding a history variable $h$ which records the entire state history. Now $SPEC$ can be rephrased as $SPEC =$ "always ($x = 4$ implies $\langle 2 \rangle \in h$)" or, equivalently:

$$SPEC = \text{"never } (x = 4 \text{ and } \langle 2 \rangle \notin h)\text{"}$$

Now we can identify a set of bad transitions which must be prevented, e.g., from state $x = 3 \wedge h = \langle 1 \rangle$ to state $x = 4 \wedge h = \langle 1, 3 \rangle$. In this way bad transitions are prevented and the modified system satisfies $SPEC$ in the presence faults.

*Problems with History Variables.* Adding a history variable $h$ in the previous example adds states to the state space of the system. In fact, defining the domain of $h$ as the set of all sequences over $\{0, 1, 2, 3, 4\}$ adds infinitely many states. Clearly this can be reduced by the observation that if faults do not corrupt $h$, then $h$ will only take on five different values ($\langle \rangle$, $\langle 1 \rangle$, $\langle 1, 2 \rangle$, $\langle 1, 2, 3 \rangle$, and $\langle 1, 2, 3, 4 \rangle$). But still, the state space has been increased from five states to $5^2 = 25$ states.

Note that $\Sigma_2$ has redundant states and $\Sigma$ is not redundant at all. So the redundancy is due to the history variable $h$. But even if the domain of $h$ has cardinality 5, the redundancy is in a certain sense not minimal, as we now explain.

Consider the program $\Sigma_3$ depicted in Figure 2. It tolerates the fault $f$ by adding only *one* state to the state space of $\Sigma$ (namely, $x = 5$). Note that $\Sigma_3$ has only one redundant state, so $\Sigma_3$ can be regarded as redundancy-minimal with respect to $SPEC$. The metric used for minimality is the number of redundant states. We want to exploit this observation to deal with the general case.

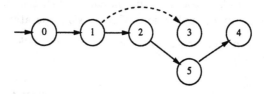

**Fig. 2.** A redundancy-minimal version fault-tolerant program. The specification is "always ($x = 4$ implies that previously $x = 2$)".

## 4   Beyond Fusion Closure

Although the automated procedures of [8,9] were developed for fusion-closed specifications, they (may) still work for specifications which are not fusion closed only if the fault model has a certain pleasant form. For example, consider the system in Figure 3 and the specification

$$SPEC = \text{``($e$ implies previously $c$) and (never $g$)''}$$

Obviously, the fault model $F$ can be tolerated using the known transformation methods because $F$ does not "exploit" the part of the specification which is not fusion closed.

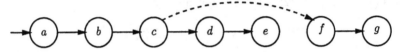

**Fig. 3.** The fail-safe transformation can be successful even if the specification is not fusion closed. The specification in this case is "($e$ implies previously $c$) and (never $g$)".

*Exploiting Non-Fusion Closure.* Now we formalize what it means for a fault model to "exploit" the fact that a specification is not fusion-closed (we call this property *non-fusion closure*). First we define what it means for a trace to be the fusion of two other traces.

**Definition 2 (fusion and fusion point of traces).** *Let $s$ be a state and $\alpha = \alpha_{pre} \cdot s \cdot \alpha_{post}$ and $\beta = \beta_{pre} \cdot s \cdot \beta_{post}$ be two traces in which $s$ occurs. Then we define*

$$fusion(\alpha, s, \beta) = \alpha_{pre} \cdot s \cdot \beta_{post}$$

*If $fusion(\alpha, s, \beta) \neq \alpha$ and $fusion(\alpha, s, \beta) \neq \beta$ we call $s$ a* fusion point *of $\alpha$ and $\beta$.*

**Lemma 1.** *For the fusion of three traces $\alpha, \beta, \gamma$ holds: If $s$ occurs before $s'$ in $\beta$ then*

$$fusion(\alpha, s, fusion(\beta, s', \gamma)) = fusion(fusion(\alpha, s, \beta), s', \gamma)$$

*and*

$$fusion(\gamma, s', fusion(\alpha, s, \beta)) = fusion(\gamma, s', \beta)$$

If *SPEC* is a set of traces, we recursively define an operator to generate the fusion closure of *SPEC*, denoted by *fusion-closure(SPEC)*. It produces a set which is closed under finite applications of the *fusion* operator.

**Definition 3 (fusion closure).** *Given a specification SPEC, a trace $\sigma$ is in fusion-closure(SPEC) iff*

1. *$\sigma$ is in SPEC, or*
2. *$\sigma = fusion(\alpha, s, \beta)$ for traces $\alpha, \beta \in fusion\text{-}closure(SPEC)$ and a state $s$ in $\alpha$ and $\beta$.*

Lemma 1 guarantees that every trace in *fusion-closure(SPEC)* which is not in *SPEC* has a "normal form", i.e., it can be represented uniquely as the sequence of fusions of traces in *SPEC*. This is shown in the following theorem.

**Theorem 1.** *For every trace $\sigma \in$ fusion-closure(SPEC) which is not in SPEC there exists a sequence of traces $\alpha_0, \alpha_1, \alpha_2, \ldots$ and a sequence of states $s_1, s_2, s_3, \ldots$ such that*

1. *for all $i \geq 0$, $\alpha_i \in SPEC$,*
2. *for all $i \geq 1$, $s_i$ is a fusion point of $\alpha_{i-1}$ and $\alpha_i$, and*
3. *$\sigma$ can be written as $\sigma = $ fusion(fusion($\ldots$ fusion($\alpha_0, s_1, \alpha_1$), $s_2, \alpha_2$), $s_3, \alpha_3$), $\ldots$).*

*Proof.* The proof is by induction on the structure of how $\sigma$ evolved from traces in *SPEC*. Basically this means an induction on the number of fusion points in $\sigma$. The induction step assumes that $\sigma$ is the fusion of two traces which have at most $n$ fusion points and depending on their relative positions uses the rules of Lemma 1 to construct the normal form for $\sigma$. □

Now consider the system depicted in Figure 4. The corresponding specification is: *SPEC* = "*f* implies previously *d*". The system may exhibit the following two traces in the absence of faults, namely $\alpha = a \cdot b \cdot c$ and $\beta = a \cdot d \cdot e \cdot f$. In the presence of faults, a new trace is possible, namely $\gamma = a \cdot b \cdot e \cdot f$. Observe that $\gamma$ violates *SPEC* and that $\gamma$ is the fusion of two traces $\alpha, \beta \in SPEC$ (the state which plays the role of *s* in Definition 2 is state *e*). In such a case we say that fault model *F* exploits the non-fusion closure of *SPEC*.

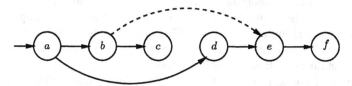

**Fig. 4.** Example where the non-fusion closure of a specification is exploited by a fault model. The specification is "*f* implies previously *d*".

**Definition 4 (exploiting non-fusion closure).** *Let $\Sigma$ satisfy SPEC. Then $F(\Sigma)$ exploits the non-fusion closure of SPEC iff there exists a trace $\sigma \in F(\Sigma)$ such that $\sigma \notin SPEC$ and $\sigma \in$ fusion-closure(SPEC).*

Intuitively, exploiting the non-fusion closure means that there exists a bad computation ($\sigma \notin SPEC$) that can potentially "impersonate" a good computation ($\sigma \in$ *fusion-closure(SPEC)*). Definition 4 states that *F* causes a violation of *SPEC* by constructing a fusion of two (allowed) traces. Given a fault model *F* such that $F(\Sigma)$ exploits the non-fusion closure of *SPEC*, then also we say that *the non-fusion closure of SPEC is exploited for $\Sigma$ in the presence of F*.

Obviously, if for some specification *SPEC* and system $\Sigma$ such an *F* exists, then *SPEC* is not fusion closed. Similarly trivial to prove is the observation that no fault model $F$ can exploit the non-fusion closure of a specification which is fusion closed.

On the other hand, if the non-fusion closure of $SPEC$ cannot be exploited, this does not necessarily mean that $SPEC$ is fusion closed. To see this consider Figure 5. The correctness specification $SPEC$ of the program is "$c$ implies previously $a$". Obviously, a fault model can only generate traces that begin with $a$. Since $a$ is an initial state and we assume that initial states are not changed by $F$, no $F$ can exploit the non-fusion closure. But $SPEC$ is not fusion closed.

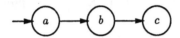

**Fig. 5.** Example where the non-fusion closure cannot be exploited but the specification is not fusion closed. The specification is "$c$ implies previously $a$".

*Preventing the Exploitation of Non-Fusion Closure.* The fact that a fault model may not exploit the non-fusion closure of a specification will be important in our approach to solve the general fail-safe transformation problem (Def. 1). A method to solve this problem, i.e., that of finding a fault-tolerant version $\Sigma_2$, should be a generally applicable method, which constructs $\Sigma_2$ from $\Sigma_1$ (this is depicted in the top part of Figure 6). Instead of devising such a method from scratch, our aim is to reuse the existing transformations to add fail-safe fault tolerance which are based on fusion-closed specifications [8, 9]. This approach is shown in the bottom part of Figure 6. Starting from $\Sigma_1$, we construct some intermediate program $\Sigma_2'$ and some intermediate fusion-closed specification $SPEC_2$ to which we apply one of the above mentioned methods for fusion-closed specifications [8, 9]. The construction of $\Sigma_2'$ and $SPEC_2$ must be done in such a way that the resulting program satisfies the properties of the general transformation problem stated in Definition 1. How can this be done?

The idea of our approach is the following: First, choose $SPEC_2$ to be the fusion closure of $SPEC_1$, i.e., choose $SPEC_2 = \textit{fusion-closure}(SPEC_1)$ and construct $\Sigma_2'$ from $\Sigma_1$ in such a way that $F(\Sigma_2')$ does not exploit the non-fusion closure of $SPEC_1$. More precisely, $\Sigma_2'$ results from applying an algorithm (which we give below) which ensures that

- $\Sigma_2'$ extends $\Sigma_1$ using some state projection $\pi$ and
- $F(\Sigma_2')$ does not exploit the non-fusion closure of $SPEC_1$.

Our claim, which we formally prove later, is that the program $\Sigma_2$ resulting from applying (for example) the algorithms of [8, 9] to $\Sigma_2'$ with respect to $SPEC_2$ in fact satisfies the requirements of Definition 1, i.e., $\Sigma_2$ is in fact an $F$-tolerant version of $\Sigma_1$ with respect to $SPEC_1$.

*Bad Fusion Points.* For a given system $\Sigma$ and a specification $SPEC$, how can we tell whether or not the nature of $SPEC$ is exploitable by a fault model? For

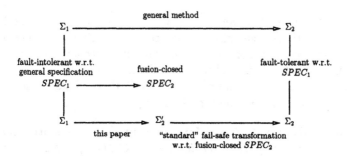

**Fig. 6.** Overview of transformation problem (top) and our approach (bottom). Algorithm 1 described in this paper offers a solution to the first step (i.e., $\Sigma_1 \to \Sigma_2'$).

the negative case (where it can be exploited), we give a sufficient criterion. It is based on the notion of a *bad fusion point*.

**Definition 5 (bad fusion point).** *Let $\Sigma$ be F-intolerant with respect to SPEC. State s of $\Sigma$ is a* bad fusion point *of $\Sigma$ for SPEC in the presence of F iff there exist traces $\alpha, \beta \in SPEC$ such that*

1. *s is a fusion point of $\alpha$ and $\beta$,*
2. *fusion$(\alpha, s, \beta) \in F(\Sigma)$, and*
3. *fusion$(\alpha, s, \beta) \notin SPEC$.*

Intuitively, a bad fusion point is a state in which "multiple pasts" may have happened, i.e., there may be two different execution paths passing through $s$, and from the point of view of the specification it is important to tell the difference. We now give several examples of bad fusion points.

As an example, consider Fig. 4 where $e$ is a bad fusion point. To instantiate the definition, take $\alpha = a \cdot b \cdot e \in F(\Sigma)$ and $\beta = a \cdot d \cdot e \cdot f \in F(\Sigma)$. The fusion at $e$ yields the trace $a \cdot b \cdot e \cdot f$ which is not in *SPEC*.

**Theorem 2 (bad fusion point criterion).** *The following two statements are equivalent:*

1. *$\Sigma$ has no bad fusion point for SPEC in the presence of F.*
2. *$F(\Sigma)$ does not exploit the non-fusion closure of SPEC.*

*Proof.* The main difficulty is to prove that if *SPEC* has no bad fusion point then $F(\Sigma)$ cannot exploit the non-fusion closure. We prove this by assuming that $F(\Sigma)$ exploits the non-fusion closure and using Theorem 1 to construct a bad fusion point.                                                                   □

*Removal of Bad Fusion Points.* Theorem 2 states that it is both necessary and sufficient to remove all bad fusion points from $\Sigma$ to make its structure robust against fault models that exploit the non-fusion closure of *SPEC*. So how can we get rid of bad fusion points?

Recall that a bad fusion point is one which has multiple pasts, and from the point of view of the specification, it is necessary to distinguish between those pasts. Thus, the basic idea of our method is to introduce additional states which split the fusion paths. This is sketched in Figure 7. Let $\Sigma_1 = (C_1, I_1, T_1)$ be a system. If $s$ is a bad fusion point of $\Sigma_1$ for $SPEC$, there exists a trace $\beta \in SPEC$ and a trace $\alpha \in F(\Sigma)$ which both go through $s$.

**Algorithm 1 (Removal of Bad Fusion Points)** *To remove bad fusion points, we now construct an extension $\Sigma_2 = (C_2, I_2, T_2)$ of $\Sigma_1$ in the following way:*

- $C_2 = C_1 \cup \{s'\}$ *where $s'$ is a "new" state,*
- $I_2 = I_1$, *and*
- $T_2$ *results from $T_1$ by "diverting" the transitions of $\beta$ to and from $s'$ instead of $s$.*

*The extension is completed by defining the state projection function $\pi$ to map $s'$ to $s$. Observe that $s$ is not a bad fusion point regarding $\alpha$ and $\beta$ anymore because $\alpha$ now contains $s$ and $\beta$ a different state $s'$ which cannot be fused. So this procedure gets rid of one bad fusion point. Also, it does not by itself introduce a new one, since $s'$ is an extension state which cannot be referenced in SPEC. So we can repeatedly apply the procedure and incrementally build a sequence of extensions $\Sigma_1, \Sigma_2, \ldots$ where in every step one bad fusion point is removed and an additional state is added. However, $F$ may cause new bad fusion points to be created during this process by introducing new faults, transitions defined on the newly added states. But since the fault model is finite it will do this only finitely often. Hence, repeating this construction for every bad fusion point will terminate because we assume that the state space is finite.*

*Note that in the extension process, certain states can be extended multiple times because they might be bad fusion points for different combinations of traces.*

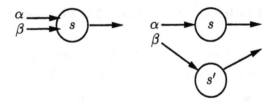

**Fig. 7.** Splitting fusion paths.

We now prove that the above method results in a program with the desired properties.

**Lemma 2.** *Let $\Sigma_1$ be $F$-intolerant with respect to a general specification $SPEC_1$. The program $\Sigma_2'$ which results from applying Algorithm 1 satisfies the following properties:*

1. $\Sigma'_2$ extends $\Sigma_1$ using some state projection $\pi$ and
2. $F(\Sigma'_2)$ does not exploit the non-fusion closure of $SPEC_1$.

*Proof.* To show the first point we argue that there exists a projection function $\pi$ (which is induced by our method) such that every fault-free execution of $\Sigma'_2$ is an execution of $\Sigma_1$. To show the second point, we argue that the method removes all bad fusion points and apply the bad fusion point criterion of Theorem 2.    □

*Correctness of the Combined Method.* Starting from a program $\Sigma_1$, Lemma 2 shows that the program $\Sigma'_2$ resulting from Algorithm 1 for removing bad fusion points enjoys certain properties (see Fig. 6). We now prove that starting off from these properties and choosing $SPEC_2$ as the fusion closure of $SPEC_1$, the program $\Sigma_2$, which results from applying the algorithms of [8, 9] on $\Sigma'_2$, has the desired properties of the transformation problem (Definition 1).

**Lemma 3.** *Given* $F$, $SPEC_1$, *and* $\Sigma_1$ *as in Lemma 2, let* $SPEC_2$ *be equal to* fusion-closure($SPEC_1$) *and let* $\Sigma_2$ *be the result of applying any of the known methods that solve the fusion-closed transformation problem to* $\Sigma'_2$ *with respect to* $F$ *and* $SPEC_2$, *where* $\Sigma'_2$ *results from* $\Sigma_1$ *through the application of Algorithm 1. Then the following statements hold:*

1. $\Sigma_2$ *extends* $\Sigma_1$ *using some state projection* $\pi$.
2. *If* $F(\Sigma_2)$ *satisfies* $SPEC_2$ *then* $F(\Sigma_2)$ *satisfies* $SPEC_1$.

*Proof.* To prove the first point we argue that a fault tolerance addition procedure only removes non-reachable transitions. Hence, every fault-free execution of $\Sigma'_2$ is also an execution of $\Sigma_2$. But since $\Sigma'_2$ extends $\Sigma_1$ so must $\Sigma_2$. To show the second point we first observe that $F(\Sigma'_2)$ does not necessarily satisfy $SPEC_1$ but not all traces for this are in $F(\Sigma_2)$ anymore (due to the removal of bad transitions during addition of fault tolerance). Next we show that any trace of $F(\Sigma_2)$ which violates $SPEC_1$ must exploit the non-fusion closure of $SPEC_1$. But this must also be a trace of $F(\Sigma')$ and so is ruled out by assumption.    □

Lemmas 2 and 3 together guarantee that the composition of the method described in Section 1 and the fail-safe transformation methods for fusion-closed specifications in fact solves the transformation problem for non-fusion closed specifications of Definition 1.

**Theorem 3.** *Let* $\Sigma_1$ *be* $F$-intolerant with respect to a general specification $SPEC_1$. The composition of Algorithm 1 and the fail-safe transformation methods for fusion-closed specifications solves the general transformation problem of Definition 1.

*Example.* We now present an example of the application of our method (more examples can be found elsewhere [6]). The top of Figure 8 (system 1) shows the original system. The augmented system is depicted at the bottom (system 4). The correctness specification for the system is "($d$ implies previously $b$) and ($e$ implies previously $c$)". There are only two bad fusion points, namely $c$ and $d$

which have to be extended. In the first step, $c$ is "removed" by splitting the fusion path which is indicated using two short lines. This results in system 2. Subsequently, $d$ is refined, resulting in system 3. Note that $d$ has to be refined twice because there are two sets of fusion paths. This results in system 4, which can be subject to the standard fail-safe transformation methods, which will remove the transitions $(c, d'')$ and $(d, e)$.

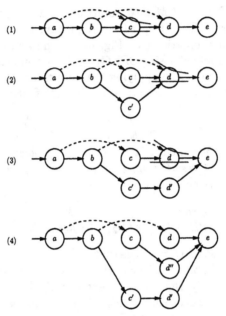

**Fig. 8.** Removing bad fusion points. The specification is "($d$ implies previously $b$) and ($e$ implies previously $c$)".

*Discussion.* The complexity of our method directly depends on the number of bad fusion points. Finding bad fusion points by directly applying Def. 5 is clearly infeasible even for moderately sized systems. However, bad fusion points are not hard to find if the specification is given as a temporal logic formula in the spirit of those used throughout this paper. For example, if specifications are given in the form "$x$ only if previously $y$" then only states which occur in traces between states $x$ and $y$ can be bad fusion points, which are states where two execution paths merge and this can easily be checked from the transition diagram of the system.

Our method requires to check every possible fusion point whether it is a bad one. So obviously, applying our method induces a larger computational overhead during the transformation process than directly adding history variables. But as can be seen in Fig. 8, the number of states is significantly less than adding a general history variable. For example, a clever addition of history variables to the system in Fig. 8 would require two bits, one to record the visit to state $b$ and one to record the visit to $c$. Overall this would result in $2 \times 2 \times 5 = 20$ states. Our method achieves the same result with a total of 8 states.

Although it can happen that states are refined multiple times, the number of bad fusion points (and hence the number of added states) only depends on the specification and the fault model whereas the number of added states using history variables depends on the size of the state space. For example, a program with $n$ states will have $2 \times n$ states after adding just one bit of history information.

In general, the worst case scenario in our scheme is when every state is a bad fusion point. Assuming there are $n$ states in the system, there are $O(n)$ bad fusion points. Assuming that faults do not affect the refined states (which, for sake of comparison is realistic since we do not assume faults to affect history variables, whenever they are used), every bad fusion point is refined, giving rise to $O(n)$ refined states. $O(n)$ bad fusion states thus give rise to $O(n^2)$ refined states. Our scheme adds an additional $O(n^2)$ states, as compared to the exponential number of additional states added by using history variables.

Note however that the resulting system in Fig. 8 is not redundancy minimal if the entire transformation problem is considered. The state $d''$ is not necessary since it may become unreachable even in the presence of faults after the fail-safe transformation is applied. This is the price we still have to pay for the modularity of our approach, i.e., adding history states does at present not "look ahead" which states might become unreachable even in the presence of faults.

In theory there are cases where our method of adding history states does not terminate because there are infinitely many bad fusion points. For this to happen, the state space must be infinite. If we consider the application area of embedded software, we can safely assume a bounded state space.

## 5   Conclusions

In this paper, we have presented ways on how to get rid of a restriction upon which procedures that add fault tolerance [8, 9] are based, namely that of fusion-closed specifications. Apart from closing a gap in the detector/corrector theory [3], our method can be viewed as a finer grained method to add history information to a given system.

As future work, it would be interesting to combine our method with one of the methods to add detectors so that the resulting method can be proven to be redundancy minimal. We are also investigating issues of non-masking fault tolerance, i.e, adding tolerance with respect to liveness properties.

## Acknowledgments

We wish to thank Sandeep Kulkarni for helpful discussions.

## References

1. M. Abadi and L. Lamport. The existence of refinement mappings. *Theoretical Computer Science*, 82(2):253–284, May 1991.

2. B. Alpern and F. B. Schneider. Defining liveness. *Information Processing Letters*, 21:181–185, 1985.
3. A. Arora and S. S. Kulkarni. Component based design of multitolerant systems. *IEEE Transactions on Software Engineering*, 24(1):63–78, Jan. 1998.
4. A. Cau and W.-P. de Roever. Specifying fault tolerance within stark's formalism. In J.-C. Laprie, editor, *Proceedings of the 23rd Annual International Symposium on Fault-Tolerant Computing (FTCS '93)*, pages 392–401, Toulouse, France, June 1993. IEEE Computer Society Press.
5. K. M. Chandy and J. Misra. *Parallel Program Design: A Foundation*. Addison-Wesley, Reading, MA, Reading, Mass., 1988.
6. F. C. Gärtner and A. Jhumka. Automating the addition of fail-safe fault-tolerance: Beyond fusion-closed specifications. Technical Report IC/2003/23, Swiss Federal Institute of Technology (EPFL), School of Computer and Communication Sciences, Lausanne, Switzerland, Apr. 2003.
7. H. P. Gumm. Another glance at the Alpern-Schneider characterization of safety and liveness in concurrent executions. *Information Processing Letters*, 47(6):291–294, 1993.
8. A. Jhumka, F. C. Gärtner, C. Fetzer, and N. Suri. On systematic design of fast and perfect detectors. Technical Report 200263, Swiss Federal Institute of Technology (EPFL), School of Computer and Communication Sciences, Lausanne, Switzerland, Sept. 2002.
9. S. S. Kulkarni and A. Arora. Automating the addition of fault-tolerance. In M. Joseph, editor, *Formal Techniques in Real-Time and Fault-Tolerant Systems, 6th International Symposium (FTRTFT 2000) Proceedings*, number 1926 in Lecture Notes in Computer Science, pages 82–93, Pune, India, Sept. 2000. Springer-Verlag.
10. L. Lamport. Proving the correctness of multiprocess programs. *IEEE Transactions on Software Engineering*, 3(2):125–143, Mar. 1977.
11. Z. Liu and M. Joseph. Specification and verification of fault-tolerance, timing and scheduling. *ACM Transactions on Programming Languages and Systems*, 21(1):46–89, 1999.
12. H. Mantel and F. C. Gärtner. A case study in the mechanical verification of fault tolerance. *Journal of Experimental & Theoretical Artificial Intelligence (JETAI)*, 12(4):473–488, Oct. 2000.

# Modeling and Verification of a Fault-Tolerant Real-Time Startup Protocol Using Calendar Automata

Bruno Dutertre[1] and Maria Sorea[2]

[1] System Design Laboratory, SRI International, Menlo Park, CA, USA
bruno@sdl.sri.com
[2] Abteilung Künstliche Intelligenz, Universität Ulm, Ulm, Germany
sorea@informatik.uni-ulm.de

**Abstract.** We discuss the modeling and verification of real-time systems using the SAL model checker. A new modeling framework based on event calendars enables dense timed systems to be described without relying on continuously varying clocks. We present verification techniques that rely on induction and abstraction, and show how these techniques are efficiently supported by the SAL symbolic model-checking tools. The modeling and verification method is applied to the fault-tolerant real-time startup protocol used in the Timed Triggered Architecture.

## 1 Introduction

SAL (Symbolic Analysis Laboratory) is a framework for the specification and analysis of concurrent systems. It consists of the SAL language [1], which provides notations for specifying state machines and their properties, and the SAL system [2] that provides model checkers and other tools for analyzing properties of state machine specifications written in SAL. These tools include a bounded model checker for infinite-state systems that relies on decision procedures for a combination of linear arithmetic, uninterpreted functions, and propositional logic. This tool enables the analysis of systems that mix real-valued and discrete state variables and can then apply to real-time systems with a dense time model.

SAL is a generalist tool, intended for the modeling and verification of discrete transition systems, and not for systems with continuous dynamics. As a consequence, existing models such as timed automata, which employ continuous clocks, do not fit the SAL framework very well. A first contribution of this paper is the definition of a new class of timed transition systems that use dense time but do not require continuously varying state variables, and are then better suited to SAL. The inspiration for these models is the concept of *event calendars* that has been used for decades in computer simulation of discrete event systems. Unlike clocks, which measure delays since the occurrence of past events, a calendar stores information about future events and the time at which they are scheduled to occur. This provides a simple mechanism for modeling time progress: time always advance to the next event in the calendar, that is, to the time where the next discrete transition is enabled. This solves the main difficulty encountered when encoding timed automata via transition systems, namely – ensuring maximal time progress.

Y. Lakhnech and S. Yovine (Eds.): FORMATS/FTRTFT 2004, LNCS 3253, pp. 199–214, 2004.

The paper shows then how the SAL infinite-state bounded-model checker – which is primarily intended for refutation and counterexample finding – can be used as a verification tool and applied to timed models. A simple technique is to use a bounded model checker to perform proof by induction. We extend this technique by applying bounded model checking (BMC) to proof by abstraction. More precisely, we use BMC for automatically proving that an abstraction is correct. This provides efficient automation to support a proof method based on disjunctive invariants proposed by Rushby [3].

The modeling approach and the verification methods have been applied to the fault-tolerant real-time startup protocol used by the Timed Triggered Architecture (TTA) [4]. We first illustrate the techniques on a simplified version of the startup algorithm, where timing and transmission delays are modeled but where faults are not considered. We then discuss the verification of a more complex version of the protocol in which both timing and node failures are modeled.

Compared to existing approaches, the framework we present lies between fully automated model checking and manual verification using interactive theorem proving. Several special-purpose model checkers (e.g., [5–8]) exist for timed automata and have been applied to nontrivial examples. However, these tools apply only to automata with finite control and, in practice, to relatively small systems. This limitation makes it difficult to apply these tools to fault-tolerant systems, as modeling faults typically leads to automata with a very large number of discrete states. Other real-time formalisms (e.g., [9, 10]) may be more expressive and general, but they have had limited tool support. In such frameworks, proofs are done by hand or, in some cases, with interactive theorem provers (e.g., [11, 12]). The modeling and verification method we discuss is applicable to a larger class of systems than timed automata, including some systems with infinite control, but it remains efficiently supported by a model-checking tool. Proofs are not completely automatic, as the user must provide auxiliary lemmas or candidate abstractions. However, the correctness of these lemmas or abstractions is checked automatically by the bounded model checker, much more efficiently than can be done using an interactive theorem prover. The method is not only efficient at reasoning about timed systems, but, as the startup example illustrates, it also copes with the discrete complexity introduced by faults.

## 2   Timed Systems in SAL

### 2.1   An Overview of SAL

SAL is a framework for the specification and analysis of traditional state-transition systems of the form $\langle S, I, \rightarrow \rangle$, where $S$ is a state space, $I \subseteq S$ is the set of initial states, and $\rightarrow$ is a transition relation on $S$. Each state $\sigma$ of $S$ is a mapping that assigns a value of an appropriate type to each of the system's state variables. The core of SAL is a language for the modular specification of such systems. The relatively abstract and high-level specification language provides many of the types and constructs found in PVS, including infinite types such as the reals, the integers, and recursive data types, and therefore allows for specifying systems and their properties in a convenient and succinct manner. The main construct in SAL is the *module*. A module contains the specification of a state machine and can be composed with other modules synchronously or asynchronously.

Several analysis tools are part of the current SAL environment [2]. These include two symbolic model checkers, a SAT-based bounded model checker for finite systems, and a bounded model checker for infinite systems. This model checker, called sal-inf-bmc, searches for counterexamples to a given property by encoding transition relation and initialization into logical formulas in the theory supported by the ICS solver. ICS is a decision procedure and satisfiability solver for a combination of quantifier-free theories that include linear arithmetic over the reals and the integers, equalities with uninterpreted function symbols, propositional logic, and others [13, 14]. sal-inf-bmc can also use other solvers, if they can decide the appropriate theories.

Although bounded model checking is primarily a refutation method, the symbolic techniques it employs can be extended to proof by induction as discussed in [15]. sal-inf-bmc can be used to prove that a system $M = \langle S, I, \rightarrow \rangle$ satisfies a formula $\Box P$, using $k$-induction, which consists of the two following stages:

- *Base case:* Show that all the states reachable from $I$ in no more than $k - 1$ steps satisfy $P$.
- *Induction step:* For all trajectories $\sigma_0 \rightarrow \ldots \rightarrow \sigma_k$ of length $k$, show that

$$\sigma_0 \models P \land \ldots \land \sigma_{k-1} \models P \implies \sigma_k \models P.$$

The usual induction rule is just the special case where $k = 1$. sal-inf-bmc also supports $k$-induction with auxiliary invariants as lemmas. This allows one to prove $\Box P$ under the assumption that a lemma $\Box Q$ is satisfied.

The $k$-induction rule can be more successful as a proof technique than standard induction, as it is a form of automated invariant strengthening. Proving the invariance of $P$ by $k$-induction is equivalent to proving the invariance of $P \land \bigcirc P \land \ldots \land \bigcirc^{k-1} P$ by one-step induction. For a sufficiently large $k$, this stronger property is more likely to be inductive than the original $P$. However, there are transition systems $M$ for which $k$-induction cannot do better than standard induction. For example, if the transition relation is reflexive, then it is easy to show that if $\Box P$ is not provable by standard induction, it is not provable either by $k$-induction with any $k > 1$.

## 2.2  Clock-Based Models

A first step in applying SAL to timed systems is to find a convenient description of such systems as state machines. One may be tempted to start from an existing formalism – such as timed automata [16] or related models (e.g., [17, 18]) – whose semantics is typically defined by means of transition systems. Encoding such models in SAL is possible and leads to what may be called *clock-based* models. A clock-based system $M$ is built from a set $C$ of real-valued state variables (the clocks) and a set $A$ of discrete variables, with $A$ and $C$ disjoint. A state $\sigma$ of $M$ is a mapping from $A \cup C$ to appropriate domains; in all initial state $\sigma$, we have $\sigma(c) = 0$ for every clock $c \in C$; and the transition relation consists of two types of transitions:

- *Time progress:* $\sigma \rightarrow \sigma'$ where, for some $\delta \geq 0$ and all clock $c$ we have $\sigma'(c) = \sigma(c) + \delta$, and, for every discrete variable $a$, we have $\sigma'(a) = \sigma(a)$.
- *Discrete transitions:* $\sigma \rightarrow \sigma'$ where $\sigma'(c) = \sigma(c)$ or $\sigma'(c) = 0$ for all clock $c$.

We have experimented with clock-based models when translating and analyzing timed automata in SAL [19, 20] but we encountered several difficulties. First, the clocks vary continuously with time. This means that $\delta$ can be arbitrarily small in a time-progress transition. As a consequence, it is difficult to ensure progress. The transition system has infinite trajectories in which no discrete transition ever occurs and time remains bounded. These undesirable trajectories cannot be easily excluded and they make it difficult to analyze liveness properties. Idle steps are possible (i.e., time-progress transitions with $\delta = 0$), which makes $k$-induction useless, except for $k = 1$. Preserving modularity is another issue, as the SAL composition operators do not match the product of timed automata.

These issues can be solved to some extent, and the analysis of timed automata in SAL is possible using various encoding tricks. A better approach is to avoid continuous clocks and develop timed models that are better suited to SAL. For this purpose, we propose a modeling method inspired from *event calendars*, a concept that has been used for decades in simulation of discrete event systems.

## 2.3   Timeout-Based Models

In discrete event simulation, a calendar (also called event list) is a data structure that stores future events and the times at which these events are scheduled to occur. Unlike a clock, which measures the time elapsed since its last reset, a calendar contains information about the future. By following this principle, we can model real-time systems as standard transition systems with no continuous dynamics. The general idea is to rely on state variables to store the time at which future discrete transitions will be taken.

A first class of models we consider are transition systems with timeouts. Their state variables include a variable $t$ that stores the current time and a finite set $T$ of *timeouts*. The variable $t$ and the timeouts are all real-valued. The initial states and transition relation satisfy the following requirements:

- In any initial state $\sigma$, we have $\sigma(t) \le \sigma(x)$ for all $x \in T$.
- If $\sigma$ is a state such that $\sigma(t) < \sigma(x)$ for all $x \in T$ then the only transition enabled in $\sigma$ is a *time progress transition*. It increases $t$ to $\min(\sigma(T)) = \min\{\sigma(x) \mid x \in T\}$ and leaves all other state variables unchanged.
- Discrete transitions $\sigma \rightarrow \sigma'$ are enabled in states such that $\sigma(t) = \sigma(x)$ for some $x \in T$ and satisfy the following conditions
  - $\sigma'(t) = \sigma(t)$
  - for all $y \in T$ we have $\sigma'(y) = \sigma(y)$ or $\sigma'(y) > \sigma'(t)$
  - there is $x \in T$ such that $\sigma(x) = \sigma(t)$ and $\sigma'(x) > \sigma'(t)$.

In all reachable states, a timeout $x$ never stores a value in the past, that is, the inequality $\sigma(t) \le \sigma(x)$ is an invariant of the system. A discrete transition can be taken whenever the time $t$ reaches the value of one timeout $x$. Such a transition must increase at least one such $x$ to a time in the future, and if it updates other timeouts than $x$ their new value must also be in the future. Whenever the condition $\forall x \in T : \sigma(t) < \sigma(x)$ holds, no discrete transition is enabled and time advances to the value of the next timeout, that is, to $\min(\sigma(T))$. Conversely, time cannot progress as long as a discrete transition is enabled.

Discrete transitions are instantaneous since they leave $t$ unchanged. Several discrete transitions may be enabled in the same state, in which case one is selected non-deterministically. Several discrete transitions may also need to be performed in sequence before $t$ can advance, but the constraints on timeout updates prevent infinite zero-delay sequences of discrete transitions.

In typical applications, the timeouts control the execution of $n$ real-time processes $p_1, \ldots, p_n$. A timeout $x_i$ stores the time at which the next action from $p_i$ must occur, and this action updates $x_i$ to a new time, strictly larger than the current time $t$, where $p_i$ will perform another transition. For example, we have used timeout-based modeling for specifying and verifying Fischer's mutual exclusion algorithm [19]. Instances of Fischer's protocol with as many as 53 processes can be verified using this method.

## 2.4   Calendar-Based Models

Timeouts are convenient for applications like Fischer's protocol, where processes communicate via shared variables that they read or write independently. Process $p_i$ has full control of its local timeout, which determines when $p_i$ performs its transitions. Other processes have no access to $p_i$'s timeout and their actions cannot impact $p_i$ until it "wakes up". To model interaction via message passing, we add *event calendars* to our transition systems.

A calendar is a finite set (or multiset) of the form $C = \{\langle e_1, t_1 \rangle, \ldots, \langle e_n, t_n \rangle\}$, where each $e_i$ is an event and $t_i$ is the time when event $e_i$ is scheduled to occur. All $t_i$s are real numbers. We denote by $\min(C)$ the smallest number among $\{t_1, \ldots, t_n\}$ (with $\min(C) = +\infty$ if $C$ is empty). Given a real $u$, we denote by $\mathrm{Ev}_u(C)$ the subset of $C$ that contains all events scheduled at time $u$:

$$\mathrm{Ev}_u(C) = \{\langle e_i, t_i \rangle \mid t_i = u \wedge \langle e_i, t_i \rangle \in C\}$$

As before, the state variables of a calendar-based system $\mathcal{M}$ include a real-valued variable $t$ that denotes the current time and a finite set $T$ of timeouts. In addition, one state variable $c$ stores a calendar. These variables control when discrete and time-progress transitions are enabled, according to the following rules:

- In all initial state $\sigma$, we have $\sigma(t) \leq \min(\sigma(T))$ and $\sigma(t) \leq \min(\sigma(c))$.
- In a state $\sigma$, time can advance if and only if $\sigma(t) < \min(\sigma(T))$ and $\sigma(t) < \min(\sigma(c))$. A time progress transition updates $t$ to the smallest of $\min(\sigma(T))$ and $\min(\sigma(c))$, and leaves all other state variables unchanged.
- Discrete transitions can be enabled in a state $\sigma$ provided $\sigma(t) = \min(\sigma(T))$ or $\sigma(t) = \min(\sigma(c))$, and they must satisfy the following requirements:
  - $\sigma(t) = \sigma'(t)$
  - for all $y \in T$ we have $\sigma'(y) = \sigma(y)$ or $\sigma'(y) > \sigma'(t)$
  - if $\sigma(t) = \min(\sigma(c))$ then $\mathrm{Ev}_{\sigma'(t)}(\sigma'(c)) \subseteq \mathrm{Ev}_{\sigma(t)}(\sigma(c))$
  - we have $\mathrm{Ev}_{\sigma'(t)}(\sigma'(c)) \subset \mathrm{Ev}_{\sigma(t)}(\sigma(c))$, or there is $x \in T$ such that $\sigma(x) = \sigma(t)$ and $\sigma'(x) > \sigma'(t)$.

These constraints ensure that $\sigma(t) \leq \min(\sigma(T))$ and $\sigma(t) \leq \min(\sigma(c))$ are invariants: timeout values and the occurrence time of any event in the calendar are never in the past.

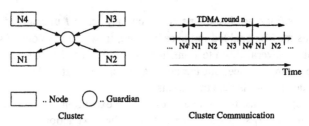

**Fig. 1.** TTA Cluster and TDMA Schedule.

Discrete transitions are enabled when the current time reaches the value of a timeout or the occurrence time of a scheduled event. The constraints on timeout are the same as before. In addition, a discrete transition may add events to the calendar, provided these new events are all in the future. To prevent instantaneous loops, every discrete transition must either consume an event that occurs at the current time or update a timeout as discussed previously.

Calendars are useful for modeling communication channels that introduce transmission delays. An event in the calendar represents a message being transmitted and the occurrence time is the time when the message will be received. The action of sending a message $m$ to a process $p_i$ is modeled by adding the event "$p_i$ receives $m$" to the calendar, which is scheduled to occur at some future time. Message reception is modeled by transitions enabled when such event occurs, and whose effects include removing the event from the calendar. From this point of view, a calendar can be seen as a set of messages that have been sent but have not been received yet, with each message labeled by its reception time.

The main benefit of timeouts and calendars is the simple mechanism they provide for controlling how far time can advance. Time progress is deterministic. There are no states in which both time-progress and discrete transitions are enabled, and any state in which time progress is enabled has a unique successor: time is advanced to the point where the next discrete transition is enabled. This semantics ensures maximal time progress without missing any discrete transitions. A calendar-based model never makes two time-progress transitions in succession and there are no idle steps. All variables of the systems evolve in discrete steps, and there is no need to approximate continuous dynamics by allowing arbitrarily small time steps.

## 3   The TTA Startup Protocol

The remainder of this paper describes an application of the preceding modeling principles to the TTA fault-tolerant startup protocol [21]. TTA implements a fault-tolerant logical bus intended for safety-critical applications such as avionics or automotive control functions. In normal operation, $N$ computers or nodes share a TTA bus using a time-division multiple-access (TDMA) discipline based on a cyclic schedule. The goal of the startup algorithm is to bring the system from the power-up state, in which the $N$ computers are unsynchronized, to the normal operation mode in which all computers are synchronized and follow the same TDMA schedule. A TTA system or "cluster"

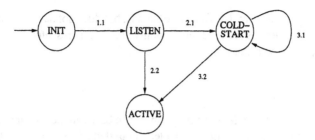

**Fig. 2.** State-machine of the TTA Node Startup Algorithm.

with four nodes and the associated TDMA schedule are depicted in Fig. 1. The cluster has a star topology, with a central hub or guardian forwarding messages from one node to the other nodes. The guardian also provides protection against node failures. It prevents faulty nodes from sending messages on the bus outside their allocated TDMA slot and, during startup, it arbitrates message collisions. A full TTA system relies on two redundant hubs and can tolerate the failure of one of them [21].

The startup algorithm executed by the nodes is described schematically in Fig. 2. When a node $i$ is powered on, it performs some internal initializations in the INIT state, and then it transitions to the LISTEN state and listens for messages on the bus. If the other nodes are already synchronized, they each send an *i-frame* during their TDMA slot. If node $i$ receives such a frame while in the LISTEN state, it can immediately synchronize with the other nodes and moves to the ACTIVE state (transition 2.2). After a delay $\tau_i^{\text{listen}}$, if $i$ has not received any message, it sends a *cs-frame* (coldstart frame) to initiate the startup process and moves to the COLDSTART state (transition 2.1). Node $i$ also enters COLDSTART if it receives a cs-frame from another node while in the LISTEN state. In COLD-START, node $i$ waits for messages from other nodes. If $i$ receives either an i-frame or a cs-frame, then it synchronizes with the sender and enters the ACTIVE state. Otherwise, if no frame is received within a delay $\tau_i^{\text{coldstart}}$, then $i$ sends a cs-frame and loops back to COLDSTART (transition 3.1). The ACTIVE state represents normal operation. Every node in this state periodically sends an i-frame, during its assigned TDMA slot. The goal of the protocol is to ensure that all nodes in the ACTIVE state are actually synchronized and have a consistent view of where they are in the TDMA cycle.

The correctness of the protocol depends on the relative values of the delays $\tau_i^{\text{listen}}$ and $\tau_i^{\text{coldstart}}$. These timeouts are defined as follows:

$$\tau_i^{\text{listen}} = 2\tau^{\text{round}} + \tau_i^{\text{startup}}$$
$$\tau_i^{\text{coldstart}} = \tau^{\text{round}} + \tau_i^{\text{startup}}$$

where $\tau^{\text{round}}$ is the round duration and $\tau_i^{\text{startup}}$ is the start of $i$'s slot in a TDMA cycle. Nodes are indexed from 1 to $N$. We then have $\tau_i^{\text{startup}} = (i-1).\tau$ and $\tau^{\text{round}} = N.\tau$ where $\tau$ is the length of each slot (this length is constant and all nodes have TDMA slots of equal length).

## 4   A Simplified Startup Protocol in SAL

We now consider the SAL specification of a simplified version of the startup protocol, where nodes are assumed to be reliable. Under this assumption, the hub has a limited role. It forwards messages and arbitrates collisions, but does not have any fault masking function. Since the hub has reduced functionality, it is not represented by an active SAL module but by a shared calendar.

## 4.1 Calendar

In TTA, there is never more than one frame in transit between the hub and any node. To model the hub, it is then sufficient to consider a bounded calendar that contains at most one event per node. To simplify the model, we also assume that the transmission delays are the same for all the nodes. As a consequence, a frame forwarded by the hub reaches all the nodes (except the sender) at the same time. All events in the calendar have then the same occurrence time and correspond to the same frame. These simplifications allow us to specify the calendar as shown in Fig. 3.

```
IDENTITY: TYPE = [1 .. N];
TIME: TYPE = REAL;
message: TYPE = { cs_frame, i_frame };

calendar: TYPE = [#
    flag: ARRAY IDENTITY OF bool,
    content: message,
    origin: IDENTITY,
    send, delivery: TIME
#];

empty?(cal: calendar): bool = FORALL (i: IDENTITY): NOT cal.flag[i];
...
i_frame_pending?(cal: calendar, i: IDENTITY): bool =
    cal.flag[i] AND cal.content = i_frame;
...
bcast(cal: calendar, m: message, i: IDENTITY, t: TIME): calendar =
    IF empty?(cal) THEN
        (# flag := [[j: IDENTITY] j /= i],
            content := m,
            origin := i,
            send := t,
            delivery := t + propagation #)
    ELSE cal WITH .flag[i] := false
    ENDIF;

consume_event(cal: calendar, i: IDENTITY): calendar =
    cal WITH .flag[i] := false;
```

**Fig. 3.** Calendar Encoding for the Simplified Startup Protocol.

A calendar stores a frame being transmitted (content), the identity of the sender (origin), and the time when the frame was sent (send) and when it will be delivered (delivery). The boolean array flag represents the set of nodes that are scheduled to receive the frame. Example operations for querying and updating calendars are shown in Fig. 3. Function bcast is the most important. It models the operation "node $i$ broadcasts frame $m$ at time $t$" and shows how collisions are resolved by the hub. If the calendar is empty when $i$ attempts to broadcast, then frame $m$ is stored and scheduled for delivery at time $t + propagation$, and all nodes except $i$ are scheduled to receive $m$. If the calendar is not empty, then the frame from $i$ collides with a frame $m'$ from another node, namely, the one currently stored in the calendar. The collision is resolved by giving priority to $m'$ and dropping $i$'s frame. In addition, node $i$ is removed from the set of nodes scheduled to receive $m'$ because channels between hub and nodes are half-duplex: since $i$ is transmitting a frame $m$, it cannot receive $m'$.

## 4.2  Nodes

Figure 4 shows fragments of a node's specification in SAL. The node module is parameterized by a node identity $i$. It reads the current time via an input state variable, has access to the global calendar cal that is shared by all the nodes, and exports three output variables corresponding to its local timeout, its current state pc, and its view of the current TDMA slot. The transitions specify the startup algorithm as discussed previously using SAL's guarded command language. The figure shows two examples of transitions: listen_to_coldstart is enabled when time reaches node[i]'s timeout while the node is in the LISTEN state. The node enters the COLDSTART state, sets its timeout to ensure that it will wake up after a delay $\tau_i^{coldstart}$, and broadcasts a cs-frame. The other transition models the reception of a cs-frame while node[i] is in the COLDSTART state. Node $i$ synchronizes with the frame's sender: it sets its timeout to the start of the next slot, compensating for the propagation delay, and sets its slot index to the identity of the cs-frame sender.

```
PC: TYPE = { init, listen, coldstart, active };

node[i: IDENTITY]: MODULE =
  BEGIN
    INPUT  time: TIME
    OUTPUT timeout: TIME, slot: IDENTITY, pc: PC
    GLOBAL cal: calendar
  INITIALIZATION
    pc = init;
    timeout IN { x: TIME | time < x AND x < max_init_time};
    ...
  TRANSITION
    ...
    [] listen_to_coldstart:
       pc = listen AND time = timeout -->
         pc' = coldstart;
         timeout' = time + tau_coldstart(i);
         cal' = bcast(cal, cs_frame, i, time)
    ...
    [] cs_frame_in_coldstart:
       pc = coldstart AND cs_frame_pending?(cal, i) AND time = event_time(cal, i) -->
         pc' = active;
         timeout' = time + slot_time - propagation;
         slot' = frame_origin(cal, i);
         cal' = consume_event(cal, i)
    ...
```

**Fig. 4.** Node Specification.

## 4.3  Full Model

The complete startup model is the asynchronous composition of $N$ nodes and a clock module that manages the time variable. The clock's input includes the shared calendar and the timeout variable from each node. The module makes time advances when no discrete transition from the nodes is enabled, as discussed in Sect. 2.4.

Since time cannot advance beyond the calendar's delivery time, pending messages are all received. For example, transition cs_frame_in_coldstart of Fig. 4 is enabled when time is equal to the frame reception time event_time(cal, i). Let $\sigma$ be a system state where this transition is enabled. Since the delivery times are the same for all nodes, the same transition is likely to be enabled for other nodes, too. Let's then assume that cs_frame_in_coldstart is also enabled for node $j$ in state $\sigma$. In general, enabling a transition does not guarantee that it will be taken. However, the model prevents time from advancing as long as the frame destined for $i$ or the frame destined for $j$ is pending. This forces transition cs_frame_in_coldstart to be taken in both node $i$ and node $j$. Since nodes are composed asynchronously, the transitions of node $i$ and $j$ will be taken one after the other from state $\sigma$, in a nondeterministic order. For the same reason, transitions that are enabled on a condition of the form time = timeout are all eventually taken. Timeouts are never missed.

# 5  Protocol Verification

## 5.1  Correctness Property

The goal of the startup protocol is to ensure that all the nodes that are in the ACTIVE state are synchronized (safety) and that all nodes eventually reach the ACTIVE state (liveness). We focus on the safety property. Our goal is to show that the startup model satisfies the following LTL formula with linear arithmetic constraints:

```
synchro: THEOREM
  system |-
    G(FORALL (i, j: IDENTITY): pc[i] = active AND pc[j] = active AND
        time < time_out[i] AND time < time_out[j] =>
          time_out[i] = time_out[j] AND slot[i] = slot[j])
```

This says that any two nodes in state ACTIVE have the same view of the TDMA schedule: they agree on the current slot index and their respective timeouts are set to the same value, which is the start of the next slot. Because nodes are composed asynchronously, agreement between $i$ and $j$ is not guaranteed at the boundary between two successive slots, when time = time_out[i] or time = time_out[j] holds.

## 5.2  Proof by Induction

A direct approach to proving the above property is the $k$-induction method supported by sal-inf-bmc. A first attempt with $k = 1$ immediately shows that the property is not inductive. Increasing $k$ does not seem to help. The smallest possible TTA system has two nodes, and the corresponding SAL model has 13 state variables (5 real variables, 6 boolean variables, and 2 bounded integer variables)[1]. On this minimal TTA model, $k$-induction at depth up to $k = 20$ still fails to prove the synchronization property.

However, as long as the number of nodes remains small, we can prove the property using $k$-induction and a few auxiliary lemmas:

---

[1] The variable slot of each process stores an integer in the interval $[1, N]$.

```
time_aux1: LEMMA
    system |- G(FORALL (i: IDENTITY): time <= time_out[i]);

time_aux2: LEMMA
    system |- G(empty?(cal) OR
                (cal.send <= time AND time <= cal.delivery));

delivery_delay1: LEMMA
    system |- G(FORALL (i: IDENTITY):
                    event_pending?(cal, i) =>
                        event_time(cal, i) = cal.send + propagation);
```

The first two lemmas are invariants that hold for any calendar-based model, the other is an obvious relation between the transmit and reception time of messages. These lemmas are all inductive; they can be proved automatically by sal-inf-bmc using $k$-induction at depth 1.

For $N = 2$, we can then show that the synchronization property holds with the following command:

```
sal-inf-bmc -v 3 -d 8 -i -l time_aux1 -l time_aux2
    -l delivery_delay1 simple_startup4 synchro
...
proved.
total execution time: 258.71 secs
```

This instructs sal-inf-bmc to perform a proof by $k$-induction at depth 8 using the three lemmas. With $N = 3$, an inductive proof at depth 14 with the same lemmas fails; the execution time is of the order of 2 hours. With higher depths, sal-inf-bmc runs out of memory, or the user runs out of patience.

## 5.3    Proof via Abstraction

The previous verification uses only induction and is straightforward, but it has a major limitation: it works only for $N = 2$. The last step in the proof is not scalable, as the induction depth required increases with the number of nodes. To analyze the protocol with a larger number of nodes, we need a less expensive proof method. Since all we can do is proof by induction, our strategy is to strengthen the invariant. We are looking for an invariant $\phi$ that implies property synchro, and can be proved with sal-inf-bmc using induction at depth 1.

To obtain an appropriate $\phi$, we use the method proposed by Rushby [3]. Given a transition system $M = \langle S, I, \rightarrow \rangle$, this method amounts to constructing an abstraction of $M$ (or verification diagram [22]) based on $n$ state predicates $A_1(\sigma), \ldots, A_n(\sigma)$. The abstraction is a transition system $M_0 = \langle S_0, I_0, \rightarrow_0 \rangle$ with state space $S_0 = \{a_1, \ldots, a_n\}$. The abstract states are in a one-to-one correspondence with the $n$ predicates. Then, the system $M_0$ is a correct abstraction of $M$ if two properties are satisfied:

- For all state $\sigma$ of $I$, there is an abstract state $a_i$ of $I_0$ such that $A_i(\sigma)$ is satisfied.
- For every abstract state $a_i$, the following formula holds:

$$\forall \sigma \in S, \sigma' \in S : A_i(\sigma) \wedge \sigma \rightarrow \sigma' \implies A_{j_1}(\sigma') \vee \ldots A_{j_k}(\sigma'),$$

where $a_{j_1}, \ldots, a_{j_k}$ are the successors of $a_i$ in $M_0$.

Less formally, the abstract system makes statements about $\mathcal{M}$ of the form "if $A_i$ is true in the current state, then the next state will satisfy $A_{j_1}$ or ... or $A_{j_k}$". It also states that some of the predicates $A_1, \ldots, A_n$ are true in all the initial states of $\mathcal{M}$. If the abstraction is correct, then clearly the disjunction $A_1 \vee \ldots \vee A_n$ is an inductive invariant of $\mathcal{M}$.

This form of abstraction has two interests for our purposes. First, it is often relatively easy for the user to find adequate predicates $A_1, \ldots, A_n$ by "tracing" the execution of $\mathcal{M}$. Second, it is possible to prove that a candidate abstraction is correct using sal-inf-bmc. We illustrate this approach on the simplified startup algorithm.

*Discovering the Abstraction.* By examining how the startup protocol works, one can decompose its execution into successive phases, as shown below:

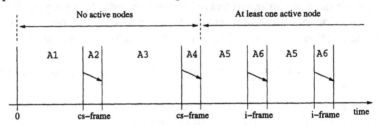

In the first phase, A1, all nodes are either in the INIT or LISTEN states and no frame is sent. Phase A2 starts when one node enters COLDSTART and broadcasts a cs-frame, and ends when that frame is transmitted. Collisions may occur in phase A2 as several nodes may broadcast a cs-frame at approximately the same time. In phase A3, at least one node is in the COLDSTART state, and all nodes are waiting. In A4 a second cs-frame is sent. By definition of the delays $\tau_i^{\text{coldstart}}$, no collision can occur in A4. After A4, all the nodes that have received the second cs-frame become active. This leads to phase A5, in which at least one node is active. Phase A6 corresponds to the transmission of an i-frame by an active node. After A6, the system returns to phase A5, and so forth.

The six phases A1 to A6 form the basis of our abstraction. For example, the abstraction predicate A2 is defined in SAL as a boolean state variable as follows:

```
A2 = cs_frame?(cal) AND pc[cal.origin] = coldstart
     AND (FORALL (i: IDENTITY):
             pc[i] = init OR pc[i] = listen OR pc[i] = coldstart)
     AND (FORALL (i: IDENTITY): pc[i] = coldstart =>
             NOT event_pending?(cal, i)
             AND time_out[i] - cal.send >= tau_coldstart(i)
             AND time_out[i] - time <= tau_coldstart(i))
     AND (FORALL (i: IDENTITY): pc[i] = listen =>
             event_pending?(cal, i)
             OR time_out[i] >= cal.send + tau_listen(i));
```

Figure 5 shows the abstract system derived from A1 to A6. The transitions specify which phases may succeed each other. Every abstract state is also its own successor but we omit self loops from the diagram for clarity.

*Proving That the Abstraction Is Correct.* Several methods can be used for proving in SAL that the diagram of Fig. 5 is a correct abstraction of the startup model. The

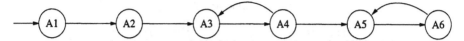

**Fig. 5.** Verification Diagram for the Simplified Startup.

most efficient technique is to build a monitor module that corresponds to the candidate abstraction extended with an error state. The monitor is defined in such a way that the error state is reached whenever the startup model performs a transition that, according to the abstraction, should not occur. For example, the monitor includes the following guarded command which specifies the allowed successors of abstract state a2:

```
state = a2 -->
    state' = IF A2' THEN a2 ELSIF A3' THEN a3 ELSE bad ENDIF
```

where bad is the error state. This corresponds to the diagram of Fig. 5: a2 and a3 are the only two successors of a2 in the diagram. The abstraction is correct if and only if the error state is not reachable, that is, if the property state /= bad is invariant. Furthermore, if the abstraction is correct, this invariant is inductive and can be proved automatically with sal-inf-bmc using $k$-induction at depth 1. This requires the same auxiliary lemmas as previously and an additional lemma per abstract state.

To summarize, our proof of the startup protocol is constructed as follows:

- An abstractor module defines the boolean variables A1 to A6 from the state variables of the concrete tta module.
- A monitor module whose input variables are A1 to A6 specifies the allowed transitions between abstract states.
- We then construct the synchronous composition of the tta, abstractor, and monitor modules.
- We show that this composition satisfies the invariant property G(state /= bad), by induction using sal-inf-bmc.
- Finally, using sal-inf-bmc again, we show that the previous invariant implies the correctness property synchro.

### 5.4 Results

Table 1 shows the runtime of sal-inf-bmc when proving the correctness of the simplified TTA startup protocol, for different numbers of nodes. The runtimes are given in seconds and were measured on a Dell PC with a Pentium 4 CPU (2 GHz) and 1 Gbyte of RAM. The numbers are grouped in three categories: proof of all auxiliary lemmas, proof of the abstraction, and proof of the synchronization property. For small numbers of nodes (less than 5), proving the lemmas is the dominant computation cost, not because the lemmas are expensive to prove but because there are several of them. For larger numbers of nodes, checking the abstraction dominates.

Using the same modeling and abstraction method, we have also formalized a more complex version of the startup algorithm. This version includes an active hub that is assumed to be reliable, but nodes may be faulty. The verification was done under the

**Table 1.** Verification Times.

| | Simplified Startup | | | | Fault-Tolerant Startup | | | |
|---|---|---|---|---|---|---|---|---|
| $N$ | lemmas | abstract. | synchro | total | lemmas | abstract. | synchro | total |
| 2 | 34.85 | 4.91 | 3.97 | 43.73 | 166.82 | 31.19 | 10.60 | 208.61 |
| 3 | 55.38 | 14.13 | 7.02 | 76.53 | 234.53 | 71.44 | 25.38 | 331.35 |
| 4 | 87.56 | 31.56 | 10.76 | 129.88 | 324.94 | 154.50 | 67.45 | 546.89 |
| 5 | 111.23 | 117.89 | 17.86 | 246.98 | 432.71 | 456.42 | 168.75 | 1057.88 |
| 6 | 154.92 | 334.31 | 26.53 | 515.76 | 547.51 | 731.60 | 346.35 | 1625.46 |
| 7 | 197.62 | 642.72 | 33.41 | 873.75 | 739.17 | 1143.48 | 648.49 | 2531.14 |
| 8 | 255.07 | 1400.34 | 45.08 | 1700.49 | 921.85 | 1653.10 | 1100.38 | 3675.33 |
| 9 | 316.36 | 2892.85 | 56.84 | 3266.05 | 1213.51 | 3917.37 | 1524.91 | 6655.79 |
| 10 | 378.89 | 4923.45 | 84.79 | 5387.13 | 1478.82 | 4943.18 | 3353.97 | 9775.97 |

assumption that a single node is Byzantine faulty, and may attempt to broadcast arbitrary frames at any time. With a TTA cluster of 10 nodes, the model contains 99 state variables, of which 23 variables are real-valued. The simplified protocol is roughly half that size. For a cluster of 10 nodes, it contains 52 state variables, of which 12 are reals[2].

Other noticeable results were discovered during the proofs. In particular, the frame propagation delay must be less than half the duration of a slot for the startup protocol to work. This constraint had apparently not been noticed earlier. Our analysis also showed that the constants $\tau_i^{\text{listen}}$ do not need to be distinct for the protocol to work, as long as they are all at least equal to two round times.

# 6  Conclusion

We have presented a novel approach to modeling real-time systems based on calendars and timeouts. This approach enables one to specify dense-timed models as standard state-transition systems with no continuous dynamics. As a result, it is possible to verify these timed models using general-purpose tools such as provided by SAL. We have illustrated how the SAL infinite-state bounded model checker can be used as a theorem prover to efficiently verify timed models. Two main proof techniques were used: proof by $k$-induction and a method based on abstraction and verification diagrams. By decomposing complex proofs in relatively manageable steps, these techniques enable us to verify a nontrivial example of fault-tolerant real-time protocol, namely, the TTA startup algorithm, with as many as ten nodes.

This analysis extends previous work by Steiner, Rushby, Sorea, and Pfeifer [21] who have verified using model checking a discrete-time version of the same algorithm. They modeled a full TTA cluster with redundant hubs, and their analysis showed that the startup protocol can tolerate a faulty node or a faulty hub. This analysis went beyond previous experiments in model-checking fault-tolerant algorithms such as [23] and [24] by vastly increasing the number of scenarios considered. It achieved sufficient performance to support design exploration as well as verification.

---

[2] The full specifications are available at http://www.sdl.sri.com/users/bruno/sal/.

Lönn and Pettersson [25] consider startup algorithms for TDMA systems similar to TTA, and verify one of them using UPPAAL [26]. Their model is restricted to four nodes and does not deal with faults. Lönn and Pettersson note that extending the analysis to more than four nodes will be very difficult, as the verification of a four-node system was close to exhausting the 2 Gbyte memory of their computer, and because of the exponential blowup of model checking timed automata when the number of clocks increases.

The model and verification techniques presented in this paper can be extended in several directions, including applications to more complex versions of the TTA startup algorithm with redundant hubs, and verification of liveness properties. Other extensions include theoretical studies of the calendar-automata model and comparison with timed automata.

# References

1. Bensalem, S., Ganesh, V., Lakhnech, Y., Muñoz, C., Owre, S., Rueß, H., Rushby, J., Rusu, V., Saïdi, H., Shankar, N., Singerman, E., Tiwari, A.: An overview of SAL. In: Fifth NASA Langley Formal Methods Workshop, NASA Langley Research Center (2000) 187–196

2. de Moura, L., Owre, S., Rueß, H., Rushby, J., Shankar, N., Sorea, M., Tiwari, A.: Tool presentation: SAL 2. In: Computer-Aided Verification (CAV 2004), Springer-Verlag (2004)

3. Rushby, J.: Verification diagrams revisited: Disjunctive invariants for easy verification. In: Computer-Aided Verification (CAV 2000). Volume 1855 of Lecture Notes in Computer Science, Springer-Verlag (2000) 508–520

4. Steiner, W., Paulitsch, M.: The transition from asynchronous to synchronous system operation: An approach for distributed fault- tolerant systems. The 22nd International Conference on Distributed Computing Systems (ICDCS 2002) (2002)

5. Larsen, K.G., Pettersson, P., Yi, W.: UPPAAL: Status and developments. In: Computer-Aided Verification (CAV'97). Volume 1254 in Lecture Notes in Computer Science, Springer–Verlag (1997) 456–459

6. Bozga, M., Daws, C., Maler, O., Olivero, A., Tripakis, S., Yovine, S.: Kronos: A model-checking tool for real-time systems. In: Computer Aided Verification (CAV'98). Volume 1427 of Lecture Notes in Computer Science, Springer-Verlag (1998) 546–550

7. Wang, F.: Efficient verification of timed automata with BDD-like data-structures. In: 4th International Conference on Verification, Model Checking, and Abstract Interpretation. Volume 2575 of Lecture Notes in Computer Science, Springer-Verlag (2003) 189–205

8. Beyer, D., Lewerentz, C., Noack, A.: Rabbit: A tool for BDD-based verification of real-time systems. In: Computer-Aided Verification (CAV 2003), Volume 2725 of Lecture Notes in Computer Science, Springer-Verlag (2003) 122–125

9. Kaynar, D., Lynch, N., Segala, R., Vaandrager, F.: Timed I/O automata: A mathematical framework for modeling and analyzing real-time systems. In: Real-Time Systems Symposium (RTSS'03). IEEE Computer Society (2003) 166–177

10. Chaochen, Z., Hansen, M.R.: Duration Calculus: A Formal Approach to Real-Time Systems. Springer-Verlag (2004)

11. Skakkebæk, J.U., Shankar, N.: Towards a duration calculus proof assistant in PVS. In: Formal Techniques in Real-time and Fault-Tolerant Systems, Volume 863 of Lecture Notes in Computer Science, Springer-Verlag, (1994)

12. Archer, M., Heitmeyer, C.: Mechanical verification of timed automata: A case study. Technical Report NRL/MR/5546-98-8180, Naval Research Laboratory, Washington, DC (1998)

13. Filliâtre, J.C., Owre, S., Rueß, H., Shankar, N.: ICS: Integrated canonizer and solver. In: Computer-Aided Verification (CAV 2001), Volume 2102 of Lecture Notes in Computer Science, Springer-Verlag (2001) 246–249
14. de Moura, L., Rueß, H.: Lemmas on demand for satisfiability solvers. In: Fifth International Symposium on the Theory and Applications of Satisfiability Testing, (2002)
15. de Moura, L., Rueß, H., Sorea, M.: Bounded model checking and induction: From refutation to verification. In: Computer-Aided Verification (CAV 2003). Volume 2725 of LNCS., Springer-Verlag (2003) 14–26
16. Alur, R., Dill, D.L.: A theory of timed automata. Theoretical Computer Science **126** (1994) 183–235
17. Henzinger, T.A., Manna, Z., Pnueli, A.: Temporal proof methodologies for timed transition systems. Information and Computation **112** (1994) 273–337
18. Lynch, N., Vaandrager, F.: Forward and backward simulations for timing-based systems. In: REX Workshop. Real-Time: Theory and Practice. Volume 600 of Lecture Notes in Computer Science, Springer-Verlag (1991) 397–446
19. Dutertre, B., Sorea, M.: Timed systems in SAL. Technical report, SRI-SDL-04-03, SRI International, Menlo Park, CA (2004)
20. Sorea, M.: Bounded model checking for timed automata. Electronic Notes in Theoretical Computer Science **68** (2002) http://www.elsevier.com/locate/entcs/volume68.html
21. Steiner, W., Rushby, J., Sorea, M., Pfeifer, H.: Model checking a fault-tolerant startup algorithm: From design exploration to exhaustive fault simulation. DSN 2004 (2004)
22. Manna, Z., Pnueli, A.: Temporal verification diagrams. In: International Symposium on Theoretical Aspects of Computer Software (TACS'94). Volume 789 of Lecture Notes in Computer Science, Springer-Verlag (1994) 726–765
23. Yokogawa, T., Tsuchiya, T., Kikuno, T.: Automatic verification of fault tolerance using model checking. In: 2001 Pacific Rim International Symposium on Dependable Computing, Seoul, Korea (2001)
24. Bernardeschi, C., Fantechi, A., Gnesi, S.: Model checking fault tolerant systems. Software Testing, Verification and Reliability **12** (2002) 251–275
25. Lönn, H., Pettersson, P.: Formal verification of a TDMA protocol start-up mechanism. In: Pacific Rim International Symposium on Fault-Tolerant Systems (PRFTS '97), IEEE Computer Society (1997) 235–242
26. Larsen, K.G., Pettersson, P., Yi, W.: Uppaal in a nutshell. Int. Journal on Software Tools for Technology Transfer **1** (1997) 134–152

# Static Fault-Tolerant Real-Time Scheduling with "Pseudo-topological" Orders

Cătălin Dima[1], Alain Girault[2], and Yves Sorel[3]

[1] Université Paris 12, 61 av du Général de Gaulle, 94010 Créteil cedex, France
[2] INRIA Rhône-Alpes, 655 Av. de l'Europe, 38334 Saint-Ismier cedex, France
[3] INRIA Rocquencourt, B.P. 105, 78153 Le Chesnay cedex, France

**Abstract.** We give a graph-theoretical model for off-line fault-tolerant scheduling of dataflow algorithms onto multiprocessor architectures with distributed memory. Our framework allows the modeling of both processor and communication channel failures of the "fail silent" type (either transient or permanent), and failure masking is achieved by replicating operations and data communications. We show that, in general, the graph representing a fault-tolerant scheduling may have circuits; hence, the classical computation of starting and ending times of the operations and communications, based upon a topological order, is inapplicable. We thus provide a notion of "pseudo-topological order" that permits the computation of the starting and ending times even in the case of cyclic graphs. We also derive algorithms for computing the timeouts that are used for failure detection.

## 1 Introduction

Embedded systems are systems built for controlling physical hardware in a changing environment, and therefore are required to react to environmental stimuli within limited time. Therefore, the design of such systems requires a thorough temporal analysis of the expected reactions. On the other hand, limitations on hardware reliability may require additional fault-tolerance design techniques and may need distributed architectures.

The complexity of the design of such a system is usually coped with by decomposing the problem into subproblems. The fault-tolerance problem is the hardest one to address: one solution is to handle it at the level of hardware; see [14, 13, 19], to cite only a few. This solution has been extensively studied in the past decade and is very useful for ensuring reliable data transmission, failsignal, fail-silent "processor blocks", fault masking with "Byzantine" components and membership protocols. This approach is important as it hides a wealth of mechanisms for fault-tolerance from the software design; however, the types of failures it cannot handle need to be coped with at the design level.

Another solution is to combine scheduling strategies with fault detection mechanisms [8, 9, 16, 15]. Such a solution is suited to system architectures in which communications are supposed to be reliable and communication costs are small. Moreover, dynamic schedulers require the existence of a reliable "master" component. All these requirements induce some limitations on the applicability of these techniques for embedded systems.

Y. Lakhnech and S. Yovine (Eds.): FORMATS/FTRTFT 2004, LNCS 3253, pp. 215–230, 2004.
© Springer-Verlag Berlin Heidelberg 2004

A third solution is to introduce redundancy levels at the design phase [18, 11, 2]. Fault masking strategies like primary/backup or triple modular redundancy (multiple if more than one failure has to be tolerated), voting components, or membership protocols are then designed for failure masking. The scheduling strategies take into account durations of communications, and therefore this approach seems to be the most appropriate to embedded systems, in which limited computational power of part of the processors is combined with tight real-time constraints at the response level. The drawback of this solution is that it does not take into account channel failures.

Taking into account both processor and communication channel failures is crucial in critical and/or non-maintainable embedded systems, like autonomous vehicles or satellites. There exist methods based on the active replication of operations (resp. data dependences) onto the processors (resp. communication channels), but they usually adopt a fixed software redundancy level, therefore resulting in a sometimes high overhead [10]. We would like a general framework for relating more accurately the software redundancy to the hardware redundancy.

To achieve this, we propose a theoretical model for the problem of fault-tolerant static scheduling onto a distributed architecture. The basic idea is that the user will provide a set of *hardware failure patterns* to be toleared; then, a fault-tolerant scheduling will be the *union of several non-fault tolerant schedulings*, one for each possible failure pattern. Our model uses only basic notions from graph theory and a calculus with mins and maxs for computing the starting and ending times.

We consider distributed architectures whose memory is distributed too. Our model does not include any centralised control for detecting failures, nor membership protocol for exchanging information about failure occurrences. Also, we work with fail-silent components, an assumption that hides the mechanisms for achieving such behaviour (recent studies on modern processors have shown that fail-silence can be acheived at a reasonable cost [1]). This is a first step is relating the software redundancy to the hardware redundancy.

We use timeouts in order to detect failures of data communications, but also in order to propagate failure information. The reason is that, in our replication technique, the replicas of the same data transmission do not necessarily have the same source, the same destination, or the same route. Therefore, some replicas of the same task may "starve" because their needed input data do not arrive, and therefore they will not be able to send their data as well, propagating further this starvation to other tasks. This propagation is achieved with timeouts.

The theoretical problem raised by this approach is that, due to the need of redundant routings, we may have to schedule non-acyclic graphs. In classical scheduling theory, cyclic graphs raise the problem of the *existence* of a scheduling. Thanks to the construction principles of our fault-tolerant schedulings, this will not be the case in our framework, and this forms the core of our work and hence one of our original contributions.

We solve this problem by introducing an original notion of *pseudo-topological order*, which models the "state-machine" arbitration mechanism between replicas of the same operation. We show that a scheduling with replication can be ordered pseudo-topologically, and therefore there exists a minimal execution of it. We also prove the existence of the minimal timeout mapping, which associates to each scheduled operation (resp. data dependences) the latest time when it should start its execution in any of the failure patterns that must be tolerated +1 (all the execution times are expressed in time units, i.e., integers, hence the "+1"). These results are based upon two algorithms that can be seen as a basic technique for constructing a fault-tolerant scheduling.

Though we have named it a "static scheduling" model, the behaviour of each processor is quite dynamic as we construct "decision makers" on each component, capable of choosing at run time the sequence of operations to be performed on that component. Moreover, both processor and channel failures are treated uniformly in our model, it is only at the implementation that they will differ.

Finally, let us mention that this paper gives the theoretical framework for the heuristics studied in a previously published paper [3].

The paper is organised as follows: in the second section we define the problem of non-fault-tolerant scheduling of a set of tasks with precedence relations. The third section contains our graph-theoretic model of fault-tolerant scheduling, together with its principles of execution, formalised in the form of a min-max calculus of starting and ending times. The fourth section deals with the formalisation of the failure detection and propagation mechanisms. The core of this section is the computation of the *minimal timeout mapping*, used for failure detection. We end with some conclusions and future work.

## 2    Plain Schedulings

This section is a brief review of some well-known results from scheduling theory, presented in a perhaps different form in order to be further generalised to fault-tolerant scheduling [12]. For reasons of convenience in defining and manipulating schedulings, and especially due to the possibility of having data dependencies routed through several channels, we chose to represent programs as bipartite *dags* (directed acyclic graphs):

**Definition 1.** *A* **task dag** *is a bipartite dag* $G_A = (O_A, D_A, E_A)$.

Nodes in $O_A$ are tasks and nodes in $D_A$ are data dependencies between tasks; e.g., $(t_1, d_1), (d_1, t_2) \in E_A$, with $t_1, t_2 \in O_A$ and $d_1 \in D_A$ means that the task $t_1$, at the end of its execution, sends data to the task $t_2$, which waits for the reception of this data before starting its execution.

**Definition 2.** *An* **architecture graph** *is a bipartite undirected graph* $G_S = (P_S, C_S, E_S)$.

Nodes in $P_S$ are processors, nodes in $C_S$ are communication channels, and edges in $E_S$ always connect a processor to a channel.

Figure 1(left) represents an example of task dag. Here, $O_A = \{A, B, C, D\}$ and $D_A = \{A{\rightarrow}B, A{\rightarrow}C, B{\rightarrow}D, C{\rightarrow}D\}$. Figure 1(right) represents an example of an architecture graph. Here, $P_S = \{P_1, P_2, P_3, P_4\}$ and $C_S = \{C_1, C_2\}$.

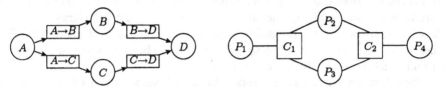

**Fig. 1.** Left: a task dag; Right: an architecture graph.

In the field of data-flow scheduling, each operation is placed onto some processor and each data dependency onto some channel, hence yielding a kind of copy of the task dag $G_A$, in which it is possible to have some data dependencies routed through several channels between their source and destination. Here we will call such a "placement" a *plain scheduling* and define it as follows:

**Definition 3.** *A **plain scheduling** of a task dag $G_A = (O_A, D_A, E_A)$ is a labelled dag $G = (V, E, \lambda)$ with $\lambda : V \longrightarrow O_A \cup D_A$, satisfying the following properties:*

**S1** *For each $v \in V$ such that $\lambda(v) = a \in O_A$, for each $b$ such that $(b, a) \in E_A$, there exists $v' \in V$ with $\lambda(v') = b$ and $(v', v) \in E$. That is, each scheduled operation must receive all its incoming data dependencies.*

**S2** *For each $v \in V$ such that $\lambda(v) = a \in D_A$, for each $b$ such that $(b, a) \in E_A$, there exists a sequence $v_1, \ldots, v_k \in V$ with $v_k = v$, $\lambda(v_1) = b$, $\lambda(v_2) = \ldots = \lambda(v_k) = a$ and $(v_i, v_{i+1}) \in E$ for all $1 \leq i \leq k - 1$. That is, data transmissions may be routed through several channels from their source to their destination.*

**S3** *For each $a \in O_A$ there exists exactly one $v \in V$ such that $\lambda(v) = a$. That is, each operation is scheduled exactly once.*

**S4** *For each $a \in D_A$, the set $\{v \in V \mid \lambda(v) = a\}$ forms a linear subgraph in $G$ (and is nonempty by condition S2). That is, the routings of any given data dependency go directly from the source operation to the destination operation.*

*Given an architecture graph $G_S = (P_S, C_S, E_S)$ and a mapping $\pi : V \longrightarrow P_S \cup C_S$, we say that the pair $(G, \pi)$ is a **plain scheduling onto** $G_S$ if $\pi$ satisfies the following condition:*

$$\forall v \in V, \lambda(v) \in O_A \implies \pi(v) \in P_S$$

Several clarifications and comments are needed concerning this definition. Firstly, the *scheduling order* on each processor is abstracted as edges $(v, v')$ for which $(\lambda(v), \lambda(v')) \notin E$ and $\lambda(v) \neq \lambda(v')$.

Then observe that properties S1 and S2 show the difference between how operations and data dependencies are scheduled, hence the "bipartite dag" model for task dags. Finally, note that there can be nodes $v \in V$ such that $\lambda(v) \in D_A$

(that is, carrying a data dependency) and $\pi(v) \in P$ (that is, scheduled onto some processor). These nodes model two things: reroutings between adjacent channels, and intra-processor transmissions of data.

Figure 2 represents *one* plain scheduling of the task dag of Figure 1(left) onto the architecture graph of Figure 1(right). The notation "$A/P_4$" means that $\pi(A) = P_4$; ovals are operations scheduled onto some processor (e.g., $A/P_4$); square rectangles are data dependencies scheduled onto some communication channel (e.g., $A{\to}B/C_1$); and rounded rectangles are data dependencies scheduled onto some processor for re-routing (e.g., $A{\to}B/P_3$). A plain scheduling, in our sense, is the *result* of some static scheduling algorithm. The restrictions on the placement of tasks or data dependencies, which guide the respective algorithm, are not visible here – we only have the result produced by such restrictions.

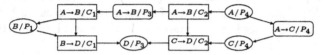

**Fig. 2.** A plain scheduling of the task dag onto the architecture graph of Figure 1.

Once a plain scheduling is created and we know the execution time of each task and the duration of sending each data dependency onto its respective channel, we may compute the starting time for each of them by a least fix-point computation, based upon the following definition of an execution:

An **execution** of a plain scheduling onto a distributed architecture is governed by the following three principles:

P1 Each task is executed only after receiving all the data dependencies it needs.

P2 Each data dependency is executed only after the task issuing it terminates.

P3 Each operation (task or data-dependency) is executed only after all the operations that precede it on the same architecture component are finished.

This worst-case computation is based on the knowledge of *maximal* duration of execution for each task, resp. data dependency, when it is scheduled onto some processor, resp. channel. The mapping $d$ is constructed from this information in the straightforward manner. As an example, our scheduling in Figure 2 may give the minimal execution represented graphically in the figure at the left, where the duration of execution of each node in $G$ is equal to the height of its corresponding box.

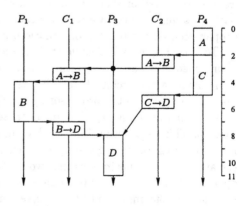

Formally, given a function $d : V \longrightarrow \mathbb{N}$, denoting the *duration of executing each scheduled task and data dependency*, we define two applications $\alpha, \beta : V \longrightarrow \mathbb{N}$, called resp. the *starting* and the *ending time*, by the two following equations:

$$\forall v \in V, \quad \alpha(v) = \max\left\{\beta(v') \mid (v', v) \in E\right\}, \quad \beta(v) = \alpha(v) + d(v) \qquad (1)$$

The computation of $\alpha$ and $\beta$ lies on the notion of *topological order*, which says that each dag $G = (V, E)$ can be linearly ordered, such that each node has a bigger index than all of its predecessors in $G$. Placements that satisfy all the four requirements S1 to S4 of a plain scheduling, failing only on the requirement to be *acyclic*, cannot be executed: the system of equations (1) has no solution, which means that the schedule is deadlocked.

It is important to note that the way such a plain scheduling (hence non fault-tolerant) is obtained is outside the scope of our article. There exist numerous references on this problem, e.g. [20, 5, 7, 4, 12].

Before ending this section, let us remind the union operation on graphs: given two graphs $G = (V, E)$ and $G' = (V', E')$, their *union* is the graph $G'' = (V \cup V', E \cup E')$. Note that the two sets of nodes might not necessarily be disjoint, and in this case the nodes in the intersection $V \cap V'$ might be connected through edges that are in $E$ or in $E'$.

## 3    Schedulings with Replication

Our view of a static scheduling that tolerates *several* failure patterns is as a *family* of plain schedulings, one for each failure pattern which must be tolerated. This informal definition captures the simplest procedure one can design to obtain a fault tolerant scheduling: compute a plain scheduling for each failure pattern, then put all the plain schedulings together.

There may be several ways to put together the plain schedulings, each one corresponding to a decision mechanism for switching between them in the presence of failures. For example, we may have a table giving the sequence of operations to be executed on each processor in the presence of each failure pattern. But this choice corresponds to a centralised failure detection mechanisms. And, as we are in a distributed environment and therefore the information on the failure pattern is quite sparse, we would rather have some distributed mechanisms for propagating failure pattern information, based on a local decision mechanism.

To this end, we will assume that, in our family of plain schedulings, any two plain schedulings are not "contradictory" on the ordering they impose on each component in the architecture. That is, if in one plain scheduling $G_1$ a task $a$ precedes a task $b$ on the processor $p$, and both tasks are scheduled onto $p$ in another plain scheduling $G_2$, then in $G_2$ these two tasks must be in the same order as on $p$. This assumption implies that, in the combination of all plain schedulings, each task or data dependency occurs at most once on each component in the architecture. This implies that we do not mask failures by rescheduling some operations and/or re-sending some data dependency. The propagation mechanism is then the impossibility to receive some data dependency within a bounded amount of time – that is, a timeout mechanism on each processor.

Consider, for example, the case of the task dag and the architecture graph given in Figure 1, and suppose that we want to tolerate either one failure for each channel, or one failure for each processor, with the exception of $P_3$ (say, an actuator whose replication cannot be supported at scheduling). Suppose also that task $D$ must always be on processor $P_3$. We will consider the plain scheduling of Figure 2(c) (it supports the failure of $P_2$), and the plain schedulings of Figures 3(a) (for the failures of $P_1$ and/or $C_1$), and 3(b) (for the failures of $P_4$ and/or $C_2$). We will then combine these three plain schedulings into the *scheduling with replication* of Figure 3(c).

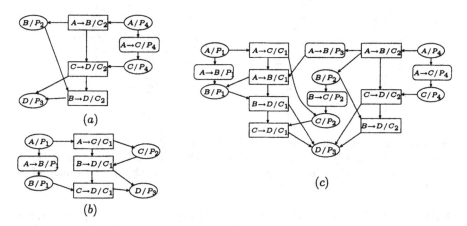

**Fig. 3.** (a) A plain scheduling tolerating the failures of $P_1$ and $C_1$. (b) A plain scheduling tolerating the failures of $P_4$ and/or $C_2$. (c) The scheduling with replication resulting from the combination of the two plain schedulings (a), (b) and the one from Figure 2.

This approach hides the following theoretical problem: the graphs that model such fault-tolerant schedulings *may contain circuits*. Formally, the process of "putting together" several plain schedulings must be modelled as a union of graphs, due to the requirement that, on each processor, each operation is scheduled at most once. But *unions of dags are not necessarily dags*. An example is provided in Figure 4. We have a symmetric "diamond" architecture, given in Figure 4(a), on which we want to tolerate two failure patterns: $\{C_1, C_5\}$ and $\{C_2, C_4\}$. We want to schedule the simple task dag of Figure 4(d), but with the constraint that $A$ must be put on $P_1$ and $B$ must be put on $P_4$ (say, because these processors are dedicated). The two failure patterns yield respectively the two reduced architectures of Figures 4(c) and (d). For both reduced architectures, we obtain respectively the plain schedulings of Figures 4(e) and (f). When combined, we obtain the scheduling with replication of Figure 4(g). More precisely, on the middle channel $C_3$, the data dependency $A \rightarrow B$ may flow in both directions! However none of the circuits obtained in the union of graphs really come into play in a real execution – they are there only because such a scheduling models the *set* of all possible executions.

The sequel of this section is dedicated to showing that the existence of circuits is not harmful when computing the execution of a scheduling with replication. We start with the formalisation of the notion of scheduling with replication.

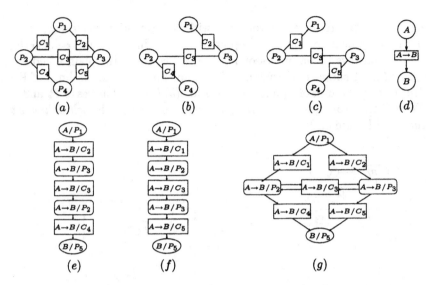

**Fig. 4.** (a) An architecture graph. (b−c) The two reduced architectures corresponding to the failure patterns $\{C_1, C_5\}$ and $\{C_2, C_4\}$. (d) The task dag to be scheduled. (e−f) The two plain schedulings of (d) onto (b) and (c) respectively. (g) The union of (e) and (f), which is not a dag!

**Definition 4.** *A scheduling with replication of a task dag $A = (O_A, D_A, E_A)$ is a labelled dag $G = (V, E, \lambda)$, with $\lambda : V \longrightarrow O_A \cup D_A$ satisfying the properties S1 and S2 of Definition 3, and the following additional property:*

**S5** *For each circuit $v_1, \ldots, v_k, v_{k+1} = v_1$ of $G$, there exists $d \in D_A$ s.t. for all $1 \leq i \leq k$, $\lambda(v_i) = d$. That is, the only allowed circuits in $G$ are those labelled with the same symbol, which must be in $D_A$.*

Since in schedulings with replication some operations might occur on several processors and some data dependencies might be routed through different paths to the same destination, the principles of execution stated in the previous section need to be relaxed. It is especially the first and the second principles that need to be restated as follows:

An **execution** of a plain scheduling onto a distributed architecture is governed by the following three principles:

**P1'** Each task can be executed only after it has received *at least one copy* of each data dependency it needs.

**P2'** Each data dependency can be transmitted only after *one of the replicas* of the tasks which may issue it has finished its execution, and hence has produced the corresponding data.

**P3'** Same as principle P3.

We use a mapping $d : V \longrightarrow \mathbb{N}$, which denotes the duration of executing each node of the task dag (resp. from $O_A$ or $D_A$) onto each component of the architecture (resp. processor or communication channel). We accept that some of the nodes may have zero duration of execution: it is the case with intra-processor data transmission; sometimes, even routings of some data dependencies between two adjacent channels may be considered as taking zero time. However we will consider that each complete routing of data through one or more channels takes at most one time unit. We will also impose a technical restriction on mappings $d$: for each circuit in $G$, if we sum up all the durations of nodes in the circuit, we get a strictly positive integer. This technical requirement will be essential in the proof of the existence of the minimal timeout mapping in the next section. Mappings $d : V \longrightarrow \mathbb{N}$ satisfying this requirement will be called *duration constraints*.

**Definition 5.** *An **execution** of a scheduling $G = (V, E, \lambda)$, with duration constraints $d : V \longrightarrow \mathbb{N}$, is a pair of functions $f = (\alpha, \beta)$, with $\alpha, \beta : V \longrightarrow \mathbb{N}$, respectively called starting time and ending time, and defined as follows:*

1. *Any task must start after it has received the first copy of each needed data dependencies: for each $a \in O_A$ and $v \in V$ with $(a, \lambda(v)) \in E_A$,*
$$\alpha(v) \geq \min \left\{ \beta(v') \mid \lambda(v') = a, (v', v) \in E \right\}$$

2. *Any data dependency starts after the termination of at least one of the tasks issuing it: for each $a \in D_A$ and $v \in V$ with $(a, \lambda(v)) \in E_A$,*
$$\alpha(v) \geq \min \left\{ \beta(v') \mid (v', v) \in E, \lambda(v') = \lambda(v) \text{ or } \lambda(v') = a \right\}$$

3. *Any task or data-dependency starts after the termination of all operations preceding it on the same architecture component:*
   *for each $v, v' \in V$ with $(v', v) \in E$ and $(\lambda(v'), \lambda(v)) \notin E_A, \alpha(v) \geq \beta(v')$*

4. *The ending time of any given task or data-dependency is equal to its starting time plus its duration: for each $v \in V$, $\beta(v) = \alpha(v) + d(v)$.*

Executions can be compared componentwise, i.e., given two executions $f_1 = (\alpha_1, \beta_1)$ and $f_2 = (\alpha_2, \beta_2)$, we put $f_1 \leq f_2$ if, for each node $v \in V$, $\alpha_1(v) \leq \alpha_2(v)$ and $\beta_1(v) \leq \beta_2(v)$.

We may then prove that the set of executions associated to a scheduling with replication forms a *complete lattice* w.r.t. this order, that is, an *infimum* and a *supremum* exists for any set of executions. Definition 5 is in fact a fixpoint definition in the lattice of executions. But we have not yet showed that this lattice is nonempty – fact which would imply that there exists a least element in it, which will be called the **minimal execution**.

For plain schedulings, the existence of an execution is a corollary of the acyclicity of the graph $G$. As schedulings with replication may have cycles, we need to identify a weaker property that assures the existence of executions. The searched-for property is the following:

**Definition 6.** *A **pseudo-topological order** of a scheduling $G = (V, E, \lambda)$ is a bijection $\phi : V \longrightarrow [1 \ldots n]$ (where $n = \text{card}(V)$), such that for all $v \in V$, the following properties hold:*

1. *If $\lambda(v) \in O_A$, then for each $d \in D_A$ for which $(d, \lambda(v)) \in E_A$, there exists $v' \in V$ such that $\lambda(v') = d$, $(v', v) \in E$, and $\phi(v') < \phi(v)$.*

2. If $\lambda(v) \in D_A$, then there exists $v' \in V$ with $(v', v) \in E$ and $\phi(v') < \phi(v)$, such that either $\lambda(v') = \lambda(v)$ or $(\lambda(v'), \lambda(v)) \in E_A$.
3. For each $v' \in V$, if $(v', v) \in E$, $(\lambda(v'), \lambda(v)) \notin E_A$, and $\lambda(v') \neq \lambda(v)$, then $\phi(v') < \phi(v)$.

**Lemma 1.** *Any scheduling $G = (V, E, \lambda)$ has a pseudo-topological order .*

The proof of this lemma is constructive: we consider the following algorithm, whose entry is a scheduling $G = (V, E, \lambda)$ of a graph $A = (O_A, D_A, E_A)$ and whose output is a bijection $\phi_n : V \longrightarrow [1 \ldots n]$ which represents a pseudo-topological order of $G$:

**Algorithm 1** Pseudo-topological order
```
1   begin
2       k := 1; X_0 := ∅;
3       while k ≤ n do
4           Choose some node w ∈ V such that:
```
    ❖ For all $w'' \in V$ such that $(w'', w) \in E$, $\lambda(w'') \neq \lambda(w)$, and $(\lambda(w''), \lambda(w)) \notin E_A$, we have $w'' \in X_{k-1}$;
    ❖ If $\lambda(w) \in D_A$, then $\exists\, w' \in X_{k-1} \cap V$ with either $\lambda(w') = \lambda(w)$ or $(\lambda(w'), \lambda(w)) \in E_A$ and such that $(w', w) \in E$;
    ❖ If $\lambda(w) \in O_A$, then $\forall\, b \in D_A$ with $(b, \lambda(w)) \in E_A$, $\exists\, w' \in X_{k-1}$ such that $\lambda(w') = b$ and $(w', w) \in E$;
```
5           X_k := X_{k-1} ∪ {w};
6           φ(k) := w;
7           k := k + 1;
8       end while
9   end
```

*Claim.* The choice step at line 4 can be applied for any $k \leq card(V)$.

This claim can be proved by contradiction, since the impossibility to make the choice step in the algorithm would imply the existence of a circuit in the graph, whose nodes would be labeled with different symbols from $O_A \cup D_A$, in contradiction with requirement S5.

It follows that the algorithm terminates, that is, $X_n = V$. Therefore, the application $\phi : V \longrightarrow [1 \ldots n]$ defined by $\phi(v) = k$ iff $v$ is the node chosen at the $k$-th step, is a pseudo-topological order on $V$. This fact proves Lemma 1.

**Theorem 1.** *The set of executions associated to any scheduling $G = (V, E, \lambda)$ is nonempty.*

*Proof.* First, we use our Algorithm 1 to construct a pseudo-topological order $\phi : V \longrightarrow [1 \ldots n]$ of the scheduling $G$. Then, we construct an execution $(\alpha^\phi, \beta^\phi)$ inductively as follows:

We start with the pair of totally undefined partial functions $\alpha_0^\phi, \beta_0^\phi : V \dashrightarrow [1 \ldots n]$. That is, both $\alpha_0^\phi(v)$ and $\beta_0^\phi(v)$ are undefined for any node $v \in V$.

Suppose then, by induction, that we have built the pair of partial functions $(\alpha_{k-1}^\phi, \beta_{k-1}^\phi)$, such that $\alpha_{k-1}^\phi : V \dashrightarrow [1 \ldots n]$ (resp. $\beta_{k-1}^\phi$) associates to each vertex $v \in V$ with $\phi(v) \leq k - 1$ the *starting* execution time (resp. the *ending* execution time). We then extend these partial functions to a new pair $(\alpha_k^\phi, \beta_k^\phi)$ with $\alpha_k^\phi, \beta_k^\phi : V \multimap [1 \ldots n]$, by defining $\alpha_k^\phi(v_k)$ and $\beta_k^\phi(v_k)$ (where $v_k$ is the $k$-th node of the pseudo-topological order, i.e., $\phi(v_k) = k$) as follows:

1. First, we compute the two following numbers:

$$x_1(v_k) = \max\left\{\beta_{k-1}^\phi(v') \mid (v', v_k) \in E \text{ and } (\lambda(v'), \lambda(v_k)) \notin E_A, \phi(v') < \phi(v_k)\right\}$$

$$x_2(v_k) = \begin{cases} \max\left\{\min\left\{\beta_{k-1}^\phi(v') \mid (v', v_k) \in E, \lambda(v') = b\right\} \mid \right. \\ \quad \left. b \in D_A, (b, \lambda(v_k)) \in E_A, \phi(v') < \phi(v_k)\right\} & \text{if } \lambda(v_k) \in O_A, \\ \min\left\{\beta_{k-1}^\phi(v') \mid (v', v_k) \in E, \phi(v') < \phi(v_k)\right. \\ \quad \left. \text{and either } \lambda(v') = \lambda(v_k) \text{ or } (\lambda(v'), \lambda(v_k)) \in E_A\right\} & \text{if } \lambda(v_k) \in D_A \end{cases}$$

Note that, by the assumption that $\phi$ is a pseudo-topological order, all the sets involved in the above computations are nonempty.

2. We then take $\alpha_k^\phi(v_k) = \max\left(x_1(v_k), x_2(v_k)\right)$ and $\beta_k^\phi(v_k) = \alpha_k(v_k) + d(v_k)$.

It is then routine to check that $\alpha_n$ and $\beta_n$ are indeed executions.     $\square$

**Corollary 1.** *There exists a minimal execution associated to any scheduling* $G = (V, E, \lambda)$.

*Proof.* The minimal execution is defined as follows: for each $v \in V$,

$$\alpha_{min}(v) = \min\left\{\alpha_n^\phi(v) \mid \phi \text{ pseudo-topological order of } G\right\}$$
$$\beta_{min}(v) = \alpha_{min}(v) + d(v).$$     $\square$

The figure here on the right gives the minimal execution for the scheduling in Figure 4 (in the absence of failures). The duration constraints are given by the vertical dimension of each rectangle, while the arrows without any target indicate lost arbitration between replicas.

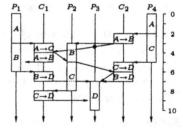

## 4   Schedulings with Replication and Failures

The fault detection mechanism described in Section 3 uses timeouts on the scheduled task and data communications. This section is concerned with the formalisation of this mechanism. Again, we will make use of the notion of pseudo-topological order: it will help us in computing the timeouts. Note that computing the timeout of a scheduled operation as the max of the ending times of all the operations that precede it in the scheduling might not work, because of the possible existence of circular dependencies: this is the same problem emphasised in Section 2, and which required the introduction of the notion of pseudo-topological order.

A **failure pattern** in a scheduling $G = (V, E, \lambda)$ is just a subset $F \subseteq V$ of nodes. In general, we will consider a set of failure patterns $\mathcal{F} \subseteq \mathcal{P}(V)$. The result of removing a set $F$ of nodes from a scheduling $G = (V, E, \lambda)$ is simply a labelled graph $G_F = (V_F, E_F, \lambda_F)$ with $E_F = E \cap (V_F \times V_F)$ and $\lambda_F = \lambda\big|_{V_F}$. $G_F$ might not be a scheduling – some nodes may fail to satisfy the requirements S1 or S2 of Definition 4. This models the situation in which some operation does not receive one or more data that it needs. We will then say that $G_F$ is a **scheduling reduced by the failure pattern** $F$.

If this graph *contains* a scheduling, i.e., there exists a scheduling $\overline{G}_F = (\overline{V}_F, \overline{E}_F, \overline{\lambda}_F)$ with $\overline{V}_F \subseteq V_F$ and $\overline{\lambda}_F = \lambda_F\big|_{\overline{V}_F}$, then we say that $G$ **tolerates the failure pattern** $F$. Note that if $G$ tolerates a failure pattern $F$, then it tolerates any failure pattern $F' \subseteq F$. On the other hand, if $G$ tolerates two failure patterns $F_1$ and $F_2$, then in general it *does not* tolerate $F_1 \cup F_2$. Hence, what we give as failure patterns are *maximal* combination of faulty components.

Graphs like $G_F$ cannot be "executed" using the principles given in Section 3 since some nodes may not receive all their data – we call such nodes as *starving*. Starving operations and data dependencies are not executed and, in order to prevent the system from being blocked, the component should try executing the next operation in its own scheduling. This is precisely how our obtained schedules mask the failures. Hence, components detect only a limited part of the "failure scenario", namely the subgraph which leads to the starving node.

We will formally say that even starving nodes are executed, but imposing that their duration of execution be zero. We will also require that, when an operation receives all its data (i.e., is not starving), it must be started before its timeout expires – just to avoid going into "philosophical" problems about the feasibility of several "instantaneous actions" in zero time:

**Definition 7.** *An **execution** of a scheduling reduced by a failure pattern $G_F = (V_F, E_F, \lambda_F)$, with duration constraints $d : V_F \longrightarrow \mathbb{N}$ and timeout mapping $\theta : V_F \longrightarrow \mathbb{N}$ is a tuple of functions $f = (\alpha, \beta, \varepsilon)$, with $\alpha, \beta : V_F \longrightarrow \mathbb{N}$ (the starting, resp. ending times) and $\varepsilon : V_F \longrightarrow \{0, 1\}$ (the execution bit), having the following properties:*

1. *For each $v \in V_F$, if we denote*
   $$U_v^F = \{\beta(v') \mid v' \in V_F, (v', v) \in E_F, \text{ and } (\lambda(v'), \lambda(v)) \notin E_A, \lambda(v') \neq \lambda(v)\}$$
   *then $\alpha(v) \geq \max U_v^F$.*
2. *For each $v \in V_F$ such that $\lambda(v) \in O_A$ and for each $a \in D_A$ such that $(a, \lambda(v)) \in E_A$, if we denote:*
   $$T_{v,a}^F = \{\beta(v') \mid v' \in V_F, \lambda(v') = a, (v', v) \in E_F, \text{ and } \varepsilon(v') = 1\}$$
   *then $\alpha(v) \geq \min\left(\theta(v), \max_{a \in D_A}(\min T_{v,a}^F)\right)$.*
3. *For each $v \in V_F$ such that $\lambda(v) \in D_A$, if we denote*
   $$T_v^F = \{\beta(v') \mid v' \in V_F, \varepsilon(v') = 1 \text{ and either } (\lambda(v'), \lambda(v)) \in E_A \text{ or } \lambda(v') = \lambda(v)\} \text{ then } \alpha(v) \geq \min\left(\theta(v), \min T_v^F\right).$$
4. *For each $v \in V_F$, $\beta(v) = \alpha(v) + d(v) \cdot \varepsilon(v)$ where $\varepsilon(v) = \begin{cases} 1 & \text{if } \alpha(v) < \theta(v) \\ 0 & \text{otherwise} \end{cases}$*

Using the notion of pseudo-topological order (with slight modifications), we may prove that, for each timeout mapping $\theta$, the set of executions of $G_F$ is nonempty. Moreover, we may prove that the **minimal execution** of $G_F$, denoted $(\alpha_F, \beta_F, \varepsilon_F)$ exists and can be computed as the least fix point of the following system of equations (here, minimality refers only to the tuple $(\alpha_F, \beta_F)$):

1. For each $v \in V_F$ such that $\lambda(v) \in O_A$ and for each $a \in D_A$ such that $(a, \lambda(v)) \in E_A$, $\alpha_F(v) = \max\left( \min\left(\theta(v), \max_{a \in D_A}(\min T_{v,a}^F)\right), \max U_v^F \right)$
2. For each $v \in V'$ with $\lambda(v) \in D_A$, $\alpha_F(v) = \max\left( \min\left(\theta(v), \min T_v^F\right), \max U_v^F \right)$.
3. And for each $v \in V$, $\beta_F(v) = \alpha_F(v) + d(v) \cdot \varepsilon_F(v)$, where $\varepsilon_F(v) = 1$ if $\alpha_F(v) < \theta(v)$, $\varepsilon_F(v) = 0$ otherwise.

Here $T_{v,a}^F$, $T_v^F$, and $U_v^F$ are the notations from Definition 7.

However, a bad choice of a timeout mapping may induce that some operations that may receive all their data be not executed, because the wait for the reception of the respective data is greater than the timeout. We will therefore call an execution *correct* if this situation does not occur, that is:

**Definition 8.** *An execution $(\alpha, \beta, \varepsilon)$ of $G_F$ is* **correct** *provided that it satisfies the following property: for each $v \in V_F$, if $\max\limits_{a \in D_A}(\min T_{v,a}^F) \neq \infty$ then $\varepsilon(v) = 1$.*

Then, the **minimal timeout** ensures that the minimal execution of the scheduling $G = (V, E, \lambda)$ reduced by any of the failure patterns from $\mathcal{F}$ is correct. We will construct this minimal timeout by repeatedly computing the minimal execution of each $G_F$ in which non-starving nodes have an infinite timeout, whereas starving nodes share the same timeout for different failure patterns $F$.

Our algorithm starts with a zero timeout for all nodes, $\theta_0(v) = 0$. At each step $i$ and for each failure pattern $F$, we utilize the timeout mapping $\overline{\theta}_i^F$ defined by $\overline{\theta}_i^F(v) = \theta_{i-1}(v)$ if $v$ is starving, and $\overline{\theta}_i^F(v) = \infty$ otherwise. We compute the minimal execution $(\alpha_F, \beta_F, \varepsilon_F)$ induced by this timeout mapping, and then we compute $\theta_i(v)$ as the maximum of the starting times for $v$ in each reduced graph $G_F$ in which $v$ is non-starving. In the following we denote $\overline{G}_F = (\overline{V}_F, \overline{E}_F, \overline{\lambda}_F)$ the *maximal* scheduling included in the graph $G_F$, assumed to exist for all $F \in \mathcal{F}$.

**Algorithm 2** Timeout mapping computation
```
1   begin
2       forall v ∈ V do θ₀(v) := 0;
3       i := 0;
4       repeat
5           i := i + 1;
6           forall F ∈ F do
7               put θ̄ᵢᶠ(v) = { θᵢ₋₁(v)   if v ∉ V̄_F (i.e., v is starving)
                               { ∞         otherwise
8               (αᵢᶠ, βᵢᶠ, εᵢᶠ) := the minimal execution induced by θ̄ᵢᶠ;
9           end for
10          forall v ∈ V do θᵢ(v) := max_{F∈F}{αᵢᶠ(v) + 1 | v ∈ V_F}.
11      until θᵢ = θᵢ₋₁
12  end
```

**Proposition 1.** *For each $i \in \mathbb{N}$, $\theta_i \geq \theta_{i-1}$.*

The proof runs by induction on $i$, using the fact that mins and maxs commute with inequalities and that for each $F \in \mathcal{F}$, $\overline{\theta}_0^F$ is the smallest timeout mapping for which $\theta(v) = \infty$ for non-starving nodes $v$.

**Proposition 2.** *Algorithm 2 terminates, i.e., there exists $i \in \mathbb{N}$ with $\theta_i = \theta_{i-1}$.*

*Proof.* Remind that a path in a graph is called *simple* if it has no loop. We call the *weight* of a path $p = (v_1, \ldots, v_k)$ the sum $w(p) = \sum_{1 \leq i \leq k} d(v_i)$. For each $v \in V$, denote $M(v)$ the max of the weights of all simple paths in $G$ ending in $v$.

We may prove by induction on $i$ that $\beta_i^F(v) \leq M(v)$ for each $v \in V$, fact which would end our proof since the mapping $M$ would then provide an upper bound for the increments on $\theta_i$. To this end, denote $p = (v_1, \ldots, v_k)$ the path that ends in some node $v = v_k$ and that is defined by the property that $\beta_i^F(v_j) = \alpha_i^F(v_{j-1})$. Hence, $p$ consists of nodes on a "critical path" that ends in $v$.

Two cases may occur: either $v_1$ has no predecessor in $V$ or is a starving node, hence is "executed" (actually, skipped) when its timeout expires. No other case is possible since $(\alpha_i^F, \beta_i^F, \varepsilon_i^F)$ is a minimal execution.

In the first case, the claim is trivially proved, since $p$ is a path that does not contain any circuit (again by definition of an execution).

In the second case, we will assume that $v_1$ is the only starving node in $p$ and, moreover, that there does not exist another non-starving node $v'$ which leads us to the first case. We have that

$$\alpha_i^F(v_2) = \beta_i^F(v_1) = \alpha_i^F(v_1) = \theta_{i-1}(v_1) = \alpha_{i-1}^{F'}(v_1) + 1$$

for some failure pattern $F'$. Since we have considered that the duration of any node is greater than 1 time unit, we then have that $\alpha_i^F(v_2) = \beta_i^F(v_1) \leq \beta_{i-1}^{F'}(v_1)$. On the other hand, by the induction hypothesis, $\beta_{i-1}^{F'}(v_1) \leq M(v_1)$. Therefore,

$$\beta_i^F(v) = \beta_i^F(v) - \alpha_i^F(v_2) + \beta_i^F(v_1) \leq w(p) + M(v_1)$$

Observe now that we must have $(\lambda(v_1), \lambda(v_2)) \notin E_A$. This follows from the assumption that $v_1$ is starving, $v_2$ is non-starving, and there exists no other non-starving node $v'$ with $\beta_i^F(v') = \alpha_i^F(v_2)$. But then, the concatenation of any simple path that ends in $v_1$ with $p$ cannot have circuits by requirement S5 in the definition of schedulings with replication. This means that $w(p) + M(v_1) \leq M(v)$, fact which ends our proof.                                                                $\square$

**Proposition 3.** *The timeout mapping $\theta_i$ which is computed by the algorithm is correct for all failure patterns and is the minimal timeout mapping with this property.*

*Proof.* The correctness of the timeout mapping is ensured by the exit condition of the loop – we may only exit the loop when, for each node, the computed timeout $\theta_i(v)$ exceeds all the starting times in each failure pattern, and hence only starving nodes may reach their timeout. The second property follows by showing, by induction on $i$, that for each correct execution $(\alpha, \beta, \varepsilon)$ we have $(\alpha_i^F, \beta_i^F) \leq (\alpha, \beta)$.                                                                $\square$

As an example, for the scheduling with replication given in Figure 3, the minimal timeout mapping is the following:

$$\theta(A/P_1) = \theta(A/P_4) = 1$$
$$\theta(B/P_1) = \theta(B/P_2) = \theta(A{\to}C/C_2) = 4$$
$$\theta(C/P_2) = \theta(C{\to}D/C_2) = 6$$
$$\theta(C{\to}D/C_1) = \theta(D/P_3) = 9$$

$$\theta(C/P_4) = \theta(A{\to}B/C_2) = 3$$
$$\theta(A{\to}B/C_1) = 5$$
$$\theta(B{\to}D/C_1) = \theta(B{\to}D/C_2) = 7$$

## 5   Conclusions

We have presented some results on the fundamentals of a theory of static fault-tolerant scheduling. The main problem we have investigated is the presence of circuits in unions of plain schedulings. We have introduced a notion of scheduling with replication, which models the loading of a system which is supposed to tolerate a family of failure patterns. We have also introduced the notion of execution of such a scheduling, which models some natural principles concerning the arbitration between replicas. We have also provided the notions of pseudo-topological order and of timeout mapping, which assure the existence and the correctness of minimal executions of a scheduling with replication.

Our work is only on the theoretical side, and the complexity of the algorithms in our paper is rather important for a practical use. In fact, all the problems treated here are NP-complete problems [6]. But we think that this theoretical layout may help developing heuristics for special architectures and/or special types of task dags, as it has been done in [17], and eventually compare the static scheduling performances with other techniques of fault-tolerant scheduling which take into account both processor and channel failures. Another possible approach for the fault-tolerant scheduling problem, that can tolerate both processor and channel failures, can be the combination of the redundancy techniques for processor failures with the fault-tolerant routing techniques. However, this combination seems not to have been given attention up to now.

## References

1. M. Baleani, A. Ferrari, L. Mangeruca, M. Peri, S. Pezzini, and A. Sangiovanni-Vincentelli. Fault-tolerant platforms for automotive safety-critical applications. In *International Conference on Compilers, Architectures and Synthesis for Embedded Systems, CASES'03*, San Jose, USA, November 2003. ACM.
2. J. Bannister and K. Trivedi. Task allocation in fault-tolerant distributed systems. *Acta Informatica*, 20:261–281, 1983.
3. C. Dima, A. Girault, C. Lavarenne, and Y. Sorel. Off-line real-time fault-tolerant scheduling. In *Proceedings of 9th Euromicro Workshop PDP'2001*, pages 410–417. IEEE Computer Society Press, 2001.
4. G. Fohler and K. Ramamritham. Static scheduling of pipelined periodic tasks in distributed real-time systems. In *Euromicro Workshop on Real-Time Systems, EWRTS'97*, Toledo, Spain, June 1997. IEEE Computer Society Press.

5. M.R. Garey and D.S. Johnson. Complexity bounds for multiprocessor scheduling with resource constraints. *SIAM J. Computing*, 4(3):187–200, 1975.
6. M.R. Garey and D.S. Johnson. *Computers and Intractability, a Guide to the Theory of NP-Completeness*. W. H. Freeman Company, San Francisco, 1979.
7. A. Gerasoulis and T. Yang. A comparison of clustering heuristics for scheduling directed acyclic graphs on multiprocessors. *Journal of Parallel and Distributed Computing*, 16(4):276–291, December 1992.
8. S. Ghosh. *Guaranteeing Fault-Tolerance through Scheduling in Real-Time Systems*. Phd thesis, University of Pittsburgh, 1996.
9. S. Ghosh, R. Melhem, D. Mossé, and J. Sansarma. Fault-tolerant, rate-monotonic scheduling. *Real-Time Systems Journal*, 15(2), 1998.
10. A. Girault, H. Kalla, and Y. Sorel. A scheduling heuristics for distributed real-time embedded systems tolerant to processor and communication media failures. *International Journal of Production Research*, 2004. To appear.
11. A. Girault, C. Lavarenne, M. Sighireanu, and Y. Sorel. An algorithm for automatically obtaining distributed and fault-tolerant static schedules. In *International Conference on Dependable Systems and Networks, DSN'03*, San-Francisco, USA, June 2003. IEEE.
12. T. Grandpierre, C. Lavarenne, and Y. Sorel. Optimized rapid prototyping for real-time embedded heterogeneous multiprocessors. In *Proceedings of 7th International Workshop on Hardware/Software Co-Design, CODES'99*, Rome, Italy, May 1999.
13. H. Kopetz. TTP/A - the fireworks protocol. Research Report 23, Institut für Technische Informatik, Technische Universität Wien, Wien, Austria, 1994.
14. H. Kopetz, A. Damm, Ch. Koza, M. Mulazzani, W. Schwabl, Ch. Senft, and R. Zainlinger. Distributed fault-tolerant real-time systems: The MARS Approach. *MICRO*, 9:25–40, 1989.
15. Y. Oh and S.H. Son. Enhancing fault-tolerance in rate-monotonic scheduling. *Real-Time Systems*, 7:315–330, 1993.
16. Y. Oh and S.H. Son. Scheduling hard real-time tasks with tolerance of multiple processor failures. Technical Report CS–93–28, Unversity of Virginia, May 1993.
17. C. Pinello, L. Carloni, and A. Sangiovanni-Vincentelli. Fault-tolerant deployment of embedded software for cost-sensitive real-time feedback-control applications. In *Design, Automation and Test in Europe, DATE'04*, Paris, February 2004. IEEE.
18. K. Ramamritham. Allocation and scheduling of precedence-related periodic tasks. *IEEE Trans. on Parallel and Distributed Systems*, 6:412–420, 1995.
19. F.B. Schneider. Byzantine generals in action: Implementing fail-stop processors. *ACM Transactions on Computer Systems*, 2:145–154, 1984.
20. J.D. Ullman. Polynomial complete scheduling problems. In *Fourth ACM Symposium on Operating System Principles*, pages 96–101, New-York, USA, 1973.

# The Influence of Durational Actions on Time Equivalences

Harald Fecher*

Christian-Albrechts-University Kiel, Germany
hf@informatik.uni-kiel.de

**Abstract.** The hierarchy of untimed equivalences is well understood for action-based systems. This is not the case for timed systems, where it is, for example, possible to detect concurrency by single timed action execution. To clarify the connection between equivalences in timed systems, a timed version of configuration structures is introduced together with timed equivalence notions adapted from untimed equivalences. There actions (events) have an occurrence time and a duration. The result of this paper is that all timed versions of the equivalences from [15] have the same relative discriminating power as in the untimed case, except that interleaving and step (for trace and bisimulation) equivalences coincide if systems are considered where every action must have a positive duration.

## 1 Introduction

Action-based formalisms are used to model systems at an abstract level. But nearly all those formalisms are too concrete in the sense that the same system can be described in many different ways. Therefore, equivalences are introduced to identify those descriptions that have the same observation. Since there are many notions of observations (e.g., linear/branching, interleaving/true concurrent, ...), different equivalences are investigated. In order to relate the level of abstraction of the equivalences, their discriminating power is examined. This is done, for example, for untimed equivalences in [15, 11, 13, 12].

Timed systems have much more observation possibilities, since observations concerning the occurrence time and the duration of actions are possible. This allows, for example, to detect some concurrency by action traces, in the case when ill-timed traces, i.e., traces where the occurrence time of actions may decrease inside a trace, are allowed [2, 1].

The observation that a certain degree of concurrency can be detected in timed systems leads to the question whether the inclusion relations of untimed equivalences are different for the timed versions, in particular, do some timed equivalence notions coincide? The advantage of the collapsing of equivalences is that the verification techniques, axiom systems and results existing for one of them can be used for the other. Furthermore, it can reduce the state spaces that have to be considered to verify the equivalences of processes; for example, when

---

* The work started when the author worked at the University of Mannheim, Germany.

Y. Lakhnech and S. Yovine (Eds.): FORMATS/FTRTFT 2004, LNCS 3253, pp. 231–245, 2004.
© Springer-Verlag Berlin Heidelberg 2004

single action execution (interleaving) bisimilarity coincides with step bisimilarity, it is enough to consider only the transition system consisting of single action executions and not also the step executions in order to verify that processes are step bisimilar.

Another question is whether the hierarchy of the timed equivalences are different when the considered system is restricted. For example do some equivalences coincide when every action has a positive duration and/or when no action may idle (i.e., an action can only be executed at the time when it becomes enabled). Systems where no action may idle, are called *urgent* systems in this paper.

The aim of this paper is to present answers to these questions. In order to have the possibility to compare equivalences, we have to define them on a common abstract domain. Configuration structures were used for this purpose in the untimed case [15]. We introduce a timed version of them, called durational configuration structures, where an event has also an occurrence time and a duration. These structures have to satisfy some well formed condition relating the causality and the occurrence time of events (an event that causes another event $e$ has to occur earlier than $e$). We introduce timed equivalences, which are extensions of untimed equivalences, in durational configuration structures. These equivalences are compared with respect to their level of abstraction. We point out that the hierarchy of all considered equivalences are the same in the untimed and the timed case, except that interleaving and step (for trace and bisimulation) equivalences coincide if every event (action) must have a positive duration. In particular, the restriction to urgent systems does not have any influence on the equivalence hierarchy.

The structure of the paper is the following: In Section 2 durational configuration structures are investigated. The timed equivalences are defined on them in Section 3. In Section 4, we introduce a simple timed process algebra in order to obtain a more readable notation for our counterexamples. The equivalences are examined with respect to their discriminating power in Section 5. The paper is concluded in Section 6.

## 2    Durational Configuration Structures

Configuration structures [14, 16, 15] are a more general event-oriented model of untimed concurrent systems, which is more general than, e.g., event structures [28]. They usually consist of a family of finite sets (the configurations) and a labelling function which maps the elements that occur in a configuration to a set of action names. A configuration can be considered as a collection of events that can appear at some stage of the system run. The labelling function indicates which actions are observable when the events happen. Sometimes configuration structures also contain a termination predicate (a subset of configurations) [16, 15], which indicates terminated configurations. Since termination is not relevant for our approach, we do not consider termination predicates. It is straightforward to transform our result to termination sensitive equivalences.

In timed systems, it is possible to observe at which time the events (actions) happen and also how long their duration is, see for example [23, 9, 8]. We make an atomicity assumption, in the sense that the termination time of an event (action) is known as soon as this event starts to execute, i.e., the duration (and also non-termination) of events is known a priory[1]. The occurrence and the duration time information can not be encoded in a configuration structure by an additional global function, as the labelling function, since the same event may happen at different times (and with different durations) in different system runs. Therefore, we encode configurations as partial functions from the set of events to the set of their possible occurrence times together with their possible duration. In our case, these will be partial functions into $\mathbb{R}_0^{+\infty} = \mathbb{R}_0^+ \times (\mathbb{R}_0^+ \cup \{\infty\})$, where the duration $\infty$ denotes that the event will never terminate.

In the following, $f : M_1 \rightharpoonup M_2$ denotes that $f$ is a *partial function* from $M_1$ to $M_2$. Partial functions are sometimes considered as sets, hence the partial function that is everywhere undefined is given by $\emptyset$. The *domain* of $f$, denoted by $\mathrm{dom}(f)$, is the set $\{m \in M_1 \mid f(m) \text{ is defined}\}$. The restriction of $f$ to set $M_1' \subseteq M_1$ is $f \upharpoonright M_1 = f \cap (M_1' \times M_2)$. Partial functions from $M_1$ to $M_2$ are ordered pointwise, denoted by $\sqsubseteq$, i.e., $f \sqsubseteq g$ iff $f \subseteq g$.

**Definition 1.** *A labelled durational configuration structure over an alphabet Act with respect to set $E$ is a tuple $\mathcal{C} = (C, l)$ such that*

$$C \subseteq \{f : E \rightharpoonup \mathbb{R}_0^+ \times \mathbb{R}_0^{+\infty} \mid |\mathrm{dom}(f)| < \infty\}$$
$$l : E \rightarrow \mathcal{A}ct.$$

An element $f$ of $C$ is called a durational configuration. Furthermore, $\pi_t$ denotes the projection to the occurrence time and $\pi_d$ denotes the projection to the duration, i.e., if $f(e) = (t, d)$ then $\pi_t(f(e)) = t$ (the absolute time when event $e$ happens in $f$) and $\pi_d(f(e)) = d$ (the duration of event $e$ in $f$). Hereafter, $\mathcal{C}$ is considered to be $(C, l)$, $E$ is assumed to be a fixed set of event names, and $\mathcal{A}ct$ be a fixed set of action names. Furthermore, if $M \subseteq E$ then $\overline{M}$ denotes the *complement* of $M$, i.e., $\overline{M} = \{e \in E \mid e \notin M\}$.

*Remark 2.* The untimed configuration structures of [15] can be modelled as durational configuration structures, where all events occur at time 0 and all events have duration 0, i.e., by assigning an untimed configuration structure $X \subseteq E$ to the durational configuration structure $f_X$, where $\mathrm{dom}(f_X) = X$ and $\forall e \in X : f_X(e) = (0, 0)$.

In the untimed case, a subset of configuration structures is characterized by the property that the causal dependencies in configurations can faithfully be represented by means of partial orders. It turned out that these are exactly the configuration structures associated with stable event structures [15]. In the following definition, we define the analogous property for durational configuration structures.

---

[1] This atomicity assumption has the consequence that the ST-equivalence [17] does not fit into our setting.

**Definition 3.** *A durational configuration structure $C$ is*

- rooted *iff $\emptyset \in C$,*
- connected *iff $\forall g \in C : g \neq \emptyset \Rightarrow \exists e \in \mathrm{dom}(g) : g \upharpoonright \overline{\{e\}} \in C$,*
- closed under bounded unions *iff $\forall f, g, h \in C : (f \sqsubseteq h \wedge g \sqsubseteq h) \Rightarrow f \cup g \in C$,*
- closed under bounded intersections *iff $\forall f, g, h \in C : (f \sqsubseteq h \wedge g \sqsubseteq h) \Rightarrow f \cap g \in C$.*

*$C$ is stable iff it is rooted, connected, closed under bounded unions, and closed under bounded intersections.*

The causality relation on events describes which event occurrences are necessary for other event occurrences and the concurrency relation describes which event occurrences are independent from each other. These relations are defined with respect to configurations, i.e., the event dependencies may vary in different configurations (system runs). The relations are adapted to durational configuration structures as follows:

**Definition 4.** *Let $C$ be a durational configuration and let $g \in C$.*
*The* causality relation *$<_g^C \subseteq \mathrm{dom}(g) \times \mathrm{dom}(g)$ on $g$ is given by $e' <_g^C e$ iff $e' \leq_g^C e$ and $e' \neq e$, where $e' \leq_g^C e \iff (\forall f \in C : (f \sqsubseteq g \wedge e \in \mathrm{dom}(f)) \Rightarrow e' \in \mathrm{dom}(f))$.*
*The* concurrency relation *$\|_g^C \subseteq \mathrm{dom}(g) \times \mathrm{dom}(g)$ on $g$ is given by $e' \|_g^C e$ iff $\neg(e' <_g^C e \vee e <_g^C e')$.*

We write $<_g$ ($\|_g$) rather than $<_g^C$ (respectively, $\|_g^C$) if $C$ is clear from the context. If an event $e'$ is a causality of $e$, i.e., $e' <_g e$, then $e'$ has to occur earlier than $e$. More precisely, $e$ has to occur later than the termination of $e'$. This is formalized in the following definition, where also further time properties of configuration structures are specified.

**Definition 5.** *A durational configuration structure $C$ is* time stable *iff $C$ is stable and $\forall g \in C : e' <_g e \Rightarrow \pi_t(g(e')) + \pi_d(g(e')) \leq \pi_t(g(e))$. Let $\mathbb{C}$ be the set of all time stable durational configuration structures.*

- *$C \in \mathbb{C}$ has* only durational action *iff $\forall g \in C, e \in \mathrm{dom}(g) : \pi_d(g(e)) > 0$.*
- *$C \in \mathbb{C}$ is* urgent *iff $\forall g \in C, e \in \mathrm{dom}(g) : \pi_t(g(e)) > 0 \Rightarrow \exists e' : e' <_g e \wedge \pi_t(g(e')) + \pi_d(g(e')) = \pi_t(g(e))$.*

*Let $\mathbb{C}^d$ be $\mathbb{C}$ restricted to those configuration structures that have only durational action and let $\mathbb{C}^u$ be $\mathbb{C}$ restricted to those configuration structures that are urgent. Finally, $\mathbb{C}^{du}$ denotes the set of all configuration structures that have only durational action and are urgent, i.e., $\mathbb{C}^{du} = \mathbb{C}^d \cap \mathbb{C}^u$.*

If a durational configuration structure is urgent, then time must not pass between actions[2], i.e., time may only pass by action execution. Urgent systems are, for example, most generative systems, where the environment has no influence on the action execution. Durational configuration structures that have only

---

[2] In some approaches, e.g., [27, 21], urgency is only enforced on internal actions.

durational actions are generated by most physical processes, since an action has to consume time in real systems. In these systems actions are sometimes abstracted and are considered durationless. But such kind of abstractions are not always reasonable. Hence, we just motivated that the restriction to durational configuration structures that are urgent and/or have only durational actions is reasonable for applications.

*Example 6.* The durational configuration structure

$$\tilde{\mathcal{C}} = (\{\{(e_0, 0, 1)\}, \{(e_1, 0, 2)\}, \{(e_0, 0, 1), (e_1, 0, 2)\}, \{(e_1, 0, 2), (e_2, 2, 1)\},$$
$$\{(e_0, 0, 1), (e_1, 0, 2), (e_2, 2, 1)\}\} , \{(e_0, a), (e_1, b), (e_2, c)\})$$

is time stable, has only durational action, and is urgent.

## 3    Timed Equivalences

In this section, we adapt equivalence notions of the untimed case to the timed case, where we concentrate on truly concurrent equivalences (i.e., those equivalences presented in [15]), since we rather expect a change in the hierarchical structure of truly concurrent equivalences. For simplicity, we only consider strong equivalences, i.e., we do not abstract from internal actions.

In order to define the equivalences, we introduce different kinds of action (not event) executions with respect to time. One concerns single action execution. Another one concerns simultaneous action execution (multisets over $\mathcal{A}ct$). A third one concerns the execution of sets of ordered actions, which are called pomsets. In all these executions, the occurrence time and the duration of the executed event is taken into account.

**Definition 7.** *Define $\mathcal{L} = \mathcal{A}ct \times \mathbb{R}_0^+ \times \mathbb{R}_0^{+\infty}$. The isomorphism class of partially ordered sets labelled by $\mathcal{L}$ are called* pomsets *over $\mathcal{L}$. The isomorphism class of a partially ordered set $u$ is denoted by $[u]$. Let $\mathcal{P}$ be the set of all pomsets over $\mathcal{L}$ where the underlying sets have to be subsets of $E$.*

Suppose $l : E \rightharpoonup \mathcal{A}ct$ and $g : E \rightharpoonup \mathbb{R}_0^+ \times \mathbb{R}_0^{+\infty}$ such that $\mathrm{dom}(l) = \mathrm{dom}(g)$, then $l \times g : E \rightharpoonup \mathcal{L}$ is defined by $\mathrm{dom}(l \times g) = \mathrm{dom}(l)$ and $\forall e \in \mathrm{dom}(l) :$ $(l \times g)(e) = (l(e), g(e))$.

**Definition 8.** *Suppose $C \in \mathbb{C}$.*
*Define the action execution relation $\longrightarrow_C \subseteq C \times \mathcal{L} \times C$, where $f \xrightarrow{(a,t)}_d C$ $g$ abbreviates $(f, (a, t, d), g) \in \longrightarrow_C$, by*

$$f \xrightarrow{(a,t)}_d C\ g \ iff \ \exists e : e \notin \mathrm{dom}(f) \land g = f \cup \{(e, t, d)\} \land l(e) = a.$$

*Define the step execution relation $\longmapsto_C \subseteq C \times (\mathcal{L} \to \mathbb{N}) \times C$ by*

$$f \xrightarrow{\gamma}_C\ g \ iff \ f \sqsubseteq g \land \exists H : H = \mathrm{dom}(g) \setminus \mathrm{dom}(f) \land (\forall e, e' \in H : e\|_g e') \land$$
$$\gamma(a, t, d) = |\{e \in H \mid l(e) = a \land g(e) = (t, d)\}|.$$

*Define the pomset execution relation $\hookrightarrow_C \subseteq C \times \mathcal{P} \times C$ by*

$$f \xrightarrow{u}_C g \text{ iff } f \sqsubseteq g \wedge \exists H : H = \mathrm{dom}(g) \setminus \mathrm{dom}(f) \wedge$$
$$u = [H, <_g \cap (H \times H), l \restriction H \times g \restriction H].$$

*Example 9.* Consider the durational configuration structures $\tilde{C}$ from Example 6. Then

$$\{(e_1, 0, 2)\}$$

$$\emptyset \quad \xrightarrow{\tilde{u}}_{\tilde{C}} \quad \{(e_0, 0, 1), (e_1, 0, 2), (e_2, 2, 1)\}$$

where $\tilde{\gamma} = \{((a, 0, 1), 1), ((c, 2, 1), 1)\}$
and $\tilde{u} = [\{e_0, e_1, e_2\}, \{(e_1, e_2)\}, \{(e_0, a), (e_1, b), (e_2, c)\}]$.

Many equivalences are based on the trace or the bisimulation technique:

**Definition 10.** *Let $C, C' \in \mathbb{C}$ and $\longrightarrow \subseteq C \times M \times C$ and $\longrightarrow' \subseteq C' \times M \times C'$ for some set of labels $M$. An element $(m_0, ..., m_{n-1}) \in M^*$ is a trace of $C$ with respect to $\longrightarrow$ if there exists $f_0, ..., f_n \in C$ with $\emptyset = f_0$ and $\forall i < n : f_i \xrightarrow{m_i} f_{i+1}$. The set of all traces of $C$ with respect to $\longrightarrow$ is denoted by $T_{(C, \longrightarrow)}$. $(C, \longrightarrow)$ and $(C', \longrightarrow')$ are trace equivalent iff $T_{(C, \longrightarrow)} = T_{(C', \longrightarrow')}$.*

**Definition 11.** *Let $C, C' \in \mathbb{C}$ and $\longrightarrow \subseteq C \times M \times C$ and $\longrightarrow' \subseteq C' \times M \times C'$ for some set of labels $M$. A relation $R \subseteq C \times C'$ is called a bisimulation between $(C, \longrightarrow)$ and $(C', \longrightarrow')$ iff $(\emptyset, \emptyset) \in R$ and if $(f, f') \in R$ then*

- $f \xrightarrow{m} g \Rightarrow \exists g' : f' \xrightarrow{m} g' \wedge (g, g') \in R$,
- $f' \xrightarrow{m} g' \Rightarrow \exists g : f \xrightarrow{m} g \wedge (g, g') \in R$.

*$(C, \longrightarrow)$ and $(C', \longrightarrow')$ are bisimilar iff there is a bisimulation between $(C, \longrightarrow)$ and $(C', \longrightarrow')$.*

In the following, the *interleaving trace equivalence* [20], *interleaving bisimilarity* [22], *step trace equivalence* [24], *step bisimilarity* [24], *pomset trace equivalence* [7], *pomset bisimilarity* [7], *weak history-preserving equivalence* [10], *history-preserving equivalence* [25] and *hereditary history-preserving equivalence* [3] are adapted to time, i.e., defined on durational configuration structures.

**Definition 12 (Interleaving trace).** *The durational configuration structures $C$ and $C'$ are interleaving trace equivalent, denoted by $C \approx_{it} C'$, iff $(C, \longrightarrow_C)$ and $(C', \longrightarrow_{C'})$ are trace equivalent.*

**Definition 13 (Interleaving bisimilarity).** *The durational configuration structures $C$ and $C'$ are interleaving bisimilar, denoted by $C \approx_{ib} C'$, iff $(C, \longrightarrow_C)$ and $(C', \longrightarrow_{C'})$ are bisimilar.*

**Definition 14 (Step trace).** *The durational configuration structures $C$ and $C'$ are step trace equivalent, denoted by $C \approx_{st} C'$, iff $(C, \longmapsto_C)$ and $(C', \longmapsto_{C'})$ are trace equivalent.*

**Definition 15 (Step bisimilarity).** *The durational configuration structures $C$ and $C'$ are step bisimilar, denoted by $C \approx_{sb} C'$, iff $(C, \longmapsto_C)$ and $(C', \longmapsto_{C'})$ are bisimilar.*

**Definition 16 (Pomset trace).** *The durational configuration structures $C$ and $C'$ are pomset trace equivalent, denoted by $C \approx_{pt} C'$, iff $(C, \hookrightarrow_C)$ and $(C', \hookrightarrow_{C'})$ are trace equivalent.*

It is easily seen that the definition of pomset trace equivalence can be restricted to single element traces, i.e.,

$$C \approx_{pt} C' \text{ iff } \forall u \in \mathcal{P} : (\exists g : \emptyset \xrightarrow{u}_C g) \Leftrightarrow (\exists g' : \emptyset \xrightarrow{u}_{C'} g').$$

**Definition 17 (Pomset bisimilarity).** *The durational configuration structures $C$ and $C'$ are pomset bisimilar, denoted by $C \approx_{pb} C'$, iff $(C, \hookrightarrow_C)$ and $(C', \hookrightarrow_{C'})$ are bisimilar.*

**Definition 18 (Weak history-preserving).** *The durational configuration structures $C$ and $C'$ are weak history-preserving equivalent, denoted by $C \approx_{wh} C'$, iff there is a bisimulation $R$ between $(C, \longrightarrow_C)$ and $(C', \longrightarrow_{C'})$ such that there is an isomorphism between the two partially ordered, labelled sets $(\mathrm{dom}(f), <_f, l \upharpoonright \mathrm{dom}(f) \times f)$, and $(\mathrm{dom}(f'), <_{f'}, l \upharpoonright \mathrm{dom}(f') \times f')$ for every $(f, f') \in R$.*

**Definition 19 (History-preserving).** *Let $C, C' \in \mathbb{C}$. A relation $R \subseteq C \times C' \times (E \to E)$ is called a history-preserving bisimulation between $C$ and $C'$ iff $(\emptyset, \emptyset, \emptyset) \in R$ and if $(f, f', \iota) \in R$ then*

- *$\mathrm{dom}(\iota) = \mathrm{dom}(f)$ and $\iota$ is an isomorphism between the two partially ordered, labelled sets $(\mathrm{dom}(f), <_f, l \upharpoonright \mathrm{dom}(f) \times f)$, and $(\mathrm{dom}(f'), <_{f'}, l \upharpoonright \mathrm{dom}(f') \times f')$,*
- *$f \xrightarrow[d]{(a,t)}_C g \Rightarrow \exists g', \kappa : f' \xrightarrow[d]{(a,t)}_{C'} g' \wedge (g, g', \kappa) \in R \wedge \kappa \upharpoonright \mathrm{dom}(f) = \iota$,*
- *$f' \xrightarrow[d]{(a,t)}_{C'} g' \Rightarrow \exists g, \kappa : f \xrightarrow[d]{(a,t)}_C g \wedge (g, g', \kappa) \in R \wedge \kappa \upharpoonright \mathrm{dom}(f) = \iota$.*

*$C$ and $C'$ are history-preserving equivalent, denoted by $C \approx_h C'$, iff there exists an history-preserving bisimulation between $C$ and $C'$.*

**Definition 20 (Hereditary history-preserving).** *The durational configuration structures $C$ and $C'$ are hereditary history-preserving equivalent, denoted by $C \approx_{hh} C'$, iff there is a history-preserving bisimulation $R$ between $C$ and $C'$ such that $\forall f, f', g, \iota, a, t, d : ((f, g, \iota) \in R \wedge f' \xrightarrow[d]{(a,t)}_C f) \Rightarrow (f', \iota(f'), \iota \upharpoonright \mathrm{dom}(f')) \in R$, where $\iota(f')_{(e')} = f'(\iota^{-1}(e'))$.*

## 4 Process Algebra

In order to describe easily some durational configuration structures (e.g., to present counterexamples for the non-inclusion of equivalences), we introduce a simple event-based timed process algebra. The event-based approach is encoded in the syntax of our Process Algebra and becomes visible in the operational semantics. The process algebra expressions Expr are defined by the following BNF-grammar:

$$B ::= a_d \mid B + B \mid B; B \mid B\|_A B \mid B\backslash\!\backslash_d A \mid B[a \mapsto b] \mid d : B \mid \lceil B\rceil_i,$$

where $i \in \{1, 2\}$, $d \in \mathbb{R}_0^{+\infty}$, $a, b \in \mathcal{A}ct$, and $A \subseteq \mathcal{A}ct$. For reasons of simplicity, we do not consider recursion or further time-specific operators here, since these are not needed for our counterexamples given in the next section. Our process algebra can be straightforwardly extended with these constructs. A non-event-based process algebra, which only speak about actions and not events, can be straightforwardly deduced from our by removing the $\lceil_-\rceil_i$ operators and neglecting the events in the operational semantics.

The expressions, which we sometimes call processes, have the following intuitive meaning: $a_d$ is the process that executes $a$ with duration $d$ at time 0 (terminates at time $d$), $B_1 + B_2$ is the choice operator, $B_1; B_2$ is the sequential composition and $B_1\|_A B_2$ is a parallel composition, where the processes have to synchronize on actions from $A$. An action may idle by waiting for synchronization. The restriction process $B\backslash\!\backslash_d A$ does not allow actions from $A$ to be executed and termination may not happen before time point $d$. $B[a \mapsto b]$ is the relabelling operator. $d : B$ behaves like $B$ except that every occurrence time is increased by $d$. In particular, $\infty : B$ cannot execute anything. Processes $\lceil B\rceil_i$ have the same behavior as $B$. They are only used for event renaming.

The event-based operational semantics of processes is given by a transition system (Expr, $\longrightarrow$), where $\longrightarrow \subseteq$ Expr $\times ((E \times \mathbb{R}_0^+ \times \mathbb{R}_0^+) \times (\mathcal{A}ct \times \mathbb{R}_0^+)) \times$ (Expr $\cup \{\sqrt{d} \mid d \in \mathbb{R}_0^{+\infty}\}$). The transition $B \xrightarrow{(e,t,d)}_{a,s} B'$ indicates that $B$ executes action $a$ with identity $e$ at time $t$ and this action has duration $d$. Furthermore, this execution happens $s$ times after the enabling of $e$. The transition $B \xrightarrow{(e,t,d)}_{a,s} \sqrt{d'}$ indicates that $B$ terminates at time $d'$ by execution of the action. This termination predicate is a timed version of the untimed one presented, for example, in [4]. The transition rules are presented in Figure 1. For technical reasons, we assume that $\bullet \in E$, $\star \notin E$ and for all $e, e' \in E$ we have $(e, e'), (\star, e), (e, \star) \in E$. These restriction are necessary to guarantee the uniqueness and the existence of events in process executions.

The durational configuration structure of process $B$, denoted by $\mathcal{C}_B$, is obtained by collecting all labels (neglecting the action name information) of a trace of $B$ where the last component of the label is always zero (execution may not idle) to obtain a configuration of $\mathcal{C}_B$. The value on $e$ of the labelling function of $\mathcal{C}_B$ is determined by the corresponding action label of a trace of $B$ that contains $e$ (where a fixed action name is used if such a trace does not exist).

*Example 21.* Consider the process $\tilde{B} = a_1\|_\emptyset(b_2; c_1)$. Then $\mathcal{C}_{\tilde{B}}$ is equal to the durational configuration structure $\tilde{C}$ from Example 6 where $e_0 = (\bullet, \star)$, $e_1 = (\star, (\bullet, \star))$ and $e_2 = (\star, (\star, \bullet))$.

We present the following proposition without proof:

$$\frac{}{a_d \xrightarrow[a,s]{(\bullet,s,d)} \sqrt{}_{d+s}}$$

$$\frac{B_1 \xrightarrow[a,s]{(e,t,d)} B'}{\begin{array}{l} B_1 + B_2 \xrightarrow[a,s]{((e,\star),t,d)} \lceil B'\rceil_1 \\ B_2 + B_1 \xrightarrow[a,s]{((\star,e),t,d)} \lceil B'\rceil_2 \end{array}}$$

$$\frac{B_1 \xrightarrow[a,s]{(e,t,d)} \sqrt{}_{d'}}{\begin{array}{l} B_1 + B_2 \xrightarrow[a,s]{((e,\star),t,d)} \sqrt{}_{d'} \\ B_2 + B_1 \xrightarrow[a,s]{((\star,e),t,d)} \sqrt{}_{d'} \end{array}}$$

$$\frac{B_1 \xrightarrow[a,s]{(e,t,d)} B_1'}{B_1; B_2 \xrightarrow[a,s]{((e,\star),t,d)} B_1'; B_2}$$

$$\frac{B_1 \xrightarrow[a,s]{(e,t,d)} \sqrt{}_{d'}}{B_1; B_2 \xrightarrow[a,s]{((e,\star),t,d)} d' : \lceil B_2\rceil_2}$$

$$\frac{B_1 \xrightarrow[a,s]{(e,t,d)} B_1' \quad a \notin A}{\begin{array}{l} B_1\|_A B_2 \xrightarrow[a,s]{((e,\star),t,d)} B_1'\|_A B_2 \\ B_2\|_A B_1 \xrightarrow[a,s]{((\star,e),t,d)} B_2\|_A B_1' \end{array}}$$

$$\frac{B_1 \xrightarrow[a,s]{(e,t,d)} \sqrt{}_{d'} \quad a \notin A}{\begin{array}{l} B_1\|_A B_2 \xrightarrow[a,s]{((e,\star),t,d)} (\lceil B_2\rceil_2)\backslash\backslash_{d'} A \\ B_2\|_A B_1 \xrightarrow[a,s]{((\star,e),t,d)} (\lceil B_2\rceil_1)\backslash\backslash_{d'} A \end{array}}$$

$$\frac{B_1 \xrightarrow[a,s_1]{(e_1,t,d)} B_1' \quad B_2 \xrightarrow[a,s_2]{(e_2,t,d)} B_2' \quad a \in A \quad s = \min\{s_1,s_2\}}{B_1\|_A B_2 \xrightarrow[a,s]{((e_1,e_2),t,d)} B_1'\|_A B_2'}$$

$$\frac{B_1 \xrightarrow[a,s_1]{(e_1,t,d)} \sqrt{}_{d'} \quad B_2 \xrightarrow[a,s_2]{(e_2,t,d)} B_2' \quad a \in A \quad s = \min\{s_1,s_2\}}{\begin{array}{l} B_1\|_A B_2 \xrightarrow[a,s]{((e_1,e_2),t,d)} (\lceil B_2'\rceil_2)\backslash\backslash_{d'} A \\ B_2\|_A B_1 \xrightarrow[a,s]{((e_2,e_1),t,d)} (\lceil B_2'\rceil_1)\backslash\backslash_{d'} A \end{array}}$$

$$\frac{B_1 \xrightarrow[a,s_1]{(e_1,t,d)} \sqrt{}_{d_1} \quad B_2 \xrightarrow[a,s_2]{(e_2,t,d)} \sqrt{}_{d_2} \quad a \in A \quad s = \min\{s_1,s_2\}}{B_1\|_A B_2 \xrightarrow[a,s]{((e_1,e_2),t,d)} \sqrt{}_{\max\{d_1,d_2\}}}$$

$$\frac{B \xrightarrow[a,s]{(e,t,d)} B' \quad a \notin A}{B\backslash\backslash_{d'} A \xrightarrow[a,s]{(e,t,d)} B'\backslash\backslash_{d'} A}$$

$$\frac{B \xrightarrow[a,s]{(e,t,d)} \sqrt{}_{d''} \quad a \notin A}{B\backslash\backslash_{d'} A \xrightarrow[a,s]{(e,t,d)} \sqrt{}_{\max\{d',d''\}}}$$

$$\frac{B \xrightarrow[a,s]{(e,t,d)} B' \quad a' \neq a}{\begin{array}{l} B[a \mapsto b] \xrightarrow[b,s]{(e,t,d)} B'[a \mapsto b] \\ B[a' \mapsto b] \xrightarrow[a,s]{(e,t,d)} B'[a' \mapsto b] \end{array}}$$

$$\frac{B \xrightarrow[a,s]{(e,t,d)} \sqrt{}_{d'} \quad a' \neq a}{\begin{array}{l} B[a \mapsto b] \xrightarrow[b,s]{(e,t,d)} \sqrt{}_{d'} \\ B[a' \mapsto b] \xrightarrow[a,s]{(e,t,d)} \sqrt{}_{d'} \end{array}}$$

$$\frac{B \xrightarrow[a,s]{(e,t,d)} B' \quad t' \neq \infty}{t' : B \xrightarrow[a,s]{(e,t+t',d)} t' : B'}$$

$$\frac{B \xrightarrow[a,s]{(e,t,d)} \sqrt{}_{d'} \quad t' \neq \infty}{t' : B \xrightarrow[a,s]{(e,t+t',d)} \sqrt{}_{t'+d'}}$$

$$\frac{B \xrightarrow[a,s]{(e,t,d)} B'}{\begin{array}{l} \lceil B\rceil_1 \xrightarrow[a,s]{((e,\star),t,d)} \lceil B'\rceil_1 \\ \lceil B\rceil_2 \xrightarrow[a,s]{((\star,e),t,d)} \lceil B'\rceil_2 \end{array}}$$

$$\frac{B \xrightarrow[a,s]{(e,t,d)} \sqrt{}_{d'}}{\begin{array}{l} \lceil B\rceil_1 \xrightarrow[a,s]{((e,\star),t,d)} \sqrt{}_{d'} \\ \lceil B\rceil_2 \xrightarrow[a,s]{((\star,e),t,d)} \sqrt{}_{d'} \end{array}}$$

**Fig. 1.** Transition Rules.

**Proposition 22.** *Let $B \in$ Expr. Then $C_B \in \mathbb{C}$. Furthermore, if for every action $a_d$ that occurs in $B$ $d > 0$ holds, then $C_B \in \mathbb{C}^d$. Moreover, if $B$ does not contain subexpressions of the form $d : B'$ or $B \backslash\backslash_d A$, then $C_B \in \mathbb{C}^u$.*

The above proposition illustrates, for example, that the concept of durational configuration structures is a reasonable one, since it can be naturally used for presenting a denotational semantics of timed process algebras.

## 5    Relations Between the Equivalences

The following theorem illustrates that there exists only a difference between the hierarchy of time equivalences versus the hierarchy of untimed equivalences, when only durational actions are allowed. In this case the step equivalences cannot be distinguished from the interleaving equivalences. All other inclusion of the equivalences are unaffected.

**Theorem 23.** *Let $\bowtie_{it}, \bowtie_{ib}, \bowtie_{st}, \bowtie_{sb}, \bowtie_{pt}, \bowtie_{pb}, \bowtie_{wh}, \bowtie_h, \bowtie_{hh}$ denote the corresponding equivalences restricted to $\mathbb{C}^u$, e.g., $\bowtie_{it} = \approx_{it} \cap \mathbb{C}^u \times \mathbb{C}^u$, let $\sim_{it}, \sim_{ib}, \sim_{st}, \sim_{sb}, \sim_{pt}, \sim_{pb}, \sim_{wh}, \sim_h, \sim_{hh}$ denote the corresponding equivalences restricted to $\mathbb{C}^d$, and let $\asymp_{it}, \asymp_{ib}, \asymp_{st}, \asymp_{sb}, \asymp_{pt}, \asymp_{pb}, \asymp_{wh}, \asymp_h, \asymp_{hh}$ denote the corresponding equivalences restricted to $\mathbb{C}^{du}$. Then all valid inclusion-relations between the equivalences are presented in Figure 2: If two equivalences are connected via a line, then the lower one identifies more elements than the upper one. Identical equivalences are separated by a comma.*

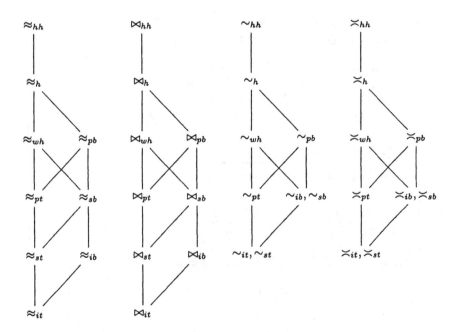

**Fig. 2.** Hierarchy of the Equivalences.

The rest of this section contains the proof of Theorem 23, where explicit counterexamples for the non-inclusions are presented.

## 5.1   Proof of the Inclusions

It is easily seen that $\approx_{hh} \subseteq \approx_h \subseteq \approx_{wh}$ and $\approx_{pb} \subseteq \approx_{sb} \subseteq \approx_{ib}$ and $\approx_{pt} \subseteq \approx_{st} \subseteq \approx_{it}$ and $\approx_{pb} \subseteq \approx_{pt}$ and $\approx_{sb} \subseteq \approx_{st}$ and $\approx_{ib} \subseteq \approx_{it}$. The proof of $\approx_h \subseteq \approx_{pb}$ can be carried out analogously to the proof of the untimed case [15] and the proof of $\approx_{wh} \subseteq \approx_{pt}$ and $\approx_{wh} \subseteq \approx_{sb}$ can also be carried out analogously to the untimed case [11].

In order to verify the inclusions $\sim_{it} \subseteq \sim_{st}$ and $\sim_{ib} \subseteq \sim_{sb}$, we introduce the following lemma. This lemma states that an ill-timed trace (a trace where time does not increase) can be replaced by a step execution only if durational actions are considered.

**Lemma 24.** *Suppose $C \in \mathbb{C}^d$ and $f_1, f_2, f_3 \in C$ such that $f_1 \overset{\gamma}{\longmapsto}_C f_2 \overset{(a,t)}{\longrightarrow}_C f_3$ and $\forall (a', t', d') \in \mathcal{L} : \gamma(a', t', d') \neq 0 \Rightarrow t' \geq t$. Then*

$$f_1 \overset{\gamma'}{\longmapsto}_C f_3 \text{ where } \gamma'(a', t', d') = \begin{cases} \gamma(a', t', d') + 1 & \text{if } (a', t', d') = (a, t, d), \\ \gamma(a', t', d') & \text{otherwise} . \end{cases}$$

*Proof.* The only non-trivial fact to show is that $e \|_{f_3} e'$ holds for every $e, e' \in (\text{dom}(f_3) \setminus \text{dom}(f_1))$. We proceed with the following case analysis:

$e, e' \in \text{dom}(f_2) \setminus \text{dom}(f_1)$: From $f_1 \overset{\gamma}{\longmapsto}_C f_2$ we get $e \|_{f_2} e'$. This implies $e \|_{f_1} e'$, which is easily checked.

$e \in \text{dom}(f_3) \setminus \text{dom}(f_2)$: Without loss of generality $e' \in \text{dom}(f_2) \setminus \text{dom}(f_1)$. Suppose $e <_{f_3} e'$. Then by the definition of $<_{f_3}$ we get $e \in \text{dom}(f_2)$, since $f_2 \sqsubseteq f_3 \wedge e' \in \text{dom}(f_2)$. Contradiction.

Suppose $e' <_{f_3} e$ then $\pi_t(f_3(e')) + \pi_d(f_3(e')) \leq \pi_t(f_3(e))$, since $C$ is time stable. Moreover, $\pi_t(f_3(e')) < \pi_t(f_3(e))$, since $C$ has only durational action. Furthermore, $\gamma(l(e'), t', d') \neq 0$ where $(t', d') = f_3(e')$. Thus from the assumption, we get $\pi_t(f_3(e')) \geq t$. This is a contradiction, since $t = \pi_t(f_3(e))$.   □

**Lemma 25.** $\sim_{it} \subseteq \sim_{st}$.

*Proof.* Suppose $C \approx_{it} C'$. Let $(\gamma_0, ..., \gamma_{n-1}) \in \mathcal{T}_{(C, \longmapsto_C)}$. The other case follows analogously. By definition, there are $f_0, .., f_n \in C$ with $\forall i < n : f_i \overset{\gamma_i}{\longmapsto}_C f_{i+1}$ and $\emptyset = f_0$. Take $q : \mathbb{N} \to \mathbb{N}$ and $e_1^i, ... e_{q(i)}^i$ for $i < n$ such that all $e_j^i$ are pairwise distinct and $\text{dom}(f_{i+1}) \setminus \text{dom}(f_i) = \{e_1^i, ..., e_{q(i)}^i\}$ and $\forall i < n : \forall j < q(i) - 1 : \pi_t(f_{i+1}(e_{j+1}^i)) \geq \pi_t(f_{i+1}(e_{j+2}^i))$. Then it is easily checked that $(\alpha_1^0, ..., \alpha_{q(1)}^0, \alpha_1^1, ..., \alpha_{q(n-1)}^{n-1}) \in \mathcal{T}_{(C, \longrightarrow_C)}$, with $\alpha_j^i = (l(e_j^i), f_1(e_j^i))$. From $C \approx_{it} C'$ we obtain $(\alpha_1^0, ..., \alpha_{q(n-1)}^{n-1}) \in \mathcal{T}_{(C', \longrightarrow_{C'})}$. From Lemma 24 we obtain $(\gamma_0, ..., \gamma_{n-1}) \in \mathcal{T}_{(C', \longmapsto_{C'})}$, as required.   □

**Lemma 26.** $\sim_{ib} \subseteq \sim_{sb}$.

*Proof.* Suppose $C \approx_{ib} C'$. Then there is a bisimulation $R$ between $(C, \longrightarrow_C)$ and $(C', \longrightarrow_{C'})$. In the following we show that $R$ is also a step bisimulation between $C$ and $C'$. Let $(f, f') \in R$, then

$$\forall \gamma, g : f \stackrel{\gamma}{\longmapsto}_C g \Rightarrow \exists g' : f' \stackrel{\gamma}{\longmapsto}_C g' \wedge (g, g') \in R. \tag{1}$$

This is verified by induction on $|\sum_{\ell \in \mathcal{L}} \gamma(\ell)|$, which has to be finite, since only finite configurations are allowed. In the case $|\sum_{\ell \in \mathcal{L}} \gamma(\ell)| = 0$, we obtain $f = f'$ and therefore $g'$ can be chosen to be $g$.

Suppose $|\sum_{\ell \in \mathcal{L}} \gamma(\ell)| > 0$. Choose $(a, t, d)$ such that $\gamma(a, t, d) > 0$ and that it is minimal in the sense that $\forall (a', t', d') : \gamma(a', t', d') > 0 \Rightarrow t' \geq t$. It is easily checked that there is $\tilde{f}$ such that $f \stackrel{\gamma'}{\longmapsto}_C \tilde{f} \stackrel{(a,t)}{\underset{d}{\longrightarrow}}_C g$ with

$$\gamma'(a', t', d') = \begin{cases} \gamma(a', t', d') - 1 & \text{if } (a', t', d') = (a, t, d), \\ \gamma(a', t', d') & \text{otherwise .} \end{cases}$$

Then there exists $\tilde{f}'$ such that $f' \stackrel{\gamma'}{\longmapsto}_C \tilde{f}' \wedge (\tilde{f}, \tilde{f}') \in R$ by induction. Since $R$ is an interleaving bisimulation, there exists $g'$ such that $\tilde{f}' \stackrel{(a,t)}{\underset{d}{\longrightarrow}}_C g' \wedge (g, g') \in R$. Furthermore, $f' \stackrel{\gamma}{\longmapsto}_C g'$ by Lemma 24.

Equation (1) also holds for the symmetrical case, thus $R$ is also a bisimulation between $(C, \longmapsto_C)$ and $(C', \longmapsto_{C'})$. Hence, $C \sim_{sb} C'$, as required. □

The other inclusions follow immediately from set theory, since $\mathbb{C}^{du} \subseteq \mathbb{C}^d \subseteq \mathbb{C}$ and $\mathbb{C}^{du} \subseteq \mathbb{C}^u \subseteq \mathbb{C}$.

## 5.2   Proof of the Non-inclusions

In the following examples, we illustrate some non-inclusions. The other non-inclusions can be derived from these counterexamples.

*Example 27* ($\bowtie_{ib} \not\subseteq \bowtie_{st}$). Let $B_1 = a_0 \|_\emptyset b_0$ and $B_1' = a_0; b_0 + b_0; a_0$. Obviously $C_{B_1} \bowtie_{ib} C_{B_1'}$ and $C_{B_1} \not\bowtie_{st} C_{B_1'}$.

Please note that it is essential in the counterexample presented in Example 27 that actions do not need to have a duration. In particular, the processes $\tilde{B}_1 = a_1 \|_\emptyset b_1$ and $\tilde{B}_1' = a_1; b_1 + b_1; a_1$ are distinguishable in $\bowtie_{ib}$, since in $\tilde{B}_1'$ there is a trace where $b$ happens at time 1, which cannot be the case in $\tilde{B}_1$ [2, 1].

*Example 28* ($\asymp_{pt} \not\subseteq \asymp_{ib}$). Let $B_2 = a_1; (b_1 + c_1)$ and $B_2' = a_1; b_1 + a_1; c_1$. Then it is easily seen that $C_{B_2} \asymp_{pt} C_{B_2'}$ and $C_{B_2} \not\asymp_{ib} C_{B_2'}$.

*Example 29* ($\asymp_{sb} \not\subseteq \asymp_{pt}$). Let $B_3 = a_1 \|_\emptyset (b_1; c_1) + (a_1; c_1) \|_\emptyset b_1$ and $B_3' = B_3 + (a_1 \|_\emptyset b_1); c_1$. Then it is easily seen that $C_{B_3} \asymp_{sb} C_{B_3'}$. Furthermore, $C_{B_3} \not\asymp_{pt} C_{B_3'}$, since the pomset $\begin{smallmatrix} a_\circ \\ \\ b_\circ \end{smallmatrix} \!\!\!\longrightarrow\!\! \circ c$ can only be executed by $B_3'$.

*Example 30 ($\asymp_{wh} \not\subseteq \asymp_{pb}$).* The untimed counterexample from [15] is adapted to time as follows. Let $B_4 = ((a_1; c_1) \|_{\{c\}} (a_1; b_1 + (a_1 \|_\emptyset c_1)))[c \mapsto b]$ and $B_4' = ((a_1; b_1) \|_\emptyset (a_1; b_1 + a_1)) \|_{\{b\}} b_1$. Then $\mathcal{C}_{B_4} \asymp_{wh} \mathcal{C}_{B_4'}$ and $\mathcal{C}_{B_4} \not\asymp_{pb} \mathcal{C}_{B_4'}$, which is argued similarly as in the untimed case [15].

*Example 31 ($\asymp_{pb} \not\subseteq \asymp_{wh}$).* Here, we modify the counterexample of [15] such that it applies to $\mathbb{C}^{du}$. Let $B_5 = (a_1 \|_\emptyset a_1'); (b_1 + c_1) + a_1 \|_\emptyset (a_1'; b_1) + (a_1; b_1) \|_\emptyset a_1' + (a_1 \|_\emptyset a_1'); b_1$ and $B_5' = (a_1 \|_\emptyset a_1'); (b_1 + c_1) + a_1 \|_\emptyset (a_1'; b_1) + (a_1; b_1) \|_\emptyset a_1'$.
Then $\mathcal{C}_{B_5} \asymp_{pb} \mathcal{C}_{B_5'}$, which can be seen as follows. The only non-obvious case is to match execution from $(a_1 \|_\emptyset a_1'); b_1$. Execution of $\{a\}$ is matched by $a_1 \|_\emptyset (a_1'; b_1)$, the execution of $\{a'\}$ and $\{a, a'\}$ are matched by $(a_1; b_1) \|_\emptyset a_1'$, and the execution of $\{a, a', b\}$ is matched by $(a_1 \|_\emptyset a_1'); (b_1 + c_1)$.
But $\mathcal{C}_{B_5} \not\asymp_{wh} \mathcal{C}_{B_5'}$, since the execution of $a$ in $(a_1 \|_\emptyset a_1'); b_1$ has to be matched by $a_1 \|_\emptyset (a_1'; b_1)$ in order to be bisimilar. But then after the executions of $a'$ and $b$ the obtained configuration structures are not isomorphic, since in only one case $a$ is a causality of $b$.

*Example 32 ($\asymp_h \not\subseteq \asymp_{hh}$).* The untimed counterexample from [15] can be immediately be used, since no sequential composition is used there. The counterexample is: $B_6 = (b_1 \|_\emptyset (a_1 + c_1)) + (a_1 \|_\emptyset b_1) + (a_1 \|_\emptyset (b_1 + c_1))$ and $B_6' = (b_1 \|_\emptyset (a_1 + c_1)) + (a_1 \|_\emptyset (b_1 + c_1))$. See [15] for the arguments that $\mathcal{C}_{B_5} \asymp_h \mathcal{C}_{B_5'}$ and $\mathcal{C}_{B_5} \asymp_{hh} \mathcal{C}_{B_5'}$.

The other non-inclusions can be derived by the set theory from the above examples or from the fact that $\mathbb{C}^{du} \subseteq \mathbb{C}^d \subseteq \mathbb{C}$ and $\mathbb{C}^{du} \subseteq \mathbb{C}^u \subseteq \mathbb{C}$.

## 6 Conclusion

We have presented durational configuration structures, where events have an occurrence time and a duration. On these structures timed equivalences are introduced. We have shown that they have the same discriminating power except for durational configuration structures where every event has a positive duration. In this case interleaving and step equivalences coincide. Consequently, if one can restrict to systems where all actions have positive duration, then it is enough to consider only single action execution in order to show step equivalence, i.e., the considered transition steps are reduced, since no step execution have to be taken into account. Furthermore, we showed that no advantage results from restricting to urgent systems, since this has no influence on the hierarchy of the discriminating power.

There are many papers that introduces timed equivalences. Among them we want to mention [19], where ill-time sensitive timed bisimilarity is compared with non timed sensitive equivalences. In [26] timed configuration, where events have an occurrence time but no duration (which is the interesting aspect in our approach), are derived from a timed version of event structures. They introduce interleaving, step, and pomset trace/bisimulation equivalences. The discriminating power of these equivalences is examined on those timed configurations that are obtained from their timed event structures (and also from restricted kinds of their timed event structures).

In our paper, we only examine ill-time sensitive equivalences, i.e., the occurrence time of the events of an execution may be less than the occurrences time of a previous event. A future task is to place equivalence notions that do not allow negative time steps into the hierarchical structure of the discriminating power. Another task is to examine the equivalences where it is not a priory known how long the actions' duration will be. Such equivalences, for example the ST-equivalence [17], are especially of interest for reactive systems and/or action refinement [18]. Of course, it is also of interest to consider weak equivalences, which abstract from internal executions.

## Acknowledgment

I thank Rob van Glabbeek for fruitful comments and suggestions. Furthermore, I thank Willem-Paul de Roever, Mila Majster-Cederbaum and the reviewers.

## References

1. L. Aceto and D. Murphy. On the ill-timed but well-caused. In Best [6], pages 97–111.
2. L. Aceto and D. Murphy. Timing and causality in process algebra. *Acta Informatica*, 33:317–350, 1996.
3. M. A. Bednarczyk. Hereditary history preserving bisimulation or what is the power of the future perfect in program logics. Technical report, Institute of Computer Science, Polish Academy of Science, 1991.
4. J. A. Bergstra, W. Fokkink, and A. Ponse. Process algebra with recursive operations. In Bergstra et al. [5], pages 333–389.
5. J. A. Bergstra, A. Ponse, and S. A. Smolka, editors. *Handbook of Process Algebra*. North-Holland, 2001.
6. E. Best, editor. *CONCUR '93*, volume 715 of *LNCS*. Springer-Verlag, 1993.
7. G. Boudol and I. Castellani. On the semantics of concurrency: Partial orders and transition systems. In H. Ehrig, R. Kowalski, G. Levi, and U. Montanari, editors, *TAPSOFT '87 (Volume 1)*, volume 249 of *LNCS*, pages 123–137. Springer-Verlag, 1987.
8. X. J. Chen and F. Corradini. On the specification and verification of performance properties for a timed process algebra. In M. Johnson, editor, *Algebraic Methodology and Software Technology*, volume 1349 of *LNCS*, pages 123–137. Springer-Verlag, 1997.
9. F. Corradini. Absolute versus relative time in process algebras. *Information and Computation*, 156:122–172, 2000.
10. P. Degano, R. D. Nicola, and U. Montanari. Observational equivalences for concurrency models. In M. Wirsing, editor, *Formal Description of Programming Concepts – III, Proceedings of the 3^{th} IFIP WG 2.2 working conference*, Ebberup 1986, pages 105–129. North-Holland, 1987.
11. H. Fecher. A completed hierarchy of true concurrent equivalences. *Information Processing Letters*, 89(5):261–265, 2004.
12. R. v. Glabbeek. The linear time–branching time spectrum II: The semantics of sequential systems with silent moves (extended abstract). In Best [6], pages 66–81.

13. R. v. Glabbeek. The linear time–branching time spectrum I. The semantics of concrete, sequential processes. In Bergstra et al. [5], pages 3–99.

14. R. v. Glabbeek and U. Goltz. Refinement of actions in causality based models. In J. W. de Bakker, W.-P. de Roever, and G. Rozenberg, editors, *Stepwise Refinement of Distributed Systems. Models, Formalisms, Correctness*, volume 430 of *LNCS*, pages 267–300. Springer-Verlag, 1990.

15. R. v. Glabbeek and U. Goltz. Refinement of actions and equivalence notions for concurrent systems. *Acta Informatica*, 37:229–327, 2001.

16. R. v. Glabbeek and G. D. Plotkin. Configuration structures. In *Proceedings of the 10th Annual IEEE Symposium on Logic in Computer Science*, pages 199–209. IEEE Computer Society Press, 1995.

17. R. v. Glabbeek and F. Vaandrager. Petri net models for algebraic theories of concurrency. In J. de Bakker, A. Nijman, and P. Treleaven, editors, *PARLE, Parallel Architectures and Languages Europe (Volume II)*, volume 259 of *LNCS*, pages 224–242. Springer-Verlag, 1987.

18. R. Gorrieri and A. Rensink. Action refinement. In Bergstra et al. [5], pages 1047–1147.

19. R. Gorrieri, M. Roccetti, and E. Stancampiano. A theory of processes with durational actions. *Theoretical Computer Science*, 140:73–94, 1995.

20. C. A. R. Hoare. *Communications Sequential Processes*. International Series in Computer Science. Prentice Hall, 1985.

21. J.-P. Katoen, R. Langerak, D. Latella, and E. Brinksma. On specifying real-time systems in a causality-based setting. In B. Jonsson and J. Parrow, editors, *Formal Techniques in Real-Time and Fault-Tolerant Systems*, volume 1135 of *LNCS*, pages 385–404. Springer-Verlag, 1996.

22. R. Milner. Calculi for synchrony and asynchrony. *Theoretical Computer Science*, 25:267–310, 1983.

23. D. Murphy. Time and duration in noninterleaving concurrency. *Fundamenta Informaticae*, 19:403–416, 1993.

24. L. Pomello. Some Equivalence Notions for Concurrent Systems. An Overview. In G. Rozenberg, editor, *Advances in Petri Nets 1985*, volume 222 of *LNCS*, pages 381–400. Springer-Verlag, 1986.

25. A. Rabinovich and B. A. Trakhtenbrot. Behavior structures and nets. *Fundamenta Informaticae*, 11(4):357–404, 1988.

26. I. B. Virbitskaite. Observational semantics for timed event structures. In D. Bjørner, M. Broy, and A. Zamulin, editors, *PSI 2001*, volume 2244 of *LNCS*, pages 214–224. Springer-Verlag, 2001.

27. Y. Wang. CCS+time = an interleaving model for real time systems. In J. Leach Albert, B. Monien, and M. Rodríguez, editors, *Automata, Languages and Programming*, volume 510 of *LNCS*, pages 217–228. Springer-Verlag, 1991.

28. G. Winskel. An introduction to event structures. In J. de Bakker, W.-P. de Roever, and G. Rozenberg, editors, *Linear Time, Branching Time and Partial Order in Logics and Models for Concurrency*, volume 354 of *LNCS*, pages 364–397. Springer-Verlag, 1989.

# Bounded Model Checking for Region Automata[*]

Fang Yu, Bow-Yaw Wang, and Yao-Wen Huang

Institute of Information Science, Academia Sinica
Nankang, Taipei 115, Taiwan
{yuf,bywang,ywhuang}@iis.sinica.edu.tw

**Abstract.** For successful software verification, model checkers must be capable of handling a large number of program variables. Traditional, BDD-based model checking is deficient in this regard, but bounded model checking (BMC) shows some promise. However, unlike traditional model checking, for which time systems have been thoroughly researched, BMC is less capable of modeling timing behavior – an essential task for verifying many types of software. Here we describe a new bounded model checker we have named *xBMC*, which we believe solves the reachability problem of dense-time systems. In xBMC, regions and transition relations are represented as Boolean formulae using discrete interpretations. In an experiment using well-developed model checkers to verify Fischer's protocol, xBMC outperformed both traditional (Kronos [8], Uppaal [16], and Red [26]) and bounded (SAL [21]) model checkers by being able to verify up to 22 processes, followed by Red with 15 processes. Therefore, although xBMC is less efficient in guaranteeing system correctness, it provides an effective and practical method for timing behavior verification of large systems.

## 1 Introduction

The successful use of model checking for software verification requires the ability to handle a large number of program variables. Because of problems associated with state explosion, this remains a difficult problem for conventional, BDD-based model checkers. SAT-based bounded model checking (BMC) [7][9] is showing some promise in this regard. A recent comparison [5] of the two techniques shows that the first requires more space and the second more time. Therefore, as Nierbert et al. [22] suggested, even though BMC is less efficient in guaranteeing the correctness of software systems, it has benefits in terms of bug hunting, especially for systems too large for complete verification. Furthermore, since numerous proposals for improving SAT solver efficiency have been made [17][19], BMC's drawback, i.e. its speed, can be improved. Due to these factors, BMC has recently gained acceptance for software verification purposes [10][13]. However, an important deficiency with BMC is its lack of support for timing behavior modeling, considered essential for verifying many types of software (e.g., embedded systems and protocol implementations). This deficiency is the focus of this paper.

---

[*] This work is partially supported by National Science Council NSC 92-2213-E-001 -023-.

Y. Lakhnech and S. Yovine (Eds.): FORMATS/FTRTFT 2004, LNCS 3253, pp. 246–262, 2004.
© Springer-Verlag Berlin Heidelberg 2004

In model checking, the verification of most temporal safety properties can be reduced to reachability analysis [6][8]. Yovine [28] has defined the reachability problem as a question of (given two dense-time system states) whether there exists an execution that starts in one state and reaches another. Our emphasis here is on solving the reachability problem of dense-time systems.

Timed automata are state transition graphs augmented with a finite set of clocks. Alur, Courcoubetis and Dill [1][2] defined finite equivalent classes, called *regions*, to represent infinite states, and used region automata to represent exact states. They thus proved the complexity of the reachability problem, but failed to provide a region automata implementation – a task that few researchers have attempted.

Biere et al. [7] have proposed a BMC-based approach for solving the reachability problem within bounded steps; their efforts have served as a catalyst for many studies on enhancing verification performance (e.g., [5][9][18][20][22][23][24][25]). In BMC, an initial state and a transition relation are transformed into SAT formulae. At each iteration, a copy of the transition relation (expressed in the following state variables) is added, and an efficient SAT solver is used to iteratively solve the expanding formulae.

We apply BMC techniques to region automata to make feasible the explicit implementation of regions. Göllü et al. [11] have proposed discretizations of dense time automata and have shown that a discrete time trajectory traverses the same timer region sequence as its corresponding dense time trajectory. This provides us with a sound base. In this project we not only characterize regions as combinations of discrete interpretations, but also precisely encode these interpretations' settings as Boolean formulae. To eliminate discretization side effects such as those induced in Göllü et al., we suggest using an exceptional successor formula that prevents timing behavior distortions.

We prove that solving these Boolean formulae's satisfiability is the equivalent of solving the forward reachability problem of dense-time systems. We attempt to incorporate these ideas into our *xBMC*, a bounded model checker that cooperates with zChaff [19], an efficient SAT solver. Our experimental results support that xBMC is more scalable for bug hunting than both traditional (Kronos [8], Uppaal [16], and Red [26]) and bounded (SAL [21]) model checkers by being able to verify Fischer's protocol up to 22 processes, followed by Red with 15 processes.

The rest of this paper is structured as follows. In Section 2 we briefly describe time automata with both discrete and clock variables. In Section 3 we provide details about our novel method that uses discrete interpretation formulae to encode exact behaviors of region automata. An explanation of the Boolean encoding of discrete interpretation formulae is given in Section 4. A reachability analysis is given in Section 5, and experimental results are summarized in Section 6. After discussing related works in Section 7, we offer our conclusions in Section 8.

## 2  Timed Automata

A timed automaton (TA) [1][2] is an automaton together with a finite set of clock variables. Its behavior consists of a) alternating discrete transitions that are constrained by guarded conditions among discrete and clock variables and b) time passages in which the automaton remains in one state while clock values increase at a uniform rate. To represent these behaviors using discrete interpretations, we define a TA that considers both discrete and clock variables, rather than one that only considers the discrete parts as locations.

## 2.1  Constraint and Interpretations

For a set $D$ of discrete variables and a set $X$ of clock variables, set $\Phi(D,X)$ of both constraints $\varphi$ is defined by the grammar $\varphi := ff \mid d = q \mid x \triangleleft c \mid \neg \varphi \mid \varphi_1 \vee \varphi_2$ , where $d \in D$ and $q \in dom(d)$, $x \in X$ , $\triangleleft \in \{<, \leq, =\}$ , and $c \in N$ is a natural number. Typical short forms are $tt \equiv \neg ff, \varphi_1 \wedge \varphi_2 \equiv \neg((\neg \varphi_1) \vee (\neg \varphi_2))$ and $\varphi_1 \rightarrow \varphi_2 \equiv \neg \varphi_1 \vee \varphi_2$ .

A discrete interpretation $s$ assigns to each discrete variable a non-negative integer that represents one value from its predefined domain (i.e., $s : D \mapsto N$ ). A clock interpretation $v$ assigns a non-negative real value to each clock (i.e., $v : X \mapsto R^+$ ). We say that an interpretation pair $(s,v)$ for $D \cup X$ satisfies constraint $\varphi$ over $D \cup X$ if and only if $\varphi$ is evaluated as being true according to the values given by $(s,v)$.

## 2.2  Time Automata

A TA is a tuple of $\langle D, X, A, I, E \rangle$ , where

1) $D$ is a finite set of discrete variables, with each $d \in D$ having a predefined finite domain denoted by $dom(d)$,
2) $X$ is a finite set of clock variables,
3) $A$ is an action set, which is a finite set of discrete variable assignments,
4) $I$ specifies an initial condition, and
5) $E \subseteq \Phi(D,X) \times A^* \times 2^X$ is a set of edges. An edge $\langle \varphi, a, \lambda \rangle$ represents a transition, with $\varphi$ acting as a triggering condition of $\Phi(D,X)$ that specifies where and when the transition can be fired. $a \in A^*$ is an action sequence that performs a series of discrete variable assignments. $\lambda \subseteq X$ is a set of clocks that are reset when the transition fires.

For some action $a \in A^*$ , $s[a]$ denotes the discrete interpretation after applying $a$ to $s$. For $\delta \in R^+$, $v + \delta$ denotes a clock interpretation that maps each clock $x$ to the value $v(x) + \delta$. For $\lambda \subseteq X$ , $v[\lambda := 0]$ denotes the clock interpretation that assigns 0 to each $x \in \lambda$ and that agrees with $v$ over the rest of the clocks.

The semantics of a TA is a transition system $\langle Q, \rightarrow \rangle$ , where $Q$ is the set of *states* and $\rightarrow$ is the *transition relation*. A *state* of a TA is a pair $(s,v)$ such that $s$ is a discrete interpretation of $D$ and $v$ is a clock interpretation of $X$. A state $(s,v)$, where $s$

maps discrete variables to values that satisfy $I$ and $v(x)=0$ for all $x \in X$, is an initial state of a TA. There are two types of $\rightarrow$:

1) For a state $(s,v)$ and an increment $\delta \in R^+$, $(s,v) \rightarrow_\delta (s, v+\delta)$.

2) For a state $(s,v)$ and an edge $<\varphi, \tau, \lambda>$ such that $(s,v)$ satisfies $\varphi$, $(s,v) \rightarrow_e (s[\tau], v[\lambda := 0])$.

A run $r$ of a TA is an infinite sequence of states and transitions $r = (s_0, v_0) \rightarrow (s_1, v_1) \rightarrow \cdots$, where for all $i \in N, (s_i, v_i) \in Q$. An arbitrary interleaving of the two transition types is permissible. $Run(s,v)$ denotes a set of runs starting at $(s,v) \in Q$. A state $(s',v')$ is reachable from $(s,v)$ if it belongs to some run starting at $(s,v)$. We define $Reach(s,v)$, where

$Reach(s,v) = \{(s',v') | \exists r = (s_0, v_0) \rightarrow \cdots \in Run(s,v), \exists i \in N.(s_i, v_i) = (s',v')\}$, to be the set of states reachable from $(s,v)$.

## 3 Discrete Interpretations of Region Automata

In this section we give a brief description of region automata based on [1][2], and then propose a robust encoding method using discrete interpretations.

### 3.1 Paired Interpretations of Equivalent Classes

System states change as time progresses, but some changed states are not distinguished by constraints. Based on this observation, Alur et al. [1] defined clock interpretation equivalence and proposed the use of region graphs for the verification of timed automata. For each $x \in X$, let $c_x$ be the largest constant that x is compared to within any triggering condition. For $t \in R^+$, let $\lfloor t \rfloor$ denote $t$'s integral part and $frac(t)$ denote $t$'s fraction, which equals $t - \lfloor t \rfloor$. A formal definition of clock interpretation equivalence is given as:

**Definition 1.** *For clock interpretations $v$ and $v'$ in a TA, $v \cong v'$ if and only if*

*1) For each clock $x \in X$, either $\lfloor v(x) \rfloor$ and $\lfloor v'(x) \rfloor$ are the same, or $v(x)$ and $v'(x)$ are both greater than $c_x$.*

*2) For each pair of clocks, $x, y \in X$ such that $v(x) \leq c_x$ and $v(y) \leq c_y$, $frac(v(x)) \leq frac(v(y))$ if and only if $frac(v'(x)) \leq frac(v'(y))$, and $frac(v(x)) = 0$ if and only if $frac(v'(x)) = 0$.*

We represent the set of clock assignments belonging to an equivalent class as a pair of discrete interpretations $v_d$ and $v_\gamma$, respectively mapping integral parts of clock assignments and fraction pair orderings. Given an equivalent class $[v]$, integral parts of the clock assignments stand for the discrete interpretation $v_d$ in (1), which maps each clock $x \in X$, where $v(x) = t$, into an integer representing an interval from $\{[0,0], (0,1), [1,1], \cdots, (c_x - 1, c_x), [c_x, c_x], (c_x, \infty)\}$.

$$v_d(x) = \begin{cases} 2\lfloor t \rfloor, & \text{if } \lfloor t \rfloor \le c_x \wedge frac(t) = 0 \\ 2\lfloor t \rfloor + 1, & \text{if } \lfloor t \rfloor \le c_x \wedge frac(t) \ne 0 \\ 2c_x + 1, & \text{otherwise} \end{cases} \tag{1}$$

We say $v(x)$ falls into a *singular* interval when $v_d(x)$ is even and into an *open* interval when $v_d(x)$ is odd; in addition, $v(x)$ falls into a *maximal* interval when $v_d(x)$ is $2c_x + 1$. Given a discrete interpretation $v_d$, let $O(v_d) \subseteq X$ denote the set of clocks whose values are both odd and less than $2c_x + 1$. Then, the discrete interpretation $v_\gamma$ in (2) maps each clock pair $(x, y)$, where $x, y \in O(v_d)$ and $x < y$, into a relation from $\{\prec, \succ, \approx\}$, which stands for pair orderings of fractions of an equivalent class $[v]$.

$$v_\gamma(x, y) = \begin{cases} \prec, & \text{if } frac(v(x)) < frac(v(y)) \\ \succ, & \text{if } frac(v(x)) > frac(v(y)) \\ \approx, & \text{if } frac(v(x)) = frac(v(y)) \end{cases} \tag{2}$$

A pair $(v_d, v_\gamma)$ denotes a clock assignment $v$ such that $v_d$ and $v_\gamma$ follow (1) and (2), respectively. For example, an equivalent class $(1 < x < y < 2) \wedge z = 1$ is represented by the pair $(v_d, v_\gamma)$, where $v_d(x) = 3 \wedge v_d(y) = 3 \wedge v_d(z) = 2 \wedge v_\gamma(x, y) = \prec$. The equivalence of two discrete interpretation pairs is defined as:

**Definition 2.** *Two pairs of interpretations are equivalent (denoted as* $(v_d, v_\gamma) \equiv (v'_d, v'_\gamma)$ *) if and only if the following conditions hold.*

1) *For each clock* $x \in X$, $v_d(x) = v'_d(x)$.

2) *For each pair (x,y), where* $x, y \in O(v_d)$ *and* $x < y$, $v_\gamma(x, y) = v'_\gamma(x, y)$.

Note that the first condition implies that $O(v_d) = O(v'_d)$.

**Lemma 1.** $v \equiv v' \leftrightarrow (v_d, v_\gamma) \equiv (v'_d, v'_\gamma)$.

**Proof:** ($\Rightarrow$) For the first condition of Definition 2, if each clock $x \in X$, while $v(x)$ and $v'(x)$ are both greater than $c_x$, $v_d(x) = v'_d(x) = 2c_x + 1$; if $\lfloor v(x) \rfloor$ and $\lfloor v'(x) \rfloor$ are the same, since $frac(v(x)) = 0$ if and only if $frac(v'(x)) = 0$, $v_d(x) = v'_d(x) = 2\lfloor v(x) \rfloor$ or $2\lfloor v(x) \rfloor + 1$. To prove the second condition of Definition 2, it is crucial to note that

a) $(frac(v(x)) \le frac(v(y)) \wedge frac(v(y)) \le frac(v(x))) \leftrightarrow v_\gamma(x, y) = \approx$,

b) $\left(frac\big(v(x)\big)\leq frac\big(v(y)\big)\wedge\neg\big(frac\big(v(y)\big)\leq frac\big(v(x)\big)\big)\right)\leftrightarrow v_\gamma(x,y)=\prec$ , and

c) $\left(\neg\big(frac\big(v(x)\big)\leq frac\big(v(y)\big)\big)\wedge frac\big(v(y)\big)\leq frac\big(v(x)\big)\right)\leftrightarrow v_\gamma(x,y)=\succ$ . Since for each

pair of clocks, where $x,y\in O(v_d)$ and $x<y$ , $frac\big(v(x)\big)\leq frac\big(v(y)\big)$ if and only if $frac\big(v'(x)\big)\leq frac\big(v'(y)\big)$, it follows that $v_\gamma(x,y)=v'_\gamma(x,y)$. ($\Leftarrow$) The proof follows in a similar way. ∎

As shown in Lemma 1, sets constrained by equivalent discrete interpretation pairs are in the same equivalent class, and each equivalent class is represented by an equivalent discrete interpretation pair. Accordingly, a *region* $\big(s,[v]\big)$ can be precisely

represented as a tuple $\big(s,v_d,v_\gamma\big)$, where three discrete interpretations

$s:D\mapsto N, v_d:X\mapsto N$ , and $v_\gamma:X\times X\mapsto\{\prec,\succ,\approx\}$ are involved.

### 3.2 Successor

A successor relation that captures a region moving into a subsequent region due to time passage is defined as:

**Definition 3.** *Let* $\alpha,\beta$ *be two distinct regions of a TA.* $\beta$ *is the successor of* $\alpha$ *, written as* $succ(\alpha)=\beta$ *, if and only if for each* $v\in\alpha$ *, there exists a positive* $\delta\in R^+$ *such that a)* $v+\delta\in\beta$ *, and b)* $v+\delta'\in\alpha\cup\beta$ *for all* $\delta'<\delta$ *.*

A region $\alpha$ is said to be out of bounds if and only if for each $v\in\alpha$ and $x\in X, v(x)>c_x$ . For an out-of-bound region $\alpha$ , its successor relation is defined as $succ(\alpha)=\alpha$ . Given a TA with $X=\{x,y\}$ , regions can be separated into nine types according to x and y evaluations: point $(\bullet)$, slash $(\diagup)$, vertical line $(|)$, horizontal line $(\_)$, triangle $(\blacktriangle)$, back triangle $(\blacktriangledown)$, vertical rectangle $(\blacksquare)$, horizontal rectangle $(\blacksquare)$ and square $(\blacksquare)$. Respective discrete interpretation conditions and successor relations of these are shown in Table 1.

Accordingly, it is possible to define a formula for the two-clock successor $\phi_{x,y}$ in (3) using the conditions of current and succeeding discrete interpretations (see Table 1). Lemma 2 shows the correctness of encoding a two-clock successor as $\phi_{x,y}$ .

$$\phi_{x,y}\equiv\bigvee_{1\leq i\leq9}\psi_i\wedge\psi_i' \tag{3}$$

**Lemma 2.** *Given a two-clock TA and a region* $\alpha$ *represented by* $\big(s,v_d,v_\gamma\big)$*,* $succ(\alpha)$

*is represented by* $\big(s,v'_d,v'_\gamma\big)$ *if and only if* $\phi_{x,y}$ *is evaluated as true according to the*

*values given by* $\big(v_d,v_\gamma,v'_d,v'_\gamma\big)$*.*

Table 1. Successor conditions in the two-clock system.

| $I$ | type<br>type' | $\psi_i$<br>$\psi'_i$ |
|---|---|---|
| 1 | • / ■ | $v_d(x)$ is *even* and $v_d(y)$ is *even*<br>$v'_d(x) = v_d(x) + 1, v'_d(y) = v_d(y) + 1, v'_\gamma(x,y) = \approx$ |
| 2 | ▮ ▰▪▰ | $v_d(x)$ is *even* and $v_d(y)$ is *odd*<br>$v'_d(x) = v_d(x) + 1, v'_d(y) = v_d(y), v'_\gamma(x,y) = \prec$ |
| 3 | ▰▪▰ | $v_d(x)$ is *odd* and $v_d(y)$ is *even*<br>$v'_d(x) = v_d(x), v'_d(y) = v_d(y) + 1, v'_\gamma(x,y) = \succ$ |
| 4 | ▰ ▮ | $v_d(x)$ is *odd*, $v_d(x) < 2c_x + 1, v_d(y)$ is *odd*, $v_d(y) < 2c_y + 1, v_\gamma(x,y) = \succ$<br>$v'_d(x) = v_d(x) + 1, v'_d(y) = v_d(y)$ |
| 5 | ▰ — | $v_d(x)$ is *odd*, $v_d(x) < 2c_x + 1, v_d(y)$ is *odd*, $v_d(y) < 2c_y + 1, v_\gamma(x,y) = \prec$<br>$v'_d(x) = v_d(x), v'_d(y) = v_d(y) + 1$ |
| 6 | ╱ • | $v_d(x)$ is *odd*, $v_d(x) < 2c_x + 1, v_d(y)$ is *odd*, $v_d(y) < 2c_y + 1, v_\gamma(x,y) = \approx$<br>$v'_d(x) = v_d(x) + 1, v'_d(y) = v_d(y) + 1$ |
| 7 | ▮ ▮ | $v_d(x)$ is *odd*, $v_d(x) < 2c_x + 1, v_d(y) = 2c_y + 1$<br>$v'_d(x) = v_d(x) + 1, v'_d(y) = v_d(y)$ |
| 8 | ▬ — | $v_d(x) = 2c_x + 1, v_d(y)$ is *odd*, $v_d(y) = 2c_y + 1$<br>$v'_d(x) = v_d(x), v'_d(y) = v_d(y) + 1$ |
| 9 | ▬ ▬ | $v_d(x) = 2c_x + 1$ and $v_d(y) = 2c_y + 1$<br>$v'_d(x) = v_d(x), v'_d(y) = v_d(y)$ |

**Proof Sketch:** The correctness of this insight is shown by the conditions in Table 1. All possible cases are considered, since $\vee_{1 \le i \le 9}\psi_i$ is true. Since $\forall i \ne j, \psi_i \wedge \psi_j$ is false, each case presents a unique type. Finally, in all cases the condition of the current equivalent class and its successor is specified by $\psi_i \wedge \psi'_i$. ∎

In order to generalize $\phi_{x,y}$ into multi-clock systems, instead of inspecting all clock values each time, the entire consensus is derived by intersecting two-clock formulae. Our initial attempt detailed intersecting the $\phi_{x,y}$ of each distinct clock pair, but this raises contradictions. For example, given a region $1 < x < y < 2 \wedge z = 1$ represented by $v_d(x) = 3 \wedge v_d(y) = 3 \wedge v_d(z) = 2 \wedge v_\gamma(x,y) = \prec$, the conjunction of $\phi_{x,y}$ for each distinct clock pair implies

$$\left(v'_d(x) = 3 \wedge v'_d(y) = 4\right)$$
$$\wedge\left(v'_d(x) = 3 \wedge v'_d(z) = 3 \wedge v'_\gamma(x,z) = \succ\right)$$
$$\wedge\left(v'_d(y) = 3 \wedge v'_d(z) = 3 \wedge v'_\gamma(y,z) = \succ\right)$$

which is contradictory because $v'_d(y)=3 \wedge v'_d(y)=4$. The contradiction occurs because $y$ needs to increase when compared to $x$, but needs to remain the same value when compared to $z$. To prevent contradiction, we make the following observations. Contradictions arise from clocks falling into open (but not maximal) intervals. Clocks that have even values must increase. If none are found, clocks having the largest fraction of all clocks must increase. Based on these observations, we add an auxiliary case in which clocks that might produce contradictions are allowed to stutter.

**Table 2.** Stuttering condition.

| type<br>type' | $\psi_s$<br>$\psi'_s$ |
|---|---|
| ◢/◥▮▮<br>◢/◥▮▮ | $v_d(x)$ is $odd, v_d(y)$ is $odd, (v_d(x) < 2c_x + 1) \vee (v_d(y) < 2c_y + 1)$<br>$v'_d(x) = v_d(x), v'_d(y) = v_d(y), v'_\gamma(x,y) = v_\gamma(x,y)$ |

After the addition, the stuttering two-clock formula is $\phi^s_{x,y}$ in (4).

$$\phi^s_{x,y} = \phi_{x,y} \vee (\psi_s \wedge \psi'_s) \tag{4}$$

For the same example, given a region $1 < x < y < 2 \wedge z = 1$, the conjunction of $\phi^s_{x,y}$ for each distinct clock pair implies that

$$\left((v'_d(x)=3 \wedge v'_d(y)=4) \vee (v'_d(x)=3 \wedge v'_d(y)=3 \wedge v'_\gamma(x,y)=\prec)\right)$$
$$\wedge \left(v'_d(x)=3 \wedge v'_d(z)=3 \wedge v'_\gamma(x,z)=\succ\right)$$
$$\wedge \left(v'_d(y)=3 \wedge v'_d(z)=3 \wedge v'_\gamma(y,z)=\succ\right)$$

This is equal to
$v'_d(x)=3 \wedge v'_d(y)=3 \wedge v'_d(z)=3 \wedge v'_\gamma(x,y)=\prec \wedge v'_\gamma(x,z)=\succ \wedge v'_\gamma(y,z)=\succ$ , a precise representation of the successor, $1 < z < x < y < 2$. However, while all of these clocks have odd values (i.e., falling in an open interval), auxiliary stuttering may incur distorted timing behavior in which all clocks refuse to increase. This can be prevented by adding a negation clause of all clocks stuttering. The successor condition for general cases is:

$$\phi \equiv \bigwedge_{x,y \in X, x < y} \phi^s_{x,y} \wedge \neg \left( \bigwedge_{x,y \in X, x < y} \psi_s \wedge \psi'_s \right) \tag{5}$$

**Lemma 3.** *Given a TA and a region $\alpha$ represented by $(s, v_d, v_\gamma)$, $succ(\alpha)$ is represented by $(s, v'_d, v'_\gamma)$ if and only if $\phi$ is evaluated to true according to the values given by $(v_d, v_\gamma, v'_d, v'_\gamma)$.*

**Proof Sketch:** ($\Rightarrow$) It is easy to see that $succ(\alpha)$ implies that, for each pair of clocks, $\phi_{x,y}^s$ is evaluated to true (according to Lemma 2), and not all stuttering cases are allowed (according to Definition 3).

($\Leftarrow$) Let $\chi = \{x \mid x \in X, v'_d(x) = v_d(x) + 1 \text{ or } v_d(x) = 2c_x + 1\}$. If $\phi$ is evaluated to true according to the values given by $(v_d, v_\gamma, v'_d, v'_\gamma)$, there exists at least one pair of clocks such that $\phi_{x,y}$ is evaluated to true, which implies that $\chi$ is not empty. If $\forall x \in \chi, v_d(x) = 2c_x + 1$, then $succ(\alpha) = \alpha$. If $\exists x \in \chi, v_d(x) < 2c_x + 1$, in the following, we prove that all cases satisfy Definition 3.

a) If $\exists x \in \chi, v_d(x)$ is even, then $\forall x \in \chi, v_d(x)$ is even. It can be seen as follows. Assume that there exists $y \in \chi$ and that $v_d(y)$ is odd. Then there exists some clock $x$ such that $v_d(x)$ is even and $\phi_{x,y}^s$ is false, which implies that $\phi$ cannot be evaluated to true. If $\forall x \in \chi, v_d(x)$ is even, then for each $v \in (v_d, v_\gamma)$, there exists a positive $\delta \in R^+$ such that i) $v + \delta \in (v'_d, v'_\gamma)$ and ii) $v + \delta' \in (v_d, v_\gamma) \cup (v'_d, v'_\gamma)$ for all $\delta' < \delta$.

b) If $\forall x \in \chi, v_d(x)$ is odd, then $\forall x \in \chi$, $x$ has the largest fraction part. It can be seen as follows. Assume that there exists $y \in \chi$ and that $y$ has a not-largest fraction part. Then there exists some clock $x$ such that $x$ has a larger fraction part than $y$ and $\phi_{x,y}^s$ is false, which implies that $\phi$ cannot be evaluated to true. If $\forall x \in \chi$, $x$ has the largest fraction part, then for each $v \in (v_d, v_\gamma)$, there exists a positive $\delta \in R^+$ such that $v + \delta \in (v'_d, v'_\gamma)$, and $v + \delta' \in (v_d, v_\gamma) \cup (v'_d, v'_\gamma)$ for all $\delta' < \delta$. ∎

## 3.3  Discrete Transitions

In this sub-section, we describe how to trigger an edge using discrete interpretations. Since we use discrete intervals to represent clock values, the first step here is to transform $\varphi$ into a discrete constraint (denoted as $Dis(\varphi)$) by replacing all clock constraints $x \triangleleft c$ with $v_d(x) \triangleleft 2c$. The set $\Phi_d(D, X)$ of discrete constraints $Dis(\varphi)$ is defined by the grammar $Dis(\varphi) := ff \mid d = q \mid v_d(x) \triangleleft 2c \mid \neg Dis(\varphi) \mid Dis(\varphi_1) \vee Dis(\varphi_2)$.

Actions of transitions include a) applying an assignment sequence $\tau$ (denoted as $s[\tau]$), and b) resetting a set of clocks $\lambda$ (denote as $v[\lambda := 0]$). Let $v_d[\lambda := 0]$ denote the discrete interpretation for $X$ that a) assigns 0 to each $x \in \lambda$ and b) agrees with $v_d$ over the rest of the clocks. Since the domain of $v_\gamma$ depends on $O(v_d)$, we remove the reset clocks from $v_\gamma$. Let $v_\gamma[O(v_d)]$ denote the discrete interpretation that a) agrees with $v_\gamma$ over the pair $(x, y)$, where both $x, y \in O(v_d)$, and b) discards other pairs.

Given an edge $\langle \varphi, \tau, \lambda \rangle$, the transition condition over discrete interpretations is defined as:

$$T_{tran} \equiv Dis(\varphi) \wedge s' = s[\tau] \wedge v'_d = v_d[\lambda := 0] \wedge v'_\gamma = v_\gamma[O(v'_d)] \tag{6}$$

**Lemma 4.** *Given a TA and two states $(s,v)$ and $(s',v')$, $(s,v) \rightarrow_e (s',v')$ if and only if $T_{tran}$ is evaluated to true according to values given by $(s,v_d,v_\gamma,s',v'_d,v'_\gamma)$, where $(v_d,v_\gamma)$ represents [v] and $(v'_d,v'_\gamma)$ represents [v'].*

### 3.4 Transition Systems

A TA's transition system is represented by a finite discrete interpretation graph $\langle Q_\cong, \rightarrow_\cong \rangle$, where $Q_\cong$ is the set of *interpretation states* and $\rightarrow_\cong$ is the *interpretation transition relation*. An interpretation state $(s,v_d,v_\gamma)$ is a triple of discrete interpretations. There are two types of $\rightarrow_\cong$ :

1) For a state $(s,v_d,v_\gamma)$, $(s,v_d,v_\gamma) \rightarrow_{\cong_s} (s,v'_d,v'_\gamma)$, such that $T_{time}$ in (7) is evaluated to true according to the values given by $(s,v_d,v_\gamma,s',v'_d,v'_\gamma)$.

2) For a state $(s,v_d,v_\gamma)$ and an edge $\langle \varphi, \tau, \lambda \rangle$, $(s,v_d,v_\gamma) \rightarrow_{\cong_e} (s',v'_d,v'_\gamma)$, such that $T_{tran}$ is evaluated to true according to the values given by $(s,v_d,v_\gamma,s',v'_d,v'_\gamma)$.

$$T_{time} \equiv (s = s') \wedge \phi \tag{7}$$

$$T \equiv T_{tran} \vee T_{time} \tag{8}$$

A step condition $T$ of $\rightarrow_\cong$ in (8) is the disjunction of (6) and (7). We define the steps and reachable states of a discrete interpretation graph in Definition 4.

**Definition 4.** *We say $(s,v_d,v_\gamma)$ can reach $(s',v'_d,v'_\gamma)$ in one step, denoted as $(s,v_d,v_\gamma) \rightarrow_\cong (s',v'_d,v'_\gamma)$, if and only if $T$ is evaluated to true according to values given by $(s,v_d,v_\gamma,s',v'_d,v'_\gamma)$. We define $Reach(s,v_d,v_\gamma)$ to be the set of interpretation states reachable from $(s,v_d,v_\gamma)$.*

$$Reach(s,v_d,v_\gamma) = \{ (s',v'_d,v'_\gamma) | (s,v_d,v_\gamma) \rightarrow_\cong^* (s',v'_d,v'_\gamma) \},$$

*where $\rightarrow_\cong^*$ is the reflexive and transitive closure of $\rightarrow_\cong$.*

The reachability problem of dense-time systems (e.g., whether one state $(s',v')$ is reachable from another state $(s,v)$) can then be solved by following Lemma 5.

**Lemma 5.** *Given a TA and two states* $(s,v)$ *and* $(s',v')$, $(s',v') \in Reach(s,v)$ *if and only if* $\left(s',v'_d,v'_\gamma\right) \in Reach\left(s,v_d,v_\gamma\right)$.

Since regions are finite, we can perform complete reachability analysis by solving bounded reachability problems (detailed in Section 5).

## 4  Boolean Encoding

Before delving into the reachability analysis, we first describe here how we encode discrete interpretation formulae as CNF Boolean ones.

### 4.1  State Variables

The definition of our state variables $B$ is given in (9), in which a set of bit vectors is used to encode an interpretation state. Given each discrete variable's domain and each clock's largest constraint value, $|B|$ is

$\Sigma_{d \in D} \lceil \lg|dom(d)| \rceil + \Sigma_{x \in X} \lceil \lg(2c_x + 2) \rceil + |X||X - 1|$ . To perform bounded model checking, we add a copy of $B_i$ to the set of state variables at the $i$th iteration.

$$B = \left\{ b_d^k \mid d \in D, 0 \le k \le \lceil \lg|dom(d)| \rceil \right\} \cup \left\{ b_x^k \mid x \in X, 0 \le k \le \lceil \lg(2c_x + 2) \rceil \right\} \qquad (9)$$
$$\cup \left\{ b_{xy}^k \mid x, y \in X, x < y, k = 0 \text{ or } 1 \right\}$$

### 4.2  Discrete Interpretation Encoding

Using state variables $B$, an interpretation state $\left(s, v_d, v_\gamma\right)$ is encoded into a Boolean formula $\beta(B)$, where $\beta(B)$ is the conjunction of discrete, interval and relation sub-formulae given in (10). Following standard bit encoding, sub-formulae are built with regard to their individual discrete interpretations. Note that an even-valued clock $x$ (the $0^{\text{th}}$ bit is zero) will be encoded with $\neg b_x^0$, making it possible to encode a condition such as "$v_d(x)$ is even" using one literal. This characteristic significantly reduces the complexity in solving the successor formulae described in Section 3.2.

$$\beta(B) = \bigwedge_{d \in D, 0 \le k \le \lceil \lg|dom(d)| \rceil} \begin{cases} b_d^k, & \text{if the } k\text{th bit of the value of } s(d) \text{ is } 1 \\ \neg b_d^k, & \text{otherwise} \end{cases} \qquad (10)$$
$$\bigwedge_{x \in X, 0 \le k \le \lceil \lg|2c_x + 2| \rceil} \begin{cases} b_x^k, & \text{if the } k\text{th bit of the value of } v_d(x) \text{ is } 1 \\ \neg b_x^k, & \text{otherwise} \end{cases}$$
$$\bigwedge_{x, y \in O(v_d), x < y} \begin{cases} \neg b_{xy}^1 \wedge b_{xy}^0, & \text{if } v_\gamma(x, y) = \prec \\ b_{xy}^1 \wedge \neg b_{xy}^0, & \text{if } v_\gamma(x, y) = \succ \\ b_{xy}^1 \wedge b_{xy}^0, & \text{if } v_\gamma(x, y) = \approx \end{cases}$$

## 4.3 Formula Encoding

We reserve our Boolean state variables using a bit-vector. The translation of a bit-vector logic (used to build the equation for a concrete transition relation) into conjunctive normal form (CNF) is straight forward: we build a circuit representation and then translate it into CNF.

# 5 Reachability Analysis

In this section, we describe how we deal with the reachability problem by iteratively solving the satisfiability of an expanding Boolean formula. We also prove that our procedure provides a sound and complete solution when we reach a big enough bound. Let $Reach_k\left(s,v_d,v_\gamma\right)$ denote the set of states reachable from $\left(s,v_d,v_\gamma\right)$ by unfolding exactly $k$ steps. Lemma 6 proves that all regions of a given TA can be reached within constant steps.

**Lemma 6.** *Given a TA having n regions, $\left(s',v'_d,v'_\gamma\right)\in Reach_k\left(s,v_d,v_\gamma\right)$ and $k>n$ implies the existence of some $k'<k$ such that $\left(s',v'_d,v'_\gamma\right)\in Reach_{k'}\left(s,v_d,v_\gamma\right)$.*

**Proof:** If $\left(s',v'_d,v'_\gamma\right)\in Reach_k\left(s,v_d,v_\gamma\right)$ and k>n, then there exists some region that was reached more than once. Assume we reached the region in the $i$th and the $j$th steps, we can derive a new path by removing steps $i+1$ to $j$. This implies the existence of some $k'<k$ such that $\left(s',v'_d,v'_\gamma\right)\in Reach_{k'}\left(s,v_d,v_\gamma\right)$. ∎

Let $T(i)$ denote $\underline{T}$ in (8) over state variables $B_i$ and $B_{i+1}$, and $\beta_{s,v_d,v_\gamma}(i)$ denote $\beta(B)$ in (10) according to the interpretation state $\left(s,v_d,v_\gamma\right)$ over state variables $B_i$. Lemma 7 shows that the bounded reachability problem is equivalent to the satisfiability problem.

**Lemma 7.** $\left(s',v'_d,v'_\gamma\right)\in Reach_k\left(s,v_d,v_\gamma\right)$ *if and only if*

$$SAT\left(\beta_{s,v_d,v_\gamma}(0)\wedge T(0)\wedge\cdots\wedge T(k-1)\wedge\beta_{s',v'_d,v'_\gamma}(k)\right).$$

Given an initial condition, a risk condition, a transition condition and an integer bound, we iteratively solve the bounded reachability problem by calling the SAT solver for bounded forward reachability analyses. We unfold the interpretation transition relation until the SAT solver returns a truth assignment or reaches the bound. Let $I(i)$ and $R(i)$ respectively denote the CNF formulae of the given initial and risk conditions over $B_i$. The implementation of BoundedFwdReach() is given in Fig. 1. By conjoining the formula with the negation clause of the risk condition, each iteration's result is saved for use in later iterations.

```
BoundedFwdReach(I, R, T, MaxBound)
  var i: 0.. MaxBound;
begin
    k := 0; F := I(i);
    loop forever
      if(SAT(F∧R(i)))return reachable;
      if(i=MaxBound)return unreachable within MaxBound;
      F := F∧¬R(i)∧T(i);
      i := i+1;
end.
```

**Fig. 1.** BoundedFwdReach() implementation.

**Theorem.** *Given a TA having n regions,* BoundedFwdReach *() is sound and complete when* MaxBound $\geq n$.

If the risk state is reachable, the formula will be satisfied at some step, and a truth assignment will be returned by zChaff. The procedure will then terminate and generate a counterexample. The formula will keep on expanding if a risk state is not reached. Therefore, if the risk state is unreachable, the procedure terminates when either MaxBound is reached or memory is exhausted. Given a TA having $n$ regions, the final formula will contain $n|B|$ branching variables. Since $n$ is exponential to both a) the number of clocks and b) each clock's largest constant, the threshold is usually prohibitively expensive.

## 6  Experimental Results

*xBMC 2.0* is written in C and makes use of zChaff [19]. Experiments were run against Fischer's mutual exclusion protocol, which consists of $n$ timed automata with each automaton modeling an individual process (Fig 2). Mutual exclusion property was considered violated when A<B. The largest constraint for the local clock of each process was adjusted by increasing the value of $B$ and keeping A=1.

We compare our model checker with Kronos [8], Uppaal [16], Red [26] and SAL 2 (infBMC) [21]. The first three tools support full TCTL verification of timed systems, but use different data structures for system state representation. Kronos and Uppaal use DBMs (Difference Bounded Matrices) [15], while Red uses CRDs (Clock Restriction Diagrams) [26]. infBMC is a bounded model checker included in SAL 2 [21], a suit of tools developed by the SRI's Symbolic Analysis Laboratory for analyzing state machines. infBMC supports verification of infinite state systems using a special decision procedure [20] that solves the satisfiability of combinations of real and integer linear arithmetic.

Performance results are shown in Table 3. All verification processes that did not crash reached a violated state. When *B=2*, Kronos failed to construct the product automaton of the system while verifying 6 processes. Uppaal ran efficiently until the number of processes reached 14. Red demonstrated an exceptional data sharing capability and outperformed the other tools in terms of memory utilization and successfully checked 15 processes. infBMC reported all counterexamples at the 10th iterations, but its internal decision procedure crashed while verifying 6 processes. xBMC was capable of reporting all counterexamples within 14 iterations and successfully checked 22 processes. When $B=4000$, the increased number of variables limited xBMC to handling up to 13 processes. On the other hand, performance among the other tools was not significantly affected by increasing values of constraint constants.

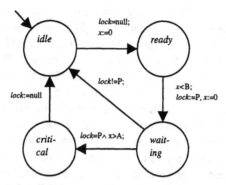

**Fig. 2.** Each process in Fischer's protocol has one local clock $x$ and one discrete variable $l$ (denoting location), where dom$(l)=\{idle, ready, waiting, critical\}$. Processes can access the global pointer $lock$ (e.g., assigning the pointer to itself $[lock:=P]$). Initially, all processes are in $idle$ and $lock$ points to none of them.

**Table 3.** Process number impact on each tool's performance when checking mutual exclusion violations of Fischer's protocol. "O/M" indicates that the model checker ran out of memory. All experiments were performed on a Pentium IV 1.7 GHz computer with 256MB of RAM running the Linux operating system.

| # | Kronos 2.5.2 $B=2$ | Kronos 2.5.2 $B=4000$ | Uppaal 3.5.1 $B=2$ | Uppaal 3.5.1 $B=4000$ | Red 5.0 $B=2$ | Red 5.0 $B=4000$ | SAL 2.1 (infBMC) $B=2$ | SAL 2.1 (infBMC) $B=4000$ | xBMC 2.0 $B=2$ | xBMC 2.0 $B=4000$ |
|---|---|---|---|---|---|---|---|---|---|---|
| 4 | 0.12s | 0.11s | 0.03s | 0.02s | 0.57s | 0.56s | 86.98s | 95.45s | 3.28s | 20.31s |
| 5 | 0.52s | O/M | 0.03s | 0.04s | 1.95s | 1.95s | 420.98s | 275.82s | 10.49s | 37.32s |
| 6 | O/M | | 0.06s | 0.06s | 5.70s | 4.82s | O/M | O/M | 14.66s | 47.63s |
| 7 | | | 0.16s | 0.17s | 14.47s | 12.90s | | | 16.83s | 47.04s |
| 9 | | | 1.17s | 1.21s | 75.5s | 74.31s | | | 46.90s | 91.35s |
| 11 | | | 5.08s | 9.35s | 321.04s | 353.61s | | | 129.46s | 200.84s |
| 13 | | | 12.21s | O/M | 1129.18s | 1345.08s | | | 111.59s | 447.39s |
| 14 | | | O/M | | 2005.23s | 2471.07s | | | 237.89s | O/M |
| 15 | | | | | 4234.41s | 4238.34s | | | 531.73s | |
| 16 | | | | | O/M | O/M | | | 453.83s | |
| 17 | | | | | | | | | 414.29s | |
| 19 | | | | | | | | | 528.66s | |
| 21 | | | | | | | | | 641.27s | |
| 22 | | | | | | | | | 587.01s | |
| 23 | | | | | | | | | O/M | |

# 7  Related Work and Discussion

Due to the many advantages described in Section 1, SAT-based model checking has recently gained considerable favor among software verification researchers. Clarke et al. [10] developed a SAT-based bounded model checker for ANSI C, and we used xBMC to verify Web application code security in an earlier project [13]. Although both projects were successful, neither supported timing behavior modeling.

The verification of timed automata via satisfiability checking has been the focus of several investigations, with most researchers encoding atomic constraint evaluations rather than regions themselves. Niebert et al. [22] represented the bounded reachability problem in Boolean variables and numerical constraints of Pratt's difference logic, but faced difficulties. The difficulty lay in solving the mixed constraints, which was done by their in-house solver. Audemard et al. [5] treated clocks as real variables and reduced bounded verification of timed systems to the satisfiability of a math formula with linear mathematical relations involving real variables. They demonstrated this approach by implementing a new solver, MATHSAT. They also showed that bounded verification was considerably improved by using symmetry reductions. Moura et al. [20] also used real variables to represent infinite state systems. In [25], Sorea checked full LTL formulae based on predicate abstraction to extend BMC capabilities. Compared to encoding abstract predicates, encoding regions themselves provides at least two advantages – simplicity and an intrinsic bound.

The approach closest to ours was described by Penczek, Wozna and Zbrzezny in [23][27]. Based on Numerical Decision Diagrams (NDDs) [4], they obtained the set of a region's representatives by dividing each unit interval into $2n$ segments ($n$ = number of clocks). Compared to our method, which encodes an exact region based on fraction order and that region's successor in one step, theirs incurs more discrete time steps. In [27], they considerably improved their performance by applying forward projection. According to their reported experimental results, our xBMC demonstrated compatible performance (in fact, better than their original explicit discretization encoding without applying forward projection) while verifying Fischer's protocol in similar conditions.

To our best knowledge on previous works concerning BMC application to timed automata (based on either discretization or general polyhedra/zones), our approach is the first that uses region graphs. One obvious drawback with region graphs is their prohibitive size, which grows exponentially with the number of clocks and with each clock's maximal constant. In particular, when applying standard model checking techniques to region graphs, verification becomes infeasible even for moderately-sized systems. However, our results appear promising and shows that region graph encoding may be feasible in practice because: a) using regions (as opposed to general zones/polyhedra) implies simple transition relations, and b) SAT-based BMC is applicable to very large systems and is efficient when the transition relations are not too complex.

## 8  Conclusion and Future Work

It is well known BMC is more efficient in identifying bugs and verifying systems with a large number of program variables. However, it is difficult for BMC to model timing behavior. To address this problem, we used a robust method to explicitly encode regions, reducing the reachability problems of dense-time systems to satisfiability problems. The results of our experiments indicate that even without enhancements (e.g., symmetry reduction, forward projection, and abstraction), our region encoding is more efficient in verifying timing behavior of large systems when compared with other well-developed tools. However, as with all bounded model checkers, xBMC is not as effective as the other tools for guaranteeing correctness. Therefore, one of our follow-up works [29] is to apply ground decision procedures based on induction to support complete computations without threshold requirements. Other future work includes: a) applying enhancements to further improve efficiency, and b) to integrate xBMC with WebSSARI [13] in an effort to verify the timing behavior of real-world Web applications.

# References

1. Alur, R., Courcoubetis, C. and Dill, D.,"Model-checking for Real-time Systems." In IEEE 5th Annual Symposium on Logic In Computer Science (LICS), Philadelphia, June 1990.
2. Alur, R. and D. L. Dill, "A Theory of Timed Automata." Theoretical Computer Science 126, pp. 183-235, 1994
3. Amla, N., Kurshan, R., McMillan, K. and Medel, R. K., "Experimental Analysis of Different Techniques for Bounded Model Checking." In Proc. TACAS'03, LNCS, Poland, 2003.
4. Asarin, E., Bozga, M., Kerbrat, A., Maler, O., Pnueli, A. and Rasse, A., "Data-structures for the Verification of Timed Automata." In Proc. HART'97, LNCS 1201, pp. 346-360, 1997.
5. ⊺Audemard, G., Cimatti, A., Korniowicz, A. and Sebastiani, R., "Bounded Model Checking for Timed Systems." In Doron Peled and Moshe Y. Vardi, editors, Formal Techniques for Networked and Distributed Systems - FORTE'02, LNCS 2529, pp. 243-259, 2002.⊺
6. Beer, I., Ben-David, S. and Landver, A., "On-the Fly Model Checking of RCTL Formulas." In Proc. of the 10P$^{th P}$ CAV, LNCS 818, 1998.
7. Biere, A., Cimatti, A., Clarke, E.M., Fujita, M., Zhu, Y., "Symbolic Model Checking Using SAT Procedures Instead of BDDs." In Proc. DAC'99, pp. 317-320, 1999.⊺
8. Bozga, M., Daws, C., Maler, O., Olivero, A., Tripakis, S. and Yovine, S., "Kronos: a Model-Checking Tool for Real-Time Systems." In Proc. of the 10th Conference on Computer-Aided Verification, CAV'98. LNCS 1427, Springer-Verlag, 1998.⊺
9. Clarke, E., Biere, A., Raimi, R.,and Zhu, Y., "Bounded Model Checking Using Satisfiability Solving." In Formal Methods in System Design, July 2001.
10. Clarke, E., Kroening, D., Yorav, K., "Behavioral Consistency of C and Verilog Programs using Bounded Model Checking." In Proc. DAC'03, Session 23.3, Anaheim, CA, 2003.
11. Göllü, A., Puri, A., and Varaiya, P., "Discretization of timed automata." In Proc. of the 33rd IEEE conferene on decision and control, pp. 957-958, 1994.
12. Henzinger, T.A., Nicollin, X., Sifakis, J. and Yovine, S., "Symbolic Model Checking for Real-Time Systems." Information and Computation, Vol. 111, pp. 193-244, 1994.
13. Huang, Y.-W., Yu, F., Hang, C., Tsai, C.-H., Lee, D.-T. and Kuo, S.-Y., "Verifying Web Applications Using Bounded Model Checking." In Proc. DSN'04, Italy, June, 2004.
14. Laroussinie, F., Larsen, K. G. and Weise, C., "From timed automata to logic - and back." In Proc. MFCS'95, LNCS 969, pp. 529-539
15. Larsen, K. G., Pettersson, P., and Wang, Y., "Compositional and Symbolic Model Checking of Real-time System." In Proc. RTSS'95, Pisa, Italy, 1995.

16. Larsen, K. G., Pettersson, P., and Wang, Y., "UPPAAL in a Nutshell." In Int. Journal on Software Tools for Technology Transfer 1(1-2), pp. 134-152, 1998.

17. Lu, Feng, Wnag, Li-C., Cheng, Kwang-Ting, Huan, Ric C-Y, "A Circuit SAT Solver With Signal Correlation Guided Learning." In Proc. DATE'03, March, 2003.

18. Moller, M. O., Rue, H., and Sorea, M., "Predicate Abstraction for Dense Real-time Systems." in Theory and Practice of Timed Systems (TPTS'2002), 2002.

19. Moskewicz, M.W., Madigan, C.F., Zhao, Y., Zhang, L. and Malik, S., "Chaff: Engineering an Efficient SAT Solver." In Proc. DAC'01, June 2001.

20. de Moura, L., Rueß, H. and Sorea, M., "Lazy Theorem Proving for Bounded Model Checking over Infinite Domains." In Proc. CADE'02, LNCS 2392, pp. 438-455, 2002.

21. de Moura, L., Owre, S., Rueß, H., Rushby, J., Shanker, N. and Sorea, M., "SAL 2." In Proc. CAV'04, 2004.

22. Niebert, P., Mahfoudh, M., Asarin, E., Bozga, M., Jain, N., and Maler, O., "Verification of Timed Automata via Satisfiability Checking." In Proc. FTRTFT'02, LNCS 2469, 2002.

23. Penczek, W., Wozna, B. and Zbrzezny, A., "Towards Bounded Model Checking for the Universal Fragment of TCTL." In Proc. FTRTFT'02, LNCS 2469, pp. 265-288, 2002.

24. Seshia, S. A., BryantT, TR. E., T"Unbounded, Fully Symbolic Model Checking of Timed Automata using Boolean Methods." In Proc.T CAV'03. LNCS 2725, Springer-Verlag, 2003.

25. Sorea, M.,"Bounded Model Checking for Timed Automata." CSL Technical Report SRI-CSL-02-03, 2002.

26. Wang, F., "Efficient Verification of Timed Automata with BDD-like Data-Structures." In Proc. VMCAI'03, LNCS 2575, Springer-Verlag, 2003.

27. Wozna, B., Penczek, W. and Zbrzezny, A., "Checking Reachability Properties for Timed Automata via SAT." Fundamenta Informaticae, Vol. 55(2), pp. 223-241, 2003.

28. Yovine, S., "Model-checking Timed Automata." Embedded Systems, LNCS 1494, 1998.

29. Yu, F. and Wang, B.-Y. "Toward Unbounded Model Checking for Region Automata." Paper Submitted.

# Some Progress in Satisfiability Checking
# for Difference Logic*

Scott Cotton[1], Eugene Asarin[2], Oded Maler[1], and Peter Niebert[3]

[1] VERIMAG, 2 Av. de Vignate, 38610 Gières, France
{Scott.Cotton,Oded.Maler}@imag.fr
[2] LIAFA, Université Paris 7, 2 place Jussieu, 75251 Paris, France
asarin@liafa.jussieu.fr
[3] Laboratoire d'Informatique Fondamentale
CMI, 39 rue Joliot-Curie, 13453 Marseille Cedex 13, France
niebert@cmi.univ-mrs.fr

**Abstract.** In this paper we report a new SAT solver for *difference logic*, a propositional logic enriched with timing constraints. The main novelty of our solver is a tighter integration of the incremental analysis of numerical conflicts with the process of Boolean conflict analysis. This and other improvements lead to significant performance gains for some classes of problems.

## 1 Introduction

The development of increasingly stronger Boolean satisfiability (SAT) solvers such as [MS99,MMZ+01,GN02] made satisfiability checking an important ingredient in verification and synthesis of finite-state systems. Recently there is a growing interest in extending the scope of SAT-based methods to reason about systems admitting variables ranging over infinite domains such as integers and reals. To this end, new satisfiability checking methods should be developed for propositional logic extended with numerical constraints that are rich enough to capture the dynamics (transition relation) of the systems in question.

*Difference logic*, also known as *separation logic*, is one of the simplest extensions of propositional logic which has recently attracted a lot of attention. In addition to propositional variables, the atoms of this logic consist of inequalities of the form $x - y < c$ for real-valued variables $x$, $y$ and an integer constant $c$. The popularity of this logic is due to the following: 1) It is rich enough to express bounded reachability for timed automata, feasibility of scheduling problems, existence of paths in digital circuits with bounded delays and other timing related problems; 2) The satisfiability of a conjunction of difference constraints can be reduced to the absence of negative cycles in finite weigthed graphs, a procedure more efficient than general linear (and, of course nonlinear) constraints satisfaction.

In the last couple of years, several groups developed independently solvers for DL [ACG99,MNAM02,S02,NMA+02,F02,ACKS02,SSB02,WZP03] or for richer logics that contain it [ABC+02,MRS02,BDS+02]. These solvers use different approaches for

---

* This work was partially supported by the EC project IST-2001-35302 AMETIST (Advanced Methods for Timed Systems).

Y. Lakhnech and S. Yovine (Eds.): FORMATS/FTRTFT 2004, LNCS 3253, pp. 263–276, 2004.

the crucial problem of managing the *interaction* between the *propositional* and *numerical* parts of the problem. In this work we introduce yet another solver, DLSAT, which is inspired by our previous solver MX-SOLVER reported in [MNAM02,NMA+02,M03] and also by some ideas in [SSB02]. The main novelty of this solver is in a more efficient algorithm for detecting numerical contradictions and in a tighter integration of this procedure with the conflict analysis and learning mechanisms used for the propositional part. We report some significant performance gains on some non toy problems.[1]

The rest of the paper is organized as follows. In Section 2 we define DL, and briefly present the process of Boolean SAT solving. In Section 3 we discuss the various approaches for combining propositional and numerical satisfiability and position our approach in this landscape. In Section 4 we discuss the process of discovering numerical contradictions using negative cycles detection in weighted graphs and present our procedure based on Goldberg's heuristic improvement of the Bellman-Ford algorithm [GR93]. Additional implementation details are described in Section 5 followed by experimental results and a discussion of future work.

## 2  Preliminaries

### 2.1  Difference Logic

**Definition 1 (Difference Logic).** *Let* $\mathcal{P} = \{p_1, p_2, \ldots p_n\}$ *be a set of propositional (Boolean) variables and* $\mathcal{X} = \{x_1, x_2, \ldots x_m\}$ *be a set of numerical variables. The set of atomic formulae of* $DL(\mathcal{P}, \mathcal{X})$ *consists of the propositions in* $\mathcal{P}$ *and numerical constraints of the following forms:*

$$x_i - x_j \leq c \ \text{ and } \ x_i - x_j < c$$

*with* $c \in \mathbb{Z}$. *The set* $\mathcal{F}$ *of all DL formulae is the smallest set containing the atomic formulae which is closed under negation and conjunction:*

- $\varphi \in \mathcal{F}$ *implies* $\neg\varphi \in \mathcal{F}$.
- $\varphi \in \mathcal{F}$ *and* $\psi \in \mathcal{F}$ *implies* $\varphi \wedge \psi \in \mathcal{F}$.

*Remaining Boolean connectives* $\vee, \wedge, \rightarrow, \ldots$ *may be defined in the usual ways in terms of conjunction and negation.*

A $(\mathcal{P}, \mathcal{X})$-*valuation* consists of two functions (overloaded with the name $v$) $v : \mathcal{P} \rightarrow \{\text{T}, \text{F}\}$ and $v : \mathcal{X} \rightarrow \mathbb{R}$. The valuation $v$ is extended to all $DL(\mathcal{P}, \mathcal{X})$ formulae by letting

$$v(x_i - x_j \leq c) = \text{T iff } v(x_i) - v(x_j) \leq c$$

and applying the obvious rules for the Boolean connectives. A partial valuation $v$ is a valuation defined over a subset of the variables. We denote by $\varphi[v]$ the formula obtained from $\varphi$ by substituting $v(p)$ and $v(x)$ (when they are defined) in $p$ and $x$, respectively. A formula $\varphi$ is satisfied by a valuation $v$ iff $v(\varphi) = \text{T}$ (we denote it also by $v \models \varphi$). A formula $\varphi$ is satisfiable if it has a satisfying valuation. The satisfiability problem for $DL(\mathcal{P}, \mathcal{X})$ is NP-complete.

Like most SAT solvers we work with formulae in conjunctive normal form:

---

[1] I.e. no Fisher's protocol.

**Definition 2 (CNF).** *A Boolean literal is a formula of the form $p$ or $\neg p$ with $p \in \mathcal{P}$. A numerical literal is a formula of the form $x - y \leq c$ or $x - y < c$. A clause is a disjunction $C = L_1 \vee L_2 \vee \ldots L_l$ of literals. A DL formula is in CNF if it is a conjunction $C_1 \wedge C_2 \wedge \ldots \wedge C_k$ of clauses.*

As in propositional logic (see [T70]), efficient translations from arbitrary formulae to CNF can be done using auxiliary Boolean variables.

## 2.2   Basics of SAT Solving

In order to be self-contained we sketch briefly the principles underlying contemporary SAT solvers as applied to Boolean satisfiability, a special case of DL with $\mathcal{X} = \emptyset$. The DPLL-based procedure for SAT can be seen as an intelligent search in the space of valuations, accompanied by formula simplification and learning. The search is conducted by iteratively generating partial valuations and extending them. Extension is performed with simplification rules which are applied after substituting the valuation in the variables. Literals are removed that evaluate to F. Clauses are removed that evaluate to T, and variables are inferred that appear in unit clauses. The result of simplification of a formula $\varphi[v]$ can thus be either T, F or an extended valuation $v'$. The search for a satisfying assignment should be continued from $\varphi[v']$.

Learning is a process, where after some $\varphi[v]$ simplifies to F, a subset $v_{con}$ of $v$ is identified as a sufficient cause for unsatisfiability, and its negation $\neg v_{con}$ is added as an additional clause to $\varphi$ in order to prune the search tree and prevent exploration of partial assignments that extend $v_{con}$. The whole procedure is sketched below where the formula $\varphi$ is a global variable and the partial valuation $v$ is an argument to the recursive procedure *Solve*, initially called with $v = \emptyset$:

**procedure** *Solve(v)*

$(v', \varphi') := Simplify(\varphi[v])$
**if** $\varphi' = $ T
   **return**(yes)
**else if** $\varphi' = $ F
   $v_{con} := Conflict(\varphi, v)$
   $\varphi := \varphi \wedge \neg v_{con}$
   **return**(no)
**else**
   pick a variable $p$ not appearing in $v$
   **if** $Solve(v \cup \{p = $ T$\})$
      **return**(yes)
   **else**
      **return**$(Solve(v \cup \{p = $ F$\}))$

Modern SAT solvers employ a myriad of optimizations and of course utilize an iterative version of this procedure. Since SAT solvers spend most of their time simplifying the formula [Zha95], a notable optimization is *two literal watching* [MMZ+01,ZH96], which reduces to two the number of literals the procedure must scan in a clause while identifying whether a clause is solved, empty, or unit. Additionally, various variable ordering heuristics are employed, most of which are based on the frequency of variable occurrences in the formula. Finally, non chronological backtracking is often employed upon analyzing a conflict, in which the procedure either jumps back to the smallest assignment which leaves the conflicting clause unit. This process prevents the solver from searching a larger number unsatisfiable subtrees that it would otherwise.

Perhaps the most interesting point (and one which can yield a great degree of variance on the performance) is exactly what clause(s) a solver decides to learn upon coming across a conflict. All the different approaches make use of an *implication graph* in which literals are vertices, and those which are deduced via unit resolution are implied by the false literals in the unit clause. One of the more successful methods of examining this graph backtracks through the implications until it finds a *unique implication point*, or a literal $l$ which lies between the literals in the empty clause and the guessed literals in such a way that every path from the guessed literals to those in the empty clause passes through $l$.

Taken together, these methods, heuristics, and optimizations have pushed the performance of Boolean SAT solvers up by a few orders of magnitude. On the other hand, the extension of these techniques to formulae with numeric atoms has not seen such improvements. In the next section, we will review some methods of leveraging and extending these techniqes for solving SAT for DL.

## 3    Approaches to DL SAT Solving

In the last couple of years several approaches for checking satisfiability of DL were introduced. The approach of [WZP03] is restricted to integer solutions (discrete time semantics). The clock variables are interpreted as integer variables encoded in binary, and the whole problem is transformed into a Boolean SAT problem on the bits of the numbers, which can then be submitted to one's favorite solver. This approach has been tried already in the context of BDD-based verification of timed automata [ABK+97] and its disadvantage is that the arithmetical content of numerical constraints is lost when they are coded in binary. The rest of the approaches known to us can be classified into the following three categories:

### 3.1    The Lazy Approach

This approach, used for example in [ABC+02], consists of transforming a formula $\varphi$ into a purely Boolean formula $\varphi'$ by replacing every numerical constraint of the form $x - y < c$ by a new propositional variable $p_{xyc}$. The formula $\varphi'$ is "easier" to satisfy, because the new variable are not interpreted and the implications between them are not visible to the Boolean solver. Consequently if $\varphi'$ is found to be unsatisfiable we can conclude that so is $\varphi$. On the other hand, whenever a satisfying assignment $v'$ is found, an additional feasibility check should be performed to see whether $v'$ can be transformed into an assignment $v$ for $\varphi$. This is done by constructing a conjunction of all numerical constraints $x - y < c$ such that $p_{xyc} = \text{T}$ and $\neg(x - y < c)$ such that $p_{xyc} = \text{F}$ in $v'$. This conjunction is then submitted to a numerical solver and if it is feasible then

$\varphi$ is satisfiable; otherwise $v'$ is declared unsatisfying and the enumeration of satisfying assignments for $\varphi'$ continues. Additionally, learning clauses from the feasibility checks and adding them to $\varphi'$ is usually performed.

This approach is very easy to implement as, with the exception of learning, the Boolean and numerical parts are kept separate. This is also the reason for its practical weakness for problems with many numerical implications as there is a limited flow of information between these parts. Typically the algorithm can check many assignments to $\varphi'$ until it finds one which can be transformed to an assignment for $\varphi$ or until it concludes that no such assignment exists.

## 3.2   The Preprocessing Approach

This approach, first suggested in [SSB02] is the opposite one. Although it is also based on introducing propositional variables for the numerical constraints, it computes all the intrinsic dependencies between the numeric variables, encoding the dependencies as Boolean constraints and adding these constraints to $\varphi'$. The advantage of this approach is that, by construction, each assignment to the augmented formula can be transformed into a satisfying assignment for the original formula. There are two major shortcomings: 1) As noted in [SSB02], some classes of sets of numerical constraints lead to an exponential blow-up in the size of the formula when their implications are added; 2) This procedure may need to compute dependencies between numerical constraints mentioned in $\varphi$ that, due to the structure of $\varphi$, will never have to be considered simultaneously.

## 3.3   Incremental Approaches

This class consists of approaches that try to check feasibility constraints somewhere between the above cited approaches. This is the case of our previous solver MX-SOLVER [NMA+02] and also that of [MRS02] where it was called "lemmas on demand". In [NMA+02] the following strategy is used: a conjunction of numerical constraints that need to be satisfied under the current assignment is maintained, represented as a DBM (Difference Bound Matrix). Whenever a Boolean variable $p_{xyc}$ is assigned to T or F, its corresponding numerical constraint is added to the DBM, which is tested for feasibility using the Floyd-Warshall algorithm (more on the structure of difference constraints in the next section). If the set of constraints is found infeasible at a partial assignment $v'$, there is no need to explore extension of $v'$. This approach has an obvious advantage over the lazy approach which needs to wait until a satisfying assignment for $\varphi'$ is found and an advantage over the preprocessing approach by not checking feasibility of all combinations of constraints, only those that need to be satisfied simultaneously in some explored branch of the search tree. However, in the absence of a learning mechanism, this expensive procedure is invoked too often.

## 3.4   Our Approach

The solver described in the present paper is another variant of the incremental approach with the following features:

1. An integrated solver that treats DL formulae and CNF Boolean formulae with two literal watching, conflict analysis (first unique implication point), as well as Boolean and numeric variable ordering heuristics.
2. Transformation to CNF is done using the more efficient construction of Wilson [W90] rather than the classical Tseitin translation [T70].
3. Equal treatment of Boolean and numerical literals in terms of branching (unlike [NMA$^+$02] where branching was applied only to Booleans).
4. Optimizations for reducing the number of feasibility checks: We omit feasibility checks upon assigning a truth value to a new numerical constraint in two cases: when all the clauses where the new constraint appears are already solved (simplified to true), and when the constraint involves a "new" numeric variable not mentioned in the constraints assigned so far.
5. A more efficient algorithm for checking feasibility of a conjunction of difference constraints. We detect cycles using a depth-first variant of the Bellman-Ford-Moore algorithm [GR93] which has much better average case complexity in practice.
6. Integration of difference constraint feasibility checks with the conflict analysis mechanism. Inconsistent sets of difference constraints are analyzed with respect to their implication graph, and the procedure learns a "reason" for the inconsistency.

In the next section we discuss numerical feasibility checks in general and present the algorithm that we use.

## 4    The Fine Structure of Sets of Difference Constraints

### 4.1    Feasibility

While conjunctions of difference constraints are a special case of linear inequalities, their structure is much simpler. We can describe the satisfiability problem of conjunctions of difference constraints using transitivity:

$$x - y < c_1 \wedge y - z < c_2 \Rightarrow x - z < c_1 + c_2$$

If a conjunction of difference constraints implies that $x - x < 0$ for some $x$, then it is infeasible, otherwise it is is feasible. It is sometimes illustrative to consider the case where each constant is 0, as all the difference constraints then take the form $x < y$. In particular in this case it is easy to see that any cycle $x < y < \ldots < z < x$ is false. In the more general case, we have that $(x_1 - x_2 < c_1) \wedge (x_2 - x_3 < c_2) \wedge \ldots \wedge (x_n - x_1 < c_n)$ is false just in case $\Sigma_{i=1}^n c_i \leq 0$.

One can easily express the negation of a difference constraint as a difference constraint: $\neg(x - y < c) \iff (x - y \geq c) \iff (y - x \leq -c)$. However, this situation requires that the logic allow for both strict and non strict constraints. As a result, we need to extend the notion of feasibility to accommodate strict and non strict constraints. Letting $\prec \in \{<, \leq\}$, the infeasibility condition becomes $(x_1 - x_2 \prec_1 c_1) \wedge (x_2 - x_3 \prec_2 c_2) \wedge \ldots \wedge (x_n - x_1 \prec_n c_n)$ is false just in case $\Sigma_{i=1}^n c_i < 0$ or $\Sigma_{i=1}^n c_i = 0$ and at least one $\prec_i$ is strict.

With such mixed constraints, it is convenient to speak of *bounds*, or pairs $(\prec, c)$, representing either the interval $(-\infty, c)$ or the interval $(-\infty, c]$. We refer to the set of bounds as $B$. Additionally, we define an order $<_B$ on bounds with $(\prec, c) <_B (\prec', c')$ whenever $c < c'$ or when $c = c'$, $\prec$ is $<$ and $\prec'$ is $\leq$. Finally, we define addition for bounds with $(\prec, c) + (\prec', c') = (\prec'', c + c')$ with $\prec''$ strict just in case either $\prec$ or $\prec'$ are strict.

A natural data structure for describing sets of difference constraints is a *bound weighted graph* in which the vertices are variables and edges represent constraints between variables:

**Definition 3 (Constraint Graph).** *The constraint graph of a set (or conjunction) of difference constraints $\Gamma$ is a graph $G = (V, E, \xi)$ with one vertex per numeric variable occurring in some difference constraint in $\Gamma$, edges $E = \{(x, y) : (x - y \prec c) \in \Gamma \text{ for some } (\prec, c) \in B\}$, and a function $\xi : E \to B$ defined by $(x, y) \mapsto \min\{(\prec, c) : (x - y \prec c) \in \Gamma\}$.*

A well known data structure for storing a constraint graph is a Difference Bound Matrix (DBM), in which a $|V| \times |V|$ matrix stores the implied relationship between each pair of variables, and each cell $x, y$ without an associated edge in the constraint graph is initialized to $(<, \infty)$.

## 4.2 Finding Shortest Paths and Negative Cycles

Under any constraint graph representation, a feasibility check reduces to the detection of a negative cycle, or any cycle where the edge bounds sum to a value less than $(\leq, 0)$. Normally negative cycles are detected as a side effect of a shortest path algorithm. Timed automata verification tools apply the Floyd-Warshall all pairs shortest path algorithm to normalize the set of constraints and the detection of negative cycles (which imply that the DBM is normalized to the empty set) is obtained as a side effect of the algorithm. Unlike the case of reachability computation for timed automata, where the DBMs are rather small, in DL solving, one can easily obtain sets with hundreds of numeric variables and a more efficient algorithm is needed. We will use a single source shortest path algorithm to do the feasibility checks.

Shortest path algorithms, either single-source or all-pairs, function by iteratively approximating the minimum distance between vertices, where a distance from $x$ to $y$ is taken to be the sum of the edge bounds on a path from $x$ to $y$. In the context of a single source shortest path algorithm, the distance estimates are represented by a function $\delta : V \to B$ indicating a bound on the distance from a distinguished source vertex. Distance functions $(\delta_0, \delta_1, \ldots)$ are successively approximated by taking any edge $(s, t)$ such that $\delta_i(s) + \xi(s, t) < \delta_i(t)$ and letting $\delta_{i+1}(t) = \min_s(\delta_i(s) + \xi(s, t))$. Following [GR93] we can use such a sequence of functions to filter out all the positive cycles whose edge bounds sum to a value greater than $(\leq, 0)$:

**Definition 4.** Given a distance function $\delta : V \to B$, an edge $(s, t)$ such that $\delta(s) + \xi(s, t) \leq \delta(t)$ is called *admissible*. The *admissible subgraph* of a constraint graph $G$, written $G_a$, is the subgraph of $G$ containing all of its admissible edges.

**Proposition 1.** Given a constraint graph $G$ and a series of distance estimating functions $(\delta_0, \delta_1, \ldots)$, $G$ has a negative or zero weight cycle if and only if $G_a$ has a cycle under some distance estimate $\delta_k$.

*Proof.* It is well known that the distance estimation will converge to a fixed point if and only if the graph has no negative cycle [CLRS01]. If it does not converge, then there is a stage $k$ for which all $\delta_k(v) = \delta_{k+1}(v)$ for all $v \in V$ except some $V'$, some of which are in negative cycles. Let $x_0 \rightarrow x_1 \ldots x_n \rightarrow x_0$ be such a cycle. Then $\delta(x_i) + \xi(x_i, x_{i+1}) < \delta(x_{i+1})$ for some[2] $i$ and $\exists v' \in V' . v' \in \{x_0, \ldots, x_n\}$. For sufficiently large $k$, the remaining edges in the cycle must be admissible, for otherwise the process would converge. Hence $G_a$ will contain the cycle.

Suppose the process converges at $\delta_k$ and $G$ contains a cycle $x_0 \rightarrow x_1 \ldots x_n \rightarrow x_0$ whose edge bounds sum to $(\leq, 0)$. Since the process converges, $\delta(x_i) + \xi(x_i, x_{i+1}) \geq \delta(x_{i+1})$. But if $\delta(x_i) + \xi(x_i, x_{i+1}) > \delta(x_{i+1})$ then there must be some $j \neq i$ such that $\delta(x_j) + \xi(x_j, x_{j+1}) < \delta(x_{j+1})$ since the edge bounds sum to $(\leq, 0)$. However, this implies the process has not converged and we have arrived at a contradiction. We can then conclude that each edge in the cycle must satisfy $\delta(x_i) + \xi(x_i, x_{i+1}) \leq \delta(x_{i+1})$ and so the cycle is in $G_a$.

In the other direction, if there is a cycle in $G_a$ then each edge in the cycle must satisfy $\delta(s) + \xi(s, t) \leq \delta(t)$. Hence $\Sigma_i \delta(x_i) + \xi(x_i, x_{i+1}) \leq \Sigma_i \delta(x_i)$, and so $\Sigma_i \xi(x_i, x_{i+1}) \leq (\leq, 0)$. ◼

The problem of detecting negative cycles can be reduced to checking for cycles in $G_a$ which contain an edge with a strict bound (in the form $(<, c)$) or an edge $(s, t)$ such that $\delta(s) + \xi(s, t) < \delta(t)$. This in turn can be accomplished via a depth first search which keeps track of the location of such edges.

This algorithm provides a significant advantage over that of Floyd-Warshall used in [NMA+02]. On a graph with $n$ nodes and $m$ edges, Floyd-Warshall takes $n^3$ time for a full canonicalization and $n^2$ time for a single incremental update on *every* execution. Bellman Ford's runtime is bounded by $nm$, and in this setting typically runs in $m$ time. Additionally, all the formulae associated with problems known to us have $m \ll 10n$. If we assume the graph is sparse with $m = 10n$, then our typical run requires less than $10n$ steps, our worst case run time is $10n^2$, a significant improvement over $n^3$ full canonicalization or even the $n^2$ incremental canonicalization on each run.

## 5    Implementation

The solver, including parsing and CNF translation, is implemented in 3500 lines of C++. Here we discuss some of the features of the solver.

### 5.1    Numeric Conflict Analysis

To explain numeric conflict analysis let us emphasize that such conflicts may appear in a richer set of circumstances than ordinary Boolean conflicts which always appear during simplification of the formula. Numerical conflicts can, in addition, appear when guessing or flipping a truth value for a numeric constraint. Our observations indicated that numeric conflicts arising outside of the simplification process occurred with less

---

[2] We take $i + 1$ modulo $n$.

frequency on the harder satisfiable problems, presumably because the number of clauses was sufficient to induce more simplification.

When the solver arrives at an inconsistent set of difference constraints, two types of analysis and learning are performed. First, a small such inconsistent set of constraints is identified and its negation is encoded as a clause. Second, if the numeric conflict appears as a result of simplification, the implication graph of the literals in the conflict clause is analyzed in order to find a reason for the inconsistency.

However the actual frequency with which the implication graphs of numericly induced conflict clauses were analyzed varied widely from never (for example in the scheduling problem FT06 described in 6.1) to roughly half (for example in the circuit problems described in 6.3). Nonetheless this process allows the solver to learn reasons for numeric conflicts which include settings of strictly Boolean variables (and vice versa). The analysis mechanism itself is a straightforward implementation of Chaff style [MMZ+01] first unique implication point (1UIP) cut of the implication graph. As with Boolean SAT solving, experiments with other mechanisms such as a decision-only cut or performing analysis on all conflicts did not perform as well as the 1UIP scheme.

The introduction of such learning into the DPLL algorithm requires a minor but essential change to the conflict resolution mechanism as it occurs in the Boolean case. This can be explained as follows. The backtracking mechanism is responsible for finding a point in the search tree to jump back to. Once this point in found, the assignment for the variable $v$ associated with this node in the search tree is flipped and the alternative subtree is explored. In the presence of numerical constraints, this assignment can of course introduce a numeric conflict. In the Boolean case, this assignment will not by itself introduce an empty clause, for otherwise $\neg v$ would have been deduced by unit resolution at a previous decision level, or higher in the search tree. Thus the conflict resolution process in the numeric case needs to be sensitive to conflicts which arise *as a result of resolving conflicts*. This suggests that conflict resolution can be made recursive for this case. However, our solver simply adds a clause representing the negation of such a numeric conflict to the clause database and continues backtracking, without analyzing the implication graph associated with the numeric conflict. As this case was rare in practice, this seems like a reasonable course of action.

## 5.2 Reducing Feasibility Checks

In an incremental setting, feasibility checks occur with high frequency. In problems dominated by numeric constraints this becomes a bottleneck. We employ two optimizations for reducing the number of required feasibility checks. First, we do not trigger feasibility checks when branching on difference constraints which do not solve any clauses. Thus at the end of the solving process, if the problem is satisfiable we will have checked that the difference constraints in a prime implicant of the problem are feasible. Second, we observe that a feasible set of difference constraints cannot be made infeasible by adding a single constraint which mentions an otherwise unconstrained numeric variable. Our observations showed that these optimizations reduced the number of feasibility checks by one third on hard problems dominated by numeric constraints.

## 6   Experimental Results

In this section we report the performance results of DLSAT on several classes of benchmark problems.

### 6.1   Job Shop Scheduling

The problem of finding optimal schedules for the job shop problem [JM99] is a hard combinatorial optimization problem whose constraints express very naturally in DL. The optimization is converted into a decision (satisfiability) problem of the form "is there a schedule whose length is smaller than $d$?" As observed in [NMA$^+$02], when $d$ is much larger or much smaller than the length of the optimal schedule for the problem, the solver finds the negative (resp. positive) answer quickly, but as we approach the optimum things become harder.

**Table 1.** Comparison of DLSAT with ICS and MX-SOLVER on the FT06 problem whose optimal schedule is of length 55.

| $d$ Solver | 50 | 51 | 52 | 53 | 54 | 55 | 56 | 57 | 58 | 59 | 60 |
|---|---|---|---|---|---|---|---|---|---|---|---|
| ICS | 1.88 | 2.95 | 3.41 | 21.90 | 38.00 | 174.00 | 85.00 | 68.00 | 95.00 | 69.00 | 0.11 |
| MX-SOLVER | 0.14 | 0.14 | 0.14 | 1.79 | 7.67 | 21.47 | 1.31 | 0.20 | 0.92 | 1.88 | 0.21 |
| DLSAT | 0.09 | 0.10 | 0.12 | 0.24 | 0.29 | 0.69 | 0.86 | 0.50 | 0.69 | 0.36 | 0.37 |

**Table 2.** Comparison of DLSAT with MX-SOLVER on the hard ABZ5 problem whose optimal schedule is of length 1234. Time is given in seconds and t/o means more than 5 minutes.

| $d$ Solver | 950 | 975 | 980 | 990 | 1000 | 1100 | 1234 | 1300 | 1390 | 1395 | 1400 | 1600 | 1800 | 3000 |
|---|---|---|---|---|---|---|---|---|---|---|---|---|---|---|
| MX-SOLVER | 4.6 | 4.7 | 4.9 | 1709.0 | t/o | t/o | t/o | t/o | t/o | 17.2 | 17.2 | 10.4 | 10.8 | 11.7 |
| DLSAT | 0.5 | 0.5 | 0.6 | 0.9 | 0.8 | 30.2 | t/o | 62.0 | 47.3 | 6.1 | 12.1 | 0.6 | 0.5 | 0.6 |

Table 1 compares the performance results of DLSAT with those of MX-SOLVER [NMA$^+$02] and ICS [FORS01] on the FT06 job shop problem with 6 machines and 6 jobs. The optimal schedule is of length 55 and DLSAT finds it within 0.69 seconds compared to 21.47 with MX-SOLVER and almost 3 minutes with ICS. This problem consists of 132 clauses, 222 difference constraints and 37 numeric variables. It is not surprising that ICS does not perform as well as MX-SOLVER or DLSAT because ICS uses a method for combining decision procedures and can hence solve more complex problems. Nevertheless we keep it as a point of reference for more general techniques. Table 2 compares DLSAT and MX-SOLVER on the hard ABZ5 problem [ABZ88] with 10 machines and 10 jobs whose optimum is 1234. Bounding execution time to 5 minutes for each query, MX-Solver can deduce that the optimum is somewhere in the interval (990, 1395] while DLSAT can conclude that it is in (1100, 1300]. Yet none of them can find the exact optimum. The problem is made up of 560 clauses over 1010 difference constraints and 101 numeric variables.

Note that we restrict the comparison to MX-SOLVER because on this type of problems, dominated by numerical constraints, it already had a much better performance than solvers that use the lazy or preprocessing approaches.

## 6.2  Diamond Problems

The diamond problems were introduced by Strichman as benchmarks for the preprocessing approach. These are sets of difference constraints whose graphical representation is a series of diamond-like shapes with an additional back-edge from the last node to the first (see Figure 1). These graphs are parametrized by the length $d$ of each side of the diamond and the number $n$ of diamonds. The corresponding DL formula is generated to require the existence of a cycle in the diamond. Such graphs have $2nd + 1$ edges and $2^n$ cycles, hence they pose a challenge to numerical feasibility checks.

The problems are partitioned into three classes, unsatisfiable, satisfiable and tightly satisfiable, i.e. with only one satisfying assignment. As Table 3 shows, DLSAT is much superior to the preprocessing approach of [SSB02] on satisfiable instances, but much inferior on unsatisfiable ones. On the satisfiable problems, DLSAT only considers combinations of difference constraints necessary to get a satisfiable answer, and hence is able to reduce the required processing of the constraints to a level far below that of the preprocessing approach. On the other hand, the approach of [SSB02] acts relatively independently of the satisfiability of the problem, since it spends by far most of its time coding the DL formula into an equivalent Boolean one, rather than solving the resulting Boolean formula. Hence its performance remains relatively constant accross the satisfiable and unsatisfiable diamond problems. Also, as this coding process examines all the possible constraints in a single step rather than piecewise (as in DLSAT), it is able to globally analyze the structure of the set of all constraints and compress the representation of the resulting Boolean formula by chordalizing the graph which represents all the possible constraints. The advantage of this global analysis is more prominent in the unsatisfiable problems because there is no satisfying subset to which DLSAT can restrict its attention.

## 6.3  Circuit Timing Analysis

The last set of benchmarks is concerned with bounded model checking of timed automata that model digital circuits using the bi-bounded delay model [BS94,MP95]. We use models of $n$-bit adders constructed from gates where changes are propagated from inputs to outputs within $t \in [l, u]$ time and would like to find the maximal stabilization time of the circuit. We assume that the circuit starts from a stable state and the inputs

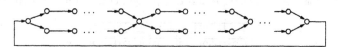

**Fig. 1.** A constraints graph having the form of diamond concatenation.

**Table 3.** A comparison of the performance DLSAT with the approach of [SSB02] (column SEP) on benchmark diamond problems with $d = 5$ (t/o means more than 4 minutes).

| $n$ | sat | | one-sat | | unsat | |
|---|---|---|---|---|---|---|
| | DLSAT | SEP | DLSAT | SEP | DLSAT | SEP |
| 5 | 0.01 | 0.17 | 0.01 | 0.17 | 15.10 | 0.17 |
| 10 | 0.03 | 0.16 | 0.01 | 0.17 | t/o | 0.17 |
| 20 | 0.03 | 0.51 | 0.03 | 0.50 | t/o | 0.50 |
| 20 | 0.03 | 0.51 | 0.03 | 0.50 | t/o | 0.50 |
| 30 | 0.04 | 1.21 | 0.06 | 1.23 | t/o | 1.25 |
| 40 | 0.06 | 2.60 | 0.10 | 2.60 | t/o | 2.60 |
| 50 | 0.20 | 5.21 | 0.14 | 5.10 | t/o | 5.30 |
| 100 | 0.20 | 45.30 | 0.50 | 44.20 | t/o | 47.60 |
| 200 | 0.70 | t/o | 2.40 | t/o | t/o | t/o |
| 500 | 4.90 | t/o | 21.90 | t/o | t/o | t/o |

change at time zero and then remain constant, consequently there is a finite number of transitions in the circuit. We submit to the solver queries, parametrized by $d$ and $k$, of the form "is there a run of the automaton with $k$ transitions which remains in an unstable state after $d$ time?". The parameter $k$ defines the number of unfolding of the transition relation of the automaton and hence the size of the DL formula. An upper-bound on $d$ can be computed by methods of static timing analysis (summing the delays along the longest path in the circuit), and also each $k$ gives an upper bound on the metric length of runs with $k$ steps. The reader may look at [BBM04] for more details on the problem definition and at [NMA+02] for the formulation of bounded reachability of timed automata in DL. Readers familiar with SAT based methods for circuit verification should bear in mind that we are dealing here with a much richer model of the circuits, with one clock variable per gate.

Table 4 shows the execution time for different queries for a 3-bit adder with 10 gates while Table 5 shows similar results for a 4-bit adder with 16 gates. The results constitute and enormous progress for DL SAT solving (MX-SOLVER could not treat any of these problems) but still they are very far from coping with the size of real problems. The DL formula corresponding to 12 unfoldings of the 4-bit adder (before conversion

**Table 4.** The time (in seconds) to answer $(k, d)$ queries for a 3-bit adder (10 gates).

| | k=4 | k=5 | k=6 | k=7 | k=8 | k=9 | k=10 |
|---|---|---|---|---|---|---|---|
| d=10 | 2.10 | 4.02 | 8.85 | 19.38 | 45.09 | 51.18 | 186.01 |
| d=15 | 2.43 | 4.03 | 8.86 | 15.86 | 39.81 | 116.00 | 376.10 |

**Table 5.** The time (in minutes) to answer $(k, d)$ queries for a 4-bit adder (16 gates).

| | k=8 | k=9 | k=10 | k=11 | k=12 |
|---|---|---|---|---|---|
| d=25 | 1:29 | 3:42 | 9:23 | 28:33 | 18:52 |
| d=35 | 1:24 | 3:38 | 9:22 | 28:04 | 17:58 |

to CNF) has 624 Boolean variables, 222 numeric variables, and 1381 difference constraints. After conversion to CNF the number of Boolean variables increases to 19463, and the formula has 31516 clauses.

## 7   Conclusions

This work represents a step forward in DL SAT solving and hence a step in the same direction for exporting bounded model checking for timed systems. For most of the problem classes we considered, our new solver performs much better than other solvers, and we attribute this to the efficient numerical feasibility checks and their integration with learning. Another direction that we explored but not report on the current version is that of *aggressive learning* where the idea is to use the result of numerical feasibility checks to encode (in a compact manner) *all* the negative cycles in the constraint graph and learn their negation. For this purpose we have derived a compact CNF formula to represent the set of all sub-graphs which have no negative cycles. Unfortunately, this formula requires auxiliary variables which could not be shared across feasibility checks. Consequently it had a negative effect on the performance. Some more experimentation and fine tuning are needed in order to assess this technique.

Another future direction of attack is a more efficient encoding of bounded reachability properties for timed automata and circuits. The size of the DL formulae after conversion to CNF is very big, even for small problem and this may be improved by more sophisticated encoding scheme (e.g. the asynchronous time approach mentioned in [NMA$^+$02]) or by extending the solver to work with non CNF formulae.

## Acknowledgments

Our understanding of SAT benefited from discussions with K. Sakallah and O. Strichman. We thank Moez Mahfoudh for his thesis through which we all took our first lessons in the domain.

## References

[ABZ88]     J. Adams, E. Balas and D. Zawack, The Shifting Bottleneck Procedure for Job Shop Scheduling, *Management Science* 34, 391-401, 1988.

[ACG99]     A. Armando, C. Castellini and E. Giunchiglia, SAT-based Procedures for Temporal Reasoning, *Proc. ECP'99*, LNCS, Springer, 1999.

[ABK$^+$97]  E. Asarin, M. Bozga, A. Kerbrat, O. Maler, A. Pnueli, and A. Rasse, Data Structures for the Verification of Timed Automata, *Proc. Hybrid and Real-Time Systems*, 346-360, LNCS 1201, Springer, 1997.

[ABC$^+$02]  G. Audemard, P. Bertoli, A. Cimatti, A. Kornilowics and R. Sebastiani, A SAT-Based Approach for Solving Formulas over Boolean and Linear Mathematical Propositions, in *Proc. CADE'02*, 193-208, LNCS 2392, Springer, 2002.

[ACKS02]    G. Audemard, A. Cimatti, A. Kornilowics and R. Sebastiani, Bounded Model Checking for Timed Systems, Technical report ITC-0201-05, IRST, Trento, 2002.

[BDS$^+$02]  C. W. Barrett, D. L. Dill, A. Stump, Checking Satisfiability of First-Order Formulas by Incremental Translation to SAT, in *Proc CAV'02*, 236-249.

[BBM04]     R. Ben Salah, M. Bozga and O. Maler, On Timing Analysis of Combinational Circuits, *Proc. FORMATS'03*, 2004.

[BS94]      J.A. Brzozowski and C-J.H. Seger, *Asynchronous Circuits*, Springer, 1994.
[CLRS01]    T. Cormen, C. Leiserson, R. Rivest, and C. Stein. *Introduction to Algorithms*. MIT Press, McGraw-Hill, 2001.
[F02]       Martin Fränzle, Take It NP-Easy: Bounded Model Construction for Duration Calculus *Proc. FTRTFT'02*, of 226-243, LNCS 2469, Springer-Verlag, 2002.
[FORS01]    J-C. Filliâtre, S. Owre, H. Rueß and N. Shankar, ICS: Integrated Canonizer and Solver, *Proc. CAV'01*, 246-250, 2001.
[GN02]      E. Goldberg and Y. Novikov: BerkMin, a Fast and Robust SAT-solver, *Proc. DATE '02*, 142-149, 2002.
[GR93]      A. V. Goldberg and T. Radzik,  A Heuristic Improvement of the Bellman-Ford Algorithm, In *Applied Mathematics Letters* 6, 1993.
[H00]       J. Hooker, *Logic-Based Methods for Optimization: Combining Optimization and Constraint Satisfaction*, Wiley, 2000
[JM94]      J. Jaffar and M. J. Maher. Constraint Logic Programming: A Survey,  *Journal of Logic Programming*, 19/20, 503-581, 1994.
[JM99]      A.S. Jain and S. Meeran, Deterministic Job-Shop Scheduling: Past, Present and Future, *European Journal of Operational Research* 113, 390-434, 1999.
[M03]       M. Mahfoudh, *On Satisfaiblity Checking for Difference Logic*, PhD Thesis, Univeristé Joseph Fourier, Grenoble, 2003.
[MNAM02]    M. Mahfoudh, P. Niebert, E. Asarin and O. Maler, A Satisfiability Checker for Difference Logic, *Proc. SAT'2002*, 2002.
[MP95]      O. Maler and A. Pnueli, Timing Analysis of Asynchronous Circuits using Timed Automata, *Proc. CHARME'95*, 189-205, LNCS 987, Springer, 1995.
[MS99]      J.P. Marques-Silva and K.A. Sakallah, GRASP: A Search Algorithm for Propositional Satisfiability, *IEEE Transactions on Computers* 48, 506-21, 1999.
[MMZ$^+$01] M. Moskewicz, C. Madigan, Y. Zhao, L. Zhang and S. Malik, Chaff: Engineering an Efficient SAT Solver, *Proc. DAC 2001*, 2001.
[MRS02]     L. de Moura, H. Rueß and M. Sorea, Lazy Theorem Proving for Bounded Model Checking over Infinite Domains, *Proc. CADE'02*, 437-453, LNCS 2392, Springer, 2002.
[NMA$^+$02] P. Niebert, M. Mahfoudh, E. Asarin, M. Bozga, N. Jain and O. Maler, Verification of Timed Automata via Satisfiability Checking, *Proc. FTRTFT'02*, 225-244, LNCS 2469, Springer, 2002.
[S02]       M. Sorea, Bounded Model Checking for Timed Automata, *Proc. MTCS'02*, 2002.
[SSB02]     O. Strichman, S.A. Seshia, and R.E. Bryant, Deciding Separation Formulas with SAT, in *Proc. CAV'2002*, Springer, 2002.
[Tar72]     R. Tarjan. Depth-first Search and Linear Graph Algorithms. *SIAM J. Comput.* 1, 146-160, 1972.
[T70]       G. Tseitin, On the Complexity of Derivation in Propositional Calculus, in *Studies in Constructive Mathematics and Mathematical Logic* 2, 115-125, Consultants Bureau, New York, 1970.
[W90]       J.M. Wilson, Compact normal forms in propositional logic and integer programming formulations, *Computers and Operation Research*, 309-314, 1990.
[WZP03]     B. Wozna, A. Zbrzezny and W. Penczek, Checking Reachability Properties for Timed Automata via SAT, *Fundamenta Informaticae* 55, 223-241, 2003.
[Zha95]     G. Zhang. The Davis-Putnam Resolution Procedure, In *Advances in Logic Programming and Automated Reasoning*, volume 2. Ablex Publishing Corporation, 1995.
[ZH96]      H. Zhang and M. Stickel: An Efficient Algorithm for Unit Propogation, In Proceedings of the Fourth International Symposium on Artificial Intelligence and Mathematics. 1996.

# Model-Checking for Weighted Timed Automata[*]

Thomas Brihaye[1], Véronique Bruyère[1], and Jean-François Raskin[2]

[1] Institut d'Informatique, Université de Mons-Hainaut
Avenue du Champ de Mars 6, B-7000 Mons, Belgium
[2] Département d'Informatique, Université Libre de Bruxelles
Boulevard du Triomphe CP 212, B-1050 Bruxelles, Belgium

**Abstract.** We study the model-checking problem for weighted timed automata and the weighted CTL logic by the bisimulation approach. Weighted timed automata are timed automata extended with costs on both edges and locations. When the costs act as stopwatches, we get stopwatch automata with the restriction that the stopwatches cannot be reset nor tested. The weighted CTL logic is an extension of TCTL that allow to reset and test the cost variables. Our main results are *(i)* the undecidability of the proposed model-checking problem for discrete and dense time, *(ii)* its PSPACE-COMPLETENESS in the discrete case for a slight restriction of the logic, *(iii)* the precise frontier between finite and infinite bisimulations in the dense case for the subclass of stopwatch automata.

## 1  Introduction

During the last decade, hybrid automata have been widely studied and especially the reachability problem for hybrid automata. In this article, we study a model-checking problem for a particular class of hybrid automata. Our motivation is the important open problem of model-checking timed automata extended with stopwatches used as observers [1].

We consider the model of *weighted timed automata*, which is an extension of timed automata with *tuples of costs* on both edges and locations. This model has been independently introduced in [6] and [7] (with single costs instead of tuples of costs).

The properties of weighted timed automata that we want to check are formalized by formulas of the *weighted CTL logic*, WCTL for short. This logic is close to the DTL logic of [8] and the ICTL logic of [2].

Our approach is a systematic study of the tool *bisimulation* as done in the works [10] and [11]. Indeed when the transition system of an hybrid automaton has a finite bisimulation that can be constructed effectively, the reachability problem and the model-checking problem are decidable. For instance this technique has been successfully applied to timed automata thanks to the region graph. However the converse does not hold in general.

[*] Supported by the FRFC project "Centre Fédéré en Vérification" funded by the Belgian National Science Foundation (FNRS) under grant nr 2.4530.02.

Y. Lakhnech and S. Yovine (Eds.): FORMATS/FTRTFT 2004, LNCS 3253, pp. 277–292, 2004.
© Springer-Verlag Berlin Heidelberg 2004

*Related Works.* There are few results on the model-checking of hybrid automata. Indeed the wide study of the particular case of the reachability problem has identified a frontier between decidability and undecidability. Among the numerous results about this problem, let us mention the following ones. The important class of *initialized rectangular automata* has a decidable reachability problem; however several slight generalizations of these automata lead to an undecidable reachability problem, in particular for timed automata augmented with one stopwatch [14]. The reachability problem is already undecidable for the simple class of *constant slope hybrid systems* which are timed automata augmented with integrators; the reachability problem becomes decidable when the integrators are used as *observers* (they are neither reset nor tested) [15]. The latter case has also been studied in [1]. Of course the well-known class of timed automata has a decidable reachability problem [5]. Recently the *minimum-cost* reachability problem has been introduced, that is, determine the minimum cost of runs of a weighted timed automaton from an initial location to a target location. This problem has been proved decidable independently in [6] and [7].

Concerning the model-checking problem of hybrid systems, let us mention two references. In [2], a model-checking procedure and its implementation in the HYTECH tool are proposed for linear hybrid automata and the ICTL logic. This procedure is not guaranteed to terminate. In [8], the model-checking problem is proved to be decidable for some fragments of the DTL logic and a restrictive class of weighted timed automata.

*Our Contribution.* In this paper, we investigate the WCTL model-checking problem for weighted timed automata. The weighted timed automata can be seen as constant slope hybrid systems where the integrators are used as observers and the edges have been enriched with costs. We have chosen this class of hybrid automata since they have a decidable reachability problem, even in the case of minimum cost. We also focus on the subclass of *automata with stopwatch observers*, which are weighted timed automata such that every integrator is a stopwatch. The WCTL logic is similar to the ICTL logic. Formulas allow the two actions forbidden in the weighted timed automata : to reset integrators and to test them. This logic is a natural extension of the TCTL logic to formulate properties about integrators instead of the total elapsed time.

Our first result is the *undecidability* of the model-checking problem. This proves that there are situations where the model-checking procedure of [2] will never terminate, even for classes of hybrid automata with a decidable reachability problem. What is surprising is that the undecidability holds even for the *discrete* time, a case where positive results usually happen. The proof is based on the halting problem for 2-counter machines, with its reduction distributed to *both* a weighted timed automaton and a WCTL formula. To the best of our knowledge, this approach is new[1]. This proof works for automata with stopwatch observers equipped with 1 clock and 3 integrators and for WCTL formulas where two integrators are compared.

---

[1] with the exception of reference [9] where we have followed the same approach.

In the sequel of the paper, we limit our study to the $WCTL_r$ logic, that is, WCTL where integrators can only be compared with *constants*. One way to prove that the model-checking problem is decidable is the effective construction of a finite bisimulation for weighted timed automata. This is the approach already proposed in [10] and [11]. The effectiveness is always guaranteed as our automata are particular linear hybrid automata. It should be noted that the existence of a finite bisimulation is sufficient but not necessary for decidability of the model-checking problem.

For *discrete* time, when working with the $WCTL_r$ logic, we show that the bisimulations are always finite. It follows that the $WCTL_r$ model checking problem for weighted timed automata is PSPACE-COMPLETE.

However for *dense* time, the panorama completely changes. In this case, we identify the *precise frontier* between finite and infinite bisimulations for automata with *stopwatch observers*. Our results are the following. There exist automata with stopwatch observers that have no finite bisimulations already with 2 clocks and 1 integrator, or with 1 clock and 2 integrators. This is no longer true with 1 clock and 1 integrator. It was a difficult task to find automata with stopwatch observers with a small number of clocks and integrators for which no finite bisimulation exists; our proofs are involved. The reason is that stopwatches cannot be reset nor tested in these automata.

## 2   Weighted Timed Automata

In this section, we introduce the notion of weighted timed automaton, which is an extension of timed automata with costs on both locations and edges. We begin with the usual notations on timed automata.

*Notations.* Let $X = \{x_1, \ldots, x_n\}$ be a set of $n$ clocks. The same notation $x = (x_1, \ldots, x_n)$ is used for the clock *variables* and for an *assignment* of values to these variables. Depending on whether the time is *dense* or *discrete*, the values are taken in domain $\mathbb{T}$ equal to the set $\mathbb{R}^+$ of nonnegative reals or to the set $\mathbb{N}$ of natural numbers. Given a clock assignment $x$ and $\tau \in \mathbb{T}$, $x + \tau$ is the clock assignment $(x_1 + \tau, \ldots, x_n + \tau)$. The set $\mathcal{G}$ denotes the set of *guards* which are finite conjunctions of atomic guards of the form $x_i \sim c$ where $x_i$ is a clock, $c \in \mathbb{N}$ is an integer constant, and $\sim$ is one of the symbols $\{<, \leq, =, >, \geq\}$. Notation $x \models g$ means that the clock assignment $x$ satisfies the guard $g$. A *reset* $r \in 2^X$ indicates which clocks are reset to 0, that is, $x' = [x_i := 0]_{x_i \in r} x$. We use notation $\Sigma$ for the set of *atomic propositions*.

**Definition 1.** *A* weighted timed automaton $\mathcal{A} = (L, E, \mathcal{I}, \mathcal{L}, \mathcal{C})$ *has the following components: (i) $L$ is a finite set of* locations, *(ii) $E \subseteq L \times \mathcal{G} \times \mathcal{P}(X) \times L$ is a finite set of* edges, *(iii) $\mathcal{I} : L \to \mathcal{G}$ assigns an* invariant *to each location, (iv) $\mathcal{L} : L \to 2^\Sigma$ is the* labeling function *and (v) $\mathcal{C} : L \cup E \to \mathbb{N}^m$ assigns a $m$-uple of costs to both locations and edges.*

*An* automaton with stopwatch observers *is a* weighted timed automaton *such that for every location $l$, $\mathcal{C}(l) \in \{0, 1\}^m$ (instead of $\mathbb{N}^m$).*

The concept of weighted timed automata has been independently introduced in [6] and [7] (with single costs instead of $m$-uples of costs). In the previous definition, we say that $\mathcal{C}(l)$ (resp. $\mathcal{C}(e)$) is the cost of location $l$ (resp. edge $e$). We will sometimes use the notation $\dot{z}_1 = d_1, \ldots, \dot{z}_m = d_m$ at location $l$ instead of $\mathcal{C}(l) = (d_1, \ldots, d_m)$; the variables $z = (z_1, \ldots, z_m)$ are called *cost variables*[2]. Note that the variables $z_1, \ldots, z_m$ cannot be reset nor tested in weighted timed automata, they are just *observers*. When an edge $e$ or a location $l$ has null costs, that is, $\mathcal{C}(e) = (0, \ldots, 0)$ or $\mathcal{C}(l) = (0, \ldots, 0)$, we say that it has *no cost*. When an edge has no cost, nor reset and a guard that is always true, it is called an *empty* edge.

**Definition 2.** *The semantics of a weighted timed automaton $\mathcal{A}$ is defined as a transition system $T_{\mathcal{A}} = (Q, \rightarrow)$ with a set of states $Q$ equal to $\{(l, x, z) \mid l \in L, x \in \mathbb{T}^n, x \models \mathcal{I}(l), z \in \mathbb{T}^m\}$ and a transition relation $\rightarrow = \bigcup_{\tau \in \mathbb{T}} \xrightarrow{\tau}$ defined as follows*

$$(l, x, z) \xrightarrow{\tau} (l', x', z')$$

- *case $\tau > 0$ (elapse of time at location $l$) : $l = l'$, $x' = x + \tau$ and $z' = z + \mathcal{C}(l) \cdot \tau$,*
- *case $\tau = 0$ (instantaneous switch) : $(l, g, r, l') \in E$, $x \models g$, $x' = [x_i := 0]_{x_i \in r} x$ and $z' = z + \mathcal{C}(e)$.*

In the previous definition, note that the value of $\tau$ (strictly positive, or null) indicates an elapse of time or an instantaneous switch. The $m$-tuple $z$ of a state $(l, x, z)$ indicates global *costs* that accumulate the individual costs described by the function $\mathcal{C}$ : either the cost rate of staying in a location (per time unit), or the cost of an edge. A transition $(l, x, z) \xrightarrow{\tau} (l', x', z')$ is shortly denoted by $q \rightarrow q'$ (given $q$ and $q'$, it is easy to compute the unique $\tau$ such that $q \xrightarrow{\tau} q'$). When $\tau > 0$, we also shortly denote by $q + \tau$ the state $q'$ of the transition $q \xrightarrow{\tau} q'$.

**Definition 3.** *Given a transition system $T_{\mathcal{A}}$, a run $\rho = (q_i)_{i \geq 0}$ is an infinite path in $T_{\mathcal{A}}$*

$$\rho = q_0 \xrightarrow{\tau_0} q_1 \xrightarrow{\tau_1} q_2 \cdots q_i \xrightarrow{\tau_i} q_{i+1} \cdots$$

*such that $\Sigma_{i \geq 0} \tau_i = \infty$ (divergence of time). A finite run $\rho = (q_i)_{0 \leq i \leq j}$ is any finite path in $T_{\mathcal{A}}$. A position in $\rho$ is any state $q_i$ or $q_i + \tau$ with $0 < \tau < \tau_i$. The set of positions in $\rho$ can be totally ordered.*

We illustrate the definitions with the classical example of the gas burner system.

*Example 1.* The weighted timed automaton of Figure 1 represents a gas burner system with two locations $l$ and $l'$, one where the system is leaking and the other where it is not leaking. There is 1 clock variable $x$ to express that a continuous leaking period cannot exceed 1 time unit and two consecutive leaking periods are separated by at least 30 time units. There are 3 costs variables $z_1, z_2, z_3$ such that $z_1$ describes the total elapsed time, $z_2$ the accumulated leaking time and $z_3$ the number of leaks.

---

[2] This notation comes from automata with integrators, the variables $z_1, \ldots, z_m$ being the integrators, see for instance [15].

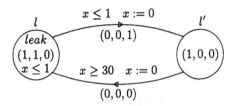

**Fig. 1.** The gas burner system.

# 3   Weighted CTL Logic and Model-Checking

In this section, we introduce the weighted CTL logic, WCTL logic for short (close to the ICTL logic of [2]). Two logics, discrete and dense, are proposed according to discrete or dense time.

*Notations.* As done previously for clocks, the same notation $z = (z_1, \ldots, z_m)$ is used for the cost variables and for an assignment of values to these variables. A *cost constraint* $\pi$ is of the form $z_i \sim c$ or $z_i - z_j \sim c$ where $z_i, z_j$ are cost variables and $c \in \mathbb{N}$ is an integer constant. Notation $z \models \pi$ means that the cost assignment $z$ satisfies the cost constraint $\pi$. Notation $\sigma$ means any atomic proposition $\sigma \in \Sigma$.

**Definition 4.** *The syntax of the discrete WCTL logic is given by the following grammar*

$$\varphi ::= \sigma \mid \pi \mid \neg\varphi \mid \varphi \vee \varphi \mid \exists \bigcirc \varphi \mid \varphi \exists U \varphi \mid \varphi \forall U \varphi \mid z_i \cdot \varphi$$

*Dense WCTL formulae are defined in the same way, except that operator $\exists\bigcirc$ is forbidden.*

The WCTL logic uses freeze quantifiers "$z_i \cdot$" on the cost variables $z_i$, $1 \leq i \leq m$. This logic allows to reset such variables and to test them. These actions are forbidden in weighted timed automata, where the cost variables are only observers. Note that the TCTL logic [4] is a particular case of WCTL when each cost variable $z_i$ describes the total elapsed time.

We restrict ourselves to *closed* WCTL formulas, i.e. formulas $\varphi$ such that every occurrence of a cost variable $z_i$ in $\varphi$ is bound by a freeze quantifier. We also impose that different freeze quantifiers bind different cost variables, i.e. two occurrences of the freeze quantifier $z_i \cdot$ are forbidden in the same formula. For convenience, we use the following abbreviations: $\exists\Diamond\varphi \equiv \top\exists U\varphi$, $\forall\Diamond\varphi \equiv \top\forall U\varphi$, $\exists\Box\varphi \equiv \neg\forall\Diamond\neg\varphi$, and $\forall\Box\varphi \equiv \neg\exists\Diamond\neg\varphi$.

We now give the semantics of WCTL.

**Definition 5.** *Suppose $\mathbb{T} = \mathbb{N}$. Let $\mathcal{A}$ be a weighted timed automaton and $q = (l, x, z)$ be a state of the transition system $T_{\mathcal{A}}$ of $\mathcal{A}$. Let $\varphi$ be a discrete WCTL formula. Then the satisfaction relation $q \models \varphi$ is defined inductively as indicated below. In case $\mathbb{T} = \mathbb{R}^+$ and $\varphi$ is a dense WCTL formula, the satisfaction relation is defined in the same way, except that $q \models \exists\bigcirc\varphi$ does not exist.*

- $q \models \sigma$ iff $\sigma \in \mathcal{L}(l)$;
- $q \models \pi$ iff $z \models \pi$;
- $q \models \neg\varphi$ iff $q \not\models \varphi$;
- $q \models \varphi \vee \psi$ iff $q \models \varphi$ or $q \models \psi$;
- $q \models \exists\bigcirc\varphi$ iff there exists a run $\rho = (q_i)_{i\geq0}$ in $T_{\mathcal{A}}$ with $q = q_0$ and $q_0 \xrightarrow{\tau} q_1$ satisfying $\tau = 0$ or $\tau = 1$, such that $q_1 \models \varphi$;
- $q \models \varphi \exists U \psi$ iff there exists a run $\rho = (q_i)_{i\geq0}$ in $T_{\mathcal{A}}$ with $q = q_0$, there exists a position $p$ in $\rho$ such that $p \models \psi$ and $p' \models \varphi$ for all $p' < p$;
- $q \models \varphi \forall U \psi$ iff for any run $\rho = (q_i)_{i\geq0}$ in $T_{\mathcal{A}}$ with $q = q_0$, there exists a position $p$ in $\rho$ such that $p \models \psi$ and $p' \models \varphi$ for all $p' < p$;
- $q \models z_i \cdot \varphi$ iff $(l, x, [z_i := 0]z) \models \varphi$.

Let us come back to the gas burner system of Example 1 and formalize some properties by WCTL formulas.

*Example 2.* Consider the first property "there exists a run with an average leaking time always bounded by 0.5" (in other words, $2z_2 \leq z_3$). Since the cost constraints $\pi$ allowed in WCTL are of the form $z_i \sim c$ or $z_i - z_j \sim c$, we replace the cost $\mathcal{C}(l) = (1, 1, 0)$ by $(1, 2, 0)$ in the automaton of Figure 1. The WCTL formula for the given property is therefore

$$z_2 \cdot z_3 \cdot (\exists\Box z_2 \leq z_3).$$

The next property we want to formalize is "in any time interval longer than 60 time units, the accumulated leaking time is at most 5% of the interval length" (that is, $z_1 \geq 60 \Rightarrow 20z_2 \leq z_1$). Again we have to modify the automaton by replacing $\mathcal{C}(l)$ by $(1, 20, 0)$. The related WCTL formula is

$$z_1 \cdot z_2 \cdot (\forall\Box(z_1 \geq 60 \Rightarrow z_2 \leq z_1)).$$

Finally, the property "there exists a run such that the accumulated leaking time is at most 5% of the time interval length and the average leaking time is bounded by 0.5, until the system never leaks" is formalized as

$$z_1 \cdot z_2 \cdot z_3 \cdot ((z_2 \leq z_1 \wedge z_2 \leq z_3)\, \exists U\, (\forall\Box\neg leak))$$

if $\mathcal{C}(l)$ is replaced by $(1, 20, 0)$ and $\mathcal{C}(l, x \leq 1, x := 0, l')$ by $(0, 0, 10)$.

The problem that we want to study in this article is the following *model-checking* problem, for discrete and dense time.

*Problem 1.* Given a weighted timed automaton $\mathcal{A}$ and a state $q$ of $T_{\mathcal{A}}$, given a WCTL formula $\varphi$, does $q \models \varphi$ hold ? ($\mathbb{T} = \mathbb{N}$ or $\mathbb{T} = \mathbb{R}^+$)

The next theorem states that this problem is undecidable, already for automata with stopwatch observers.

**Theorem 1.** *In both cases of discrete and dense time, the WCTL model-checking problem for automata with stopwatch observers is undecidable.*

**Corollary 1.** *Problem 1 is undecidable.*

*Proof.* (of Theorem 1) The proof is based on a reduction of the halting problem for a 2-counter machine. We recall that a machine with 2 counters $C_1$ and $C_2$ can be described by a linear labeled program allowing the following basic instructions:

- $k$ :  **goto** $k'$ ;
- $k$ :  **if** $C_i > 0$ **then goto** $k'$ **else goto** $k''$ ;
- $k$ :  $C_i := C_i + 1$ ;
- $k$ :  $C_i := C_i - 1$ (this operation is not defined if $C_i = 0$) ;
- $k$ :  **stop** .

The emulation of the 2-counter machine is done partly by an automaton with stopwatch observers $\mathcal{A}$ and partly by a WCTL formula $\varphi$. Suppose that the first label of the program is $k_0$ and the last instruction is a **stop** instruction labeled by $k_t$. The 2 counters are encoded by 3 cost variables as follows

$$C_1 = z_1 - z_2, \quad C_2 = z_1 - z_3.$$

The automaton $\mathcal{A} = (L, E, \mathcal{I}, \mathcal{L}, \mathcal{C})$ has 1 clock $x$ and no cost on its edges. The set $\Sigma$ of atomic propositions labeling $L$ contains an atomic proposition $\sigma_k$ for each label $k$ of the program and 4 additional atomic propositions $\rho_1$, $\rho'_1$, $\rho_2$ and $\rho'_2$. The set $L$ contains a location for each label $k$ of the program, which is labeled by $\sigma_k$; it contains additional locations.

The **goto** and **stop** instructions are easily encoded in $\mathcal{A}$. The instruction for incrementing counter $C_1$ is encoded by the subautomaton given in Figure 2. The

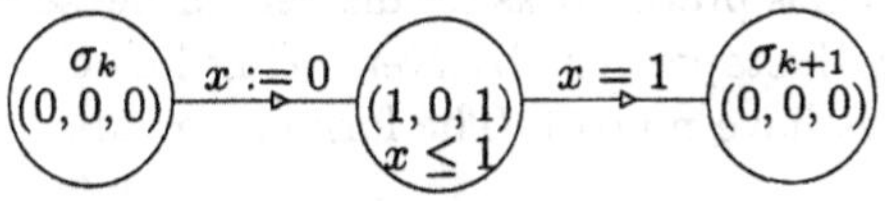

**Fig. 2.** Incrementing counter $C_1$.

subautomaton for incrementing $C_2$ is similar except that the cost of the central state is $(1, 1, 0)$.

The instruction for decrementing counter $C_1$ is encoded in Figure 3. The atomic proposition $\rho_1$ is a witness that $C_1 > 0$ while $\rho'_1$ is a witness that $C_1 = 0$. Since the automaton $\mathcal{A}$ is not allowed to test its cost variables, the formula $\varphi$ will check if $C_1 = 0$ or $C_1 > 0$ depending on the values of $z_1$ and $z_2$. A similar subautomaton is given for counter $C_2$ with atomic propositions $\rho_2$ and $\rho'_2$.

The **if** instruction is encoded similarly to the decrementation instruction, see Figure 4. Again $\varphi$ will check which case occurs.

Let us now give formula $\varphi$ :

$$\sigma_{k_0} \wedge z_1 \cdot z_2 \cdot z_3 \cdot \left( \begin{pmatrix} \rho_1 \Rightarrow z_1 - z_2 > 0 \wedge \rho'_1 \Rightarrow z_1 - z_2 = 0 \\ \wedge \rho_2 \Rightarrow z_1 - z_3 > 0 \wedge \rho'_2 \Rightarrow z_1 - z_3 = 0 \end{pmatrix} \exists U \, \sigma_{k_t} \right).$$

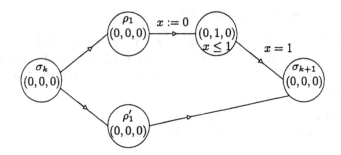

Fig. 3. Decrementing counter $C_1$.

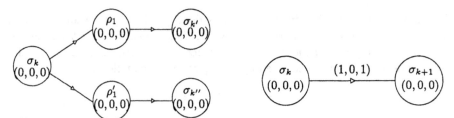

Fig. 4. If instruction with test on $C_1$.

Fig. 5. Incrementing counter $C_1$ with no cost in the locations.

Clearly, the 2-counter machine halts on the instruction **stop** labeled by $k_t$ iff $q \models \varphi$ for the state $q$ equal to $(l_0, 0, 0, 0, 0)$ where $l_0$ is the location labeled by $k_0$. It follows that the model-checking problem is undecidable.          □

*Comments.* The previous proof works for discrete or dense time. The automaton $\mathcal{A}$ is an automaton with stopwatch observers using 1 clock $x$ and 3 cost variables $z_1, z_2, z_3$. All its edges have no cost. The formula $\varphi$ uses cost constraints of the form $z_i - z_j \sim 0$.

The proof can be easily adapted if one prefers an automaton with all its locations having no cost. In this case, $\mathcal{A}$ has no clock and again 3 cost variables. In Figure 5 an incrementation of counter $C_1$ is depicted. The formula $\varphi$ remains identical. One can imagine a third proof with 1 clock and 3 cost variables, as a mix of both previous approaches, such that there exist non null costs on certain locations and on certain edges.

In the sequel of the article, we will work with the WCTL logic restricted to cost constraints $\pi$ of the form $z_i \sim c$. It is denoted WCTL$_r$. The related model-checking problem is the following one.

*Problem 2.* Given a weighted timed automaton $\mathcal{A}$ and a state $q$ of $T_\mathcal{A}$, given a WCTL$_r$ formula $\varphi$, does $q \models \varphi$ hold ? ($\mathbb{T} = \mathbb{N}$ or $\mathbb{T} = \mathbb{R}^+$)

*Example 3.* For the gas burner system of Example 1, the property "if the number of leaks is less than 5, then the leaking time is strictly bounded by 5" is formalized in WCTL$_r$ by the next formula

$$z_2 \cdot z_3 \cdot \forall\Box(z_3 < 5 \Rightarrow z_2 < 5).$$

The next property "at each position of every run, the number of leaks does not exceed 2 in any time interval less than 100 time units" is formalized by

$$\forall\Box(z_1 \cdot z_3 \cdot \forall\Box(z_1 \leq 100 \Rightarrow z_3 \leq 2)).$$

## 4   Bisimulations

In the sequel of the article, we want to study Problem 2 via bisimulations. We recall in this section useful notions on time abstracting bisimulations (see [10] or [3]).

**Definition 6.** *Let $A$ be a weighted timed automaton and $T_A = (Q, \rightarrow)$ its transition system. A bisimulation of $A$ is an equivalence relation $\approx \subseteq Q \times Q$ such that for all $q_1, q_2 \in Q$, $q_1 \approx q_2$,*

- *whenever $q_1 \xrightarrow{0} q_1'$ with $q_1' \in Q$, there exists $q_2' \in Q$ such that $q_2 \xrightarrow{0} q_2'$ and $q_1' \approx q_2'$ ;*
- *whenever $q_1 \xrightarrow{\tau} q_1'$ with $\tau > 0$ and $q_1' \in Q$, there exist $\tau' > 0$ and $q_2' \in Q$ such that $q_2 \xrightarrow{\tau'} q_2'$ and $q_1' \approx q_2'$.*

A bisimulation $\approx$ is *finite* if it has a finite number of equivalence classes. It is said to *respect a partition* $\mathcal{P}$ of the set $Q$ if any $P \in \mathcal{P}$ is a union of equivalence classes of $\approx$. A set $P \subseteq Q$ will be sometimes called a *region*.

Given a region $P \subseteq Q$, the set $Pre(P)$ of predecessor states of $P$ is defined as $Pre_0$ or $Pre_{>0}$ according to both kinds of transitions : instantaneous switch or elapse of time, by

$$Pre_0(P) = \{q \in Q \mid \exists q' \in P \; q \xrightarrow{0} q'\};$$

$$Pre_{>0}(P) = \{q \in Q \mid \exists q' \in P \; \exists \tau > 0 \; q \xrightarrow{\tau} q'\}.$$

A crucial property of a bisimulation $\approx$ is that for every equivalence class $P$ of $\approx$, the predecessor $Pre(P)$ is a union of equivalence classes. It follows that the *coarsest* bisimulation respecting a partition $\mathcal{P}_0$ can be computed by the next procedure.

**Procedure Bisim.**
  **Initially** $\mathcal{P} := \mathcal{P}_0$ ;
  **While** there exist $P, P' \in \mathcal{P}$ such that $\emptyset \subsetneq P \cap Pre(P') \subsetneq P$, do
        $P_1 := P \cap Pre(P'), \; P_2 := P \setminus Pre(P')$
        $\mathcal{P} := (\mathcal{P} \setminus \{P\}) \cup \{P_1, P_2\}$ ;
  **Return** $\mathcal{P}$ .

**Proposition 1.** *Let $A$ be a weighted timed-automaton. The procedure Bisim terminates iff the coarsest bisimulation of $A$ that respects a partition $\mathcal{P}$ is finite.*

An important property of bisimulations is that they preserve $WCTL_r$ formulas if they respect a well-chosen initial partition. We omit the proof since it is similar to the proof given in [4] for timed automata and the TCTL logic.

**Proposition 2.** *Let $A$ be a weighted timed automaton and $\varphi$ be a $WCTL_r$ formula. If $A$ has a bisimulation $\approx$ that respects the partition $\mathcal{P}$ induced by*

1. *the atomic propositions $\sigma$ labeling the locations of $A$,*
2. *the cost constraints $\pi$ appearing in $\varphi$,*
3. *the reset of the cost variables in $\varphi$ (operator $z\cdot$),*

*then for any states $q, q'$ of $T_A$ such that $q \approx q'$, we have $q \models \varphi$ iff $q' \models \varphi$.*

As a consequence of this proposition, it can be proved that if each step of Procedure `Bisim` is *effective* and if this procedure *terminates*, then Problem 2 is decidable. Note that the effectiveness hypothesis is not necessary since weighted timed automata are linear hybrid automata for which the effectiveness of Procedure `Bisim` is known [10].

**Corollary 2.** *If a weighted timed automaton $A$ has a finite bisimulation respecting the partition of Proposition 2, then the $WCTL_r$ model-checking problem is decidable[3].*

To conclude this section, let us recall the classical bisimulation $\approx_t$ for timed automata [5]. Let $T_A$ be the transition system of a timed automaton $A$. Let $C \in \mathbb{N}$ be the supremum of all constants $c$ used in guards of $A$. For $\tau \in \mathbb{T}$, $\overline{\tau}$ denotes its fractional part and $\lfloor \tau \rfloor$ its integral part.

**Definition 7.** *Two states $q = (l, x)$, $q' = (l', x')$ of $T_A$ are equivalent, $q \approx_t q'$, iff the following conditions hold*

- *$l = l'$ ;*
- *For any $i$, $1 \leq i \leq n$, either $\lfloor x_i \rfloor = \lfloor x'_i \rfloor$ or $x_i, x'_i > C$ ;*
- *For any $i \neq j$, $1 \leq i, j \leq n$ such that $x_i, x_j \leq C$, $\overline{x}_i \leq \overline{x}_j$ iff $\overline{x}'_i \leq \overline{x}'_j$ ;*
- *For any $i$, $1 \leq i \leq n$ such that $x_i \leq C$, $\overline{x}_i = 0$ iff $\overline{x}'_i = 0$.*

Note that for discrete time, only the first two conditions have to be considered in this definition. Thus given a clock $x_i$, its possible values in an equivalence class are $1, 2, \ldots, C$ and $C^+ = \{n \in \mathbb{N} \mid n > C\}$.

## 5   Frontier Between Finite and Infinite Bisimulations

In this section, we study Problem 2 with the approach of Corollary 2. We begin with the simple case of discrete time before studying the more complex case of dense time.

---

[3] The same result holds for WCTL (instead of $WCTL_r$) if the cost constraints in Condition 2 of Proposition 2 are general constraints $z_i \sim c$ or $z_i - z_j \sim c$.

## 5.1   Discrete Time

**Theorem 2.** *Let $\mathbb{T} = \mathbb{N}$. Any weigthed timed automaton has a finite bisimulation respecting the partition $\mathcal{P}$ of Proposition 2.*

*Proof.* (Sketch) This result is proved in [13] for more general automata which are the discrete-time rectangular automata, but without costs on the edges. However, the proposed bisimulation remains valid for weighted timed automata. It is the usual bisimulation of timed automata (see Definition 7) adapted as follows : the cost variables are treated as clock variables, and constant $C$ is the supremum of the constants used in the guards of $\mathcal{A}$ and in the cost constraints of $\varphi$.   □

**Corollary 3.** *Let $\mathbb{T} = \mathbb{N}$. The $WCTL_r$ model-checking problem for weigthed timed automata is* PSPACE-COMPLETE.

*Proof.* (Sketch). The PSPACE-HARDNESS is a direct consequence of the fact that TCTL model-checking on timed automata is PSPACE-COMPLETE [4]. The PSPACE-EASINESS is established using classical arguments, see [4]. First note that the number of equivalence classes of the bisimulation given in the proof of Theorem 2 is bounded by an exponential in the size of the input of the model-checking problem (sum of the sizes of the automaton and the formula). We can turn the usual labeling algorithm used for CTL-like logics into a nondeterministic algorithm that uses polynomial space and computes the labels of regions as they are required. By Savitch's theorem, we know that there also exists a deterministic version of this algorithm that uses polynomial space.   □

## 5.2   Dense Time

For dense time, the panorama is completely different. We will identify the *precise frontier* between finite and infinite bisimulations for the subclass of *automata with stopwatch observers*. We will conclude with some comments on the entire class of weighted timed automata.

**Automata with Stopwatch Observers.** By the proof of Theorem 1, for WCTL, we know that there exist automata with stopwatch observers using 1 clock and 3 cost variables for which any bisimulation respecting the partition $\mathcal{P}$ of Proposition 2 is infinite. The next theorem states that, for $WCTL_r$, it is already the case with 1 clock and 2 cost variables, as well as with 2 clock and 1 cost variables[4].

**Theorem 3.** *Let $\mathbb{T} = \mathbb{R}^+$. There exists an automaton with stopwatch observers $\mathcal{A}$ using either 1 clock and 2 cost variables, or 2 clock and 1 cost variables, and a $WCTL_r$ formula $\varphi$ such that no bisimulation respecting the partition $\mathcal{P}$ of Proposition 2 is finite.*

---

[4] We were able to establish this result partly with experiments performed with the HyTECH tool [12].

*Proof.* The two automata that we are going to consider are given in Figures 6 and 7. Note that these automata have empty edges and no labeling of the locations by atomic propositions.

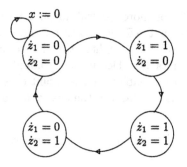

**Fig. 6.** 1 clock and 2 cost variables.     **Fig. 7.** 2 clocks and 1 cost variables.

The proof is based on Procedure Bisim and Proposition 1 with the initial partition $\mathcal{P}$ given in Proposition 2. Note that Condition 1 of Proposition 2 is trivially satisfied.

Let us begin with the case of 1 clock variable $x$ and 2 cost variables $z_1, z_2$. As initial partition $\mathcal{P}$, we take the partition induced by the bisimulation given in Definition 7. The following discussion justifies this choice.

At location of Figure 6 where $\dot{z}_1 = \dot{z}_2 = 1$ (we denote this location by $l$), the behavior of $z_1, z_2$ is the one of a clock. We have thus 3 clocks $x$, $z_1$, $z_2$ at location $l$. As shown in [5], if $x$, $z_1$ and $z_2$ are compared with constant 1, then Procedure Bisim leads to the bisimulation $\approx_t$ of Definition 7 in the cube $[0, 1]^3$ and in location $l$. A way to get these comparisons with constant 1 is simply to add some guard or invariant $x = 1$ in the automaton of Figure 6 and to consider some WCTL$_r$ formula $\varphi$ with the two cost constraints $\pi_1$ and $\pi_2$ respectively equal to $z_1 = 1$ and $z_2 = 1$. Again by Procedure Bisim, the bisimulation $\approx_t$ is transfered to the other locations by applying $Pre_0$ on the empty edges of the automaton. Therefore, as announced before, we can take as partition $\mathcal{P}$ the partition of the cube $[0, 1]^3$ induced by $\approx_t$.

(1) *1 clock variable $x$ and 2 cost variables $z_1, z_2$.*

Let us show that Procedure Bisim does not terminate because it generates an infinite number of regions $R_n$, $n \geq 1$, each containing exactly one triple $(x, z_1, z_2)$ such that[5]

$$(x, z_1, z_2) = (0, \frac{1}{3^n}, \frac{3^n + 1}{2 \cdot 3^n}).$$

(a) We need to work with a particular region generated by the procedure (see Figure 8)

$$S : \quad 0 = x < z_1 < z_2 < 1, \quad 2z_2 - z_1 = 1.$$

---

[5] When speaking about the constructed regions, we can omit the locations since the empty edges transfer the information to each location.

It is constructed as (see Figure 9)

- $S' = Pre_{>0}(P_1) \cap P_2$ with $P_1 : \; 0 < z_1 = z_2 < x = 1$, $P_2 : \; 0 < z_1 < z_2 = x < 1$, and $\dot{z}_1 = 1, \dot{z}_2 = 0$,
- $S = Pre_{>0}(S') \cap P_3$ with $P_3 : \; 0 = x < z_1 < z_2 < 1$, and $\dot{z}_1 = \dot{z}_2 = 0$.

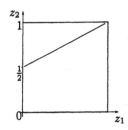

Fig. 8. Region $S$ $(x = 0)$.

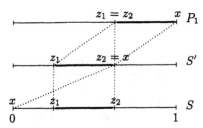

Fig. 9. Its construction.

Looking at the bold intervals in Figure 9, we see that on line $S$, we have $z_2 - z_1 = 1 - z_2$. It follows that $2z_2 - z_1 = 1$ must be satisfied in $S$.

(b) The first region $R_1 = \{0, \frac{1}{3}, \frac{2}{3}\}$ is then constructed as (see Figures 10 and 11)

- $R'_1 = Pre_{>0}(P_1) \cap P_2$ with $P_1 : \; 0 < x = z_1 < z_2 = 1$, $P_2 : \; 0 = x < z_1 < z_2 < 1$, and $\dot{z}_1 = 0, \dot{z}_2 = 1$,
- $R_1 = Pre_0(R'_1) \cap S$.

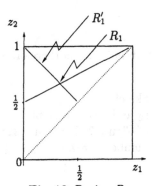

Fig. 10. Region $R_1$.

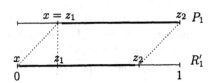

Fig. 11. Its construction.

Looking at the bold intervals in Figure 11, one verifies that $R'_1$ is the region

$$R'_1 : \quad 0 = x < z_1 < z_2 < 1, \quad z_1 + z_2 = 1.$$

In Figure 10, the intersection of $R'_1$ and $S$, which is nothing else than $R_1 = Pre_0(R'_1) \cap S$, is the point $(0, \frac{1}{3}, \frac{2}{3})$.

(c) It remains to explain how to construct $R_{n+1}$ from $R_n$. It is done as follows (see Figures 12 and 13)

- $S_1' = Pre_0(R_n) \cap P_1$ with $P_1 : 0 < z_1 < z_2 < x = 1$,
- $S_2' = Pre_{>0}(S_1') \cap P_2$ with $P_2 : 0 < x = z_1 < z_2 < 1$, and $\dot{z}_1 = 0$, $\dot{z}_2 = 0$,
- $S_3' = Pre_{>0}(S_2') \cap P_3$ with $P_3 : 0 < x < z_1 < z_2 < 1$, and $\dot{z}_1 = 0$, $\dot{z}_2 = 1$,
- $R_{n+1}' = Pre_{>0}(S_3') \cap P_4$ with $P_4 : 0 = x < z_1 < z_2 < 1$, and $\dot{z}_1 = 1$, $\dot{z}_2 = 0$,
- $R_{n+1} = Pre_0(R_{n+1}') \cap S$.

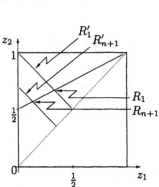

Fig. 12. Region $R_{n+1}$.

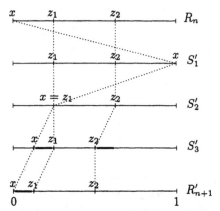

Fig. 13. Its construction from $R_n$.

Recall that $R_n = (0, \frac{1}{3^n}, \frac{3^n+1}{2 \cdot 3^n})$. Thus looking at the bold intervals of Figure 13 (in particular at lines $R_{n+1}'$, $S_3'$ and $R_n$)), the next equality must hold on $R_{n+1}'$

$$z_1 + z_2 = \frac{3^n + 1}{2 \cdot 3^n}.$$

On Figure 12, the intersection of $R_{n+1}'$ and $S$, which is $R_{n+1}$, is therefore the point $(0, \frac{1}{3^{n+1}}, \frac{3^{n+1}+1}{2 \cdot 3^{n+1}})$.

(2) 2 clock variables $x_1, x_2$ and 1 cost variable $z$. (Sketch)

The proof for the case of 2 clock variables $x_1, x_2$ and 1 cost variable $z$ is in the same vein as before. The automaton is the one of Figure 7. Procedure Bisim does not terminate because it generates an infinite number of regions $R_n$, $n \geq 1$, each formed by the unique triple

$$(x_1, x_2, z) = (0, 1 - \frac{1}{2^n}, \frac{1}{2^n}).$$

□

Any timed automaton has a finite bisimulation respecting the partition $\mathcal{P}$ of Proposition 2 (see Definition 7). Thus the remaining case to establish a precise frontier between finite and infinite bisimulations is the case of automata with stopwatch observers using 1 clock and 1 cost variables.

**Theorem 4.** *Let* $\mathbb{T} = \mathbb{R}^+$. *Let* $\mathcal{A}$ *be an automaton with stopwatch observers using 1 clock and 1 cost variables* $x$ *and* $z$. *Then* $\mathcal{A}$ *has a finite bisimulation respecting the partition* $\mathcal{P}$ *of Proposition 2.*

*Proof.* (Sketch) The proposed bisimulation is the one of Definition 7, where $z$ is treated as a clock. □

**Corollary 4.** *The WCTL$_r$ model-checking problem for automata with stopwatch observers using 1 clock and 1 cost variables is decidable.*

**Comments on Weighted Timed Automata.** All the results of the previous paragraph are concerned with automata with stopwatch observers. If we consider weighted timed automata, the frontier between finite and infinite bisimulations is easily established. There exist weighted timed automata with 1 clock and 1 cost variables $x$ and $z$ such that $\dot{z} = d_1$, $\dot{z} = d_2$, with $d_1, d_2 > 0$ two integer constants, for which no finite bisimulation exists [11] (see Figure 14). If for automata with 1 clock and 1 cost variables $x$ and $z$, we impose that there exists an integer constant $d > 0$ such that $\dot{z} \in \{0, d\}$ in each location, then a finite bisimulation exists. It is the bisimulation of Definition 7, where $z$ is treated as a clock and each diagonal $z - x = c$ is replaced by $z - dx = c$ (see Figure 15). Note

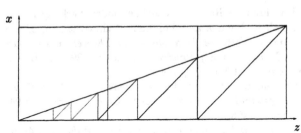

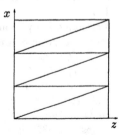

**Fig. 14.** Infinite bisimulation when $d_1 = 1, d_2 = 3$.

**Fig. 15.** Finite bisimulation when $d = 3$.

that a finite bisimulation still exists if we allow to add to the variables $x$ and $z$ additional cost variables $z_2, \ldots, z_m$ having a null cost on the locations and an arbitrary cost on the edges. In Example 1, $z_3$ is such a variable. The required finite bisimulation is a direct product of the bisimulation given before for $x$ and $z$ with the bisimulation of Definition 7 applied to the variables $z_2, \ldots, z_m$ treated as clocks.

Note that Problem 2 remains unanswered for dense time (except in the case of Corollary 4) since the existence of a finite bisimulation is sufficient but not necessary for decidability of the model-checking problem. For instance, in the particular case of weighted timed automata with one cost variable, the cost-bounded reachability problem is shown to be decidable in [1] while there is no finite bisimulation as mentioned above.

# References

1. R. Alur, C. Courcoubetis, and T.A. Henzinger. Computing accumulated delays in real-time systems. In *CAV 93: Computer-Aided Verification*, Lecture Notes in Computer Science 697, pages 181–193. Springer-Verlag, 1993.

2. R. Alur, T.A. Henzinger, and P.-H. Ho. Automatic symbolic verification of embedded systems. *IEEE Transactions on Software Engineering*, 22:181–201, 1996.

3. R. Alur, T.A. Henzinger, G. Lafferriere, and G.J. Pappas. Discrete abstractions of hybrid systems. *Proceedings of the IEEE*, 88:971–984, 2000.

4. Rajeev Alur, Costas Courcoubetis, and David L. Dill. Model-checking in dense real-time. *Information and Computation*, 104(1):2–34, 1993.

5. Rajeev Alur and David L. Dill. A theory of timed automata. *Theoretical Computer Science*, 126(2):183–235, 1994.

6. Rajeev Alur, Salvatore La Torre, and George J. Pappas. Optimal paths in weighted timed automata. In *Proceedings of the 4th International Workshop on Hybrid Systems:Computation and Control (HSCC'01)*, volume 2034 of *Lecture Notes in Computer Science*, pages 49–62. Springer-Verlag, 2001.

7. Gerd Behrmann, Ansgar Fehnker, Thomas Hune, Kim Larsen, Paul Pettersson, Judi Romijn, and Frits Vaandrager. Minimum-cost reachability for priced timed automata. In *Proceedings of the 4th International Workshop on Hybrid Systems:Computation and Control (HSCC'01)*, volume 2034 of *Lecture Notes in Computer Science*, pages 147–161. Springer-Verlag, 2001.

8. Ahmed Bouajjani, Rachid Echahed, and Joseph Sifakis. On model checking for real-time properties with durations. In *Logic in Computer Science*, pages 147–159, 1993.

9. Véronique Bruyère and Jean-François Raskin. Real-time model-checking: Parameters everywhere. In Paritosh K. Pandya and Jaikumar Radhakrishnan, editors, *FST TCS 2003: Foundations of Software Technology and Theoretical Computer Science, 23rd Conference, Mumbai, India, Proceedings*, number 2914 in Lecture Notes in Computer Science, pages 100–111. Springer, 2003.

10. T.A. Henzinger. Hybrid automata with finite bisimulations. In *ICALP 95: Automata, Languages, and Programming*, Lecture Notes in Computer Science 944, pages 324–335. Springer-Verlag, 1995.

11. T.A. Henzinger. The theory of hybrid automata. In *Proceedings of the 11th Annual Symposium on Logic in Computer Science*, pages 278–292. IEEE Computer Society Press, 1996.

12. T.A. Henzinger, P.-H. Ho, and H. Wong-Toi. A user guide to HyTech. In *TACAS 95: Tools and Algorithms for the Construction and Analysis of Systems*, Lecture Notes in Computer Science 1019, pages 41–71. Springer-Verlag, 1995.

13. T.A. Henzinger and P.W. Kopke. Discrete-time control for rectangular hybrid automata. In *ICALP 97: Automata, Languages, and Programming*, Lecture Notes in Computer Science 1256, pages 582–593. Springer-Verlag, 1997.

14. T.A. Henzinger, P.W. Kopke, A. Puri, and P. Varaiya. What's decidable about hybrid automata? In *Proceedings of the 27th Annual Symposium on Theory of Computing*, pages 373–382. ACM Press, 1995.

15. Yonit Kesten, Amir Pnueli, Joseph Sifakis, and Sergio Yovine. Decidable integration graphs. *Information and Computation*, 150(2):209–243, 1999.

# Symbolic Model Checking
# for Probabilistic Timed Automata*

Marta Kwiatkowska[1], Gethin Norman[1], Jeremy Sproston[2], and Fuzhi Wang[1]

[1] School of Computer Science, University of Birmingham
Birmingham B15 2TT, UK
{M.Z.Kwiatkowska,G.Norman,F.Wang}@cs.bham.ac.uk
[2] Dipartimento di Informatica, Università di Torino, 10149 Torino, Italy
sproston@di.unito.it

**Abstract.** Probabilistic timed automata are an extension of timed automata with discrete probability distributions, and can be used to model timed randomized protocols or fault-tolerant systems. We present symbolic model-checking algorithms for verifying probabilistic timed automata against properties of PTCTL (Probabilistic Timed Computation Tree Logic). The algorithms operate on zones, which are sets of valuations of the probabilistic timed automaton's clocks, and therefore avoid an explicit construction of the state space. Furthermore, the algorithms are restricted to system behaviours which guarantee the divergence of time with probability 1. We report on a prototype implementation of the algorithms using Difference Bound Matrices, and present the results of its application to the CSMA/CD and FireWire root contention protocol case studies.

## 1 Introduction

Systems exhibiting both *timed* and *probabilistic* characteristics are widespread, in application contexts as diverse as home entertainment, medicine and business. For example, timing constraints are often vital to the correctness of embedded digital technology, whereas probability exhibits itself commonly in the form of statistical estimates regarding the environment in which a system is embedded. Similarly, protocol designers often exploit the combination of time and probability to design correct, efficient protocols, such as the IEEE 1394 FireWire root contention protocol [13]. The diffusion of such systems has led to methods for obtaining formal correctness guarantees, for instance, adaptations of model checking. *Symbolic model checking* refers to model-checking techniques in which implicit representations – such as BDDs – are used to represent both the transition relation of the system model and the state sets that are computed during the execution of the model-checking algorithm.

In this paper, we consider the modelling formalism of *probabilistic timed automata* [18], an extension of timed automata [3] with discrete probability distributions. This formalism has been shown to be suitable for the description of

* Supported in part by EPSRC grants GR/N22960 and GR/S46727, FORWARD and MIUR-FIRB Perf.

Y. Lakhnech and S. Yovine (Eds.): FORMATS/FTRTFT 2004, LNCS 3253, pp. 293–308, 2004.

timed, randomized protocols, such as the backoff strategy of the IEEE 802.11 standard [20], and the link-local address selection protocol of the IPv4 standard [17]. As a requirement specification language for probabilistic timed automata we consider PTCTL (Probabilistic Timed Computation Tree Logic). The logic PTCTL combines the probabilistic threshold operator of the probabilistic temporal logic PCTL [11] with the timing constraints of the timed temporal logic TCTL [1, 12], in order to express properties such as 'with probability at least 0.99, the system elects a leader within 1 second'. Model checking of probabilistic timed automata against PTCTL was shown to be decidable in [18] via an adaptation of the classical region-graph construction [3, 1]. Unfortunately, the region-graph construction (and digital clocks approach [17]) can result in huge state spaces if the maximal constant used in the description of the automaton is large. Instead, the practical success of *symbolic, zone*-based techniques for non-probabilistic timed automata [4, 8] suggests that a similar symbolic approach may also be employed for the verification of probabilistic timed automata against PTCTL properties. We answer this hypothesis affirmatively in this paper.

The non-trivial cases of our model-checking algorithm concern PTCTL formulae referring to a temporal modality and a probability threshold. In general, PTCTL properties may have thresholds with arbitrary probability values; we refer to such properties as *quantitative*. Properties which express statements such as '$\varphi$ is true with probability below 0.95' impose a bound on the *maximal* probability of $\varphi$; analogously, properties such as '$\varphi$ is true with probability at least 0.01' impose a bound on the *minimal* probability of $\varphi$. In previous work, we presented a zone-based algorithm for the verification of properties referring to maximal probabilities [19]. The aim of this previous algorithm was to construct a finite-state, untimed probabilistic system which has sufficient information to compute the maximum probability using well-established model-checking methods for finite-state probabilistic systems [5]. In this paper, we extend that result by presenting algorithms for probabilistic properties referring to minimal probability of satisfaction, hence permitting verification of arbitrary PTCTL properties.

In order to verify properties of real-world behaviour, it is vital that model-checking algorithms for real-time systems incorporate a notion of *time divergence*. The issue of time divergence is of importance to our algorithms for verifying properties referring to minimal probabilities. For example, to compute the minimum probability of reaching a certain set $F$, for any state not in $F$, the probabilistic timed automaton could exhibit behaviour in which the amount of time elapsed converges before $F$ is reached, or even in which no time elapses. Clearly, such behaviours where time does not progress beyond a bound are pathological, and should be disregarded during model checking. We present an algorithm for computing minimum reachability probabilities which considers *only time-divergent behaviour*, based on the non-probabilistic precedent of [12]. The algorithm is based on computing maximum probabilities for the dual formula while restricting attention to time-divergent behaviours. Because it is possible that a probabilistic timed automaton contains states from which it is impossible for time to diverge with probability 1 (constituting a modelling error), based on [12] we present an algorithm to check for and eliminate such states.

Finally, we report on a prototype implementation of the techniques of this paper using Difference Bound Matrices (DBMs) [10]. We apply this implementation to two case studies: the first concerns the CSMA/CD (Carrier Sense, Multiple Access with Collision Detection) communication protocol [14], whereas the second considers the IEEE 1394 FireWire root contention protocol [13].

The paper proceeds as follows. We review a number of preliminary concepts in Section 2, and in Section 3 we revisit the definitions of probabilistic timed automata and PTCTL. In Section 4, we introduce the model-checking algorithms for PTCTL. Section 5 summarises our prototype implementation of these algorithms. In Section 6, we present the application of the prototype implementation to the case studies, and we conclude the paper in Section 7.

## 2  Preliminaries

In this section, for the sake of completeness, we recall the definitions of probabilistic and timed probabilistic systems needed to give semantics to probabilistic timed automata. Variants of these were originally introduced in [5, 24, 18].

A (discrete probability) *distribution* over a finite set $Q$ is a function $\mu : Q \rightarrow [0, 1]$ such that $\sum_{q \in Q} \mu(q) = 1$. For an uncountable set $Q'$, let $\mathsf{Dist}(Q')$ be the set of distributions over finite subsets of $Q'$. The point distribution $\mu_q$ denotes the distribution which assigns probability 1 to $q$.

**Definition 1.** *A* probabilistic system, PS, *is a tuple* $(S, Steps, \mathcal{L})$ *where* $S$ *is a set of* states, $Steps \subseteq S \times \mathsf{Dist}(S)$ *is a probabilistic transition relation, and* $\mathcal{L} : S \rightarrow 2^{AP}$ *is a labelling function assigning atomic propositions to states.*

A *probabilistic transition* $s \xrightarrow{\mu} s'$ is made from a state $s$ by nondeterministically selecting a distribution $\mu \in \mathsf{Dist}(S)$ such that $(s, \mu) \in Steps$, and then making a probabilistic choice of target state $s'$ according to $\mu$, such that $\mu(s') > 0$.

We consider two ways in which a probabilistic system's computation may be represented. A *path*, representing a particular resolution of both nondeterminism *and* probability, is a non-empty sequence of transitions: $\omega = s_0 \xrightarrow{\mu_0} s_1 \xrightarrow{\mu_1} \cdots$. We denote by $\omega(i)$ the $(i{+}1)$th state of $\omega$ and $last(\omega)$ the last state of $\omega$ if it is finite. The set of infinite (respectively, finite) paths starting in the state $s$ are denoted by $Path_{ful}(s)$ (respectively, $Path_{fin}(s)$).

In contrast to a path, an *adversary* represents a particular resolution of nondeterminism *only*. Formally, an adversary $A$ is a function mapping every finite path $\omega$ to a distribution $\mu$ such that $(last(\omega), \mu) \in Steps$. For any adversary $A$ and state $s$, we let $Path_{ful}^A(s)$ (respectively, $Path_{fin}^A(s)$) denote the subset of $Path_{ful}(s)$ (respectively, $Path_{fin}(s)$) which corresponds to $A$ and, using classical techniques [15], we can define the probability measure $Prob_s^A$ over $Path_{ful}^A(s)$.

We now consider the definition of timed probabilistic systems.

**Definition 2.** *A* timed probabilistic system, TPS, *is a tuple* $(S, Steps, \mathcal{L})$ *where:* $S$ *and* $\mathcal{L}$ *are as in Definition 1 and* $Steps \subseteq S \times \mathbb{R} \times \mathsf{Dist}(S)$ *is a timed prob-*

abilistic transition relation, *such that, if $(s, t, \mu) \in Steps$ and $t>0$, then $\mu$ is a point distribution.*

The component $t$ of a tuple $(s, t, \mu)$ is called a *duration*. As for probabilistic systems, we can introduce paths and adversaries for timed probabilistic systems, except transitions are now labelled by duration-distribution pairs and an adversary maps each finite path to a duration-distribution pair.

We restrict attention to *time-divergent adversaries*; a common restriction imposed in real-time systems so that unrealisable behaviour (corresponding to time not advancing beyond a bound) is disregarded during analysis. For any path $\omega = s_0 \xrightarrow{t_0, \mu_0} s_1 \xrightarrow{t_1, \mu_1} \cdots$ of a timed probabilistic system, the duration up to the $n+1$th state of $\omega$, denoted $\mathcal{D}_\omega(n+1)$, equals $\sum_{i=0}^n t_i$, and we say that a path $\omega$ is *divergent* if for any $t \in \mathbb{R}$, there exists $j \in \mathbb{N}$ such that $\mathcal{D}_\omega(j)>t$.

**Definition 3.** *An adversary $A$ of a timed probabilistic system* TPS *is divergent if and only if for each state $s$ of* TPS *the probability under* $Prob_s^A$ *of the divergent paths of* $Path_{ful}^A(s)$ *is 1. Let* $Adv_{TPS}$ *be the set of divergent adversaries of* TPS.

For motivation on why we consider *probabilistic* divergence, as opposed to the stronger notion where an adversary is divergent if and only if all its paths are divergent, see [18]. A restriction we impose on probabilistic timed systems is that of *non-zenoness*, which stipulates that there does not exist a state from which time cannot diverge, as we consider this situation to be a modelling error.

**Definition 4.** *A probabilistic timed system* TPS *is non-zeno if it has at least one divergent adversary.*

## 3     Probabilistic Timed Automata

In this section we review the definition of probabilistic timed automata [18], a modelling framework for real-time systems exhibiting both nondeterministic and stochastic behaviour. The formalism is derived from classical timed automata [3, 12] extended with discrete probability distributions over edges.

### 3.1     Clocks and Zones

Let $\mathcal{X}$ be a finite set of variables called *clocks* which take values from the time domain $\mathbb{R}$ (non-negative reals). A point $v \in \mathbb{R}^{\mathcal{X}}$ is referred to as a *clock valuation*. For any clock $x \in \mathcal{X}$, we use $v(x)$ to denote the value $v$ assigns to $x$. For any $v \in \mathbb{R}^{\mathcal{X}}$ and $t \in \mathbb{R}$, we use $v+t$ to denote the clock valuation defined as $v(x)+t$ for all $x \in \mathcal{X}$. We use $v[X:=0]$ to denote the clock valuation obtained from $v$ by resetting all of the clocks in $X \subseteq \mathcal{X}$ to 0.

The set of *zones* of $\mathcal{X}$, written $Zones(\mathcal{X})$, is defined inductively by the syntax:

$$\zeta ::= x \leqslant d \,|\, c \leqslant x \,|\, x + c \leqslant y + d \,|\, \neg\zeta \,|\, \zeta \vee \zeta$$

where $x, y \in \mathcal{X}$ and $c, d \in \mathbb{N}$. The clock valuation $v$ *satisfies* the zone $\zeta$, written $v \triangleright \zeta$, if and only if $\zeta$ resolves to true after substituting each clock $x \in \mathcal{X}$ with the corresponding clock value $v(x)$ from $v$.

We only consider canonical zones [26] ensuring equality between their syntactic and semantic (subsets of $\mathbb{R}^{\mathcal{X}}$ which satisfy the zone) representations. This enables us to use the above syntax interchangeably with set-theoretic operations. We require the following classical operations on zones [12, 26]. For any zones $\zeta, \zeta' \in Zones(\mathcal{X})$ and subset of clocks $X \subseteq \mathcal{X}$, let:

$$\swarrow_{\zeta'} \zeta \stackrel{\text{def}}{=} \{v \mid \exists t \geqslant 0. (v + t \triangleright \zeta \wedge \forall t' \leqslant t. (v + t' \triangleright \zeta \vee \zeta'))\}$$
$$[X := 0]\zeta \stackrel{\text{def}}{=} \{v \mid v[X := 0] \triangleright \zeta\}.$$

## 3.2   Syntax and Semantics of Probabilistic Timed Automata

**Definition 5.** *A* probabilistic timed automaton *is a tuple* $(L, \mathcal{X}, inv, prob, \mathcal{L})$ *where: $L$ is a finite set of* locations; *the function* $inv : L \to Zones(\mathcal{X})$ *is the* invariant condition; *the finite set* $prob \subseteq L \times Zones(\mathcal{X}) \times \text{Dist}(2^{\mathcal{X}} \times L)$ *is the* probabilistic edge relation; *and* $\mathcal{L} : L \to 2^{AP}$ *is a* labelling function *assigning atomic propositions to locations.*

A *state* of a probabilistic timed automaton PTA is a pair $(l, v) \in L \times \mathbb{R}^{\mathcal{X}}$ such that $v \triangleright inv(l)$. Informally, the behaviour of a probabilistic timed automaton can be understood as follows. In any state $(l, v)$, there is a nondeterministic choice of either making a *discrete transition* or letting *time pass*. A discrete transition can be made according to any $(l, g, p) \in prob$ with source location $l$ which is *enabled*; that is, zone $g$ is satisfied by the current clock valuation $v$. Then the probability of moving to the location $l'$ and resetting all clocks in $X$ to 0 is given by $p(X, l')$. The option of letting time pass is available only if the invariant condition $inv(l)$ is satisfied while time elapses.

   An *edge* of PTA is a tuple $(l, g, p, X, l')$ such that $(l, g, p) \in prob$ and $p(X, l') > 0$. Let edges denote the set of all edges and $edges(l, g, p)$ the edges of $(l, g, p)$.

   We now give the semantics of probabilistic timed automata defined in terms of timed probabilistic systems.

**Definition 6.** *Let* PTA $= (L, \mathcal{X}, inv, prob, \mathcal{L})$ *be a probabilistic timed automaton. The semantics of* PTA *is defined as the timed probabilistic system* $\text{TPS}_{\text{PTA}} = (S, Steps, \mathcal{L}')$ *where:* $S \subseteq L \times \mathbb{R}^{\mathcal{X}}$ *such that* $(l, v) \in S$ *if and only if* $v \triangleright inv(l)$; $((l, v), t, \mu) \in Steps$ *if and only if one of the following conditions holds:*

**[time transitions]** $t \geqslant 0$, $\mu = \mu_{(l, v+t)}$ *and* $v + t' \triangleright inv(l)$ *for all* $0 \leqslant t' \leqslant t$
**[discrete transitions]** $t = 0$ *and there exists* $(l, g, p) \in prob$ *such that* $v \triangleright g$ *and for any* $(l', v') \in S$: $\mu(l', v') = \sum_{X \subseteq \mathcal{X} \wedge v' = v[X:=0]} p(X, l')$.

*Finally,* $\mathcal{L}'(l, v) = \mathcal{L}(l)$ *for all* $(l, v) \in S$.

We say that PTA is non-zeno if and only if $\text{TPS}_{\text{PTA}}$ is non-zeno.

## 3.3   Probabilistic Timed Computation Tree Logic (PTCTL)

We now describe the probabilistic timed logic PTCTL which can be used to specify properties of probabilistic timed automata. As in TCTL [1, 12], PTCTL employs a set of *formula clocks*, $\mathcal{Z}$, disjoint from the clocks $\mathcal{X}$ of the probabilistic timed automaton. Formula clocks are assigned values by a *formula clock valuation* $\mathcal{E} \in \mathbb{R}^{\mathcal{Z}}$. Timing constraints can be expressed using such clocks and the reset quantifier $z.\phi$. As in PCTL [11], PTCTL includes the probabilistic quantifier $\mathcal{P}_{\sim\lambda}[\cdot]$.

**Definition 7.** *The syntax of* PTCTL *is defined as follows:*

$$\phi ::= a \mid \zeta \mid \neg\phi \mid \phi \vee \phi \mid z.\phi \mid \mathcal{P}_{\sim\lambda}[\phi \, \mathcal{U} \, \phi]$$

*where* $a \in AP$, $\zeta \in Zones(\mathcal{X} \cup \mathcal{Z})$, $z \in \mathcal{Z}$, $\sim \in \{\leqslant, <, >, \geqslant\}$ *and* $\lambda \in [0,1]$.

In PTCTL we can express properties such as 'with probability at least 0.95, the system clock $x$ does not exceed 3 before 8 time units elapse', which is represented as the formula $z.\mathcal{P}_{\geqslant 0.95}[(x \leqslant 3) \, \mathcal{U} \, (z = 8)]$.

We write $v, \mathcal{E}$ to denote the composite clock valuation in $\mathbb{R}^{\mathcal{X} \cup \mathcal{Z}}$ obtained from $v \in \mathbb{R}^{\mathcal{X}}$ and $\mathcal{E} \in \mathbb{R}^{\mathcal{Z}}$. Given a state and formula clock valuation pair $(l,v), \mathcal{E}$, zone $\zeta$ and duration $t$, by abuse of notation we let $(l,v), \mathcal{E} \rhd \zeta$ denote $v, \mathcal{E} \rhd \zeta$, and $(l,v)+t$ denote $(l,v+t)$.

**Definition 8.** *Let* TPS $= (S, Steps, \mathcal{L}')$ *be the timed probabilistic system associated with the probabilistic timed automaton* PTA. *For any state* $s \in S$, *formula clock valuation* $\mathcal{E} \in \mathbb{R}^{\mathcal{Z}}$ *and PTCTL formula* $\theta$, *the satisfaction relation* $s, \mathcal{E} \models \theta$ *is defined inductively as follows:*

$$
\begin{aligned}
s, \mathcal{E} &\models a & &\Leftrightarrow a \in \mathcal{L}'(s) \\
s, \mathcal{E} &\models \zeta & &\Leftrightarrow s, \mathcal{E} \rhd \zeta \\
s, \mathcal{E} &\models \phi \vee \psi & &\Leftrightarrow s, \mathcal{E} \models \phi \text{ or } s, \mathcal{E} \models \psi \\
s, \mathcal{E} &\models \neg\phi & &\Leftrightarrow s, \mathcal{E} \not\models \phi \\
s, \mathcal{E} &\models z.\phi & &\Leftrightarrow s, \mathcal{E}[z := 0] \models \phi \\
s, \mathcal{E} &\models \mathcal{P}_{\sim\lambda}[\phi \, \mathcal{U} \, \psi] & &\Leftrightarrow p^A_{s,\mathcal{E}}(\phi \, \mathcal{U} \, \psi) \sim \lambda \text{ for all } A \in Adv_{\text{TPS}}
\end{aligned}
$$

*where* $p^A_{s,\mathcal{E}}(\phi \, \mathcal{U} \, \psi) = Prob^A_s\{\omega \in Path^A_{ful}(s) \mid \omega, \mathcal{E} \models \phi \, \mathcal{U} \, \psi\}$, *and, for any path* $\omega \in Path_{ful}(s)$: $\omega, \mathcal{E} \models \phi \, \mathcal{U} \, \psi$ *if and only if there exists* $i \in \mathbb{N}$ *and* $t \leqslant \mathcal{D}_\omega(i+1) - \mathcal{D}_\omega(i)$ *such that*

- $\omega(i)+t, \mathcal{E}+\mathcal{D}_\omega(i)+t \models \psi$;
- *if* $t' < t$, *then* $\omega(i)+t', \mathcal{E}+\mathcal{D}_\omega(i)+t' \models \phi \vee \psi$;
- *if* $j < i$ *and* $t' \leqslant \mathcal{D}_\omega(j+1) - \mathcal{D}_\omega(j)$, *then* $\omega(j)+t', \mathcal{E}+\mathcal{D}_\omega(j)+t' \models \phi \vee \psi$.

In the following sections we will also consider the dual of the sub-formula $\phi \, \mathcal{U} \, \psi$, namely the release formula $\neg\phi \, \mathcal{V} \, \neg\psi$. In the standard manner, we refer to $\phi \, \mathcal{U} \, \psi$ and $\phi \, \mathcal{V} \, \psi$ as *path formulae*, and use the abbreviation $true \, \mathcal{U} \, \phi = \Diamond\phi$.

## 4   Symbolic PTCTL Model Checking

In this section, we show how a probabilistic timed automaton may be model checked against PTCTL formulae. In order to represent the state sets computed

> **algorithm** PTCTLModelCheck(PTA, $\theta$)
> **output:** set of symbolic states $[\![\theta]\!]$ **such that**
> $\qquad [\![a]\!] := \{(l, inv(l)) \mid l \in L \text{ and } l \in \mathcal{L}(a)\};$
> $\qquad [\![\zeta]\!] := \{(l, inv(l) \wedge \zeta) \mid l \in L\};$
> $\qquad [\![\neg\phi]\!] := \{(l, inv(l) \wedge \neg \bigvee_{(l,\zeta) \in [\![\phi]\!]} \zeta) \mid l \in L\};$
> $\qquad [\![\phi \vee \psi]\!] := [\![\phi]\!] \vee [\![\psi]\!];$
> $\qquad [\![z.\phi]\!] := \{(l, [\{z\}{:=}0]\zeta) \mid (l, \zeta) \in [\![\phi]\!]\};$
> $\qquad [\![\mathcal{P}_{\sim\lambda}[\phi \,\mathcal{U}\, \psi]]\!] := \text{Until}([\![\phi]\!], [\![\psi]\!], \sim \lambda);$

**Fig. 1.** Symbolic PTCTL model-checking algorithm.

during the model-checking process, we use the concept of *symbolic state*: a symbolic state is a pair $(l, \zeta)$ comprising a location and a zone over $\mathcal{X} \cup \mathcal{Z}$. The set of state and formula clock valuation pairs corresponding to a symbolic state $(l, \zeta)$ is $\{(l, v), \mathcal{E} \mid v, \mathcal{E} \triangleright \zeta\}$, while the state set corresponding to a set of symbolic states is the union of those corresponding to each individual symbolic state. In the manner standard for model checking, we progress up the parse tree of a PTCTL formula, recursively calling the algorithm PTCTLModelCheck, shown in Figure 1, to compute the set of symbolic states which satisfy each subformula. Handling atomic propositions and Boolean operations is classical, and therefore we only consider only computing $\text{Until}([\![\phi_1]\!], [\![\phi_2]\!], \sim\lambda)$, which arises when we check probabilistically quantified formula. Our technique relies on the comparison of maximum or minimum probabilities with $\lambda$, since, from the semantics of PTCTL (Definition 8):

$$\{s, \mathcal{E} \mid s, \mathcal{E} \models \mathcal{P}_{\sim\lambda}[\phi \,\mathcal{U}\, \psi]\} = \begin{cases} \{s, \mathcal{E} \mid p_{s,\mathcal{E}}^{\max}(\phi \,\mathcal{U}\, \psi) \sim \lambda\} \text{ if } \sim \in \{<, \leqslant\} \\ \{s, \mathcal{E} \mid p_{s,\mathcal{E}}^{\min}(\phi \,\mathcal{U}\, \psi) \sim \lambda\} \text{ if } \sim \in \{\geqslant, >\} \end{cases} \quad (1)$$

where for any PTCTL path formula $\varphi$:

$$p_{s,\mathcal{E}}^{\max}(\varphi) \stackrel{\text{def}}{=} \sup_{A \in Adv_{\text{TPS}}} p_{s,\mathcal{E}}^{A}(\varphi) \quad \text{and} \quad p_{s,\mathcal{E}}^{\min}(\varphi) \stackrel{\text{def}}{=} \inf_{A \in Adv_{\text{TPS}}} p_{s,\mathcal{E}}^{A}(\varphi).$$

We begin by introducing operations on symbolic states. In Section 4.2, we review algorithms for calculating maximum probabilities, while in Section 4.3 we present new algorithms for calculating minimum probabilities. Proofs of the key results, and specialised algorithms for *qualitative* formulae ($\lambda \in \{0, 1\}$), for which verification can be performed through an analysis of the underlying graph, are available in [22].

## 4.1   Operations on Symbolic States

In this section we extend the *time predecessor* and *discrete predecessor* functions tpre and dpre of [12, 26] to probabilistic timed automata. For any sets of symbolic states $\mathsf{U}, \mathsf{V} \subseteq L \times Zones(\mathcal{X} \cup \mathcal{Z})$, clock $x \in \mathcal{X} \cup \mathcal{Z}$ and edge $(l, g, p, X, l')$:

$$x.\mathsf{U} \stackrel{\text{def}}{=} \{(l, [\{x\}{:=}0]\zeta_{\mathsf{U}}^{l}) \mid l \in L\}$$
$$\text{tpre}_{\mathsf{U}}(\mathsf{V}) \stackrel{\text{def}}{=} \{(l, \swarrow_{\zeta_{\mathsf{U}}^{l} \wedge inv(l)} (\zeta_{\mathsf{V}}^{l} \wedge inv(l))) \mid l \in L\}$$
$$\text{dpre}((l, g, p, X, l'), \mathsf{U}) \stackrel{\text{def}}{=} \{(l, g \wedge ([X := 0]\zeta_{\mathsf{U}}^{l'}))\}.$$

where $\zeta_U^l = \bigvee\{\zeta \mid (l, \zeta) \in U\}$, i.e $\zeta_U^l$ is the zone such that $v, \mathcal{E} \rhd \zeta_U^l$ if and only if $(l, v), \mathcal{E} \in u$ for some $u \in U$. Furthermore, we define the conjunction and disjunction of sets of symbolic states as follows:

$$U \wedge V \stackrel{\text{def}}{=} \{(l, \zeta_U^l \wedge \zeta_V^l) \mid l \in L\} \text{ and } U \vee V \stackrel{\text{def}}{=} \{(l, \zeta_U^l \vee \zeta_V^l) \mid l \in L\}.$$

Finally, let $[\![\text{false}]\!] = \varnothing$ and $[\![\text{true}]\!] = \{(l, inv(l)) \mid l \in L\}$, the sets of symbolic states representing the empty and full state sets respectively.

## 4.2   Computing Maximum Probabilities

In this section we review the methods for calculating the set of states satisfying a formula of the form $\mathcal{P}_{\leq\lambda}[\phi\,\mathcal{U}\,\psi]$ which, from (1), reduces to the computation of $p_{s,\mathcal{E}}^{\max}(\phi\,\mathcal{U}\,\psi)$ for all state and formula clock valuation pairs $s, \mathcal{E}$. Note that, since we consider only non-zeno automata, when calculating these sets we can ignore the restriction to divergent adversaries: letting time diverge can only make reaching $\psi$ less likely. This is similar to verifying (non-probabilistic) non-zeno timed automata against formulae of the form $\phi\,\exists\mathcal{U}\,\psi$ ('there exists a divergent path which satisfies $\phi\,\mathcal{U}\,\psi$') [12].

To compute maximum probabilities, we adopt the algorithm of [19] (see Figure 2). The key observation is that to preserve the probabilistic branching one must take the conjunctions of symbolic states generated by edges from the same distribution. Lines 1–4 deal with the initialisation of Z, which is set equal to the set of time predecessors of V, and the set of edges $E_{(l,g,p)}$ associated with each probabilistic edge $(l, g, p) \in prob$. Lines 5–20 generate a finite-state graph, the nodes of which are symbolic states, obtained by iterating timed and discrete predecessor operations (line 8), and taking conjunctions (lines 12–17). The edges of the graph are partitioned into the sets $E_{(l,g,p)}$ for $(l, g, p) \in prob$, with the intuition that $(z, (X, l'), z') \in E_{(l,g,p)}$ corresponds to a transition from any state in $z$ to some state in $z'$ when the outcome $(X, l')$ of the probabilistic edge $(l, g, p)$ is chosen. The graph edges are added in lines 11 and 15. The termination of lines 5–20 is guaranteed (see [19]). Line 21 describes the manner in which the probabilistic edges of the probabilistic timed automaton are used in combination with the computed edge sets to construct the probabilistic transition relation *Steps*. Finally, in line 22, model checking is performed on the resulting finite-state probabilistic system PS to obtain $MaxProbReach(z, \text{tpre}_{U\vee V}(V))$, the maximum probability of reaching $\text{tpre}_{U\vee V}(V)$ from $z$, for each $z \in Z$. Note that we write $z \neq \varnothing$ if and only if $z$ encodes at least one state and formula clock valuation pair. The following proposition states the correctness of this algorithm.

**Proposition 1.** *For any probabilistic timed automaton* PTA *and PTCTL formula* $\mathcal{P}_{\leq\lambda}[\phi\,\mathcal{U}\,\psi]$, *if* PS $= (Z, Steps)$ *is the probabilistic system generated by* MaxU($[\![\phi]\!], [\![\psi]\!], \gtrsim \lambda$), *then for any* $s, \mathcal{E} \in S \times \mathbb{R}^{\mathcal{Z}}$: $p_{s,\mathcal{E}}^{\max}(\phi\,\mathcal{U}\,\psi) > 0$ *if and only if* $s, \mathcal{E} \in \text{tpre}_{[\![\phi\vee\psi]\!]}(Z)$, *and if* $p_{s,\mathcal{E}}^{\max}(\phi\,\mathcal{U}\,\psi) > 0$, *then* $p_{s,\mathcal{E}}^{\max}(\phi\,\mathcal{U}\,\psi)$ *equals*

$$\max\left\{ MaxProbReach(z, \text{tpre}_{[\![\phi\vee\psi]\!]}[\![\psi]\!]) \mid z \in Z \text{ and } s, \mathcal{E} \in \text{tpre}_{[\![\phi\vee\psi]\!]}(z) \right\}.$$

Based on the above we set Until($[\![\phi]\!], [\![\psi]\!], \lesssim \lambda$) = $[\![\text{true}]\!] \setminus$ MaxU($[\![\phi]\!], [\![\psi]\!], \gtrsim \lambda$).

**algorithm** MaxU($U, V, \gtrsim \lambda$)
1.   $Z := \text{tpre}_{UVV}(V)$
2.   **for** $(l, g, p) \in prob$
3.     $E_{(l,g,p)} := \varnothing$
4.   **end for**
5.   **repeat**
6.     $Y := Z$
7.     **for** $y \in Y \wedge (l, g, p) \in prob \wedge e = (l, g, p, X, l') \in \text{edges}(l, g, p)$
8.       $z := U \wedge \text{dpre}(e, \text{tpre}_{UVV}(y))$
9.       **if** $(z \neq \varnothing) \wedge (z \notin \text{tpre}_{UVV}(V))$
10.        $Z := Z \cup \{z\}$
11.        $E_{(l,g,p)} := E_{(l,g,p)} \cup \{(z, (X, l'), y)\}$
12.        **for** $(\bar{z}, (\bar{X}, \bar{l'}), \bar{y}) \in E_{(l,g,p)}$
13.          **if** $(z \wedge \bar{z} \neq \varnothing) \wedge ((\bar{X}, \bar{l'}) \neq (X, l')) \wedge (z \wedge \bar{z} \notin \text{tpre}_{UVV}(V))$
14.            $Z := Z \cup \{z \wedge \bar{z}\}$
15.            $E_{(l,g,p)} := E_{(l,g,p)} \cup \{(z \wedge \bar{z}, (X, l'), \bar{y}), (z \wedge \bar{z}, (\bar{X}, \bar{l'}), y)\}$
16.          **end if**
17.        **end for**
18.       **end if**
19.     **end for**
20.   **until** $Z = Y$
21.   construct $PS = (Z, Steps)$ where $(z, \rho) \in Steps$ if and only if
      there exists $(l, g, p) \in prob$ and $E \subseteq E_{(l,g,p)}$ such that
      $- ((z', e, z'') \in E \Rightarrow z' = z) \wedge ((z, e, z'') \neq (z, e', z'') \in E \Rightarrow e \neq e')$
      $- \rho(z') = \sum \{\!| p(X, l') | (z, (X, l'), z') \in E |\!\} \ \ \forall z' \in Z$
22.   **return** $\bigvee \{\text{tpre}_{UVV}(z) \mid z \in Z \wedge MaxProbReach(z, \text{tpre}_{UVV}(V)) \gtrsim \lambda\}$

**Fig. 2.** Algorithm MaxU($\cdot, \cdot, \gtrsim \lambda$).

### 4.3   Computing Minimum Probabilities

We now consider verifying formulae of the form $\mathcal{P}_{\geq \lambda}[\phi \, \mathcal{U} \, \psi]$ which, using (1), reduces to computing $p_{s,\mathcal{E}}^{\min}(\phi \, \mathcal{U} \, \psi)$ for all state and formula clock valuation pairs $s, \mathcal{E}$. In contrast to the case for maximal probability, the computation of minimal probabilities should be restricted to time-divergent adversaries, in the same way as universally-quantified path formulae of non-probabilistic timed automata should be restricted to time-divergent paths. For example, for any formula clock $z \in \mathcal{Z}$, under divergent adversaries the minimum probability of reaching $z > 1$ is 1; however, if we remove the restriction to time divergent adversaries the minimum probability is 0 (by letting time converge before $z$ exceeds 1).

The techniques we introduce here are based on the result of [12] that verifying $\phi \, \forall \mathcal{U} \, \psi$ ('all divergent paths satisfy $\phi \, \mathcal{U} \, \psi$') reduces to computing the fixpoint:

$$\mu X.(\psi \vee \neg z.((\neg X) \, \exists \mathcal{U} \, (\neg(\phi \vee X) \vee (z > c)))) \tag{2}$$

for any $c(> 0) \in \mathbb{N}$. The important point is that the universal quantification over paths has been replaced by an existential quantification, which, together with the constraint $z > c$, allows one to ignore the restriction to time divergence

```
algorithm MaxV≥1(c, U, V)
Z:=[true]
repeat
    Y:=Z
    Z:=V ∧ z.MaxU≥1(Y, (U∧Y) ∨ [z>c])
until Z = Y
return Z
```

```
algorithm NonZeno
Z:=[true]
repeat
    Y:=Z
    Z:=z.MaxU≥1([true], Y ∧ [z=1])
until Z = Y
return Z₀
```

**Fig. 3.** $\mathsf{MaxV}_{\geq 1}(c, \cdot, \cdot)$ and $\mathsf{NonZeno}$ algorithms.

in the verification procedure. Using the duality $\phi \, \mathcal{U} \, \psi \equiv \neg(\neg\phi \, \mathcal{V} \, \neg\psi)$, we have, for any state $s$ of $\mathsf{TPS_{PTA}}$ and formula clock valuation $\mathcal{E}$:

$$p^{\min}_{s,\mathcal{E}}(\phi \, \mathcal{U} \, \psi) = 1 - p^{\max}_{s,\mathcal{E}}(\neg\phi \, \mathcal{V} \, \neg\psi),$$

and hence, to verify $\mathcal{P}_{\geq\lambda}[\phi \, \mathcal{U} \, \psi]$, it suffices to calculate $p^{\max}_{s,\mathcal{E}}(\neg\phi \, \mathcal{V} \, \neg\psi)$ for all state and formula clock valuation pairs. Now, although we have reduced the problem to calculating a maximum probability, we cannot ignore time divergence when calculating such probabilities. For example, consider the formula $\mathtt{false} \, \mathcal{V} \, \phi$, meaning 'always $\phi$' ($\square\phi$): the probability of this formula is 1 within states satisfying $\phi$ by always taking time transitions with duration 0.

Proposition 2 below shows that we can reduce the computation of the maximum probability of satisfying a release formula to that of computing the maximum probability of an until operator within which a *qualitative* release formula is nested. As issues of time divergence are irrelevant to the computation of the maximum probabilities of until formulae, the proposition permits us to focus our attention on incorporating time divergence within the verification of the qualitative release formula.

**Proposition 2.** *For any timed probabilistic system* $\mathsf{TPS_{PTA}} = (S, Steps, \mathcal{L}')$, $s \in S$, *formula clock valuation* $\mathcal{E} \in \mathbb{R}^{\mathcal{Z}}$ *and PTCTL formulae* $\phi, \psi$:

$$p^{\max}_{s,\mathcal{E}}(\phi \, \mathcal{V} \, \psi) = p^{\max}_{s,\mathcal{E}}(\psi \, \mathcal{U} \, \neg\mathcal{P}_{<1}[\phi \, \mathcal{V} \, \psi]).$$

Since we have already introduced an algorithm for calculating the maximum probability of satisfying until formulae, it remains to consider a method for calculating the set of states satisfying $\neg\mathcal{P}_{<1}[\phi \, \mathcal{V} \, \psi]$; that is, $\{s, \mathcal{E} \mid p^{\max}_{s,\mathcal{E}}(\phi \, \mathcal{V} \, \psi) \geq 1\}$. Based on (2) we obtain the following proposition.

**Proposition 3.** *For any positive* $c \in \mathbb{N}$ *and PTCTL formulae* $\phi, \psi$, *if* $z \in \mathcal{Z}$ *does not appear in either* $\phi$ *or* $\psi$, *then the set* $\{s, \mathcal{E} \mid p^{\max}_{s,\mathcal{E}}(\phi \, \mathcal{V} \, \psi) \geq 1\}$ *is given by the fixpoint* $\nu X.(\psi \wedge z.\neg\mathcal{P}_{<1}[X \, \mathcal{U} \, ((X \wedge \phi) \vee z{>}c)])$.

The algorithm $\mathsf{MaxV}_{\geq 1}$ for calculating the set $\{s, \mathcal{E} \mid p^{\max}_{s,\mathcal{E}}(\phi \, \mathcal{V} \, \psi) \geq 1\}$ follows from Proposition 3 and is given in Figure 3. The algorithm calls $\mathsf{MaxU}_{\geq 1}([\phi], [\psi])$, given in Figure 4, which computes the set of states $\{s, \mathcal{E} \mid p^{\max}_{s,\mathcal{E}}(\phi \, \mathcal{U} \, \psi) \geq 1\}$ and is based on a similar algorithm for finite-state probabilistic systems [9]. Putting this together, and letting $\gtrsim \Rightarrow$ and $\precsim \Rightarrow \geq$, we set

$$\mathsf{Until}([\phi], [\psi], \gtrsim \lambda) = [\mathtt{true}] \setminus \mathsf{MaxU}([\neg\psi], \mathsf{MaxV}_{\geq 1}(c, [\neg\phi], [\neg\psi]), \precsim 1 - \lambda).$$

```
algorithm pre1(U, V)
Y := [false]
for (l, g, p) ∈ prob
    Y₀ := [true]
    Y₁ := [false]
    for e ∈ edges(l, g, p)
        Y₀ := dpre(e, U) ∧ Y₀
        Y₁ := dpre(e, V) ∨ Y₁
    end
    Y := (Y₀ ∧ Y₁) ∨ Y
end
return Y
```

```
algorithm MaxU≥1(U, V)
Z₀ := [true]
repeat
    Y₀ := Z₀
    Z₁ := [false]
    repeat
        Y₁ := Z₁
        Z₁ := V ∨ (U ∧ pre1(Y₀, Y₁))
        Z₁ := Z₁ ∨ tpre_UVV(Y₀ ∧ Y₁)
    until Z₁ = Y₁
    Z₀ := Z₁
until Z₀ = Y₀
return Z₀
```

**Fig. 4.** $\mathsf{MaxU}_{\geqslant 1}(\cdot, \cdot)$ algorithm.

### 4.4 Checking Non-zenoness

In the non-probabilistic case [12] checking non-zenoness corresponds to finding the greatest fixpoint $\nu X.(z.(\exists\Diamond\,((z{=}1)\wedge X)))$. For probabilistic timed automata, we can replace $\exists$ with $\neg\mathcal{P}_{<1}[\cdot]$, i.e replace 'there exists a path that reaches $(z{=}1)\wedge X$' with 'there exists an adversary which reaches $(z{=}1)\wedge X$ with probability 1'. Following this approach, the algorithm for calculating the set of non-zeno states is given in Figure 3. Formally, we have the following proposition.

**Proposition 4.** *A probabilistic timed automaton* PTA *is non-zeno if and only if* $\{(l, inv(l) \mid l \in L\}$ *equals the fixpoint* $\nu X.(z.\neg\mathcal{P}_{<1}[\Diamond((z{=}1) \wedge X)])$.

Similarly to [12], the algorithm can be used to convert a 'zeno' probabilistic timed automaton into a non-zeno automaton by strengthening invariants.

## 5 Implementation

In this section we briefly summarise our prototype implementation of the model-checking algorithms given in Section 4. It is important to note that the aim of our implementation is to validate the algorithms presented for model checking probabilistic timed automata against PTCTL, rather than to devise an efficient implementation; the latter will be the subject of future work. Note that, to perform the final step of the algorithm MaxU (line 22 of Figure 2), that is compute maximum reachability probabilities on a finite-state probabilistic system, we export the problem to the probabilistic symbolic model checker PRISM [16, 23].

The main step in the implementation of our techniques is the representation of (sets of) symbolic states and the operations required on them; more precisely, since a symbolic state is a pair $(l, \zeta)$ where $l \in L$ and $\zeta$ is a zone, we require a method for representing zones and performing operations on zones.

Difference Bound Matrices (DBMs) [10] are a well known data-structure for the representation of convex zones and are used in the model checkers UPPAAL [4] and KRONOS [8]. As the operations required by our algorithm can introduce non-convexity, we also represent non-convex zones. Following the approach presented in [26], we represent non-convex zones by lists of DBMs, that is, we represent a non-convex zone $\zeta$ by a list of convex zones $\zeta_1, \ldots, \zeta_n$ such that $\zeta = \zeta_1 \cup \cdots \cup \zeta_n$. It thus follows that a symbolic state can be represented by a location and a list of DBMs. This representation is clearly not canonical: there are many ways of decomposing a non-convex zone into a set of convex zones. However, [26] presents algorithms (used by KRONOS [6]) for the operations we require when zones are represented as lists of DBMs. Based on [26], we have implemented, in Java, a prototype DBM package and the operations on lists of DBMs required by our model-checking algorithms. Note that the equality checking performed by the algorithms MaxV$_{\geqslant 1}$, MaxU$_{\geqslant 1}$ and NonZeno reduces to an inclusion test based on whether a least or greatest fixpoint is being performed.

## 6    Case Studies

In this section we report on the results of our prototype implementation applied to two case studies: the CSMA/CD communication protocol [14], and the IEEE1394 FireWire root contention protocol [13]. Due to space limitations, we include the results for the generation of the finite-state probabilistic system, and not the verification of this system which is performed by PRISM, and is therefore standard; further details are available from the PRISM web page [23].

We test both the maximum and minimum probability algorithms, in each case confirming the results with those obtained using the digital clocks approach in PRISM [17, 21] and, when possible, the forward reachability approach [18, 7]. This comparison is feasible since the models are 'closed' and 'diagonal-free' (they do not feature either strict inequalities or comparisons between clocks), but our algorithms are applicable to general probabilistic timed automata. When calculating minimum probabilities of deadline properties, for comparison we also use the alternative method introduced in [21], as explained by the following remark.

*Remark 1.* We observe that certain deadline properties referring to minimum probability can be expressed in terms of properties referring to maximum probability. Consider a property $z.\mathcal{P}_{\geqslant \lambda}[\Diamond(\phi \wedge z \leqslant D)]$ and assume that $\phi$ is reachable with probability 1 for all adversaries and states. We adjust the model so that states in which $\phi$ is true are forced to make a transition to a sink-location; furthermore, we allow the model to make a transition to a different, "deadline exceeded" sink-location, denoted exceeded, as soon as the value of the clock $z$ exceeds $D$ [21] (provided that we are not in a state satisfying $\phi$). Because this location is a sink, $\phi$ cannot become true after it is entered. Then, given any adversary $A$, state $s$ and formula clock valuation $\mathcal{E}$, we have that $p_{s,\mathcal{E}}^{A}(\Diamond(\phi \wedge z \leqslant D)) = 1 - p_{s,\mathcal{E}}^{A}(\Diamond \text{ exceeded})$. Hence, we are able to reduce the computation of a minimum probability to a maximum probability.

**Table 1.** Statistics for MaxV$_{\geqslant 1}$ as $c$ varies, when verifying the CSMA/CD protocol.

| $c$ | $\mathcal{P}_{\geqslant 1}[\lozenge \text{ done}]$ | | | $z.\mathcal{P}_{\geqslant \lambda}[\lozenge(\text{done} \wedge z \leqslant 2000)]$ | | |
|---|---|---|---|---|---|---|
| | time (sec) | MaxV$_{\geqslant 1}$ iters | MaxU$_{\geqslant 1}$ iters | time (sec) | MaxV$_{\geqslant 1}$ iters | MaxU$_{\geqslant 1}$ iters |
| 10 | 119 | 99 | 583 | 56.4 | 15 | 97 |
| 26 | 56.2 | 40 | 261 | 31.3 | 9 | 83 |
| 50 | 37.6 | 22 | 156 | 24.0 | 6 | 65 |
| 100 | 136 | 13 | 120 | 720 | 8 | 94 |
| 808 | 11,240 | 4 | 89 | 23,276 | 5 | 115 |

**Table 2.** Model sizes (and generation times in seconds) for CSMA/CD protocol.

| $D$ ($\mu s$) | $z.\mathcal{P}_{\sim \lambda}[\lozenge(\text{done} \wedge z \leqslant D)]$ | | | | $\mathcal{P}_{\leqslant \lambda}[\lozenge \text{exceeded}]$ | | digital clocks [20] |
|---|---|---|---|---|---|---|---|
| | maximum $[\sim\ =\ \leqslant]$ | | minimum $[\sim\ =\ \geqslant]$ | | | | |
| 1600 | 431 | (83.8) | 451 | (58.2) | 362 | (18.6) | 4,501,705 |
| 2000 | 725 | (125) | 691 | (75.6) | 562 | (29.4) | 6,570,692 |
| 2400 | 997 | (153) | 1,075 | (151) | 882 | (77.2) | 8,654,692 |
| 2800 | 1,263 | (205) | 1,435 | (284) | 1,182 | (158) | 10,738,692 |

**CSMA/CD Protocol.** The CSMA/CD (Carrier Sense, Multiple Access with Collision Detection) protocol is designed for networks with a single channel and specifies the behaviour of stations with the aim of minimising simultaneous use of the channel (data collision). The basic structure of the protocol is as follows: when a station has data to send, it listens to the medium, after which, if the medium was free (no one transmitting), the station starts to send its data. On the other hand, if the medium was sensed busy, the station waits a random amount of time and then repeats this process. For the case study we have supposed that the random choice is a uniform choice between two delays. Further details are available from the PRISM web page [23].

The first property we check is that the minimum probability that both stations correctly deliver their packets is 1; that is, we verify $\mathcal{P}_{\geqslant 1}[\lozenge \text{ done}]$. The algorithm MaxV$_{\geqslant 1}$ returns no symbolic states, which implies that the minimum probability is 1. In Table 1 we give the model-checking statistics for MaxV$_{\geqslant 1}$ as we vary the parameter $c$ (26 and 808 are the smallest and largest non-zero constants appearing in the model). As in the non-probabilistic case [27], further investigations and case studies are needed to establish if there is any way of finding a 'good' choice for the parameter $c$ in advance.

The remaining properties we consider are the maximum and minimum probabilities that both stations deliver their packets by time $D$, that is, the property $z.\mathcal{P}_{\sim \lambda}[\lozenge(\text{done} \wedge z \leqslant D)]$. Using the observation given in Remark 1 and the results for $\mathcal{P}_{\geqslant 1}[\lozenge \text{ done}]$, we also compute the minimum probabilities via a translation into a computation of maximum probabilities. In Table 2 we have presented the model sizes (and generation times) of the finite-state probabilistic system generated by our implementation and, for comparison, the size of the model constructed using the digital clocks approach [17, 21] (there are no generation times in this case as the digital semantics leads directly to a finite-state system).

**Table 3.** Statistics for $\text{MaxV}_{\geqslant 1}$ as $c$ varies, when verifying $I_1^P$.

| $c$ | $\mathcal{P}_{\geqslant 1}[\lozenge \text{ elect}]$ | | | $z.\mathcal{P}_{\geqslant \lambda}[\lozenge(\text{elect} \wedge z \leqslant 10000)]$ | | |
|---|---|---|---|---|---|---|
| | time (sec) | $\text{MaxV}_{\geqslant 1}$ iters | $\text{MaxU}_{\geqslant 1}$ iters | time (sec) | $\text{MaxV}_{\geqslant 1}$ iters | $\text{MaxU}_{\geqslant 1}$ iters |
| 10 | 21.26 | 372 | 1,492 | 13.3 | 85 | 373 |
| 100 | 2.63 | 39 | 162 | 3.96 | 18 | 95 |
| 360 | 1.22 | 13 | 67 | 1.84 | 7 | 55 |
| 1,670 | 0.646 | 5 | 30 | 1.76 | 5 | 46 |
| 5,000 | 0.479 | 3 | 24 | 1.07 | 3 | 34 |
| 10,000 | 0.571 | 3 | 31 | 1.19 | 3 | 41 |

**Table 4.** Model sizes and (generation times in seconds) when verifying $I_1^P$.

| $D$ ($10^3$ns) | $z.\mathcal{P}_{\geqslant \lambda}[\lozenge(\text{elect} \wedge z \leqslant D)]$ | | $\mathcal{P}_{\leqslant \lambda}[\lozenge \text{exceeded}]$ | | forwards [7] | digital clocks [20] |
|---|---|---|---|---|---|---|
| 2 | 15 | (1.09) | 25 | (0.197) | 53 (0.00) | 68,056 |
| 4 | 25 | (1.20) | 47 | (0.280) | 131 (0.00) | 220,565 |
| 8 | 81 | (1.38) | 126 | (0.615) | 372 (0.02) | 530,965 |
| 10 | 126 | (1.65) | 183 | (1.09) | 526 (0.03) | 686,165 |
| 20 | 528 | (12.2) | 643 | (19.3) | 1,876 (0.09) | 1,462,165 |
| 40 | 2,168 | (886) | 2,395 | (1,333) | 7,034 (0.46) | 3,014,165 |

The results show a significant decrease in the model size when compared to the digital clocks approach. Comparing the results for $z.\mathcal{P}_{\geqslant \lambda}[\lozenge(\text{done} \wedge z \leqslant D)]$ and $\mathcal{P}_{\leqslant \lambda}[\lozenge \text{exceeded}]$, we see that using Remark 1 can decrease both the states and generation time. Table 1 includes the model-checking statistics for the $\text{MaxV}_{\geqslant 1}$ algorithm when verifying $z.\mathcal{P}_{\sim \lambda}[\lozenge(\text{done} \wedge z \leqslant 2000)]$.

**FireWire Root Contention Protocol.** We consider the abstract probabilistic timed automaton model $I_1^P$, which is a probabilistic extension of the classical timed automaton $I_1$ of [25], as studied in [7, 21]. The timing constraints are derived from those given in the standard when the communication delay is 360ns. The properties we consider concern the minimum probability to elect a leader with and without a deadline, that is, the properties $\mathcal{P}_{\geqslant \lambda}[\lozenge \text{ elect}]$ and $z.\mathcal{P}_{\geqslant \lambda}[\lozenge(\text{elect} \wedge z \leqslant D)]$.

When verifying $\mathcal{P}_{\geqslant \lambda}[\lozenge \text{ elect}]$, the algorithm $\text{MaxV}_{\geqslant 1}$ returns no symbolic states, which implies that the minimum probability is 1. In Table 3 we give the model-checking statistics for the $\text{MaxV}_{\geqslant 1}$ algorithm as the value of $c$ changes (360 and 1670 are the smallest and largest non-zero constants appearing in the model). In Table 4 we have reported on the size and generation times in seconds when verifying $z.\mathcal{P}_{\geqslant \lambda}[\lozenge(\text{elect} \wedge z \leqslant D)]$ for a range of deadlines. As for the CSMA/CD case study, we can use Remark 1 and instead verify $\mathcal{P}_{\leqslant \lambda}[\lozenge \text{exceeded}]$ on a modified model. Additionally, in Table 4 we include the results obtained when applying the forwards approach [18, 7] and using digital clocks [21]. Note that the approach of [18, 7] cannot be used to calculate the minimum probability of eventually electing a leader. The results show that the use of the algorithms presented in this paper leads to a smaller state space than the other approaches.

The generation times for our prototype implementation are considerably greater than those obtained with the forwards approach as these are generated with the optimized tool KRONOS. Comparing the results obtained when verifying $z.\mathcal{P}_{\geqslant\lambda}[\Diamond(\text{elect} \wedge z\leqslant D)]$ and $\mathcal{P}_{\leqslant\lambda}[\Diamond\text{exceeded}]$, we see that the direct approach leads to a smaller state space and, for large deadlines, is faster than the approach based on Remark 1.

## 7    Conclusions

We have presented the theoretical foundations for the symbolic model checking of probabilistic timed automata and PTCTL and validated them through a prototype implementation using DBMs. For quantitative formulae, our algorithm is expensive, as, in the worst case, the MaxU algorithm constructs the powerset of the region graph, which itself is exponential in the largest constant used in zones and the number of clocks. However, for the case studies considered, we observe much smaller state spaces than this upper bound, which confirms that the algorithms are feasible in practice. Note that we do not construct a partition of the state space (as in [2], for example), but rather a (property dependent) set of overlapping symbolic states to avoid potentially expensive disjunction operations on zones within MaxU.

Future work will address the efficient symbolic implementation of the presented algorithms, adaptations to probabilistic polyhedral hybrid automata and symbolic probabilistic systems [19], and a comparison of our approach with state partitioning techniques, for example [2], extended to the probabilistic setting.

## References

1. Alur, R., Courcoubetis, C., and Dill, D. Model checking in dense real time. *Information and Computation*, 104(1):2–34, 1993.
2. Alur, R., Courcoubetis, C., Dill, D. L., Halbwachs, N., and Wong-Toi, H. Minimization of timed transition systems. In *Proc. CONCUR'92*, volume 630 of *LNCS*. Springer, 1992.
3. Alur, R. and Dill, D. L. A theory of timed automata. *Theoretical Computer Science*, 126(2):183–235, 1994.
4. Behrmann, G., David, A., Larsen, K., Möller, O., Pettersson, P., and Yi, W. UPPAAL - present and future. In *Proc. CDC'01*. IEEE, 2001.
5. Bianco, A. and de Alfaro, L. Model checking of probabilistic and nondeterministic systems. In *Proc. FST&TCS'95*, volume 1026 of *LNCS*, pages 499–513. Springer, 1995.
6. Daws, C. Private communication. 2004.
7. Daws, C., Kwiatkowska, M., and Norman, G. Automatic verification of the IEEE 1394 root contention protocol with KRONOS and PRISM. *International Journal on Software Tools for Technology Transfer*, 5(2–3):221–236, 2004.
8. Daws, C., Olivero, A., Tripakis, S., and Yovine, S. The tool KRONOS. In *Proc. Hybrid Systems III*, volume 1066 of *LNCS*, pages 208–219. Springer, 1996.
9. de Alfaro, L. *Formal Verification of Probabilistic Systems*. PhD thesis, Stanford University, 1997.

10. Dill, D. Timing assumptions and verification of finite-state concurrent systems. In *Proc. Automatic Verification Methods for Finite State Systems*, volume 407 of *LNCS*, pages 197–212. Springer, 1990.

11. Hansson, H. and Jonsson, B. A logic for reasoning about time and reliability. *Formal Aspects of Computing*, 6(4):512–535, 1994.

12. Henzinger, T., Nicollin, X., Sifakis, J., and Yovine, S. Symbolic model checking for real-time systems. *Information and Computation*, 111(2):193–244, 1994.

13. IEEE 1394-1995. High Performance Serial Bus Standard. 1995.

14. IEEE 802.3-2002. Carrier Sense Multiple Access with Collision Detection (CSMA/CD) Standard. 2002.

15. Kemeny, J., Snell, J., and Knapp, A. *Denumerable Markov Chains*. Springer, 1976.

16. Kwiatkowska, M., Norman, G., and Parker, D. PRISM: Probabilistic symbolic model checker. In *Proc. TOOLS'02*, volume 2324 of *LNCS*, pages 200–204. Springer, 2002.

17. Kwiatkowska, M., Norman, G., Parker, D., and Sproston, J. Performance analysis of probabilistic timed automata using digital clocks. In *Proc. FORMATS'03*, volume 2791 of *LNCS*, pages 105–120. Springer, 2003.

18. Kwiatkowska, M., Norman, G., Segala, R., and Sproston, J. Automatic verification of real-time systems with discrete probability distributions. *Theoretical Computer Science*, 282:101–150, 2002.

19. Kwiatkowska, M., Norman, G., and Sproston, J. Symbolic computation of maximal probabilistic reachability. In *Proc. CONCUR '01*, volume 2154 of *LNCS*, pages 169–183. Springer, 2001.

20. Kwiatkowska, M., Norman, G., and Sproston, J. Probabilistic model checking of the IEEE 802.11 wireless local area network protocol. In *Proc. PAPM/PROBMIV'02*, volume 2399 of *LNCS*, pages 169–187. Springer, 2002.

21. Kwiatkowska, M., Norman, G., and Sproston, J. Probabilistic model checking of deadline properties in the IEEE 1394 FireWire root contention protocol. *Formal Aspects of Computing*, 14:295–318, 2003.

22. Kwiatkowska, M., Norman, G., and Sproston, J. Symbolic model checking for probabilistic timed automata. Technical Report CSR-03-10, School of Computer Science, University of Birmingham, 2003.

23. PRISM Web site. www.cs.bham.ac.uk/~dxp/prism.

24. Segala, R. *Modelling and Verification of Randomized Distributed Real Time Systems*. PhD thesis, Massachusetts Institute of Technology, 1995.

25. Simons, D. and Stoelinga, M. Mechanical verification of the IEEE 1394a root contention protocol using Uppaal2k. *Springer International Journal of Software Tools for Technology Transfer*, 3(4):469–485, 2001.

26. Tripakis, S. *L'Analyse Formelle des Systèmes Temporisés en Pratique*. PhD thesis, Université Joseph Fourier, 1998.

27. Wang, F., Hwang, G.-D., and Yu, F. TCTL inevitability analysis of dense-time systems. In *Proc. CIAA'03*, volume 2759 of *LNCS*, pages 176–187. Springer, 2003.

# Structured Modeling
# of Concurrent Stochastic Hybrid Systems*

Mikhail Bernadsky, Raman Sharykin, and Rajeev Alur

University of Pennsylvania

**Abstract.** We propose a modeling language for structured specification of interacting components with both hybrid and stochastic dynamics. The behavior of a stochastic hybrid agent is described using a hybrid automaton whose dynamics is specified by stochastic differential equations and probabilistic jumps. Stochastic hybrid agents interact with other agents using shared variables. The operations of parallel composition, instantiation and hiding are defined to allow hierarchical descriptions of complex agents. We report on a stochastic extension of the modeling environment CHARON for hybrid systems, a simulation tool, and case studies using the tool.

## 1 Introduction

Hybrid systems models combine discrete dynamics expressed using extended state machines with continuous dynamics expressed using algebraic and differential equations (see [15, 1, 14, 3] for sample models). In many applications, from embedded avionics controllers to biomolecular gene regulatory networks, there is some uncertainty inherent in the physical world that can be most appropriately described using stochastic concepts. In this paper, we extend the hybrid systems modeling with stochastic constructs for both continuous evolution and discrete switching.

Stochastic modeling is an extensively studied area. Models such as Piecewise Deterministic Markov Processes [6], Switched Diffusion Processes [8], and Stochastic Hybrid Systems [11] allow integrating discrete switching, continuous dynamics, and stochastic behavior in some manner (see [20] for a recent overview). The previous research in this area has focussed on mathematical properties such as computing the distributions for switching times. Our motivation is orthogonal, namely, developing a modeling language that will allow modular descriptions of complex systems. Modular descriptions with compositional semantics has been a central theme in concurrency theory dating back to process algebras such as CCS [17] and CSP [10]. Modularity has been studied, and exploited by analysis tools, for hybrid systems (for example, Charon [2], hybrid I/O automata [14]), and for timed probabilistic systems (c.f. [13, 5]). However, we are not aware of any concurrency formalisms that allow continuous evolution using stochastic differential equations.

* This research was supported by NSF award ITR/SY 0121431.

Y. Lakhnech and S. Yovine (Eds.): FORMATS/FTRTFT 2004, LNCS 3253, pp. 309–324, 2004.
© Springer-Verlag Berlin Heidelberg 2004

We develop our model by extending the modeling language CHARON, a design environment for specification and analysis of embedded systems [3, 2]. In CHARON, the building block for describing the system architecture is an *agent* that communicates with its environment via shared variables. The language supports the operations of *composition* of agents to model concurrency, *hiding* of variables to restrict sharing of information, and *instantiation* of agents to support reuse. The stochastic extension of CHARON retains this hierarchical structure. A stochastic agent has private, output, and input variables, and its behavior is described using modes. A mode is annotated with stochastic differential equations that specify the continuous evolution of variables, and invariants that specify the region of the state-space where the current dynamics is valid. Mode switches are triggered when the invariant is violated, and are specified by probabilistic jumps with discrete distributions over the target modes and continuous distributions over the updated states.

In Section 2, we present our notion of a stochastic hybrid agent, define the underlying stochastic process for closed agents, and define the operations on agents. In Section 3, we describe the prototype implementation in CHARON, along with the simulation tool. In Section 4, we present two modeling case studies and simulation-based analysis. The first example, inspired by the case study in [9], involves maneuvers by two aircrafts, and we estimate the minimum distance between them using simulations. The second example, inspired by the case study in [18], models power management strategy in a hard drive, and we use simulations to estimate the average power consumption.

## 2     Model

In this section we give a definition of an *agent* – a formal description of a component in a hybrid system, define its execution, specify conditions when execution is a stochastic process, and state the properties of this process.

Let $\mathbb{R}^n$, $n \geq 1$ be the $n$-dimensional space of reals. For a finite set $X$ of variables, each of which ranges over $\mathbb{R}$, $V(X) = \mathbb{R}^{|X|}$ is the valuation space of $X$, and $\Delta(X)$ is the set of all open convex sets in $V(X)$. Given a set $U$, we denote by $\partial U$ its boundary. Our modeling of continuous-time stochastic evolution builds on standard models of white noise: we use $W_t^n$ to denote the $n$-dimensional standard Wiener process, the generalized derivative of this process is called the *Gaussian white noise*.

To be able to define *probability measures* on the state space of an agent, let us briefly review some terminology. Suppose that $\Omega$ is a set and $\mathcal{T}$ is a topology on $\Omega$. Then for the topological space $(\Omega, \mathcal{T})$ the minimal $\sigma$-algebra which is generated by the open sets of $\mathcal{T}$ is called the *Borel $\sigma$-algebra* and denoted by $\mathcal{B}(\Omega)$. Recall that for $\mathbb{R}^n$ there exists the *usual topology* $\mathcal{T}_{\mathbb{R}^n}$ induced by all open rectangles in $\mathbb{R}^n$, and that for any finite set $Q$ we can consider the *discrete topology* $\mathcal{T}_Q$ such that every subset of $Q$ is, by definition, open in $\mathcal{T}_Q$. We denote by $\mathcal{B}(\mathbb{R}^n)$ and $\mathcal{B}(Q)$ Borel $\sigma$-algebras of $(\mathbb{R}^n, \mathcal{T}_{\mathbb{R}^n})$ and $(Q, \mathcal{T}_Q)$ respectively. Now we define $\mathcal{B}(Q \times \mathbb{R}^n)$ to be the *product topology* $\mathcal{T}_{Q \times \mathbb{R}^n} =$

$\{U_1 \times U_2 : U_1 \text{ is open in } \mathcal{T}_Q, U_2 \text{ is open in } \mathcal{T}_{\mathbb{R}^n}\}$. The space $Q \times \mathbb{R}^n$ and its $\sigma$-algebra $\mathcal{B}(Q \times \mathbb{R}^n)$ form a *measurable space* and therefore we can define probability measures on $(Q \times \mathbb{R}^n, \mathcal{B}(Q \times \mathbb{R}^n))$ in the standard way (c.f. [6]).

**Definition 1.** *An agent $A$ is a tuple $(Q, X^p, X^o, X^e, Inv, F, G, Init, Jump)$ where*

- *$Q$ is a finite set of modes;*
- *$X^p$ is a finite set of private variables;*
- *$X^o$ is a finite set of observable variables (or outputs); let $X^c = X^p \cup X^o$ be the set of controlled variables;*
- *$X^e$ is a finite set of external variables (or inputs); let $X = X^c \cup X^e$ be the set of all variables.*
- *$Inv : Q \to \Delta(X)$ maps each mode $q$ to an invariant on the variables of the agent.*
  *Let $S = Q \times V(X)$ be the set of all states, $S^c = Q \times V(X^c)$ be the set of controlled states, and $D = \cup_{q \in Q}(q \times Inv(q))$, $D \subseteq S$ be the set of states satisfying the invariant.*
- *$F = \{f_x : D \to \mathbb{R} | x \in X^c\}$ and $G = \{g_x : D \to \mathbb{R}^{|X^c|} | x \in X^c\}$ are sets of functions specified for every variable in $X^c$. Each $f_x(\cdot, \cdot) \in F$ and $g_x(\cdot, \cdot) \in G$ is bounded and Lipschitz continuous in the second argument;*
- *$Init : \mathcal{B}(S^c) \to [0,1]$ is an initial probability measure on $(S^c, \mathcal{B}(S^c))$;*
- *$Jump : S \setminus D \to (\mathcal{B}(S^c) \to [0,1])$ is called jump measure and maps every state $s$, $s \in S \setminus D$, to a probability measure on $(S^c, \mathcal{B}(S^c))$. We require that for a fixed $U \in \mathcal{B}(S^c)$, $Jump(\cdot)(U)$ is a measurable function.*

Private and observable variables are controlled by the agent. Each external variable $x \in X^e$ is an observable variable of some other agent $A_x$, and similarly the observable variables in $X^o$ may be external variables of other agents. Such shared variables allow interaction among the agents. On the other hand, the variables in $X^p$ are private, and their evolutions are hidden from the other agents. We say that a state $s \in S$ is a *flow state* if $s \in D$ and a *jump state* otherwise. An agent $A$ is called *closed* iff $X^e = \emptyset$. Notice, that in this case $S = S^c$. In Section 2.2 we introduce the *composition* operation that allows the combination of all agents of a hybrid system into a single closed agent.

The *execution* of a closed agent $A$ is the evolution of its (controlled) variables over time. Initially, the valuations for the variables in $X^c$ are chosen according to the probability measure $Init$. In a flow state $s = (q, y) \in D$ the dynamics of the variables in $X^c$ coincides with a (continuous) realization of an $n$-dimensional Itô diffusion $\bar{x}(t) = (x_1(t), \ldots, x_n(t))$, $n = |X^c|$, $x_i(t)$ corresponds to a variable $x_i \in X^c$. The diffusion is defined by the system of stochastic differential equations (SDEs):

$$dx_i(t) = f_{x_i}(q, \bar{x}(t))dt + g_{x_i}(q, \bar{x}(t))dW_t^n, \; i = 1, \ldots, n .$$

The conditions on the functions in $F$ and $G$ guarantee the existence and uniqueness of the diffusion (see, for example, [19]). Since $\bar{x}(t)$ is Markov, we can choose the initial condition to be $\bar{x}(0) = y$. During this evolution the mode $q$ stays unchanged.

If $A$ reaches a jump state $s$ then the next state $s_{new}$ is chosen according to the probability measure $Jump(s)(\cdot)$. The state $s_{new} = (q_{new}, y_{new})$ may be either a flow or a jump state. If it is a flow state then the evolution is determined, as before, by the corresponding SDEs with the initial condition $\bar{x}(0) = y_{new}$; if it is a jump state then the next state is chosen according to $Jump(s_{new})(\cdot)$. A sequence of successive jump states in an execution is called a *jump sequence*. We assume that jump sequences occur instantaneously.

To exclude aberrant executions we introduce the following definition.

**Definition 2.** *A closed agent $A$ is* well-formed *if it satisfies the following:*

- *A flow state is reachable from every jump state in a finite number of jumps with probability one. Thus every jump sequence almost surely terminates.*
- *Expectation of $N_t$, which is the number of jump sequences in $[0, t]$, is finite for all $t$. This condition guarantees time-divergence.*

There exist sufficient tests to verify the conditions above. For example, the first condition is satisfied if $\exists \varepsilon > 0$ such that for all jump states $s \in S \setminus D$, $Jump(s)(D) > \varepsilon$. The second condition is satisfied if $\exists \varepsilon, \delta : \varepsilon > 0, 0 \leq \delta < 1$ such that for every jump state $s_{jump}$, $Jump(s_{jump})(S \setminus D_\varepsilon) = 1$, where $D_\varepsilon = \{s \in D | Pr(t_*(s) < \varepsilon) > \delta\}$, $t_*(s)$ is the time required for the diffusion to reach $\partial D$ from $s$. The requirement ensures that if a flow state $s$ is reached then, with strictly positive probability, the next jump state will be reached only after the time $t_*(s) \geq \varepsilon$ elapses.

The execution of a well-formed agent $A$ can be seen as a trajectory of a stochastic process $P_A$. The state space of $P_A$ is $S$. The initial state $s_{init} = (q_{init}, y_{init})$ is chosen according to $Init$. Without loss of generality, we assume that $s_{init}$ is a flow state. Starting from $s_{init}$, the process continuously evolves in the mode $q_{init}$. Suppose there is a stopping time $T_1$ such that $\bar{x}(T_1^-) = \lim_{t \uparrow T_1} \bar{x}(t)$ and $(q_{init}, \bar{x}(T_1^-))$ is a jump state. Now $P_A$ starts a jump sequence. The jump sequences are Markov chains on the continuous space that are stopped when they reach a state in $D$. For every $s \in S \setminus D, U \in \mathcal{B}(D)$ we define transition kernel $K(s, U)$, which is the probability to reach $U$ starting from $s$. In general we may have a sequence of stopping times $T_1, \ldots, T_m, \ldots$ such that during an interval $[T_i, T_{i+1})$ the process continuously evolves in a mode $q_i$, and these continuous evolutions are "glued" together by $K(\cdot, \cdot)$. Applying results from [16] (as shown in [4]) we obtain:

**Theorem 1.** *For a well-formed stochastic hybrid agent $A$, $P_A$ is a right continuous strong Markov process.*

## 2.1   Relation to Other Models

In this section we briefly look at other stochastic hybrid models considered in [20] and show (informally) how they can be expressed in our framework. It should be noted that none of the models have a notion of inputs, outputs, and composition.

*Piecewise Deterministic Markov Processes.* A PDMP $P$ (see [6]) is a tuple $(Q, d, Inv, f, Init, \lambda, Jump)$ where $Q$ is a countable set of modes, each $q \in Q$ is associated with its invariant $Inv(q)$, which is an open set in $\mathbb{R}^{d(q)}$. Let $D = \cup_{q \in Q}(q \times Inv(q))$ then the state space of $P$ is $S = D \cup \partial D$. The initial state is chosen according to the probability measure $Init$ concentrated on $D$. A Lipschitz vector field $f : D \to \mathbb{R}^{d(\cdot)}$ gives deterministic dynamics $d\bar{x}(t) = f(q, \bar{x}(t))dt$ for $P$ in $D$. The process makes a jump in two cases: when it reaches the boundary of the invariant and according to a generalized Poisson process with a transition rate function $\lambda : S \to \mathbb{R}^+$. The state after a jump is chosen according to a probability measure $Jump : S \to (\mathcal{B}(D) \to [0, 1])$; the probability measure depends on the state before the jump and is concentrated on $D$.

For $P$ to be well-defined, Davis assumes that for any $t \geq 0$, $E(N_t) < \infty$ where $N_t$ is the number of jumps in the time interval $[0, t]$.

Our framework allows modeling of a PDMP with a finite number of modes as a well-formed agent. Modeling of $Q$, $d$, $Inv$, $f$, $Init$, and $Jump$ is straightforward. To model Poisson switches we can use the following trick inspired by [6]: Suppose we are given a Poisson process $R$ with rate function $\lambda(\bar{x}(t))$, $\bar{x}(t)$ is an $n$-dimensional flow. It is known that the survivor function for a jump time $T$ of $R$ is

$$S(t) = Pr(T > t) = e^{-\int_0^t \lambda(\bar{x}(s))ds} .$$

We can simulate a random variable $T$ with the survival function $S(t)$ by generating a random variable $U$ uniformly distributed on $[0, 1]$ and setting $T = S^{-1}(U)$. Equivalently, $T = \inf\{t : S(t) \leq U\}$ ($S(t)$ is a decreasing function). Now to simulate the time of a jump we generate $U$ and define the process $Z(t) = -U + e^{-\int_0^t \lambda(\bar{x}(s))ds}$. When $Z(t)$ hits 0, a jump occurs. We can model $Z(t)$ using an algebraic variable and $U$ by modifying the jump measure.

*Switching Diffusion Processes.* A SDP $P$ (see [8]) is a tuple $(Q, S, f, \sigma, Init, \lambda_{ij})$. The state space of $P$ is $S = Q \times \mathbb{R}^n$, $Q$ is a finite set of modes. The initial state is chosen according to the probability measure $Init$ on $S$. For each mode $q \in Q$, the evolution of $P$ is given by the continuous solution of the SDEs: $d\bar{x}(t) = f(q, \bar{x}(t))dt + \sigma(q, \bar{x}(t))dW_t^n$. Transitions between modes happen according to a compound Poisson process and the transition rate function for switching between modes $q_i$ and $q_j$ is $\lambda_{ij} : S \to \mathbb{R}^+$. Notice that switches affect only the current mode – the trajectory in $\mathbb{R}^n$ remains continuous.

$P$ can be modeled in our framework. The components $Q$, $S$, $f$, $\sigma$, $Init$ have their immediate counterparts and for $\lambda_{ij}$ we can apply the same trick as we used for PDMPs.

*Stochastic Hybrid Systems.* A SHS $P$ (see [11]) is a tuple $(Q, S, Inv, f, \sigma, Init, G, Jump)$. The state space is $S = Q \times \mathbb{R}^n$, $Q$ is a countable set of modes. The map $Inv$ assigns each $q \in Q$ with an open set $Inv(q)$ in $\mathbb{R}^n$. Let $D = \cup_{q \in Q}(q \times Inv(q))$. The initial state is chosen according to the probability measure $Init$ concentrated on $D$. The dynamics in $D$ is given by the Lipschitz, bounded vector fields $f$ and $\sigma$: $d\bar{x}(t) = f(q, \bar{x}(t))dt + \sigma(q, \bar{x}(t))dW_t^n$. The process jumps when it reaches a point in $\partial D$. For each $q$ the map $G$ partitions $\partial Inv(q)$ into disjoint measurable sets $G(q, q')$, which called guards. For each pair of $q$ and $q'$, $Jump(q, q')$ maps every point $s \in G(q, q')$ to a corresponding probability measure on $S$ which is concentrated on $q' \times Inv(q')$.

We can model $P$ with a finite number of modes as a closed agent by specializing $Jump$ in our definition.

## 2.2   Operations

In this section we define three operations on the agents to facilitate structured description of systems.

Given an agent $A$ and variables $x \in X^o \cup X^e$, $x' \notin X$, we denote by $A[x := x']$ a new agent in which all occurrences of $x$ are replaced with the variable $x'$. This operation is called *renaming* and it is used to create instances of the same definition.

Being a component of a stochastic hybrid system, an agent interacts with other agents. In our framework an agent uses its observable and external variables as interface to the other agents. Suppose that a variable $x$ is an external variable of an agent $A$ and an observable variable of some other agent $A'$, then the evolution of $x$ in $A$ is completely determined and coincides with its evolution in $A'$. Thus observable variables provide output for the other agents, and external variables serve as the inputs from the rest of the system.

Suppose that the agents $A$ and $A'$ interact using two variables $x_1 \in X_A^o \cap X_{A'}^e$ and $x_2 \in X_{A'}^o \cap X_A^e$. A typical scenario is the following. The variables of both $A$ and $A'$ are initialized and evolve over the flow states. Then $A$ first reaches a jump state, the agent updates its state according to its jump measure. The value of $x_1$ changes in $A$. The new value of $x_1$ is not in the invariant of $A'$; therefore the state of $A'$ changes according to its jump measure. As a result, variable $x_2$ obtains a new value in $A'$ and $A$. If the new value of $x_2$ does not satisfy the invariant of $A$ then a new jump occurs. In general, there may be a (finite) sequence of jumps until the agents settle for the new flow states and the evolution of their variables becomes continuous again.

Before defining composition formally, we notice that the *Jump* relation of an agent can be extended to another relation $GJump$ defined on the entire state space $S$ of the agent, i.e. $GJump : S \rightarrow (\mathcal{B}(S^c) \rightarrow [0, 1])$. Given a set of variables $Y$ and a state $s = (q, y)$ in $S$, we denote by $y[Y]$ projection of $y$ on $V(Y)$. Then for every state $s = (q, y)$ and $U \in \mathcal{B}(S^c)$:

$$GJump(s)(U) = \begin{cases} Jump(s)(U) \text{ if } s \in S \setminus D, \\ 1 \qquad \text{if } s \in D \text{ and } (q, y[X^c]) \in U, \\ 0 \qquad \text{if } s \in D \text{ and } (q, y[X^c]) \notin U \ . \end{cases}$$

Suppose we are given two agents

$$A_k = (Q_k, X_k^p, X_k^o, X_k^e, Inv_k, F_k, G_k, Init_k, Jump_k), k = 1, 2 \ .$$

We want to define an agent $A$ which is the composition of $A_1$ and $A_2$ (we use notation $A = A_1 || A_2$). We require that $X_1^c \cap X_2^c = \emptyset$.

Let $X_{1\to2}$ and $X_{2\to1}$ be the set of variables that the agents use to interact, i.e. $X_{1\to2} = X_1^o \cap X_2^e$, and $X_{2\to1} = X_2^o \cap X_1^e$. Then $A$ is the tuple $(Q, X^p, X^o, X^e, Inv, F, G, Init, Jump)$ such that:

- $Q = Q_1 \times Q_2$;
- $X^p = X_1^p \cup X_2^p$;
- $X^o = X_1^o \cup X_2^o$ and $X^c = X_1^c \cup X_2^c$;
- $X^e = (X_1^e \cup X_2^e) \backslash (X_{1\to2} \cup X_{2\to1})$.
  As before, $X_k = X_k^c \cup X_k^e$, $S_k^c = Q_k \times V(X_k^c)$, for $k = 1, 2$; $X = X^c \cup X^e$, $S^c = Q \times V(X^c)$, $S = Q \times V(X)$, and $D = \cup_{q\in Q}(q \times Inv(q))$.
- Let $s = (q, y)$ be a state in $S$, $q = (q_1, q_2)$, $q_1 \in Q_1$ and $q_2 \in Q_2$. Then $y \in Inv(q)$ iff $y[X_1] \in Inv_1(q_1)$ and $y[X_2] \in Inv_2(q_2)$;
- $F = F_1 \cup F_2$ and $G = G_1 \cup G_2$;
- Let $U = U_1 \times U_2$, $U_k \in \mathcal{B}(S_k^c)$, $k = 1, 2$. Then $Init(U) = Init_1(U_1) \times Init_2(U_2)$. It is known, that we can uniquely extend $Init(\cdot)$ to the entire $\mathcal{B}(S^c)$.
- Let $s = (q, y)$ be a state in $S \backslash D$, $q = (q_1, q_2)$, $q_1 \in Q_1$ and $q_2 \in Q_2$. Then for $U = U_1 \times U_2$, $U_k \in \mathcal{B}(S_k^c)$, $k = 1, 2$:

$$Jump(s)(U) = GJump(q_1, y[X_1])(U_1) \times GJump(q_2, y[X_2])(U_2) \ .$$

Again, we are able to uniquely extend the product probability measure $Jump(s)(\cdot)$ to the entire $\mathcal{B}(S^c)$.

**Theorem 2.** *The composition operation is associative, i.e. for any agents $A_1$, $A_2$, $A_3$, $(A_1\|A_2)\|A_3$ and $A_1\|(A_2\|A_3)$ are isomorphic.*

Finally, we consider the *hiding* operation. Given an agent $A$ and an observable variable $x$, we write $A' = Hide\ x\ in\ A$. The agent $A'$ has the same structure as $A$ except its sets of private and observable variables are changed: $X_{A'}^p = X_A^p \cup \{x\}$ and $X_{A'}^o = X_A^o \backslash \{x\}$. This operation is useful to restrict the scoping of variables.

## 3 Implementation in Charon

Charon is a language for modular specification of interacting hybrid systems based on the notions of agents and modes. The language supports the operations of agent composition for concurrency, hiding of variables for information encapsulation, and instantiation of agents for reuse. For more details please visit http://www.cis.upenn.edu/mobies/charon/.

### 3.1 Charon Extension

**Syntax Extension.** To make Charon suitable for our purposes, we extended the current version with the syntax for specifying initial probability measures, jumps, and SDEs.

The syntax for specifying an invariant is: `inv <condition>` where condition depends on the variables of the agent.

The syntax for specifying a jump is:

```
jump from <source_mode> when <guard>
( to <destination_mode> do { <update_1>; ... ;<update_k> }
  weight <weight> )+
```

where the guard depends on the variables of the agent and defines a part of
the complement of the invariant assigned to the source mode. The union of all
guards of a mode must be equivalent to the complement of the invariant of
that mode, and the guards must be pairwise disjoint. A jump may have multiple
transition branches. Each branch is specified by its destination mode, a sequence
of updates, and the weight assigned to it. The weight can depend on the variables
of the agent. The probability for a branch to be executed is proportional to its
weight:

$$Pr(branch) = \frac{weight\ of\ the\ branch}{the\ sum\ of\ the\ weights\ of\ all\ branches}\ .$$

Updates <update_1>; ... ;<update_k> are assignments of the form
variable_name = f(...) where $f$ is a random variable whose distribution can
depend on the variables of the agent. The whole sequence of updates specifies
the probability measure on the set of the variable valuations of the destination
mode.

Random variables with the following predefined distributions can be used to
construct $f$:

- randExp(parameter) specifies exponential distribution;
- randNorm(mean,variance) specifies normal distribution;
- randUniform(begin,end) specifies uniform distribution on the interval
  [begin,end];
- randPareto(parameter_a,parameter_b) specifies Pareto distribution.

Random variables with arbitrary distributions can be obtained by calling
external Java functions.

The syntax for specifying a stochastic differential equation is:

```
SDE { d(<variable name>) == f(...)*dt + g(...)*dW(t) }
```

where $f(...)$ and $g(...)$ are functions which depend on the variables of the
agent.

To specify the initial probability measure we use the following syntax:

```
jump from default when true
(to <destination_mode> do { <update_1>; ... ;<update_k> }
 weight <weight>)+
```

which is similar to jumps but with the source mode defined by the keyword
default and the trivial guard.

A sample stochastic hybrid agent coded in Charon is shown in Fig. 1. The
agent system is composed of two agents: agent1 and agent2. The agent agent1
has an observable variable $y$ which becomes an observable variable of the composite agent system. The agent agent2 controls the dynamics for the external
variable $x$ of agent1.

```
agent system() {
    private variable x;

    agent agent1 = agent1();
    agent agent2 = agent2();
}


agent agent1() {
    external variable x;
    observable variable y;
    private variable z;

    mode mode1 = agent1_mode1()
    mode mode2 = agent1_mode2()
    mode mode3 = agent1_mode3()

    jump from default when true
        to mode1
            do { y = randUniform(1,2); z=0 }
    jump from mode1 when x=<0 || x>=2
        to mode2
            do { z = randUniform(2,3) } weight 2
        to mode3
            do { z = randUniform(1,2) } weight 3
    jump from mode2 when z=<0
        to mode1
    jump from mode3 when z=<0
        to mode1
}

mode agent1_mode1() {
    SDE { d(y) == 2*dt + dW(t) }
    SDE { d(z) == 0 }
    inv x>0 && x<2
}
```

```
mode agent1_mode2() {
    SDE { d(y) == dt + 3*dW(t) }
    SDE { d(z) == -dt }
    inv z>0
}

mode agent1_mode3() {
    SDE { d(y)=0 }
    SDE { d(z) == -dt }
    inv z>0
}


agent agent2() {
    observable variable x;

    mode mode1 = agent2_mode1();
    mode mode2 = agent2_mode2();

    jump from default when true
        to mode1
            do { x = 1 + randExp(0.5) }
    jump from mode1 when x=<0
        to mode2
            do { x = randExp(1) }
    jump from mode2 when x=<0
        to mode1
            do { x = randUniform(1,3) }
}

mode agent2_mode1() {
    SDE { d(x) == -dt + dW(t) }
    inv x>0
}

mode agent2_mode2() {
    SDE { d(x) == -2*dt + 3*dW(t) }
    inv x>0
}
```

**Fig. 1.** Sample stochastic hybrid system in charon syntax.

The initial probability measure for agent1 is defined in such a way that the agent always starts in mode1, $y$ is chosen according to the uniform distribution on $[1, 2]$, and $z$ is set to zero. In mode1 the dynamics of $y$ is specified by an SDE and $z$ remains constant.

When the value of the external variable $x$ is outside of the interval $(0, 2)$, the agent jumps to either mode2 with probability 2/5 or to mode3 with probability 3/5, as specified by the weights of these two branches. With this jump the agent picks a value for $z$ according to the distribution specified in the chosen branch of the transition. In mode2, the dynamics for $y$ is specified by another SDE and $z$ plays the role of a clock. It linearly decreases, and when it hits the boundary of the invariant $z > 0$, the agent jumps back to mode1. In mode3, $y$ remains constant, and $z$ plays the same role as in mode2. When $z$ becomes zero the agent jumps to mode1.

As defined in Fig. 1, agent2 has two modes: mode1 and mode2. It always starts in mode1 and jumps from mode1 to mode2 and back when $x$ hits the boundary of the corresponding invariant, and sets the new value of $x$ according to the specified distributions. The evolution of $x$ in each mode is given by a stochastic differential equation.

## 3.2 Simulator

Charon simulator consists of two main components: the part responsible for jumps and the part responsible for modeling stochastic differential equations.

To model a jump we need to pick a branch and execute the updates associated with the branch. For this, the simulator generates a random variable $N_B$ that determines which branch to choose. $N_B$ takes its values in the set $\{1, \ldots, k\}$, where $k$ is the number of branches in the transition. The probability to pick a particular value is proportional to the weight of the corresponding branch.

When a branch is chosen, the updates associated with the branch are executed. These updates can be constructed from random variables with exponential, normal, uniform, Pareto, or user-defined distributions.

To obtain realizations of solutions of stochastic differential equations the simulator uses Euler-Maruyama method. Consider a stochastic differential equation

$$dx(t) = f(\bar{x}(t))dt + g(\bar{x}(t))dW_t^n, \quad x(0) = x_0, \quad 0 \le t \le T .$$

The Euler-Maruyama simulation scheme of this SDE, over the interval $[0, T]$ divided into $L$ subintervals of the equal length $\Delta t$, has the form

$$x_k = x_{k-1} + f(\bar{x}_{k-1})\Delta t + g(\bar{x}_{k-1}) \cdot (W_{\tau_k}^n - W_{\tau_{k-1}}^n), \quad k = 1, \ldots, L$$

where $\tau_0 = 0$, $\tau_k = \tau_{k-1} + \Delta t$. Each of the $n$ components in the vector $W_{\tau_k}^n - W_{\tau_{k-1}}^n$ is simulated as a random variable $\sqrt{\Delta t}N(0, 1)$ where $N(0, 1)$ is a random variable with the standard normal distribution.

## 4     Examples

We present two examples in which we use Stochastic Charon to model a system and perform Monte-Carlo simulations to obtain statistical information. In the first example, we model a system of two aircrafts taking off simultaneously from two airports and estimate the probability that these aircrafts will come, during their flights, to a particular minimum distance. In the second example we simulate a model of a hard drive for three different values of a parameter which determines the power management policy and estimate the probability that a service request is lost.

In the examples we use the following notation presented in Fig. 2. When we write stay for randDistr(params) in a mode, we mean that when an agent enters the mode, we pick time according to the specified distribution and jump from the mode when that time has elapsed.

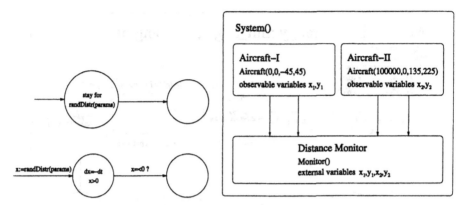

**Fig. 2.** Notation.                    **Fig. 3.** System of two aircrafts.

## 4.1   Air Traffic Control

Models for automatic air traffic management systems are important since they can be used for conflict prediction, conflict resolution, and validation of conflict detection and resolution strategies [9].

We model a pair of aircrafts flying from two airports located 100 kilometers apart. The motion of each aircraft is determined by the system of stochastic differential equations derived from the basic aerodynamics, and the stochastic part of the motion is due to the changing wind.

The aircrafts have their initial directions chosen randomly from a specified interval. During their flights each aircraft performs two turns to randomly chosen new directions. Using Monte-Carlo simulations we estimate the percentage of flights in which the minimum distance between the aircrafts reaches $r_{min}$ for $r_{min} = 1, \ldots, 50$ kilometers. The parameters of the model are realistic and taken from BADA database [7] for a particular aircraft. However, the flight trajectories are artificial and have the purpose to illustrate our framework.

**Aircraft Model.** We model Airbus A300-B4 flying at 20000 feet altitude with the speed $V = 250$ knots (130 m/sec). The system of SDEs we use to model the motion of the aircraft is due to [9]. Let $X$, $Y$, and $V$ denote the position of the aircraft and its speed. Let $\psi$ be the flight path angle, $\phi$ be the bank angle, and $\gamma$ be the angle of attack. Then the aircraft motion can be modeled by the following system of SDEs:

$$dX = V \cos(\psi) \sin(\gamma)dt + W_x dW_t$$
$$dY = V \sin(\psi) \sin(\gamma)dt + W_y dW_t$$
$$dh = V \sin(\gamma)dt$$
$$dV = (T/m - C_D S\rho V^2/2m - g\sin(\gamma))dt$$
$$d\psi = (C_L S\rho V \sin(\phi)/(2m))dt$$
$$dm = -\eta T dt$$

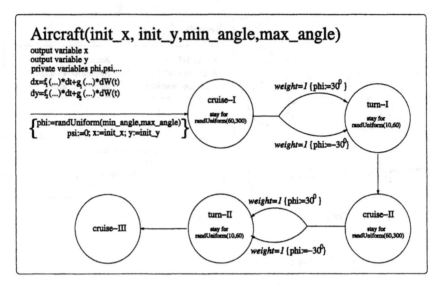

**Fig. 4.** Aircraft.

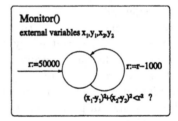

**Fig. 5.** Minimum distance monitor.

where the concrete parameters to use in the model can be found in BADA database.

Notice that the bank angle $\phi$ affects the path angle $\psi$, and therefore it can be used to change the direction of the flight.

**System.** The system is presented in Fig. 3. It consists of two instances of the same agent that models the dynamics of an aircraft. The aircrafts take off from the airports $A$ and $B$ and move towards each other. The distance between the airports is 100 kilometers. On $(x, y)$-plane the airport $A$ is located at the origin. The airport $B$ is located at $(100000, 0)$. These values are assigned to the positions of the aircrafts during instantiation of the aircraft agents in the composite agent system.

The agent that specifies the aircraft is shown in Fig. 4. It starts flying from the airport $A$ or $B$ depending on the initial parameters x_init and y_init. We consider only the flights in which the angle between the initial direction and the $x$-axis of the first aircraft is restricted to the interval $[-45^0, 45^0]$, and the angle of the second aircraft is restricted to the interval $[135^0, 225^0]$.

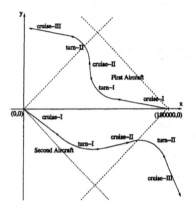

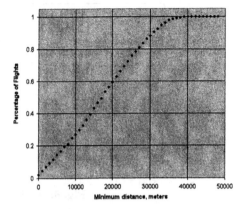

**Fig. 6.** Sample paths of the aircrafts.

**Fig. 7.** Percentage of the flights with a particular minimum distance.

After choosing the initial direction, the flight of each aircraft proceeds as follows. An aircraft flies in the cruise mode (without attempting to change the direction) for a duration of time distributed uniformly from 1 to 5 minutes. After that it performs a turn. The turn can be to the left or to the right with the equal probability. During the turn the bank angle $\phi$ is set either to $-30^0$ or to $30^0$ for the left or for the right turn respectively, as specified by BADA. The aircraft performs the turn for a random time, which is uniformly distributed from 10 to 60 seconds, providing a random new direction. After that it returns to the cruise mode and flies along the new direction for an additional duration distributed uniformly from 1 to 5 minutes. After that it performs the second identical turn and continues the final course. A sample motion of two aircrafts is depicted in Fig. 6. The Charon code for the example can be found at http://www.math.upenn.edu/~rsharyki/.

**Simulation.** The minimum distance is measured by the monitor presented in Fig. 5. It starts with the minimum distance equal to 50 kilometers and each time the distance becomes smaller than the current minimum distance the monitor updates it by subtracting one kilometer. At the end of the simulation, monitor's observable variable $r$ contains the minimum distance that appeared during the simulation. It has precision of 1 kilometer.

We performed 1000 simulation runs of the system evolving for 20 minutes to estimate the percentage of the flights during which the aircrafts will approach to a particular minimum distance.

The simulations took 3 hours on a Celeron 1.8 GHz laptop with 512 megabytes of memory. The results are presented in Fig. 7.

## 4.2   Hard Drive Modeling

Portable systems have very strict constraints on energy consumption. To reduce system's power consumption and increase the battery life, system-level dynamic

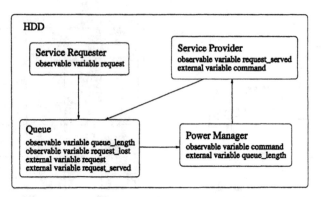

**Fig. 8.** Hard drive model.

power-management algorithms are used. These algorithms shut down idle running components and awake them when necessary.

A hard drive model presented in this section is adopted from [18]. The model in [18] uses constant jump rates between modes. To make it more precise, we specify jump rates according to the results in [21].

The structure of the system is depicted in Fig. 8. The system consists of four agents: Service Requester (SR), Queue (Q), Service Provider (SP), and Power Manager(PM). SR generates signal `request` to Q. The distribution of the time between consecutive requests is exponential. Q increases `queue_length` by one when it receives a request from SR. Q decreases `queue_length` when it receives a signal `request_served` from SP. If `queue_length` exceeds 20, the queue sets the signal `request_lost` to on. SP can be in two modes: active and stand-by. The time of the transitions from active to stand-by and from stand-by to active have uniform distributions. SP serves requests in active mode with the service time distributed exponentially. Stand-by mode is characterized by low energy consumption. PM's policy is the following one. SP starts in stand-by mode. PM watches the queue length. When the queue length reaches some particular value $Q_{on}$, PM issues command `go-to-active` to SP. When the queue length becomes zero PM issues command `go-to-standby` to SP. The Charon code for the example can be found at http://www.math.upenn.edu/~rsharyki/.

**Simulation.** We implemented the model of the hard drive described above in Charon and used Monte-Carlo simulations to estimate the percentage of the simulation runs during which a request is lost at time $t$ due to overflow of the queue for three different values of the awakening queue length parameter $Q_{on}$ of Power Manager.

The simulations took 6 hours and the results are presented in Fig. 9. The $x$-axis represents time and $y$-axis represents the estimated percentage of simulation runs during which a request has been lost up to this time. The three curves depict the results obtained for the values of the awakening queue length: $Q_{on} = 14$, $Q_{on} = 16$, and $Q_{on} = 18$. We performed 50 simulation runs for each value of

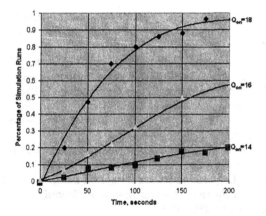

**Fig. 9.** Percentage of the simulation runs with a request lost up to a particular time.

the parameter. During the simulations the system was modeled for 200 seconds. As the results show, a slight change in the parameter $Q_{on}$ leads to considerable changes in the percentage of simulation runs during which a request has been lost.

## 5    Future Work

We have presented a modeling language that allows structured modeling of interacting stochastic hybrid components, and a prototype implementation in a simulation toolkit. Combining ideas from concurrency theory and theory of stochastic processes leads to a rich research agenda, and there are many directions for future work. First, developing a useful compositional semantics and refinement calculus in presence of all these features is a challenging problem. Second, we are investigating techniques for accurate event detection in simulating stochastic differential equations so that jumps are accurately simulated. Finally, we believe that systems biology will be a fruitful application domain for stochastic hybrid systems [12], and we are constructing models of gene regulatory processes in our toolkit.

## References

1. R. Alur, C. Courcoubetis, N. Halbwachs, T.A. Henzinger, P. Ho, X. Nicollin, A. Olivero, J. Sifakis, and S. Yovine. The algorithmic analysis of hybrid systems. *Theoretical Computer Science*, 138:3–34, 1995.
2. R. Alur, T. Dang, J. Esposito, Y. Hur, F. Ivancic, V. Kumar, I. Lee, P. Mishra, G. Pappas, and O. Sokolsky. Hierarchical modeling and analysis of embedded systems. *Proceedings of the IEEE*, 91(1), 2003.
3. R. Alur, R. Grosu, Y. Hur, V. Kumar, and I. Lee. Modular specifications of hybrid systems in CHARON. In *Hybrid Systems: Computation and Control, Third Intl. Workshop*, LNCS 1790, pages 6–19, 2000.

4. M. Bujorianu. Extended stochastic hybrid systems and their reachability problem. In *Hybrid Systems: Computation and Control, 7th Intl. Workshop*, LNCS 2993, pages 234–249, 2003.

5. P. D'Argenio, H. Hermanns, J.-P. Katoen, and R. Klaren. Modest - a modeling and description language for stochastic timed systems. In *Proc. of the PAPM-PROBMIV Joint Intl. Workshop*, LNCS 2165, pages 87–104, 2001.

6. M.H.A. Davis. *Markov processes and optimization.* Chapman & Hall, 1993.

7. Eurocontrol Experimental Centre. *User manual for the base of aircraft data (BADA) revision 3.3*, 2003.

8. M.K. Ghosh, A. Araposthasis, and S.I. Marcus. Ergodic control of switched diffusions. *SIAM Journal on Control Optimization*, 35(6):1952–1988, 1997.

9. W. Glover and J. Lygeros. A stochastic hybrid model for air traffic control simulation. In *Hybrid Systems: Computation and Control, Seventh Intl. Workshop*, LNCS 2993, pages 372–386, 2004.

10. C.A.R. Hoare. Communicating sequential processes. *Communications of the ACM*, 21(8):666–677, 1978.

11. J. Hu, J. Lygeros, and S. Sastry. Towards a theory of stochastic hybrid systems. In *Hybrid Systems: Computation and Control, Third Intl. Workshop*, LNCS 1790, pages 160–173, 2000.

12. P. Lincoln and A. Tiwari. Symbolic systems biology: Hybrid modeling and analysis of biological networks. In *Hybrid Systems: Computation and Control, 7th Intl. Workshop*, LNCS 2993, pages 660–672, 2004.

13. G. Lowe. Probabilistic and prioritized models of Timed CSP. *Theoretical Computer Science*, 138(2):315–332, 1995.

14. N.A. Lynch, R. Segala, and F.W. Vaandrager. Hybrid I/O automata. *Information and Computation*, 185(1):105–157, 2003.

15. O. Maler, Z. Manna, and A. Pnueli. From timed to hybrid systems. In *Real-Time: Theory in Practice, REX Workshop*, LNCS 600, pages 447–484, 1991.

16. P.A. Meyer. Renaissance, recollectments, mélanges, ralentissement de processus de markov. *Annales de l'institut Fourier*, 25(3-4):465–497, 1975.

17. R. Milner. *A Calculus of Communicating Systems*. LNCS 92. Springer, 1980.

18. G. Norman, D. Parker, M. Kwiatkowska, S. Shukla, and R. Gupta. Using probabilistic model checking for dynamic power management. In *Proc. of Third Workshop on Automated Verification of Critical Systems*, 2003.

19. B. Øksendal. *Stochastic Differential Equations.* Springer-Verlag, 2003.

20. G. Pola, M. Bujorianu, J. Lygeros, and M. Di Benedetto. Stochastic hybrid systems: An overview. In *Proc. of the IFAC Conference on Analysis and Design of Hybrid Systems*, pages 45–50, 2003.

21. T. Simunic, L. Behini, P. Glynn, and G. De Micheli. Dynamic power management for portable systems. In *Mobile computing and networking, 6th Intl. Conference*, 2000.

# Computing Schedules for Multithreaded Real-Time Programs Using Geometry

Philippe Gerner and Thao Dang

VERIMAG, Centre Équation, 2, av. de Vignate, 38610 Gières, France
{Philippe.Gerner,Thao.Dang}@imag.fr

**Abstract.** We describe a novel technique for computing efficient schedules for multi-threaded real-time programs. The technique makes use of abstractions which are constructed by embedding the model of the program in a geometric space and then constructing a decomposition of this space. This embedding uses the model of *PV diagrams*. We introduce a timed version for PV programs and diagrams, which allows us to define the worst-case response time of the schedules, and then to use the geometric abstractions for computing efficient schedules.

## 1 Introduction

With the decreasing cost of embedded systems, constructing "more intelligent" embedded systems becomes possible and now product designers ask for more functionalities from an embedded system. This increases the portion of the software in the system, to the point that some applications require programming with threads – that is, what was before designed as separate hardware components on a chip can now be conceived of as separate threads. These threads can then be executed on one or several (in the case of multiprocessing) hardware components. But parallel programming in the real-time context is rather new, and much work is to be done in order to be able to analyse the real-time behaviour of such programs. Indeed, simple extensions of existing analysis tools for sequential programs will not suffice: parallelism with threads involves purely parallel-specific phenomena like deadlocks. In this paper we examine the behaviour of a class of multi-threaded programs, from the point of view of the *worst-case response time* (WCRT). In order to address this complex issue, we employ a geometric approach, which enables us not only to better "see" what happens, but also to exploit the geometric nature of the model in order to deal with the problem of state explosion arising in the analysis of concurrent programs. We will also address the issue of scheduling parallel programs on a limited number of processors, using the same approach.

Our ideas of exploiting the geometry of parallel programs are inspired by the work on *PV diagrams*. This model for geometrically describing interactions of concurrent processes was introduced by Dijkstra [8]. It has been used, since the beginning of the 90's, for the analysis of concurrent programs [13,10] (see [15] for a good survey). In particular, in this paper, we follow the spirit of [10], where the geometry of the diagrams is used to construct an efficient analysis

Y. Lakhnech and S. Yovine (Eds.): FORMATS/FTRTFT 2004, LNCS 3253, pp. 325–342, 2004.

algorithm. We use the notion of *timed PV diagrams*, which can be used in the context of real-time concurrent programming. We focus on a particular problem: finding a schedule which is safe (no deadlocks), and quick – that is, though we are not looking for the quickest possible schedule, we want to find one which is as quick as possible within a reasonable computational time. The motivations for this are:

- the program under consideration might be part of a global system and subject to a deadline. However, if no precise timing analysis result is available, then to determine the worst-case response time of the program one must assume the worst case, i.e., all threads share a single protected resource (with a single access). This amounts to sequentialization of the threads, and the WCRT is the sum of the WCRT of each thread considered individually. This measure can easily be greater than the deadline, while the real worst case concurrent behaviour of the program is probably better. Here we are interested in analysing these real WCRT.
- Using our method, finding a deadlock-free schedule comes "for free" when looking for a quick schedule.
- Finally, in a more general consideration, we believe that if finding a quick schedule is computationally feasible, it is good investment to design systems using such efficient schedules. For example, by reducing the computation time one can reduce energy consumption.

The paper is structured as follows. In Section 2 we recall the concepts related to PV programs and diagrams. In the next section we describe our timed version of PV programs and diagrams, and we define the worst case response time for a schedule. In Section 4 we explain an abstraction of efficient schedules which can serve to find them. Section 5 describes how to construct this abstraction using the geometry of timed PV diagrams and a spatial decomposition method. In Section 6 the case when there are less processors than threads is treated. In Section 7 we describe some related work on timed PV diagrams and on the scheduling of concurrent programs. In Section 8 we conclude and present future work.

## 2    PV Programs and Diagrams

In this section we briefly present PV programs and PV diagrams. "P" and "V" are actions on semaphores: "P" is for "proberen", "to test" in Dutch, and "V" is for "verhogen" ("to increment"), as applied on Dijkstra semaphores. In this paper we adapt the vocabulary of PV programs to our application domain: we speak of "threads" instead of "processes", and we call a set of threads running together a "program" or a "PV program". In multithreaded programs vocabulary, P is for "lock", and V for "unlock" or "release". In PV programs, only lock and unlock actions are considered. The classical example of a PV program is shown in Fig. 1(a), where a and b are 1-semaphores. In this section and until Sec. 5 included we assume that the threads can always run concurrently, so a thread can run as soon as it gets all the shared resources it required. For example in the program of Fig. 1(a) we may assume that both threads A and B have their own processor to run on. The case were the threads have to share some processors is studied in Sec. 6.

PV programs have a geometric representation. The PV diagram of the Swiss flag program is shown in Fig. 1(b).

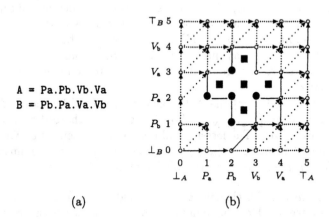

A = Pa.Pb.Vb.Va
B = Pb.Pa.Va.Vb

(a)                           (b)

**Fig. 1.** The Swiss flag program (a) and diagram (b); a schedule (b).

The meaning of the diagram is that a schedule for the program is represented by a sequence of arrows from the bottom left corner of the diagram, point $(\perp_A, \perp_B)$, to the top right corner, point $(\top_A, \top_B)$. Indeed, any possible schedule is a particular order of actions $(P$ or $V)$ of threads A and B. A schedule is shown in the diagram, drawn in solid arrows. In dotted line are all the other arrows that a schedule could follow. The black circles indicate the "forbidden points": those that are not possible in a schedule. For example, point $(2,1)$ is forbidden because its associated combination of actions $(P_b, P_b)$ means that both threads lock resource b at the same time, which is not possible since b is a 1-semaphore. The small black squares in the diagram mark "forbidden squares", which are the expansion of each forbidden point to the adjacent upper-right little square. The "Swiss flag" name of the example comes from the cross form of the union of these forbidden squares. The advantage of such diagrams is that they allow to visualize special behaviours of a program. In this example we can see two special cases: point $(1,1)$ is a *deadlock* and point $(3,3)$ is an *unreachable point*.

## 2.1   PV Programs and Diagrams: Formal Definitions

We now formalize the above explanation and provide the basis for our subsequent development of a timed version of PV programs and diagrams.

*Resources.* Shared resources are represented by a set $\Re$ of **resource names**. Each resource is protected by a **semaphore**. This is represented with a function *limit* : $\Re \to \mathbb{N}_+$. An **action** (by a thread) is the locking or unlocking of a resource $r$; such an action is denoted by $P_r$, resp. $V_r$.

*Threads.* We consider a set of $N$ **threads**, $E_1, \ldots, E_N$. Each thread $E_i$ is a total order of **events**. A thread event $e$ has one associated action, for example $P_r$. The order relation of $E_i$ is denoted by $\sqsubseteq_{E_i}$ and is also written simply $\sqsubseteq$ when no confusion is possible. Each thread $E_i$ contains at least two events: its *start event*, $\perp_{E_i}$, and its *end event*, $\top_{E_i}$, which are respectively the bottom and top elements of the order. The threads are *well-behaved*, in the sense that for each resource $r \in \Re$ the thread has form: $B^*(P_r B^* V_r)^* B^*$, where $B$ is the set of actions $P_{r'}$ or $V_{r'}$ with $r' \neq r$. We say that thread $i$ is **accessing** resource $r$ at event $e$ if and only if $P_r$ has occurred before or at $e$, and the corresponding release $V_r$ occurs (strictly) after $e$.

The running together of the $N$ threads is formalized by the product of the $N$ total orders, $\mathcal{E} = \prod_{i=1,\ldots,N} E_i$. We denote by $\preccurlyeq$ the order of $\mathcal{E}$, which is defined componentwise. The letter $\epsilon$ will denote an element of $\mathcal{E}$. We denote by $\perp$ the bottom element of $\mathcal{E}$, $(\perp_{E_1}, \ldots, \perp_{E_N})$ and by $\top$ its maximum element $(\top_{E_1}, \ldots, \top_{E_N})$. Elements of $\mathcal{E}$ are called **states**.

*Forbidden Elements.* An element $\epsilon$ of $\mathcal{E}$ is said to be *forbidden* if there is at least one resource to which the number of concurrent accesses is greater than its limit: $\exists r \in \Re \mid \sum_{i=1,\ldots,N} accessing_i(r, \epsilon) > limit(r)$, where $accessing_i(r, \epsilon) = 1$ if thread $E_i$ is accessing resource $r$ at $\epsilon_i$, 0 otherwise. We denote by $F$ the set of all forbidden elements of $\mathcal{E}$, and by $\mathcal{A}$ (for "allowed") the restriction of order $\mathcal{E}$ to non-forbidden elements.

*Strings and Schedules.* If $B$ is a partial order and $b, b' \in B$ are such that $b \sqsubseteq b'$, we call this couple of elements an "arc" or "arrow" and we denote it by $\langle b, b' \rangle$. Also, if $B$ is a total order and if $b \in B$ and $b \neq \perp_B$, then $pred_B(b)$ denotes the direct predecessor of $b$ in $B$ ($pred_B(b) \sqsubseteq b' \sqsubset b \implies b' = pred_B(b)$). When the order is clear from the context, we simply write $pred(b)$. An arrow $\langle \epsilon', \epsilon \rangle \in \preccurlyeq$ is called a *small step* if $\forall i = 1, \ldots, N$ : $pred(\epsilon_i) \sqsubseteq \epsilon'_i \sqsubseteq \epsilon_i$. For example, in the diagram of Fig. 1(b) the dotted arrows are small steps from $\preccurlyeq$.

**Definition 1.** *A* **string** *$s$ is a suborder of $\mathcal{A}$ which is total and such that for each element $\epsilon$ in $s \setminus \{\top_s\}$, arrow $\langle pred_s(\epsilon), \epsilon \rangle$ is a small step. A string $s$ with $\perp_s = \perp$ and $\top_s = \top$ is called a* **schedule**.

**Geometric Realization.** We call the mapping of a program and its schedules to a diagram and trajectories, its **geometric realization**. The idea is to map the set of schedules to trajectories inside an $N$-dimensional cube, going from the bottom left corner (for $\perp$) to the top right corner (for $\top$) of the cube. Since we want to stay in the discrete world, we describe geometric realization in $\mathbb{Z}^N$. We use notation "$\overline{\phantom{-}}$" for the mapping; hence, $\overline{s}$ is the image of string $s$ by this mapping. We map threads $E_i$ onto a subset of $\mathbb{N}$ as follows. Each event $e$ of thread $E_i$ is associated with an ordinate $c(e)$. The ordinates are defined inductively as follows:   • $c(\perp_{E_i}) = 0$.   • $c(e) = c(pred(e)) + 1$ if $e \neq \perp_{E_i}$.

The order of $E_i$ is mapped onto the order $\leq$ between the integers $c(e)$. We denote by $\overline{E_i}$ the resulting total order $(\{c(e) \mid e \in |E_i|\}, \leq)$. This mapping is clearly an isomorphism of total orders. The geometrization of $\mathcal{E}$, $\overline{\mathcal{E}}$, is defined as the product of partial orders $\prod_{i=1,\ldots,N} \overline{E_i}$, and is isomorphic to $\mathcal{E}$. Every $\epsilon = (e_1, \ldots, e_N) \in \mathcal{E}$ is sent to $\overline{\epsilon} = (c(e_1), \ldots, c(e_N))$.

The set of forbidden elements $F$ is mapped onto $\overline{F}$, which has has an intuitive form geometrically: if every point of $\overline{F}$ lends a colouring of the adjacent top right "little box", then we see a union of $N$-dimensional boxes, which we call "forbidden boxes" or forbidden regions. Any string $s$ is mapped onto a trajectory $\overline{s} \subseteq \overline{A} \subseteq \overline{\mathcal{E}}$. Geometrically schedules are trajectories that do not touch the front boundary of the forbidden boxes.

# 3   Timed PV Programs and Diagrams

In this section we present our timed version of PV programs and diagrams. This version differs from existing versions of timed PV programs and diagrams [14, 9], which are briefly presented in Section 7, where we also explain why we introduce this new version.

After defining our timed version of PV programs, our goal is to define the duration of a given schedule. And in the next sections we will aim at finding a quick schedule, in the sense of the schedule that makes the execution of all threads finish as soon as possible.

## 3.1   Timed PV Programs

Our version of timed PV programs is an enrichment of untimed PV programs with a task duration between any two consecutive events of each thread. This is motivated by considerations of practical real-time programming, where one may measure the duration of the execution of the program code between two events. Such measures are usually done to foresee the worst case, so this duration is a *worst-case execution time* (WCET). So we associate with each event $e$ in a thread $E_i$ the duration (the WCET) of the task corresponding to the part of the program code which is performed between the direct predecessor of $e$ and $e$. We denote by $E$ the union $\bigcup_{i=1,\ldots,N} |E_i|$, where $|E_i|$ is the set of events of $E_i$. The task durations are given with a function $d : E \to \mathbb{N}$. We define $d(\perp_{E_i}) = 0$ for each thread $E_i$.

As an example the following is a timed version of the Swiss flag program:

```
A = 1.Pa.1.Pb.2.Vb.5.Va.2   ,   B = 1.Pb.3.Pa.1.Va.0.Vb.1
```

The numbers between the actions are the task durations. The bottom and top elements are not represented. For example the initial 1 for thread A is the duration of the task which is to be executed between the beginning of thread A and its first action, $P_a$.

## 3.2   Geometric Realization

For the geometric realization of timed PV programs we could use in principle the geometric realization of the untimed case, since the involved orders are the same. However, it is more convenient to have a diagram where one can visualize durations. To this end, we change the ordinate function $c$ so that the distances (in the Euclidian space) visually reflect task durations. A special case is tasks with zero duration, for which a fixed length $\alpha > 0$ is chosen. The ordinates are defined inductively as follows: $c(\perp_{E_i}) = 0$; $c(e) = c(\mathrm{pred}(e)) + d(e)$ if $e \neq \perp_{E_i}$ and $d(e) \neq 0$; and $c(e) = c(\mathrm{pred}(e)) + \alpha$ if $e \neq \perp_{E_i}$ and $d(e) = 0$. The timed diagram for the timed Swiss Flag program is shown in Fig. 2 (with $\alpha = 1$).

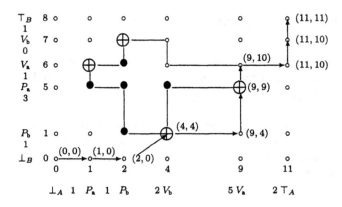

**Fig. 2.** A timed schedule.

## 3.3   3D Example: The Timed Dining Philosophers

We describe a timed version of the 3 philosophers problem. The philosophers, as usually, have to get their left and right forks for eating. Single-access to the forks is modelled with one 1-semaphore per fork. In the PV program we call these fork-semaphores a, b, and c: the left fork of philosopher A is a, its right fork is b, and so on (and the right fork of C is a). We add a 2-semaphore (which we call room) for controlling the access to a small thinking room which can contain no more than 2 philosophers at a time. Each philosopher thinks in the thinking room, then walks to the eating room and eats. Non-zero task durations are given for thinking, walking, and eating. The program is the following:

```
A = 0. P room  .5. V room .4. P a .0. P b .15. V a .0. V b .0
B = 0. P room .14. V room .6. P b .0. P c  .5. V b .0. V c .0
C = 0. P room  .9. V room .9. P c .0. P a  .2. V c .0. V a .0
```

Geometrically the trajectory of a schedule is, in the cube shown in Fig. 3(a), a sequence of small steps from the front-bottom-left corner to the back-up-right corner (marked with little white cubes for identifiying them). The boxes inside the cube are the forbidden regions. The different shadings in the figures are the shadows of the colors of the allowed boxed that result form the decomposition which is explained in Sec. 5. We use these shadings here both because they ease the visualization of the shapes (when they intersect), and because they give an idea of the decomposition.

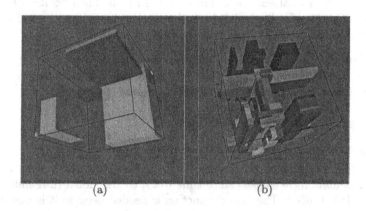

**Fig. 3.** The three philosophers: (a) simple version; (b) enriched version.

The bottom-left cube is the forbidden region for the thinking room. Let us explain that. We say that a thread $E_i$ creates an *access interval* for a resource $r$ when it accesses $r$ $(P_r)$ at an event $e$, and releases it some time after $(V_r)$, at event $e' \sqsupseteq e$. Here both threads A, B and C have an access interval for room, while the limit for room is 2 accesses. Thus the points which are in the region delimited by these 3 intervals are forbidden.

The three intersecting bars are the forbidden regions created by concurrent accesses to the 1-semaphores a, b and c. The great bar which is mainly white, for example, is for access to a by A and C. Thread B has no access interval for a, so the square defined by the concurrent accesses of A and C to a holds for all ordinates of the B axis, hence the extension of the square along this axis which results in a bar.

We show also, in Fig. 3(b), the geometry of a more complex version where the thinking room is limited to two philosophers (with a 2-semaphore); the three philosophers share a single anti-stress (through a 1-semaphore); and B and C share a single ashtray (through yet another 1-semaphore).

### 3.4 Duration of Strings

We now define the **duration** of a string (and hence of a schedule), that corresponds to the case where all the tasks take their WCET as effective duration, so it is the worst-case response time of the string. The duration of a string $s$, which we denote by $d(s)$, is computed with the following algorithm, whose goal is to find "what time is at least at $\top_s$" when time is 0 at $\bot_s$ and the string is followed from $\bot_s$ to $\top_s$. The algorithm uses $N$ **local clocks** – one for each thread –, and one **global clock**. Let H be the scalar variable for the global clock, and h the array (of size $N$) of the local clocks: h[i] is the local clock of thread $E_i$. The algorithm also uses the notion of **new events**: for a string $s$ and an element $\epsilon \in s \setminus \{\bot_s\}$, the set of new events, denoted by $new_s(\epsilon)$, that occur at $\epsilon$ is defined as $\{\epsilon_i \ (i = 1, \ldots, N) \mid (pred_s(\epsilon))_i \neq \epsilon_i\}$. The algorithm is as follows. First all clocks, global and local, are initialized to 0. Then we iterate over the sequence of states of $s$, beginning from the element just above $\bot_s$ and ending at $\top_s$ (included). For each element $\epsilon$ of the sequence do:

1. Update the global clock according to new events:
   H := max(H, h[i] + $d(\epsilon_i)$)  for all $i$ such that $\epsilon_i \in new_s(\epsilon)$.
2. Update the local clocks of all threads that have a new event:
   h[i] := H  for all $i$ such that $\epsilon_i \in new_s(\epsilon)$.
   This syncronizes these local clocks.

The algorithm returns the final value of H, which defines $d(s)$.

We explain step (1) of the algorithm. If thread $E_i$ has a new event at $\epsilon$, then $d(\epsilon_i)$ times units have elapsed since time h[i], so the global time must be now at least h[i] + $d(\epsilon_i)$. The "max" function is needed because it is possible that h[i] + $d(\epsilon_i)$ is not greater than the last H recorded: an example of this case is given below.

*Example.* The algorithm is illustrated with the schedule shown in Fig. 2. The vector-like annotations that accompany the trajectory indicate the values of the local clocks during the execution of the algorithm. (The value of the global clock is always the maximum of the values of the local clocks.) We explain what happens at some particular states. We identify states by their coordinates in the diagram.

- At state $(4, 1)$ a new event happens to thread $A$ and to thread $B$. Thread $A$ updates the global clock to 4 in step (1) of the algorithm, and thread $B$ does not update the global clock since $0 + 1 < 4$. The global clock H is now 4, and both local clocks are updated to 4. That is, the schedule states that action $P_b$ of thread $B$ must not happen before action $V_b$ of thread $A$, so since $A$ runs for 4 time units before executing $V_b$, $B$ cannot execute $P_b$ before that time point. So $B$ has a lapse of 4 time units for executing its task of duration 1. It means that if it finishes this task before $t = 4$ (for example if it began executing it at $t = 0$), it must *wait* ( for 3 time units if it began at $t = 0$) until $A$ releases resource $b$.

- At state $(11, 7)$ a new event of thread $B$ happens, but the duration of the task before this event is zero so there is no change to be made to the clocks.

The final value of the global clock, 11, defines the WCRT of this schedule.

## 4    Abstraction of Efficient Schedules

*The Scheduling Problem and Approach.* We are interested in finding a quick schedule. Let us first assume that we are looking for the quickest possible one (in the sense of a schedule which has the minimal WCRT). We observe that the approach of computing the duration for each possible schedule and then picking the schedule with the minimal duration is not feasible in general. Indeed, the combinatorial explosion comes not only from the number of possible states, but also from the total number of possible schedules from bottom to top. If we also count the forbidden schedules (which pass through forbidden regions) to simplify computations, we get the following numbers: for the timed Swiss flag example, $6 \times 6 = 36$ states and 1683 possible schedules; for the timed philosophers example, $8 \times 8 \times 8 = 512$ states and 75494983297 possible schedules; for the enriched version of the timed philosophers, $16 \times 18 \times 26 = 7488$ states and more than $5 \times 10^{30}$ possible schedules[1]. Given this complexity problem, we propose to exploit the geometry of the diagrams to construct abstractions that can make the computation of efficient schedules feasible. In this section we define these abstractions, and we will describe in the next section a method to compute them.

*Eager Strings.* We focus on a class of strings that is interesting w.r.t looking for efficient schedules: **eager strings** are the strings that make no unnecessary wait. A necessary wait for a thread is, waiting for a resource it needs to be unlocked. An example of a non-necessary wait is given in the example of Fig. 2 by a schedule that would go, for example, through points $(4, 0)$ and $(9, 0)$ before going to $(9, 1)$: this corresponds to $B$ waiting for $A$ to release resource $a$ before accessing resource $b$, while resource $b$ is already available.

Notice that while the quickest schedule is necessarily eager the converse is not true in general: in Fig. 2, a string from $\perp$ to $\top$ that would go *above* the cross could be eager, but not optimal. Indeed, since thread $A$ has to wait for resources $a$ and $b$ to be unlocked by thread $B$, the quickest string that goes above the cross has duration $5 + 1 + 9 = 15$ time units.

In the following we detail an abstraction for eager strings, which is used in the next section for (efficiently) computing efficient schedules.

*Bows: Abstractions of Wait-Free Strings.* We first define abstractions for the wait-free parts of the eager strings. For this we introduce the notion **bow**. Intuitively, a bow is an arc $\langle e, e' \rangle$ from $\mathcal{A}$ such that the longest side of the cube (in the geometric realization) whose bottom left and top right corners correspond to $e$ and $e'$ is equal to the duration of the quickest strings between $e$ and $e'$. For using arcs as abstractions of strings we introduce the following operation.

**Definition 2.** *Given any arc $\langle \epsilon, \epsilon' \rangle$ from $\mathcal{A}$, the **stringing** of $\langle \epsilon, \epsilon' \rangle$, which we denote by $\langle \epsilon, \epsilon' \rangle \searrow$, is the set of all the strings from $\epsilon$ to $\epsilon'$ that have the smallest duration.*

This set is not empty, since $\epsilon \preccurlyeq \epsilon'$ implies that there is a sequence of small steps from $\epsilon$ to $\epsilon'$ in $\mathcal{A}$. We call the **tightened length** of an arc $\langle \epsilon, \epsilon' \rangle$ from $\mathcal{A}$, the duration of any element of $\langle \epsilon, \epsilon' \rangle \searrow$. We extend notation $d$ to sets of strings that have the same duration, and we denote the tightened length of $\langle \epsilon', \epsilon \rangle$ by $d(\langle \epsilon', \epsilon \rangle \searrow)$. This measure will be compared to *distance*:

---

[1] $-5589092438965486974774900743393$, to be precise.

**Definition 3.** *The **distance** between two elements $\epsilon, \epsilon' \in \mathcal{E}$ with $\epsilon \preccurlyeq \epsilon'$ is defined as: $\|\langle \epsilon, \epsilon' \rangle\| = \max_{i=1,\ldots,N}(s(\epsilon_i) - s(\epsilon'_i))$, where for any thread $E_i$ and event $e \in E_i$: $s(e) = \sum_{\perp_{E_i} \sqsubseteq e' \sqsubseteq e} d(e)$.*

Note that $s(e) \neq c(e)$ in general: $c(e)$ is the ordinate of $e$ for the geometric realization, while $s(e)$ is the "true ordinate" of $e$ in term of the sum of the WCETs of the tasks: the difference comes from the tasks that have a duration equal to zero, and for which $\alpha > 0$ is applied in the geometric realization. Now we can define the abstractions of wait-free-strings:

**Definition 4.** *A **bow** is an arc $\langle \epsilon, \epsilon' \rangle$ from $\mathcal{A}$, such that $\epsilon \prec \epsilon'$ and $d(\langle \epsilon, \epsilon' \rangle \searrow) = \|\langle \epsilon, \epsilon' \rangle\|$.*

For example, in Fig. 2 arc $\langle (9,0), (11,6) \rangle$ is a bow, while arc $\langle (0,1), (9,8) \rangle$ is not. Indeed, the latter arc has length $\|\langle (0,1), (9,8) \rangle\| = 9$, while its tightened length is $11$ – the quickest string from $(0,1)$ to $(9,8)$ exchanges resource $b$ at point $(2,7)$, and thread $A$ has to wait for it for at least 2 time units.

*Critical Potential Exchange Points.* We define critical potential exchange points– the only points where an eager string can wait. A **potential exchange point** is an element $\epsilon \in \mathcal{A}$ where a resource can be exchanged: there exist at least one resource $r \in \Re$ and two indices $i, j$ such that $\epsilon_i = V_r$ and $\epsilon_j = P_r$. We use the term "potential" because in order to be a real exchange point, it must be the element of a string $s$ with $\epsilon_i, \epsilon_j \in new_s(\epsilon)$.

**Definition 5.** *A potential exchange point which has $accessing(r, \epsilon) = limit(r)$ for some resource $r$ is called a **critical potential exchange point** ("CPEP" for short).*

In the Swiss flag example of Fig. 2 CPEPs are indicated by circled addition symbols.

*The Abstraction Graph.* We are now ready to define our *abstraction of all the eager strings* (and hence also of all the quickest schedules). It is the graph having CPEPs, plus $\perp$ and $\top$, has nodes and bows as arrows. We call it the **abstraction graph**. We denote by $C$ the union of all CPEPs with $\{\perp, \top\}$. The abstraction graph is the weighted graph defined as the binary relation $G \subseteq C \times C$ which is characterized by: $\epsilon \, G \, \epsilon' \iff \langle \epsilon, \epsilon' \rangle$ is a bow; and each arc $(\epsilon, \epsilon')$ of $G$ has weight $\|\langle \epsilon, \epsilon' \rangle\|$.

For $\epsilon, \epsilon' \in C$ with $\epsilon \preccurlyeq \epsilon'$, we denote by $\widehat{\langle \epsilon, \epsilon' \rangle}$ the set of the shortest paths in $G$ from $\epsilon$ to $\epsilon'$. By abuse of notation, we denote by $l(\widehat{\langle \epsilon', \epsilon \rangle})$ the length of any of the paths in $\widehat{\langle \perp, \top \rangle}$. Graph $G$ has an important property:

**Theorem 1.** *The duration of a quickest schedule from $\perp$ to $\top$ is the length of a shortest path in $G$ from $\perp$ to $\top$: $d(\langle \perp, \top \rangle \searrow) = l(\widehat{\langle \perp, \top \rangle})$.*

**Proof:** The proof is long so we only sketch it here. The full proof can be found in the technical report [12].

- The abstraction of an eager string $s$ with $\perp_s, \top_s \in C$, which we denote by $s\nearrow$, is defined as the path in $G$ which is constituted of all the CPEPs contained in $s$. (Since $s$ is eager, bows exist between the CPEPs.)

- Let $\langle \epsilon, \epsilon' \rangle \in \mathcal{A}$, with $\epsilon, \epsilon' \in C$. We prove that there exists a string $s \in \langle \epsilon, \epsilon' \rangle \searrow$ which is such that $l(s\nearrow) = d(s)$. (The proof is by induction on the number of CPEPs in $s\nearrow$.)

- We then prove that for such a string, $s\nearrow$ is among the shortest paths in $G$ from $\epsilon$ to $\epsilon'$.

- Take a $\rho$ in $\langle \perp, \top \rangle \searrow$, such that $l(\rho\nearrow) = d(\rho)$ (which is possible by the first above result). By the second above result, $\rho\nearrow$ is among the shortest paths from $\perp$ to $\top$. Thus $d(\langle \perp, \top \rangle \searrow) = d(\rho) = l(\rho\nearrow) = l(\widehat{\langle \perp, \top \rangle})$. $\qquad \square$

An interesting computational implication of Theorem 1 is that the size of graph $G$ is reasonable since the number of CPEPs is much smaller than the number of elements in $\mathcal{E}$; hence the shortest paths in $G$ from $\perp$ to $\top$ can be efficiently computed. This is discussed in more detail in the following section.

# 5   Finding Efficient Schedules Using Geometric Realization

The construction of graph $G$ has two parts: 1) find the CPEPs; 2) find the bows between these points. Then the shortest path in graph $G$ from $\perp$ to $\top$ is computed. Notice that this approach automatically finds a *deadlock-free path*. Indeed, if a path in $G$ leads to a deadlock point, no bow goes from it; and a shortest path from $\perp$ to $\top$ is, above all, a path from $\perp$ to $\top$, and hence contains no deadlock.

We use geometry for the construction. Notice however that our method does not depend on the coordinates $c(e)$, in the sense that the function $c$ of the untimed case would give the same results, because we use the *structure* of the geometry of $\overline{\mathcal{E}}$ (the forbidden boxes), not the distances in the embedding: function $c$ uses $d(e)$ only for visual intuition (the "max" measure is still close to the Euclidian distance).

Notice that is it possible, after we have found a satisfying path from $\perp$ to $\top$, to actually *construct* an eager string abstracted by this path. The construction operates bow by bow: for each bow $\langle \epsilon, \epsilon' \rangle$ construct a wait-free string abstracted by it. For this, start from $\epsilon$ and follow an adjacent small step to an $\epsilon''$ which increases the least the duration, among those that have not $\epsilon''_i \sqsupset \epsilon'_i$ for some $i$, and iterate until $\epsilon'$ is reached.

## 5.1   Computing the Critical Potential Exchange Points

The CPEPs are given by some points on the boundary the forbidden regions: in dimension 2, these are the bottom-right and top-left points of the forbidden regions; in dimension 3, all points on some edges of the boundary; etc. In Fig. 2 CPEPs are indicated with the circled addition symbols.

Since the CPEPs can be determined from the forbidden regions, we compute the forbidden regions from the timed PV program. Clearly checking for each element whether it is forbidden is not a reasonable approach. We compute instead the *boundaries* of the regions, from the access intervals, as hinted in Sec. 3.3.

## 5.2    Finding the Arrows of the Abstraction Graph

We have computed the CPEPs: it remains to compute the bows between them. A simple method to determine whether an arc $\langle \epsilon, \epsilon' \rangle$ is a bow is to determine the tightened length of the arc by enumerating all the strings from $\epsilon$ to $\epsilon'$ and check the condition of Definition 4. However, this method is clearly very expensive and to remedy this we will exploit some properties of the geometric realization. We use a method which finds arcs which are necessarily bows: we use a decomposition of forbidden-point-free regions. Using this approach we may not find a quickest schedule but we can find a good schedule. This decomposition approach and the strategies for looking for the quickest schedule are discussed in the following.

*Finding Efficient Schedules Using Decomposition.* We denote $\mathcal{B} = [0, c(\mathsf{T}_1)] \times \ldots \times [0, c(\mathsf{T}_N)] \subset \mathbb{R}^N$. In $\mathbb{R}^N$, $\overline{\mathcal{E}}$, the geometric realization of the product $\mathcal{E}$ of all the threads, forms a (non-uniform) $N$-dimensional grid over the box $\mathcal{B}$. A CPEP $\epsilon$ corresponds to a grid point $\overline{\epsilon}$. The forbidden regions is a union of boxes whose vertices are grid points. This union is indeed an *orthogonal polyhedron* [5], denoted by $P_F$. Let $P_A = \mathcal{B} \backslash P_F$ denote the *allowed polyhedron*. We now make the following observation: if a box contains no forbidden points, then any two points on its boundary form a bow if they are grid points. This motivates considering a decomposition of the polyedron $P_A$.

**Definition 6.** *A decomposition of an orthogonal polyhedron $P$ is a set $\mathcal{D}_P = \{B_1, \ldots, B_k\}$ where each $B_i$ ($i \in \{1, \ldots, k\}$) is a full-dimensional box such that the following conditions are satisfied:*

1. *For all $i \in \{1, \ldots, k\}$ the vertices of $B_i$ are grid points.*
2. $P = \bigcup_{i \in \{1, \ldots, k\}} B_i$.
3. *For all $i, j \in \{1, \ldots, k\}$, $i \neq j$, the boxes $B_i$ and $B_j$ are non-overlapping, that is their interiors do not intersect with each other.*

Note that the vertices of the boxes in a decomposition are not necessarily CPEPs. If all the vertices of a box are grid points then it is called a *grid box*. Additionally, if a grid box does not contain any other grid boxes, then it is called *elementary box*. We distinguish two types of decompositions: given a decomposition $\mathcal{D}_P = \{B_1, \ldots, B_k\}$, $\mathcal{D}_P$ is called *elementary* if all $B_i$ are elementary boxes; $\mathcal{D}_P$ is called *compact* if there exists no pair of $B_i$ and $B_j$ with $i \neq j$ such that $B_i \cup B_j$ is a grid box. Intuitively, in a elementary decomposition none of its boxes can be split into smaller grid boxes, and in a compact decomposition no pair of its boxes forms a grid box. Note that there exists a unique elementary decomposition of a given orthogonal polyhedron, however there may be many different compact decompositions.

We use decompositions to construct the abstraction graph $G$. Let $\mathcal{D}_{P_A}$ be a decomposition of the allowed polyhedron $P_A$. We first recall the observation we use to reduce the complexity of the search for bows: a line segment connecting two vertices of a box $B_i \in \mathcal{D}_{P_A}$ corresponds to a bow. It is however clear that even when $\mathcal{D}_{P_A}$ is the elementary decomposition, the set of all such edges does not allow to cover all possible bows since two vertices of two different boxes might also form a bow. However, if our goal is to find a path with the shortest duration it is not necessary to construct the whole graph $G$ but we need to include all the CPEPs and bows that form such a path. It can be proved that there exists a decomposition such that the vertices of its boxes are enough to discover a shortest path. We call such a decomposition an *effective decomposition*, and it is of great interest to find such a decomposition, which is our ongoing work.

The essential idea of our current method for computing a compact decomposition of orthogonal polyhedra is as follows. From a given starting box we try to merge it with other elementary boxes, along one or more axes, so as to maximize the volume of the resulting box. To do so, we make use of the efficient algorithms for Boolean operations and membership testing developed based on a compact and canonical representation of such polyhedra (see [5]). In some cases the criterion of maximizing the volume of merged boxes may not be the best one with respect to including the shortest path in the graph. Alternative criteria are merging as many as possible boxes along a fixed axis. Intuitively, a shortest path tends to approach the diagonal between the bottom left and top right corners of the box $B$ while avoiding the forbidden regions; hence, we can combine different merging criteria depending on the relative position to the forbidden regions.

## 5.3   Experimental Results

We demonstrate in this section the effectiveness of our method. We have written a prototype which implements the exposed method. For computing the forbidden regions we use a program written in the language Maude [6]. The execution time for this computation is negligible. The program for the decomposition into allowed boxes, the construction of the abstraction graph from them, and the computation of the shortest path from $\bot$ to $\top$ in the graph is written in C++. The decomposition is rather quick, and most of the execution time for this program is spent in the construction of the graph from the allowed boxes – due to the number of vertices we use, as we explain below. We present in the table below some experiments with this program.

We first test with the philosophers problem, in 3 dimensions and more. We use $N$ forks – one per philosopher – and a thinking room which can take only $N - 1$ philosophers. Then we take the same program, but with a small thinking room ("s.th.-r") which can contain only $\lfloor N/2 \rfloor$ philosophers. Then we test with the enriched version of the philosophers problem ("enr. phil."), whose geometry is shown in Fig. 3(b). Program "enr. phil. 4D" is when a fourth philosopher is added alongside the three philosophers of the latter program. Program "more enr. phil." is when still more actions are added to the threads of "enr. phil.". We also give the results for the program of Section 6 ("3 phil. 2 procs"), whose geometry is shown in Fig. 4. In the table, "na" stands for "not available" – the computation was not finishing in less than 10 minutes. We have used a PC with a 2.40 GHz Xeon processor, 1 Go of memory and 2 Go of swap.

| program | dim | #states | #forbid | #allowed | #nodes | #edges | t (sec.) |
|---|---|---|---|---|---|---|---|
| 3 phil. | 3 | 512 | 4 | 35 | 151 | 773 | 0.58 |
| 4 phil. | 4 | 4096 | 5 | 107 | 743 | 7369 | 17.38 |
| 5 phil. | 5 | 32768 | 6 | 323 | 3632 | 67932 | 571.12 |
| 6 phil. | 6 | 262144 | 7 | 971 | na | na | na |
| 3 phil. s.th.-r. | 3 | 512 | 6 | 59 | 227 | 1271 | 1.50 |
| 4 phil. s.th.-r. | 4 | 4096 | 8 | 199 | 1147 | 13141 | 60.24 |
| 5 phil. s.th.-r. | 5 | 32768 | 15 | 1092 | na | na | na |
| 6 phil. s.th.-r. | 6 | 262144 | 21 | 3600 | na | na | na |
| enr. phil. | 3 | 7488 | 26 | 390 | 1468 | 7942 | 51.01 |
| enr. phil. 4D | 4 | 119808 | 44 | 5447 | na | na | na |
| more enr. phil. | 3 | 29568 | 137 | 1165 | 4616 | 30184 | 461.18 |
| 3 phil. 2 procs | 3 | 1728 | 12 | 78 | 352 | 2358 | 2.56 |

One can observe that the number of allowed boxes is very reasonable compared with the number of states. The number of nodes reflects the fact in our current prototype we add in the graph some of the vertices of the allowed boxes which are not CPEPs, to compensate for the fact that we do not currently include inter-allowed-box bows: thus we can find paths whose length approximate (conservatively) the weight of inter-box bows. The advantage of this approach is that any decomposition can serve to find a relatively good schedule; its inconvenient is that the number of considered vertices for a box is of order $2^N$, so that the number of threads is the main obstacle in our current implementation.

We find good schedules: in the case of the enriched 3 philosophers program of Sec. 3.3 (whose image is shown in Fig. 3(a)) the durations of the threads are 24, 25 and 20 respectively and the found schedule has duration 39, which is good. In the case of the enriched version of Fig. 3(b), the threads have respective durations 83, 94, and 95, and the found schedule has duration 160, which is also good in view of the many forbidden regions which bar the direct way.

Our future experiments will use the following heuristics: using for each allowed box only its bottom and top elements. Intuitively, quick schedules follow diagonals, so this heuristics should find efficient schedules. It addresses the main obstacle of our method – the number of vertices considered per allowed box (we descend from $2^N$ points per box to only 2). On the other hand, how close one then gets to the quickest schedule depends on the decomposition, as discussed in the previous section.

## 6   Limited Number of Available Processors

We have defined the WCRT of a schedule *assuming that the threads run concurrently*. But what does the WCRT of the schedule become when there are only $M < N$ processors available? This is treated in the present section.

The problem of mapping of the $N$ threads (or processes) onto $M$ processors has already been treated in [7]. But this is in the untimed context. We are in a timed context and we are looking for *efficient* schedules. We can distinguish two approaches: 1) first compute an efficient schedule with the method shown in Sec. 5 above; and then compute a good mapping of this schedule onto the $M$ processors. The inconvenient of this method is that the best abstract schedules do not necessarily perform well when $M$ processors are shared, while some schedules which are inefficient with $N$ processors might perform well under the constraint of $M < N$ processors. 2) Taking this constraint into account from the beginning for computing an efficient schedule. The advantage of this approach is that it is more precise. The inconvenient is that adding this constraint to the optimization problem can lead to state explosion if no care is taken. In this section we examine this solution, because it gives some geometric intuition on the mapping, and in addition, for many practical cases the complexity of the computation is reasonable.

*The Processor Semaphore.* It is not necessary in fact to modify the model: the idea is to use an $M$-semaphore to model the fact that $M$ processors are shared between the threads. This modelling assumes that the threads have no preference on which processor to run on, which is reasonable in the case of an homogeneous architecture – all the processors are identical. The advantage of using a semaphore is a drastic combinatorial simplification: knowing which $Q \leq M$ threads are running (locking the processor semaphore), among the $N$ threads, is what interests us from the point of view of scheduling, so we do not need to say which processor each of these $Q$ threads is running on. The distribution onto the processors can be done after we have determined the schedule.

The idea is that the programmer indicates in his program the releasing and re-locking of the processor semaphore, which corresponds to a *proposition of preemption*: the thread gives a chance to other threads of taking the processor. Of course if the schedule which is eventually chosen does not use this preemption opportunity, then in the implementation of the schedule the thread does not need to preempt itself. The mechanism is illustrated with the philosophers program of Sec. 3.3. Suppose that the programmer decides that a philosopher makes a proposition of preemption just before entering the thinking room. We denote by p the semaphore for the processors. The corresponding modified program of philosopher A is shown in Fig. 4(a) (the modification is similar for philosophers B and C), and the geometry of the new program is shown in Fig. 4(b). The accesses to p creates big boxes, and the propositions of premption create some "canyons" (of width $\alpha$, here 1) between these boxes. A trajectory must go through these canyons and avoid the parts of the previous forbidden regions that still emerge from the new boxes (here the bars from the forks). Notice that the forbidden box for room is now included in the bottom left p-forbidden box (and is thus invisible). Indeed, the room semaphore served to forbid concurrent access to the room by more than two philosophers, which is no longer necessary since only two processors are available.

Since each philosopher accesses 2 times a processor (through a lock of p), we get $2^3 = 8$ corresponding forbidden regions. Computationally it means that a thread should not propose preemption too often. On the other hand, finding the optimal schedule for all possible preemptions would imply proposing a

```
A =    0. Pp .
   0. P room .5. V room .4.
       Vp .0. Pp .0.
   P a .0. P b .15. V a .0. V b .0
       . Vp .0
 B = ...
 C = ...
```

(a)                              (b)

**Fig. 4.** The three philosophers problem with two processors.

preemption between each event of the original program (which can be done auto-matically). But this would induce an exponential number of forbidden regions for the processor semaphore. On the other hand, this geometric approach can give new ideas for optimizing the control of programs that run on a limited number of processors. For example, in the above example the geometry indicates that if the given preemption is implemented, then the implementation can dispense with the room semaphore.

## 7 Related Works

*Timed PV Diagrams.* Some other versions of timed PV diagrams have been proposed. We have not used them, for the reasons we explain below.

• The work [9], which presents a timed version of PV programs and diagrams, attempts to model multiple clocks, as in timed automata [3]. In the present paper we do not use the timed automaton model. Moreover, in the approach of [9] time is modeled as an additional dimension – one per clock. Thus, in the case of one clock and three threads, a 4-dimensional space is studied. In this paper we consider each thread dimension as as a "local time dimension" and define the synchronization of these local times.

• The work [14] exploits the dimension of each process as a time dimension. In this aspect, this work is close to ours. However there are important differences. First, the definitions in [14] are given in a continuous setting, and therefore topo-logical spaces are considered, such that the duration of a schedule is described with an integral. In our work we stay in the discrete domain, and the definition of the duration of a schedule is given by an algorithm on a discrete structure. Also, the fact that the definitions in [14] are tied to geometry implies, in partic-ular, that zero-delays between two consecutive actions in a process (for example two successive locks, which often happens in programs that share resources) are not possible since the two actions would be the same in the geometry. In our approach, while we exploit the geometry to construct abstractions, the notion of duration itself is not geometric. Consequently, zero-delays are possible. This is of particular interest if one considers that the practical delay, on most architectures, between two consecutive locks, is too small to be modelled as a non-zero value. We conjecture that our version of timed PV diagrams is a discretized version of the continuous version of [14] (in the case of no zero-delays in the program).

*Timed Automata.* A large class of real-time systems can be adequately modelled with *timed automata* [3], and in this framework the problem of scheduling has been addressed [4, 1, 2, 16, 17], often closely related to the context of *controller synthesis*. A timed PV program has a direct representation using timed automata: each thread is modelled as an automaton, where each node represents an event and each transition is labeled with constraint "$h \geq d(e)$" plus a reset of clock $h$. The global automaton is the product of all the thread-automata. Semaphores can be represented via variables. Such a product of automata is very close to that of [16], where the aim is also to schedule multi-threaded programs. In this work a *scheduler* is constructed to guarantee that a schedule does not go into deadlock states or deadline-breaking directions. We look for a complete schedule which is not only safe but also efficient; however our model is not as rich as the timed automata model: we have not yet included deadlines, branching, and looping.

# 8   Conclusion and Future Work

In this paper we defined a timed version of PV programs and diagrams which can be used to model a large class of multithreaded programs sharing resources. We also introduced the notion of the worst-case response time of a schedule of such programs. This framework was then used to find efficient schedules for multi-threaded programs. In particular, to tackle the complexity problem, we define an abstraction of the quickest schedules and we show how to exploit the geometry of PV diagrams to construct this abstraction and compute efficient schedules. This work demonstrates an interesting interplay between geometric approaches and real-time programming. An experimental implementation allowed us to validate the method and provided encouraging results.

Our future work will explore the following directions.

• When developing a real-time system one is often interested in the worst-case response time of the whole program, if it is part of a larger system, *for any schedule*. As a definition, this WCRT could be given as the duration of the eager schedule that has the longest duration. We conjecture that we could use abstraction graph $G$ for computing the longest eager schedule by computing the longest path in a subgraph of $G$. Defining this subgraph is a topic of our future research.

• We are currently investigating the problem of adding *deadlines* in our model. This extension is not straightforward since the "symmetry" with the lower bounds to durations of tasks (the WCET) is not trivial. We also intend to examine the possibility of lifting to the timed case the existing studies on the geometry of loops [11] or branching in PV programs.

## Acknowledgments

We thank Ph. Gaucher for introducing us to PV diagrams; B. Meister for wondering with us about time in PV diagrams; and S. Yovine, P. Caspi and S. Tripakis for useful discussions.

## References

1. Y. Abdeddaïm and O. Maler. Job-shop scheduling using timed automata. In *Proc. of the 13th Int. Conf. on Computer Aided Verification (CAV 2001), LNCS 2102*, pages 478–492. Springer, 2001.
2. K. Altisen, G. Gößler, and J. Sifakis. Scheduler modelling based on the controller synthesis paradigm. *Journal of Real-Time Systems*, (23):55–84, 2002. Special issue on control-theoretical approaches to real-time computing.
3. R. Alur and D. L. Dill. A theory of timed automata. *Theoretical Computer Science*, 126(2):183–235, 1994.
4. R. Alur, S. La Torre, and G. Pappas. Optimal paths in weighted timed automata. In *Proc. of Fourth Int. Workshop on Hybrid Systems: Computation and Control, LNCS 2034*, pages 49–62, 2001.
5. O. Bournez, O. Maler, and A. Pnueli. Orthogonal polyhedra: Representation and computation. In *Proc. of Hybrid Systems: Computation and Control (HSCC'99), LNCS 1569*, 1999.
6. M. Clavel, F. Durán, S. Eker, P. Lincoln, N. Martí-Oliet, J. Meseguer, and C. Talcott. *Maude 2.0 Manual*. SRI International, 2003.
7. R. Cridlig and E. Goubault. Semantics and analysis of Linda-based languages. In *Proc. of WSA'93, LNCS 724*. Springer, 1993.
8. E. W. Dijkstra. Co-operating sequential processes. In F. Genuys, editor, *Programming Languages*, pages 43–110. Academic Press, 1968.
9. U. Fahrenberg. The geometry of timed PV programs. In *Electronic Notes in Theoretical Computer Science*, volume 81. Elsevier, 2003.
10. L. Fajstrup, E. Goubault, and M. Raussen. Detecting deadlocks in concurrent systems. In *Proc. CONCUR'98*, pages 332–347, 1998.
11. L. Fajstrup and S. Sokolowski. Infinitely running concurrent processes with loops from a geometric viewpoint. In *Electronic Notes in Theoretical Computer Science*, volume 39. Elsevier, 2001.
12. Ph. Gerner and T. Dang. Computing schedules for multithreaded real-time programs using geometry. Technical Report TR-2004-08, Verimag, March 2004.
13. E. Goubault. Schedulers as abstract interpretations of higher-dimensional automata. In *Proc. of PEPM'95 (La Jolla)*, 1995.
14. E. Goubault. Transitions take time. In *Proc. of ESOP'96, LNCS 1058*, pages 173–187. Springer, 1996.
15. E. Goubault. Geometry and concurrency: A user's guide. *Mathematical Structures in Computer Science*, 10(4), August 2000.
16. Chr. Kloukinas, Ch. Nakhli, and S. Yovine. A methodology and tool support for generating scheduled native code for real-time java applications. In R. Alur and I. Lee, editors, *Proc. of the Third Int. Conf. on Embedded Software (EMSOFT 2003), LNCS 2855*, 2003.
17. J. I. Rasmussen, K. G. Larsen, and K. Subramani. Resource-optimal scheduling using priced timed automata. In *Proc. of the 10th Int. Conf. on Tools and Algorithms for the Construction and Analysis of Systems (TACAS 2004)*, pages 220–235, 2001.

# Forward Reachability Analysis of Timed Petri Nets

Parosh Aziz Abdulla, Johann Deneux, Pritha Mahata, and Aletta Nylén

Uppsala University, Sweden
{parosh,johannd,pritha,aletta}@it.uu.se

**Abstract.** We consider verification of safety properties for concurrent real-timed systems modelled as timed Petri nets, by performing symbolic forward reachability analysis. We introduce a formalism, called *region generators* for representing sets of markings of timed Petri nets. Region generators characterize downward closed sets of regions, and provide exact abstractions of sets of reachable states with respect to safety properties. We show that the standard operations needed for performing symbolic reachability analysis are computable for region generators. Since forward reachability analysis is necessarily incomplete, we introduce an acceleration technique to make the procedure terminate more often on practical examples. We have implemented a prototype for analyzing timed Petri nets and used it to verify a parameterized version of Fischer's protocol and a producer-consumer protocol. We also used the tool to extract finite-state abstractions of these protocols.

## 1 Introduction

*Timed Petri nets (TPNs)* are extensions of Petri nets in the sense that each token has an "age" which is represented by a real valued clock (see [Bow96] for a survey). TPNs are computationally more powerful than timed automata [AD90], since they operate on a potentially unbounded number of clocks. This implies that TPNs can, among other things, model parameterized timed systems (systems consisting of an unbounded number of timed processes) [AN01].

A fundamental problem for TPNs (and also for standard Petri nets) is that of *coverability*: check whether an upward closed set of *final markings* is reachable from a set of initial markings. Using standard techniques [VW86], several classes of safety properties for TPNs can be reduced to the coverability problem where final markings represent violations of the safety property. To solve coverability, one may either compute the set of *forward reachable markings*, i.e., all the markings reachable from the initial markings; or compute *backward reachable markings*, i.e., all the markings from which a final marking is reachable.

While backward and forward analysis seem to be symmetric, they exhibit surprisingly different behaviours in many applications. For TPNs, even though the set of backward reachable states is computable [AN01], the set of forward reachable states is in general not computable. Therefore any procedure for performing forward reachability analysis on TPNs is necessarily incomplete. However, forward analysis is practically very attractive. The set of forward reachable states contains much more information

Y. Lakhnech and S. Yovine (Eds.): FORMATS/FTRTFT 2004, LNCS 3253, pp. 343–362, 2004.

about system behaviour than backward reachable states. This is due to the fact that forward closure characterizes the set of states which arises during the execution of the system, in contrast to backward closure which only describes the states from which the system may fail. This implies for instance that forward analysis can often be used for constructing a symbolic graph which is a finite-state abstraction of the system, and which is a simulation or a bisimulation of the original system (see e.g. [BLO98,LBBO01]).

**Contribution:** We consider performing forward reachability analysis for TPNs. We provide an abstraction of the set of reachable markings by taking its *downward closure*. The abstraction is exact with respect to coverability (consequently with respect to safety properties), i.e, a given TPN satisfies any safety property exactly when the downward closure of the set of reachable states satisfies the same property. Moreover, the downward closure has usually a simpler structure than the exact set of reachable states.

The set of reachable markings (and its downward closure) is in general infinite. So, we introduce a symbolic representation for downward closed sets, which we call *region generators*. Each region generator denotes the union of an infinite number of *regions* [AD90]. Regions are designed for timed automata (which operate on a finite number of clocks), and are therefore not sufficiently powerful to capture the behaviour of TPNs. We define region generators hierarchically as languages where each word in the language is a sequence of multisets over an alphabet. The idea is that elements belonging to the same multiset correspond to clocks with equal fractional parts while the ordering among multisets in a word corresponds to increasing fractional parts of the clock values.

We show that region generators allow the basic operations in forward analysis, i.e, checking membership, entailment, and computing the post-images with respect to a single transition. Since forward analysis is incomplete, we also give an acceleration scheme to make the analysis terminate more often. The scheme computes, in one step, the effect of an arbitrary number of firings of a single discrete transition interleaved with timed transitions.

We have implemented the forward reachability procedure and used the tool to compute the reachability set for a parameterized version of Fischer's protocol and for a simple producer/consumer protocol. Also, we used the tool for generating finite state abstractions of these protocols.

**Related Work:** [ABJ98] considers *simple regular expressions (SRE)* as representations for downward closed languages over a *finite* alphabet. SREs are used for performing forward reachability analysis of lossy channel systems. SREs are not sufficiently powerful in the context of TPNs, since they are defined on a finite alphabet, while in the case of region generators the underlying alphabet is infinite (the set of multisets over a finite alphabet).

Both [DR00] and [FRSB02] consider (untimed) Petri nets and give symbolic representations for upward closed sets and downward closed sets of markings, respectively. The works in [FIS00,BG96,BH97] give symbolic representation for FIFO automata. These representations are designed for weaker models (Petri nets and FIFO automata) and cannot model the behaviour of TPNs.

[AN01] considers timed Petri nets. The symbolic representation in this paper characterizes upward closed sets of markings, and can be used for backward analysis, but not for forward analysis.

**Outline:** In the next section, we introduce timed Petri nets and define the coverability problem for TPNS. In Section 3, we introduce region generators. Section 4 gives the forward reachability algorithm. Section 5 and Section 6 give algorithms for computing post-images and acceleration respectively. In Section 7 we report on some experiments with our implementation. Finally, we give conclusions and directions for future research in Section 8.

## 2  Definitions

We consider *Timed Petri Nets* (*TPNs*) where each token is equipped with a real-valued clock representing the "age" of the token. The firing conditions of a transition include the usual ones for Petri nets. Additionally, each arc between a place and a transition is labelled with an interval of natural numbers. When firing a transition, tokens which are removed (added) from (to) places should have ages in the intervals of corresponding arcs.

We use $\mathbb{N}, \mathbb{R}^{\geq 0}$ to denote the sets of natural numbers, nonnegative reals respectively. We use a set *Intrv* of intervals. An open interval is written as $(w,z)$ where $w \in \mathbb{N}$ and $z \in \mathbb{N} \cup \{\infty\}$. Intervals can also be closed in one or both directions, e.g. $[w,z)$ is closed to the left and open to the right.

For a set $A$, we use $A^*$ and $A^\circledast$ to denote the set of finite words and finite multisets over $A$ respectively. We view a multiset over $A$ as a mapping from $A$ to $\mathbb{N}$. Sometimes, we write multisets as lists, so $[2.4, 5.1, 5.1, 2.4, 2.4]$ represents a multiset $B$ over $\mathbb{R}^{\geq 0}$ where $B(2.4) = 3$, $B(5.1) = 2$ and $B(x) = 0$ for $x \neq 2.4, 5.1$. We may also write $B$ as $[2.4^3, 5.1^2]$. For multisets $B_1$ and $B_2$ over $\mathbb{N}$, we say that $B_1 \leq^m B_2$ if $B_1(a) \leq B_2(a)$ for each $a \in A$. We define addition $B_1 + B_2$ of multisets $B_1, B_2$ to be the multiset $B$ where $B(a) = B_1(a) + B_2(a)$, and (assuming $B_1 \leq^m B_2$) we define the subtraction $B_2 - B_1$ to be the multiset $B$ where $B(a) = B_2(a) - B_1(a)$, for each $a \in A$. We use $\varepsilon$ to denote both the empty multiset and the empty word.

**Timed Petri Nets.** A *Timed Petri Net (TPN)* is a tuple $N = (P, T, In, Out)$ where $P$ is a finite set of places, $T$ is a finite set of transitions and $In, Out$ are partial functions from $T \times P$ to *Intrv*.

If $In(t,p)$ $(Out(t,p))$ is defined, we say that $p$ is an *input (output) place* of $t$. A *marking* $M$ of $N$ is a multiset over $P \times \mathbb{R}^{\geq 0}$. We abuse notations and write[1] $p(x)$ instead of $(p,x)$. The marking $M$ defines the numbers and ages of tokens in each place in the net. That is, $M(p(x))$ defines the number of tokens with age $x$ in place $p$. Notice that untimed Petri nets are a special case in our model where all intervals are of the form $[0, \infty)$.

For a marking $M$ of the form $[p_1(x_1), \ldots, p_n(x_n)]$ and $x \in \mathbb{R}^{\geq 0}$, we use $M^{+x}$ to denote the marking $[p_1(x_1 + x), \ldots, p_n(x_n + x)]$.

---

[1] Later, we shall use a similar notation. For instance, we write $p(n)$ instead of $(p,n)$ where $n \in \mathbb{N}$, and write $p(I)$ instead of $(p, I)$ where $I \in Intrv$.

**Transitions:** There are two types of transitions : *timed* and *discrete* transitions. A *timed transition* increases the age of each token by the same real number. Formally, for $x \in \mathbb{R}^{\geq 0}$, $M_1 \longrightarrow_x M_2$ if $M_2 = M_1^{+x}$. We use $M_1 \longrightarrow_{Time} M_2$ to denote that $M_1 \longrightarrow_x M_2$ for some $x \in \mathbb{R}^{\geq 0}$.

We define the set of *discrete transitions* $\longrightarrow_{Disc}$ as $\bigcup_{t \in T} \longrightarrow_t$, where $\longrightarrow_t$ represents the effect of firing the transition $t$. More precisely, $M_1 \longrightarrow_t M_2$ if the set of input arcs $\{p(I) \mid In(t,p) = I\}$ is of the form $\{p_1(I_1), \ldots, p_k(I_k)\}$, the set of output arcs $\{p(I) \mid Out(t,p) = I\}$ is of the form $\{q_1(\mathcal{J}_1), \ldots, q_\ell(\mathcal{J}_\ell)\}$, and there are multisets $B_1 = [p_1(x_1), \ldots, p_k(x_k)]$ and $B_2 = [q_1(y_1), \ldots, q_\ell(y_\ell)]$ such that the following holds:
- $B_1 \leq^m M_1$
- $x_i \in I_i$, for $i : 1 \leq i \leq k$.
- $y_i \in \mathcal{J}_i$, for $i : 1 \leq i \leq \ell$.
- $M_2 = (M_1 - B_1) + B_2$.

Intuitively, a transition $t$ may be fired only if for each incoming arc to the transition, there is a token with the "right" age in the corresponding input place. These tokens will be removed when the transition is fired. The newly produced tokens have ages belonging to the relevant intervals.

We define $\longrightarrow = \longrightarrow_{Time} \cup \longrightarrow_{Disc}$ and use $\stackrel{*}{\longrightarrow}$ to denote the reflexive transitive closure of $\longrightarrow$. We say that $M_2$ is *reachable* from $M_1$ if $M_1 \stackrel{*}{\longrightarrow} M_2$. We define $Reach(M)$ to be the set $\left\{ M' \mid M \stackrel{*}{\longrightarrow} M' \right\}$.

**Remark:** Notice that we assume a lazy (non-urgent) behaviour of TPNS. This means that we may choose to "let time pass" instead of firing enabled transitions, even if that disables a transition by making some of the needed tokens "too old".

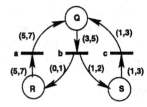

**Fig. 1.** A small timed Petri net.

*Example 1.* Figure 1 shows an example of a TPN where $P = \{Q, R, S\}$ and $T = \{a, b, c\}$. For instance, $In(b, Q) = (3,5)$ and $Out(b, R) = (0,1)$ and $Out(b, S) = (1,2)$.

**Regions.** We define an ordering on markings which extends the equivalence relation on markings induced by the classical region graph construction of [AD90]. Let *max* be the maximum natural number which appears (in the intervals) on the arcs of the TPN. A *region* defines the integral parts of clock values up to *max* (the exact age of a token is irrelevant if it is greater than *max*), and also the ordering of the fractional parts among clock values. For TPNs, we need to use a variant which also defines the place in which each token (clock) resides. Following Godskesen [God94] we represent a region by a triple $(B_0, w, B_{max})$ where

- $B_0 \in (P \times \{0, \ldots, max\})^{\circledast}$. $B_0$ is a multiset of pairs. A pair of the form $p(n)$ represents a token with age exactly $n$ in place $p$.
- $w \in \left((P \times \{0, \ldots, max-1\})^{\circledast}\right)^*$. $w$ is a word over the set $(P \times \{0, \ldots, max-1\})^{\circledast}$, i.e., $w$ is a word where each element in the word is a multiset over $P \times \{0, \ldots, max-1\}$. The pair $p(n)$ represents a token in place $p$ with age $x$ such that $x \in (n, n+1)$. Pairs in the same multiset represent tokens whose ages have equal fractional parts. The order of the multisets in $w$ corresponds to the order of the fractional parts.
- $B_{max} \in P^{\circledast}$. $B_{max}$ is a multiset over $P$ representing tokens with ages strictly greater than $max$. Since the actual ages of these tokens are irrelevant, the information about their ages is omitted in the representation.

Formally, each region characterizes an infinite set of markings as follows. Assume a marking $M = [p_1(x_1), \ldots, p_n(x_n)]$ and a region $r = (B_0, B_1 B_2 \cdots B_m, B_{m+1})$. Let $B_j$ be of the form $\left[q_{j1}(y_{j1}), \ldots, q_{j\ell_j}(y_{j\ell_j})\right]$ for $j : 0 \le j \le m$ and $B_{m+1}$ is of the form $\left[q_{m+1 \, 1}, \ldots, q_{m+1 \, l_{m+1}}\right]$. We say that $M$ *satisfies* $r$, written $M \models r$, if there is a bijection $h$ from the set $\{1, \ldots, n\}$ to the set of pairs $\{(j,k) \mid (0 \le j \le m+1) \wedge (1 \le k \le \ell_j)\}$ such that the following conditions are satisfied:

- $p_i = q_{h(i)}$. Each token should have the same place as that required by the corresponding element in $r$.
- If $h(i) = (j,k)$ then $j = m+1$ iff $x_i > max$. Tokens older than $max$ should correspond to elements in multiset $B_{m+1}$. The actual ages of these tokens are not relevant.
- If $x_i \le max$ and $h(i) = (j,k)$ then $\lfloor x_i \rfloor = y_{jk}$. The integral part of the age of tokens should agree with the natural number specified by the corresponding elements in $w$.
- If $x_i \le max$ and $h(i) = (j,k)$ then $fract(x_i) = 0$ iff $j = 0$. Tokens with zero fractional parts correspond to elements in multiset $B_0$.
- If $x_{i_1}, x_{i_2} < max$, $h(i_1) = (j_1, k_1)$ and $h(i_2) = (j_2, k_2)$ then $fract(x_{i_1}) \le fract(x_{i_2})$ iff $j_1 \le j_2$. Tokens with equal fractional parts correspond to elements in the same multiset (unless they belong to $B_{m+1}$). The ordering among multisets inside $r$ reflects the ordering among fractional parts in clock values.

We let $[\![r]\!] = \{M \mid M \models r\}$.

The region construction defines an equivalence relation $\equiv$ on the set of markings such that $M_1 \equiv M_2$ if, for each region $r$, it is the case that $M_1 \in [\![r]\!]$ iff $M_2 \in [\![r]\!]$. It is well-known [AD90] that $\equiv$ is a congruence on the set of markings, i.e, if $M_1 \longrightarrow M_2$ and $M_1 \equiv M_3$ then there is an $M_4$ such that $M_2 \equiv M_4$ and $M_3 \longrightarrow M_4$.

**Ordering.** Now we define an ordering $\preceq$ on the set of markings such that $M_1 \preceq M_2$ if there is an $M_2'$ with $M_1 \equiv M_2'$ and $M_2' \le^m M_2$. In other words, $M_1 \preceq M_2$ if we can delete a number of tokens from $M_2$ and as a result obtain a new marking which is equivalent to $M_1$. We let $M_1 \prec M_2$ denote that $M_1 \preceq M_2$ and $M_1 \not\equiv M_2$.

A set M of markings is said to be *upward closed* if $M_1 \in$ M and $M_1 \preceq M_2$ implies $M_2 \in$ M. We define the *upward closure* M $\uparrow$ to be the set $\{M \mid \exists M' \in$ M $: M' \preceq M\}$. Downward closed sets and downward closure M $\downarrow$ of a set M are defined in a similar manner.

Next, we consider the following lemma which states that $\longrightarrow$ is *monotonic* with respect to the ordering $\preceq$.

**Lemma 1.** *If $M_1 \longrightarrow M_2$ and $M_1 \preceq M_3$ then there is an $M_4$ such that $M_2 \preceq M_4$ and $M_3 \longrightarrow M_4$.*

*Example 2.* Consider the TPN $N$ in Figure 1 where $max = 7$. Here is an example of a region $r = ([R(2)], [S(5)] \ \ [R(1), S(5), S(2)], [Q])$. Markings $M_1 = [R(2.0), S(5.5), R(1.7), S(5.7), S(2.7), Q(8.9)]$ and $M_2 = [R(2.0), S(5.7), R(1.8), S(5.8), S(2.8), Q(9.9)]$ of $N$ satisfy the above region. Notice that $M_1 \equiv M_2$. Let $M_3 = M_2 + [R(1.2), Q(14.2)]$. Since $M_2 \leq^m M_3$ and $M_1 \equiv M_2$, we have $M_1 \preceq M_3$.

### Coverability Problem for TPNs

**Instance:** A set of initial markings $M_{init}$ and a finite set $M_{fin}$ of final markings.
**Question:** $Reach(M_{init}) \cap (M_{fin} \uparrow) = \emptyset$ ?

The coverability problem is interesting from the verification point of view, since checking safety properties (e.g, mutual exclusion properties) can almost always be reduced to coverability[VW86]. We use the set $M_{fin} \uparrow$ to represent a set of "bad markings" which we do not want to occur during the execution of the system. Safety is then equivalent to non-reachability of $M_{fin} \uparrow$.

In fact, from Lemma 1 it follows immediately that analyzing coverability will not be affected by taking the downward closure of the set of reachable markings.

**Lemma 2.** *For a set of markings $M_{init}$ and an upward closed set $M$ of markings, we have $Reach(M_{init}) \cap M = \emptyset$ iff $(Reach(M_{init})) \downarrow \cap M = \emptyset$.*

Since $M_{fin} \uparrow$ (in the definition of the coverability problem) is upward closed by definition, it follows from Lemma 2 that taking downward closure of $Reach(M_{init})$ gives an exact abstraction with respect to coverability.

**Infeasibility of the Karp-Miller Algorithm.** The Karp-Miller algorithm [KM69] is the classical method used for checking coverability in untimed Petri nets. However, it is not obvious how to extend the algorithm to TPNs. [KM69] constructs a reachability tree starting from an initial marking. It detects paths in the reachability tree which leads from a marking $M_1$ to a larger marking $M_2$. In such a case, it makes an over-approximation of the set of reachable markings by putting $\omega$ (interpreted as "unboundedly many tokens") in each place $p$ with $M_1(p) < M_2(p)$. This over-approximation preserves safety properties.

In the case of TPNs, if $M_1 \prec M_2$ (in fact even if $M_1 < M_2$) the only conclusion we can draw is that we will generate unboundedly many tokens with ages greater than *max*. Even if all such tokens are abstracted by $\omega$, an unbounded number of tokens with ages less than *max* may still appear in the analysis. Termination is therefore not guaranteed.

## 3   Region Generators

In this section we introduce *region generators* which we define in a hierarchical manner. First, we introduce *multiset* and *word language generators* and then describe how a region generator characterizes a potentially infinite set (language) of regions.

**Mlgs.** We define *multiset language generator (mlgs)*, each of which characterizes a language which consists of multisets over a finite alphabet.

Let $A$ be a finite alphabet. A *multiset language* (over $A$) is a subset of $A^{\circledast}$. We will consider multiset languages which are downward closed with respect to the relation $\leq^m$ on multisets. If $L$ is downward closed then $B_1 \in L$ and $B_2 \leq^m B_1$ implies $B_2 \in L$. Recall that $\leq^m$ is the ordering defined on multisets (Section 2).

We define *(downward-closed) multiset language generators* (or *mlgs* for short) over the finite alphabet $A$. Each mlg $\phi$ over $A$ defines a multiset language over $A$, denoted $L(\phi)$, which is downward closed. The set of mlgs over $A$ and their languages are defined as follows

- An *expression* over $A$ is of one of the following two forms:
  - an *atomic expression* $a$ where $a \in A$. $L(a) = \{[a], \varepsilon\}$.
  - a *star expression* of the form $S^{\circledast}$ where $S \subseteq A$. $L(S^{\circledast}) = \{[a_1, \ldots, a_m] \mid m \geq 0 \wedge a_1, \ldots, a_m \in S\}$.
- An *mlg* $\phi$ is a (possibly empty) sequence $e_1 + \cdots + e_{\ell}$ of expressions. $L(\phi) = \{B_1 + \cdots + B_{\ell} \mid B_1 \in L(e_1), \cdots, B_{\ell} \in L(e_{\ell})\}$. We denote an empty mlg by $\varepsilon$ and assume that $L(\varepsilon) = \{\varepsilon\}$.

We also consider sets of mlgs which we interpret as unions. If $\Phi = \{\phi_1, \cdots, \phi_m\}$ is a set of mlgs, then $L(\Phi) = L(\phi_1) \cup \cdots \cup L(\phi_m)$. We assume $L(\emptyset) = \emptyset$.

Sometimes we identify mlgs with the languages they represent, so we write $\phi_1 \subseteq \phi_2$ (rather than $L(\phi_1) \subseteq L(\phi_2)$), and $B \in \phi$ (rather than $B \in L(\phi)$), etc.

An mlg $\phi$ is said to be in *normal form* if it is of the form $e + e_1 + \cdots + e_k$ where $e$ is a star expression and $e_1, \ldots, e_k$ are atomic expressions and for each $i : 1 \leq i \leq k$, $e_i \not\subseteq e$. A set of mlgs $\{\phi_1, \cdots, \phi_m\}$ is said to be *normal* if $\phi_i$ is in *normal form* for each $i : 1 \leq i \leq m$, and $\phi_i \not\subseteq \phi_j$ for each $i, j : 1 \leq i \neq j \leq m$.

**Wlgs.** We consider languages where each word is a sequence of multisets over a finite alphabet $A$, i.e., each word is a member of $(A^{\circledast})^*$. The language is then a subset of $(A^{\circledast})^*$. Notice that the underlying alphabet, namely $A^{\circledast}$ is infinite.

For a word $w \in L$, we use $|w|$ to denote the length of $w$, and $w(i)$ to denote the $i^{th}$ element of $w$ where $1 \leq i \leq |w|$. We observe that $w(i)$ is a multiset over $A$. We use $w_1 \bullet w_2$ to denote the concatenation of the words $w_1$ and $w_2$.

We define the ordering $\leq^w$ on set of words such that $w_1 \leq^w w_2$ if there is a strictly monotonic injection $h : \{1, \ldots, |w_1|\} \to \{1, \ldots, |w_2|\}$ where $w_1(i) \leq^m w_2(h(i))$ for $i : 1 \leq i \leq |w_1|$.

We shall consider languages which are downward closed with respect to $\leq^w$. In a similar manner to mlgs, we define downward closed *word language generators (wlgs)* and (word) languages as follows.

- A *word expression* over $A$ is of one of the following two forms:
  - a *word atomic expression* is an mlg $\phi$ over $A$. $L(\phi) = \{B \mid B \in \phi\} \cup \{\varepsilon\}$.
  - a *word star expression* of the form $\{\phi_1, \cdots, \phi_k\}^*$, where $\phi_1, \ldots, \phi_k$ are mlgs over $A$.
    $L(\{\phi_1, \cdots, \phi_k\}^*) = \{B_1 \bullet \cdots \bullet B_m \mid (m \geq 0) \text{ and } B_1, \ldots, B_m \in L(\phi_1) \cup \cdots \cup L(\phi_k)\}$.

- A *word language generator (wlg)* $\psi$ over $A$ is a (possibly empty) concatenation $e_1 \bullet \cdots \bullet e_\ell$ of word expressions $e_1, \ldots, e_\ell$. $L(\psi) = \{w_1 \bullet \cdots \bullet w_\ell \mid w_1 \in L(e_1) \wedge \cdots \wedge w_\ell \in L(e_\ell)\}$.

Notice that the concatenation operator is associative, but not commutative (as is the operator $+$ for multisets). Again, we denote the empty wlg by $\varepsilon$. For a set $\Psi = \{\psi_1, \cdots, \psi_m\}$ of wlgs, we define $L(\Psi) = L(\psi_1) \cup \cdots \cup L(\psi_m)$.

A *word atomic expression* $e$ of the form $\phi$ is said to be in normal form if $\phi$ is a normal mlg. A *word star expression* $\{\phi_1, \ldots, \phi_k\}^*$ is said be in normal form if the set of mlgs $\{\phi_1, \ldots, \phi_k\}$ is in normal form.

A wlg $\psi = e_1 \bullet \cdots \bullet e_\ell$ is said to be *normal* if (a) $e_1, \ldots, e_\ell$ are normal, (b) $e_i \bullet e_{i+1} \not\subseteq e_i$ and (c) $e_i \bullet e_{i+1} \not\subseteq e_{i+1}$, for each $i : 1 \leq i < \ell$. A set of wlgs $\{\psi_1, \cdots, \psi_m\}$ is said to be *normal* if $\psi_1, \ldots, \psi_m$ are normal and $\psi_i \not\subseteq \psi_j$ for each $i, j : 1 \leq i \neq j \leq m$.

**Lemma 3.** *For each set of wlgs (mlgs) $\Psi$, there is a unique normal set of wlgs (mlgs) $\Psi'$ such that $L(\Psi) = L(\Psi')$.*

From now on, we assume always that (sets of) mlgs and wlgs are in normal form.

**Entailment.** Given two (sets of) mlgs $\Phi_1, \Phi_2$, we say that $\Phi_1$ entails $\Phi_2$ to denote that $\Phi_1 \subseteq \Phi_2$. We define entailment for (sets of) wlgs in a similar manner. The following theorem describes complexity of entailment on mlgs and wlgs.

**Theorem 1.** *Entailment of sets of mlgs and wlgs can be computed in quadratic time and cubic time, respectively.*

The next theorem relates mlgs and wlgs to downward closed languages.

**Theorem 2.** *For each downward closed word (multiset) language $L$, there is a finite set $\Psi$ of wlgs (mlgs) such that $L = L(\Psi)$.*

**Region Generators.** A *region generator* $\theta$ is a triple $(\phi_0, \psi, \phi_{max})$ where $\phi_0$ is an mlg over $P \times \{0, \ldots, max\}$, $\psi$ is a wlg over $P \times \{0, \ldots, max-1\}$, and $\phi_{max}$ is an mlg over $P$. The language $L(\theta)$ contains exactly each region of the form $(B_0, w, B_{max})$ where $B_0 \in \phi_0$, $w \in \psi$, and $B_{max} \in \phi_{max}$. We observe that if $\theta_1 = (\phi_0^1, \psi^1, \phi_{max}^1)$ and $\theta_2 = (\phi_0^2, \psi^2, \phi_{max}^2)$ then $\theta_1 \subseteq \theta_2$ iff $\phi_0^1 \subseteq \phi_0^2$, $\psi^1 \subseteq \psi^2$, and $\phi_{max}^1 \subseteq \phi_{max}^2$. In other words entailment between region generators can be computed by checking entailment between the individual elements.

For a region generator $\theta$, we define $[\![\theta]\!]$ to be $\cup_{r \in L(\theta)} [\![r]\!]$. In other words, a region generator $\theta$: (a) defines a language $L(\theta)$ of regions; and (b) denotes a set of markings, namely all markings which belong to the denotation $[\![r]\!]$ for some region $r \in L(\theta)$. A finite set $\Theta = \{\theta_1, \ldots, \theta_m\}$ of region generators denotes the union of its elements, i.e, $[\![\Theta]\!] = \cup_{1 \leq i \leq m} [\![\theta_i]\!]$.

Given a marking $M$ and a region generator $\theta$, it is straightforward to compute whether $M \in [\![\theta]\!]$ from the definition of $[\![r]\!]$ and $[\![\theta]\!]$.

We define an ordering $\leq^r$ on regions such that if $r_1 = (B_0^1, w^1, B_{max}^1)$ and $r_2 = (B_0^2, w^2, B_{max}^2)$ then $r_1 \leq^r r_2$ iff $B_0^1 \leq^m B_0^2$, $w^1 \leq^w w^2$, and $B_{max}^1 \leq^m B_{max}^2$.

By Theorem 2 it follows that for each set $R$ of regions which is downward closed with respect to $\leq^r$, there is a finite set of region generators $\Theta$ such that $L(\Theta) = R$. Also, by definition, it follows that if $r_1 \leq^r r_2$ then $M_1 \preceq M_2$ for each $M_1 \in [\![r_1]\!]$ and $M_2 \in [\![r_2]\!]$.

From this we get the following

**Theorem 3.** *For each set* M *of markings which is downward closed with respect to* $\preceq$ *there is a finite set of region generators* $\Theta$ *such that* M $= [\![\Theta]\!]$.

*Example 3.* Consider again the TPN in Figure 1 with *max* $= 7$. Examples of mlgs over $\{Q,R,S\} \times \{0,\ldots,7\}$ are $R(2)$, $\{S(5),R(1),S(2)\}^{\circledast}$, $Q(3)$, etc. $\{\{S(5),R(1),S(2)\}^{\circledast}\}^* \bullet Q(3)$ is an example of a wlg over $\{Q,R,S\} \times \{0,\ldots,7\}$ and $Q+R$ is an mlg over $\{Q,R,S\}$. Finally, an example of region generator is given by $\theta = (R(2), \{\{S(5),R(1),S(2)\}^{\circledast}\}^* \bullet Q(3), Q+R)$. Notice that the region $r$, given in Example 2, is in $L(\theta)$.

## 4  Forward Analysis

We present a version of the standard symbolic forward reachability algorithm which uses region generators as a symbolic representation. The algorithm inputs a set of region generators $\Theta_{init}$ characterizing the set $M_{init}$ of initial markings, and a set $M_{fin}$ of final markings and tries to answer whether $[\![\Theta_{init}]\!] \cap M_{fin} \uparrow = \emptyset$. The algorithm computes the sequence $\Theta_0, \Theta_1, \ldots$ of sets of region generators s.t $\Theta_{i+1} = \Theta_i \cup succ(\Theta_i)$ with $\Theta_0 = \Theta_{init}$. If $[\![\Theta_i]\!] \cap M_{fin} \uparrow \neq \emptyset$ (amounts to checking membership of elements of $M_{fin}$ in $[\![\Theta]\!]$), or if $\Theta_{i+1} = \Theta_i$, then the procedure is terminated. We define $succ(\Theta)$ to be $Post_{Time}(\Theta) \cup \bigcup_{t \in T}(Post_t(\Theta) \cup Step_t(\Theta))$. $Post_{Time}$ and $Post_t$, defined in Section 5, compute the effect of timed and discrete transitions respectively. $Step_t$, defined in Section 6, implements acceleration. Also, whenever there are two region generators $\theta_1, \theta_2$ in a set of region generators such that $\theta_1 \subseteq \theta_2$, we remove $\theta_1$ from the set.

Even if we know by Theorem 3 that there is finite set $\Theta$ of region generators such that $Reach([\![\Theta_{init}]\!]) = [\![\Theta]\!]$, it is straightforward to apply the techniques presented in [May00] to show the following.

**Theorem 4.** *Given a region generator* $\theta_{init}$ *we cannot in general compute a set* $\Theta$ *of region generators such that* $Reach([\![\Theta_{init}]\!]) = [\![\Theta]\!]$.

The aim of acceleration is to make the forward analysis procedure terminate more often.

## 5  Computing *Post*

In this section, we consider the post-image of a region generator $\theta$ with respect to timed and discrete transitions respectively.

### *Post*$_{Time}$

For an input region generator $\theta$, we shall characterize the set of all markings which can be reached from a marking in $[\![\theta]\!]$ through the passage of the time. We shall compute $Post_{Time}(\theta)$ as a finite set of region generators such that $[\![Post_{Time}(\theta)]\!] = \{M' | \exists M \in [\![\theta]\!]. M \longrightarrow_{Time} M'\}$.

First, we analyze informally the manner in which a marking changes through passage of time. Then, we translate this analysis into a number of computation rules on region generators. Consider a marking $M$ and a region $r = (B_0, w, B_{max})$ such that $M \models r$. Three cases are possible:

**1.** If $B_0 = \varepsilon$, i.e., there are no tokens in $M$ with ages whose fractional parts are equal to zero. Let $w$ be of the form $w_1 \bullet B_1$. The behaviour of the TPN from $M$ due to passage of time is decided by a certain subinterval of $\mathbb{R}^{\geq 0}$ which we denote by $stable(M)$. This interval is defined by $[0 : 1 - x)$ where $x$ is the highest fractional part among the tokens whose ages are less than $max$. Those tokens correspond to $B_1$ in the definition of $r$. We call $stable(M)$ the *stable period* of $M$.

Suppose that time passes by an amount $\delta \in stable(M)$. If $M \longrightarrow_{\delta} M_1$ then $M_1 \models r$, i.e., $M_1 \equiv M$. In other words, if the elapsed time is in the stable period of $M$ then all markings reached through performing timed transitions are equivalent to $M$. The reason is that, although the fractional parts have increased (by the same amount), the relative ordering of the fractional parts, and the integral parts of the ages are not affected.

As soon as we leave the stable period, the tokens which originally had the highest fractional parts (those corresponding to $B_1$) will now change: their integral parts will increase by one while fractional parts will become equal to zero. Therefore, we reach a marking $M_2$, where $M_2 \models r_2$ and $r_2$ is of the form $\left(B_1^{+1}, w_1, B_{max}\right)$. Here, $B_1^{+1}$ is the result of replacing each pair $p(n)$ in $B_1$ by $p(n+1)$.

**2.** If $B_0 \neq \varepsilon$, i.e., there are some tokens whose ages do not exceed $max$ and whose fractional parts are equal to zero. We divide the tokens in $B_0$ into two multisets: *young tokens* whose ages are strictly less than $max$, and *old tokens* whose ages are equal to $max$. The stable period $stable(M)$ here is the point interval $[0 : 0]$. Suppose that we let time pass by an amount $\delta : 0 < \delta < 1 - x$, where $x$ is the highest fractional part of the tokens whose ages are less than $max$. Then the fractional parts for the tokens in $B_0$ will become positive. The young tokens will still have values not exceeding $max$, while the old tokens will now have values strictly greater than $max$. This means that if $M \longrightarrow_{\delta} M_1$ then $M_1 \models r_1$ where $r_1$ is of the form $(\varepsilon, young \bullet w, B_{max} + old)$. Here, $young$ and $old$ are sub-multisets of $B_0$ such that $young(p(n)) = B_0(p(n))$ if $n < max$, and $old(p) = B_0(p(max))$. Since the fractional parts of the tokens in $young$ are smaller than all other tokens, we put $young$ first in the second component of the region. Also, the ages of the tokens in $old$ are now strictly greater than $max$, so they are added to the third component of the region.

**3.** If $B_0 = \varepsilon, w = \varepsilon$, all tokens have age greater than $max$. Now, if we let time pass by any amount $\delta \geq 0$ and $M \longrightarrow_{\delta} M_1$, then $M_1 \models r$. When all tokens reach age of $max$, aging of tokens becomes irrelevant.

Notice that in cases 1 and 2, the stable period is the largest interval during which the marking does not change the region it belongs to. Markings in case 3 never change their regions and are therefore considered to be "stable forever" with respect to timed transitions. Also, we observe that each of first two cases above corresponds to "rotating" the multisets in $B_0$ and $w$, sometimes also moving them to $B_{max}$.

Now, we formalize the analysis above as a number of computation rules on region generators. First, we introduce some notations. Let $\phi$ be an mlg of the form $\{a_1, \ldots, a_k\}^{\circledast} + a_{k+1} + \cdots + a_{k+\ell}$. Notice that, by the normal form defined in Section 3, we can always write $\phi$ in this form. We define $\#\phi$ to be the pair $(B, B')$ where $B = [a_1, \ldots, a_k]$ and $B' = [a_{k+1}, \ldots, a_{k+\ell}]$.

Let $\phi$ be an mlg over $P \times \{0, \ldots, max\}$ with $\#\phi = (B, B')$. We define $young(\phi)$ and $old(\phi)$ to be mlgs over $P \times \{0, \ldots, max-1\}$ and $P$ respectively such that the following holds: let $\#young(\phi) = (B_1, B'_1)$ and $\#old(\phi) = (B_2, B'_2)$ such that

- $B(p(n)) = B_1(p(n))$ and $B'(p(n)) = B'_1(p(n))$ if $n < max$.
- $B(p(max)) = B_2(p)$ and $B'(p(max)) = B'_2(p)$.

In other words, from $\phi$, we obtain an mlg given by $young(\phi)$ which characterizes tokens younger than $max$ and an mlg $old(\phi)$ which characterizes tokens older than $max$.

Let $\phi$ be an mlg over $P \times \{0, \ldots, max-1\}$ of the form $\{p_1(n_1), \ldots p_k(n_k)\}^{\circledast} + p_{k+1}(n_{k+1}) + \cdots + p_{k+\ell}(n_{k+\ell})$. We use $\phi^{+1}$ to denote the mlg $\{p_1(n_1+1), \cdots, p_k(n_k+1)\}^{\circledast} + p_{k+1}(n_{k+1}+1) + \cdots + p_{k+\ell}(n_{k+\ell}+1)$. That is, we replace each occurrence of a pair $p(n)$ in the representation of $\phi$ by $p(n+1)$.

We are ready to define the function $Post_{Time}(\theta_{in})$ for some input region generator $\theta_{in}$. We start from $\theta_{in}$ and perform an iteration, maintaining two sets $V$ and $W$ of region generators. Region generators in $V$ are already analyzed and those in $W$ are yet to be analyzed. We pick (also remove) a region generator $\theta$ from $W$, add it to $V$ (if it is not already included in $V$). We update $W$ and $V$ with new region generators according to the rules described below. We continue until $W$ is empty. At this point we take $Post_{Time}(\theta_{in}) = V$. Depending on the form of $\theta$, we update $W$ and $V$ according to one of the following cases.

- If $\theta$ is of the form $(\phi_0, \psi, \phi_{max})$, where $\phi_0 \neq \varepsilon$. We add a region generator $(\varepsilon, young(\phi_0) \bullet \psi, \phi_{max} + old(\phi_0))$ to $W$. This step corresponds to one rotation according to case 2 in the analysis above.
- If $\theta$ is of the form $(\varepsilon, \psi \bullet \phi, \phi_{max})$. Here the last element in the second component of the region generator is an atomic expression (an mlg). We add the region generator $(\phi^{+1}, \psi, \phi_{max})$ to $W$. This step corresponds to one rotation according to case 1 in the analysis above.
- If $\theta$ is of the form $(\varepsilon, \psi \bullet \{\phi_1, \ldots, \phi_k\}^*, \phi_{max})$. Here, the last expression in the second component of the region generator is a star expression. This case is similar to the previous one. However, the tokens corresponding to $\{\phi_1, \ldots, \phi_k\}^*$ now form an unbounded sequence with strictly increasing fractional parts. We add

$$\left( \phi_i^{+1}, \{young(\phi_1^{+1}), \ldots, young(\phi_k^{+1})\}^* \bullet \psi \bullet \{\phi_1, \ldots, \phi_k\}^*, \phi_{max} + Old^{\circledast} \right)$$

to $V$, and

$$\left( \phi_i^{+1}, \{young(\phi_1^{+1}), \ldots, young(\phi_k^{+1})\}^* \bullet \psi, \phi_{max} + Old^{\circledast} \right)$$

to $W$, for $i : 1 \leq i \leq k$. Here, $Old$ is the union of the sets of symbols occurring in the set of mlgs $\{old(\phi_1^{+1}), \ldots, old(\phi_k^{+1})\}$. This step corresponds to performing a sequence of rotations of the forms of case 1 and case 2 above.

Notice that we add one of the newly generated region generators directly to $V$ (and its "successor" to $W$). This is done in order to avoid an infinite loop where the same region generator is generated all the time.

- If $\theta$ is of the form $(\varepsilon, \varepsilon, \phi_{max})$, i.e., all tokens have ages which are strictly greater than $max$, then we do not add any element to $W$.

The termination of this algorithm is guaranteed due to the fact that after a finite number of steps, we will eventually reach a point where we analyze region generators which will only characterize tokens with ages greater than $max$ (i.e. will be of the form $(\varepsilon, \varepsilon, \phi_{max})$).

### $Post_t$

For an input region generator $\theta$, we compute (the downward closure of) the set of all markings which can be reached from a marking in $[\![\theta]\!]$ by firing a discrete transition $t$, i.e we compute $Post_t(\theta)$ as a finite set of region generators s.t $[\![Post(\theta)]\!] = \{M'| \exists M \in [\![\theta]\!].M \longrightarrow_t M'\}$.

Notice that from a downward closed set of markings, when we execute a timed transition, the set of markings reached is always downward-closed. But this is not the case for discrete transitions. Therefore, we consider the downward closure of the set of reachable markings in the following algorithm.

To give an algorithm for $Post_t$, we need to define an *addition* and a *subtraction* operation for region generators. An addition (subtraction) corresponds to adding (removing) a token in a certain age interval. These operations have hierarchical definitions reflecting the hierarchical structure of region generators.

We start by defining addition and subtraction for mlgs, defined over a finite set $P \times \{0, \ldots, max\}$.

Given a *normal* mlg $\phi = S^{\circledast} + a_1 + \cdots + a_\ell$ and a pair $p(n)$ where $p$ is a place and $n$ denotes the integral part of the age of a token in $p$, we define the *addition* $\phi \oplus p(n)$ to be the mlg $\phi + p(n)$.

The subtraction $\phi \ominus p(n)$ is defined by the following three cases.

- If $p(n) \in S$, then $\phi \ominus p(n) = \phi$. Intuitively, the mlg $\phi$ describes markings with an unbounded number of tokens each with an integral part equal to $n$, and each residing in place $p$. Therefore, after removing one such a token, we will still be left with an unbounded number of them.
- If $p(n) \notin S$ and $a_i = p(n)$ for some $i : 1 \le i \le \ell$ then $\phi \ominus p(n) = S^{\circledast} + a_1 + \cdots + a_{i-1} + a_{i+1} + \cdots + a_\ell$.
- Otherwise, the operation is undefined.

Addition and subtraction from mlgs over $P$ is similar where instead of $p(n)$, we simply add (subtract) $p$.

Now, we extend the operations to wlgs defined over mlgs of the above form.

The addition $\psi \oplus p(n)$ is a wlg $\psi$ consisting of the following three sets of wlgs.

1. For each $\psi_1$, $\psi_2$, and $\phi$ with $\psi = \psi_1 \bullet \phi \bullet \psi_2$, we have
   $\psi_1 \bullet (\phi \oplus p(n)) \bullet \psi_2 \in (\psi \oplus p(n))$.
2. For each $\psi_1$, $\psi_2$ and $\psi = \psi_1 \bullet \{\phi_1, \cdots, \phi_k\}^* \bullet \psi_2$, we have for $i : 1 \le i \le k$,
   $\psi_1 \bullet \{\phi_1, \cdots, \phi_k\}^* \bullet (\phi_i \oplus p(n)) \bullet \{\phi_1, \cdots, \phi_k\}^* \bullet \psi_2 \in (\psi \oplus p(n))$.

3. For each $\psi_1$ and $\psi_2$ with $\psi = \psi_1 \bullet \psi_2$, we have
   $\psi_1 \bullet p(n) \bullet \psi_2 \in (\psi \oplus p(n))$.

Intuitively, elements added according to the first two cases correspond to adding a token with a fractional part equal to that of some other token. In the third case the fractional part differs from all other tokens.

We define the subtraction $\psi \ominus p(n)$, where $\psi$ is a wlg, to be a set of wlgs, according to the following two cases.

– If there is a star expression $e = \{\phi_1, \cdots, \phi_k\}^*$ containing the token we want to re-move, i.e., if $\psi$ is of the form $\psi_1 \bullet e \bullet \psi_2$, and if any of the operations $\phi_i \ominus p(n)$ is defined for $i : 1 \le i \le k$, then $\psi \ominus p(n) = \{\psi\}$.
– Otherwise, the set $\psi \ominus p(n)$ contains wlgs of the form $\psi_1 \bullet \phi' \bullet \psi_2$ such that $\psi$ is of the form $\psi_1 \bullet \phi \bullet \psi_2$ and $\phi' \in (\phi \ominus p(n))$.

Now we describe how to use the addition and subtraction operations for computing $Post_t$. Addition and subtraction of pairs of the form $p(n)$ can be easily extended to pairs of the form $p(N)$ where $N \subseteq \{0, \ldots, max\}$, e.g $\psi \ominus p(N) = \{\psi \ominus p(n)| n \in N\}$.

We recall that, in a TPN, the effect of firing a transition is to remove tokens from the input places and add tokens to the output places. Furthermore, the tokens which are added or removed should have ages in the corresponding intervals. The effect of of firing transitions from the set of markings characterized by a region generator $\theta = (\phi_0, \psi, \phi_{max})$ can therefore be defined by the following operations.

First, we assume an interval $I$ of the form $(x, y)$. The subtraction $\theta \ominus p(I)$ is given by the union of the following sets of region generators.

– $(\phi_0 \ominus p(N), \psi, \phi_{max})$ where each $n \in N$ is a natural number in the interval $I$. In-tuitively, if the age of the token that is removed has a zero fractional part, then $N$ contains the valid choices of integral part.
– $(\phi_0, \psi', \phi_{max})$ such that $\psi' \in \psi \ominus p(N)$, where $N = \{n| n \in \mathbb{N} \wedge x \le n < y\}$ i.e., each $n$ is a valid choice of integral part for the age of the token if it has a non-zero fractional part.
– $(\phi_0, \psi, \phi_{max} \ominus p)$ if $I$ is of the form $(x, \infty)$, i.e., the age of the token may be greater than $max$.

Addition is defined in a similar manner. The addition and subtraction operations will be similar if the interval is closed to the left. But if the interval is closed to the right, the last rule is undefined in that case.

We extend definition of subtraction and addition for subtracting a set of tuples $p(I)$ in the obvious manner. For a set of region generators $\Theta$, we define $\Theta \oplus p(I) = \bigcup_{\theta \in \Theta} (\theta \oplus p(I))$. Subtraction for a set of region generators is defined in a similar manner.

Let $\mathcal{A}_{in}(t)$ be the set of input arcs given by $\{p(I)| In(t,p) = I\}$ and the set of output arcs $\mathcal{A}_{out}(t)$ be given by $\{p(I)| Out(t,p) = I\}$.

We define,

$$Post_t(\theta) = (\theta \ominus \mathcal{A}_{in}(t)) \oplus \mathcal{A}_{out}(t)$$

## 6    Acceleration

In this section, we explain how to accelerate the firing of a single transition interleaved with timed transitions from a region generator. We give a criterion which characterizes when acceleration can be applied. If the criterion is satisfied by an input region generator $\theta_{in}$ with respect to a transition $t$, then we compute a finite set $Accel_t(\theta_{in})$ of region generators such that $[\![Accel_t(\theta_{in})]\!] = \{M' | \exists M \in [\![\theta_{in}]\!].\ M(\longrightarrow_{Time} \cup \longrightarrow_t)^* M'\}$. We shall not compute the set $Accel_t(\theta_{in})$ in a single step. Instead, we will present a procedure $Step_t$ with the following property: for each region generators $\theta_{in}$ there is an $n \geq 0$ such that $Accel_t(\theta) = \bigcup_{0 \leq i \leq n} (Post_{Time} \circ Step_t)^i(\theta)$. In other words, the set $Accel_t(\theta)$ will be fully generated through a finite number of applications of $Post_{Time}$ followed by $Step_t$. Since the reachability algorithm of Section 4 computes both $Post_{Time}$ and $Step_t$ during each iteration, we are guaranteed that all region generators in $Accel_t(\theta_{in})$ will eventually be produced.

To define $Step_t$ we need some preliminary definitions.

For a word atomic expression (mlg) $\phi = \{a_1, \ldots, a_k\}^{\circledast} + a_{k+1} + \cdots + a_{k+\ell}$, we define $sym(\phi)$ as the set of symbols given by $\{a_1, \ldots, a_{k+\ell}\}$. For a word star expression $e = \{\phi_1, \ldots, \phi_k\}^*$, $sym(e) = \bigcup_i sym(\phi_i)$ for $i : 1 \leq i \leq k$.

Given a symbol $a \in A$ and an mlg $\phi$ over $A$ of the form $S^{\circledast} + a_1 + \cdots + a_\ell$, we say that $a$ is a $\circledast - symbol$ in $\phi$ if $a \in S$. Intuitively, $a$ is a $\circledast - symbol$ in an mlg $\phi$ if it can occur arbitrarily many times in the multisets in $\phi$.

Given a wlg $\psi = e_1 \bullet \cdots \bullet e_l$ over $A$, we say that a symbol $a \in A$ is a

- $\circledast - symbol$ in $\psi$ if there is an $i : 1 \leq i \leq l$ such that $a$ is a $\circledast - symbol$ for some mlg $\phi$ occurring in wlg $\psi$.
- $* - symbol$ in $\psi$ if there is an $i : 1 \leq i \leq l$ such that $a \in sym(e_i)$ and $e_i$ is a word star expression.

Intuitively, $a$ is a $* - symbol$ in $\psi$ if it can occur an arbitrary number of times in arbitrarily many consecutive multisets in a word given by the wlg $\psi$.

In this section, we show how to perform acceleration when intervals are open, i.e of the form $(x, y)$. It is straightforward to extend the algorithms to closed intervals (see [ADMN03] for details).

To compute the effect of acceleration, we define an operation $\uplus$.

**Accelerated addition** $\uplus$ corresponds to repeatedly adding an arbitrary number of tokens of the form $p(n)$ (with all possible fractional parts) to a region generator $\theta$.

First we define the operation $\uplus$ for mlgs. Given a mlg $\phi$ and a pair $p(n)$, the accelerated addition $\phi \uplus p(n)$ is given by an mlg $\phi + \{p(n)\}^{\circledast}$.

Given a wlg $\psi$, $\psi \uplus p(n)$ can be inductively defined as follows.

- If $\psi = \varepsilon$, then $\psi \uplus p(n) = \{\{p(n)\}^{\circledast}\}^*$.
- If $\psi = \phi \bullet \psi'$, then $\psi \uplus p(n) = \{\{p(n)\}^{\circledast}\}^* \bullet (\phi \uplus p(n)) \bullet (\psi' \uplus p(n))$
- If $\psi = \{\phi_1, \cdots, \phi_n\}^* \bullet \psi'$, then $\psi \uplus p(n) = \{\phi_1 \uplus p(n), \cdots, \phi_n \uplus p(n)\}^* \bullet (\psi' \uplus p(n))$

Accelerated addition can be extended to sets of pairs of the form $\{p(n_1), \ldots, p(n_k)\}$. Given a wlg $\psi$, we define $\psi \uplus \{p(n_1), \ldots, p(n_k)\} = \psi \uplus p(n_1) \uplus \cdots \uplus p(n_k)$.

Given a region generator $\theta = (\phi_0, \psi, \phi_{max})$ and a pair $p(I)$ where $I = (x, y)$, we define

$$\theta \uplus p(I) = \left(\phi_0 + S_1^{\circledast}, \; \psi \uplus S_2, \; \phi_{max} + \{p_{max}\}^{\circledast}\right) \text{ where}$$

- $S_1 = \{p(n) \mid n \in \mathbb{N} \wedge x < n < y\}$.
- $S_2 = \{p(n) \mid n \in \mathbb{N} \wedge x \leq n < y\}$.
- $p_{max} = p$ if $y = \infty$, $p_{max} = \varepsilon$ otherwise.

For a set of pairs, $\mathcal{A} = \{p_1(I_1), \cdots, p_k(I_k)\}$, we define $\theta \uplus \mathcal{A} = \theta \uplus p_1(I_1) \uplus \cdots \uplus p_k(I_k)$.

**Acceleration Criterion:** For a discrete transition $t$, to check whether we can fire $t$ arbitrarily many times interleaved with timed transitions, first we categorize the input places of $t$ with respect to a region generator $\theta = (\phi_0, \psi, \phi_{max})$ and the transition $t$.

**Type 1 place** An input place $p$ of $t$ is said to be of *Type 1* if one of the following holds. Given $In(t, p) = (x, y)$,

  - there is an integer $n$ such that $x < n < y$ and $p(n)$ is a $\circledast - symbol$ in $\phi_0$.
  - there is an integer $n$ such that $x \leq n < y$ and $p(n)$ is a $\circledast - symbol$ or a $* - symbol$ in $\psi$.
  - $p$ is a $\circledast - symbol$ in $\phi_{max}$ and $y = \infty$.

Intuitively, unbounded number of tokens with the "right age" are available in an input place $p$ of Type 1.

**Type 2 place** An input place $p$ of $t$ is of *Type 2* if it is not of Type 1, but it is an output place and both the following holds.

  1. Given $In(t, p) = I$, $\theta \ominus p(I) \neq \emptyset$. Intuitively, for a Type 2 place, there is initially at least one token of the "right age" for firing $t$.
  2. $In(t, p) \cap Out(t, p)$ is a non-empty interval. Intuitively, a token generated as output in any firing may be re-used as an input for the next firing.

We accelerate if each input place of $t$ is a Type 1 place or a Type 2 place.

**Acceleration:** Let $\mathcal{A}_{in}(t), \mathcal{A}_{out}(t)$ be the set of input and output arcs as defined in Section 5. Now, given a region generator $\theta$, we describe acceleration in steps.

  - First we subtract input tokens from all input places. Then we add tokens to Type 2 places (places which always re-use an output token as an input for next firing). Formally we compute a set of region generators $\Theta = (\theta \ominus \mathcal{A}_{in}(t)) \oplus T_2$ where $T_2 = \{p(I) \mid p \text{ is of Type } 2 \wedge p(I) \in \mathcal{A}_{out}(t)\}$ is the set of output arcs from Type 2 places.
  - Next, we accelerate addition for each region generator in $\Theta$ and add tokens of all possible ages in the output places which are not of Type 2 (Type 2 places re-use input tokens, therefore do not accumulate tokens), i.e, we compute

$$Step_t(\theta) = \bigcup_{\theta' \in \Theta} \theta' \uplus (\mathcal{A}_{out}(t) \setminus T_2)$$

**Theorem 5.** *If the acceleration criterion holds from a region generator $\theta$ with respect to a transition $t$ in a TPN, there is an $n \geq 0$ such that $Accel_t(\theta) = \bigcup\limits_{0 \leq i \leq n} (Post_{Time} \circ$*

$Step_t)^i(\theta)$.

# 7  Experimental Results

We have implemented a prototype based on our algorithm and used it to verify two protocols.

**Parameterized Model of Fischer's Protocol.** Fischer's protocol is intended to guarantee mutual exclusion in a concurrent system consisting of arbitrary number of processes trying to get access to a shared variable (see e.g. [AN01] for more details). The

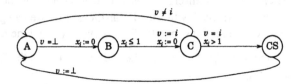

**Fig. 2.** One process in Fischer's Protocol for Mutual Exclusion

protocol consists of processes running a code, which is graphically described in Figure 2. Each process $i$ has a local clock, $x_i$, and a control state, which assumes values in the set $\{A, B, C, CS\}$ where $A$ is the initial state and $CS$ is the critical section. The processes read from and write to a shared variable $v$, whose value is either $\perp$ or the index of one of the processes. Our aim is to show that this protocol allows at most one process to enter the critical section $CS$. Figure 3 shows a timed Petri net model

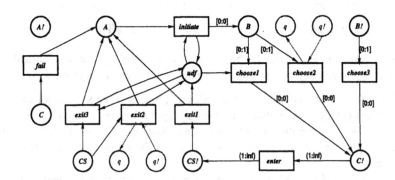

**Fig. 3.** TPN model for Parameterized version of Fischer's Protocol for Mutual Exclusion.

[AN01] of the parameterized protocol. Tokens in the places $A$, $B$, $C$, $CS$, $A!$, $B!$, $C!$ and $CS!$ represent processes running the protocol. In the figure, We use $q$ to denote any of the process states $A, B, C, CS$. The places marked with ! represent that the value of the shared variable is the index of the process modeled by the token in that place. We use a place $udf$ to represent that the value of the shared variable is $\perp$. The critical section is modelled by the places $CS$ and $CS!$, so mutual exclusion is violated when the total number of tokens in those places is at least two. In order to prove the mutual exclusion property, we specify markings with two tokens in $CS, CS!$ as the bad markings. We use $\left( \{A(0), A(1)\}^\circledast + udf(0), \{\{A(0)\}^\circledast\}^*, \{A\}^\circledast \right)$ as the initial region generator $\theta_{init}$. $\theta_{init}$ characterizes arbitrarily many processes in $A$ having any clock value (age) and one token in $udf$ with age 0. Furthermore, to prove that mutual exclusion is guaranteed, we checked the membership of the bad markings (characterizing an upward closed set of bad states) in the computed set of region generators.

**Producer-Consumer System[NSS01].** We consider the producer/consumer system mentioned in [NSS01][2]. Figure 4 shows a timed Petri net model of the pro-

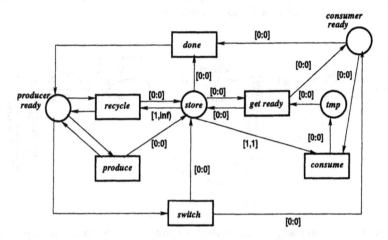

**Fig. 4.** TPN model for Producer/Consumer System.

ducer/consumer system. A token in the place *producer_ready* means that the producer can produce *items*; firing transition *produce* creates new *items* in place *store*. The consumer consumes items of age 1 if the place *consumer_ready* has a token. Old items (of age greater than 1) are recycled by the producer using the transition *recycle*. Control is switched between the producer and the consumer by transitions *switch* and *done*. We use $(producer\_ready(0), \varepsilon, \varepsilon)$ as the initial region generator $\theta_{init}$ which characterizes a single token in place "*producer_ready*" with age 0.

Our program computes the reachability set for both protocols (the set of computed region generators are shown in Appendix). The procedure fails to terminate without the use of acceleration in both cases. It took 35MB memory and 26s to analyse Fischer's protocol, and 3.25MB memory and 3s to analyse producer/consumer system on a 1 GHz processor with 256 MB RAM.

**Abstract Graph.** Using forward analysis of a TPN, our tool also generates a graph $\mathcal{G}$ which is a finite-state abstraction of the TPN. Each state in $\mathcal{G}$ corresponds to a region

---

[2] [NSS01] considers a TPN model with local time in each place.

generator in the reachability set. Edges of $G$ are created as follows. Consider two region generators $\theta_1, \theta_2$ in the reachability set. If there is a region generator $\theta_2' \in Post_t(\theta_1)$ such that $\theta_2' \subseteq \theta_2$, then we add an edge $\theta_1 \xrightarrow{t} \theta_2$ to $G$. Similarly, if there is a region generator $\theta_2' \in Post_{Time}(\theta_1)$ such that $\theta_2' \subseteq \theta_2$, then we add an edge $\theta_1 \xrightarrow{\tau} \theta_2$. Notice that each region generator in the post-image should be included in some region generator in the computed set. It is straightforward to show that the abstract graph simulates the corresponding TPN model.

The graph obtained by the above analysis contains 12 states and 54 edges in the case of Fischer's protocol; and 11 states and 21 edges in the case of producer/consumer system. Furthermore, we use *The Concurrency Workbench* [CPS89] to minimize the abstract graphs modulo weak bisimilarity. Figure 5 shows the minimized finite state labelled transition systems for the above protocols.

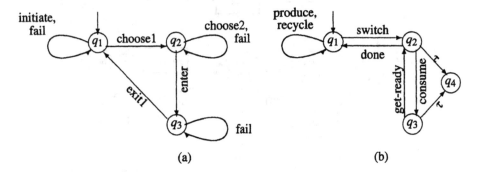

**Fig. 5.** Minimized abstract graph for (a) Fischer's protocol. (b) Producer/Consumer System.

## 8   Conclusions and Future Research

We have described how to perform forward analysis augmented with acceleration for timed Petri nets, using a symbolic representation called *region generators*. There are a number of interesting directions for future research. Firstly, we show how to accelerate with respect to single discrete transition interleaved with timed transitions. A remaining challenge is to extend the technique and consider accelerations of *sequences* of discrete transitions. It is not clear to us whether such accelerations are computable in the first place. Secondly, we assume a lazy behaviour of TPNS. It is well-known that checking safety properties is undecidable for TPNs with *urgent* behaviours even if the net is safe (bounded). Therefore, designing acceleration techniques is of particular interest for urgent TPNs. Notice that downward closure is no longer an exact abstraction if the behaviour is urgent. Thirdly, we use *region generators* for symbolic representation. We want to investigate designing efficient data structures (e.g . *zone generators* corresponding to a large number of region generators). *Zones* are widely used in existing tools for verification of timed automata [LPY97,Yov97]. Intuitively, a zone generator will correspond to a state in each minimized automaton in Figure 5. Finally, We aim at developing generic methods for building downward closed languages, in a similar manner to the methods we have developed for building upward closed languages in [AČJYK00]. This would give a general theory for forward analysis of infinite state systems, in the same way the work in [AČJYK00] is for backward analysis. Simple regular expressions of [ABJ98] and the region generators of this paper are examples of data structures which might be developed in a systematic manner within such a theory.

# References

[ABJ98]    Parosh Aziz Abdulla, Ahmed Bouajjani, and Bengt Jonsson. On-the-fly analysis of systems with unbounded, lossy fifo channels. In *Proc. CAV'98*, volume 1427 of *LNCS*, pages 305–318, 1998.

[AČJYK00] Parosh Aziz Abdulla, Karlis Čerāns, Bengt Jonsson, and Tsay Yih-Kuen. Algorithmic analysis of programs with well quasi-ordered domains. *Information and Computation*, 160:109–127, 2000.

[AD90]     R. Alur and D. Dill. Automata for modelling real-time systems. In *Proc. ICALP '90*, volume 443 of *LNCS*, pages 322–335, 1990.

[ADMN03]   Parosh Aziz Abdulla, Johann Deneux, Pritha Mahata, and Aletta Nylén. Forward reachability analysis of timed petri nets. Technical Report 2003-056, Dept. of Information Technology, Uppsala University, Sweden, 2003. http://user.it.uu.se/~pritha/Papers/tpn.ps.

[AN01]     Parosh Aziz Abdulla and Aletta Nylén. Timed Petri nets and BQOs. In *Proc. ICATPN'2001*, volume 2075 of *LNCS*, pages 53 –70, 2001.

[BG96]     B. Boigelot and P. Godefroid. Symbolic verification of communication protocols with infinite state spaces using QDDs. In *Proc. CAV'96*, volume 1102 of *LNCS*, pages 1–12, 1996.

[BH97]     A. Bouajjani and P. Habermehl. Symbolic reachability analysis of fifo-channel systems with nonregular sets of configurations. In *Proc. ICALP'97*, volume 1256 of *LNCS*, 1997.

[BLO98]    S. Bensalem, Y. Lakhnech, and S. Owre. Computing abstractions of infinite state systems automatically and compositionally. In *Proc. CAV'98*, volume 1427 of *LNCS*, pages 319–331, 1998.

[Bow96]    F. D. J. Bowden. Modelling time in Petri nets. In *Proc. Second Australian-Japan Workshop on Stochastic Models*, 1996.

[CPS89]    R. Cleaveland, J. Parrow, and B. Steffen. A semantics-based tool for the verification of finite-state systems. In Brinksma, Scollo, and Vissers, editors, *Protocol Specification, Testing, and Verification IX*, pages 287–302. North-Holland, 1989.

[DR00]     G. Delzanno and J. F. Raskin. Symbolic representation of upward-closed sets. In *Proc. TACAS'00*, volume 1785 of *LNCS*, pages 426–440, 2000.

[FIS00]    A. Finkel, S. Purushothaman Iyer, and G. Sutre. Well-abstracted transition systems. In *Proc. CONCUR'00*, pages 566–580, 2000.

[FRSB02]   A. Finkel, J.-F. Raskin, M. Samuelides, and L. Van Begin. Monotonic extensions of petri nets: Forward and backward search revisited. In *Proc. Infinity'02*, 2002.

[God94]    J.C. Godskesen. *Timed Modal Specifications*. PhD thesis, Aalborg University, 1994.

[KM69]     R.M. Karp and R.E. Miller. Parallel program schemata. *Journal of Computer and Systems Sciences*, 3(2):147–195, May 1969.

[LBBO01]   Y. Lakhnech, S. Bensalem, S. Berezin, and S. Owre. Symbolic techniques for parametric reasoning about counter and clock systems. In *Proc. TACAS'01*, volume 2031 of *LNCS*, 2001.

[LPY97]     K.G. Larsen, P. Pettersson, and W. Yi. UPPAAL in a nutshell. *Software Tools for Technology Transfer*, 1(1-2), 1997.

[May00]     R. Mayr. Undecidable problems in unreliable computations. In *Theoretical Informatics (LATIN'2000)*, volume 1776 of *LNCS*, 2000.

[NSS01]     M. Nielson, V. Sassone, and J. Srba. Towards a distributed time for petri nets. In *Proc. ICATPN'01*, pages 23–31, 2001.

[VW86]     M. Y. Vardi and P. Wolper. An automata-theoretic approach to automatic program verification. In *Proc. LICS'86*, pages 332–344, June 1986.

[Yov97]     S. Yovine. Kronos: A verification tool for real-time systems. *Journal of Software Tools for Technology Transfer*, 1(1-2), 1997.

# Lazy Approximation for Dense Real-Time Systems[*]

Maria Sorea[**]

Universität Ulm, Abteilung Künstliche Intelligenz, Germany
sorea@informatik.uni-ulm.de

**Abstract.** We propose an effective and complete method for verifying safety and
liveness properties of timed systems, which is based on predicate abstraction for
computing finite abstractions of timed automata and TCTL formulas, finite-state
CTL model checking, and successive refinement of finite-state abstractions. Starting with some coarse abstraction of the given timed automaton and the TCTL
formula we define a finite sequence of refined abstractions that converges to the
region graph of the real-time system. In each step, new abstraction predicates
are selected nondeterministically from a finite, predetermined basis of abstraction predicates. Symbolic counterexamples from failed model-checking attempts
are used to heuristically choose a small set of new abstraction predicates for incrementally refining the current abstraction. Without sacrificing completeness,
this algorithm usually does not require computing the complete region graph to
decide model-checking problems. Abstraction refinement terminates quickly, as
a multitude of spurious counterexamples is eliminated in every refinement step
through the use of symbolic counterexamples for TCTL.

## 1 Introduction

*Timed Automata* [2] are state-transition graphs augmented with a finite set of real-valued
clocks. The clocks proceed at a uniform rate and constrain the times at which transitions
may occur. Given a timed automaton and a property expressed in a (timed) temporal
logic, model checking answers the question whether the timed automaton satisfies the
given formula. The fundamental graph-theoretic model checking algorithm by Alur,
Courcoubetis and Dill [1] constructs a finite quotient, the so-called *region graph*, of the
infinite state graph corresponding to the timed automaton. Algorithms directly based on
the explicit construction of such a partition of states are inefficient since the number of
equivalence classes of states of the region graph grows exponentially with the largest
time constant and the number of clocks that are used to specify timing constraints.

In [19] we propose a novel method for verifying safety and liveness properties of
timed systems based on predicate abstraction [14] for timed automata, finite-state model
checking, and counterexample-guided abstraction refinement. We define a set of so-
called *basis predicates*, which are expressive enough for distinguishing between any
two clock regions. This set of predicates determines a strongly preserving abstraction

---

[*] This work was supported by SRI International, by NSF grants CCR-ITR-0326540 and CCR-
ITR-0325808.

[**] Currently at Stanford University. This research has been mainly conducted while the author
was visiting SRI International.

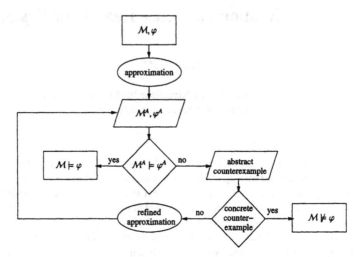

**Fig. 1.** Lazy approximation.

in the sense that a timed automaton validates a $\mu$-calculus formula iff the corresponding finite abstraction validates this formula. The control structure of the timed automaton is preserved in the abstract system. The abstracted systems no longer refer to the real-time nature of computations, and finite-state model checkers can be used to establish safety and liveness properties in the abstracted system.

In many cases it is not necessary to compute the exact abstraction using the entire basis of predicates, since a coarser approximation of this is sufficient for proving or refuting the desired property. Since we consider safety and liveness properties we maintain both under- and over-approximations of the given timed system. Existential formulas have to be established in the under-approximation, while over-approximations are necessary for universal formulas. These approximations are computed via an iterative abstraction-refinement process that starts with some coarse approximations of the timed system and computes a sequence of approximations until the one necessary for proving or refuting the property is obtained. In each refinement step new abstraction predicates are selected from the finite set of basis predicates and new, more detailed approximations are computed. Hereby, the choice of predicates is guided by counterexamples from failing model-checking attempts. We call this method *lazy approximation*. This process of abstracting and refining approximations is illustrated in Figure 1. When using the entire basis of predicates for computing the approximations, the under- and over-approximation are identical, yielding therefore a strongly property preserving abstraction of the timed system. Since the sequence of approximations converges toward the region graph of the real-time systems, the method of lazy approximation is complete [19]. The main advantage of this approach is that finite time-abstractions are computed lazily. This results in substantial savings in computation whenever coarse abstractions are sufficient to prove the property at hand. Standard benchmark examples for timed automata such as train gate controller and a version of Fischer's mutual exclusion protocol can be proved using only a few abstraction predicates.

In this paper we extend our previous results [19] in several directions. First, we consider TCTL [1] for expressing qualitative and quantitative properties of timed systems, instead of the untimed logic considered in [19]. We define an abstraction function for TCTL that maps a TCTL formula to a CTL formula, together with the inverse operation of concretization. The predicates necessary for the abstraction are extracted from the time-bounded operators of the TCTL formula. For extracting the predicates we introduce for every time-bounded operator of a given TCTL formula $\varphi$ a new clock variable $z_i$. Now, the set of abstraction predicates $\Psi_\varphi$ with respect to $\varphi$ consists of all the formulas $z_i {\sim} c$ with free variables $z_i$, where ${\sim} c$ denotes the time bound of the temporal operators occurring in $\varphi$. For examples, the abstraction predicates corresponding to the TCTL formula $\varphi = \mathbf{EG}_{<2}\, p\, \wedge\, \mathbf{A}[q\, \mathbf{U}_{\leq 4}\, r]$, with $p$, $q$, $r$ atomic propositions, are given as $\psi_1 \equiv z_1 < 2$, $\psi_2 \equiv z_2 \leq 4$. The resulting abstract CTL formula is now obtained using these predicates as $\varphi^A = \mathbf{EG}(p \wedge \psi_1) \wedge \mathbf{A}[q\, \mathbf{U}\, (r \wedge \psi_2)]$.

Second, in contrast to the previous version of our algorithm [19], where refined approximations are recomputed from scratch, we compute abstraction refinements in an incremental fashion, following the approach outlined by Das and Dill [8] for the untimed case.

Third, we introduce a symbolic form of counterexamples for the full TCTL logic, as sequences over sets of states. These symbolic structures are timed extensions of the symbolic counterexamples for (untimed) CTL [21]. We use symbolic counterexamples in the abstraction-refinement algorithm as a heuristic for selecting new abstraction predicates from the given set of basis predicates. Symbolic counterexamples make the refinement process converge more quickly compared to the use of linear counterexamples, as a multitude of spurious counterexamples are discarded in every refinement step. Moreover, since we define symbolic counterexamples for the full TCTL, the method of lazy approximation is applicable for full TCTL, and not only for a fragment of universal formulas as it is the case when using linear counterexamples.

The main contributions of our paper are

1. A definition of abstraction functions for timed automata and TCTL based on predicate abstraction.
2. A definition of symbolic counterexamples for full TCTL.
3. An incremental abstraction refinement algorithm for computing finite approximations of timed automata and TCTL formulas.
4. A proof for termination, soundness and completeness of the abstraction refinement algorithm.

**Related Work.** The abstract interpretation framework [7] has been used earlier in the context of real-time systems for formalizing approximations of safety properties [23, 12, 9]. In contrast, the techniques proposed in [19] and extended in this paper, also allow for verifying liveness. Whereas verification techniques for infinite-state systems based on predicate abstraction [14, 5, 20, 15] are usually used in an incomplete way for proving safety properties, our verification method for timed systems is even complete for liveness properties.

There is a direct correspondence between our notions of approximations and three-valued abstractions [13] of modal transition system (MTS) [17]. A MTS contains two kinds of transitions, may and must. May transitions correspond to the transitions in the over-approximation, while must transitions are those in the under-approximation.

Counterexample-guided refinement has been studied by many researchers, and recent work includes [6, 8, 16, 15]. In contrast to these approaches, we use counterexamples only as a heuristic for selecting good pivot predicates from a fixed, predetermined pool of abstraction predicates to speed convergence of the approximation process.

Dill and Wong-Toi [12] also use an iteration of both over- and under-approximations of the reachable state set of timed automata, but their techniques are limited to proving invariants. Daws and Tripakis [9] propose several abstractions that reduce the state space of a timed system, while preserving reachability properties. Tripakis and Yovine [22] show how to abstract dense real time to obtain time-abstracting, finite bisimulations. Behrmann, Bouyer, Larsen and Pelánek [4] propose zone based abstractions with respect to the minimal and maximal constants to which clocks are compared, obtaining a sound and complete verification method for reachability. Whenever it suffices to compute rather coarse abstractions, we expect to obtain much smaller transition systems by means of lazy approximation. Alur, Itai, Kurshan, and Yannakakis [3] present a technique based on over-approximations: the method consists in attempting to prove a property on an abstract system, where some clocks are ignored; if this attempt fails, clocks are reintroduced progressively until either the property is proved on the abstract system, or all the clocks have been reintroduced. The method still requires exact computation of the region graph for each abstracted system.

Henzinger, Jhala, Majumdar, and Sutre [15] present an abstraction-refinement algorithm for model checking safety properties that integrates the construction of the abstract model with the verification process. The abstract model is constructed on demand during verification, by refining only parts of the current abstract model. However, this method allows for checking only reachability properties, whereas our approach can be used to verify or refute any kind of TCTL properties.

All the above-described approaches use linear counterexamples during the refinement process. In contrast, symbolic counterexamples make the refinement process converge more quickly compared to the use of linear counterexamples, since several spurious counterexamples are discarded in one refinement step.

**Organization.** The remainder of this paper is organized as follows. Section 2 reviews the basic notions of timed automata and TCTL. Finite over- and under-approximations of timed automata are defined in the first part of Section 3, while the second part contains definitions of abstraction and concretization functions for TCTL. Symbolic counterexamples for TCTL as sequences over sets of states are introduced in Section 4. In Section 5, we define the iterative abstraction refinement algorithm and show termination and completeness thereof. Finally, Section 6 contains some concluding remarks.

## 2   Preliminaries

Given a set of clocks $C$, the set of *timing (or clock) constraints Constr* comprises tt, $x \sim d$, and $x - y \sim d$, where $x, y \in C$, $d \in \mathbb{N}$, $\sim \in \{\leq, <, =, >, \geq\}$. The set *Inv* is the subset of *Constr*, where $\sim$ is chosen from $\{\leq, <\}$. For a positive integer $\gamma$, *Constr*$(\gamma)$ is the finite subset of all clock constraints $x \sim \gamma$, $x - y \sim \gamma$, where $x, y \in C$.

A *timed automaton* [2] is a tuple $S = \langle L, P, C, E, L_0, I \rangle$, where

- $L$ is a nonempty finite set of locations.
- $P : L \rightarrow \mathcal{P}(\mathbf{AP})$ maps each location to a set of propositional symbols $\mathbf{AP}$.
- $C$ is a finite set of clocks.
- $E \subseteq L \times \mathcal{P}(Constr) \times \mathcal{P}(C) \times L$ is a transition relation; we write $l \xrightarrow{g,r} l'$ for $\langle l, g, r, l' \rangle \in E$.
- $L_0 \subseteq L$ is the set of initial locations.
- $I : L \rightarrow \mathcal{P}(Inv)$ assigns a set of downward closed clock constraints to each location $l$; the elements of $I(l)$ are the *invariants* for location $l$.

A function $v : C \rightarrow \mathbb{R}_{\geq 0}$ is a *clock valuation*, and the set of clock valuations is collected in $\mathcal{V}_C$. $\mathcal{V}_0$ denotes the set of initial clock valuations that assigns to every clock the value 0. The clock valuation $(v + \delta)$ is obtained by adding $\delta$ to the value of each clock in $v$. For $X \subseteq C$, $v[X := 0]$ denotes the clock valuation that updates every clock $x \in X$ to zero, and leaves all the other clock values unchanged. The value $gv$ of a clock constraint $g$ with respect to the clock valuation $v$ is obtained by substituting the clocks $x$ in $g$ with the corresponding value $v(x)$. If $gv$ simplifies to the true value, $v$ satisfies $g$ and we write $v \models g$. A set $X \subseteq \mathcal{V}_C$ of clock valuations satisfies $g \in Constr$, written as $X \models g$, if and only if $v \models g$ for all $v \in X$. A pair $(l, v) \in L \times \mathcal{V}_C$ is called a *timed configuration*, if it satisfies the invariants $I(l)$; formally, $v \models I(l)$ iff $v \models g$ for every invariant $g \in I(l)$. A *clock region* [2] is a set $X \subseteq \mathcal{V}_C$ of clock valuations, such that for all timing constraints $g \in Constr(\gamma)$ and for any two $v_1, v_2 \in X$ it is the case that $v_1 \models g$ if and only if $v_2 \models g$. In this case we write $v_1 \cong v_2$.

A *timed step* is either a *delay step*, where time advances by some positive real-valued $\delta$, or an instantaneous *state transition step*. For $\delta > 0$, we say that the timed configuration $(l, v + \delta)$ is obtained from $(l, v)$ by a *delay step* $(l, v) \overset{\delta}{\Rightarrow} (l, v + \delta)$, if the invariant constraint $v + \delta \models I(l)$ holds. A *state transition step* $(l, v) \overset{g,r}{\Rightarrow} (l', v')$ occurs if there exists a $l \xrightarrow{g,r} l' \in E$, and $v \models g$, $v' := v[r := 0]$, and $v' \models I(l')$.

The lazy approximation method, we present here, allows for verifying not only safety properties, but also liveness properties. Liveness in dense real time is complicated by the possible sequences of infinitesimally decreasing delay steps; they constitute a degenerated behavior of a system, a behavior that has to be disallowed. As in [19], we eliminate this undesired behavior by restricting the model of timed automata to delay steps that force a clock to step beyond integer bounds when all fractional clock values are not zero. We have shown [19] that such a restriction does not change the possible observations of the model with respect to $\mu$-calculus formulas. The proof can easily be adapted to TCTL formulas. A *restricted delay step* [19] is a delay step $(l, v) \overset{\delta}{\Rightarrow} (l, v + \delta)$ for all positive, real-valued $\delta$, such that

$$\exists x \in C. \exists k \in \{0, \ldots, \gamma\}. \ v(x) = k \vee (v(x) < k \wedge v(x) + \delta \geq k).$$

In this paper we consider timed systems with restricted delay steps only. The *transition relation* $\Rightarrow$ of a timed system $S$, is now the union of restricted delay and state transition steps, that is, $\Rightarrow := \overset{\delta}{\Rightarrow} \cup \overset{g,r}{\Rightarrow}$.

The (restricted) semantics of a timed system $S = \langle L, L_0, C, I, P, E \rangle$ is given by associated with it a transition system $M = \langle \mathbf{S}, \mathbf{S_0}, \mathbf{P}, \mathbf{N} \rangle$, where $\mathbf{S} = L \times \mathcal{V_C}$, $\mathbf{S_0} = L_0 \times \mathcal{V_0} \subseteq \mathbf{S}$ are the initial states, $\mathbf{P} = P$, and $\mathbf{N}$ is the timed transition relation $\Rightarrow$ introduced above. For $(s, s') \in \mathbf{N}$, we also write $s' \in \mathbf{N}(s)$, and if $S \subseteq \mathbf{S}$, then $\mathbf{N}(S)$ is $\cup_{s \in S} \mathbf{N}(s)$. The converse transition relation $\widetilde{\mathbf{N}}$ is defined by $\widetilde{\mathbf{N}}(s, s') \Longleftrightarrow \mathbf{N}(s', s)$. We assume that the transition relation $\mathbf{N}$ is total, that is, every state has a successor. A *path* $\pi$ is a finite or infinite sequence of configurations $\pi = (s_0, s_1, \ldots)$ such that $s_{i+1} \in \mathbf{N}(s_i)$ for all $i \geq 0$. We sometimes denote a path by $s_0 \Rightarrow s_1 \Rightarrow \ldots$.

Given a set $S \subseteq \mathbf{S}$ and the transition relation $\mathbf{N}$, we define three *predicate transformers* from $2^{\mathbf{S}}$ to $2^{\mathbf{S}}$; $post(\mathbf{N})(S) = \mathbf{N}(S)$, $pre(\mathbf{N})(S) = \widetilde{\mathbf{N}}(S)$, and $\widetilde{pre}(\mathbf{N})(S) = \{s \in \mathbf{S} \mid \mathbf{N}(s) \subseteq S\}$. The *postcondition* function $post(\mathbf{N})(S)$ computes for a given set $S$ of states, the set of states that can be reached in one step from some state in $S$. The *preimage* function $pre(\mathbf{N})(S)$ returns the set of states that can reach $S$ in a single step. The *precondition* function $\widetilde{pre}(\mathbf{N})(S)$ returns the set of those states that have no successors outside of $S$.

The logic TCTL [1] is a dense real-time extension of CTL with time-bounded temporal operators and is defined by the grammar ($p \in \mathbf{AP}$)

$$\varphi := p \mid \neg\varphi \mid \varphi_1 \wedge \varphi_2 \mid \mathbf{E}[\varphi_1 \, \mathbf{U}_{\sim c} \, \varphi_2] \mid \mathbf{A}[\varphi_1 \, \mathbf{U}_{\sim c} \, \varphi_2] \,.$$

The semantics of TCTL formulas is given in the usual way, with respect to a transition system. The notions of *s-path* and TCTL-structure are as in [1].

## 3  Abstraction Functions

### 3.1  Abstracting Timed Systems

**Definition 1 (Abstraction Predicates [19]).**  Given a set of clocks $C$, an *abstraction predicate* with respect to $C$ is any formula with the set of free variables in $C$. Similarly to timing constraints, the value of an abstraction predicate $\psi$ with respect to a clock valuation $v$, where both free and bound variables are interpreted in the domain $C$, is denoted by the juxtaposition $\psi v$. Whenever $\psi v$ evaluates to true, we write $v \models \psi$.

A *basis* is a set of abstraction predicates that is expressive enough to distinguish between two clock regions.

**Definition 2 (Basis [19]).**  Let $S$ be a timed automaton with clock set $C$ and let $\Psi$ be a set of abstraction predicates. Then $\Psi$ is a *basis* with respect to $S$ iff for all clock valuations $v_1, v_2 \in \mathcal{V_C}$: $[\, (\forall \psi \in \Psi. \, v_1 \models \psi \Leftrightarrow v_2 \models \psi) \implies v_1 \cong v_2 \,]$.

For a timed automaton $S$ with clock set $C$ and largest constant $\gamma$ the (infinite) set of clock constraints *Constr*, the (infinite) set of invariant constraints *Inv*, the (finite) set of clock constraints *Constr($\gamma$)*, and the (finite) set of membership predicates for the quotient $\mathcal{V_C}$ modulo $\cong$ are all basis sets. Since the set of predicates *Constr($\gamma$)* is finite, there is a finite basis for every timed automaton. Notice, however, that this basis is not necessarily minimal. For example, a basis for a timed automaton with two clock $x, y$

and largest constant 1, is given as $\Psi = \{x = 0, y = 0, x = 1, y = 1, x < 1, x > 1, y < 1, y > 1, x > y, x < y, x = y\}$.

A set of abstraction predicates $\Psi = \{\psi_0, \cdots, \psi_{n-1}\}$ determines an *abstraction function* $\alpha$, which maps clock valuations $v$ to a *bitvector* $b$ of length $n$, such that the $i$-th component of $b$ is set if and only if $\psi_i$ holds for $v$. Here, we assume that bitvectors of length $n$ are elements of the set $B_n$, which are functions of domain $\{0, \cdots, n-1\}$ and codomain $\{0, 1\}$. The inverse image of $\alpha$, that is, the *concretization function* $\gamma$, maps a bitvector to the set of clock valuations that satisfy all $\psi_i$ whenever the $i$-th component of the bitvector is set. Thus, a set of concrete states $(l, v)$ is transformed by the abstraction function $\alpha$ into the abstract state $\alpha(l, v)$, and an abstract state $(l, b)$ is mapped by $\gamma$ to a set of concrete states $\gamma(l, b)$.

**Definition 3 (Abstraction/Concretization [19]).** Let $C$ be a set of clocks and $\mathcal{V}_C$ the corresponding set of clock valuations. Given a finite set of predicates $\Psi = \{\psi_0, \cdots, \psi_{n-1}\}$, the *abstraction function* $\alpha : L \times \mathcal{V}_C \to L \times B_n$ is defined by $\alpha(l, v)(i) := (l, \psi_i v)$ and the *concretization function* $\gamma : L \times B_n \to L \times \mathcal{P}(\mathcal{V}_C)$ is defined by $\gamma(l, b) := \{(l, v) \in L \times \mathcal{V}_C \mid I(l) \wedge \bigwedge_{i=0}^{n-1} \psi_i v \equiv b(i)\}$.

We also use the notations $\alpha(S) := \{\alpha(l, v) \mid (l, v) \in S\}$ and $\gamma(S^a) := \{\gamma(l, b) \mid (l, b) \in S^a\}$. Now, the abstraction/concretization pair $(\alpha, \gamma)$ forms a Galois connection.

An abstract state $(l, b)$ is *feasible* if and only if its concretization is not empty, that is, $\gamma(l, b) \neq \emptyset$.

**Definition 4 (Over-/Under-approximation [19]).** Given a (concrete) transition system $M = \langle S^c, S^c_0, \mathbf{P}, \Rightarrow \rangle$, where $S^c = L \times \mathcal{V}_C$, $S^c_0 = L_0 \times \mathcal{V}_0$, and a set $\Psi$ of abstraction predicates, we construct two (abstract) transition systems $M^+_\Psi = \langle S^a, S^a_0, \mathbf{P}, \Rightarrow^+ \rangle$, and $M^-_\Psi = \langle S^a, S^a_0, \mathbf{P}, \Rightarrow^- \rangle$, as follows:

- $S^a := L \times B_n$
- $(l, b) \Rightarrow^+ (l', b')$ iff $\exists v, v' \in \mathcal{V}_C$ s.t. $(l, v) \in \gamma(l, b) \wedge (l', v') \in \gamma(l', b')$. $(l, v) \Rightarrow (l', v')$
- $(l, b) \Rightarrow^- (l', b')$ iff $(l, b)$ feasible, and
    $\forall v \in \mathcal{V}_C$ s.t. $(l, v) \in \gamma(l, b)$. $\exists v' \in \mathcal{V}_C$ s.t. $(l', v') \in \gamma(l', b')$. $(l, v) \Rightarrow (l', v')$
- $S^a_0 := \{(l_0, b_0) \mid l_0 \in L_0, \text{ and } b_0(i) = 1 \text{ iff } v_0 \models \psi_i\}$.

$M^+_\Psi$ is called an *over-approximation*, and $M^-_\Psi$ an *under-approximation* of $M$. Obviously, we have that $\Rightarrow^- \subseteq \Rightarrow^+$.

Definition 4 does not allow the incremental computation of over- and under-approximations. When adding new predicates to $\Psi$, new approximations have to be constructed from scratch starting from the initial transition system. We modify Definition 4 such that successive approximations can be computed incrementally from previously obtained approximations by adding new predicates from the basis.

We introduce the following notations. A bitvector of length $k$ is denoted by $b[0 : k-1]$, and corresponds to the set $\Psi_k = \{\psi_0, \ldots, \psi_{k-1}\}$ of abstraction predicates. The abstraction and concretization functions determined by $\Psi_k$ are denoted by $\alpha_k$, $\gamma_k$, respectively. The finite over-approximation of $M$ with respect to $\Psi_k$ is denoted by $M^+_{\Psi_k}$ and is the tuple $\langle S^a_k, S^a_{0_k}, \mathbf{P}, \Rightarrow^+_k \rangle$. Similarly, the finite under-approximation of $M$ with respect to $\Psi_k$ is denoted by $M^-_{\Psi_k} = \langle S^a_k, S^a_{0_k}, \mathbf{P}, \Rightarrow^-_k \rangle$. Note that the mapping function $\mathbf{P}$ does not depend on the abstraction predicates, merely on the finite control structure $L$.

**Definition 5 (Incremental Over-/Under-approximation).** For a timed system $S$, with corresponding transition system $M$, and a TCTL formula $\varphi$, let $\Psi$ be the corresponding basis of abstraction predicates, $M_{\Psi_k}^+ = \langle S_k^a, S_{0_k}^a, \mathbf{P}, \Rightarrow_k^+ \rangle$ and $M_{\Psi_k}^- = \langle S_k^a, S_{0_k}^a, \mathbf{P}, \Rightarrow_k^- \rangle$ the over-approximation and under-approximation of $M$ obtained in step $i$ with respect to a set $\Psi_k \subset \Psi$ of abstraction predicates, respectively. Let $\Psi_{k'}$ be the set of predicates obtained from the failed model-checking attempt in step $i$. The over-approximation $M_{\Psi_m}^+ = \langle S_m^a, S_{0_m}^a, \mathbf{P}, \Rightarrow_m^+ \rangle$ respectively under-approximation $M_{\Psi_m}^- = \langle S_m^a, S_{0_m}^a, \mathbf{P}, \Rightarrow_m^- \rangle$ obtained in step $i + 1$ with respect to the set of predicates $\Psi_m = \Psi_k \cup \Psi_{k'}$, is derived from $M_{\Psi_k}^+$, respectively $M_{\Psi_k}^-$, as follows. ($\hat{\psi}_j$ denotes $\psi_j$ if $b[j] = 1$, and $\neg\psi_j$ if $b[j] = 0$).

- $S_m^a = \{(l, b[0 : m - 1]) \mid (l, b[0 : k - 1]) \in S_k^a$ and
  $\quad \forall i = k, \ldots, k + k' - 1.\ b[i] = 1$ if $\hat{\psi}_0 \wedge \ldots \wedge \hat{\psi}_{k-1} \wedge \psi_i = $ true, else $b[i] = 0\}$
- $(l, b[0 : m - 1]) \Rightarrow_m^+ (l', b'[0 : m - 1])$ iff
  - $(l, b[0 : k - 1]) \Rightarrow_k^+ (l', b'[0 : k - 1])$ and
  - $\exists v_m, v'_m \in \mathcal{V}_C$ s.t. $(l, v_m) \in \gamma_m(l, b[0 : m - 1])$ and $(l', v'_m) \in \gamma_m(l, b'[0 : m - 1])$ with $v_m = v_k \cap \{v \in \mathcal{V}_C \mid \Psi_{k'} v \equiv 1\}$ and $v'_m = v'_k \cap \{v' \in \mathcal{V}_C \mid \Psi_{k'} v \equiv 1\}$ such that $(l, v_m) \Rightarrow (l', v'_m)$.
- $(l, b[0 : m - 1]) \Rightarrow_m^- (l', b'[0 : m - 1])$ iff
  - $(l, b[0 : k - 1]) \Rightarrow_k^- (l', b'[0 : k - 1])$ and
  - $\forall v_m$ s.t. $(l, v_m) \in \gamma_m(l, b[0 : m - 1])$, $\exists v'_m \in \mathcal{V}_C$ s.t. $(l', v'_m) \in \gamma_m(l', b'[0 : m - 1])$. $v_m = v_k \cap \{v \in \mathcal{V}_C \mid \Psi_{k'} v \equiv 1\}$ and $v'_m = v'_k \cap \{v' \in \mathcal{V}_C \mid \Psi_{k'} v \equiv 1\} \longrightarrow (l, v_m) \Rightarrow (l', v'_m)$.

The set $S_m^a$ can also be defined as in Definition 4 as the product of $L$ and $B_m$, where $B_m$ is the set of all bitvectors of length $m$. However, the above definition is more restrictive, in the sense that a smaller set of abstract states than $L \times B_m$ is obtained, since infeasible states are discarded. The above Definition will be used in the incremental abstraction-refinement algorithm in Section 5, for refining under- and over-approximations. An example will also be given in Section 5.

In the sequel we abstract TCTL formulas to CTL formulas, which have to be interpreted in the abstract transition systems $M_{\Psi}^+$ and $M_{\Psi}^-$, respectively.

**Definition 6 (Predicate Abstracted Semantics of CTL).** Let $\varphi$ be a CTL formula, $M = \langle S, S_0, \mathbf{P}, \Rightarrow \rangle$ a transition system, and $\Psi$ a set of abstraction predicates. Consider, as given in Definition 4, the over-approximation $M_{\Psi}^+ = \langle S^a, S_0^a, \mathbf{P}, \Rightarrow^+ \rangle$, and the under-approximation $M_{\Psi}^- = \langle S^a, S_0^a, \mathbf{P}, \Rightarrow^- \rangle$ of $M$. Then, the *predicate abstracted* semantics $[\![\varphi]\!]^{M_{\Psi}^\sigma}$, where $\sigma$ is either $+$ or $-$, of the CTL formula $\varphi$ with respect to the finite-state transition systems $M_{\Psi}^\sigma$ is defined in a mutually inductive way. The notation $\bar{\sigma}$ is used to toggle the sign $\sigma$.

$$[\![\text{tt}]\!]^{M_{\Psi}^\sigma} := S^a \qquad [\![p]\!]^{M_{\Psi}^\sigma} := \{(l, b) \in S^a \mid p \in \mathbf{P}(l)\}$$

$$[\![\neg\varphi]\!]^{M_{\Psi}^\sigma} := S^a \setminus [\![\varphi]\!]^{M_{\Psi}^{\bar{\sigma}}} \qquad [\![\varphi_1 \vee \varphi_2]\!]^{M_{\Psi}^\sigma} := [\![\varphi_1]\!]^{M_{\Psi}^\sigma} \cup [\![\varphi_2]\!]^{M_{\Psi}^\sigma}$$

$$[\![\mathbf{E}[\varphi_1 \,\mathbf{U}\, \varphi_2]]\!]^{M_{\Psi}^\sigma} := \{s \in S^a \mid \text{for some path } \pi = (s_0 \Rightarrow^\sigma s_1 \Rightarrow^\sigma \ldots) \text{ with } s_0 = s,$$
$$\text{for some } i \geq 0,\ s_i \in [\![\varphi_2]\!]^{M_{\Psi}^\sigma} \text{ and } s_j \in [\![\varphi_1]\!]^{M_{\Psi}^\sigma} \text{ for } 0 \leq j < i\}$$

$$[\![\mathbf{A}[\varphi_1 \,\mathbf{U}\, \varphi_2]]\!]^{M_{\Psi}^\sigma} := \{s \in S^a \mid \text{for every path } \pi = (s_0 \Rightarrow^{\bar{\sigma}} s_1 \Rightarrow^{\bar{\sigma}} \ldots) \text{ with } s_0 = s,$$
$$\text{for some } i \geq 0,\ s_i \in [\![\varphi_2]\!]^{M_{\Psi}^\sigma} \text{ and } s_j \in [\![\varphi_1]\!]^{M_{\Psi}^\sigma} \text{ for } 0 \leq j < i\}$$

We also write $M^\sigma, (l, b) \models^a \varphi$, to denote that $(l, b) \in [\![\varphi]\!]^{M_{\Psi}^\sigma}$.

## 3.2  TCTL Abstraction

We define abstractions and concretizations functions for TCTL formulas based on a set of abstraction predicates $\Psi_\varphi$. The predicates are extracted from the time-bounded temporal operators of the formulas. Following a similar approach as in [1] for model checking TCTL formulas, we introduce for every time-bounded operator of a given formula $\varphi$ a new clock variable $z_i$. These clocks are used for keeping track of the time elapsed in traversing a sequence of states of the underlying TCTL-structure starting in the initial state.

Now, the set of abstraction predicates $\Psi_\varphi$ with respect to $\varphi$ consists of all the formulas $z_i{\sim}c$ with free variables $z_i$, where $\sim c$ denotes the timed bound of the temporal operators occurring in $\varphi$. For example, the abstraction predicates corresponding to the formula $\varphi = \mathbf{EG}_{<2}\, p \wedge \mathbf{A}[q\,\mathbf{U}_{\leq 4}\, r]$, with $p$, $q$, $r$ atomic propositions, are given as $\psi_1 \equiv (z_1 < 2)$ and $\psi_2 \equiv (z_2 \leq 4)$. The abstraction yields the CTL formula $\varphi^A = \mathbf{EG}(p \wedge \psi_1) \wedge \mathbf{A}[q\,\mathbf{U}\,(r \wedge \psi_2)]$.

**Definition 7 (TCTL Abstraction Predicates).**  Given a TCTL formula $\varphi$. A TCTL *abstraction predicate* is a formula $z_i{\sim}c_i$, with $z_i$ a free variable and $\sim c_i$ the time bound of the $i$-th bounded temporal operator in $\varphi$. The TCTL abstraction predicates corresponding to a formula $\varphi$ are collected in the set $\Psi_\varphi$. If $\varphi$ does not contain any time bounds, then $\Psi_\varphi$ is empty.

**Definition 8 (TCTL Abstraction/Concretization).**  Given a TCTL formula $\varphi$, and a set $\Psi_\varphi$ of abstraction predicates. Furthermore, let $\psi \equiv z{\sim}c$ be a predicate in $\Psi_\varphi$, corresponding to the bounded operator $\mathbf{U}_{\sim c}$. The *abstraction function* $\alpha_\varphi : TCTL \to CTL$ is defined inductively over the structure of $\varphi$. The interesting cases are those for the time-bounded $\mathbf{U}$ operator.

$$\alpha_\varphi(\mathbf{E}[\varphi_1\,\mathbf{U}_{\sim c}\,\varphi_2] := \mathbf{E}[\alpha_\varphi(\varphi_1)\,\mathbf{U}\,(\alpha_\varphi(\varphi_2) \wedge \psi)]$$
$$\alpha_\varphi(\mathbf{A}[\varphi_1\,\mathbf{U}_{\sim c}\,\varphi_2] := \mathbf{A}[\alpha_\varphi(\varphi_1)\,\mathbf{U}\,(\alpha_\varphi(\varphi_2) \wedge \psi)]$$

The *concretization function* $\gamma_\varphi : CTL \to TCTL$ maps a CTL formula to a TCTL formula, and is the inverse operation to $\alpha_\varphi$, that is $\gamma_\varphi(\varphi) = \alpha_\varphi^{-1}(\varphi)$.

Now, given a timed automaton $S$ with a set of clocks $C$, and a TCTL formula $\varphi$, we add the clocks $z_i$ corresponding to the bounded operators of $\varphi$ to $C$, and define the abstraction predicates with respect to the new set of clocks. All $z_i$ are initially zero and are updated consistently with the other clocks. Clocks corresponding to nested subformulas are reset on every transition in the given timed automaton. The largest constants, which the $z_i$ clocks are even compared to are given by the constants $c_i$, appearing in the time bounds of $\varphi$.

Let $\Psi$ be the set of abstraction predicates corresponding to $S$ and $\varphi$. If $\varphi$ does not contain any time bounds, then $\Psi$ consists only of the predicates with respect to the automaton clocks, as in Definition 1.

The following Theorems and the Corollary are taken from [19] with the slightly difference that we consider here TCTL instead of the (untimed) $\mu$-calculus. The proofs in [19] can easily be adapted to TCTL formulas.

**Theorem 1 (Soundness of Abstraction).** Let $M = \langle S, S_0, P, \Rightarrow \rangle$ be a transition system, $\Psi$ a set of abstraction predicates, and $M_\Psi^+$, $M_\Psi^-$ the over-approximation and under-approximation of $M$ with respect to $\Psi$. Then, for any TCTL formula $\varphi$,

$$\gamma([\![\alpha_\varphi(\varphi)]\!]^{M_\Psi^-}) \subseteq [\![\varphi]\!]^M \subseteq \gamma([\![\alpha_\varphi(\varphi)]\!]^{M_\Psi^+}).$$

Here, $\alpha_\varphi$ is the abstraction function for TCTL formulas from Definition 8, and $\gamma$ the concretization function from Definition 3.

If a basis, as introduced in Definition 2, is used for predicate abstraction, then the approximation is exact with respect to the TCTL logic, that is, the approximation is property-preserving.

**Theorem 2.** Let $S$ be a timed automaton, $M$ the corresponding transition system, and $\varphi$ a TCTL formula. Furthermore, let $C$ be the set of clocks corresponding to $S$ and $\varphi$, and $\gamma$ the largest constant, which these clocks are compared to. Let $\Psi$ be a basis with respect to $C$, and $M_\Psi^-$, $M_\Psi^+$ the under- and over-approximation of $S$ with respect to $\Psi$. Then, for any TCTL formula $\varphi$, it follows that $[\![\alpha_\varphi(\varphi)]\!]^{M_\Psi^-} = [\![\alpha_\varphi(\varphi)]\!]^{M_\Psi^+}$.

**Corollary 1 (Basis Completeness).** Let $S = \langle L, L_0, C, I, P, E \rangle$, be a timed automaton, and $M$ the corresponding transition system. Then, for any TCTL formula $\varphi$, and initial state $l_0 \in L_0$ ($\Psi$ is a basis for $S$ and $\varphi$),

$$(l_0, b_0) \in [\![\alpha_\varphi(\varphi)]\!]^{M_\Psi^-} \;\Leftrightarrow\; (l_0, v_0) \in [\![\varphi]\!]^M \;\Leftrightarrow\; (l_0, b_0) \in [\![\alpha_\varphi(\varphi)]\!]^{M_\Psi^+}.$$

## 4   Symbolic Counterexamples for TCTL

Given a Kripke structure $M$, with $S_0$ initial states, and a TCTL formula $\varphi$, a *symbolic counterexample* carries a justification that $M, S_0 \not\models \varphi$. When we write $X$, we mean a list of elements of the form $[X_0, \ldots]$, and $X^m$ implies that the list $X$ is of length $m+1$, that is, of the form $[X_0, \ldots, X_m]$. We write $c \vdash M, C \not\models \varphi$ to denote that $c$ is a counterexample, which demonstrates that for every state $s \in C$, $M, s \not\models \varphi$. As in Subsection 3.2 we introduce additional clocks $z_i$ corresponding to the bounded temporal operators of the TCTL formula.

Before giving the formal definition of symbolic counterexamples for TCTL formulas, we explain them using an example. Consider the timed automaton $S$ from the left side of Figure 2, and the TCTL property $EG_{\leq 2}\, p$. Obviously, the property does not hold on $S$, since there is no path on which $p$ holds globally during the first 2 time units. A counterexample, $c$, for the validity of $EG_{\leq 2}\, p$ in $S$, is given by the list $[X_0, X_1, X_2]$, where[1] $X_0 = (l_2, z \leq 2 \wedge x \leq 1) \cup (l_3, z \leq 2 \wedge x \leq 1)$, $X_1 = X_0 \cup (l_1, z \leq 1, x \leq 1)$, and $X_2 = X_1 \cup (l_0, z \leq 1 \wedge x \leq 1)$. Note that $X = X_2$ is the least fixpoint of $\mu Z.X_0 \vee \widetilde{pre}(N)(Z)$. This example illustrates a typical situation in which trace-like counterexamples cannot be given in such a compact way. One would need to enumerate all paths starting in $s_0 = (l_0, x = 0, z = 0)$ that lead to a state, reachable within two time units, where $p$ does not hold, and also to prove that there are no other paths that have not been considered. In contrast, the symbolic counterexample describes all the possible failure states of the system.

---

[1] To simplify the notation we denote sets of concrete states such as $\{(l, v) \mid l = l_0 \wedge v(x) < 1 \wedge v(z) \leq 2\}$ by $(l_0, x < 1 \wedge z \leq 2)$.

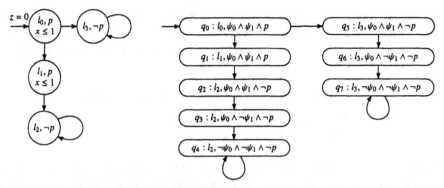

**Fig. 2.** Timed automaton (left) and under-approximation with $\psi_0 \equiv (z \leq 2)$, $\psi_1 \equiv (x \leq 1)$ (right) for Example 1.

**Definition 9.** Let $M = \langle S, S_0, P, N \rangle$ be a transition system, $\varphi$ a TCTL formula with time bound $\sim c$ and $z$ the corresponding clock of $\varphi$. An atomic proposition $\zeta$ holds on a state $s \in S$ iff the value of $z$ in $s$ satisfies $\sim c$.

**Definition 10 (Symbolic Counterexamples).** [2] Let $M = \langle S, S_0, P, N \rangle$ be a transition system, where $S = L \times \mathcal{V}_C$, $S_0 \subseteq S$, and $N$ is the transition relation. For a TCTL formula $\varphi$, and a set of states $C \subseteq S_0$, a symbolic counterexample $c$ justifying $M, C \not\models \varphi$ has the form $X^m$, and is defined as follow.

1. A counterexample $c \vdash M, C \not\models \mathbf{EG}_{\sim c} \varphi$ is a list $c = X^m$, such that $\exists C' \subseteq S$ with (a) $M, C' \not\models \varphi \wedge \zeta$, (b) $X_0 \subseteq C'$, (c) $X_{i+1} \subseteq X_i \cup \widetilde{pre}(N)(X_i)$, for $i < m$, (d) $C = X_m$.
2. A counterexample $c \vdash M, C \not\models \mathbf{AG}_{\sim c} \varphi$ is a list $c = X^m$, such that $\exists C' \subseteq S$ with (a) $M, C' \not\models \varphi \wedge \zeta$, (b) $X_0 \subseteq C'$, (c) $X_{i+1} \subseteq X_i \cup pre(N)(X_i)$, for $i < m$, (d) $C = X_m$.
3. A counterexample $c \vdash M, C \not\models \mathbf{EF}_{\sim c} \varphi$ is a list $c = X^m$, such that $\exists C' \subseteq S$ with (a) $M, C' \not\models \varphi \wedge \zeta$, (b) $X_0 \subseteq C'$, (c) $X_{i+1} \subseteq X_i$, for $i < m$, (d) $C = X_m \subseteq \widetilde{pre}(N)(X_m)$.
4. A counterexample $c \vdash M, C \not\models \mathbf{AF}_{\sim c} \varphi$ is a list $c = X^m$, such that $\exists C' \subseteq S$ with (a) $M, C' \not\models \varphi \wedge \zeta$, (b) $X_0 \subseteq C'$, (c) $X_{i+1} \subseteq X_i$, for $i < m$, (d) $C = X_m \subseteq pre(N)(X_m)$.

*Example 1.* We use predicate abstraction for refuting the property $\mathbf{EG}_{\leq 2}\, p$ of the timed system from Figure 2, left side. A given basis for this system and this property is $\Psi = \{x = 0, z = 0, x = 1, z = 1, x = 2, z = 2, x < 1, x > 1, z < 1, z > 1, x < 2, x > 2\}$. The transition system with the initial under-approximation using the abstraction predicates $\psi_0 \equiv (z \leq 2)$ and $\psi_1 \equiv (x \leq 1)$ is shown in the right side of Figure 2. Model checking the abstract formula $\varphi = \alpha_\varphi(\mathbf{EG}_{\leq 2}\, p) = \mathbf{EG}(p \wedge \psi_0)$ on the transition system $M^-_{\{\psi_0, \psi_1\}}$ returns **false**. The finite-state model-checking algorithm WMC [11, 21] returns the symbolic counterexample $[X_0, X_1, X_2]$, where $X_0 = \{q_2, q_5\}$, $X_1 = \{q_1, q_2, q_5\}$, and $X_2 = \{q_0, q_1, q_2, q_5\}$. Recall the meaning of this counterexample list: the set $X_0$ consists of those states that do not satisfy the subformula $p \wedge \psi_0$, $X_1$ are the states in $X_0$ plus those states that can reach only states in $X_0$ in one step, and so forth. According

---

[2] For lack of space we define here only counterexamples for $\mathbf{EG}_{\sim c}$, $\mathbf{AG}_{\sim c}$, $\mathbf{EF}_{\sim c}$, and $\mathbf{AF}_{\sim c}$. Similar definition can be given for the other temporal operators.

to Theorem 1 an abstract counterexample does not necessarily induce a concrete one. Therefore, we have to concretize the abstract counterexample and to check if we obtain indeed a counterexample in the concrete system. The concretization yields $[X_0^c, X_1^c, X_2^c]$ where $X_i^c \subseteq_v \gamma(X_i)$ for all $i = 0, 1, 2$.

$$\gamma(X_0) = (l_2, z \leq 2 \wedge x \leq 1) \cup (l_3, z \leq 2 \wedge x \leq 1)$$
$$\gamma(X_1) = \gamma(X_0) \cup (l_1, z \leq 2 \wedge x \leq 1)$$
$$\gamma(X_2) = \gamma(X_1) \cup (l_0, z \leq 2 \wedge x \leq 1)$$

The sets of states $X_i^c$ are exactly those presented at the beginning of this section. Since all four conditions from Definition 10 (1) are satisfied (this can be checked using a decision procedure for linear arithmetic with quantifier elimination), we conclude that $\mathbf{EG}_{\leq 2}\, p$ does not hold on our timed automaton.

In the above example the concretization of the abstract counterexample yielded a concrete counterexample. This is not always the case. The abstract counterexample can be spurious, which means the current approximation is too coarse, and has to be refined. This process is illustrated in the next Section.

## 5   Incremental Abstraction-Refinement Algorithm

**Definition 11 (Set Inclusion w.r.t. Clock Valuations).** For two sets of states $S = \{(l_1, v_1), \dots, (l_m, v_m)\}$ and $S' = \{(l'_1, v'_1), \dots, (l'_n, v'_n)\}$, the *set inclusion with respect to clock valuations* relation $S \subseteq_v S'$ is defined as:
$$S \subseteq_v S' \text{ iff } [n = m,\ l_i = l'_i, \text{ and } v_i \subseteq v'_i, \text{ for all } 0 \leq i \leq m].$$

Before we present the abstraction-refinement algorithm, we explain it with an example.

*Example 2.* Consider the timed automaton from the upper part in Figure 3. We want to prove that location $l_2$ is never reached, specified as $\varphi = \mathbf{AG}(\neg at\_l_2)$, where the atomic (boolean) proposition $at\_l_2$ is true if the system is in location $l_2$. Note that $\varphi$ is actually a CTL formula, and therefore does not need to be abstracted. A given basis for this system is $\Psi = \{x = 0, y = 0, x = 1, y = 1, x < 1, x > 1, y < 1, y > 1, x > y, x < y, x = y\}$. The transition system of the initial approximations with the single abstraction predicate $\psi_0 \equiv (x = 0)$ is shown in the lower left part of Figure 3. Dashed transitions are not present in the under-approximation. Model checking $\varphi = \mathbf{AG}(\neg at\_l_2)$ on the over-approximation returns a symbolic counterexample in form of the list $[X_0, X_1, X_2, X_3]$, with $X_0 = \{q_4\}$, $X_1 = \{q_3, q_4\}$, $X_2 = \{q_1, q_2, q_3, q_4\}$, $X_3 = \{q_0, q_1, q_2, q_3, q_4\}$. The concretization of this counterexample yields

$$\gamma(X_0) = (l_2, x > 0 \wedge y \geq 0)$$
$$\gamma(X_1) = (l_1, x > 0 \wedge y \geq 0) \cup (l_2, x > 0 \wedge y \geq 0)$$
$$\gamma(X_2) = (l_0, x > 0 \wedge y \geq 0) \cup (l_1, x \geq 0 \wedge y \geq 0) \cup (l_2, x > 0 \wedge y \geq 0)$$
$$\gamma(X_3) = (l_0, x \geq 0 \wedge y \geq 0) \cup (l_1, x \geq 0 \wedge y \geq 0) \cup (l_2, x > 0 \wedge y \geq 0)$$

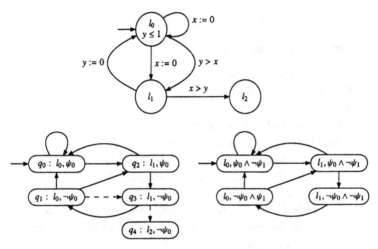

**Fig. 3.** Timed automaton and over-approximations (reachable fragments) with $\psi_0 \equiv (x = 0)$ (lower left part) and $\Psi = \{x = 0, x > y\}$ (lower right part) for Example 2.

Now, we have to check if there is a corresponding symbolic counterexample on the concrete system, that is, there exists $[X_0^c, X_1^c, X_2^c, X_3^c]$, with $X_i^c \subseteq_v \gamma(X_i)$, for all $i = 0, \ldots, 3$. This is the case if the following formula is valid:

$$\phi = \exists X_0^c \subseteq_v \gamma(X_0), \ldots, X_3^c \subseteq_v \gamma(X_3).$$

$$(X_0^c \Rightarrow \neg at\_l_2) \wedge \bigwedge_{i=0}^{2} (X_{i+1}^c \Rightarrow (X_i^c \vee pre(N)(X_i^c))) \,.$$

Here, $\phi$ is not satisfiable, since on the concrete transition system $X_2^c \not\subseteq (X_1^c \cup pre(N)(X_1^c))$ does not hold. $X_1^c \cup pre(N)(X_1^c) = (l_2, x > 0 \wedge y \geq 0) \cup (l_1, x > y \geq 0)$ does not contain a state with location $l_0$, but according to Definition 11 and the fact that $X_2^c \subseteq_v \gamma(X_2)$, $X_2^c$ must contain a state with a $l_0$ location, and therefore $X_2^c \not\subseteq (X_1^c \cup pre(N)(X_1^c))$.

Now, we have to choose new abstraction predicates from $\Psi$ to disallow the transition from $q_3$ to $q_4$ in the abstract system (recall that $q_4$ is the "bad" state, i.e., the state that invalidates $\varphi^A$). This is achieved through a preimage computation on the concretization of $q_4$ (i.e. $X_0^c$): $pre(N)(X_0^c) = \{(l_1, v) \mid v(x) > v(y)\}$. From this set we extract the guard $x > y$ as a new abstraction predicate, say $\psi_1$. A new under- and over-approximation are computed incrementally, according to Definition 5. For example a state $(l_0, \psi_0 \wedge \psi_1)$ is not contained in the new set of abstract states, since it is infeasible and therefore discarded according to Definition 5. Also, the transition from $q_1$ to $q_3$ in the first approximation is eliminated, since, when considering the new predicate $\psi_1 \equiv (x > y)$, there is no corresponding transition in the concrete system from $(l_0, x > 0 \wedge x > y)$ to $(l_0, x > 0 \wedge x \leq y)$ (which is required by Definition 5 to preserve the transition).

Figure 3 (lower right part) shows the reachable fragment of the resulting approximation of $M$ with $\Psi = \{\psi_0, \psi_1\}$. Note that here the under- and over-approximation w.r.t. $\Psi$ coincide. Model checking the formula $\varphi = AG(\neg at\_l_2)$ on the new, refined approximation succeeds, since $s_0 = (l_0, \psi_0 \wedge \neg\psi_1) \in \gamma(\llbracket \varphi \rrbracket^{M^-_{\{\psi_0, \psi_1\}}})$.

The abstraction-refinement algorithm is displayed in Figure 4. The variables $\Psi_n$ and $\Psi_a$ store the currently unused (new) and used (actual) abstraction predicates, re-

**Algorithm:** *abstract_and_refine*
**Input:**      $M, S, s_0, N, \varphi, \Psi$
**Output:**     answer to model checking query "$M, s_0 \models \varphi$ ?"

$$\textbf{choose } \Psi' = \{\psi_1, \ldots, \psi_i\} \text{ from } \Psi; \tag{1}$$

$$\Psi_n := \Psi \setminus \Psi'; \quad \Psi_a := \Psi'; \tag{2}$$

**loop** (3)

$\quad$ **if** $s_0 \in \gamma(\llbracket \alpha_\varphi(\varphi) \rrbracket^{M_{\Psi_a}^-})$ **then return** true $\qquad$ (4)

$\quad$ **else let** $[X_0, X_1, \ldots, X_n]$ be a counterexample in $M_{\Psi_a}^\sigma$ $\qquad$ (5)

$\qquad$ **if** there exists $[X_0^c, X_1^c, \ldots, X_n^c]$ s.t. $X_i^c \subseteq_v \gamma(X_i)$ for all $0 \le i \le n$ $\qquad$ (6)

$\qquad$ and $[X_0^c, X_1^c, \ldots, X_n^c]$ is counterexample in $M$ $\qquad$ (7)

$\qquad$ **then return** false $\qquad$ (8)

$\qquad$ **else let** $k$ s.t. $X_{k+1}^c \not\subseteq X_k^c \cup pre(N)(X_k^c); \ S = pre(N)(X_{k-1}^c) \subseteq S$ $\qquad$ (9)

$\qquad\quad$ **choose** feasible[3] $\Psi' = \{\psi_1, \ldots, \psi_i\} \subseteq \Psi_n$ s.t. $\exists (l, v) \in S. \ v \models \psi_i;$ $\qquad$ (10)

$\qquad\quad$ $\Psi_a := \Psi_a \cup \Psi'; \quad \Psi_n := \Psi_n \setminus \Psi'$ $\qquad$ (11)

$\qquad$ **endif** $\qquad$ (12)

$\quad$ **endif** $\qquad$ (13)

**endloop** $\qquad$ (14)

**Fig. 4.** Iterative abstraction-refinement algorithm.

spectively. Initially, $\Psi_a$ contains those predicates from the basis that correspond to the time bounds of $\varphi$, and possibly some predicates derived from the timing constraints of the automaton, and $\Psi_n$ contains the remaining predicates (lines (1)-(2)). First, it is checked if $s_0 \in \gamma(\llbracket \alpha_\varphi(\varphi) \rrbracket^{M_{\Psi_a}^-})$ by calling a finite-state CTL model checker that generates symbolic evidence, as for example the WMC model checker [11, 21]. If indeed the under-approximation satisfies the abstracted formula $\alpha_\varphi(\varphi)$, then, by Theorem 1, $M$ also satisfies $\varphi$ and the algorithm returns **true** (line (4)). Otherwise (line (5)), the CTL model checker returns a counterexample in the form of an abstract list of sets of states $[X_0, X_1, \ldots, X_n]$, where the initial state of $M_{\Psi_a}^\sigma$ is contained in $X_n$. Here, $\sigma = +$ if $\varphi$ is a universal formula, while $\sigma = -$ for an existential formula. If for the abstract list of sets of states there exists a corresponding list of concrete sets of states, which is indeed a counterexample for the concrete transition system and given (TCTL) formula, then we obtain a counterexample for the concrete model-checking problem (lines (6)-(8)). This requires checking the satisfiability of a Boolean formula with linear arithmetic constraints, which in turns requires quantifier elimination, and can be performed using, for example, DDDs [18]. In case the abstract counterexample is spurious, there exists a smallest index $k$ such that $X_{k+1}^c \not\subseteq X_k^c \cup pre(N)(X_k^c)$ (line (9)). $k$ is the index of the list of states $X_k^c$ that can reach in one step states in $X_{k-1}^c$, but which can no longer be reached from the states in $X_{k+1}^c$. Now, we have to choose those predicates from the basis that are satisfied by the valuations $v$ of some states $(l, v) \in S$, the preimage of $X_{k-1}^c$ (lines (9)-(10)). We add the selected predicates to $\Psi_a$ and compute incrementally, according to Definition 5, new under- and over-approximations. Notice that the concretization function $\gamma$ actually depends on the current set $\Psi_a$ of abstraction predicates. The iter-

---

[3] A set of predicates is feasible, if the conjunction of the predicates is satisfiable.

ative abstraction-refinement algorithm terminates after a finite number of refinements, yielding a sound and complete decision procedure for checking whether or not a timed automaton satisfies a given TCTL formula.

**Theorem 3 (Termination, Soundness, and Completeness).** Let $\mathcal{M}$ be a transition system with a corresponding finite basis $\Psi$, and $\varphi$ a TCTL formula. Then the algorithm in Figure 4 always terminates. Moreover, if it terminates with **true**, then $\mathcal{M} \models \varphi$, and if the result is **false**, then $\mathcal{M} \not\models \varphi$.

**Proof.** Let $n$ be the cardinality of the basis $\Psi$. Every execution of the loop (line (3)) adds at least one new predicate from the basis to the set $\Psi_a$ (line (12)). After at most $n$ iterations, according to Theorem 2, $[\![\alpha_\varphi(\varphi)]\!]^{\mathcal{M}_\Psi^-} = [\![\alpha_\varphi(\varphi)]\!]^{\mathcal{M}_\Psi^+}$. By Theorem 1, $\gamma([\![\alpha_\varphi(\varphi)]\!]^{\mathcal{M}_\Psi^-}) = [\![\varphi]\!]^{\mathcal{M}} = \gamma([\![\alpha_\varphi(\varphi)]\!]^{\mathcal{M}_\Psi^+})$, and by Corollary 1, $\mathcal{M}_\Psi^+$ satisfies the formula $\alpha_\varphi(\varphi)$ if and only if $\mathcal{M}$ satisfies $\varphi$. Thus, the algorithm terminates, since either $\varphi$ can be established or a concrete counterexample can be derived. □

# 6 Conclusion

We have defined symbolic counterexamples for the full TCTL logic, and used them for developing a verification algorithm for timed automata based on predicate abstraction, untimed model checking, and decision procedures for the Boolean combination of linear arithmetic constraints. The main advantage of this approach is that finite state abstractions are computed lazily and incrementally. Using symbolic counterexamples makes it possible to apply the abstraction refinement paradigm to the full TCTL logic.

Dual to the notion of symbolic counterexamples, we can also define symbolic witnesses for the full TCTL, as extensions of symbolic witnesses for CTL [21]. These witnesses and counterexamples can be seen as proofs for the judgment that the timed automaton does or does not satisfy the given TCTL formula, and can be independently verified using a satisfiability checker that can decide the theory of linear arithmetic with reals. Moreover, explicit linear or tree-like witnesses and counterexamples can be extracted from these symbolic evidence, following the approach in [21] for CTL.

During the refinement process we add predicates to all the locations of the timed automaton. As in [15], we could optimize the process by performing local refinement, where predicates are added only to some locations.

The method of lazy approximation is also applicable to other real-time logics. Moreover, this technique can readily be extended to also apply to richer models than timed automata, such as parameterized timed automata, timed automata with other infinite data types, or even to hybrid systems. The price to pay is that such extensions are necessarily incomplete.

Work in progress investigates the combination of lazy approximation with the approach to controller synthesis for finite-state systems presented in [21], for synthesizing real-time controllers.

# Acknowledgment

I would like to thank the anonymous referees for their helpful comments, and N. Shankar for the useful inputs he provided.

# References

1. R. Alur, C. Courcoubetis, and D. Dill. Model checking in dense real-time. *Information and Computation*, 104(1):2–34, 1993.
2. R. Alur and D. L. Dill. A theory of timed automata. *Theoretical Computer Science*, 126(2):183–235, 25 April 1994.
3. R. Alur, A. Itai, R.P. Kurshan, and M. Yannakakis. Timing verification by successive approximation. *Information and Computation*, 118(1):142–157, 1995.
4. G. Behrmann, P. Bouyer, K. G. Larsen, and R. Pelánek. Lower and upper bounds in zone based abstractions of timed automata. *LNCS*, 2988:312–326, 2004.
5. S. Bensalem, Y. Lakhnech, and S. Owre. Computing abstractions of infinite state systems compositionally and automatically. *LNCS*, 1427:319–331, 1998.
6. E. Clarke, O. Grumberg, S. Jha, Y. Lu, and H. Veith. Counterexample-guided abstraction refinement. *LNCS*, 1855:154–169, 2000.
7. P. Cousot and R. Cousot. Abstract interpretation: a unified lattice model for static analysis. *4th ACM Symposium on Principles of Programming Languages*, January 1977.
8. S. Das and D. Dill. Successive approximation of abstract transition relations. In *Proc. of Logic in Computer Science (LICS '01)*, 2001.
9. C. Daws and S. Tripakis. Model checking of real-time reachability properties using abstractions. *LNCS*, 1384:313–329, 1998.
10. L. de Moura, S. Owre, H. Rueß, J. Rushby, and N. Shankar. The ICS decision procedures for embedded deduction. *LNCS*, 3097:218–222, 2004.
11. L. de Moura, S. Owre, H. Rueß, J. Rushby, N. Shankar, M. Sorea, and A. Tiwari. SAL 2. In *16th Conference on Computer Aided Verification*, LNCS. Springer-Verlag, 2004. Tool description.
12. D. Dill and H. Wong-Toi. Verification of real-time systems by successive over and under approximation. *LNCS*, 939:409–422, 1995.
13. P. Godefroid, M. Huth, and R. Jagadeesan. Abstraction-based model checking using modal transition systems. *LNCS*, 2154:426–440, 2001.
14. S. Graf and H. Saïdi. Construction of abstract state graphs with PVS. *LNCS*, 1254:72–83, 1997.
15. T.A. Henzinger, R. Jhala, R. Majumdar, and G. Sutre. Lazy abstraction. In *Symposium on Principles of Programming Languages*, pages 58–70, 2002.
16. Y. Lachnech, S. Bensalem, S. Berezin, and S. Owre. Incremental verification by abstraction. *LNCS*, 2031:98–112, 2001.
17. K. G. Larsen. Modal specifications. In *Proceedings of the international workshop on Automatic verification methods for finite state systems*, pages 232–246. Springer-Verlag New York, Inc., 1990.
18. J. Møller, J. Lichtenberg, H. R. Andersen, and H. Hulgaard. Difference decision diagrams. In *Computer Science Logic*, The IT University of Copenhagen, Denmark, September 1999.
19. M. O. Möller, H. Rueß, and M. Sorea. Predicate abstraction for dense real-time systems. *ENTCS*, 65(6), 2002. http://www.elsevier.com/locate/entcs/volume65.html.
20. H. Saïdi and N. Shankar. Abstract and model check while you prove. *LNCS*, 1633:443–454, 1999.
21. N. Shankar and M. Sorea. Counterexample-driven model checking. Technical Report SRI-CSL-03-04, SRI International, 2003. http://www.csl.sri.com/users/sorea/reports/wmc.ps.gz.
22. S. Tripakis and S. Yovine. Analysis of timed systems using time-abstracting bisimulations. *Formal Methods in System Design*, 18(1):25–68, 2001. Kluwer Academic Publishers.
23. H. Wong-Toi. *Symbolic Approximations for Verifying Real-Time Systems*. PhD thesis, Stanford University, November 1994.

# Learning of Event-Recording Automata

Olga Grinchtein, Bengt Jonsson, and Martin Leucker*

Department of Computer Systems, Uppsala University, Sweden
{olgag,bengt,leucker}@it.uu.se

**Abstract.** We extend Angluin's algorithm for on-line learning of regular languages to the setting of *timed systems*. We consider systems that can be described by a class of deterministic *event-recording automata*. We present two algorithms that learn a description by asking a sequence of membership queries (does the system accept a given timed word?) and equivalence queries (is a hypothesized description equivalent to the correct one?). In the constructed description, states are identified by sequences of symbols; timing constraints on transitions are learned by adapting algorithms for learning hypercubes. The number of membership queries is polynomially in the minimal zone graph and in the biggest constant of the automaton to learn for the first algorithm. The second algorithm learns a (usually) smaller representation of the underlying system.

## 1   Introduction

Research during the last decades have developed powerful techniques for using *models of reactive systems* in specification, automated verification (e.g., [9]), test case generation (e.g., [12,24]), implementation (e.g., [16]), and validation of reactive systems in telecommunication, embedded control, and related application areas. Typically, such models are assumed to be developed *a priori* during the specification and design phases of system development. In practice, however, often no formal specification is available, or becomes outdated as the system evolves over time. One must then construct a model that describes the behavior of an existing system or implementation. In software verification, techniques are being developed for generating abstract models of software modules by static analysis of source code (e.g., [10,19]). However, peripheral hardware components, library modules, or third-party software systems do not allow static analysis. In practice, such systems must be analyzed by observing their external behavior. In fact, techniques for constructing models by analysis of externally observable behavior (black-box techniques) can be used in many situations.

- To create models of hardware components, library modules, that are part of a larger system which, e.g., is to be formally verified or analyzed.
- For regression testing, a model of an earlier version of an implemented system can be used to create a good test suite and test oracle for testing subsequent versions. This has been demonstrated, e.g., by Hungar et al. [15,20]).

---

* This author is supported by the European Research Training Network "Games".

Y. Lakhnech and S. Yovine (Eds.): FORMATS/FTRTFT 2004, LNCS 3253, pp. 379–395, 2004.

- Black-box techniques, such as adaptive model checking [14], have been developed to check correctness properties, even when source code or formal models are not available.

- Tools that analyze the source code statically depend heavily on the implementation language used. Black-box techniques are easier to adapt to modules written in different languages.

The construction of models from observations of system behavior can be seen as a learning problem. For finite-state reactive systems, it means to construct a (deterministic) finite automaton from the answers to a finite set of *membership queries*, each of which asks whether a certain word is accepted by the automaton or not. There are several techniques (e.g., [4, 13, 21, 23, 5]) which use essentially the same basic principles; they differ in how membership queries may be chosen and in exactly how an automaton is constructed from the answers. The techniques guarantee that a correct automaton will be constructed if "enough" information is obtained. In order to check this, Angluin and others also allow *equivalence queries* that ask whether a hypothesized automaton accepts the correct language; such a query is answered either by *yes* or by a counterexample on which the hypothesis and the correct language disagree. Techniques for learning finite automata have been successfully used for regression testing [15] and model checking [14] of finite-state systems for which no model or source code is available.

In this paper, we extend the learning algorithm of Angluin and others to the setting of timed systems. One longer-term goal is to develop techniques for creating abstract timed models of hardware components, device drivers, etc. for analysis of timed reactive systems; there are many other analogous applications. To the best of our knowledge, this is the first work on learning of timed systems; it is not an easy challenge, and we will therefore in this first work make some idealizing assumptions. We assume that a learning algorithm observes a system by checking whether certain actions can be performed at certain moments in time, and that the learner is able to control and record precisely the timing of the occurrence of each action. We consider systems that can be described by a timed automaton [2], i.e., a finite automaton equipped with clocks that constrain the possible absolute times of occurrences of actions. Since timed automata can not in general be determinized [2], we restrict consideration to a class of *event-recording automata* [3]. These are timed automata that, for every action $a$, use a clock that records the time of the last occurrence of $a$. Event-recording automata can be determinized, and are sufficiently expressive to model many interesting timed systems; for instance, they are as powerful as timed transition systems [17, 3], another popular model for timed systems.

In this work, we further restrict event-recording automata to be event-deterministic in the sense that each state has at most one outgoing transition per action (i.e., the automaton obtained by removing the clock constraints is deterministic). Under this restriction, timing constraints for the occurrence of an action depend only on the past sequence of actions, and not on their relative timing; learning such an automaton becomes significantly more tractable, and allows us to adapt the learning algorithm of Angluin to the timed setting.

We present two algorithms, LSGDERA and LDERA, for learning deterministic event-recording automata. LSGDERA learns a so-called *sharply guarded* deterministic event-recording automaton. We show that every deterministic event-recording automaton can be transformed into a unique sharply guarded one with at most double exponentially more locations. We then address the problem of learning a smaller, not necessarily sharply guarded version of the system. The algorithm LDERA achieves this goal by *unifying* the queried information when it is "similar" which results in merging states in the automaton construction.

We show that the number of membership queries of LSGDERA is polynomial in the size of the biggest constant appearing in guards and in the number $n$ of locations of the sharply guarded deterministic event-recording automaton. Furthermore, we show that every deterministic event-recording automaton can be transformed into a sharply guarded one with at most double exponentially more locations. The number of equivalence queries is at most $n$. LDERA exceeds these bounds in the worst case, however, in practice it can be expected that it behaves better than LSGDERA.

We are not aware of any other work on learning of timed systems or timed languages. However, several papers are concerned with finding a definition of timed languages which is suitable as a basis for learning. There are several works that define determinizable classes of timed automata (e.g., [3, 25]) and right-congruences of timed languages (e.g., [22, 18, 26]), motivated by testing and verification.

The paper is structured as follows. After preliminaries in the next section, we define deterministic event-recording automata (DERA) in Section 3. In Section 4, we present our techniques for learning DERAs and their timing constraints. Section 5 gives a short example and shows the differences of both algorithms.

## 2   Preliminaries

We write $\mathbb{R}^{\geq 0}$ for the set of nonnegative real numbers, and $\mathbb{N}$ for the set of natural numbers. Let $\Sigma$ be a finite alphabet of size $|\Sigma|$. A *timed word* over $\Sigma$ is a finite sequence $w_t = (a_1, t_1)(a_2, t_2) \ldots (a_n, t_n)$ of symbols $a_i \in \Sigma$ that are paired with nonnegative real numbers $t_i$ such that the sequence $t_1 t_2 \ldots t_n$ of time-stamps is nondecreasing. We use $\lambda$ to denote the empty word. A *timed language* over $\Sigma$ is a set of timed words over $\Sigma$.

An event-recording automaton contains for every symbol $a \in \Sigma$ a clock $x_a$, called the *event-recording clock* of $a$. Intuitively, $x_a$ records the time elapsed since the last occurrence of the symbol $a$. We write $C_\Sigma$ for the set $\{x_a | a \in \Sigma\}$ of event-recording clocks.

A *clock valuation* $\gamma$ is a mapping from $C_\Sigma$ to $\mathbb{R}^{\geq 0}$. A *clock constraint* is a conjunction of atomic constraints of the form $x \sim n$ or $x - y \sim n$ for $x, y \in C_\Sigma$, $\sim \in \{\leq, \geq\}$, and $n \in \mathbb{N}$. We use $\gamma \models \phi$ to denote that the clock valuation $\gamma$ satisfies the clock constraint $\phi$. A clock constraint is *K-bounded* if it contains no constant larger than $K$. A clock constraint $\phi$ *identifies* a $|\Sigma|$-dimensional *poly-hedron* $[\![\phi]\!] \subseteq (\mathbb{R}^{\geq 0})^{|\Sigma|}$ viz. the vectors of real numbers satisfying the constraint. A *clock guard* is a clock constraint whose conjuncts are only of the form $x \sim n$ (for $x \in C_{\Sigma}$, $\sim \in \{\leq, \geq\}$), i.e., comparison between clocks is not permitted. The set of clock guards is denoted by $G$. A clock guard $g$ *identifies* a $|\Sigma|$-dimensional *hypercube* $[\![g]\!] \subseteq (\mathbb{R}^{\geq 0})^{|\Sigma|}$. Thus, for every guard $g$ that is satisfiable, we can talk of its *smallest corner*, denoted by $sc(g)$, using the notions from the cube identified by $g$. If furthermore $K$ is the biggest constant appearing in $g$, we call a valuation $\gamma$ a *biggest corner* of $g$, if $\gamma$ is maximal in the dimensions where $[\![g]\!]$ is bounded and exceeds $K$ in the others. The set of all biggest corners for a guard $g$ is denoted by $bc(g)$. Sometimes, when convenient, we identify all values greater than $K$ and denote them by $\infty$. Furthermore, we use *true* (*false*) to denote constraints that are always (never, respectively) satisfiable. Sometimes, the context requires $x = true$ to mean $x \geq 0 \wedge x \leq \infty$ and $x = false$ to mean $x \leq 0 \wedge x \geq \infty$.

Clock constraints can efficiently and uniquely be represented using difference bound matrices (DBMs, [11]). Furthermore, DBMs allow efficient operations on clock constraints like intersection, checking equality etc.

A *clocked word* $w_c$ is a sequence $w_c = (a_1, \gamma_1)(a_2, \gamma_2) \ldots (a_n, \gamma_n)$ of symbols $a_i \in \Sigma$ that are paired with event-clock valuations. Each timed word $w_t = (a_1, t_1)(a_2, t_2) \ldots (a_n, t_n)$ can be naturally transformed into a clocked word $CW(w_t) = (a_1, \gamma_1)(a_2, \gamma_2) \ldots (a_n, \gamma_n)$ where for each $i$ with $1 \leq i \leq n$,

- $\gamma_i(x_a) = t_i$ if $a_j \neq a$ for $1 \leq j < i$,
- $\gamma_i(x_a) = t_i - t_j$ if there is a $j$ with $1 \leq j < i$ and $a_j = a$, such that $a_k \neq a$ for $j < k < i$.

A *guarded word* $w_g$ is a sequence $w_g = (a_1, g_1)(a_2, g_2) \ldots (a_n, g_n)$ of symbols $a_i \in \Sigma$ that are paired with clock guards. Note that we identify an empty conjunction with *true*. For a clocked word $w_c = (a_1, \gamma_1)(a_2, \gamma_2) \ldots (a_n, \gamma_n)$ we use $w_c \models w_g$ to denote that $\gamma_i \models g_i$ for $1 \leq i \leq n$. For a timed word $w_t$ we use $w_t \models w_g$ to denote that $CW(w_t) \models w_g$.

A guarded word $w_g = (a_1, g_1)(a_2, g_2) \ldots (a_n, g_n)$ is called a *guard refinement* of $a_1 a_2 \ldots a_n$, and $a_1 a_2 \ldots a_n$ is called the word *underlying* $w_g$. The word $w$ underlying a timed word $w_t$ is defined in a similar manner.

A *deterministic finite automaton* (DFA) $\mathcal{A} = \langle \Gamma, L, l_0, \delta \rangle$ over the alphabet $\Gamma$ consists of states $L$, initial state $l_0$, and a partial transition function $\delta : L \times \Gamma \to L$. A *run* of $\mathcal{A}$ over the word $w = a_1 a_2 \ldots a_n$ is a finite sequence

$$l_0 \xrightarrow{a_1} l_1 \xrightarrow{a_2} \cdots \xrightarrow{a_n} l_n$$

of states $l_i \in L$ such that $l_0$ is the initial state and $\delta(l_{i-1}, a_i)$ is defined for $1 \leq i \leq n$, with $\delta(l_{i-1}, a_i) = l_i$. In this case, we write $\delta(l_0, w) = l_n$, thereby extending the definition of $\delta$ in the natural way. The language $\mathcal{L}(\mathcal{A})$ comprises all words $a_1 a_2 \ldots a_n$ over which a run exists[1].

---

[1] Usually, DFAs are equipped with accepting states. We are only interested in prefix-closed languages. For these languages, DFAs with partial transition function and every state assumed to be accepting suffice.

# 3    Deterministic Event-Recording Automata

**Definition 1.** *A deterministic event-recording automaton (DERA)*
$D = \langle \Sigma, L, l_0, \delta, \eta \rangle$ *consists of a finite input alphabet $\Sigma$, a finite set $L$ of loca-tions, an initial location $l_0 \in L$, a transition function $\delta : L \times \Sigma \to L$, which is a partial function that for each location and input symbol potentially prescribes a target location, a guard function $\eta : L \times \Sigma \to G$, which is a partial function that for each location and input symbol prescribes a clock guard, whenever $\delta$ is defined for this pair.*

In order to define the language accepted by a DERA, we first understand it as a DFA.

Given a DERA $D = \langle \Sigma, L, l_0, \delta, \eta \rangle$, we define $dfa(D)$ to be the DFA $\mathcal{A}_D = \langle \Gamma, L, l_0, \delta' \rangle$ over the alphabet $\Gamma = \Sigma \times G$ where $\delta' : L \times \Gamma \to L$ is defined by $\delta'(l, (a, g)) = \delta(l, a)$ if and only if $\delta(l, a)$ is defined and $\eta(l, a) = g$, otherwise $\delta'(l, (a, g))$ is undefined. Note that $D$ and $dfa(D)$ have the same number of locations/states. Further, note that this mapping from DERAs over $\Sigma$ to DFAs over $\Sigma \times G$ is injective, meaning that for each DFA $\mathcal{A}$ over $\Sigma \times G$, there is a unique (up to isomorphism) DERA over $\Sigma$, denoted $dera(\mathcal{A})$, such that $dfa(dera(\mathcal{A}))$ is isomorphic to $\mathcal{A}$.

The language $\mathcal{L}(D)$ accepted by a DERA $D$ is defined to be the set of timed words $w_t$ such that $w_t \models w_g$ for some guarded word $w_g \in \mathcal{L}(dfa(D))$. We call two DERAs $D_1$ and $D_2$ equivalent iff $\mathcal{L}(D_1) = \mathcal{L}(D_2)$, and denote this by $D_1 \equiv_t D_2$, or just $D_1 \equiv D_2$. A DERA is $K$-*bounded* if all its guards are $K$-bounded.

From the above definitions, we see that the language of a DERA $D$ can be characterized by a prefix-closed set of guarded words $(a_1, g_1)(a_2, g_2) \ldots (a_n, g_n)$ in $\mathcal{L}(dfa(D))$ such that each $a_1 a_2 \ldots a_n$ occurs in at most one such guarded word. Thus, we can loosely say that $D$ imposes on each untimed word $a_1 a_2 \ldots a_n$ the timing constraints represented by the conjunction of the guards $g_1 g_2 \ldots g_n$.

*Example 1.* The event-recording automaton shown in Figure 1 uses three event-recording clocks, $x_a$, $x_b$, and $x_c$. Location 0 is the start location of the automaton. Clock constraint $x_b \geq 3$ that is associated with the edge from location 1 to 4 ensures that the time difference between $b$ and the subsequent $a$ is greater or equal to 3.    □

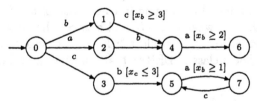

**Fig. 1.** An event-recording automaton.

A central idea in Angluin's construction of finite automata is to let each state be identified by the words that reach it from the initial state (such words are called *access strings* in [5]). States are equivalent if, according to the queries submitted so far, the same continuations of their access strings are accepted. This idea is naturally based on the nice properties of Nerode's right congruence (given a language $L$, two words $u, v \in \Sigma^*$ are equivalent if for all $w \in \Sigma^*$ we have $uw \in L$ iff $vw \in L$) which implies that there is a unique minimal DFA accepting $L$. In other words, for DFAs, every state can be characterized by the set of words accepted by the DFA when considering this state as an initial state, and, every string leads to a state in a unique way.

For timed languages, it is not obvious how to generalize Nerode's right congruence. In general there is no unique minimal DERA which is equivalent to a given DERA. Consider Figure 1, assuming for a moment the $c$-transition from location 7 to 5 is missing, then the language of the automaton does not change when changing the transition from 1 to 4 to 1 to 5, although the language accepted from 4 is different then the one from 5. Furthermore, we can reach location 4 by two guarded words: $(b, true)(c, x_b \geq 3)$ as well as $(a, true)(b, true)$. Although they lead to the same state, they admit different continuations of event-clock words: action $a$ can be performed with $x_b = 2$ after $(a, true)(b, true)$ but not after $(b, true)(c, x_b \geq 3)$. The complication is that each past guarded word has a post-condition, which constrains the values of clocks that are possible at the occurrence of future actions.

For a guarded word $w_g$, we introduce the *strongest postcondition* of $w_g$, denoted by $sp(w_g)$, as the constraint on clock values that are induced by $w_g$ on any following occurrence of a symbol. Postcondition computation is central in tools for symbolic verification of timed automata [8, 6], and can be done inductively as follows:

- $sp(\lambda) = \bigwedge_{a,b \in \Sigma} x_a = x_b$,
- $sp(w_g(a, g)) = ((sp(w_g) \wedge g)[x_a \mapsto 0]) \uparrow$,

where for clock constraint $\phi$ and clock $x$,

- $\phi[x \mapsto 0]$ is the condition $x = 0 \wedge \exists x.\phi$,
- $\phi \uparrow$ is the condition $\exists d.\phi'$, where $d$ ranges over $\mathbb{R}^{\geq 0}$ and where $\phi'$ is obtained from $\phi$ by replacing each clock $y$ by $y - d$.

Both operations can be expressed as corresponding operations on clock constraints. We will also introduce the $K$-approximation $Approx(\phi)_K$ of $\phi$ as the clock constraint obtained by changing in constraints of the form $x - y \leq c$ the constant $c$ to $-(K + 1)$ when $c < -K$ and $c$ to $\infty$ when $c > K$. For example, $x \leq K + 2$ is changed to $x \leq \infty$ while $x \geq K + 2$ is changed to $x \geq K + 1$.

Let us now define a class of DERAs that admit a natural definition of right congruences.

**Definition 2.** *A DERA $D$ is sharply guarded if for all guarded words $w_g(a, g) \in \mathcal{L}(dfa(D))$, we have that $g$ is satisfiable and*

$$g = \bigwedge \{g' \in G \mid sp(w_g) \wedge g' = sp(w_g) \wedge g\}$$

We remark that whether or not a DERA is sharply guarded depends only on $\mathcal{L}(dfa(D))$. In other words, a DERA is called sharply guarded if whenever a run of $\mathcal{L}(dfa(D))$ has reached a certain location $l$, then the outgoing transitions from $l$ have guards which cannot be strengthened without changing the timing conditions under which the next symbol will be accepted. This does not mean that these guards are "included" in the postcondition (see also Figure 2), but at least their smallest and biggest corners:

**Lemma 1.** *If $w_g(a, g) \in \mathcal{L}(dfa(D))$, where $D$ is a sharply guarded DERA, then*

1. *there is a timed word $w_t(a, t) \in \mathcal{L}(D)$ such that*
   $CW(w_t(a, t)) = (a_1, \gamma_1) \ldots (a_n, \gamma_n)(a, \gamma_g) \models w_g(a, g)$ *and* $\gamma_g \in bc(g)$.
2. *there is a timed word $w_t(a, t) \in \mathcal{L}(D)$ such that*
   $CW(w_t(a, t)) = (a_1, \gamma_1) \ldots (a_n, \gamma_n)(a, \gamma_g) \models w_g(a, g)$ *and* $\gamma_g = sc(g)$.

*Proof.* The claim follows easily from the definition of sharply guarded.    □

Every DERA can be transformed into an equivalent DERA that is sharply guarded using the zone-graph construction [1].

**Lemma 2.** *For every DERA there is an equivalent DERA that is sharply guarded.*

*Proof.* Let the DERA $D = \langle \Sigma, L, l_0, \delta, \eta \rangle$ be $K$-bounded. We define an equivalent sharply guarded DERA $D' = \langle \Sigma, L', l'_0, \delta', \eta' \rangle$ based on the so-called zone automaton for $D$. We sketch the construction, details can be found in [1,7]. The set of locations of $D'$ comprises pairs $(l, \phi)$ where $l \in L$ and $\phi$ is a $K$-bounded clock constraint. The intention is that $\phi$ is the postcondition of any run from the initial location to $(l, \phi)$. For any symbol $a$ such that $\delta(l, a)$ is defined and $\phi \wedge \eta(l, a)$ is satisfiable, let $\delta'((l, \phi), a)$ be defined as $(\delta(l, a), \phi'')$ where $\phi'' = Approx\,((( \phi \wedge \eta(l, a))[x_a \mapsto 0]) \uparrow)_K$. We set $\eta'((l, \phi), a) = g'$ with $g' = \bigwedge \{g'' \mid \phi \wedge g'' = \phi \wedge \eta(l, a)\}$. It is routine to show that the part of the automaton reachable from the initial location $(l_0, true)$ is sharply guarded.    □

The important property of sharply guarded DERAs is that equivalence coincides with equivalence on the corresponding DFAs.

**Definition 3.** *We call two sharply guarded DERAs $D_1$ and $D_2$ dfa-equivalent, denoted by $D_1 \equiv_{dfa} D_2$, iff $dfa(D_1)$ and $dfa(D_2)$ accept the same language (in the sense of DFAs).*

**Lemma 3.** *For two sharply guarded DERAs $D_1$ and $D_2$, we have*

$$D_1 \equiv_t D_2 \text{ iff } D_1 \equiv_{dfa} D_2$$

*Proof.* The direction from right to left follows immediately, since $\mathcal{L}(D_i)$ is defined in terms of $\mathcal{L}(dfa(D_i))$. To prove the other direction, assume that $D_1 \not\equiv_{dfa} D_2$. Then there is a shortest $w_g$ such that $w_g \in \mathcal{L}(dfa(D_1))$ but $w_g \notin \mathcal{L}(dfa(D_2))$ (or the other way around). By Lemma 1 this implies that there is a timed word $w_t$ such that $w_t \in \mathcal{L}(D_1)$ but $w_t \notin \mathcal{L}(D_2)$, i.e., $D_1 \not\equiv_t D_2$.    □

We can now prove the central property of sharply guarded DERAs.

**Theorem 1.** *For every DERA there is a unique equivalent minimal sharply guarded DERA (up to isomorphism).*

*Proof.* By Lemma 2, each DERA $D$ can be translated into an equivalent DERA $D'$ that is sharply guarded. Let $\mathcal{A}_{min}$ be the unique minimal DFA which is equivalent to $dfa(D')$ (up to isomorphism). Since (as was remarked after Definition 2) whether or not a DERA is sharply guarded depends only on $\mathcal{L}(dfa(D))$, we have that $D_{min} = dera(\mathcal{A}_{min})$ is sharply guarded. By Lemma 3, $D_{min}$ is the unique minimal sharply guarded DERA (up to isomorphism) such that $D_{min} \equiv D'$, i.e., such that $D_{min} \equiv D$.                                                    $\square$

## 4   Learning DERAs

Let us now turn to the problem of learning a timed language $\mathcal{L}(D)$ accepted by a DERA $D$. In this setting, we assume

- to know an upper bound $K$ on the constants occurring in guards of $D$,
- to have a *Teacher* who is able to answer two kinds of queries:
  - A *membership query* consists in asking whether a timed word $w_t$ over $\Sigma$ is in $\mathcal{L}(D)$.
  - An *equivalence query* consists in asking whether a hypothesized DERA $H$ is correct, i.e., whether $\mathcal{L}(H) = \mathcal{L}(D)$. The *Teacher* will answer *yes* if $H$ is correct, or else supply a counterexample $u$, either in $\mathcal{L}(D) \setminus \mathcal{L}(H)$ or in $\mathcal{L}(H) \setminus \mathcal{L}(D)$.

Based on the observations in the previous section, our solution is to learn $\mathcal{L}(dfa(D))$, which is a regular language and can therefore be learned in principle using Angluin's learning algorithm. However, Angluin's algorithm is designed to query (untimed) words rather than timed words. Let us recall Angluin's learning algorithm, before we present our solution in more detail.

### 4.1   Learning a DFA

Angluin's learning algorithm is designed for learning a regular (untimed) language, $\mathcal{L}(\mathcal{A}) \subseteq \Gamma^*$, accepted by a minimal deterministic finite automaton (DFA) $\mathcal{A}$ (when adapted to the case that $\mathcal{L}(\mathcal{A})$ is prefix-closed). In this algorithm a so called *Learner*, who initially knows nothing about $\mathcal{A}$, is trying to learn $\mathcal{L}(\mathcal{A})$ by asking queries to a *Teacher*, who knows $\mathcal{A}$. There are two kinds of queries:

- A *membership query* consists in asking whether a string $w \in \Gamma^*$ is in $\mathcal{L}(\mathcal{A})$.
- An *equivalence query* consists in asking whether a hypothesized DFA $\mathcal{H}$ is correct, i.e., whether $\mathcal{L}(\mathcal{H}) = \mathcal{L}(\mathcal{A})$. The *Teacher* will answer *yes* if $\mathcal{H}$ is correct, or else supply a counterexample $w$, either in $\mathcal{L}(\mathcal{A}) \setminus \mathcal{L}(\mathcal{H})$ or in $\mathcal{L}(\mathcal{H}) \setminus \mathcal{L}(\mathcal{A})$.

The *Learner* maintains a prefix-closed set $U \subseteq \Gamma^*$ of prefixes, which are candidates for identifying states, and a suffix-closed set $V \subseteq \Gamma^*$ of suffixes, which are used to distinguish such states. The sets $U$ and $V$ are increased when needed during the algorithm. The *Learner* makes membership queries for all words in $(U \cup U\Gamma)V$, and organizes the results into a *table* $T$ which maps each $u \in (U \cup U\Gamma)$ to a mapping $T(u) : V \mapsto \{\text{accepted, not accepted}\}$. In [4], each function $T(u)$ is called a *row*. When $T$ is *closed* (meaning that for each $u \in U$, $a \in \Gamma$ there is a $u' \in U$ such that $T(ua) = T(u')$) and *consistent* (meaning that $T(u) = T(u')$ implies $T(ua) = T(u'a)$), then the *Learner* constructs a hypothesized DFA $\mathcal{H} = \langle \Gamma, L, l_0, \delta \rangle$, where $L = \{T(u) \mid u \in U\}$ is the set of distinct rows, $l_0$ is the row $T(\lambda)$, and $\delta$ is defined by $\delta(T(u), a) = T(ua)$, and submits $\mathcal{H}$ in an equivalence query. If the answer is *yes*, the learning procedure is completed, otherwise the returned counterexample is used to extend $U$ and $V$, and perform subsequent membership queries until arriving at a new hypothesized DFA, etc.

### 4.2  Learning a Sharply Guarded DERA

Given a timed language that is accepted by a DERA $D$, we can assume without loss of generality that $D$ is the unique minimal and sharply guarded DERA that exists due to Theorem 1. Then $D$ is uniquely determined by its symbolic language of $\mathcal{A} = dfa(D)$, which is a regular (word) language. Thus, we can learn $\mathcal{A}$ using Angluin's algorithm and return $dera(\mathcal{A})$. However, $\mathcal{L}(\mathcal{A})$ is a language over guarded words, but the *Teacher* in the timed setting is supposed to deal with timed words rather than guarded words.

Let us therefore extend the *Learner* in Angluin's algorithm by an *Assistant*, whose role is to answer a membership query for a guarded word, posed by the *Learner*, by asking several membership queries for timed words to the (timed) *Teacher*. Furthermore, it also has to answer equivalence queries, consulting the timed *Teacher*.

*Learning Guarded Words.* To answer a membership query for a guarded word $w_g$, the *Assistant* first extracts the word $w$ underlying $w_g$. It thereafter determines the unique guard refinement $w'_g$ of $w$ that is accepted by $\mathcal{A}$ (if one exists) by posing several membership queries to the (timed) *Teacher*, in a way to be described below. Note that each word $w$ has at most one guard refinement accepted by $\mathcal{A}$. Finally, the *Assistant* answers the query by *yes* iff $w'_g$ equals $w_g$.

The guard refinement of $w$ accepted by $\mathcal{A}$ will be determined inductively, by learning the guard under which an action $a$ is accepted, provided that a sequence $u$ of actions has occurred so far. Letting $u$ range over successively longer prefixes of $w$, the *Assistant* can then learn the guard refinement $w'_g$ of $w$. Let $u = a_1 a_2 \ldots a_n$, and assume that for $i = 1, \ldots, n$, the *Assistant* has previously learned the guard $g_i = \eta(a_1 \ldots a_{i-1}, a_i)$ under which $a_i$ is accepted, given that the sequence $a_1 \ldots a_{i-1}$ has occurred so far. He can then easily compute the strongest postcondition $sp((a_1, g_1) \ldots (a_n, g_n)) =: sp(u)$. A typical situation for two clocks is depicted in Figure 2. The *Assistant* must now determine the strongest guard $g_a$ such that $a$ is accepted after $u$ precisely when

$\phi_a \equiv sp(u) \wedge g_a$ holds. In other words, he establishes the hypercube identified by guarding the polyhedron identified by $\phi_a$ in which $a$ is accepted. As before, the constraint $\phi_a$ for $a$ depends only on the sequence of symbols in $u$, not on the timing of their occurrence.

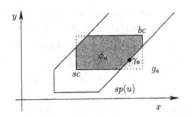

The guard $g_a$ is determined by inquiring whether a set of clock valuations $\gamma_a$ satisfies $\phi_a$. Without loss of generality, the *Assistant* works only with integer valuations. For each $\gamma_a$ that satisfies the postcondition $sp(u)$, he can make a membership query by constructing a timed word $w_t$ that satisfies the guarded word $(a_1, g_1)(a_2, g_2)\ldots(a_n, g_n)(a, g(\gamma_a))$, where $g(\gamma_a) \equiv \bigwedge_b (x_b = \gamma_a(x_b))$ constrains the clocks to have the values given by $\gamma_a$. Note that such a $w_t$ exists precisely when $\gamma_a \models sp(u)$. In other words, he can ask the (timed) *Teacher* for every point in the zone $sp(u)$ whether it is in $\phi_a$ (see Figure 2).

Let us now describe how clock valuations $\gamma_a$ are chosen in membership queries in order to learn the guard $g_a$ for $a$.

As mentioned before, we assume that the *Assistant* knows the maximal constant $K$ that can appear in any guard. This means that if a clock valuation $\gamma$ with $\gamma(x) > K$ satisfies $g$, then clock $x$ has no upper bound in $g$. Thus, a guard $g$ is uniquely determined by some biggest corner and its smallest corner.

Let us consider how to find a maximal clock valuation that satisfies $g_a$. Suppose first that the *Assistant* knows some clock valuation $\gamma_a$ that satisfies $\phi_a$. The *Assistant* will then repeatedly increase the clock values in $\gamma_a$ until $\gamma_a$ becomes the maximal clock valuation satisfying $g_a$. At any point in time, let $Max$ be the set of clocks for which *Assistant* knows that they have reached a maximum, and let $\overline{Max} = C_\Sigma \setminus Max$ be the clocks for which a maximum value is still searched. Initially, $Max$ is empty and $\overline{Max} = C_\Sigma$. At each iteration, the *Assistant* increases the clocks in $\overline{Max}$ by the same amount $k \in \{1, \ldots, K+1\}$ such that $\gamma_a[\overline{Max} \oplus k] \models \phi_a$, but $\gamma_a[\overline{Max} \oplus (k+1)] \not\models \phi_a$, and then sets $\gamma_a := \gamma_a[\overline{Max} \oplus k]$. Here, $\gamma[C \oplus k]$ is defined as $\gamma(x) + k$ for $x \in C$ and $\gamma(x)$ otherwise. This can be done by binary search using at most $\log K$ queries. For all clocks $x$ with $\gamma_a(x) \geq K+1$ he concludes that $x$ has no upper bound in $\phi_a$. These clocks are moved over from $\overline{Max}$ to $Max$. If $\gamma_a(x) \leq K$ for some clock $x \in \overline{Max}$ then among these a clock $x$ must be found that cannot be increased, and this will be moved over from $\overline{Max}$ to $Max$.

Let us examine how to find a clock $x$ that cannot be increased, i.e., for all $\gamma'$ with $\gamma'(x) > \gamma_a(x)$ we have $\gamma' \not\models \phi_a$. The particularity to handle is that it might be possible to increase $x$ but only together with other clocks, since $sp(u)$ must be satisfied (e.g., $\gamma_a$ as in Figure 2 requires both $x$ and $y$ to be incremented to stay in $sp(u)$). We define $d(x) = \bigcap \{C \mid x \in C \text{ and } \gamma_a[C \oplus 1] \models sp(u)\}$ as the clocks dependent on $x$. In other words, if $x$ is incremented in $\gamma_a$ so should be the clocks in $d(x)$ since otherwise $sp(u)$ is not satisfied. Note that $x \in d(x)$. Now, he queries for every clock $x$ whether $\gamma_a[d(x) \oplus 1] \models \phi_a$. If not, he moves $x$ to $Max$.

This can be optimized in the following way. The dependency graph of $sp(u)$ has nodes $\overline{Max}$ and edges $x \to y$ iff $y \in d(x)$. We define its initial nodes as nodes of strongly connected components that have no incoming edge. He can then use a divide-and-conquer technique to find initial nodes that cannot be incremented using $\log |C_\Sigma|$ queries.

If such a clock $x$ is found then the loop continues and another $k$ is computed. Otherwise, a maximal valuation is found.

Thus, all in all, determining the upper bound of a guard $g_a$ needs at most $|C_\Sigma|$ binary searches, since in every loop at least one clock is moved to $Max$. Each uses at most $\log K + \log |C_\Sigma|$ membership queries. He can use the same idea to find the minimal clock valuation that satisfies $\phi_a$. $g_a$ is given by the $K$-approximation of the guard that has the minimal clock valuation as smallest corner and the maximal clock valuation as biggest corner, which can easily be formulated given these two points. Thus, the *Assistant* needs at most $2|C_\Sigma|(\log K + \log |C_\Sigma|)$ membership queries to learn a guard $g_a$, if initially it knows a valuation which satisfies $\phi_a$.

Suppose now that the *Assistant* does not know a clock valuation $\gamma_a$ that satisfies $\phi_a$. In principle, $\phi_a$ and therefore $g_a$ could specify exactly one valuation, meaning that the *Assistant* essentially might have to ask membership queries for all $\binom{|\Sigma|+K}{|\Sigma|}$ integer points that could be specified by $\phi_a$. This is the number of non-increasing sequences of $|\Sigma| = |C_\Sigma|$ elements, where each element has values among $0$ to $K$, since $sp(u)$ defines at least an ordering on the clocks.

Thus, the *Assistant* can answer a query for a guarded word $w_g$ using at most $|w|\binom{|\Sigma|+K}{|\Sigma|}$ (timed) membership queries.

*The Final Algorithm.* To complete the learning algorithm, we have to explain how the *Assistant* can answer equivalence queries to the *Learner*. Given a DFA $\mathcal{H}$, the *Assistant* can ask the (timed) *Teacher*, whether $dera(\mathcal{H}) = D$. If so, the *Assistant* replies *yes* to the *Learner*. If not, the *Teacher* presents a timed word $w_t$ that is in $\mathcal{L}(D)$ but not in $\mathcal{L}(dera(\mathcal{H}))$ (or the other way round). For the word $w$ underlying $w_t$, we can obtain its guard refinement $w_g$ as described in the previous paragraph. Then $w_g$ is in $\mathcal{L}(dfa(D))$ but not in $\mathcal{L}(\mathcal{H})$ (or the other way round, respectively). Thus, the *Assistant* can answer the equivalence query by $w_g$ in this case.

We call the algorithm outlined in the section LSGDERA.

*Complexity.* For Angluin's algorithm it is known that the number of membership queries can be bounded by $O(kn^2m)$, where $n$ is the number of states, $k$ is the size of the alphabet, and $m$ is the length of the longest counterexample. The rough idea is that for each entry in the table $T$ a query is needed, and $O(knm)$ is the number of rows, $n$ the number of columns.

In our setting, a single membership query for a guarded word $w_g$ might give rise to $|w|\binom{|\Sigma|+K}{|\Sigma|}$ membership queries to the (timed) *Teacher*. While the alphabet of the DFA $dfa(D)$ is $\Sigma \times G$, a careful analysis shows that $k$ can be bounded by $|\Sigma|$ in our setting as well. Thus, the query complexity of LSGDERA for a sharply guarded DERA with $n$ locations is

$$O\left(kn^2ml\binom{|\Sigma|+K}{|\Sigma|}\right)$$

where $l$ is the length of the longest guarded word queried. Since the longest word queried and the longest counterexample can be bounded by $O(n)$, we get at most polynomially many membership queries, in the number of locations as well in the size of the biggest constant $K$. The number of equivalence queries remains at most $n$. Note that, in general a (non-sharply guarded) DERA $D$ gives rise to a sharply guarded DERA with double exponentially more locations, while the constants do not change.

### 4.3   Learning Non-sharply Guarded DERAs

Learning a sharply guarded DERA allows to transfer Angluin's setting to the timed world. However, in practice, one might be interested in a smaller non-sharply guarded DERA rather than its sharply guarded version. In this section, we describe to learn a usually smaller, non-sharply guarded version. The idea is to identify states whose futures are "similar". While in the worst-case, the same number of membership queries is needed, we can expect the algorithm to converge faster in practice.

Let us now define a relationship on guarded words, which will be used to merge states whose futures are "similar", taking the postcondition into account.

Let $PG = \{\langle\phi_1,(a_1,g_{11})\ldots(a_n,g_{1n})\rangle,\ldots,\langle\phi_k,(a_1,g_{k1})\ldots(a_n,g_{kn})\rangle\}$ be a set of $k$ pairs of postconditions and guarded words with the same sequences of actions. We say that the guarded word $(a_1,\hat{g}_1)\ldots(a_n,\hat{g}_n)$ *unifies* $PG$ if for all $j \in \{1,\ldots,k\}$ and $i \in \{1,\ldots,n\}$

$$g_{ji} \wedge sp(\phi_j,(a_1,g_{j1})\ldots(a_{i-1},g_{j(i-1)})) \equiv \hat{g}_i \wedge sp(\phi_j,(a_1,\hat{g}_1)\ldots(a_{i-1},\hat{g}_{i-1}))$$

Then, the set $PG$ is called *unifiable* and $(a_1,\hat{g}_1)\ldots(a_n,\hat{g}_n)$ is called a *unifier*. Intuitively, the guarded words with associated postconditions can be unified if there is a unifying, more liberal guarded word, which is equivalent to all guarded words in the context of the respective postconditions. Then, given a set of guarded words with postconditions among $\{\phi_1,\ldots,\phi_k\}$, these guarded words can be considered to yield the same state, provided that the set of future guarded actions together with the respective postcondition is unifiable.

It is easy to check, whether $PG$ is unifiable, using the property that the guards in the $PG$ are tight in the sense of Definition 2. The basic idea in each step is to take the weakest upper and lower bounds for each variable. Assume the guard $g_{ji}$ is given by its upper and lower bounds:

$$g_{ji} = \bigwedge_{a\in\Sigma}(x_a \leq c^{\leq}_{a,ji} \wedge x_a \geq c^{\geq}_{a,ji})$$

For $i = 1,\ldots,n$, define the candidate $\hat{g}_i$ as

$$\hat{g}_i = \bigwedge_a\left(x_a \leq \max_j\{c^{\leq}_{a,ji}\}\right) \wedge \bigwedge_a\left(x_a \geq \min_j\{c^{\geq}_{a,ji}\}\right)$$

and check whether the guarded word $(a_1, \hat{g}_1) \ldots (a_n, \hat{g}_n)$ obtained in this way is indeed a unifier. It can be shown that if $PG$ is unifiable, then this candidate is the strongest possible unifier.

The learning algorithm using the idea of unified states works similar as the one for DERAs. However, we employ a slightly different observation table. Let $\Gamma = \Sigma \times G$. Rows of the table are guarded words of a prefix-closed set $U \subseteq \Gamma^*$. Column labels are untimed words from a suffix-closed set $V \subseteq \Sigma^*$. The entries of the table are sequences of guards describing under which values the column label extends the row label. Thus, we define a *timed observation table* $T : U \cup U\Gamma \rightarrow (V \rightarrow G^*)$, where $T(u)(v) = g_1 \ldots g_n$ implies $|v| = n$. We require the initial observation table to be defined over $U = \{\lambda\}$ and $V = \Sigma \cup \{\lambda\}$.

A *merging* of the timed observation table $T$ consists of a partition $\Pi$ of the guarded words $U \cup U\Gamma$, and an assignment of a clock guard $CG(\pi, a)$ to each block $\pi \in \Pi$ and action $a \in \Sigma$, such that for each block $\pi \in \Pi$ we have

- for each suffix $v \in V$, the set $\{\langle sp(u), (a_1, g_1) \ldots (a_n, g_n) \rangle \mid u \in U', T(u)(v) = g_1 \ldots g_n\}$ is unifiable, and
- $(a, CG(\pi, a))$ is the unifier for $\{\langle sp(u), (a, g') \mid u \in \pi, u(a, g') \in U\Gamma\}$ for each $a \in \Sigma$.

Intuitively, a merging defines a grouping of rows into blocks, each of which can potentially be understood as a state in a DERA, together with a choice of clock guard for each action and block, which can be understood as a guard for the action in the DERA. For each table there are in general several possible mergings, but the number of mergings is bounded, since the number of partitions is bounded, and since the number of possible unifiers $GC(\pi, a)$ is also bounded.

A merging $\Pi$ is *closed* if for every $\pi \in \Pi$ there exists $u \in \Pi$ and $u \in U$, i.e., at least one representative of each block is in the upper part of the table. A merging $\Pi$ is *consistent* if for all blocks $\pi$, whenever $u, u' \in \Pi$, then for all $a \in \Sigma$, for which there there are clock guards $g$ and $g'$ such that $T(u(a, g)) \neq false$ and $T(u'(a, g')) \neq false$, i.e., there is an $a$-successor, there is a block $\pi'$ such that $u(a, g) \in \pi'$ and $u'(a, g') \in \pi'$. A *coarsest merging* of the timed observation table $T$ is a merging with a minimal number of blocks.

Given a merging $(\Pi, GC)$ of a closed and consistent timed observation table $T$, one can construct the DERA $\mathcal{H} = \langle \Sigma, L, l_0, \delta, \eta \rangle$ as

- $L = \Pi$ comprises the blocks of $\Pi$ as locations,
- $l_0 = \pi \in \Pi$ with $\lambda \in \pi$ is the initial location,
- $\delta$ is defined by $\delta(\pi, a) = \pi'$, where for $u \in \pi$, $u \in U$, $u(a, g) \in \pi'$ and we require $T(u, (a, g)) \neq false$ if such $u$ and $g$ exist.
- $\eta$ is defined by $\eta(\pi, a) = GC(\pi, a)$.

The algorithm *LDERA* for learning (non-sharply guarded) DERAS is as LS-GDERA, except that the new notions of closed and consistent are used. This implies that rows are unified such that the number of blocks is minimal. One further modification is that the hypothesis is constructed as described in the previous paragraph, using the computed merging. The rest of the algorithm remains unchanged.

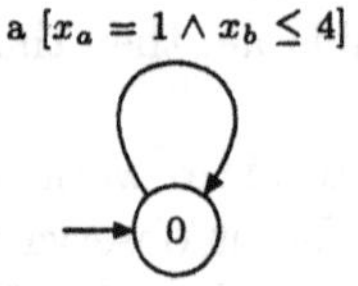

a $[x_a = 1 \wedge x_b \leq 4]$

(a) Automaton $A_1$

| $T$ | $\lambda$ | $a$ |
|-----|-----------|-----|
| $u_1$ | true | $x_a = 1 \wedge x_b = 1$ |
| $u_2$ | true | $x_a = 1 \wedge x_b = 2$ |
| $u_3$ | true | $x_a = 1 \wedge x_b = 3$ |
| $u_4$ | true | $x_a = 1 \wedge x_b = 4$ |
| $u_5$ | true | $false$ |

(b) Table $T$

**Fig. 3.** A DERA to learn and an observation table.

**Lemma 4.** *The algorithm LDERA terminates.*

*Proof.* Assume that we have a machine to learn. We assume a model $\mathcal{A}$ of it that is a sharply guarded DERA. Suppose the algorithm for learning non-sharply guarded DERAs does not terminate. Then it will produce an infinite sequence of closed and consistent observation tables $T_1, \ldots,$, each $T_i : U_i \cup U_i \Gamma \rightarrow (V_i \rightarrow (G^* \cup \{\text{not accepted}\}))$. Every step of LDERA increases the number of states of the automaton or creates a new automaton with the same number of states, because a (equivalence) query either introduces new states or changes the accepted language. Since the number of different automata with the same number of states is finite, the sequence $T_1, \ldots$ defines a sequence of hypothesis of $\mathcal{A}$ with an increasing number of states.

On the other hand, a table $T_i$ can also be understood as a an observation table suitable for the algorithm of learning sharply guarded DERAs: Let $V_w$ be the set of all possible guarded words over $w \in V_i$, and, let $V_i' = \cup_{w \in V_i} V_w$. Such an observation table is coincides all with $\mathcal{A}$ on all strings listed in the table. As such, it can be used as an initial table for LSGDERA, which, would make it closed and consistent as a first step, yielding $T_i''$.

The automaton corresponding to $T_i''$ has at least as many states as the automaton that corresponds to the one by table $T_i$, since in the latter, states are merged. When continuing LSGDERA on $T_i''$, it will terminate with table $T_{r_i}'$ as the table that corresponds to $\mathcal{A}$. Thus, the automaton corresponding to $T_i''$ has less states than $\mathcal{A}$. Thus, all automata corresponding to $T_i$ have less states than $\mathcal{A}$. Therefore, the sequence cannot exist.  □

Roughly, LDERA can be understood as LSGDERA plus merging. Therefore, in the worst case, more steps and therefore queries are needed as in LSGDERA. However, when a small non-sharply guarded DERA represents a large sharply guarded DERA, LDERA will terminate using less queries. Therefore, a better performance can be expected in practice.

## 5   Example

In this section, we illustrate the algorithms LDERA and LSGDERA on a small example. Let the automaton $A_1$ shown in Figure 3(a) be the DERA to learn.

We assume that initially clocks $x_a$ and $x_b$ are equal to 0. After a number of queries of the algorithm LDERA, we obtain the observation table $T$ shown in Figure 3(b), where the guarded words $u_1$ - $u_5$ are defined by

$$u_1 = (\lambda, x_a = 0 \wedge x_b = 0)$$
$$u_2 = (a, x_a = 1 \wedge x_b = 1)$$
$$u_3 = (a, x_a = 1 \wedge x_b = 1)(a, x_a = 1 \wedge x_b = 2)$$
$$u_4 = (a, x_a = 1 \wedge x_b = 1)(a, x_a = 1 \wedge x_b = 2)(a, x_a = 1 \wedge x_b = 3)$$
$$u_5 = (a, x_a = 1 \wedge x_b = 1)(a, x_a = 1 \wedge x_b = 2)(a, x_a = 1 \wedge x_b = 3)(a, x_a = 1 \wedge x_b = 4)$$

It turns out that all rows of $T$ are unifiable. Define $PG$ by

$$PG = \{ \ \langle sp(u_1), (a, x_a = 1 \wedge x_b = 1) \rangle,$$
$$\langle sp(u_2), (a, x_a = 1 \wedge x_b = 2) \rangle,$$
$$\langle sp(u_3), (a, x_a = 1 \wedge x_b = 3) \rangle,$$
$$\langle sp(u_4), (a, x_a = 1 \wedge x_b = 4) \rangle,$$
$$\langle sp(u_5), (a, false) \rangle \}$$

It can be checked that the guarded word $(a, x_a = 1 \wedge x_b \leq 4)$ unifies $PG$. We will use the merging of the observation table $T$ as the partition which consists of exactly one block, and equipping the action $a$ with the guard $x_a = 1 \wedge x_b \leq 4$. The automaton obtained from this mergings is the automaton $A_1$ which consists of exactly one state. In contrast, the algorithm LSGDERA, which does not employ unification, would construct the sharply guarded DERA $A_2$ shown in Figure 4. The automaton $A_2$ has 5 states, since table $T$ has 5 different rows.

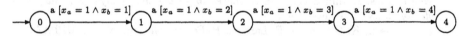

**Fig. 4.** Automaton $A_2$.

## 6    Conclusion

In this paper, we presented a technique for learning timed systems that can be represented as event-recording automata. By considering the restricted class of event-deterministic automata, we can uniquely represent the automaton by a regular language of guarded words, and the learning algorithm can identify states by access strings that are untimed sequences of actions. This allows us to adapt existing algorithms for learning regular languages to the timed setting. The main additional work is to learn the guards under which individual actions will be accepted. Without the restriction of event-determinism, learning becomes significantly less tractable, since we must also learn timing constraints of past actions under which guards on current actions are relevant. This might be possible in principle, representing the language by a regular language of guarded words, e.g., as in [22], but would lead to an explosion in the number of possible access strings.

The complexity of our learning algorithm is polynomial in the size of the minimal zone graph. In general, this can be doubly exponentially larger than a minimal DERA automaton representing the same language, but for many practical systems the zone graph construction does not lead to a severe explosion, as exploited by tools for timed automata verification [8,6]. Furthermore, we discussed learning of not necessarily sharply guarded DERAs directly to quickly obtain smaller representations of the system to learn. It would be interesting to establish lower bounds of the learning problem for timed systems.

## Acknowledgments

We thank Paul Pettersson and Rafał Somla for insightful discussions, and Oded Maler for sending his paper [22].

## References

1. R. Alur. Timed automata. In *Proc. 11th International Computer Aided Verification Conference*, LNCS 1633, p. 8–22. Springer, 1999.
2. R. Alur and D. Dill. A theory of timed automata. *Theoretical Computer Science*, 126:183–235, 1994.
3. R. Alur, L. Fix, and T. Henzinger. Event-clock automata: A determinizable class of timed automata. *Theoretical Computer Science*, 211:253–273, 1999.
4. D. Angluin. Learning regular sets from queries and counterexamples. *Information and Computation*, 75:87–106, 1987.
5. J. L. Balcázar, J. Díaz, and R. Gavaldá. Algorithms for learning finite automata from queries: A unified view. In *Advances in Algorithms, Languages, and Complexity*, p. 53–72. Kluwer, 1997.
6. J. Bengtsson, K. G. Larsen, F. Larsson, P. Pettersson, and W. Yi. UPPAAL: a tool suite for the automatic verification of real-time systems. In R. Alur, T. A. Henzinger, and E. D. Sontag, editors, *Hybrid Systems III*, LNCS 1066, p. 232–243. Springer, 1996.
7. P. Bouyer. Untameable timed automata. In H. Alt and M. Habib, editors, *Symp. on Theoretical Aspects of Computer Science*, LNCS 2607. Springer, 2003.
8. M. Bozga, C. Daws, O. Maler, A. Olivero, S. Tripakis, and S. Yovine. Kronos: A model-checking tool for real-time systems. In A. J. Hu and M. Y. Vardi, editors, *Proc. 10th International Conference on Computer Aided Verification, Vancouver, Canada*, LNCS 1427, p. 546–550. Springer, 1998.
9. E. Clarke, O. Grumberg, and D. Peled. *Model Checking*. MIT Press, Dec. 1999.
10. J. Corbett, M. Dwyer, J. Hatcliff, S. Laubach, C. Pasareanu, Robby, and H. Zheng. Bandera : Extracting finite-state models from Java source code. In *Proc. 22nd Int. Conf. on Software Engineering*, June 2000.
11. D. Dill. Timing assumptions and verification of finite-state concurrent systems. In J. Sifakis, editor, *Automatic Verification Methods for Finite-State Systems*, LNCS 407. Springer, 1989.
12. J.-C. Fernandez, C. Jard, T. Jéron, and C. Viho. An experiment in automatic generation of test suites for protocols with verification technology. *Science of Computer Programming*, 29, 1997.
13. E. M. Gold. Language identification in the limit. *Information and Control*, 10:447–474, 1967.

14. A. Groce, D. Peled, and M. Yannakakis. Adaptive model checking. In J.-P. Katoen and P. Stevens, editors, *Proc. TACAS '02, 8th Int. Conf. on Tools and Algorithms for the Construction and Analysis of Systems*, LNCS 2280. Springer, 2002.

15. A. Hagerer, H. Hungar, O. Niese, and B. Steffen. Model generation by moderated regular extrapolation. In R.-D. Kutsche and H. Weber, editors, *Proc. FASE '02, 5th Int. Conf. on Fundamental Approaches to Software Engineering*, LNCS 2306, p. 80–95. Springer, 2002.

16. D. Harel, H. Lachover, A. Naamad, A. Pnueli, M. Politi, R. Sherman, A. Shtull-Trauring, and M. Trakhtenbrot. STATEMATE: A working environment for the development of complex reactive systems. *IEEE Trans. on Software Engineering*, 16(4):403–414, April 1990.

17. T. Henzinger, Z. Manna, and A. Pnueli. Temporal proof methodologies for timed transition systems. *Information and Computation*, 112:173–337, 1994.

18. T. Henzinger, J.-F. Raskin, and P.-Y. Schobbens. The regular real-time languages. In K. Larsen, S. Skuym, and G. Winskel, editors, *Proc. ICALP '98, 25th International Colloquium on Automata, Lnaguages, and Programming*, LNCS 1443, p. 580–591. Springer, 1998.

19. G. Holzmann. Logic verification of ANSI-C code with SPIN. In *SPIN Model Checking and Software Verification: Proc. 7th Int. SPIN Workshop*, LNCS 1885, p. 131–147, Stanford, CA, 2000. Springer.

20. H. Hungar, O. Niese, and B. Steffen. Domain-specific optimization in automata learning. In *Proc. 15th Int. Conf. on Computer Aided Verification*, 2003.

21. M. Kearns and U. Vazirani. *An Introduction to Computational Learning Theory*. MIT Press, 1994.

22. O. Maler and A. Pnueli. On recognizable timed languages. In *Proc. FOSSACS04, Conf. on Foundations of Software Science and Computation Structures*, LNCS. Springer, 2004. Available from http://www-verimag.imag.fr/PEOPLE/Oded.Maler/.

23. R. Rivest and R. Schapire. Inference of finite automata using homing sequences. *Information and Computation*, 103:299–347, 1993.

24. M. Schmitt, M. Ebner, and J. Grabowski. Test generation with Autolink and Testcomposer. In *Proc. 2nd Workshop of the SDL Forum Society on SDL and MSC - SAM'2000*, June 2000.

25. J. Springintveld and F. Vaandrager. Minimizable timed automata. In B. Jonsson and J. Parrow, editors, *Proc. FTRTFT'96, Formal Techniques in Real-Time and Fault-Tolerant Systems, Uppsala, Sweden*, LNCS 1135, p. 130–147. Springer, 1996.

26. T. Wilke. Specifying timed state sequences in powerful decidable logics and timed automata. In H. Langmaack, W. P. de Roever, and J. Vytopil, editors, *Proc. FTRTFT'94, Formal Techniques in Real-Time and Fault-Tolerant Systems, Lübeck, Germany*, LNCS 863, p. 694–715. Springer, 1994.

# Author Index

# Lecture Notes in Computer Science

For information about Vols. 1–3117

please contact your bookseller or Springer

Vol. 3173: F. Yin, J. Wang, C. Guo (Eds.), Advances in Neural Networks – ISNN 2004. XXXV, 1041 pages. 2004.

Vol. 3172: M. Dorigo, M. Birattari, C. Blum, L. M. Gambardella, F. Mondada, T. Stützle (Eds.), Ant Colony, Optimization and Swarm Intelligence. XII, 434 pages. 2004.

Vol. 3170: P. Gardner, N. Yoshida (Eds.), CONCUR 2004 - Concurrency Theory. XIII, 529 pages. 2004.

Vol. 3166: M. Rauterberg (Ed.), Entertainment Computing – ICEC 2004. XXIII, 617 pages. 2004.

Vol. 3163: S. Marinai, A. Dengel (Eds.), Document Analysis Systems VI. XI, 564 pages. 2004.

Vol. 3162: R. Downey, M. Fellows, F. Dehne (Eds.), Parameterized and Exact Computation. X, 293 pages. 2004.

Vol. 3160: S. Brewster, M. Dunlop (Eds.), Mobile Human-Computer Interaction – MobileHCI 2004. XVII, 541 pages. 2004.

Vol. 3159: U. Visser, Intelligent Information Integration for the Semantic Web. XIV, 150 pages. 2004. (Subseries LNAI).

Vol. 3158: I. Nikolaidis, M. Barbeau, E. Kranakis (Eds.), Ad-Hoc, Mobile, and Wireless Networks. IX, 344 pages. 2004.

Vol. 3157: C. Zhang, H. W. Guesgen, W.K. Yeap (Eds.), PRICAI 2004: Trends in Artificial Intelligence. XX, 1023 pages. 2004. (Subseries LNAI).

Vol. 3156: M. Joye, J.-J. Quisquater (Eds.), Cryptographic Hardware and Embedded Systems - CHES 2004. XIII, 455 pages. 2004.

Vol. 3155: P. Funk, P.A. González Calero (Eds.), Advances in Case-Based Reasoning. XIII, 822 pages. 2004. (Subseries LNAI).

Vol. 3154: R.L. Nord (Ed.), Software Product Lines. XIV, 334 pages. 2004.

Vol. 3153: J. Fiala, V. Koubek, J. Kratochvíl (Eds.), Mathematical Foundations of Computer Science 2004. XIV, 902 pages. 2004.

Vol. 3152: M. Franklin (Ed.), Advances in Cryptology – CRYPTO 2004. XI, 579 pages. 2004.

Vol. 3150: G.-Z. Yang, T. Jiang (Eds.), Medical Imaging and Augmented Reality. XII, 378 pages. 2004.

Vol. 3149: M. Danelutto, M. Vanneschi, D. Laforenza (Eds.), Euro-Par 2004 Parallel Processing. XXXIV, 1081 pages. 2004.

Vol. 3148: R. Giacobazzi (Ed.), Static Analysis. XI, 393 pages. 2004.

Vol. 3146: P. Érdi, A. Esposito, M. Marinaro, S. Scarpetta (Eds.), Computational Neuroscience: Cortical Dynamics. XI, 161 pages. 2004.

Vol. 3144: M. Papatriantafilou, P. Hunel (Eds.), Principles of Distributed Systems. XI, 246 pages. 2004.

Vol. 3143: W. Liu, Y. Shi, Q. Li (Eds.), Advances in Web-Based Learning – ICWL 2004. XIV, 459 pages. 2004.

Vol. 3142: J. Diaz, J. Karhumäki, A. Lepistö, D. Sannella (Eds.), Automata, Languages and Programming. XIX, 1253 pages. 2004.

Vol. 3140: N. Koch, P. Fraternali, M. Wirsing (Eds.), Web Engineering. XXI, 623 pages. 2004.

Vol. 3139: F. Iida, R. Pfeifer, L. Steels, Y. Kuniyoshi (Eds.), Embodied Artificial Intelligence. IX, 331 pages. 2004. (Subseries LNAI).

Vol. 3138: A. Fred, T. Caelli, R.P.W. Duin, A. Campilho, D.d. Ridder (Eds.), Structural, Syntactic, and Statistical Pattern Recognition. XXII, 1168 pages. 2004.

Vol. 3137: P. De Bra, W. Nejdl (Eds.), Adaptive Hypermedia and Adaptive Web-Based Systems. XIV, 442 pages. 2004.

Vol. 3136: F. Meziane, E. Métais (Eds.), Natural Language Processing and Information Systems. XII, 436 pages. 2004.

Vol. 3134: C. Zannier, H. Erdogmus, L. Lindstrom (Eds.), Extreme Programming and Agile Methods - XP/Agile Universe 2004. XIV, 233 pages. 2004.

Vol. 3133: A.D. Pimentel, S. Vassiliadis (Eds.), Computer Systems: Architectures, Modeling, and Simulation. XIII, 562 pages. 2004.

Vol. 3132: B. Demoen, V. Lifschitz (Eds.), Logic Programming. XII, 480 pages. 2004.

Vol. 3131: V. Torra, Y. Narukawa (Eds.), Modeling Decisions for Artificial Intelligence. XI, 327 pages. 2004. (Subseries LNAI).

Vol. 3130: A. Syropoulos, K. Berry, Y. Haralambous, B. Hughes, S. Peter, J. Plaice (Eds.), TeX, XML, and Digital Typography. VIII, 265 pages. 2004.

Vol. 3129: Q. Li, G. Wang, L. Feng (Eds.), Advances in Web-Age Information Management. XVII, 753 pages. 2004.

Vol. 3128: D. Asonov (Ed.), Querying Databases Privately. IX, 115 pages. 2004.

Vol. 3127: K.E. Wolff, H.D. Pfeiffer, H.S. Delugach (Eds.), Conceptual Structures at Work. XI, 403 pages. 2004. (Subseries LNAI).

Vol. 3126: P. Dini, P. Lorenz, J.N.d. Souza (Eds.), Service Assurance with Partial and Intermittent Resources. XI, 312 pages. 2004.

Vol. 3125: D. Kozen (Ed.), Mathematics of Program Construction. X, 401 pages. 2004.

Vol. 3124: J.N. de Souza, P. Dini, P. Lorenz (Eds.), Telecommunications and Networking - ICT 2004. XXVI, 1390 pages. 2004.

Vol. 3123: A. Belz, R. Evans, P. Piwek (Eds.), Natural Language Generation. X, 219 pages. 2004. (Subseries LNAI).

Vol. 3122: K. Jansen, S. Khanna, J.D.P. Rolim, D. Ron (Eds.), Approximation, Randomization, and Combinatorial Optimization. IX, 428 pages. 2004.

Vol. 3121: S. Nikoletseas, J.D.P. Rolim (Eds.), Algorithmic Aspects of Wireless Sensor Networks. X, 201 pages. 2004.

Vol. 3120: J. Shawe-Taylor, Y. Singer (Eds.), Learning Theory. X, 648 pages. 2004. (Subseries LNAI).

Vol. 3119: A. Asperti, G. Bancerek, A. Trybulec (Eds.), Mathematical Knowledge Management. X, 393 pages. 2004.

Vol. 3118: K. Miesenberger, J. Klaus, W. Zagler, D. Burger (Eds.), Computer Helping People with Special Needs. XXIII, 1191 pages. 2004.